THE WALL STREET JOURNAL.

GUIDE TO

WHO'S WHO
&
WHAT'S WHAT
ON
WALL STREET

THE WALL STREET JOURNAL.

GUIDE TO

WHO'S WHO
&
WHAT'S WHAT
ON
WALL STREET

BY THE EDITORS OF

THE WALL STREET JOURNAL.

BALLANTINE BOOKS · NEW YORK

A Ballantine Book
Published by The Ballantine Publishing Group

Copyright © 1998 by Dow Jones & Company, Inc.

http://www.randomhouse.com

LIBRARY OF CONGRESS CATALOGING-IN-PUBLICATION DATA
The Wall Street Journal guide to who's who and what's what on Wall Street /
the editors of the Wall Street Journal.
p.   cm.
ISBN 0-345-41483-7 (alk. paper)
1. Wall Street. 2. Securities industry—United States. 3. Stockbrokers—
United States.   I. Wall Street Journal (Firm).
HG4572.W28   1998
332.6'2'0973—dc21   97-32816
CIP

Manufactured in the United States of America
First Edition: March 1998

10 9 8 7 6 5 4 3 2 1

TABLE OF CONTENTS

INTRODUCTION

Wall Street—the short street, that is, that cuts across lower Manhattan—isn't very impressive. It isn't grand like Fifth Avenue or busy like Broadway. The street is too narrow and the buildings too closely packed to create any sense of awe. About the best that can be said of it is that the buildings lining the street provide a nice framework for Trinity Church for pedestrians walking west.

But the other Wall Street—the collection of brokerage firms, investment banks and trading houses that together are the nation's securities industry—is endlessly fascinating. This Wall Street stretches coast-to-coast, from Manhattan to San Francisco, and encompasses the giants, firms with household names like Merrill Lynch, as well as the obscure. It includes white-shoe investment banks like Goldman Sachs that can put together giant mergers or arrange arcane financings anywhere in the world. It also includes seedy little bucket shops in Fort Lauderdale intent on fleecing retirees of their pension money. And Wall Street isn't confined to money-making companies. It includes the places many of those companies do business—the New York Stock Exchange and the National Association of Securities Dealers. It also includes the government agencies that monitor and regulate that business—the Securities and Exchange Commission and the Federal Reserve.

What we have tried to do in this book is give the reader a sense of the creative energy, the financial power and the ceaseless change that is Wall Street. Rather than offer a superficial survey of all that is Wall Street, we have chosen instead to present a more complete picture of the largest, most powerful firms, the two major trading institutions and the two most powerful regulators. Taken together these firms, institutions and agencies encompass almost every facet of the nation's securities industry (including plenty of the bad stuff). We don't mean to imply that firms like A. G. Edwards or Donaldson, Lufkin & Jenrette aren't important parts of Wall Street. Neither do we dismiss the important role that institutions and agencies like the American Stock Exchange and the Commodity Futures Trading Commission play in creating the environment in which Wall Street operates. But as newspeople who deal daily with deadlines and space constraints, we're acutely aware that the more topics and subjects we introduce, the less we can say about each of them. We think we have struck the best balance, one that will appeal to the Wall Street professional as much as to the merely curious individual investor or student who wants to know more about this enormously powerful, complex industry.

We think the reader will come away with a better understanding of how Wall Street works by examining the structure, culture and strategies of the firms chosen. And by focusing on recent events more than on history, we hope to impart a sense of immediacy and to capture what may well be an important turning point in Wall Street's development. The bull market that began in 1990 amid a modest recession and the beginning of the Persian Gulf War has been unprecedented in both its length and strength. It also has been unprecedented in the participation by individual investors of all stripes. Today an estimated four Americans in ten own stocks in one form or another, twice the number in 1980. The mind-boggling growth of the mutual fund industry—there are more mutual funds available to the individual investor than there are stocks on the New York Stock Exchange—is altering forever the traditional role of the retail brokerage house. The little guy and his money has also forced every firm to rethink its long-term strategy. Such a rethinking led to the merger between Morgan Stanley, the august investment bank, and Dean Witter, purveyor of stocks to the little guy. The idea of ever pairing such wildly different firms would have been laughable only a few years ago.

But the story of Wall Street isn't confined to the retail investor and the bull market. It's also about the global reach of the American securities industry. That became very apparent a few years ago as *Wall Street Journal* editors and reporters discussed what was happening to the securities industry in Europe. Virtually every deal we talked about and every financial strategy we mentioned had behind it an American investment bank. It suddenly dawned on us that all the chatter about the *globalization* of finance was wrong. It is the *Americanization* of finance that we have witnessed in this decade.

In our increasingly knowledge-based economy it is often said that a company's assets go down the elevator every night. Certainly that is true of Wall Street. The great firms we discuss in this book would be nothing without the people who inhabit their trading desks, their hushed conference rooms and their brokerage offices across America. One of our particular goals in preparing this guide to Wall Street was to identify some of the most powerful and creative minds in the securities business. Wall Street being what it is, where talent is measured in millions of dollars in annual bonuses and loyalty is a mile wide and an inch deep, some of the people you'll read about in this book already will have left one firm and gone to another. But don't worry. Their talent will be undiminished. Just figure that they will bring the same energy and creativity with them.

As newspeople we've tried to be as current as we can given the vastly different publication schedules required to produce a book rather than a daily newspaper. And certainly events of the past year or so have kept us busily updating each chapter. The mergers of Morgan Stanley with Dean Witter and Salomon with Smith Barney, the unprecedented overhaul of the National Association of Securities Dealers and its Nasdaq Stock Market, and the Federal Reserve's efforts to rein in economic growth and fend off inflation are only the most dramatic events of many that changed the face of Wall Street in the past year or so. We hope our efforts to explain and describe the securities industry will meet a reception that allows us to bring out regular revisions of this work to stay abreast of the changes that will continue to shake Wall Street.

The format of this book is simple enough. We begin with chapters describing the biggest and most diversified of Wall Street firms. Not surprisingly, we start with Merrill Lynch, the one firm that historically has been everything to everyone. This is a company that takes in more than $250 million *every day*. It is the only firm that has been able over the years to nurture within its own framework a powerful investment banking operation as well as a vast network of retail brokers. Yet its dominance is being challenged. Sanford Weill, chief of Salomon Smith Barney's parent, would dearly love to be able to boast of fielding a bigger nationwide brokerage army than Merrill.

Next we deal with the predominantly retail firms, the big brokerage firms that are critically dependent upon getting an ever-larger share of the little guys' money under management. PaineWebber and Prudential Securities, both of which have had their share of legal woes from soured partnerships in the recent years, are trying to find their niche in Wall Street's new order. Meantime, at least the bull market has buoyed their financial results, which had long been disappointing.

Then come the gunslingers, the trading houses that are confident enough—and reckless enough—to put vast sums of their own money at risk in the markets. Salomon Brothers, Bear Stearns, and, to a lesser extent, Lehman Brothers, best exemplify this rough-and-tumble trading culture. Salomon—now part of Salomon Smith Barney—and Bear boast among the Street's fattest paychecks for their top talent. But Salomon has had a devil of a time keeping its top traders, partly because of a botched attempt to scale back huge bonuses. Salomon, of course, still hasn't recovered from the 1991 bond trading scandal that led to the ouster of its top executives. Bear has its share of critics, too, who question the firm's willingness to clear trades for some smaller brokerages that are, at the least, of questionable ethics. But Bear's unique culture allows it to forge ahead in that and other trading businesses even as its top executives keep an eagle eye on every penny spent to insure that Bear doesn't become like its wasteful brethren on Wall Street.

From the high-rolling cult of traders we move in the opposite direction, to the white-shoe investment banks. These prestigious firms live by their brains, not by their brawn, although their asset bases make them plenty powerful in a world in which power is measured by money. Even as it mints money, though, Goldman Sachs struggles with the problems inherent in being the only remaining private partnership among the big players on Wall Street. How long it can— or wants to—remain private isn't clear. But the transition, when it comes, won't be easy. Meanwhile, Credit Suisse First Boston, as its name implies, wrestles with its own identity crisis as the only major Wall Street player owned by foreigners.

Finally, there are the giant commercial banks that have virtually abandoned their role as banks to pursue a place of their own in the securities industry. J. P. Morgan has over the past decade transformed itself from a somewhat staid commercial bank into a trading and dealmaking powerhouse. With its global reach, high credit rating and huge assets, it has been and will continue to be a major force on Wall Street. Bankers Trust, in the meantime, set out a few years ago to become a nimble and creative financier, but it stumbled in the pursuit of that goal when it let the art of the deal become paramount at the expense of its clients. After acrimonious legal wrangling, a much chastened Bankers Trust has set about reinventing itself while struggling to stay out of the clutches of other predatory firms. The purchase last year of Alex. Brown Inc., the Baltimore-based investment bank, will go a long way to move Bankers Trust toward its goal of remaining an independent power broker on Wall Street.

Part VI of the book deals with the venues in which Wall Street does much of its business: the New York Stock Exchange and the Nasdaq Stock Market. The two have been locked in mortal combat for a decade. Those of us who have been covering Wall Street for more than a few years remember the cocky Nasdaq advertisements that sported the slogan "The Stock Exchange for the Next 100 Years." But that was before some academics did a study that demonstrated how Nasdaq dealers were siphoning billions of dollars from investors by keeping "spreads"—the difference between the prices at which they would buy and sell stocks to investors—artificially wide. The study touched off investigations by the SEC and the Justice Department and resulted in a wholesale shake-up of the National Association of Securities Dealers, Nasdaq's parent. Not only did the structure and leadership of the NASD change radically, so did the rules by which its traders must play. The new rules give the individual investor much more clout in setting prices. The Big Board, although refraining from gloating during its competitors' travails, nevertheless pressed home its efforts to lure more publicly traded companies away from the NASD's electronic market and into its own auction market.

Unlike other companies that make, say, automobiles or airplanes or software, Wall Street cuts straight to the chase: it makes money. And in the pursuit of that single-minded goal, the firms and players sometimes extend the bounds of propriety or even legality. Keeping them in check is the role of the regulators, most prominent of which are the Securities and Exchange Commission and the Federal Reserve. The SEC played a crucial role in engineering the overhaul of the NASD to clean up its abuses. It has also been the force behind investigations of "pay-to-play" deals in the municipal finance industry and in setting new regulations governing what mutual fund companies can and can't do. The Federal Reserve has been the focus of attention not so much for its regulatory role, but for its role in monetary policy. Nevertheless, when necessary the Fed has come down hard on firms that it believes are jeopardizing the sanctity of the nation's financial system. Just ask the former heads of Salomon Brothers or Daiwa Bank. The close call Salomon had with losing its cherished role as a primary dealer in the Treasury bond market was scary enough; it doesn't compare to what happened to Daiwa for concealing information from the Fed: It was literally booted out of the country.

Throughout the book we have included, where appropriate, news and feature stories from *The Wall Street Journal* that we think will add some perspective to the profiles you're reading. Each firm, institution or agency has its own fascinating story. We invite you to dip into them at your leisure; any chapter can be read as a stand-alone profile. But only a full reading of the book can capture the power, the greed and the glory of Wall Street.

PART ONE

THE FULL SERVICE FIRMS

Merrill Lynch & Co.

•

Morgan Stanley, Dean Witter & Co.

•

Salomon Smith Barney Holdings Inc.

MERRILL LYNCH & CO.

ALL THINGS TO ALL CLIENTS

Big and Smart

I t wasn't long ago that Merrill Lynch & Co. was a Wall Street laughing-stock. Saddled with bloated costs and poor investments, the nation's biggest brokerage firm sank deep into the red. The firm's bumbling ways led analysts to joke that the "thundering herd"—Merrill's nickname since the 1940s—had become the "blundering herd."

A 1996 advertising campaign summed up how much perceptions can change. The ads featured a prominent display of the Codex Leicester, the scientific manuscript bequeathed to the world by the Renaissance master Leonardo da Vinci. The message was deliberate: We're no longer dumb. "We want to position ourselves as a wisdom company, not a muscle company," said David Komansky, who became Merrill's chief executive in 1996.

Yet no one doubts that Merrill also has plenty of muscle to back up its new wisdom. As one Wall Street firm after another flopped in trying to build financial supermarkets, Merrill has plunged into nearly every sector of financial services. After spelling disaster in the 1980s, Merrill's sheer diversity now consistently translates into huge profits and lots of clout on Wall Street. Indeed, the Merrill story shows that a financial firm can thrive with a broad array of products.

The firm shows no signs of stopping. In November 1997, Merrill made its boldest bet yet that it can export the kind of mania for stocks and mutual funds that has fueled the 1990s bull market. In the firm's biggest acquisition ever, Merrill bought Mercury Asset Management, a London money manager, for $5.3 billion in cash. Though the price was steep, the deal catapulted Merrill to fourth place among global asset managers with about $450 billion in assets under management, trailing only Fidelity Investments, France's Group Axa, and Barclays Bank PLC's Barclays Global Investors. And Merrill wants still more: Just after completing the Mercury deal, the firm entered into talks to buy Hambrecht & Quist, a San Francisco-based technology investment bank, for more than $1 billion, before scuttling those talks. Meanwhile, Merrill in February 1998 made a big plunge into the retail-securities market in Japan, taking over about thirty branches across the country once owned by Yamaichi Securities Co., which collapsed in late 1997. As part of the deal, Merrill set plans to hire one-third of Yamaichi's 6,000 former employees to staff its new nationwide branch network, which it aims to open by June 1998.

The Merrill machine is formidable: Its client assets now exceed $1 trillion— 2.85 percent of all U.S. household-financial assets. On each business day in recent years, Merrill takes in an astounding average of $250 million-plus in new assets. In October 1997, Merrill became the first brokerage firm to trade more than 1 billion shares for institutional clients in a single month. Unlike many rivals, whose earnings rise and fall with the markets, Merrill's earnings have been consistently strong for several years. In some quarters, Merrill has posted net income about equal to the combined net income of the next six largest publicly traded securities firms.

Merrill has the nation's largest brokerage force, with 13,700 "financial consultants," and 5.86 million client accounts. It is among the nation's largest mutual-fund companies, overseeing $272 billion in fund assets, and the largest vendor of money-market funds.

It manages $134 billion in individual retirement accounts. It is the top trader of exchange-listed stocks. In investment banking, it is the biggest underwriter of stocks and bonds—and has been since 1989. Merrill helps bring to market more than 16 percent of all new U.S. stock and bond issues, earning $1.35 billion in underwriting fees in 1997. It has $18.2 billion of insurance assets, making it the nation's thirty-eighth-largest insurer, and services $9.6 billion of home-mortgage loans. In short, Merrill does it all and does much of it very well.

Merrill also has been making a big push to move into the top tier of managers of defined-contribution retirement plans. In 1997, for instance, Merrill bought a division of Barclays Global Investors that administers $16 billion in 401(k) plan assets. The transaction still left Merrill fourth among the nation's managers of 401(k) retirement plans, but closed the gap with Fidelity Investments, Vanguard Group and State Street Global Advisors.

Merrill has thrived by developing a culture far different than that of most Wall Street firms. Unlike some old-line firms with Anglo-Saxon pedigrees (such as Morgan Stanley), Merrill revels in its Roman Catholic heritage. Several years ago Joseph Grano, a top-ranking brokerage executive at Merrill, told Daniel Tully, the former Merrill chairman, he was planning to leave the firm for rival PaineWebber Inc. In an effort to keep Mr. Grano, Mr. Tully, perhaps hoping for divine intervention, urged him to go to church to think it over. Mr. Grano went to church, but decided to leave Merrill anyway. He wound up president of PaineWebber.

Even Mr. Komansky, whose heritage is half-Jewish, half-Catholic, plays along.

When Mr. Tully was in Italy on an investment-banking pitch, he got a call in his hotel room, advising him that the Pope wanted to meet him. The meeting conflicted with the banking appointment, so Mr. Tully called Mr. Komansky to fly out and fill in for him on the banking meeting. "The 'Big Guy' wants to see me," Mr. Tully explained. Joked Mr. Komansky: "Is that important?"

Merrill rarely hires stars from rivals, preferring to train its own brokers and investment bankers. Employees are expected to sublimate their egos to "Mother Merrill." Merrill executives often have compared the firm to the Penn State football team, which doesn't put names on its jerseys—and whose coach, Joe Paterno, is an old friend of former Merrill Chairman William Schreyer. The result is a firm that sports few superstars, but that can field a team of excellent people working together for the firm.

Merrill has become so big that executives sometimes scoff at being compared with other brokerage firms. Instead, Merrill wants to create a franchise akin to McDonald's Corp. or Procter & Gamble Co., that elevates it above Wall Street into broader brand-name identity. "We've tried not to look over our shoulders" at competitors, according to Mr. Komansky. "On Wall Street there are very few firms where brand name is a corporate advantage, and we think ours is one of them."

Merrill believes the 1997 megadeals that created Morgan Stanley, Dean Witter, Discover & Co. and Salomon Smith Barney Holdings Inc. only validated its long strategy of having dual franchises of brokerage and investment banking. Indeed, the firm is determined to do far more. And it has paid off: Merrill Lynch Credit Corp. received the 1997 Malcolm Baldrige National Quality Award, the most prestigious honor a U.S. company can get for business excellence.

Merrill has undergone wrenching change to get where it is today. The changes began in earnest in 1989 with an intense cost-cutting crusade. Sticky little red dots became a symbol of the crusade as Mr. Tully stalked the halls of Merrill's New York headquarters, slapping the dots on any equipment he deemed excess, including stock-quote machines, desks and telephones. "People hid from me," Mr. Tully recalled. "They were afraid I'd put a red dot on their forehead."

He didn't use red dots, but Mr. Tully did pare the bloated staff by 20 percent in less than four years. Then he began cutting compensation, Merrill's biggest single expense. The biggest move on that front was a pay plan concocted by Herbert Allison, then the firm's chief financial officer, and now its president, that tied employee bonuses to return-on-equity targets.

Not surprisingly, that plan met stiff resistance. After all, employees' 1990 bonus checks were coming from a firm that showed an embarrassing ROE of just 5.8 percent compared to ROEs of 14 percent and 12 percent at Morgan Stanley and Bear Stearns, respectively. Merrill staffers derided their paltry checks as "Herbies." Now, with Merrill's ROE topping 20 percent for ten consecutive quarters and ranking among the best on Wall Street, bonuses have soared. Employees now speak more respectfully of their bonus checks, hailing them as "Mr. Allisons" or even "Sir Herberts."

And Merrill's new profitability isn't just the result of a booming stock market over the past few years. Merrill executives, who review the firm's annual budget every six to eight weeks, privately projected in 1997 a return on its $7.8 billion equity of 23 to 24 percent if business remains robust. Should the bull market ease, the firm's "baseline" budget calls for a ROE of 19 to 22 percent. And even if Wall Street suffers a significant decline in business, the result of perhaps a prolonged bear market, Merrill still expects a return of 16 to 17 percent.

A significant part of Merrill's strategy calls for a broadening of its revenue base. In recent years the firm has managed to penetrate banking and other non-brokerage businesses, such as insurance and secured loans like home mortgages, home-equity loans and mortgage refinancings. Though such penetration isn't deep, Merrill doesn't care; it uses those new businesses as a bridge to funnel new customers to its core brokerage operations. A case in point: The Whitney Group, an executive search firm, turned to Merrill a few years ago after banks balked at granting the firm a $1 million credit line. Soon, Merrill was arranging Whitney's term loans, managing its retirement business and setting up money-market accounts for its executives. "They really grab you with everything," said Gary Goldstein, Whitney's president. "Merrill has become a traditional banker to us."

Not every foray beyond securities has worked, of course. Merrill sold its lackluster real-estate brokerage and telecommunications operations in 1990. A few years ago it also unwound a $1 billion portfolio of small-business loans that led to a $200 million write-down in 1992.

And because of its sheer size, Merrill is bracing for a big hit from administrative costs stemming from the "Year 2000 Problem." The new millennium is expected to throw mainframe computers into chaos by switching the digits to 20— from 19—. The software makeover to avert such a disaster will cost Merrill about $300 million, an amount that Merrill executives say is already being budgeted.

Moreover, Merrill's breadth has helped thrust it deeply into the spectacular financial collapse of Orange County, California. In June 1997, Merrill paid $30 million in a settlement with the Orange County district attorney that ended the county's criminal investigation into Merrill's role in the matter. In a statement, Merrill said: "We continue to believe that we acted properly and professionally in all facets of our relationship with Orange County, and have entered into this settlement to resolve this matter in a way that avoids the substantial cost and distraction of protracted litigation." In December 1997, Merrill agreed to pay $1.9 million to settle a securities-fraud class-action suit brought on behalf of Orange County bondholders, charging Merrill and other firms with misleading investors about the financial health and risks of the county investment pool. Merrill still is fighting a $3 billion lawsuit the county filed in federal court in Santa Ana, California, accusing the brokerage firm of promoting a highly risky investment strategy for a public fund. The county alleges that Merrill "wantonly and callously" sold risky investments to the fund, whose $1.7 billion loss pushed the fund and the county into bankruptcy court in December 1994.

Merrill's deep embroilment in the case stemmed partly from its many roles: The brokerage firm acted as broker for the county; its investment-banking group arranged new securities underwritten by the county; its repurchase desk lent billions to the county's investment fund; and its swaps desk helped sell securities to the fund. (Merrill repeatedly has said it did nothing wrong.)

Meanwhile, Merrill is making a big push to broaden its mergers-and-acquisitions business and global operations, not, of course, without opposition from other Wall Street firms and from foreign securities firms. Its international businesses are being run by Winthrop H. Smith Jr., whose father ran Merrill between 1940 and 1961. Since 1995 Merrill has bought all or part of seven investment-banking businesses abroad.

And Merrill believes it can smooth out earnings bumps by further reducing its dependence on trading commissions. The highly cyclical commissions once brought in more than half its net revenue; they now account for about 29 percent. "The fee-based revenue stream provides some sort of offset" to volatile trading commissions, according to Mr. Komansky, who added that though Merrill has made progress, "We have a long way to go."

But that smacks of too much modesty. The strategy already is paying big dividends. In 1994, when some Wall Street firms had losses amid a bond-market crash, Merrill generated net income exceeding $1 billion—a feat that amazed many of its rivals. Merrill aims to cover all its fixed costs with fee-based revenue by the end of the decade, in a bid to keep its profitability in any market cycle.

A few years back, John "Launny" Steffens, Merrill's brokerage chief, predicted that Merrill would hit $1 trillion in client assets in this decade. (Merrill hit that milestone in October 1997.) And Mr. Allison, the firm's president, has said Merrill can be the "most important financial intermediary in the world by 2000."

There aren't many on Wall Street—or, for that matter, in traditional banking and insurance companies—who are betting against it.

Continued Expansion Amid Huge Profits and New Leaders

Merrill has boldly expanded its operations in recent years even as it continues its roll of record profits and dominance amid new leadership and nagging woes from the Orange County bankruptcy.

The firm's biggest strategic maneuver in 1997 was the purchase of Mercury Asset Management. The move could help the brokerage giant stay ahead of Wall Street rivals that have been attempting to mimic its successful strategy of marrying securities businesses catering to institutional investors with those catering to individuals, whose mutual-fund appetite has dominated the U.S. bull market. With the purchase, Merrill made a different gamble, betting that its greatest growth in the financial-services business won't come in the domestic arena, but on the largely untapped global stage. "Merrill quite rightly is looking beyond this bull market to see what the next wave of growth is going to be, and it's international," said Sallie Krawcheck, an analyst at Sanford C. Bernstein.

But Merrill executives acknowledged that the price was steep. To acquire Mercury, Merrill paid about 3 percent of assets under management, which is higher than the industry average for asset-management deals in the United Kingdom of 2 percent to 2.5 percent. "It was a negotiated transaction, albeit a painfully negotiated transaction as evidenced by the price we paid for the company," Mr. Komansky said at the time.

Though analysts cringed at the price, they grudgingly applauded the move. "We like this deal strategically, but wish it hadn't been so expensive," a report by Raphael Soifer at Brown Brothers Harriman & Co. said. "Yet, quality does not come cheaply. In our view, the combination of Mercury with Smith New Court (bought by Merrill in 1995), Merrill Lynch Asset Management and the Merrill Lynch global brokerage network should give this firm an unparalleled opportunity to achieve a leading position among European asset management firms, as well as providing tangible benefits to Merrill Lynch in the U.S., Japan and elsewhere in the world."

Discussions between Merrill and Mercury executives began in the summer of 1997, with negotiations intensifying in early November as Merrill bankers shuttled to London to do due diligence on the deal. The code name for Merrill in the deal was Mars, while Mercury was known as the Messenger, an allusion to Mercury's role in mythology as the messenger of the gods. The two parties reached an agreement in principle on November 18 when Mr. Komansky met with Mercury executives in the Dorchester Hotel in London. "It happened to be the exact same suite that I stayed in and reached a deal with Smith New Court," Mr. Komansky said. He said he ordered "the same wines, and the same food," including Peking duck, as he had ordered during the Smith New Court talks. Quipped Mr. Komansky: "I guess I'm superstitious."

Merrill's purchase of Mercury capped a more-than-yearlong hunt for an asset-management firm. Merrill had serious discussions in 1996 to acquire Wells Fargo & Co.'s index-fund business and to buy RCM Capital Management, according to people familiar with the situation. And Merrill executives throughout late 1996 and 1997 had reviewed and run numbers on a list of about a dozen asset-management acquisition targets, including Alliance Capital Management, a unit of Equitable Cos., and Los Angeles-based Capital Guardian Trust.

With the stock market hitting new records in 1997, Merrill recorded its most profitable year ever. The firm had net income of $1.9 billion, topping the prior record of $1.6 billion in 1996, and marking the fifth consecutive year of profits topping $1 billion.

But the profit run masks big underlying changes. Merrill named a new chairman and president in 1997, breaking earlier molds in the process. The big move: elevating Mr. Komansky, one of Merrill's most powerful trading executives, to be chairman. Mr. Komansky became the first Merrill chairman to have extensive experience on both sides of the company, its retail operation catering to individual investors and its increasingly important securities-trading and underwriting businesses.

The elevation of Mr. Komansky, who replaced Mr. Tully, is the latest confirmation of Merrill's shift since the 1980s to emphasizing not only its retail-brokerage operations, but capital markets, or trading and underwriting. Indeed, Mr. Komansky played key roles in Merrill's transformation to a global investment bank from a company focused on selling stocks and bonds to investors.

Mr. Allison, who had overseen the firm's investment-banking and capital-markets operations, was elected Merrill's president a month after Mr. Komansky's selection as chairman. Mr. Allison's speedy selection as No. 2 surprised Wall Street. After all, Mr. Tully and his two predecessors, Mr. Schreyer and Roger Birk, had stretched out the transition period, waiting at least a year before naming their successors as president.

The board "saw no reason to wait," said Mr. Komansky, comparing his relationship with Mr. Allison to that with Mr. Tully. Mr. Allison "will be the perfect partner for me."

Mr. Allison's likely selection as the eventual chairman of a firm that has long been run by retail brokerage executives signals the growing importance of investment banking in Merrill's strategy. The odd man out in the equation was Mr. Steffens, Merrill's longtime brokerage chief. Some Wall Street executives had expected Mr. Steffens to be Merrill's next president, and he was an early front-runner for the post. Instead, Mr. Steffens was named a Merrill vice chairman.

The move "is appropriate recognition both of Launny's more than two decades of strategic leadership at the corporate level and in our (brokerage) business, as well as the continuing core importance of this business to our global strategy," Merrill said in a statement. Merrill executives insist that Mr. Steffens told them he was happy with running the firm's brokerage operations.

"Launny is very determined to see that business achieve the goals and stature he has dreamt about for many years," Mr. Komansky said. "He truly is a visionary."

Merrill, like the rest of Wall Street, was nicked by the one-day 554-point market drop on October 27, 1997, dubbed "Bloody Monday." But through the rout—Mr. Komansky's first major leadership test—he impressed Wall Street. No big deal, Mr. Komansky said in an interview, throwing up his hands. "I've been doing this for 30 years," he shrugged. "Been there, seen this, done that, didn't like it then, don't like it now, don't know what to do about it."

It was early Monday when Hong Kong's market plunge showed signs of triggering stock mayhem in the United States and elsewhere. Huddling in Merrill's headquarters overlooking the Hudson River at 7 A.M. Monday, Mr. Komansky and members of the firm's executive committee went into crisis mode. Edward Sheridan, the firm's sales chief, told the executives that Merrill's clients weren't big sellers and there were no major mutual-fund redemptions.

But Mr. Komansky discovered the firm's greatest exposure wasn't in stocks, but in emerging-market bonds. The bad news: Russia's securities markets essentially never traded; markets in Latin America, central Europe, Southeast Asia, though theoretically open, were trading very thinly.

As the meeting broke, Mr. Komansky exhorted his managers. "Get out of your offices, be visible," walk the floors, calm the troops. Still, the carnage was everywhere: The stock market plunged 7 percent, with even bigger losses in many stock and bond markets abroad. Merrill ended Monday with about $50 million in losses, and marked down the value of its emerging-bond positions by as much as 25 percent, according to a Wall Street executive. (A Merrill spokesman declined to comment on the firm's performance.)

Heading into Tuesday was scary. Merrill and other firms were bracing for a plunge in U.S. stocks at the opening bell, what with sell orders piling up after the Big Board closed its market Monday when the Dow Jones Industrial Average fell 554 points. Mr. Komansky, with his relaxed gate, strolled through Merrill's trading floor, going from group to group to keep things loose. As he ambled to the emerging-markets bond desk, he encountered traders dressed in khakis, polo shirts and shoes with no socks. "What kind of way is this to come into work?" he joked to Steven Renehan, the desk's head. "Are you kidding?" Mr. Renehan retorted. "We've been here since 3 A.M."

Mr. Komansky's more serious message: "We didn't want a heroic stand by our traders to stanch the flow, if you will. But we wanted to continue making markets." He told his traders: "There won't be fingerpointing; there won't be second-guessing. Just go ahead and do your jobs the same way you do them in good markets."

About twenty minutes after the opening Tuesday, Mr. Komansky was "listening to some of the orders we were getting." It was all big blocks for sale, 100,000 shares of this or that blue-chip stock. "I had the feeling this was going to be a rout," he said. Then stock prices bounced hard off the bottom and institutional customers withdrew big sell orders and rushed in to buy big blocks of stock. "The only day I've seen like that, with that kind of euphoria, was the day" the Gulf War broke out, he said.

"Younger people never experienced anything like this," said Mr. Grano, president of PaineWebber Inc. and a former Merrill executive. "Their eyes are on the boardroom leader—how the leaders are acting has a ton to do with how they act," Mr. Grano added. "David maintained a very high profile" at Merrill that week.

Strategically, Merrill has continued to expand through acquisitions. Seeking a stronger toehold in the mammoth pension-fund business, in 1996 Merrill bought Hotchkis & Wiley, a money-management firm in Los Angeles with about $10 billion in assets, for about $200 million. The purchase marked a bold bid by Merrill to broaden its stable of fee-based businesses by building up its institutional asset-management franchise. Though Merrill has long been one of the dominant players in the asset-management business catering to individual investors, it had a far smaller presence on the institutional front. The acquisition allowed Merrill to be able to compete for the traditional defined-benefit business and use the Hotchkis & Wiley factory to create products for the defined-contribution business.

Continuing its push overseas, in 1996 Merrill bought McIntosh Securities Ltd., the third-largest securities firm in Australia, for about $94 million. The purchase was Merrill's third acquisition of a foreign brokerage in the past few years. In October 1995, Merrill paid $810 million for Smith New Court PLC, an agreement that made Merrill the biggest brokerage firm in the United Kingdom—and the largest stock organization in the world. In 1996, Merrill bought FG Inversiones Bursatiles SA, a Spanish brokerage firm, for $30 million.

The Orange County mess continues to bedevil Merrill. The Securities and Exchange Commission is investigating the way Merrill sold $14 billion in securities to investment funds and underwrote hundreds of millions of municipal-note issues for the county. In particular, the SEC is likely to focus on a $600 million taxable note underwritten by Merrill in June 1994, even as losses mounted in the investment pool. The proceeds of that offering went into the county's investment pool, but the firm made no disclosure about the pool's deteriorating condition to buyers of the notes.

The pool used the proceeds to buy more securities, some of them from Merrill. Another possible issue garnering SEC attention is whether Merrill made the proper disclosures regarding its sale of risky securities, known as structured notes, to the county pool.

Amid the legal battle, Merrill has lost ground in the closely watched muni-bond underwriting standings. Merrill moved to fourth place in the muni underwriting rankings in 1997, as lead manager of $18 billion in bond issues for an 8.4 percent market share, according to Securities Data Co., a Newark, New Jersey, firm that tracks corporate-finance activity.

That was a drop from 1995, when Merrill was the No. 2 muni underwriter, with $17 billion and an 11 percent market share. Merrill's fall-off in California alone has been even more dramatic, from No. 1 in 1995 to No. 7 in 1996 and 1997.

Orange County isn't the only pothole Merrill hit in the $1.3 trillion muni-bond marketplace. In the fall of 1995, Merrill agreed, without admitting or denying the charges, to pay $12 million to settle SEC charges that it failed to disclose a secret kickback pact with Lazard Frères & Co.

Merrill's involvement in the case: The firm paid Lazard $2.6 million between 1990 and 1992 so that Mark Ferber, then a Lazard partner—who had been hired by municipalities to give them independent financial advice on financial transactions—would recommend Merrill. This kickback arrangement, which wasn't disclosed to Mr. Ferber's clients, triggered millions of dollars of fees to Merrill and Lazard.

When Mr. Ferber was sentenced in the case in December 1996, a federal judge in Boston blasted Merrill for its role in the matter. "Once Merrill found that Mr. Ferber was ethically defective, they played him for a sucker," said U.S. District Judge William G. Young. "They played him like a patsy. When faced with criminal behavior, they were his co-conspirators."

Indeed, Judge Young was so outraged by Merrill's relatively light punishment that he reduced Mr. Ferber's sentence in the case. "I am struck by the disparity in the sanctions on Merrill," Judge Young said. "They bought their way out for twelve million dollars and none of them are going to jail. I don't think a twelve-million-dollar civil settlement caused them much pause on the way to the tennis courts or the yacht club."

Merrill's response: "We strongly disagree with the judge's characterizations, which are unfortunate and unfair."

There were other muni-bond miscues. In May 1996, a $1,000 political contribution by a Merrill executive to Indiana Lt. Gov. Frank O'Bannon put Merrill out of the business of underwriting much of the debt issued by that state. The contribution ran afoul of a 1994 rule by the Municipal Securities Rulemaking Board. Known as G-37, it is designed to end so-called pay-to-play in the muni business, a practice in which muni underwriters tried to influence the underwriting selections of state and local officials by making campaign contributions.

Merrill officials said at the time the contribution was returned, and that the firm hadn't violated contribution rules because it hadn't underwritten any Indiana state debt in recent months. The executives said the contribution, made by a Merrill brokerage official, violated company policy.

On the competitive front, Merrill is aggressively hiring to feed its growing overseas operations. Merrill hired 448 people out of graduate and undergraduate schools in 1997, up from 323 in 1996. (The firm plans to hire more than 500 in 1998.) Many of those hired will be sent overseas. "Our ability to execute our strategy will really be governed by the availability of talent," said Mr. Komansky.

That's why Merrill is increasing entry-level hiring. Its worldwide employment grew in 1997 by 5,877 people, or about 12 percent.

Moving Targets

Brokers and the Firms They Leave Battle To Keep the Clients

Litigation and Connivance Mark a Fight That Casts The Investor as a Pawn

A Welcome, Farewell Dinner

By MICHAEL SICONOLFI
Staff Reporter of THE WALL STREET JOURNAL

NEW YORK—The blizzard of '96 was a blessing in disguise for Ronald Waltemeyer.

The 33-year-old broker had just quit Merrill Lynch & Co. The day the storm hit, he was set to join rival Dean Witter Reynolds Inc. and badly wanted to keep his coveted "book" of clients.

Merrill had other ideas.

Furious at Mr. Waltemeyer's exit, it sought a court order barring him from soliciting the clients, which Merrill claims are its property and "lifeblood." Taking customers to the Dean Witter, Discover & Co. unit would be "nothing short of 'piracy,' " Merrill said in court papers.

But nearly two feet of snow closed the Baltimore federal court for three days—giving Mr. Waltemeyer time to persuade many of his clients to follow him to his new firm. The case was settled.

Behind-the-scenes battles increasingly are erupting over investor accounts when brokers leave their firms, raising the broad question: Who "owns" brokerage-firm clients? In the meantime, the nation's big brokerage houses are taking aggressive action to keep clients from leaving when brokers jump ship.

Securities firms, led by Merrill, have stepped up their practice of suing former brokers who try to take clients with them: Such cases have quintupled in the 1990s, brokerage executives say. Prudential Securities Inc. has tempted some brokers with twice their typical commissions for snaring clients of a departing colleague. Smith Barney Inc. has offered to waive fees for some clients of departing brokers—and warned them of penalties if they transfer retirement accounts.

"The premise is based on establishing a quick relationship with the departing broker's clients to entice them to stay," says John Creque, a former Prudential broker now at Interstate/Johnson Lane Inc. in Charlotte, N.C.

Wall Street firms are scrambling to keep investors amid heightened competition from mutual-fund companies, banks and other brokerage firms. The past two years "were extremely busy," says Thomas Campbell, a lawyer representing brokers in such disputes.

The Last to Know

The pawns in these tussles: brokers' clients. Many investors are unaware that brokers receive incentives to win their business or that firms are going to court to stop them from following their brokers. Few know that accounts of departing brokers are divvied up among the firms' remaining brokers. Some even find their accounts inaccessible during the battles.

Chances are that many investors eventually will confront the issue: Broker turnover ran 18% in 1994, according to the most recent data from the Securities Industry Association.

At times, brokerage chiefs get involved in the scraps. In May, an irate David Hubers, chief executive of American Express Financial Advisors Inc., shot off a letter to Merrill Chairman Daniel Tully, grousing that the nation's largest brokerage firm was "raiding" its financial planners, and thus its clients.

After several calls between Mr. Hubers and Merrill brokerage chief John "Launny" Steffens, Merrill stopped the recruiting. But the hiring soon resumed, and the American Express Co. unit yanked its trade-processing business—amounting to $30 million a year—for several weeks. This prompted a call to Mr. Hubers from Merrill President David Komansky, promising Merrill wouldn't raid the firm, people familiar with the matter say. (American Express since has resumed directing the clearing business to Merrill.)

An American Express spokesman declines to provide specifics but says, "We had a number of conversations with Merrill, and we have resolved the matter." Merrill won't comment.

Pestering Clients

More often, battles are fought in the trenches. In their quest for clients, remaining brokers sometimes are less than upfront about their former colleagues' practices and departures.

When David Bray, a Torrance, Calif., plastic surgeon, followed his Prudential broker to another firm, two Prudential brokers pestered him so much he complained to the Securities and Exchange Commission. Dr. Bray accused Martin McBroom and Thomas Murray of browbeating him by saying his pension portfolio was far too risky and his holdings could have violated government regulations.

"Neither of the above is true," Dr. Bray wrote. "I find this absolutely unacceptable behavior on the part of these two brokers . . . an attempt to retain or virtually steal accounts." (The SEC suggested he contact a private lawyer.) Messrs. McBroom and Murray decline to comment.

A more common technique: Tell clients their broker was ousted. That is what Cheryl Novotny of Gering, Neb., says a broker at Edward D. Jones & Co. did in 1994 when she wanted to follow Channing Schwartz, who had just quit Jones. In an arbitration case brought by Mr. Schwartz against Jones, Mrs. Novotny accused Jones broker John Kleager of telling her and her husband that Mr. Schwartz "was fired. . . . So, you know, you guys are making a big mistake" by doing business with him. (When she discovered Mr. Schwartz had quit on his own, she followed him to his new firm.)

Mr. Kleager declines to comment. A Jones spokeswoman says Mr. Kleager "does admit he certainly was trying to plant the seed of doubt" about Mr. Schwartz with the Novotnys, but denies having told them the former Jones broker was fired.

Higher Commissions

In a few instances, brokerage firms tempt their troops with incentives in writing. A common tactic is to jack up commissions for remaining brokers to snatch clients of recently departed colleagues. In an internal memorandum, Prudential Securities promised some brokers a whopping 70% of the commissions for a month from the client list of two departed brokers. Typically, brokers get to keep roughly one-third of their commissions.

A spokesman for the Prudential Insurance Co. of America unit says: "There's no firm policy about additional payouts of any kind, though it's perfectly possible that a local branch manager may have felt particularly under siege by a competitor raiding our brokers."

Prudential's payout offer isn't unique. "Go to work," says a Smith Barney memo to brokers of a departed partner, promising a 50% payout for three months. "I doubt there are very strong ties to [the former broker] with these clients." A spokesman for the Travelers Group unit says, "Steps are taken from time to time to retain account executives and clients." But he says such incentives "are more an exception than common practice."

Brokerage firms sometimes promise big clients of former brokers big breaks to persuade them to stay. In a form letter, Smith Barney offered 50% discounts on commissions to certain investors in its White Plains, N.Y. branch—and warned them that if they transferred individual-retirement accounts or other holdings, they could face termination fees.

A Smith Barney spokesman says such letters "aren't standard policy"; rather they are one step many brokerage firms take to keep accounts. The warning about termination fees is a helpful reminder, the spokesman adds. "We want to give our clients the opportunity to stay with the firm: of course, ultimately the client makes the final decision."

Through it all, some investors can be left in the cold, because their accounts sometimes are inaccessible until the spats are resolved. When Randall Wright's Merrill broker left for a rival firm late last year, he tried to follow her.

But he says the transfer papers for his portfolio were held up for weeks, and for a time he had no access to his funds. During a trip, he tried to withdraw $100 at Pittsburgh's airport from his $12,000 money-fund account and was told there were insufficient funds.

Merrill brokers had been fighting to get his account, he says, but "they neglected one minor detail—it's not their money." Mr. Wright, of Montoursville, Pa., says he invested with Merrill because of his broker. "If she was with Smith Barney or Joe's Consulting, it wouldn't matter," he says. A spokesman for Merrill says that Mr. Wright "never made any complaint" and that there wasn't a delay on its part in transferring his account. The firm says part of the lag stemmed from a delay in receiving transfer papers from the new firm. Mr. Wright says he got access to his money about 10 days later.

Some brokerage houses, led by Merrill, argue that the clients belong to the firms; they cite their big investment in training salespeople, among other things. "We spend a lot of resources behind the Merrill Lynch brand—and it's a huge advantage for Merrill financial consultants," says a Merrill spokesman. "As a result, the clients are the clients of the firm."

Other brokerage executives have different notions. "It is the broker's business—the customers do business with the broker," Robert F. Jerome, a Smith Barney branch manager and 26-year brokerage veteran, testified in a recent court case. "We would like to think that it is the name of the firm, but that is not true."

Sales Pitches

When brokers leave a firm, branch managers immediately hand client accounts to remaining brokers, who start making their pitches to get the business. Sometimes managers don't wait for brokers to walk out the door.

"Accounts get divvied up faster than the honk you get in New York when a light changes green," says David Robbins, a securities lawyer and former arbitration chief at the American Stock Exchange.

"Most of the time, your account goes to a baby broker" who isn't seasoned and faces greater pressure to generate commissions, says Sella Quinn, a former Smith Barney broker. The result, she says: "Your account gets experimented on—new brokers learn on your account."

At times, branch managers pass along accounts of recently departed brokers to their favorites, or to big producers. When PaineWebber Group Inc. dismissed Armando Ruiz in 1995, it passed along some of his accounts—including such celebrities as comedian Jackie Mason and singer Joan Jett—to Reuben Taub, a star broker who generated 1995 commissions of $2.6 million. (Mr. Taub is now at Bear Stearns Cos.)

Some older brokers say their firms try to oust them to grab their client books. Beverly Fanning, who is 52 and a 21-year brokerage veteran, says in a claim with the New York Stock Exchange that Merrill forced her to resign and threatened to file a damaging regulatory record in a bid to get control of her $70 million in client assets.

In a Dec. 13, 1995, letter to Merrill, Ms. Fanning accused Patrick Kelley and Donna Bobbs, two Merrill brokers, of telling her clients she "was fired because of a fight with the manager." Robin Connelly, another Merrill broker, told Ms. Fanning's clients she was "fired because she had failed to comply" with Merrill's educational and computer capabilities, the letter alleged. Ms. Bobbs and Messrs. Kelley and Connelly decline to comment.

Merrill ousted Ms. Fanning to acquire her $70 million book of business and to "obtain an advantage in the 'battle' to retain customer accounts," contends Morgan Bentley, Ms. Fanning's Newark, N.J., lawyer.

In a Dec. 14 letter, Merrill Assistant General Counsel Thomas Smith shot back: "Ms. Fanning does not have clients; Merrill Lynch has clients which were serviced by Ms. Fanning." Merrill didn't seek an "advantage" in keeping clients, he said.

Merrill "denies that there has been any defamation of Beverly Fanning by any individual" at the firm. The firm declines to elaborate because the case is pending.

A recent case involving former Merrill

broker Alan Arno underscores how frantic the scraps can be. After bolting to Smith Barney, Mr. Arno—along with a team of as many as 12 operations and support staffers—scrambled to send 250 account-transfer forms, some by Federal Express, to Mr. Arno's clients over two days, according to testimony in an arbitration case, filed by Merrill against Mr. Arno.

For his part, Mr. Arno said he had every right to the client list. Merrill "had no relationship with the customers; I had the relationship," he testified.

An arbitration panel subsequently ruled for Mr. Arno. Merrill and Mr. Arno decline to comment on the matter.

Dinner Transfer

Some brokers take extreme steps to fight back. After he left Prudential Securities one Friday in June 1994, broker Bruce Tuthill sent out limousines with invitations to 75 of his largest clients to attend a dinner that Sunday at a ritzy Hanover, Mass., restaurant. Over dessert of tiramisu and coffee, Mr. Tuthill stood up and announced he was leaving—and had his clients sign account-transfer forms on the spot to his new firm, PaineWebber.

"You have to do something to offset the countervailing power of these firms to make your life miserable," he says.

But some brokers are so concerned with having their clients snatched that they reluctantly stay put. George Schwelling says he stayed at the former Shearson Lehman Brothers Inc.'s brokerage operation (now part of Smith Barney) for a full five years after submitting a resignation letter in 1989. Shearson managers "told him if he left, they would give his clients 90% discounts" on commissions for a period of time, says Leslie Silverstone, a former Dean Witter branch manager.

Mr. Schwelling says he can't recall who made the threats. But he concedes that the warnings "had a big bearing on my staying. . . . I understood the unwritten rule—and that kept me as long as I stayed."

March 18, 1996

In the meantime, Merrill has been a recruiting target of aggressive foreign brokerage firms looking for a foothold in the United States. In particular, Deutsche Morgan Grenfell, the U.S. securities unit of Frankfurt's Deutsche Bank AG, hired sixty-eight professionals from Merrill in 1995 and 1996, including a core group of bond capital-markets managers, led by Edson Mitchell and Grant Kvalheim; Mr. Mitchell ran that group at Merrill until 1995. Merrill's Mr. Komansky noted that the target for big foreign banks will be Wall Street's stable of stock executives.

All this is putting pressure on compensation. Merrill and other big Wall Street firms have been forced to pay higher bonuses to their most cherished traders and investment bankers to keep them from jumping ship. The net result: Bonuses for 1996 were up an average of 30 percent for Merrill's traders and bankers, one of the biggest year-over-year jumps in the firm's history. With the bidding wars easing a bit in 1997, Merrill held down average pay increases to less than 20 percent across the board.

Defending the Brokerage Business

Merrill's core brokerage business remains a major spoke in its strategic wheel. Though it once generated the bulk of Merrill's earnings, the brokerage group has contributed about half the firm's profit for the past several years.

Street Fight

Merrill Lures Brokers Of Small-Town Rival With Signing Bonuses

Edward D. Jones, of St. Louis, Wants Nothing to Do With New York Giant

Report of Takeover Overture

BY MICHAEL SICONOLFI
Staff Reporter of THE WALL STREET JOURNAL

Edward D. Jones & Co., a fast-growing brokerage firm based in middle America, has something Merrill Lynch & Co. wants: middle-America investors.

For months, giant Merrill has been wooing Jones brokers in rural outposts with offers of lucrative signing bonuses. And the brokers have often brought along to Merrill their large local clientele, carefully cultivated over the years at a conservative firm that specializes in a down-home style of business. Jones isn't happy about Merrill's recruiting.

Well, there would be an easy way to put a stop to it, a Wall Street executive says Jones has been told: a Merrill Lynch takeover of Jones itself.

Merrill strenuously denies making takeover overtures to Jones. "There's never been a conversation that's been authorized" between the two firms, says John "Launny" Steffens, Merrill's brokerage chief. "The fact is, we look at all kinds of opportunities to expand businesses all the time. . . . But I'm not so sure the fit is great" between Merrill and Jones.

Third Party

The brokerage executive familiar with the situation says that while Merrill officials themselves haven't spoken to Jones, an informal overture was made in December by a third party that he is convinced was authentic. The executive says it was specifically posed as a way to end the friction between the firms stemming from Merrill's aggressive recruiting of Jones brokers.

Jones declines to comment on any specific overtures. John Bachmann, the firm's managing principal, says generally, "We're a partnership—we're not for sale. We see a great opportunity and a bright future."

Jones, based in St. Louis and operating many solo offices, contrasts sharply with high-powered, New York-based Merrill, the nation's biggest securities firm. But Jones is seen as an attractive takeover candidate as Wall Street girds for the stiffer competition to come with the eventual end of a Depression-era law separating securities from commercial banking.

Target Market

"Merrill likes the style of business that Jones has done—face-to-face management of assets vs. the wire-house 'smile and dial,'" says Greg Miller, a Merrill stockbroker in Burlington, Iowa, who jumped from Jones two weeks ago. He left Jones after 16 years and says he is taking most of his clients with him. "Merrill realizes there's a market here they've not been able to penetrate as well," Mr. Miller says.

Jones has built its business in what might be called the old-fashioned way: through personal relationships, and by urging clients to buy and hold. Jones doesn't go in for chancy investments. It has shunned selling options or commodities, as well as any stock priced at less than $1 a share.

And its stockbrokers, who often walk door-to-door to solicit customers, don't face the intense selling pressure seen at big Wall Street firms. Indeed, Jones says about 20% of its brokers aren't profitable to the firm, although that percentage has declined in the past couple of years.

Merrill, by contrast, revels in the fact that it offers a broad range of services to clients—basically, whatever they want to buy. As at other big firms, some of its brokers make unsolicited "cold calls" to drum up business; its brokers are under pressure to produce, facing sales goals and production contests.

And Merrill offers signing bonuses to coveted brokers from other firms, a practice avoided by Jones and increasingly by some other large brokerage houses as well. There is a paradox in this. An industry commission called for an end to such bonuses last year. The informal name of the industry group: the Tully Commission, so named because it was headed by the chairman of Merrill Lynch, Daniel Tully.

"It's ironic—here are the guys who are supposed to be champions" of the effort to clean up brokerage pay practices, says Peter Harrison, director at D.S. Wolf Associates Inc., a New York brokerage-recruiting firm.

Merrill says it is only right to pay brokers signing bonuses to ease the transition between firms, particularly because brokers often don't bring their entire book of client business.

The attractiveness of Jones brokers to Merrill lies partly in the clients that may follow them to Merrill. Yet Merrill has long gone to court to stop its own defecting brokers from taking their clients to their new firms. The clients belong to the firm, not the broker, and for a broker to bring them along would be "nothing short of 'piracy,' " Merrill said in a recent case.

The Securities and Exchange Commission is worried that the custom of paying upfront bonuses—by encouraging brokers to jump ship—tends to leave investors in the lurch. Mr. Steffens, the chief of Merrill's sprawling crew of brokers, denies that any conflict is created by the bonuses, which, he notes, Merrill pays only partly in cash; half the bonus comes in a 10-year deferred payout.

Mr. Steffens says this practice follows the letter of the Tully report, which also noted that some brokerage executives "made a vigorous case" for not discouraging upfront bonuses.

Merrill's broker recruitment is part of a broader strategy it put into place about two years ago. Dubbed Strategic Marketing Opportunities, it was defined as opening small offices with sometimes as few as three brokers. The idea: Instead of building large, downtown offices, go after small brokerage offices in rural outposts.

That's where Edward D. Jones comes in. "One way to manage that was to go

raid one- and two-man offices of Jones," says Joseph Klarberg, a former 20-year Merrill broker who left in January to join A.G. Edwards Inc. in Rochester, N.Y.

An oddity among investment firms, Jones—a private partnership—has largely shunned big cities as it has built its brokerage empire. Nearly every Jones office has three rooms and only a single broker, who serves only individual investors. You don't see a Jones office in New York City; you do in towns such as Guthrie, Okla., Perry, Ga., and Kenton, Ohio.

With more than 3,300 offices in 49 states, Jones has more branches than any other brokerage house. It clearly is on a growing spree. Last month alone, Jones hired 85 brokers to start new offices. The number of Jones offices has nearly tripled in the past 10 years.

Until recently, such small outposts went unnoticed by brokerage behemoths. Now, Merrill and other large investment houses realize that tapping Main Street can be profitable. The most obvious advantage: Client loyalty is strong with the face-to-face relationships common in smaller communities.

Merrill doesn't deny that its strategy sometimes leads to run-ins with Jones. "The fact is, that's life," says Mr. Steffens, the brokerage chief. "All I'm telling you is we don't have a giant controversy brewing between the two firms."

What is clear is that Merrill is seeking to expand its brokerage force of about 13,000—already the largest in the nation. Last year, Merrill hired 15 Jones brokers, although it attempted to hire far more. It offered upfront bonuses of as much as $1 million in a few cases, according to Wall Street executives who say they are familiar with the offers.

Meanwhile, Merrill says it lost 10 brokers to Jones last year. But the moves hurt Jones far more. When Jones loses a broker, it risks losing an entire office—and its presence in the community.

When Merrill hired Mr. Miller from Jones two weeks ago, the big Wall Street firm had 67 accounts in Burlington, Iowa; Mr. Miller says he had several thousand at Jones. When he switched firms, "all my clients came walking in the door" to Merrill, he says, even though he didn't send them any correspondence urging them to follow him.

Jones disputes that clients have left. It says its Burlington office now has about 1,580 accounts. Jones, after losing Mr. Miller, went out and hired Timothy Watson, who had been a Merrill broker in the past but was out of the industry temporarily. He soon will take the Burlington office's reins.

Meantime, the mood in the office is downbeat. "We're searching for customers until we get the new broker," says Robert Wieting, a Jones broker who was temporarily thrown into emergency duty at the branch when Mr. Miller left.

On a broader basis, Merrill now is the most aggressive firm in recruiting brokers, according to securities executives and recruiters. "Merrill is throwing money at brokers," says Mr. Harrison, the brokerage recruiter.

Merrill denies being the most aggres-sive. Mr. Steffens says his firm offers signing bonuses for "defensive purposes."

But its continued use of signing bonuses has caught the eye of the SEC, which sponsored the Tully report. The SEC is pleased that most firms have adopted many of the report's recommendations. But Arthur Levitt, the SEC's chairman, says he is "not satisfied" with the fact that some firms still offer up-front bonuses, and adds, "I'm hopeful that Merrill will find itself in the same position of leadership" in broker-pay practices that it is with "other parts of the business they are proud of."

A Merrill spokesman, referring to the Tully report, says: "Just because [Mr. Tully's] name was on it doesn't mean he embraced every detail. We embraced the concept of change."

April 11, 1996

But some analysts say brokerage profits at Merrill and other big "retail" houses are under siege. These full-service brokerage firms have lost about 25 percent of the individual-investor market to discount brokers, mutual-fund firms and other specialized vendors in recent years, according to Booz-Allen & Hamilton Inc., a management-consulting firm.

"The challenge for full-service brokerages to compete in this brave new world will be to identify customer segments best suited to their strengths," said Navtej Nandra, a Booz-Allen partner. "By targeting investors, full-service firms can make up cost gaps with superior investment advice and relationship management."

Merrill's Mr. Komansky countered that most of the lost business has been from "segments of the market we don't strategically focus on." He said the real question is whether a new generation of investors will continue to pay for investment advice. "Our biggest challenge is to find ways to enhance what accounts offer" clients.

One way is through Merrill's popular "Financial Foundations." Launched in 1992, the plan is designed to give Merrill clients their total financial picture in an eighty-page hardbound book for $250. The firm asks clients twenty-nine questions on issues such as salary, savings and retirement data. After a computer crunches the numbers, the plan—complete with recommendations—is presented to clients.

The Foundation is a critical part of Merrill's ambitious strategy to shift from being a brokerage firm that merely sells stocks and bonds to being a financial manager of all its clients' assets. The basic principle: A fee-based advisory business is less reliant on Wall Street's feast-or-famine business cycles. The plan also can be a marketing tool to pinpoint other Merrill products and services clients could use.

But some brokers grouse about pressure to sell the Foundations. Each Merrill broker must sell at least ten of these computerized-asset plans a year or face a steep penalty: forfeiture of membership in the elite clubs that reward top brokers for their performance and planning prowess. These clubs—"recognition circles" in brokerage parlance—reward participants with trips and deferred compensation worth as much as tens of thousands of dollars each year in broker perks.

"All contests are focused around Financial Foundations," complained Ronald Waltemeyer, a former Merrill broker who left the firm in 1996 for rival Dean Witter Reynolds Inc.

In a statement, the firm said: "The financial planning requirements include achieving financial planning designations as well as selling financial plans." Merrill's Mr. Steffens, the architect of the Foundation plan, brushed aside the broker criticism, saying "I question their commitment to the business and I question their professionalism."

There's no denying the Foundation plan's popularity with clients. Merrill's marketing surveys indicate that 87 percent of its clients believe they need a formalized financial plan, and 91 percent of those who bought Financial Foundations were pleased with them.

At the same time a broad brokerage strategy Merrill now employs is opening small offices in the hinterlands with sometimes as few as two or three brokers, rather than building large—and expensive—downtown offices.

One Merrill executive was given the task of doing nothing more than identifying cities and towns, mostly in rural America where Merrill could open such storefront offices. The result: an aggressive recruiting drive that has helped Merrill open up 220 such offices in the past few years.

This push has led to a spat with rival Edward D. Jones & Co., a St. Louis brokerage firm that has made a name for itself with one-man offices specializing in such a down-home style of business. Merrill even made a takeover overture to Jones in December 1995.

"We saw what Jones had accomplished in markets we could never get at," Mr. Komansky said, adding that Merrill had mulled the small-town strategy for several years before finally "pulling the trigger. It has worked out very well for us."

Merrill continues to boast the nation's biggest army of brokers. And an annual survey by *Registered Representative* magazine ranked the firm as having among the most satisfied salespeople in the securities business. "Merrill Lynch producers are most satisfied with the firm's image with the public, which appears to make up for the lowest payout in the industry," the magazine said.

Not all brokers are happy, however. Some brokers complain that Merrill is heavy-handed in trying to keep clients when they move to rival firms. And others grouse about pressure to push clients into high-fee based products and services.

Joseph Klarberg, who left Merrill in 1996 after twenty years to join A. G.

Edwards Inc. in Rochester, New York, summed up why in a memorandum to Merrill executives: "A realization that senior management has put ROE ahead of the customers and employees. And who benefits the most from ROE? Senior management—the value of whose bonuses, stock options, and actual stock are all tied to ROE."

In the memo Mr. Klarberg said there was "unreasonable and relentless pressure" to steer clients into products with steep fees "that are not in the client's best interest." He added that Merrill "had ceased to be an enjoyable or nice place to work. Honesty and respect were no longer part of the basic moral character of the firm." Merrill notes that Mr. Klarberg now works at a rival firm, adding: "At Merrill Lynch, we put our clients' interests first."

Merrill also has faced some criticism for continuing to offer "signing bonuses" to brokers recruited from rivals, even as regulators have called for an end to the practice. "Merrill is throwing money at brokers," said Peter Harrison, a former director at D. S. Wolf Associates Inc., a New York brokerage-recruiting firm.

Under pressure from regulators, Merrill has considered revising this controversial practice. Merrill hasn't made a final decision, and it isn't likely that the firm will entirely scrap these up-front bonuses. But Merrill has told the SEC that it is reviewing the matter.

"We are trying to work out a solution that would be acceptable to the SEC in terms of creating a program which would reduce or eliminate any conflict or appearance of a conflict of interest in providing payments to" brokers, said Mr. Steffens, Merrill's brokerage chief.

There are few issues that have divided the brokerage business as much in recent years as up-front bonuses, which at times total $1 million or more each for top brokers. In 1995, an industry commission—headed, ironically, by Mr. Tully, Merrill's former chairman—called for an end to signing bonuses and other practices that could create client conflicts. Merrill denies that there are conflicts, and says it must pay brokers for the cost of switching their business to a new firm.

The SEC, which sponsored the so-called Tully Commission, worries that paying up-front bonuses tempts brokers to jump ship and can make investors pawns as the departing brokers and their firms fight over who gets to keep client accounts. Brokers rarely disclose such bonuses to clients. The SEC has been frustrated because Merrill—despite the key role of the firm's former chairman on the industry commission—has been the most high-profile holdout in doing away with the bonuses. In late 1997, the firm said: "Merrill Lynch's practices are consistent with the best practices of the Tully Commission report in that signing bonuses are paid in the form of forgivable loans, not up front cash."

As the millennium nears, one of Merrill's biggest challenges could be integrating an on-line brokerage service with its more traditional system. After insisting that its clients weren't interested in on-line trading, Merrill is expected to offer the service to its clients by the middle of 1998. A move would be significant: Despite the popularity of the Internet, most big full-service brokerage firms have resisted the move to on-line trading, where stocks are bought and sold on the Internet, because they fear that it could cannibalize their advice-driven business.

Fighting the Funds

Merrill has taken several steps to counterattack mutual funds and financial advisers cutting into its business. In 1996, the firm launched a client-reward program that works like frequent-flyer miles.

Investors who maintain at least $100,000 in Merrill accounts now are offered a batch of commission-free stock and bond trades, financial planning and other services for one annual fee. This fee starts at 1.5 percent of assets for "bronze" customers with the rate shrinking to less than 1 percent for seven-figure "platinum" accounts.

With the program, Merrill is seeking to attract investors who might avoid full-service firms because they believe the commission structure is either too high or creates a conflict of interest between broker and client. "There is a lot of feeling out there that people want a predictable price," says J. Arthur Urciuoli, a Merrill senior vice president.

At the same time, Merrill has made a huge strategic shift in selling mutual funds. Historically, brokerage firms have sold only their own in-house funds, along with those of outside fund companies that charged "loads," or fees. But with the market share of load funds continuously shrinking—Merrill's market share slipped to 3.9 percent in 1997 from 4 percent in 1990—Merrill and its rivals in 1996 began planning to offer their clients a stable of no-load funds from outside vendors that compete with their own funds.

Merrill's long-awaited entry into the industry's no-load "supermarket" arena took place in 1997. The idea: to allow Merrill clients to trade no-load mutual funds from 29 unrelated fund companies without going outside the big brokerage house. But there was a hitch: Merrill initially had trouble persuading participating fund families to pay a higher rate to Merrill than they already pay to be in rival supermarket programs such as Charles Schwab Corp.'s.

"We feel that Merrill Lynch is the premier mutual fund opportunity because Merrill Lynch positions more mutual funds than any other distributor," the firm said in late 1997.

Meanwhile, Merrill's purchase of mutual-fund manager Hotchkis & Wiley showed early signs of strain. The problem: Some of the fund company's money managers and assets quickly left the firm, underscoring the risks in buying money-management operations these days.

Several bond-fund managers who left Hotchkis & Wiley set up shop at Metropolitan West Securities, a rival firm. A lawsuit filed in state court in Los

Angeles by Hotchkis against the managers was settled on undisclosed terms, but the damage already had been done: Defecting with the managers were eleven large clients and their $607 million in assets, or more than 5 percent of the $10 billion managed by Hotchkis.

Merrill kept a smiling face on the deal. The managers' departure "in no way diminishes the value of the Hotchkis & Wiley transaction from a strategic standpoint," Merrill said. "The franchise we bought remains virtually intact."

In 1997, Merrill made a move that rankled the brokerage industry: offering its own "index funds" to small investors. These funds, which are structured to mirror the performance of popular stock-market benchmarks, such as the Standard & Poor's 500, simply try to match the market rather than beat it. As such, they run counter to the brokerage-firm thinking that fund investors crave active money management to protect their savings amid market slumps. By their nature, index funds are much cheaper to run and thus carry lower management fees than actively managed funds. Investors tend to like the idea, especially since index funds have had better returns in recent years than the majority of actively managed funds.

The King of Underwriting

Merrill has dominated the underwriting of new stocks and bonds. The firm has led the widely watched rankings of new-issue underwritings in the United States since 1988 and globally since 1989. In 1997, Merrill again led all investment banks, underwriting $208.1 billion of new U.S. stocks and bonds, for a 16.1 percent market share, according to Securities Data. Merrill was ranked No. 1 in nine of fourteen investment categories, including preferred stock, investment-grade bonds, and international stocks and bonds.

Among its biggest underwriting coups of 1996 was being among the select group of underwriters chosen to bring to market New York City's municipal bonds. At stake were the underwriting rights on billions of dollars of city debt, and millions of dollars in fees for the Wall Street firms chosen to lead the city's various underwriting groups.

The selection was particularly sweet for Merrill, because in 1995 New York City had suspended Merrill from some of its duties as a senior manager after the firm reached a multimillion-dollar settlement with federal and state regulators for some of its muni activities with Massachusetts.

Merrill has made a particular push in arranging for foreign governments to sell shares in national conglomerates. In 1997, Merrill won the mandate to help lead-manage the $4.6 billion stock offering for Matav Rt., the Hungarian national telecommunications company, making the issuer the first central European company to be traded on the New York Stock Exchange. The same year, Merrill also lead-managed the $4.7 billion stock offering of Endesa SA, Chile's largest power producer, and a $4.1 billion bond issue for US West Inc. Merrill also was the global coordinator in 1996 offerings for the Peruvian and Portuguese telecommunications issuers, as well as taking the lead role as financial adviser in 1997 for the huge privatization offering of France Telecom.

Merrill hasn't been in every big deal, however. In 1996, Merrill tried to nose out rivals Lehman Brothers Holdings Inc. and S. G. Warburg & Co. to manage an offering taking part of the Venezuelan telephone company public; Lehman and Warburg had won the company's business five years earlier. "We made the conscious decision to dethrone Warburg and Lehman," said T. Mark Maybell, head of the global-telecommunications group at Merrill. It didn't work.

No matter: Merrill's underwriting fees still have rocketed to records. In 1997, Merrill led all other investment banks, receiving $1.35 billion in disclosed underwriting fees, for a 16 percent market share, supplanting rival Goldman, Sachs & Co. as the No. 1 underwriting fee earner for the second consecutive year.

Through it all, Merrill and other investment banks continue to face pressure from the imminent demise of the Glass-Steagall Act, the 1933 law that separates commercial and investment banking. In 1996, the Federal Reserve expanded the amount of corporate bond and stock underwriting banks can do to 25 percent of the revenue in their securities affiliates, up from 10 percent. The result: Some banks, such as J. P. Morgan, will continue to take market share away from brokerage firms in the underwriting arena.

There also will continue to be mergers between commercial and investment banks. As of January 1, 1997, banks have been allowed to invest as much as 10 percent of their capital in a brokerage firm or other financial firm, and to conduct these and other nonbanking operations through an operating unit. "For a bank the size of Citicorp or Chase, with almost $20 billion in capital apiece, this means an acquisition or merger with a nonbanking firm with capitalization of $2 billion to $4 billion could be permitted under the new regulation," wrote Charles Gabriel Jr., an analyst at Prudential Securities, in a research report.

"Some securities firms will no doubt be bought by banks," when Glass-Steagall is formally eradicated, Merrill's Mr. Komansky correctly predicted in a 1995 issue of *Investment Dealers' Digest*, a trade magazine. Merrill, with its size, won't likely be one of them. And Mr. Komansky played down the impact of the shift. "In practice, banks have already made sufficient inroads into the securities business that this should prove an evolutionary rather than a revolutionary change for the industry overall."

Topping the Mergers-and-Acquisitions Chart

Merrill's M&A team had a banner year, rising to No. 1 in 1997 among the leading U.S. merger advisers tracked by Securities Data for the second consecutive year. In 1997, Merrill advised U.S. companies on $266.7 billion in announced merger or acquisition deals, for a 29 percent market share, vaulting the firm ahead of such white-shoe banking rivals as Morgan Stanley and Goldman. That's a jump from the No. 3 ranking in 1995, and is a far cry from just a few years ago, when Merrill's mergers team was derisively referred to on the Street as the "Post Office," for its lack of innovation and stars despite its enormous size.

Three of Merrill's biggest M&A roles in 1997 involved NationsBank Corp.'s purchase of Barnett Banks Inc. ($14.8 billion), HFS's merger with CUC International Inc. ($11.3 billion), and the acquisition of Hughes Electronics' defense business by Raytheon Co. ($9.5 billion). In 1996, Merrill scored a major coup by advising Bell Atlantic Corp. in its $21.3 billion merger with NYNEX Corp., the year's biggest mergers deal. Bell Atlantic had been a Salomon Brothers Inc. client in the past, but Merrill was able to muscle in by hiring Tom Middleton, a senior Salomon investment banker amid turbulence at that firm. Merrill pocketed a hefty $30 million in fees from the Bell Atlantic/NYNEX deal alone.

Other 1996 highlights: Merrill snared the advisory role for Cisco Systems Inc.'s $4.8 billion stock swap with StrataCom Inc., and was co-adviser with J. P. Morgan in Gillette Co.'s $7.9 billion stock swap with Duracell International Inc.

Merrill's mergers team has had increasing success getting its feet in the door of many deals through the many relationships garnered by its dominance in underwriting. And it beefed up its mergers presence by hiring a spate of M&A bankers from reeling rivals, including Salomon and CS First Boston Corp. But it didn't get in every big deal: A major disappointment was getting shut out of the $14 billion Boeing Co.-McDonnell Douglas Corp. stock swap; rival J. P. Morgan got the coveted advisory role for McDonnell Douglas.

Trading's Mixed Bag

Merrill's trading operations have accounted for a sizable chunk of earnings in recent years. Revenue from stock and stock-derivatives trading, for instance, soared to more than $1 billion in the past couple of years from $534 million in 1991. Revenue from interest-rate and currency swaps more than tripled during the same period.

But one of its better trades in recent years involved selling back 10 percent of Bloomberg L.P. in 1996 for $200 million—a stake that cost just $13 million when Merrill bought it in 1985. Merrill recorded a pretax gain of about $155 million on the deal; the gain was reduced because Merrill may need to make additional payments to Bloomberg as part of an agreement to purchase services. Merrill still owns a 20 percent stake in Bloomberg, an expanding financial-information company.

Merrill's commodities trading hasn't fared as well. Revenue from futures trading has fallen sharply in recent years amid a decline in interest among investors. In 1996, Merrill pulled back from soft commodities, dropping its cocoa analyst and its coffee-brokerage business amid slack profits. In all, the firm let go seventy-five of its approximately 530 employees in its commodities division in early 1996. "With the new focus on risk-adjusted rates of return, many firms are demanding higher rates of return from businesses like commodities with higher risks," said Dean Eberling, an analyst at Prudential Securities Inc. at the time. "When those higher return thresholds aren't reached, the capital gets pulled and reallocated."

Commission revenue from Nasdaq Stock Market trading had soared in recent years, the result of robust trading volume. But new regulations designed to make the Nasdaq market fairer to small investors have pinched profits at Merrill and other big Nasdaq traders. The new Nasdaq rules will force market makers like Merrill to share their vast knowledge of what is going on at any given moment in the market for a Nasdaq stock with small investors. Without the exclusive access to such intelligence, the dealers won't be able to book as much profit on the average trade.

The result: Merrill, along with many other big Nasdaq market makers, has pulled back from making markets for infrequently traded small stocks that simply are seen as too risky given new Nasdaq rules on how stocks are priced. Merrill, for instance, slashed the number of small stocks it makes markets in to 550 in 1997 from 850 in 1996.

Merrill's biggest Nasdaq hit in 1997 came in December, when the firm was among thirty Nasdaq dealers to agree—without admitting wrongdoing—to settle a 1994 class-action lawsuit alleging that the firms unfairly priced Nasdaq stocks between 1989 and 1994. Of the $910 million settlement in the case, filed in a New York federal court, Merrill agreed to pony up the most: a hefty $100 million. "Although we believe our practices were entirely proper, it made no sense to continue litigating the merits of practices that are no longer followed when the matter could be resolved on an industry-wide basis," a Merrill spokesman said at the time. (Merrill and the other firms will be able to spread the payments over several quarters because the bulk of the money isn't due until the second half of 1998.)

Meanwhile, Merrill had a couple of commodity-related scraps in 1997. The Commodity Futures Trading Commission rebuked Merrill for not taking sufficient steps to discover misconduct by a former broker. The CFTC ruling arose out of an investigation into the broker, who ended up pleading guilty in 1994 to wire fraud in connection with a Ponzi scheme that defrauded more than 100 investors out of $8 million. Merrill contested the CFTC's conclusions, and said it had reimbursed about $3.5 million to investors who lost money through the broker.

Merrill also paid $25 million to Codelco in an out-of-court settlement that resolved a long-simmering dispute between the two firms over whether Merrill's commodities traders should or could have spotted $170 million in losses accumulated by an alleged Codelco rogue trader.

Buying An International Presence

Merrill's non-U.S. operations have blossomed in recent years. In 1997, Merrill's nondollar denominated stock business matched the firm's U.S.-dollar stock business for the first time.

On the global front, Merrill has purposely pursued a different cross-border strategy than that of arch rivals Morgan Stanley and Goldman. Unlike those firms, which are growing their own businesses abroad, Merrill is simply buying its way into foreign markets.

Indeed, Merrill has attempted to colonize the world's financial-services markets just as Coca-Cola and McDonald's have taken their brands global in soft drinks and fast food. Unlike Coke and McDonald's, Merrill is aiming to satisfy investors' appetite for stocks and bonds. This is most evident in its purchase of Mercury Asset Management, which will help boost Merrill's non-U.S. revenues to about 28 percent, compared with 21 percent in 1994 before the firm launched its big global push.

The move married Merrill, a household name among U.S. investors, with Mercury, a longstanding British money-management firm that caters to institutional investors and, at the time of the Merrill deal, had $177 billion in assets under management, along with nearly 200 fund managers and about 1,300 employees in 19 offices worldwide. While 83 percent of Merrill Lynch Asset Management's assets are in the hands of individual investors, just 12 percent of Mercury's money is controlled by retail investors. And while 94 percent of Mercury's funds had been invested outside the U.S., only 21 percent of Merrill's funds had been invested overseas. After the merger, Merrill's approximately $450 billion in assets under management were split fairly evenly between institutional and retail investors and between overseas and domestic funds.

In Britain, Merrill didn't trade any sterling securities just a few years back. But with the firm's 1995 acquisition of Smith New Court PLC, Merrill essentially bought a 20 percent share of that market, a move that Mr. Komansky said makes it easier for Merrill to "build origination capability and compete in the U.K. for U.K. business."

Merrill has pursued a similar strategy in Australia, on a smaller scale, with its purchase of McIntosh. "We have aspirations [overseas] to replicate what Merrill Lynch signifies in the U.S.," Mr. Komansky said. Other foreign markets have been more difficult to crack. In Germany, for instance, Merrill hasn't made headway butting heads with that country's three indigenous banking powerhouses.

Merrill's move to snap up Yamaichi employees and branches was another bold step. The move made Merrill the only foreign brokerage firm attempting to directly serve individual Japanese investors by selling them stocks, bonds, mutual funds and other financial products through its own retail outlets. By taking over the approximately thirty branches, Merrill instantly controlled the tenth-largest retail brokerage network in a country where individual savers hold about $10 trillion in assets, a market second only to the United States.

The challenge Merrill faces overseas: It's far more costly to do business, with profits typically slimmer than in the United States. Fees for Merrill's European investment-banking business run 30 to 40 percent less than in the United States. "Foreign business can be a short-term drag on your ROE," Mr. Komansky conceded but added: "We see global expansion as an investment in our future."

Merrill's strategy in Indonesia reflects its approach in cracking smaller markets. Merrill executives joke that five years ago, nobody at Merrill could find Indonesia on a map. But Merrill slowly built its operations—the firm now has forty-two employees there—and underwrote a few big new stock issues in the Indonesian government's privatization drive that Merrill knew would generate local attention.

Merrill's swaps business is a real driver overseas; about 60 percent of the firm's total swaps trading revenue is generated outside the United States, Merrill executives say. And analysts say Merrill in 1996 did more business in Japan than Nomura Securities Co., Japan's biggest brokerage firm.

With all its success, Merrill's international group suffered a blow in 1997, when the firm fired one of its highest producing brokers and filed fraud charges against him in Singapore and Hong Kong. The broker, Kevin Wallace, had cultivated more than 100 Asian high-rolling clients who entrusted him with chunks of their personal fortunes. Merrill accused Mr. Wallace of "unauthorized trading in certain private-client accounts," as well as misrepresenting client statements and forging client signatures. Mr. Wallace was arrested by Hong Kong authorities.

Meanwhile, Merrill moved to quickly pay clients "who had legitimate claims" against the firm, and also is fighting other suits brought by Mr. Wallace's ex-clients. A Merrill spokesman said the firm reserved $45 million to settle claims stemming from the case.

A Shy Bull

Call it the cafeteria approach to research and strategy. From soup to nuts, a Merrill Lynch client can find nearly anything he or she is looking for from the firm's six hundred–strong team of analysts and strategists. The only missing ingredient is a unanimous view of what investors should be doing with their dollars.

Take the first quarter of 1997, for instance. Merrill's chief investment strategist, Chuck Clough, was one of Wall Street's most resolute bears, urging clients to keep their holdings of U.S. stocks to 26 percent, while holding 14 percent in foreign stocks and 55 percent of their assets in bonds, with the remainder in cash. At the same time, Richard Bernstein, head of the quantitative research team at Merrill, saw no reason why stock prices couldn't climb higher still, in spite of a slowdown and profits, thanks to a more benign interest rate environment. That's where the firm's new chief economist, Bruce Steinberg, broke ranks, anticipating further rate increases. Whew.

As if that wasn't confusing enough, while Mr. Clough voiced caution about stocks as an asset class, Mr. Bernstein was sounding warning signals about technology stocks. Still, however, the firm's technology analyst remained adamant that sell-offs in some of the bellwether companies like IBM created ideal opportunities.

But Merrill's top strategists, who still adopted similar views of the market at year-end, insist that their clients welcome this diversity.

"To try to shoehorn a single view of a complicated world into our points of view would be silly," said Mr. Clough. "To help our clients, we have to let everyone express themselves and maintain the independence of our various disciplines."

Mr. Clough is the lynchpin of Merrill's research and strategy efforts—even though he grew up on the streets of Boston without knowing what the stock market was. "We were too poor to worry about that stuff," he recalled. In fact, it wasn't until he'd spent a semester in premed studies at Boston College and dabbled in prelaw, that he opted for graduate business school at the University of Chicago. Even then, he claims, he wound up on Wall Street as a fluke: he nearly pursued management consulting as a career.

After stints managing money at Donaldson, Lufkin & Jenrette Securities Corp., he moved on to Cowen & Co. and pursued his growing interest in investment strategy, still, in 1982, a fledgling discipline. "This has been so much fun, I can't believe this is a real job," he said. In 1987, he joined Merrill and has headed the team of strategists there for the last decade.

Mr. Clough's bearishness dates back to early 1996, when signs of weakness in areas like orders for nondefense capital goods led him to believe that a slowdown in economic growth, and thus profits and stock price growth, was inevitable. So far, he's been wrong, and trails his peers on asset-allocation performance. But he's sticking to his guns, and is one of the few Wall Street bears to retain a loyal following.

That's because institutional investors, in particular, like his approach to the market, which is less based on correct calls on the Dow's direction than it is on providing clients with ideas they can use.

"It's naive or worse to think you can accurately call where stocks are bound," Mr. Clough argued. "If you can bring thoughtful analysis to the table, that's critical. All you can bring to the table with portfolio managers that have access to far more information than you do is to give them some insight they hadn't thought of."

Mr. Clough tries to capture important turning points in sectors of the market, such as financial services, where he was an early advocate of buying banks and insurance companies. "We still think that has a long way to run," he said, but shuns cyclical industries, reflecting his bearish view of economic growth, a call that paid off for his clients throughout the first half of 1997.

Mr. Clough's strategy is supplemented by perhaps the largest team of technical, quantitative and global strategists on Wall Street. Mr. Bernstein, head of the extensive quantitative team, has won a growing following among clients for early calls on the technology sell-off early this year, as well as for novel approaches to the market, such as the quest for high-quality, big stocks that remain relatively inexpensive to the market. Richard McCabe, the veteran technical analyst at Merrill, is known as one of the most easily understood members of this group, often seen as specializing in translating incomprehensible jargon. Robert Farrell continues to draw a crowd for calls such as the one he made in December 1996, when he argued that 1997 would see a "reverse January effect," where large stocks would outperform their smaller counterparts, a reversal of the traditional seasonal pattern.

An army of salespeople—Merrill is Wall Street's largest retail brokerage firm—ensures that its stock analysis is well-distributed and retains a high profile. Cautionary notes on IBM released ahead of the company's earnings this spring in the midst of the rocky technology stock market, for instance, caused a twenty-minute delay in the opening of the stock and a sharp, albeit short-lived, sell-off in the stock.

In 1997, Merrill had thirty-three all-star analysts, giving them the top spot in the rankings. Among these stars are tobacco analyst Allan Kaplan, Stephen McClellan, a four-year veteran of the *Wall Street Journal*'s all-star rankings, and Steven Fleishman, lured away from Dean Witter in 1996 to cover utilities.

The retail outlets, as well as demanding the attention of Merrill's vast research department, impose demands on Mr. Clough and his group of strategists. But the calm and soft-spoken dean of the world of investment strategy isn't rattled, even though some weeks find him reviewing the same facts and materials for two entirely different groups of audiences.

"Actually having the retail investors around is a big advantage," he said. "They're a lot more sophisticated than people usually give them credit for, and it helps me keep tabs on what's going on."

More arduous are the growing demands that follow from the increased globalization of financial markets. Mr. Clough and his colleagues find themselves on planes to Asia and Europe at regular intervals to meet with clients there, and they convene an annual seminar on global investing. The 1995 merger with Britain's Smith Newcourt brokerage boosted Merrill's European presence in research and strategy "considerably," he said. Still, while the increased emphasis on global investing brings more scope to his job, "it has also made it a lot more physically taxing."

Settle Quickly and Quietly

Merrill boasts the best record among major Wall Street firms in securities arbitration: It wins 55 percent of all cases filed by clients, the average award is just $66,200 and cost per broker is $1,800, according to the *Securities Arbitration Commentator*, a Maplewood, New Jersey, newsletter. Overall, brokerage clients win 51 percent of cases filed; the average amount awarded is $81,000, according to a survey by the newsletter, which covered ten thousand awards involving Wall Street securities firms granted between May 1989 and June 1995.

One reason Merrill fares so well is its policy of quickly and quietly settling cases filed by investors. Two major cases Merrill chose to fight, however, backfired for the firm in 1996. In one instance, an arbitration panel of the National Association of Securities Dealers Inc. ordered Merrill to pay $2.1 million to a former star commodity broker who claimed that Merrill defamed her, blackballing her from the futures business. And another NASD panel ordered Merrill to pay nearly $1 million to a pair of elderly sisters whose accounts were filled with risky mortgage-backed securities.

A big legal black hole for Merrill, of course, has been Orange County. Merrill executives scoff at suggestions that Merrill could end up settling the county's civil case for several hundred million dollars. But the executives concede the matter could drag on for a while. Publicly, all Merrill will say is: "We acted properly and professionally in our relationship with Orange County."

Merrill's People

David H. Komansky, chairman and chief executive: Mr. Komansky assumed the top spot from Daniel Tully in December 1996, ensuring a smooth management transition in an industry known for its high-level coups. Mr. Komansky began his thirty-year career at Merrill as a stockbroker but has had broad business experience; before moving into the CEO suite, he had been president and head of the firm's powerful stock and bond-market groups.

As president and now CEO, a major focus of Mr. Komansky's has been on Merrill's global expansion. He has pushed for a strategy of using the firm's strong market position as a platform for penetrating key local markets. Recent acquisitions, including Smith New Court in 1995 (Britain), McIntosh Secu-

Komansky, David
Chairman & CEO-
Merrill Lynch

rities in 1996 (Australia), and the purchase of Mercury Asset Management (Britain), reflect Mr. Komansky's leadership priorities.

Mr. Komansky played key roles in Merrill's transformation into a global investment-banking powerhouse. In the mid-1980s, he ran Merrill's real-estate subsidiary, then oversaw the company's sale of that operation in 1987. He has been among Merrill's best-paid executives; he even earned a heftier 1995 pay package—valued at more than $12 million—than the then-No. 1 Mr. Tully.

As former head of Merrill's bond group, Mr. Komansky also has been a key figure in dealing with Merrill's litigation-filled woes with Orange County. "Our actions with respect to Orange County were totally proper and professional," Mr. Tully said. "Dave has taken a leadership role in managing Merrill's response to this situation."

Born in Mount Vernon, New York, and raised in the New York City borough of the Bronx, Mr. Komansky started as a broker in Merrill's branch office in Forest Hills, Queens. In 1983, he became the regional director for the retail-brokerage operations in the New York City area.

Colleagues praise Mr. Komansky's affable nature. When he was named head of the bond group in 1992, Mr. Komansky conceded he had no experience in the area. So colleagues jokingly sent him a booklet explaining what a bond was. (They said he dutifully read it.)

Herbert M. Allison Jr., president: Merrill wasted no time in naming Mr. Allison to replace Mr. Komansky as president. Mr. Allison has one of the broadest backgrounds of any Merrill executive.

Unlike Mr. Komansky, who came up through the ranks of Merrill's brokerage force, Mr. Allison has spent about three of his twenty-five years at Merrill on the retail side. After he joined Merrill in 1971 with an MBA from Stanford University, he held investment-banking jobs in Paris, Tehran, and London before moving into finance and human resources in the 1980s.

He spent three years as treasurer, then ran the human-resources department, where he updated Merrill's cost-measurement system. Mr. Allison carried that discipline over to his next stint of more than three years as chief financial officer. Mr. Allison earned notoriety within the firm for tying employee bonuses to ROE targets. Mr. Allison "played a strong role at the time of starting to layer in some corporate objectives," said Samuel Liss, an analyst at CS First Boston.

The reward for a job well-done there was that Mr. Allison was put in charge of Merrill's investment-banking operations in 1993. Two years later, he was able to consolidate his authority over the firm's stock and bond underwriting and trading operations as well. In 1995, Mr. Allison received a pay package valued at $4.8 million.

John L. Steffens, vice chairman and head of brokerage operations: When he was named to his new post in 1996, Mr. Steffens also was appointed to the Merrill board. Mr. Steffens is among the most powerful executives at the firm. Indeed, Mr. Steffens's insistence on continuing Merrill's practice of paying up-front bonuses helped persuade Mr. Tully not to back down on the practice in 1996, despite pressure from regulators.

Mr. Steffens has climbed the ladder at Merrill. Joining in 1963 as a member of its junior-executive training program, Mr. Steffens became a broker in the Merrill branch office in his hometown Cleveland. In 1970 he attended the firm's management-training program and returned to the Cleveland office as sales manager.

He came to New York in 1975 as manager of the operations-planning department. In 1981, he was appointed marketing director for Merrill Lynch Individual Sales unit, and was named senior vice president and director of national sales for Merrill in 1984. In 1995, Mr. Steffens received a pay package valued at a little more than $5 million.

Mr. Steffens also has served as chairman of the Securities Industry Association in 1994. He also held four consecutive terms as vice chairman between 1990 and 1993, and has been chairman or cochairman of the SIA tax-policy committees since 1989.

Stephen L. Hammerman, vice chairman and general counsel: Mr. Hammerman is one of the most respected legal executives on Wall Street. He is the architect of Merrill's strategy of attempting to quietly settle private cases brought against the firm rather than risking major public-relations fiascoes.

Before joining Merrill (through the 1978 merger of White, Weld & Co.), Mr. Hammerman had been an assistant U.S. attorney in the criminal division for the Southern District of New York. In 1979, he left Merrill to become New York regional administrator for the SEC. He rejoined Merrill in 1981, keeping his SEC contacts and experience, serving as Merrill's general counsel and chief administrative officer between 1985 and 1987.

In 1985, President Reagan appointed Mr. Hammerman to the board of the Securities Investors Protection Corp., which insures most brokerage accounts for up to $500,000 in cash and securities; he served at the SIPC until his term expired in 1987. Mr. Hammerman was also the 1988 chairman of the National Association of Securities Dealers' board of governors, and joined the board of the New York Stock Exchange in 1995.

Barry S. Friedberg, executive vice president and chairman of corporate and institutional-client group: Mr. Friedberg is among the most senior investment bankers on Wall Street. He also is a member of the firm's office of the chairman and executive-management committee. Mr. Friedberg had run Merrill's investment-banking operations until 1993, when the firm created the office of the chairman in a bid to bolster its client business. Mr. Friedberg over-saw a period of great growth of Merrill's banking operations.

Mr. Friedberg began his career in 1963 with Chemical Bank. The following year, he joined A. G. Becker, which was acquired by Merrill in 1984. Merrill has made great strides in its mergers operations under his tenure, and continues to dominate Wall Street's underwriting business.

Jerome P. Kenney, executive vice president, corporate strategy, bond and stock research, economics and U.S. government relations: Mr. Ken-ney is a member of Merrill's office of the chairman and its executive-management committee. Before heading capital markets in the late 1980s, he had been Mer-rill's director of securities research, director of institutional sales and marketing and head of investment banking.

Mr. Kenney came to Merrill in 1978 at the time of White Weld merger. He joined White Weld in 1967 as a research analyst and was named to the *Institu-tional Investor* All-America team in the building industry. He became research chief at White Weld and was on its board.

Born in Newton, Massachusetts, Mr. Kenney received an MBA from Northwestern University (Kellogg) Graduate School. He is a member of the New York Society of Security Analysts. In 1995, he received a pay package valued at $3.4 million, reflecting his clout at the firm.

Winthrop H. Smith Jr., chairman of Merrill Lynch International and execu-tive vice president, international private-client group: Mr. Smith also is a member of Merrill's executive committee. Before assuming his current post in 1992, Mr. Smith was senior vice president and national sales director, eastern division, in the brokerage operation. Mr. Smith was responsible for Merrill's 138 eastern-division branch offices, with 3,200 brokers and annual revenue of $1 billion.

Mr. Smith, whose dad was one of Merrill's founding fathers, started at the firm in 1974 as an investment banker. After stints managing the firm's financial analysis and budgets and compensation and benefits groups, he became vice president—at thirty, the youngest officer at Merrill at the time.

In 1980, Mr. Smith became the youngest division director as head of human resources and later the youngest executive vice president, in 1992. In his cur-rent post, Mr. Smith oversees Merrill's growing international operations, with locations in more than thirty nations.

Carol Galley, cohead of Merrill Lynch-Mercury asset-management opera-tions: Ms. Galley, former vice chairman of Mercury Asset Management, also is the only female member of Merrill's executive-management committee. Ms. Galley joined Mercury in 1971, was appointed a director of the company in 1982 and vice chairman in 1995.

Stephen Zimmerman, cohead of Merrill Lynch-Mercury asset-management operations: Mr. Zimmerman, former deputy chairman of Mercury Asset Management, is a member of Merrill's executive-management committee. Mr. Zimmerman joined Mercury in 1971, and has been involved in its management of U.K. pensions since 1974.

Hugh Stevenson, non-executive chairman of Merrill Lynch-Mercury asset-management operations: Mr. Stevenson, former chairman of Mercury, will remain in his new position until late 1998 to oversee the integration of the two businesses. Mr. Stevenson had been Mercury chairman since 1992, and director since 1986. Before entering the money-management business, he had been a lawyer with Linklater & Paine.

David Causer, executive director of Mercury asset-management group: Mr. Causer was appointed to the Mercury's board as finance director in 1995. Mr. Causer joined Mercury as chief financial officer in 1988 after serving as senior European financial officer for three U.S. financial-service firms.

Thomas H. Patrick, executive vice president: Mr. Patrick is also chairman of Merrill's special-advisory services, and a member of the office of the chairman and executive-management committee. In his special-advisory services role, Mr. Patrick is responsible for the development of proprietary products for Merrill's investment-banking clients.

Mr. Patrick previously had been chief of Merrill's stock-markets group, and head of the firm's insurance operations. He also had been chief financial officer. At Merrill, he is perhaps best known for being one of the two inventors (along with Lee Cole) of Merrill's successful LYONs, or liquid yield options note, product.

John G. Heimann, chairman of Merrill's global-financial institutions group: Mr. Heimann also is a member of the firm's office of the chairman and executive-management committee. After a career at Smith Barney Inc. and E. M. Warburg Pincus & Co. and four years as Comptroller of the Currency, Mr. Heimann joined Merrill in 1984 as vice chairman of Merrill's capital-markets group. Before his current job, he was chairman of the executive committee for Merrill's Europe/Middle East operations.

Edward L. Goldberg, executive vice president, operations, services and technology: Mr. Goldberg has management responsibility for Merrill's worldwide information services, real estate and purchasing. He also is a member of the firm's executive-management committee. Mr. Goldberg has served in administrative, sales, marketing and operations capacities since joining Merrill in 1961.

In the Beginning . . .

Ironically, the firm that is called Merrill Lynch & Co. today had that same name in 1915. Since then, though, it has gone through a series of changes that brought it back to that simple moniker only twenty-five years ago. The name Merrill Lynch & Co. was first adopted on October 15, 1915, as a successor to the firm launched by Charles E. Merrill the year before. Merrill's first recruit in 1914 was a friend, Edmund C. Lynch, whom he persuaded to take a pay cut—to $25 a week from $75 a week—to give up selling soda-fountain equipment and "learn the securities business," according to a Merrill historical guide.

Messrs. Merrill and Lynch sought to attract a broader class of customers beyond the highbrow social elite that the white-shoe Wall Street firms cozied up to. True to its plain-folks roots, the firm early on helped raise capital for the fledgling chain-store industry; its first major deal was an offering for McCrory Stores.

Merrill also was a pioneer in breaking the gender line. The firm hired Wall Street's first bond saleswoman, Annie Grimes, in 1919; "she proved a decided success in the heady 1920s," the Merrill guide gushed. In seeking to cater to its "Mr. Average Investor," the firm in May 1924 began opening its uptown New York office every weekday evening from 7 P.M. to 9 P.M.

Following the 1929 stock-market crash, Merrill Lynch in February 1930 transferred its brokerage business to E.A. Pierce & Co. In April 1940, Charles Merrill combined his firm with the Pierce concern to create a new firm called Merrill Lynch, E.A. Pierce & Cassatt. The following year, Merrill became the first Wall Street firm to publish an annual report. Also in 1941, the firm merged with Fenner & Beane to become Merrill Lynch, Pierce, Fenner & Beane.

By the mid-fifties, Merrill had become a household name for those even vaguely acquainted with Wall Street. And the firm's investment-banking group had evolved. In late 1955, Merrill was among the select group of seven managers chosen to handle the 1956 initial public stock offering of Ford Motor Co. In 1958, following the resignation of Alpheus C. Beane Jr., the firm honored senior executive Winthrop Smith by adding his name to the firm, which became Merrill Lynch, Pierce, Fenner & Smith.

Its clout grew further in 1970 amid a major trading crunch on the New York Stock Exchange. To avert a panic, Merrill stepped in and bought Goodbody & Co., then the exchange's fifth-largest member firm. On July 27, 1971, Merrill became the second brokerage firm to sell its shares to the public (the first was Donaldson, Lufkin & Jenrette Inc. in 1970). In 1973, to simplify things, the firm returned to its original name, Merrill Lynch & Co., and in 1978, Merrill bought the prestigious White, Weld & Co. investment-banking firm.

Roger M. Vasey, executive vice president and senior adviser: Mr. Vasey, a member of the firm's executive-management committee, has responsibilities for maintaining relationships with a broad base of clients. Before his current post, Mr. Vasey headed the firm's bond-markets group. Over a thirteen-year period, Mr. Vasey built the group into a global bond powerhouse.

Joseph T. Willett, senior vice president and chief financial officer: Mr. Willett, a member of the firm's executive-management committee, is responsible for Merrill's audit, controller, credit, investor relations and treasury functions. Before his current position, Mr. Willett was treasurer and controller.

Daniel T. Napoli, senior vice president, global risk management: Mr. Napoli, a member of Merrill's executive-management committee, oversees the firm's important risk-management group, which manages and controls the firm's trading exposure. Mr. Napoli also chairs the Merrill Lynch Risk Council, which reviews all risks and institutional-market controls. Since 1985, Mr. Napoli has served on the Public Securities Association special advisory committee to the U.S. Treasury and Federal Reserve.

Jeffrey Peek, president of Merrill Lynch Asset Management: Mr. Peek, a former investment banker who had been Merrill's cohead of investment banking, replaced Arthur Zeikel, Merrill's longtime asset-management chief, in late 1997. Mr. Peek took over a mutual-funds operation that had grown from less than $400 million in assets twenty years ago and didn't have a single fund carrying the Merrill name.

Arthur Zeikel, chairman of Merrill Lynch Asset Management: Mr. Zeikel is a member of the firm's executive-management committee and is a senior adviser to Merrill's president and CEO.

Patrick J. Walsh, senior vice president, human resources: Mr. Walsh, a member of the firm's executive-management committee, is responsible for Merrill's management training and development, equal-employment opportunity, employee benefits, compensation and other administrative functions. Mr. Walsh joined Merrill in 1969, holding a number of sales and management positions in Merrill's branch system.

Paul W. Critchlow, senior vice president for marketing and communications: Mr. Critchlow, a member of the firm's executive-management committee, oversees Merrill's advertising, media relations, government relations, employee communications, diversity, corporate marketing, special events, philanthropic programs and other related activities. Mr. Critchlow joined Merrill in 1985 as director of corporate communications after an extensive career in journalism and government. He was promoted to his current post in 1988.

Thomas Davis, executive vice president and cohead of corporate and institutional-client group: Mr. Davis, a member of Merrill's executive-management committee, previously had been managing director and cohead of investment banking. In his current post, he oversees the firm's investment banking, bond and stock market activities worldwide. Mr. Davis joined Merrill in 1977 as an associate in investment banking. Since then, he has held a wide variety of senior posts in Merrill's investment banking and stock operations.

E. Stanley O'Neal, executive vice president and cohead of corporate and institutional client group: Mr. O'Neal previously had been managing director and head of global capital markets, with responsibilities including both bond and stock new issue activity worldwide. Before that post, he was a managing director in Merrill's investment-banking group, heading the financing services group. Mr. O'Neal worked at General Motors Corp. before joining Merrill.

Michael J.P. Marks, deputy chairman, Merrill Lynch International, and chief operating officer, Europe/Middle East/Africa operations: Mr. Marks previously had been cohead of global stocks, and deputy chairman of Merrill Lynch International. He was chairman of Smith New Court at the time of its acquisition by Merrill in 1995.

Kevan Watts, chief operating officer, Asia Pacific region: Mr. Watts previously had been managing director and head of investment banking for Europe/ Middle East/Africa operations. Mr. Watts joined Merrill in 1981 in New York, where he worked on United States corporate-finance matters. He previously had been an official at H.M. Treasury, where he held a number of jobs and ultimately became the principal advising on export credit policy.

Richard Fuscone, chief operating officer, Latin America/Canada operations: Mr. Fuscone previously had been managing director and head of global debt markets. He is responsible for Merrill's bond, stock, investment banking, private-client and asset-management business in Latin America and Canada. Before joining Merrill in 1979, he worked with the commercial-paper group at A.G. Becker Inc.

Gregory Bundy, co-chief operating officer, Australia/New Zealand operations: Mr. Bundy had previously been managing director of international stock sales and trading. He joined Merrill in 1984, and held various trading positions in the small-stock area, including senior block trader, before heading up the firm's Japan stock-trading operation.

John Magowan, co-chief operating officer, Australia/New Zealand operations: Mr. Magowan joined Merrill with its acquisition of McIntosh Securities Ltd., where he had been chief executive officer, stockbroking. Mr. Magowan had served in a variety of capacities at McIntosh for more than ten years.

G. Stephen Thoma, senior vice president and director of Merrill Lynch's Group Employee Services division: Mr. Thoma heads a Merrill unit that provides a wide range of employee-benefit programs including retirement, 401(k), stock option, stock purchase and after-tax savings plans to businesses of all sizes. Before joining the division in 1985, Mr. Thoma was a resident vice president of four Merrill offices in Connecticut. He began his career in 1966 with Merrill as a member of the junior executive training program.

Howard Sorgen, senior vice president, chief technology officer of Merrill's private-client group: Mr. Sorgen is responsible for all technology strategy and systems development for Merrill's brokerage business. Before joining Merrill in 1988, he spent twenty-seven years with Manufacturers Hanover Corp., where he was an executive vice president.

Anthony J. Vespa, senior vice president: Mr. Vespa also is president and chief executive officer of Merrill Lynch Insurance Group Inc. This business manufactures and distributes investment-oriented variable annuities and variable life insurance products. Before his current post, Mr. Vespa was district director of the New York City district for Merrill's brokerage operations. He began his career in 1960 with Goodbody & Co., a predecessor firm.

Nassos Michas, senior vice president, Diversified Financial Services: Before his current post, Mr. Michas had been chairman of private banking for Merrill's brokerage group, heading the firm's international and domestic banking, trust and credit institutions for individual clients. Mr. Michas has held a variety of other positions at Merrill, including chief international executive of Merrill Lynch Capital Markets.

Madeline Weinstein, senior vice president and director of Merrill Lynch Strategic Professional Development: Ms. Weinstein is responsible for employing new technology to benefit Merrill private clients and the firm's brokers and for the professional development and training of brokers, branch managers and administrative staff. Ms. Weinstein joined Merrill in 1979.

Harry Allex, senior vice president, operations, services and telecommunications: Mr. Allex also is a member of Merrill's private-client executive and operating committees, and serves on the board for Merrill Lynch Trust Co. Moreover, Mr. Allex is chairman and chief executive of Merrill Lynch Financial Data Services Inc., an independent unit that provides transfer-agent services for money-market and mutual funds.

Robert Sherman, senior vice president: Mr. Sherman also is national sales director for Merrill's eastern sales division. In that post, he is responsible for one-third of Merrill's branch system with 5,000 employees in more than 140 offices in 12 states and the District of Columbia. Mr. Sherman joined Merrill in 1967.

Thomas Muller, senior vice president: Mr. Muller also is national sales director for Merrill's western sales division. He began his career with Merrill in 1966 as a broker in Merrill's Nashville, Tennessee, office. Before his current post, Mr. Muller was North Central Regional Director based in Chicago.

Arthur Urciuoli, chairman of Merrill's international private-client group: Before his current post, Mr. Urciuoli had been responsible for the strategy, account and product programs, market research and advertising for the individual-client market segments of Merrill's U.S. brokerage operations. Before his current post, Mr. Urciuoli was, among other things, director of international investment banking and president of Merrill Lynch International.

A. Bruce Brunson, chairman of Merrill Lynch Hubbard: Mr. Brunson has been senior vice president at Merrill since 1986. Before his current position, he served as, among other things, Merrill's treasurer. Before joining Merrill, he worked for nineteen years at Exxon Corp.

Christopher Reeves, chairman of Merrill Lynch Europe PLC and Merrill Lynch International: Mr. Reeves is engaged in Merrill's business in Europe, the Middle East, Africa and India. He joined Merrill in 1988 as a senior adviser to the president of Merrill Lynch Capital Markets. He became a vice chairman in 1989 and assumed his current post in 1993. Before joining Merrill, Mr. Reeves was deputy chairman and group chief executive at Morgan Grenfell Group PLC.

Peter Clarke, chairman of Asia/Pacific operations: Mr. Clarke has held this position since 1992, when he joined Merrill. He previously had been at Salomon Brothers, where he was a managing director and held management positions in Hong Kong, Tokyo and London over seventeen years.

Robert Grandy, chairman, Canadian operations: Mr. Grandy previously held a variety of posts in Merrill's Canadian operations since 1988. Before joining Merrill, Mr. Grandy worked at Wood Gundy Ltd.

Hisashi Moriya, chairman of Merrill Lynch Japan: Mr. Moriya also is a member of Merrill's global management committee. Before his current post, Mr. Moriya had been vice chairman for Merrill Lynch Japan. Before joining Merrill, he was a managing director and partner at A.G. Becker Paribas Ltd., which merged with Merrill in 1984.

Robert McCann, head of global stock markets within Merrill's corporate and institutional-client group: Mr. McCann is responsible for the trading and risk management activities of Merrill stock products. He began his career with Merrill in 1982, and has held a variety of posts in Merrill's stock desk.

Edward Sheridan, director of the institutional-client division: Mr. Sheridan is responsible for all institutional-client services globally for both stock and bond products. Mr. Sheridan joined Merrill in 1976 as a municipal-bond salesman. He has held a variety of positions in Merrill's bond group.

G. Kelly Martin, chief technology officer of Merrill's corporate and insititutional-client group: Mr. Martin's group oversees Debt and Equity Markets worldwide and Investment Banking. As Chief Technology Officer, Mr. Martin has global responsibility for applications development and settlement processing systems.

Jeffrey Gelfand, first vice president, director of finance and administration for Merrill's corporate and institutional-client group: Mr. Gelfand is responsible for all financial and administrative matters of Merrill's worldwide bond, stock and investment-banking businesses. Before joining Merrill, Mr. Gelfand worked at Peat Marwick Mitchell & Co.

Michael Quinn, managing director and head of institutional-asset management: Mr. Quinn joined Merrill in 1983 and has been head of institutional-asset management since 1995. Before his current post, Mr. Quinn was cohead of Merrill's stock division. He joined Merrill from Donaldson, Lufkin & Jenrette.

Joseph Moglia, senior vice president and director of individual financial services and middle markets within the private client group: Mr. Moglia's career includes a number of positions at Merrill and outside the industry. He joined Merrill in 1984 in Institutional Sales, where he became director of Global Fixed Income Sales in 1992. Before assuming his current position, Mr. Moglia headed Merrill's municipal division, with responsibility for all origination and trading of tax-exempt securities. Mr. Moglia spent sixteen years in his "first career" as a football coach. Before joining Merrill, he was the defensive coordinator for the Dartmouth football team, and author of a book on offensive theory.

James Kennedy, managing director, global risk-management group: Mr. Kennedy has been a member of Merrill's risk group since its inception in 1987. He joined Merrill in 1982 from Salomon Brothers, and founded Merrill's analytical systems department as manager. He also has held a variety of other responsibilities at Merrill, including posts in bond-portfolio analysis, and hedging and arbitrage.

John Breit, managing director, global risk-management group: Mr. Breit's responsibilities include complex derivatives, options and swaps, commodities, stock derivatives, foreign exchange and mortgages. Before joining Merrill, Mr. Breit was responsible for domestic risk management at Security Pacific Merchant Bank.

Andrew Ivan Butcher, director, global risk-management group in Tokyo: Mr. Butcher previously had been a director of risk management in Merrill's New York office. Before joining the firm in 1995, Mr. Butcher worked at Bankers Trust New York Corp. as a vice president of risk management.

Daniel Bayly, managing director and head of investment banking: Before his current post, Mr. Bayly had held a variety of investment-banking roles in Chicago and New York. Mr. Bayly joined Merrill in 1972 from Northwestern (Kellogg) Graduate Business School.

Rosemary T. Berkery, director of global securities research and economics: Ms. Berkery had been manager of the corporate law department, which serves as counsel to Merrill's board and senior management. Before joining Merrill in 1983, she had worked at Shearman & Sterling as a corporate and securities lawyer.

J. Michael Giles, chairman of international private banking: Mr. Giles has been in this post since 1989, responsible for Merrill's private-banking business outside the United States. He joined Merrill in 1981 from Citibank.

Allen Jones, head of private-client marketing: Before his current post, Mr. Jones had been a senior vice president in United States private-client marketing. He also has been director of individual-financial services, and president and chief executive of Merrill Lynch Insurance Co. He joined Merrill in 1973.

Andrew J. Melnick, senior vice president and director of global securities research and economics: Mr. Melnick joined Merrill in 1988 and had served as a director of global fundamental stock research before being appointed to his current post in 1997. Before joining the firm, he served in research-related roles at Woolcott & Co., L.F. Rothschild Unterberg, Tobin, and Drexel Burnham Lambert Inc.

Conrad Voldstad, managing director and cohead of global bond markets: Mr. Voldstad previously had been president and chief executive of Merrill Lynch Derivatives Products, and London-based regional head of debt markets. Before joining Merrill in 1988, he was a senior bond executive at J. P. Morgan.

Seth Waugh, managing director and cohead of global debt markets: Before his current post, Mr. Waugh had been head of the global credit trading and new issues group. Before joining Merrill in 1988, he had been on the corporate bond and international trading desks at Salomon Brothers.

Theresa Lang, senior vice president and treasurer: Ms. Lang is responsible for all short-term and long-term funding, capital planning, cash management, bank relations, insurance and risk finance for the firm. She joined Merrill in 1984.

MORGAN STANLEY, DEAN WITTER & CO.

TAKING A RUN AT THE BULL

Wall Street's New Behemoth

The 1997 megamerger between elite investment bank Morgan Stanley Group Inc. and retail-broker Dean Witter, Discover & Co. spawned a bull market in headlines to describe the marriage: BRAINS AND BRAWN. BLUE BLOOD AND BLUE COLLAR. SILK AND POLYESTER. CLASS MEETS MASS.

But in the end, the bottom line for Wall Street's biggest-ever merger was this: It made solid business sense. The two firms were clear leaders in their respective Wall Street arenas. Morgan Stanley was a top institutional player with huge market-share positions in trading, underwriting and mergers-advisory work. It also had spread its tentacles around the globe, and branched out into managing assets. Dean Witter had a narrow, and profitable, focus on the retail-brokerage business.

Their bold bet was that the future of the business lies in melding these institutional and retail camps. For years, most Wall Street franchises were cleanly divided between investment banks that provide strategic advice and underwrite stocks and bonds for corporate clients and brokerage houses selling stocks, bonds and mutual funds to small investors.

By combining, Morgan Stanley and Dean Witter took direct aim at competing more effectively with Merrill Lynch & Co., the only Wall Street firm ever to successfully bridge the two cultural camps. But Merrill accomplished this through internal growth; no Wall Street firm has ever been able to pull it off through a merger. The combined Morgan Stanley, Dean Witter (the firm dropped Discover from its name in 1998) nearly matched Merrill as the nation's largest securities firm in terms of total capital ($33.6 billion compared with Merrill's $37.5 billion). In 1997, Morgan Stanley, Dean Witter had net income of $2.59 billion for its fiscal year ended November 30, compared with $1.9 billion for Merrill.

But Merrill remained No. 1 in 1997 net revenue ($15.7 billion compared

Micro-Economics

Wall Street Wants The 'Little Guy,' and It Will Merge to Get Him

Dean Witter Deal Puts Host Of Brokers, Mutual Funds In Morgan Stanley's Orbit

New Pressure on Competitors

BY MICHAEL SICONOLFI
AND ANITA RAGHAVAN
Staff Reporters of THE WALL STREET JOURNAL

Several years back, PaineWebber Group Inc. Chairman Donald Marron preached his mantra to all who would listen: The 1990s, he said, will be the decade of the little guy.

Yesterday's megamerger announcement involving two of his major rivals showed how right he was. Blue-chip investment bank Morgan Stanley Group Inc. and Dean Witter, Discover & Co., a "retail" brokerage house catering to individual investors, confirmed that they plan a stock swap to create the nation's largest securities firm. The merger will be about a $10.22 billion deal.

Driving it was a bid to snare the burgeoning assets of small investors, particularly in mutual funds. The combined Morgan Stanley, Dean Witter, Discover & Co. will boast $271 billion in assets under management, making it the world's fifth-largest money-management concern. In a telling move, the surprise chief executive of the new goliath will be Philip Purcell, Dean Witter's CEO. Yesterday, some Wall Street executives were dubbing him Mr. Retail.

Money Flood

Behind the big trend: The little guy lately has been investing tons of money in stocks. In the past 10 years, the percentage of households' financial assets in stocks has more than doubled, to about 50%. Last year alone, investors poured more than $222 billion into stock funds, a record. For brokerage firms, managing such vast assets can mean recurring revenue streams that blunt the wild zigzags of profitability inherent in the markets. Yet traditional full-service brokerage firms have lost 25% of their business in recent years to discount brokers and mutual-fund companies, according to Booz-Allen & Hamilton Inc.

The money flood stems partly from a broad shift toward so-called defined-contribution pension plans, which give employees the task of investing retirement funds contributed by their employers. "Individual investors used to buy stocks or not, or sell stocks and buy a house," Mr. Marron says. "Now, a whole new class of investors has control over the money that is crucial to their future"—and many are turning to financial-services firms.

The irony for Mr. Marron: Yesterday's merger could leave his brokerage firm, the nation's fourth-largest, squeezed. PaineWebber and many other midsize financial-service firms will be under tremendous pressure to find partners to compete with the new Wall Street giant. "This opens the door to lots of thoughts and conversations for everybody," says Jamie Dimon, chief executive at Travelers Group's Smith Barney Inc., now the nation's second-largest brokerage firm in number of brokers.

Aiming Lower

The merger comes as several other Wall Street firms are looking at ways to reach small investors. Goldman, Sachs & Co., Wall Street's last major private partnership, is in the midst of developing more stock and bond mutual funds. Salomon Inc. agreed last month to sell stock issues it underwrites to brokerage customers of FMR Corp.'s Fidelity Investments.

Going for the little guy balances out some of the risks, because "the small investor has been less prone to overreact" to big market moves, says Richard Lipstein of consulting firm Solomon-Page Group Ltd. "Institutions are much less likely to ride through any storms."

Yesterday, executives at what will become Morgan Stanley, Dean Witter were crowing that they will unseat Merrill Lynch & Co. as the nation's biggest brokerage firm. But Morgan Stanley and Dean Witter are doing exactly what Merrill set out to do two decades ago: Cobbling together a firm with a foundation of small investors to sell investments to.

"For Dean Witter, the great benefit is the added breadth of product," Mr. Purcell says. This will come, he says, as its brokers start selling initial public stock offerings and municipal-bond issues underwritten by Morgan Stanley. For Morgan, the plus will be an army of 9,300 brokers "committed to selling those underwritings in the right way," Mr. Purcell says.

But Merrill still is a formidable rival in snaring the business of small investors. Its fleet of brokers remains the nation's largest—13,000—while its brokerage-account assets total $839 billion. And Merrill is a leader in deriving steady streams of income from managing assets: It now generates nearly two-thirds of its annual income from recurring management fees, up from less than 40% in 1990.

By contrast, asset-management fees make up just 20% of the planned Morgan Stanley, Dean Witter's pro-forma 1997 net income, people familiar with the matter say. That percentage is projected to rise to 25% to 30% over the next couple of years, they add.

"We would not trade Merrill Lynch's competitive position with any other company," Merrill told its employees yesterday. "So while they take on the challenges of merging their corporate cultures, we will face the dramatic opportunities of the years ahead from a position of established strength and clear strategic direction." Merrill declined further comment.

On-Line Service

The new firm will also move to increase its distribution of stocks through the Internet. Dean Witter recently acquired Lombard Brokerage Inc., a small San Francisco firm best known for its on-line trading service. "Over time we see a lot of Internet-based distribution," a Morgan Stanley executive says.

But Morgan Stanley and Dean Witter executives feel sure the Internet can't make brokerage firms superfluous. "We have had people say that bricks and mortars are a thing of the past, and, in some sectors of the financial industry, that is true," says Philip Duff, who will be the merged firm's chief financial officer. "But we believe that more than half of the population will continue to buy investment products with financial advice and that advice will be delivered by humans."

Brokerage firms have made a variety of moves to snare small investors in recent years. Take mutual funds: Brokers at full-service firms like Smith Barney have long put dinner on the table by imposing an up-front sales charge, or load, on every mutual fund they sell. But times are changing: Broker-sold funds have been losing market share to no-load funds, available commission-free from the fund sponsors or from discount brokerage firms.

Smith Barney and Merrill recently took the bold step of selling no-load funds themselves, in addition to their load funds—the Wall Street equivalent of sleeping with the enemy.

Brokers who steer clients into no-load funds won't go hungry. While clients of the full-service brokerage firms won't pay an up-front commission to buy some funds, they will have to pay an annual account fee of up to 1.5% of assets.

More Services

Smith Barney and Merrill are betting that with the explosion in the size of the mutual-fund industry, they can keep old clients and lure new ones by offering more services to investors who have come to expect lower costs. But by adding no-load funds to their "proprietary" mutual funds, brokerage firms are taking a risk, wagering that they won't compete against themselves to a damaging extent.

"If one product cannibalizes another, so be it," Smith Barney's Mr. Dimon said last year. "We want to do what is right for our clients."

Some brokerage firms are taking other steps to snare the little guy. Prudential Securities Inc. bought 20,000 brokerage accounts of small-fry investors from Lehman Brothers Holdings Inc. for $1 million in 1995. The move brought to Prudential the Lehman accounts that had $25,000 or less in assets. Typically, an account transfer like that occurs only when a Wall Street firm folds, is sold or jettisons its brokerage operations. The unusual agreement was a clear sign that Prudential, which now has 2.2 million customer accounts, was scrambling to offset erosion in brokers and accounts in recent years. The firm is a unit of Prudential Insurance Co. of America.

Merrill is bidding for more individual investors with a client-reward program that works like frequent-flier miles. People who keep at least $100,000 in their Merrill accounts are offered a batch of commission-free stock and bond trades, financial planning and other services for one annual fee. It starts at 1.5% of assets for "bronze" customers, with the rate shrinking to less than 1% for seven-figure "platinum" accounts.

'Index Funds'

With the program, Merrill is seeking to attract investors who might avoid full-service firms because they believe the commissions are too high or who think there is a conflict of interest between broker and client.

Now, Merrill even is offering small investors its own "index funds," mutual funds structured to mirror the performance of a benchmark such as the Standard & Poor's 500. Since index funds don't try to beat the market, they run counter to the brokerage-firm thinking that fund investors want active management to protect them amid market slumps.

In this frenzied play for individuals' wealth, the odd man out is the insurance industry. Middle-class baby boomers, concerned not just about prematurely dying but also about outliving their savings, are drawn to investment products that offer their purveyors only scant profit margins. The fees from mutual funds are a lot skinnier than those on conventional life insurance. Insurance companies, even when they have had the chance to sell directly competing products, have produced only lackluster, if not embarrassing, results.

Joining Forces

To make matters worse, securities firms are increasingly invading the in-surance industry's turf through sales of life insurance.

The insurance industry has tried to fight back. The result has been a series of mergers and acquisitions. Analysts predict further consolidation as the companies try to gain the economies of scale necessary to make money on thin-margin products. Traditional life insurers also are trying to reposition themselves as more diversified financial-services companies.

"The days of dominating sales to middle-America are gone, and insurance companies that believe they can stick to their knitting are going to get annihilated by" discount brokers such as Charles Schwab Corp., mutual-fund giants such as Fidelity, diversified financial-services companies such as American Express Co. and brokerage behemoths such as Morgan Stanley, Dean Witter, says David F. D'Alessandro, president of Boston's John Hancock Mutual Life Insurance Co.

This competitive battle will only intensify. Executives of Morgan Stanley and Dean Witter already are looking for new ways to find small investors.

Greeting Cards

In particular, they want to capitalize on investors' love affair with credit cards. "We love the [credit card] business," says John Mack, who will be president and chief operating officer of the new firm. He says the Dean Witter card-holder list is one "that we think is going to have tremendous potential for doing more business." Discover ranked No. 3 among card companies with $34.4 billion in credit-card balances outstanding as of year end, and plans are afoot to expand the operation abroad.

But the biggest allure for the marriage remains old-fashioned asset management. About $146 billion of the merged firm's assets under management will be in an array of mutual funds, including Morgan Stanley's newly acquired Van Kampen American Capital funds and Dean Witter's Intercapital funds.

Roughly 11% of Morgan Stanley's net income last year stemmed from recurring fee businesses such as asset management, people familiar with the situation say. (The total included just one month of income from Van Kampen American Capital.) Based on pro-forma projections, the asset-management and credit-card business would account for roughly 40% of the combined firm's net income this year.

Country Funds

At the same time, its executives say the merger will open new avenues for Morgan Stanley's investment-banking products. These include so-called country funds—mutual funds that invest in a narrow geographic sector—and preferred-stock issues. Both of these investments have been popular among small investors.

"We can both now be competitive for business where we couldn't be competitive before—where 90% of the buying comes from the individual," says Morgan Stanley Chairman Richard Fisher, who will be chairman of the executive committee of the new firm's board.

The move to embrace individual investors comes as investment banks catering to big institutions have slowly come to realize the declining profit margins in their business. In the early 1980s, the annual return on equity for large investment banks ranged from a high of 50% to a low of 27%, according to Sanford C. Bernstein & Co. But by the 1990s, returns for large investment banks had fallen sharply, fluctuating from minus 4% in 1994 to 22% in 1991.

Through it all, the potential of the little guy was driven home to Morgan Stanley executives by one simple statistic: In 1994, Morgan Stanley had an 8.8% return on equity. Dean Witter's? 19.6%. Says Mr. Fisher: "That really struck us."

—Leslie Scism contributed to this article
February 6, 1997

with $14.8 billion for Morgan Stanley, Dean Witter); number of brokers (about 13,700 versus 9,946); retail clients (5.8 million versus 3.5 million); and offices worldwide (969 compared with 435). Merrill also is a leader in generating steady streams of income from managing assets. The "Bull" now generates nearly two-thirds of its annual income from recurring management fees, up from less than 40 percent in 1990. By contrast, asset-management fees make up just 20 percent of the Morgan Stanley, Dean Witter's pro-forma 1997 net income, say people familiar with the matter. That percentage is expected to rise to 25–30 percent over the next couple of years, they added.

"In attempting to create a dual franchise, Morgan Stanley and Dean Witter are validating the business strategy that Merrill Lynch has had in place for two decades," Merrill sniffed in an internal memorandum the day the merger was announced. "So while they take on the challenges of merging their corporate cultures, we will face the dramatic opportunities of the years ahead from a position of established strength and clear strategic direction."

Behind the deal was a bid to snatch the ballooning assets of small investors, particularly in mutual funds. The combined Morgan Stanley, Dean Witter boasts $338 billion in assets under management, making it one of the world's largest money-management concerns. They want even more of a piece of the cascading money small investors are pouring into stocks. In the past ten years, the percentage of households' financial assets in stocks has more than doubled, to about 50 percent. In 1996 and 1997, investors purchased a total of about $250 billion of stock funds. And the newly combined firm knew all too well that managing such vast assets meant recurring revenue streams that blunt the impact of cyclical earnings inherent to Wall Street.

"There's a realization on the part of the very big houses that having both institutional and retail capability is a benefit," said Jamie Dimon, Smith Barney chairman. He predicted in February 1997 that more mergers would follow. "This opens the door to lots of thoughts and conversations—for everybody." He was prescient. Within months, the Street's foundation was rejiggered amid a flurry of mergers: Smith Barney–Salomon Inc., Bankers New York Trust Corp.–Alex Brown Inc., SBC Warburg–Dillon Read, BankAmerica Corp.–Robertson Stephens & Co., and NationsBank Corp.–Montgomery Securities.

One benefit of merging is sheer heft. "There's nothing like an $11 billion equity base to absorb the impact of a rogue trader or a merchant banking deal that goes bad or a derivatives model that fails utterly," said *Gimme Credit*, a Chicago market newsletter. "In fact, there's a good reason Merrill Lynch is the only broker we've ever recommended: We believe the business is so unpredictable and virtually unanalyzable that we only feel safety in very large numbers."

Dean Witter's chairman and chief executive, Philip Purcell, dubbed "Mr. Retail," was given the chairman title of the newly combined firm. But it was the Morgan Stanley executives who held one key measure of the power at the merged firm. These Morgan Stanley insiders, who owned 40 percent of Morgan Stanley stock in the form of restricted stock, options and other compensation, had about an 18 percent stake in the combined company when it was completed. That was more than twice the size of 6.77 percent stake held by Dean Witter employees in the new company. With Morgan Stanley insiders holding the biggest single block of stock of the new firm, it wasn't as surprising that Morgan Stanley's president, John J. Mack—widely viewed as a dynamic and hands-on manager—agreed to take what was ostensibly the No. 2 spot as president and chief operating officer of the new firm.

"The guy who owns the ball kind of dictates the game to a great extent," said New York money manager Michael Holland. Added William Benedetto, who ran Dean Witter's investment-banking operations in the early 1980s, "Eighteen percent is a big voting block. Phil is going to have to listen to that insider group more than he probably listens to his own executives because of their vote." (Morgan officials note that their stock is widely spread, diluting any impact that it could have.)

Though the merger pointed the way to the future, it also brought back a blast from the past. Bruce Wasserstein, the 1980s king of the megamerger, helped advise Dean Witter on the deal. His firm, Wasserstein Perella & Co., had been synonymous with hostile takeovers a decade ago, though more recently it has been in the thick of the mergers-advisory business. Mr. Wasserstein's longtime relationship with certain Dean Witter directors, as well as his firm's status as a specialty boutique, probably helped land the job of advising Dean Witter on the Morgan Stanley deal. "Neither side would likely have been comfortable with one of their bulge-bracket competitors understanding either firm's strategy" or inspecting either firm's books, said Fred Seegal, a partner of Mr. Wasserstein and a former Salomon Brothers Inc. executive.

The merger marked a remarkable change in strategy for white-shoe Morgan Stanley. Unlike Dean Witter, which serves mostly small investors, Morgan Stanley long has catered to Wall Street's biggest blue-chip clients. This dates back to when the firm was the investment-banking arm of J. P. Morgan & Co., before the two giant institutions were split apart during the Depression. After the stock-market crash of 1929, the Glass-Steagall Act mandated the separation of commercial banks and securities firms.

But in recent years, Morgan Stanley slowly has been cozying up to individual investors, as they have entered the stock market in droves through mutual funds. In 1996, the firm bought Van Kampen/American Capital, an Oakbrook Terrace, Illinois, asset-management firm with $39.6 billion in mutual funds sold by brokers. The acquisition, though richly priced, thrust Morgan Stanley squarely into the retail arena, forcing it to look for other ways to distribute the mutual funds. So the merger gave Morgan Stanley, with its risky investment-banking and trading businesses, a portfolio of stable franchises such as asset management and credit cards.

Dean Witter gained from the deal, too. The merger provided access to a vast array of investment-banking products, including initial public stock offerings and bond deals to sell to small investors. "For Dean Witter, the great benefit is the added breadth of product," Mr. Purcell said. Dean Witter had been part of Sears, Roebuck & Co. throughout most of the 1980s, which attempted with little success to combine the securities business with its department stores to become a financial supermarket. Sears sold a stake to the public in 1993 and then distributed its remaining 80 percent interest to Sears shareholders the same year.

Melding the securities firms' cultures over the long haul will be a challenge. The pinstriped investment bankers who thrive at Morgan Stanley by catering to CEOs historically haven't meshed well with hard-charging brokers who deal with Mom and Pop. And there are great disparities in the compensation of the two groups. Highlighting this pay gap was the 1996 pay package of Dean Witter's Mr. Purcell, who was tapped to be chairman of the newly merged firm. He was paid $4.3 million in cash and stock, less than all five of Morgan Stanley's top executives—and less than half the $10 million Morgan Stanley paid Mr. Mack, who is the merged firm's No. 2 executive. (Mr. Purcell made up the gap in 1997; he received $14.4 million in cash and restricted stock—on par with Mr. Mack—in addition to $36.4 million by exercising stock options.)

And Dean Witter has had cultural problems of its own, partly stemming from the clients it has catered to. In the 1980s, the firm made a failed push for its brokers to sell stocks in Sears stores. The plan—derisively referred to on Wall Street as "Socks and Stocks"—led Dean Witter brokers to gripe that they didn't make much money trying to sell stocks and other investments to customers shopping for shirts and vacuum cleaners.

One former Dean Witter broker recalled the embarrassment of calling clients around Christmastime from a Dean Witter booth at Sears's Jersey City, New Jersey, store—just across from the children's department. A Disney movie video was blaring in the background. Said the broker: "It sounded like I was calling them from my house with the kids screaming in the background."

Said Alan C. Synder, a former Dean Witter executive: "Sears believed that the Dean Witter client was a subset of its overall client base, but everyone may have underestimated how difficult cross-selling truly is."

Dean Witter nevertheless thrived by avoiding many of the excesses of its rivals in the 1980s. It sidestepped underwriting high-risk junk bonds and making "bridge" loans to temporarily finance corporate acquisitions. It also historically had shunned traditional Wall Street perks such as fancy offices. But in pursuing small investors, Dean Witter has generated some problems along with the profits. Like many Wall Street firms, it has pushed its brokers to sell internally managed—and thus more profitable—mutual funds, rather than competing mutual funds. Brokers thus have faced the somewhat unpleasant task of foisting on their clients funds that have had only mediocre results compared to those of competing fund families. The sensitivity over the firm's fund performance boiled over several years back when Dean Witter fired a top broker in Fort Worth, Texas, after he wrote a letter of apology to a customer over the firm's fund performance. A Dean Witter spokesman said at the time that the broker was "fired not for the (letter's) content but for violating firm policy about sending anything to a client without having it reviewed by a manager."

There's no denying that the new Morgan Stanley, Dean Witter is amply diversified. In the 1990s, the combined firm would have derived half its pro-forma earnings from institutional businesses, such as trading, underwriting and mergers-advisory work; 24 percent from retail brokerage; and 26 percent from credit services, analysts say. This split is similar to that at rival Merrill (except that half Morgan Stanley, Dean Witter's retail-type earnings would have come from credit cards). Analysts look for that split to eventually shift at the new firm to 30 percent institutional, 40 percent retail and 30 percent credit services.

The newly combined firm set annual revenue targets of between 15 percent and 20 percent. "Earnings should follow right through," said Mr. Mack, the firm's president. Morgan Stanley, Dean Witter is betting it can achieve the higher revenue-growth levels from higher broker productivity and a greater share of markets such as real-estate investment trusts, preferred-stock issues and asset-backed securities. Dean Witter's individual-investor clients like products such as high-yielding preferred stock because they provide hefty current income.

"We ought to be the leader in retail products such as real-estate investment trusts, asset-backed securities and preferred stock," Mr. Purcell, the firm's chairman, said. "There is no excuse for us not being in the top three" in these areas.

By 2001, Morgan Stanley, Dean Witter should have a "normal" return-on-equity of 19 percent according to a 1997 report by Sanford C. Bernstein & Co. (This compares with projected ROEs in 2001 of 14 percent at Morgan Stanley and 15.5 percent at Dean Witter, Bernstein said.) Thus, the combined firm's ROE would be in line with industry leader Merrill—a very lofty standard, indeed.

At the very least, some analysts said, there has been some synergy, an element missing in many past Wall Street mergers. The new firm should show higher earnings, a larger and more solid base of assets, a diversified earnings stream and impressive money-management growth, according to a report by rival Prudential Securities Inc. "We expect that the potential to cross-sell product into the Dean Witter retail system could be substantial, and with the development of Dean Witter's Internet business, opportunities could be dramatic," the Prudential report said.

Other analysts are similarly ebullient. "We expect Morgan Stanley, Dean Witter to outearn and outgrow the other retail and institutional companies," said the Bernstein report. "Earnings accretion from the merger, though limited near-term, is projected at 25–30% by 2001, taking the company's growth to mid-teen levels. The quality of the combined company's earnings is also projected to improve over time, reflecting the effects of retail order flow on the more-institutional businesses."

As usual, it is the continuing risk of colliding cultures that most threatens the long-term effectiveness of the deal. Corporate culture clashes have become the leading cause of merger failures, according to management consultants. A ten-year study of 340 major acquisitions by Mercer Management Consulting Inc. found that total shareholder returns for 57 percent of the merged concerns lagged behind their industry averages three years after the transactions.

But the cultural chasm could be smoothed at Morgan Stanley, Dean Witter because there is little overlap in the firms' businesses. Indeed, the merger led to only a few hundred job cuts, resulting in savings of about $250 million— relatively small numbers for two firms that together earned nearly $2 billion in 1996 and employed about 45,000 people.

One matter was clear from the get-go: There was little doubt the merger would go through. A major reason is that the proposed marriage would have been very expensive to walk away from. If either party ended up striking a better deal with another partner, it would cost them $250 million—representing about 2.5 percent of the deal's value. In addition to the steep breakup fee, each firm gave the other an option to acquire a big chunk of the other's stock—19.9 percent of its then-outstanding shares—if a higher bidder came along. There was nothing to worry about. The deal was approved by shareholders without a hitch.

Now, the question is what firm Morgan Stanley, Dean Witter will look to merge with next. After the merger was announced in February 1997, Morgan Stanley executives continued to prowl the Wall Street waterfront.

Meanwhile, the newly combined firm made it clear to analysts that it seeks equally strong legs in its three businesses: institutional and retail brokerage and credit cards. But Morgan Stanley, Dean Witter's credit-card operations look relatively weak. Thus, "it is our belief that the ideal next merger or joint venture partner would be American Express," said Sanford C. Bernstein in its 1997 report. "In joining the companies together in some way, they would significantly strengthen their credit cards business, their asset management business and their retail securities business."

It's only a matter of time, analysts said, before the other shoe drops.

Making the Merger Work

The new stock symbol "MWD" appeared on the Big Board in June 1997, the symbolic affirmation that the merger of Morgan Stanley and Dean Witter was complete. The new stock symbol represented each of the brands of the combined firm, with "M" standing for Morgan Stanley, "W" representing Dean Witter and "D" for Discover. ("MDD," another possible symbol for the new firm, already was taken by McDonald & Co. Investments, a Cleveland brokerage firm.)

But in the four months before their marriage was approved by shareholders, the two firms were living together quite nicely. Morgan Stanley's bankers had been underwriting securities such as high-yielding preferred stock that typically was marketed to the individual investors served by Dean Witter. In May 1997, for instance, Dean Witter's army of 9,300 brokers played an important part in selling a $150 million issue of United Dominion Realty $25 perpetual preferred yielding 8.6 percent, which Morgan Stanley comanaged. Dean Witter brokers were almost exclusively responsible for selling the shares allocated to Morgan Stanley in the deal. "We have already seen that the retail distribution capability combined with investment banking creates business," Morgan Stanley Chairman Richard Fisher said after the annual meeting in May at which shareholders of the firm approved the merger.

Morgan Stanley also used its underwriting prowess to upgrade some of Dean Witter's longstanding relationships. In May 1997, Morgan Stanley won an assignment to underwrite a $400 million issue of Bank of New York trust preferred securities. Though Dean Witter had long had a close relationship with Bank of New York, it hadn't lead-managed any securities offerings for the bank, according to Securities Data Co. In the Bank of New York deal, Morgan Stanley and Merrill jointly ran the books.

By then, Morgan Stanley already had begun leaning on Dean Witter brokers to sell other types of securities issues as well. In a 1997 Morgan Stanley underwriting of a $1.25 billion global floating-rate note for General Motors Acceptance Corp., about 40 percent of Morgan Stanley's U.S. allotment on the deal was pushed through the Dean Witter system, according to people familiar with the situation.

"We are capturing a bigger chunk of the economics" on deals because the firm can distribute more stock on its own and doesn't have to syndicate distribution to other retail-brokerage firms, Morgan Stanley Chief Financial Officer Philip Duff said at the time. (Mr. Duff relinquished his post to run the firm's Van Kampen/American Capital mutual-fund company.)

The merger seemed to pay immediate dividends. In the first calendar quarter since the union with Dean Witter was completed, Morgan Stanley waltzed to the top of the charts in some key measures of investment-banking performance. The merged firm was the No. 1 underwriter of U.S. stocks and initial public stock offerings, or IPOs. More important to its bottom line, Morgan Stanley took in the largest amount among all Wall Street firms of disclosed fees—$280 million—for underwriting stocks and bonds and advising companies on mergers and acquisitions.

In the end, while Morgan Stanley's name may have come first in the merger, Dean Witter won an important battle. In softball. Teams from the two companies squared off against each other in the 1997 Financial District Softball League best-of-five playoffs. Dean Witter took the crown by winning game five, 6–4.

There were some glitches in the merger, of course. Veteran Morgan Stanley investment banker Robert Scott, tapped to head the firm's transition team, suffered a heart attack; Mr. Scott later succeeded Mr. Duff as the firm's chief financial officer. And there were some slip-ups. The new firm didn't move quickly enough to merge research departments of the two firms, resulting in notable departures such as computer analyst Jay Stevens. Then there was the issue of musical chairs, a delicate issue in the wake of a big merger. Dean Witter officials snared some high-profile spots: In addition to the top one— Chairman Purcell—Christine A. Edwards, Dean Witter's general counsel, was appointed the top lawyer of the combined firm, over Morgan Stanley's general counsel.

The two firms first held talks regarding a possible merger for well over a year before surprising Wall Street with the news. (Since 1993, in fact, the two firms had discussed a possible joint venture or alliance between them, according to regulatory filings.) Representatives of both companies began to meet from June to October 1995 regarding a possible joint venture, and talked about the consolidation in the financial-services industry.

Morgan Stanley and Dean Witter entered into a confidentiality agreement in August 1995 and a combination of the two firms was considered in the late fall of 1995, regulatory filings show. After they decided to end talks during the first quarter of 1996, the issue simmered. Then the companies met again on December 4, 1996, discussing a possible "merger of equals." There were further meetings. All were kept secret, as the two firms exchanged financial data and began to negotiate the terms of a deal. The $10.5 billion transaction was first reported in *The Wall Street Journal*, on February 5, 1996.

After the merger was completed, in October 1997 the firm's officials scrambled to stamp out a brush fire sparked by a kiss-and-tell book. Written by a former Morgan Stanley derivatives salesman, the book, "F.I.A.S.C.O.: Blood in the Water on Wall Street," suggested that the firm frequently placed profit ahead of its clients' interests as it made an aggressive and lucrative push into the then-booming derivatives business. Morgan Stanley didn't dispute the book's claim that its derivatives-product group took in some $1 billion in fees from 1993 to 1995, but it did take issue with the book's contention that it designed complex securities with catchy names to sell to unsophisticated clients.

The book's subtitle came from a quote the author attributed to John Mack, now the merged firm's president. After a pair of big corporate clients of Bankers Trust New York Corp. suffered some highly publicized derivatives losses in early 1994, the book says, Mr. Mack exhorted his troops to take advantage of their own clients' distress, saying: "There's blood in the water. Let's go kill someone." Through a spokeswoman, Mr. Mack denied ever making the statement.

In a more significant embarrassment, a Morgan Stanley compliance officer was arrested in late 1997 on charges of selling inside information she obtained as part of her job to guard against insider trading by others at the giant securities firm. Morgan Stanley fired the officer, Marisa Baridis, who pleaded guilty in a New York federal court in December 1997 to two counts of violating federal securities laws. Ms. Baridis, who joined Morgan Stanley in April 1997, worked in the firm's legal department at a salary of about $70,000. She also was accused of selling information at her previous compliance job at Smith Barney Inc., where she worked for four years.

A federal grand jury indicted Ms. Baridis, among others outside the firm, alleging a wide-ranging conspiracy involving the stocks of thirteen companies that netted a total of more than $1 million in ill-gotten gains. Ms. Baridis's job at both Morgan Stanley and Smith Barney was to make sure brokers didn't trade on information about deals the firms' investment bankers were working on. Her title at Smith Barney was "Chinese Wall coordinator." In a scene reminiscent of the 1980s insider-trading scandal, Ms. Baridis was arrested at Morgan Stanley's midtown Manhattan offices. The twenty-nine-year-old law school graduate was summoned by supervisors to an office on the thirty-eighth floor, where she was met by investigators. Prosecutors said Ms. Baridis's supervisors at Morgan Stanley didn't know about the alleged illegal trading until they were called before arresting the woman.

A Morgan Stanley spokeswoman said the firm fired Ms. Baridis "after reviewing the grand jury indictment." The indictment quoted Ms. Baridis acknowledging the consequences of being caught in a conversation with an unidentified man that was recorded on a surveillance tape. "It's the most illegal-est thing you can do," the indictment quoted Ms. Baridis as saying.

The Spin Desk

Underwriters Set Aside IPO Stock for Officials Of Potential Customers

Coincidentally or Otherwise, Work Frequently Follows For the Investment Bank

Bribery, or Just Business?

By MICHAEL SICONOLFI
Staff Reporter of THE WALL STREET JOURNAL

Joseph Cayre was ecstatic.

Holding an investment "road show" for a firm he heads that was about to go public, Mr. Cayre reveled in the first-day stock surge of an unrelated company, Pixar Animation Studios, that had just gone public itself. He boasted that he had just turned a quick $2 million profit on 100,000 Pixar shares, witnesses to the 1995 incident say.

Where did he get a huge chunk of one of the year's most coveted initial public stock offerings, one that surged 77% on its first day of trading? Robertson Stephens Inc., Pixar's lead investment bank, had allocated the shares to Mr. Cayre's personal brokerage account.

Less than a month later, Mr. Cayre's company used Robertson Stephens for its own initial public offering. After it had become publicly held, the company, GT Interactive Software Corp., hired Robertson Stephens to advise it on acquisitions. Robertson Stephens's total fees: more than $5 million.

Mr. Cayre says there was no quid pro quo. He hired Robertson Stephens simply because he liked an investment banker at the firm, he says. But he adds that he had personally asked Robertson Stephens's chairman, Sanford Robertson, for the 100,000-share Pixar allocation. "I believe it's good business," he says.

Good Customer

Mr. Robertson, for his part, says Mr. Cayre is "a very, very good client" who has a lot of money in funds run by Robertson Stephens. "We try to run an honest business. I don't see anything wrong giving a good client a new issue," Mr. Robertson says. He, too, sees no quid pro quo. However, when an internal debate arose within the investment bank about making such a big Pixar allocation, Mr. Robertson recalls that Mr. Cayre threatened to take his business elsewhere if he didn't get all 100,000 Pixar shares.

Such is the world of Wall Street's "spin desks." Many investment banks silently allocate chunks of hot new stocks to the personal brokerage accounts they hold for corporate executives and venture capitalists—"spinning," or flipping, the shares on the day of the IPO for quick profits—in an apparent bid for business from the executives' firms.

"It's like sand on a railroad wheel," says Edward McCann, a former senior technology banker at Hambrecht & Quist LLC, which is an active spin player. "It helps you get under way sooner and faster."

Crucial Distinction

This isn't just a matter of the big players getting the breaks. It is no news that underwriters make most of the shares in hot IPOs available not to the little-guy investor but to institutions, such as mutual-fund companies and pension funds, that provide a lot of trading commissions and other business. But there is a critical difference: Spin shares don't go to the corporate customer itself—they go to individuals at the corporation who are in a position to sway the company's decisions.

"It's a bribe, no question about it," contends Robert Messih, a managing director at Salomon Inc., which doesn't have a brokerage arm or engage in spinning. "You pay them off and expect you're going to get treated in kind when they do the transaction."

Spin desks may violate regulatory rules. (The term is used by many bankers, though some say they haven't heard it.) The National Association of Securities Dealers requires investment banks to make a bona fide distribution of IPO shares and bars them from selling such shares to "any senior officer" of an "institutional-type account" who "may influence or whose activities directly or indirectly involve or are related to the function of buying or selling securities" for such institutional-type accounts.

But there hasn't been any enforcement action. In fact, officials at the NASD and Securities and Exchange Commission say they were unaware of spinning until contacted by a reporter. Roger Sherman, the NASD's enforcement chief, says such a practice "raises a host of potential problems," but each case would have to be assessed separately. NASD lawyer Gary Goldsholle adds that there could be a violation even without any finding of a quid pro quo.

No Problem

Cristina Morgan, Hambrecht & Quist's managing director of investment banking, isn't worried. The San Francisco firm is an active spin player, but she sees nothing wrong with the practice, likening it to such perks as free golf outings. "What we're talking about is trying to solicit business," Ms. Morgan says. "What do you think about taking them out to dinner? What do you think about that? We throw lavish parties with caviar. Is that not trying to influence them, their behavior? I suggest that it is." Allocating hot IPOs to corporate executives, she argues, is "not illegal. It's not immoral. It's a business decision."

In any case, it is rampant. "It's as common as water, and you can have all you want" if you are a senior executive or venture capitalist at a company that potentially will do business with Wall Street, says David Cary, chief financial officer at i2 Technologies Inc., an Irving, Texas, software company.

He should know. Mr. Cary says he and other senior i2 Technologies executives were showered with shares in hot IPOs from several investment banks, including Hambrecht & Quist, which co-managed i2 Technologies' IPO in 1996. Mr. Cary says that in 1995 H&Q let him buy 400 shares of Netscape Communications Corp. at the offering price. He cashed in for a quick $5,000 profit.

His risk was as close to zero as it gets. That's because H&Q didn't allocate the shares to Mr. Cary's personal brokerage account until after Netscape shares had begun trading and were up sharply, Mr. Cary says.

He adds that H&Q took the action without even asking him. "All I know is I'd get a phone call saying, 'Hey, we got some shares for you.' "

Mr. Cary at first couldn't comprehend how easy it was to cash in. "The first couple of times, [firms] literally explained to me what they were doing: 'I'm giving you shares at the IPO price,' " he says. "Nobody ever does that," was his reply. The response, he says: "Yes, we do."

IPO allocations were so common at i2 Technologies that the company set a policy about receiving them. "Everyone on the executive team got the same share," Mr. Cary says. "It was a very rigid rule—either give to all or none."

He says the stock didn't sway i2 Technologies' investment-bank choice when it went public. The company picked H&Q as a co-manager but used the larger Goldman, Sachs & Co. as lead manager. "A guaranteed $5,000 IPO 'friend of the firm' allocation won't do anything at all," he says. "It won't do anything to me."

Even so, Mr. Cary became uncomfortable with the practice, and last year i2 Technologies told its executives they could no longer accept spin shares.

Who Gets the Stock

Here is how the process works. Investment banks managing an IPO for a fledgling company line up buyers of the shares at the offering price. IPO shares are much sought-after, because a new stock frequently soars on its first day of trading, buoyed by buying from eager investors who didn't get in on the ground floor. Then the shares often slip back as demand abates.

The banks offer most of the shares to big institutional client companies. A small number, known as the "retail pot," are set aside for individuals, and spin shares typically come from this pot. That leaves even fewer IPO shares for the small investor with no connections.

Spinning got going in the 1980s and exploded during the 1990s bull market, as underwriters began competing fiercely to handle initial offerings. The practice "ain't going to stop," predicts A.B. "Buzzy" Krongard, a vice chairman of Bankers Trust New York Corp. "There's too much of a cause and effect."

Recently, however, Wall Street has seen a bit of a backlash. The National Venture Capital Association, a trade group, has cautioned members that taking such IPOs could lead to regulation of the venture-capital community.

And despite the easy money, a few people are just saying no. Besides Mr. Cary and others at i2 Technologies, they include officials of two venture-capital firms, Sequoia Partners in Menlo Park, Calif., and Greylock Management Corp. in Boston. "It doesn't seem to be the right thing to do," says Henry McCance, Greylock general partner.

After the Fact

Particularly bothersome to critics is the practice of providing an executive with a share allocation—together with a quick, profitable sale—after trading is under way. This is possible if a corporate executive has a discretionary account at an underwriting firm, which permits a broker there to trade for the executive.

"At its extreme," explains Frank Quattrone, chief executive of Deutsche Morgan Grenfell Inc.'s technology group in Menlo Park, "an IPO is priced Wednesday. Thursday morning, you call 25 venture capitalists and say, 'By the way, XYZ just went public at 15; it's now trading at 30. You just sold the allocation at $29^{1}/_{2}$. I hope you're happy.' That to me is smarmy."

Consider the offer made to Gregory Hinckley. In 1995, Mr. Hinckley, then the chief financial officer of VLSI Technology Inc., a publicly held San Jose, Calif., chip maker, received a call from an administrative assistant at Needham & Co. in New York. The message: 1,000 shares of Oak Technology Inc. had been "reserved in your name," say two people familiar with the matter. With the newly public Oak shares already trading and up sharply, Mr. Hinckley's immediate, guaranteed profit would total nearly $10,000. He declined the offer.

Mr. Hinckley confirms that he has been approached "periodically" with offers of spin shares, and he says they are "enough probably to influence" some executives to direct business to the investment banks. Mr. Hinckley, now chief financial officer of Mentor Graphics Corp. in Wilsonville, Ore., won't say much more about what he calls Wall Street's version of a "modern morality play." But he adds: "My view is you don't ever screw around with your integrity for pocket change—and this was pocket change. It wouldn't influence me."

Pressure on Underwriter

Unlike Mr. Hinckley, VLSI Technology Chairman Alfred Stein accepted more than 1,000 shares of Oak Technology from Needham, a person close to the transaction says. And when Salomon Brothers later arranged a stock offering for VLSI, Mr. Stein demanded that Salomon assign Needham—which was a minor member of the syndicate—more of the shares to sell, according to Salomon's Mr. Messih.

"If it were left to his doing, he would have paid Needham more than the co-managers," an incredulous Mr. Messih says. "We told him, 'You can't do that; it's not appropriate.' " Salomon didn't let Needham have the increased allocation.

Despite repeated requests, Mr. Stein will "remain unavailable for comment," says VLSI's public-relations director. As for Needham, its chairman, George Needham, says, "Those things can happen." But he adds that his firm now has formally banned spinning. "Our policy is not to do this stuff," Mr. Needham says. "The practice really smells."

Too Few Shares

Yet some investment bankers say they are penalized if they don't keep pace in allocating IPO shares to executives. Andrew "Flip" Filipowski, president and chief executive of Platinum Technology Inc. of Oakbrook Terrace, Ill., complained about his IPO allocations a few years back in a private meeting with investment bankers at Robertson Stephens. In a suite at the Stanford Court hotel in San Francisco, Mr. Filipowski told Michael McCaffery, Robertson's president and chief executive, there was a "problem" in the relationship, witnesses say.

"You're giving me 500 and 1,000 shares, and H&Q is giving me 5,000 and

10,000 shares on a deal," Mr. Filipowski told Mr. McCaffery, the witnesses say. "Even when they can't contact me, they give me stock and sell it."

Robertson Stephens—recently bought by BankAmerica Inc.—does use spin shares, but its executives contend the firm won't go so far as to allocate them at the offering price after trading has begun. Mr. McCaffery shot back: "If H&Q wants to do that for you, they can. But it's legally wrong, morally wrong, and we're not going to do it."

Bringing in DLJ

H&Q and Roberston Stephens had co-managed Platinum Technology's IPO. But after the hotel talk, Platinum reduced Robertson Stephens's role, eventually picking rival Donaldson, Lufkin & Jenrette Inc. to join H&Q as a lead manager.

Mr. McCaffery referred a call to a spokeswoman, who said the executive recalled the incident but "would never have said it wasn't legal."

Mr. Filipowski says he has no recollection of the hotel discussion, but he denies pressuring Robertson Stephens. "That uncategorically can't be," he says. He says the reason he cut Robertson Stephens's role was that it "had really dropped the ball a lot" in covering his company.

Platinum's other original co-manager, H&Q, has let Mr. Filipowski in on 20 to 25 IPOs over the years in his discretionary account there, he estimates, although he says he didn't get in on the red-hot Netscape and Pixar issues. "The last time I got a special deal as far as I can remember was 200 shares of Boston Chicken," Mr. Filipowski says, and that was from a different investment bank.

H&Q's Ms. Morgan scoffs that these deals are too small to sway an executive like Mr. Filipowski, because "Flip is worth zillions." Mr. Filipowski agrees that IPO allocations have "absolutely nothing" to do with which underwriters Platinum uses. In view of how well off executives are, "it doesn't take too many brain cells to know that 200 or 500 shares don't count for diddly squat," Mr. Filipowski says. "I don't think I've ever gotten 5,000 shares—even after begging extensively to everyone."

Still, whether by coincidence or other-wise, IPO allocations sometimes are made just before executives or directors select investment banks. In August 1995, Morgan Stanley allocated 1,000-share blocks of the Netscape IPO to some executives at Arbor Software Corp. of Sunnyvale, Calif., according to several people familiar with the matter. Arbor was about to pick an underwriter for its own IPO. It chose Morgan Stanley.

Among those who accepted a Netscape allocation from Morgan Stanley and flipped the shares for a quick profit was Stephen Imbler, Arbor's chief financial officer. He says the allocation had no effect on investment-bank selection. "There was no tie," he says. "We picked Morgan Stanley partially because they're a tier-one banker—for their marquee value."

Arbor board member Douglas Leone, a venture capitalist at Sequoia, turned down the offer to buy Netscape shares. In an interview, Mr. Leone says, "I can't speak for what the other board members did or didn't do, but I will tell you I felt uncomfortable accepting 1,000 shares of a hot stock."

He adds, "I was going into a board meeting 24, 48 hours later, where I knew a number of bankers were going to be vying for the business" of managing Arbor's own IPO. But he says Arbor's selection of Morgan Stanley wasn't "swayed" by the Netscape windfall.

A 1,000-share Netscape block gained more than $30,000 in value its first day. "As it turns out, I left a great deal of money on the table," Mr. Leone says. "But I felt good about it." A spokeswoman for Morgan Stanley, now known as Morgan Stanley, Dean Witter, Discover & Co., declines to comment.

Working with Montgomery

It helps if an executive's company does a lot of business with the investment bank. Take the relationship between Montgomery Securities and Jamie Coulter, chairman of Lone Star Steakhouse & Saloon Inc. Lone Star, of Wichita, Kan., has tapped Montgomery as sole manager of four stock offerings, including its 1992 IPO. Montgomery, now a unit of NationsBank Corp. and known as NationsBanc Montgomery Securities Inc., earned millions in fees.

Montgomery has let Mr. Coulter in on numerous IPOs. In one case, according to a former Montgomery broker, Mr. Coulter, his family and business associates were allocated as much as 15,000 shares of President Riverboat, a Davenport, Iowa, casino company whose IPO Montgomery handled. The broker says the shares were flipped for Mr. Coulter for a quick profit on the first trading day.

"How do you know that?" Mr. Coulter demanded, when asked about it. "It's a private matter. I don't know if I got that or not." Two weeks later, he called back to say his personal President Riverboat allocation was 1,500 shares, not 15,000. "He had no control over the shares allocated to the individual family-member accounts," says Mr. Coulter's assistant, Christopher Wettig.

Mr. Coulter says he has a discretionary brokerage account at Montgomery but doesn't get "an inordinate amount of IPOs." He has received "1,000 or 1,500 shares of an IPO," he says, but "can't remember getting as many as 15,000 except in one instance, and it wasn't Riverboat."

Mr. Coulter says his firm continues to tap Montgomery because of a longstanding relationship. "They handled our IPO at a time that other investment-banking firms of their stature wouldn't take us public," he says.

Thomas Weisel, chairman of NationsBanc Montgomery Securities, says, "We do allocate IPOs, hot or otherwise, to our better clients. But they're not postdated," or allocated after the stock has started trading. He says there is "zero" tie between the allocations and subsequent corporate-finance activity handled by Montgomery, adding: "What we do with Jamie Coulter for his private account is only information between him and his counterpart at Montgomery."

Occasionally, spats break out over spin shares. Mr. Cayre of GT Interactive Software got into one with Robertson Stephens before GT went public. New York-based GT was majority-owned by Mr. Cayre and his family, with significant minorities held by others, including venture capitalists. Mr. Cayre, its founder, had a commitment from Robertson Stephens for 100,000 shares of the Pixar IPO, and he was livid when the investment bank tried to pull back from the allotment at the 11th hour.

Mr. Cayre yelled at Mr. Robertson: "What kind of bank are you? How can I trust you? I expect every single share." He threatened to steer his business elsewhere if Robertson Stephens didn't play ball.

"I think I remember that," Mr. Robertson says. He concedes there was internal opposition to such a big Pixar allocation.

Actually, Mr. Cayre says, he wanted even more than the 100,000-share allocation. He says he tried to pry additional Pixar shares from Robertson Stephens for his children. He didn't get them.

But there are other deals. Over the years, the video-game CEO figures, investment banks have let him in, personally, on roughly 400 initial public offerings. "Every banker has given me great IPOs," he says.

November 12, 1997

Investment Banking: White-Shoe Morgan

The combination of Morgan Stanley and Dean Witter catapulted the new firm to the top of the investment-banking heap. On its own, Morgan Stanley in the past few years had trailed behind Merrill and Goldman in the lucrative stock-underwriting rankings. To be sure, Dean Witter didn't do much investment banking, so there won't be any dramatic change. And there won't be much impact on the bond-underwriting or mergers-advisory work, because of Dean Witter's minor presence in these areas. "It is in the equity underwriting business—particularly in the overseas markets—in which we expect some addition to earnings in the wake of the merger," according to the Sanford C. Bernstein report. This is partly because access to a big brokerage force is considered even more valuable overseas than it is in the United States.

For instance, two sizzling underwriting categories where Dean Witter quickly helped Morgan Stanley win more business have been privatizations—public offerings of stock in foreign government-owned companies—and real-estate investment trusts (REITs). Morgan Stanley previously had been hampered in winning privatizations because of the firm's lack of retail-brokerage presence. Among REITs, Morgan Stanley won four underwriting assignments before the merger was completed, based on Dean Witter's extensive research coverage of such companies. Said Mr. Duff, "Morgan Stanley wouldn't have been involved in them at all [previously] because we didn't cover the companies."

Morgan Stanley came in third in 1997's underwriting derby, following Merrill and Salomon Smith Barney. The firm helped bring to market $139.5 billion of new stocks and bonds in the United States, for a 10.8 percent market share, according to Securities Data Co. Morgan Stanley managed the $2.02 billion First Union stock offering, 1997's largest stock underwriting deal by a U.S. company. The firm also jointly led the $839.8 million stock offering of Household International and sole-managed the $577.5 million SunAmerica stock underwriting, according to Securities Data.

On the merger side, Morgan Stanley in 1997 was among the advisers to MCI Communications Corp.'s $37 billion merger with WorldCom Inc.—the largest mergers transaction ever. Morgan Stanley also advised First Union Corp. in its $17.1 billion purchase of CoreStates Financial Corp. And the firm was an adviser to Barnett Banks Inc. in its $14.8 billion purchase by Nations-Bank Corp. In all, Morgan Stanley was ranked No. 3, advising U.S. companies on $207.75 billion in announced merger or acquisition deals, for a 22.6 percent market share.

Even before the merger, Morgan Stanley was generating a pretax margin on its investment-banking business of a lofty 30 to 35 percent, analysts say. "Its strong market shares in the more lucrative areas have driven earnings levels that are above those of the industry (particularly as companies have been increasingly willing to do business at low, no, or negative levels of profitability as a means of breaking in)," the Bernstein analysis said.

But these margins could be squeezed. For one thing, Dean Witter's small banking group could crimp profit somewhat. For another, Morgan Stanley could have to dole out heftier paychecks to its much-sought-after bankers to keep them from bolting to competitors offering multi-year pay guarantees.

As business has exploded, Morgan Stanley has faced some ticklish client-relationship issues. In late 1996, Morgan's top investment bankers on the AT&T account held discussions with executives at the telephone giant to smooth out ruffled feathers stemming from Morgan's decision to help advise British Telecommunications on its talks to acquire MCI Communications—a combination that would have produced an even more formidable competitor to AT&T than MCI previously was.

The Morgan Stanley-AT&T relationship dates back to the turn of the century, when a group led by J. P. Morgan installed Theodore Vail as the leader of the modern AT&T that remained intact until the 1984 breakup. In the 1990s alone it has produced disclosed fees of more than $60 million. But that long history has collided with big changes in investment banking and telecommunications. Both businesses have gone global, multiplying the potential for such conflicts as investment banks seek to serve a wider universe of clients worldwide.

Morgan's banking group got new leadership in 1997. Less than a month before the merger, the firm promoted Joseph Perella, one of Wall Street's most well-known bankers, to head its investment-banking group. Mr. Perella, a founding partner of Wasserstein Perella & Co., had been hired by Morgan in 1993 as a senior deal maker. Mr. Perella's promotion to banking chief was part of a broader reorganization, which led to the departure of Neal Garonzik, head of Morgan's mammoth stock business, who quit after it became apparent he wouldn't be elevated in the shakeup.

Mr. Perella's elevation came as a surprise. Morgan Stanley, like Goldman, has a close-knit culture and rarely brings outsiders to top-level positions. "This is the most dramatic example of someone who has come in from the outside and has been accepted into leadership" at Morgan, said Samuel Hayes, a Harvard University investment-banking professor who taught Mr. Perella in the early 1970s.

Since joining Morgan, Mr. Perella has been credited with reviving the investment bank's relationship with Time Warner Inc., which deteriorated after Morgan advised Paramount Communications Inc. on an unsuccessful attempt to break up the acquisition of Time Inc. by Warner Communications Inc. In 1996, Morgan represented Time Warner in the acquisition of Turner Broadcasting System. And Mr. Perella's longtime relationship with Sandoz Ltd. secured Morgan a berth in the biggest merger of 1996, the combination of Sandoz with Ciba-Geigy Ltd.

Throughout 1997, Morgan Stanley's stellar M&A group shone in many areas, including real-estate deals. In a six-week period in the late summer the firm advised companies on seven transactions valued at a total of $10.5 billion.

Brokerage: Blue-Collar Dean Witter

Dean Witter caters to the low end of the retail market of individual investors. Annual commissions for its brokers average far less than $300,000, compared with more than $425,000 for those at Merrill. And there have been disappointments. In 1994, two years after announcing a much-ballyhooed partnership with NationsBank Corp. to sell Dean Witter mutual funds, the two companies parted ways. People close to Dean Witter said that NationsBank wanted to sell the funds more aggressively but Dean Witter resisted. A NationsBank spokesman in 1997 said that "one of the goals behind the partnership—namely the desire of Dean Witter to establish syndicated clearing services with other banks—did not develop as anticipated."

Over the years, Dean Witter has chided its branch managers for allowing brokers to sell too many competing mutual funds. Most Wall Street firms sell roughly equal amounts of internally and externally managed mutual funds; the split at Dean Witter historically has been 75 to 25 in favor of the in-house portfolios, known as InterCapital funds. And some investors and brokers have griped about the performance of many Dean Witter funds over the years.

Analysts expect the newly combined firm to increase its brokerage force by one thousand a year through 2001, double Dean Witter's premerger plans of hiring five hundred new brokers a year. And look for the firm to change its policy of hiring fledgling brokers straight from school, turning instead to luring more experienced brokers who can more quickly add to the firm's bottom line. "We believe Morgan Stanley, Dean Witter's goal is to move to the #1 slot in terms of account executives (retail brokers) over the next several years, overtaking Merrill Lynch," according to the 1997 Bernstein report.

Bernstein estimates that the combined firm's pro-forma return on equity for the retail-brokerage business would have been 26 percent in the 1990s. This compares with an average of 22 percent for Merrill (though Bernstein estimated that Merrill's ROE more recently rose to the mid-30 percent range) and to 34 percent for Smith Barney. Bernstein projects that the new firm's retail-securities return will be an estimated 23 percent in 2001, adding: "This will be somewhat lower than the numbers we anticipate for Merrill Lynch and Smith Barney."

The new firm also moved to increase its distribution of stocks through the Internet. Just months before the merger, Dean Witter had bought Lombard Brokerage Inc., a small San Francisco firm best known for its on-line trading service. "Industry securities growth through the Internet will be explosive [almost by definition, given its low starting base]," according to Sanford C. Bernstein. "We expect that in the short- to medium-term, business in the channel will not cannibalize that in the full-service channel." Said a Morgan Stanley executive: "Over time we see a lot of Internet-based distribution."

But not necessarily in the futures business. The firm sold its institutional-futures operations to Credit Agricole's Banque Indosuez in 1997. The sale underscored that the new giant didn't want a presence in futures as it did in other, more profitable areas. While the retail, or individual-investor, clients from Dean Witter continue to execute trades through the merged firm, Dean Witter's institutional business went to the French firm, which paid about $25 million for the business and seats on futures exchanges that went with it.

It was an unexpected move. Immediately following the merger announcement, futures executives had noted how the new firm, boasting nearly $2.5 billion in customer equity invested in commodities and futures exchanges, had vaulted Dean Witter ahead of leader Merrill. There had been high hopes. "Dean Witter has a great sales force and Morgan Stanley has a lot of product and the best research on the Street," John Damgard, president of the Futures Industry Association, said in February 1997.

Asset-Management at All Costs

Morgan Stanley aggressively sought an asset-management presence even before the Dean Witter deal. In 1996, for instance, the firm paid a lofty $745 million to buy Van Kampen/American Capital Inc. from Clayton, Dubilier & Rice Inc. Morgan also assumed Van Kampen's debt load of $430 million as part of the acquisition of the mutual-fund company. The purchase catapulted Morgan in the ranks of Wall Street money managers. And it gave Morgan a toehold in the fast-growing mutual fund business; of the $57.3 billion in assets that Van Kampen managed, $39.6 billion was in mutual funds.

But the Van Kampen funds had turned in only a ho-hum investment performance. And some Morgan Stanley competitors initially balked at selling the Van Kampen funds. About 25 percent of Van Kampen's sales were completed through brokerage firms, such as Merrill and Smith Barney, with the remainder being evenly divided among regional brokerage firms, commercial banks and financial planners.

Before the February 1997 merger announcement, Mr. Duff had been named to run Van Kampen, but later had been tapped to continue as Morgan Stanley's chief financial officer to help manage the integration of the two firms. In a shift announced just before the merger was completed, however, the new firm appointed Mr. Duff to run Van Kampen.

Dean Witter's mutual-fund business has come under fire for mediocre performance. According to data provided in 1997 by Morningstar Inc., a publisher of mutual-find information, the average five-year total return for Dean Witter's U.S. diversified stock funds was 16.56 percent, ranking them 181 out of 333 similar stock funds.

There have been some real lemons among Dean Witter mutual funds throughout the years. One such fund was the Dean Witter Premium Income Trust, which performed so poorly that Dean Witter InterCapital took the unusual step of liquidating the portfolio in 1997. In an embarrassing admission, one of the holders was the Investment Company Institute, the mutual fund industry's major trade group.

Dean Witter's push to sell proprietary funds has thrust its brokers to the fore. "The AE [account executive] is king, and has access to analysts and to portfolio managers," the Bernstein report said. "A change in the culture of Dean Witter's asset management operation certainly represents one of the key risks of the merger; for this reason, we are projecting a decline in proprietary fund sales to 50% of the total."

The combined firm initially had $260 billion in assets under management, dwarfing Merrill's $234 billion at the time. But Morgan Stanley, Dean Witter's revenues from asset management lagged behind those at Merrill. That's because 43 percent of the new firm's assets are institutional, which earn far lower management fees than do individual-investor assets.

Trading Gains

The merger is likely to bolster profit from institutional and proprietary stock trading, stemming from the new company's increased activity by individual investors. This could amount to an additional $60 million in trading revenue in 1998, according to the Bernstein study; the division's pretax margins should rise several percentage points, to 13 percent during the next few years.

The good news for Morgan Stanley, Dean Witter is that the higher margins could also be accompanied by lower volatility. That's because massive retail-trading volumes offer some relatively low-risk trading opportunities, as well as greater exposure in the small-stock market, the Bernstein analysis said.

Profit margins in the firm's bond-trading business are likely to remain high, at about 30 percent, analysts said. There isn't likely to be much change in Morgan Stanley's institutional bond business from the merger because of the corporate-client nature of the business. "We do not expect the merger to mute Morgan Stanley's risk level in institutional fixed income; rather, we expect the culture to remain one of risk-taking and therefore should have higher highs and lower lows than those of the other full-service securities firms," according to Bernstein.

Morgan Stanley's bond business has had some bumps. In July 1996, during a market swoon, the firm took a $25 million loss on a position in Office Depot Inc. zero-coupon convertible bonds. Though the loss was far from devastating, it was one of Morgan Stanley's largest ever on a single position. A Morgan Stanley spokeswoman wouldn't comment on the size of the loss, but said: "It was related to a hedge that became imperfect in a volatile market environment."

On the stock side, Morgan Stanley, Dean Witter suffered, along with the rest of the industry, in a December 1997 settlement of a high-profile class-action suit alleging price-fixing in the Nasdaq Stock Market. The firm, without admitting wrongdoing, agreed to pay $65 million (of a total of $910 million divided among thirty firms) to settle charges that dealers in small stocks improperly kept "spreads"—or the difference between a dealer's selling and buying prices—unfairly wide from May 1989 to May 1994.

A Morgan Stanley unit in late 1997 sought to bolster its position in the increasingly competitive market for repackaging real-estate loans. Morgan Stanley

Like Old Times

A Rock 'n' Roll Banker Makes Massive Bets, And Profits, at Nomura

Ethan Penner, 35, Gambles On Real-Estate Loans; 1995 Pay: $23 Million

Is the Group Being Shopped?

BY MICHAEL SICONOLFI
AND MITCHELL PACELLE
Staff Reporters of THE WALL STREET JOURNAL

NEW YORK—Growing up in blue-collar Yonkers, N.Y., Ethan Penner had no interest in white-shoe Wall Street. In college he was a journalism major who once wrote about a soccer match but forgot to include the score.

Mr. Penner knows the score now: He has emerged as one of the most powerful figures on Wall Street. In three years at the U.S. unit of Japan's Nomura Securities Co., he has almost single-handedly transformed the subsidiary from a nobody in the arena of commercial mortgages to an industry giant.

His innovation: When banks and insurance companies all but abandoned real-estate lending amid steep losses, he filled the void by making quick decisions to lend big chunks of Nomura's money. The result has been nearly $15 billion of loans in three years, loans soon chopped up into securities and resold.

Mr. Penner, 35 years old, does things the 1980s way: with big deals and big risks. Also big pay. His 1995 check was $23 million.

"The dollars he's putting at risk are phenomenal, and the profits he's ringing up are so big, he's the Mike Milken of the 1990s," says Andrew Albert, publisher of a newsletter called Asset-Backed Alert.

No Bureaucracy

Unlike rivals, he operates with near autonomy. "We don't have committees," Mr. Penner brags. "We react to change quicker than anyone else."

But he also has courted controversy. Mr. Penner holds personal stakes in partnerships controlled by a real-estate company Nomura made a loan to. Last year, he drew criticism for a Nomura ad that featured three seductive models and a real-estate developer who, it turned out, had had a run-in with the Securities and Exchange Commission. And his group once improperly told clients the details of a transaction before making a formal filing, Nomura told regulators in 1994.

Mr. Penner also is flamboyant. He hired the co-founder of a fancy restaurant as a Nomura marketing executive so his people could always get a table. To entertain clients at conferences, he hires the likes of Elton John, Bob Dylan, the Eagles and Crosby Stills and Nash. To incredulous rivals, it seems like a replay of the excesses of Drexel Burnham Lambert Inc.'s "predators' balls." Indeed, Mr. Milken, Drexel's former junk-bond chief and a hero of Mr. Penner's, was a speaker at Nomura's last conference.

Might Nomura Sell It?

Now, Nomura's rock 'n' roll banker faces a tough test. The "spreads" Nomura receives on real-estate loans have been cut in half since he went to work there in 1993, the result of increasing competition. That heightened competition among lenders has forced Nomura to make potentially riskier loans, some traders say.

And now there are indications Nomura is considering getting out at the top. It has quietly been exploring the possibility of a sale or joint venture of Mr. Penner's real-estate finance group involving other Wall Street firms, including Goldman, Sachs & Co., say people familiar with the matter. Nomura and Mr. Penner say nothing is on the table; Goldman won't comment.

Although nobody suggests that Mr. Penner's success isn't legitimate, critics say it stems from a financial high-wire act. For instance, his group unloaded many of the riskiest mortgage securities it created by providing generous financing to buyers, an arrangement that critics suggest leaves Nomura still saddled with some of the risk of those securities.

Lone Wolf

Mr. Penner's rapid rise shows that Wall Street can still celebrate the individual. Even after the disasters at Kidder, Peabody & Co., Daiwa Bank, Sumitomo Corp. and Barings International—where single traders led to huge losses—some firms allow a few individuals to roam free and take significant gambles. Mr. Penner's group recently accounted for $323 million—fully 42%—of the U.S. Nomura unit's total risk capital, according to an internal document.

The son of a rabbi, Ethan Hosea Penner grew up as a chunky kid nicknamed "Moo" who belonged to the fan club of the heavymetal group Twisted Sister. His mother reared him, and he says she instilled in him the idea that he could do anything. Still, his journalism aspirations died soon after the soccer story he wrote, sans score, for New York University's student paper. "It was NYU-Adelphi, so I don't really think anyone cared," he says.

After a switch to accounting and political science, he joined Drexel as a mortgage-bond trader, but lost money during the 1987 bond-market swoon. "It was my first experience with pain and failure," he says.

Moving to Morgan Stanley & Co., he was asked to leave following a controversial loan to a firm run by a former Drexel colleague. Mr. Penner says he was a scapegoat.

When he joined Nomura in 1993, the timing was right. The commercial-real-estate market was mired in its worst slump in decades. Banks and insurers that had flooded the industry with capital in the 1980s had abandoned it. Billions of dollars of loans were coming due, and borrowers had nowhere to go for refinancing.

But Mr. Penner was willing to write large loans quickly, using Nomura's money. Nomura collected the loans into huge pools, sliced them up into securities, had them rated, then sold them as commercial mortgage-backed securities.

Mr. Penner accumulated the loans in pools so large that rating agencies didn't penalize Nomura for concentrating risk in too few assets. He dubbed the resulting pools "megadeals."

Borrowers flocked in. Revenue before expenses for Mr. Penner's group soared to $320 million in the fiscal year ended last March 31, from $125 million in fiscal 1993, and now represents one-third of the entire revenue of Nomura's U.S. brokerage unit, Nomura Securities International Inc. The first megadeal earned Nomura a profit of $25 million, traders say.

All this has spelled millions for Mr. Penner: His contract gives him about 9% of the group's net revenue, roughly double the share other business-unit heads previously had received.

Noninvestment Grade

Mr. Penner dismisses persistent suggestions that he takes too much risk. As of Sept. 6, Nomura held $56 million in noninvestment-grade bonds on its books, according to an internal document. Though that is just 12% of the total amount of these so-called B pieces created by Nomura deals—and Nomura since has sold a big chunk of these bonds—it is still far more than rivals hold of such securities. In a distressed market, "if they had to have a fire sale, there would be some serious trouble" selling the B pieces, contends George Lucaci, a former senior Nomura bond executive.

Nonsense, says Mr. Penner—"everything" eventually gets sold. "I believe in risk management—not risk avoidance," he says. Adds Boyd Fellows, a top commercial-mortgage trader at Nomura: "Hey, we made the loans—I know these things. We're very comfortable with the risk."

Mr. Penner is used to skepticism. Max Chapman, former chief of the U.S. unit, once suggested to Nomura executives that Mr. Penner should be fired for his wild ways, according to a Nomura executive. "Gee, I don't remember," Mr. Chapman says now. "It's conceivable—Ethan can frustrate anyone."

Mr. Penner says Mr. Chapman constantly grilled him. How are you pricing these bonds? How are you hedging? How are you making money? He says that, in exasperation, he finally told Mr. Chapman: "You don't have to be a criminal to make money."

Mr. Penner is famous for his snap decisions. In 1994, executives of Starwood Capital Group, of Greenwich, Conn., met with him and his lieutenants on a Tuesday. Starwood, which was buying Westin Hotels & Resorts from Aoki Corp. of Japan, wanted a complex $425 million financing and it had to have it by that Friday. Mr. Penner's response: done.

"We needed a very funky loan," says Starwood's president, Barry Sternlicht. Among other things, Starwood could defer payments and avoid default if the hotel company's cash flow didn't measure up. "Ethan wrote a loan that only Ethan could write," Mr. Sternlicht says. "The day he wrote it, if he had to sell it, he probably would have lost 30% of his money. It was under water." Mr. Penner disputes that but agrees with Mr. Sternlicht that Nomura now "will make a ton of money on it."

Mr. Sternlicht didn't come to him as a stranger. Mr. Penner personally owns two Starwood limited partnerships and one Starwood land deal, with a combined value of as much as $700,000. He bought them the year before he joined Nomura.

To the criticism that these holdings create a conflict of interest, Nomura replies that Mr. Penner properly disclosed them. Mr. Penner himself says the investment is too small to pose a conflict. "If it did, I would have sold," he says.

The Brother

Another tie to Mr. Sternlicht's group was that Mr. Penner's brother, Joseph, worked there. And Mr. Penner further raised eyebrows by having Nomura hire his brother to work at Nomura's Los Angeles office. Nomura, defending the move, says Ethan was prevented from formally determining the size of his brother's bonus. And Ethan Penner says his brother "earned his stripes his own way." Joseph Penner recently left to start an investment fund to buy, among other things, Nomura's B pieces.

Mr. Penner's group at times has cut corners. In a rush to complete Megadeal I before the end of fiscal 1994, the group improperly sent internal data to a handful of clients before a formal prospectus was filed with regulators. This violated regulatory rules and gave other clients the right to sue to force Nomura to buy the securities back at the purchase price. Nomura went to the SEC and disclosed the problem.

Nomura asked Mr. Penner to set aside part of his $10 million fiscal 1994 bonus to offset potential suits. Mr. Penner, who says the early disclosure was inadvertent, says he refused and suggested he might sue the firm. In the end, Nomura backed off. No charges were filed by the SEC, and no clients sued Nomura. Nor did Mr. Penner.

Mr. Penner has become so powerful at Nomura that it now seems dangerous not to be a "Friend of Ethan." Consider the fate of James Finkel. Mr. Finkel, a lawyer in the Penner group, struck up a conversation with a stranger at an airport and mentioned the danger in Mr. Penner's risk-taking ways, Nomura executives say. The stranger turned out to be a Penner real-estate client, according to Mr. Penner. People at the firm say he demanded that Mr. Finkel be ousted from his group. Mr. Penner says Mr. Finkel, now at Bear Stearns Cos., broke his trust.

"It's always possible that something I said got misconstrued and passed along," Mr. Finkel says. "All I can say is, in trying to bring the allegation to a head, it was never directly stated what was said and to whom. It confused me."

High and Tight

Despite his strong reaction in the Finkel case, Mr. Penner adopts what he calls a "sophomoric" management style in the office, trying to keep things loose. He recently gave his secretary $200 to buy a catcher's mitt and mask, then cleared out the trading room and began throwing what he calls "80-mile-an-hour fastballs" to a colleague. Michael Berman, CEO of Nomura's U.S. unit, told him to cut it out.

Some of his antics have been even less well received. Once, he barged into a Nomura ladies' room and used a stall. Jean Murtha, a trading assistant who was in the restroom, complained, and Mr. Penner was called in by Mr. Berman. He explained that he had done it on a bet with a female colleague.

Now he is contrite. Ms. Murtha's "concern was: 'What if I had been standing there with my clothes off?' " Mr. Penner says. "She was offended and I apologized, and she accepted my apology. I've matured since then." Ms. Murtha declines to comment.

Early on at Nomura, Mr. Penner

decided he needed "to create an industry-wide buzz," a notion he got from "Predators' Ball," the Connie Bruck book on Drexel and Mr. Milken. Mr. Penner's group hired Elton John to play piano at its first real-estate-client conference. It wasn't cheap—$500,000—but he says clients were in tears as Mr. John left the stage.

This wasn't Mr. Penner's only marketing innovation. After seeing a two-month wait for reservations at Bouley, the exclusive Manhattan restaurant, he made an offer to Bouley co-founder Robert Wilson. The deal: "I'll hire you for $75,000 plus bonus, and if you actually do well, we'll pay you some real money." In return, "we want reservations at Bouley" at the drop of a hat.

Mr. Wilson handles Nomura's client conferences, now as a consultant for the firm. "The E-man," he says of Ethan Penner, "kind of knew what my innate talents were in terms of making noise, and it worked out very well." Bouley has closed "for renovations."

Another Penner effort to create a stir, in advertising, didn't work out quite as planned. The ads, an effort to modernize the traditional "tombstone" ad for securities offerings, featured real-estate developer Lenny Mandor seated at a linen-covered table with three alluring models. "Face it, your life probably won't change overnight," the ads read. "But it'll definitely get better when you work with Nomura."

But competitors noted with glee that Mr. Mandor had had a scrape with the SEC. In February 1995, the agency fined his Boca Raton, Fla., real-estate firm $500,000 for allegedly forging proxy documents from investors so it could merge two partnerships. (Mr. Mandor's firm neither admitted nor denied the charges.)

Nomura pulled the ads. Mr. Penner says it wasn't a big deal: "Every company involved in the business of syndication has been sued more times than they ever thought possible." He has no regrets. "I have to make things interesting," he says. "Just the fact that we're talking about it means it was a flaming success."

What baffles many on Wall Street is how the Japanese, famous for their distaste for risk-taking, allow Mr. Penner to run free. Bad real-estate investments in the 1980s nearly brought down the Japanese banking industry, and just last month, Nomura's Tokyo parent took a $3.4 billion real-estate hit from bad loans.

Although Mr. Penner's bosses dispute him, he has his own explanation: Executives at Nomura's parent never were fully aware of what he was doing until the big money began rolling in. "Otherwise, we never would have gotten started," Mr. Penner says. "By nine months, we were very big and very successful—so there was no turning back."

October 17, 1996

Mortgage Capital Inc. agreed to provide $3 billion to finance the high-flying real-estate lending operation that Nomura Holding America Inc. plans to spin off in 1998. The Nomura unit is headed by flamboyant investment banker Ethan Penner, who built a reputation as a pioneer on Wall Street by making huge bets on commercial buildings, and received a pay package totaling $47 million for the fiscal year ended March 31, 1997. Morgan Stanley will provide capital to finance the loans on commercial property made by Mr. Penner's group. The new company will bundle those loans together into bonds known as commercial mortgage-backed securities, or CMBS. In exchange for providing the line of credit, Morgan Stanley will be a joint lead manager for the first two of those bond offerings.

Credit-Card Plans; International Push

The merger was partly an attempt by Dean Witter to draw out Discover Card's promise. But credit-card operations clearly are the weakest link at the new firm. And it won't be easy to pull off. "We love the [credit-card] business," Mr. Mack said. He added that the Dean Witter cardholder list is one "that we think is going to have tremendous potential for doing more business."

Discover ranked No. 3 among card companies with $34.4 billion in credit-card balances outstanding as of year-end 1996, and plans are afoot to expand the operation abroad. For Dean Witter, the brokerage and credit-card businesses have provided a natural hedge. That's because they are countercyclical: The brokerage side thrives when interest rates are low and the stock market high, and the credit-card side does well when the economy expands.

Not all analysts are impressed with the credit-services side. "Unfortunately, the credit card business adds a disconcerting wrinkle," said the *Gimme Credit* newsletter. "This segment provides roughly half of [Dean Witter Discover's] earnings, but after years of phenomenal growth, it's recently been experiencing deteriorating asset quality and lower margins."

The firm clearly is trying to cross-sell products; it notes that there are 39 million Discover Card holders, 6.5 million of whom have a demographic profile similar to Dean Witter brokerage clients. "No one has yet figured out how to cross-market investment products to credit card customers," the Bernstein report said, "but management figures that this is only a matter of time, and they are going to try."

On the global securities front, Morgan Stanley has made great strides over the past few years. Yet it still has lagged behind Goldman and Merrill in the market share for worldwide stock and bond offerings. Morgan Stanley is betting that the merger will help win it more international banking mandates.

Morgan Stanley sought to trumpet its early and aggressive push internationally. In one full-page newspaper ad, for instance, the firm said its experience— "having worked closely over the years with government, business and financial people in Beijing, Shanghai, Hong Kong and across China—tells us to be optimistic."

In the United States, lacking a brokerage arm hasn't made much difference, Bernstein said, "with Morgan Stanley claiming to be successful in winning mandates when going head-to-head with Merrill Lynch some 75% of the time."

The Research Troika

They're known in the industry as the "troika" or the "triumvirate"—the three Morgan Stanley pundits whose pronouncements can unnerve markets.

Now Byron Wien, Barton Biggs and Stephen Roach—the investment strategist, head of global investments and chief economist, respectively—have been joined by the Dean Witter team of strategists, providing the newly merged client base of the two firms with an incredible array of opinion on the markets. The new arrivals, who tend to approach their task from a different perspective than their

Morgan Stanley counterparts, will help offset what some clients viewed as the dismaying departure of Tom McManus from the strategy group in December 1996. (Mr. McManus was noted for his analysis of industry sectors; his research provided the basis for the firm's "nifty fifty" stock index, options on which became tradable in April 1997 on the Chicago Board Options Exchange.)

Already, Morgan Stanley's weekly publication, *Investment Perspectives*, is one of the most eagerly-awaited strategy reports among institutional investors. Nearly every issue includes an essay, think piece, or piece of strategic advice from both Mr. Biggs and Mr. Wien, as well as economic musings from the firm's noted bear, Mr. Roach. Among its chief attractions are its sometimes whimsical tone: a favorite recent issue included a mock dialogue between Federal Reserve Chairman Alan Greenspan and Sigmund Freud, with the former lamenting that no one paid attention to his comments of "irrational exuberance" in financial asset values.

The remainder of the publication symbolizes Morgan Stanley's traditional approach to strategy and research (which likely will remain intact post-merger): a top-down view of the world beginning with overall investment strategy, moving on into the analysis of industries or sectors, and thence to company-specific coverage.

Just don't look for consistency among all these pundits. Mr. Wien, for instance, won kudos for calling for the Dow Jones Industrial Average to break above 6,000 during 1996 early that year, as well as predicting interest rates would top 7 percent. Both came to pass, but before they did, Mr. Wien said that May he saw a 1,000-point drop as being likely—and the Dow falling to 4500 by year-end, at which time it continued to hover around 8000. "I made my bearish call too early," he said with a shrug. He retreated from that, but has remained intermittently cautious ever since, advocating a return to market-timing, or the art of jumping in and out of stocks to capture gains and avoid declines, and still urges investors to take profits on any gains in the U.S. market.

Mr. Biggs, meanwhile, who took home a $6.3 million pay package last year as head of Morgan Stanley's asset management division, remains, as he put it memorably in a 1997 report, "an invested bear": wary of forfeiting the gains that might still lie ahead in the U.S. market, but stubborn in his belief that U.S. stocks remain the most overvalued segment of world markets. Instead, Mr. Biggs is an equally stubborn bull on emerging markets, despite the struggles and uneven track record of this segment of the market in recent years. A good call on Russia, where he advocated boosting exposure long before that market's recent astonishing gains, don't offset some of his less successful views in the eyes of some clients, but his pronouncements on such topics as what he perceives as overvalued U.S. technology stocks still have the ability to shake up the markets.

Their bearish inclinations don't mean that "B and B," as they're known to clients, operate in tandem. On one memorable occasion in early 1996, they issued diametrically opposing calls on the U.S. stock market, for instance. "It's like a car dealership deciding that people should only buy one kind of car—there's a role for this kind of dispute," says one Morgan Stanley insider. That kind of disagreement could grow now that Peter Canelo, Dean Witter's strategist, is on board. Mr. Canelo, one of Wall Street's biggest bulls, has drawn dramatically different conclusions on the market's direction in recent years.

Despite the high profile of these pundits, several clients say that while they study both men's views as provocative and intellectually interesting, they are less and less likely to base investment (as opposed to trading) decisions on their pronouncements. Mr. Biggs, insightful, often controversial, stimulates thought and debate, but isn't often right, clients note. The same is true of Mr. Wien, they add. "I hardly ever invest based on what they're saying, but what they're talking about might cause me to look at something I'd otherwise ignore," said one client.

Mr. Canelo insists that Mr. Wien is "pleased as punch" about adding him and his team to Morgan Stanley's strategy department. "We have complementary skills, and we'll be working together," he adds. "We may disagree on details, a quarter percentage point on interest rates here or fifty cents in earnings there, but Byron's been one of the best people around for pinpointing things I think are important, like the risk that's inherent in this market at these levels."

Mr. Canelo believes his interest in helping steer clients clear of "disaster areas" (like the bond market in 1994) will be useful in the newly merged firm. And the other Dean Witter strategists joining Morgan bring areas of expertise in which the latter has so far been lacking, such as quantitative and technical strategy and research. Scott Reed, for instance, has tracked corporate earnings data and flow of funds into mutual funds, while David Lipshitz is a quantitative strategist with a growing reputation.

Morgan Stanley boasts perhaps the most comprehensive international coverage of all the U.S. investment dealers. It is one of a handful of firms to do regular surveys of foreign markets, tracking the progress of financial market reform in Japan and Latin America, and offering investors a checklist monitoring Hong Kong investments as the British colony makes the transition to Chinese ownership.

With strategists in Europe and Asia, and 174 analysts in nine countries, in late 1996 the firm launched a global research product aimed at identifying the companies worldwide with the greatest competitive edge. While the glossy publication had a rocky start (25 percent of the forty top picks were replaced in April) the approach has been received with interest by clients.

Already, the combination of the two firms' research departments is producing some interesting synergies. When Morgan's steel analyst was in search of a new Coca-Cola contour can, being test-marketed in a few select regions, the word went out on Dean Witter's retail network, and the research department was inundated with sample cans for him to study.

Premerger, the firm boasted twenty-one all-star analysts in 1996 and twenty-three in 1997, including top-ranked banking and biotechnology analysts, ranking fifth in 1997 among the firms surveyed by *The Wall Street Journal*. The merger won't only boost the number of all-stars (and the number of total analysts, as Morgan retains 10 of Dean Witter's 34 analysts, adding to its own 166-strong roster pre-merger), but will also allow Morgan Stanley to expand its coverage to include areas like REITs, predominantly of interest to retail investors. Already, Morgan Stanley's research is being transmitted to Dean Witter brokers through the latter's existing investment publication, and the two firms have passed on to brokers what one official called a "huge package" of information, including profiles and photos of the analysts themselves.

Morgan Stanley, Dean Witter & Co.'s People

Purcell, Philip
Chairman & CEO-Dean Witter

Philip J. Purcell, chairman and chief executive officer: One of Wall Street's least-known chief executives, Mr. Purcell finally got his day in the sun. But it hasn't been easy. When rivals started poaching Dean Witter brokers in the early 1980s, Mr. Purcell, then Dean Witter president, made an unusual appeal. Calling on the heads of Wall Street's biggest brokerage firms, he told them that Dean Witter was struggling amid the widespread defections. "But," he warned, "we've got more capital than you do, and one day the shoe will be on the other foot."

Pretty prescient, that Mr. Purcell. Now, as chief of the nation's largest brokerage firm, at least by some measures, his clout is formidable. But you would never know it from the laconic Mr. Purcell, who has long been an overachiever. Raised in a middle-class Irish Catholic family in Salt Lake City, Utah, Mr. Purcell, son of an insurance broker, became the youngest managing director at McKinsey & Co. at age thirty-two. During his sixteen-year Wall Street career, he has transformed the firm from an also-ran into strong middle-of-the-pack brokerage house by boosting its brokerage force to more than nine thousand from 7,064 in 1990 and thrusting the firm into new areas, including credit cards and mutual funds. At the time of the merger, Dean Witter managed more than $250 billion in customer assets, more than twice the amount it managed in 1990.

Mr. Purcell hasn't had an unblemished record. As head of strategic planning at Sears, it was Mr. Purcell who led Sears to buy Dean Witter in 1981. But the "financial supermarket" Sears envisioned never caught on. Nevertheless, colleagues and friends say Mr. Purcell's strength is that he is a strategic thinker. Known for his self-deprecating style, Mr. Purcell allows colleagues to use a picture of him crouched on all fours under his desk in presentations to lighten the tone. Mr. Purcell has the last laugh: He received $4.3 million in cash and stock in 1996.

John J. Mack, president and chief operating officer: At Morgan Stanley, the hard-charging Mr. Mack effectively ran the firm day-to-day, despite his No. 2 president title. A former bond salesman, Mr. Mack is widely credited on Wall Street with building Morgan Stanley's fixed-income business into a powerful force in the securities industry. "In the early 1980s, people didn't take them seriously in fixed-income, but John proved them wrong," said Eric Gleacher, a former mergers chief at Morgan. As for Mr. Mack's style, Mr. Gleacher said: "He calls 'em real straight."

A stocky North Carolinian, Mr. Mack's forceful management style around Morgan and his once-key role in past cost-cutting drives had struck fear in some employees, who referred to Mr. Mack as "Mack the Knife." But Mr. Mack has said he considers himself a builder, not a cutter. Indeed, he has been at the forefront of Morgan's burgeoning international business.

Mr. Mack joined Morgan in 1972. He has headed Morgan's world-wide taxable bond division, and served as chairman of the operating committee. Mr. Mack, who was named president in 1993, received a 1996 paycheck of about $10 million.

Richard B. Fisher, chairman of the executive committee of the board: Mr. Fisher, one of the most well-liked Wall Street executives, in recent years had passed much of Morgan's leadership to Mr. Mack, after leading Morgan through a significant period of growth. He has held a variety of senior positions at Morgan since joining the firm in 1962 in corporate-finance. For a period of years, Mr. Fisher was responsible for the firm's bond operations, stock and research, then its entire capital-markets group. He became a managing director in 1970, president in 1984 and chairman of Morgan Stanley Group in 1991.

Thomas C. Schneider, executive vice president, chief strategic and administrative officer: Before his current post, Mr. Schneider was Dean Witter's chief financial officer. He previously had held a number of key positions at Dean Witter, including leading both the stock and bond divisions.

Philip N. Duff, president and chief executive officer of Van Kampen American Capital Inc.: Mr. Duff earlier had been Morgan's chief financial officer, and was tapped to help manage the integration of the two firms. Mr. Duff joined Morgan in 1984, became a managing director in 1993, and CFO in 1994. He previously had been head of the investment-banking group's financial institutions area. He also supervised Morgan's acquisitions of Miller Anderson &

Sherrerd LLP, Van Kampen/American Capital Inc., and the global custody business of Barclay Bank PLC.

Christine A. Edwards, executive vice president and chief legal officer: Ms. Edwards, previously Dean Witter's general counsel, won the new firm's top legal spot over Jonathan Clark, Morgan Stanley's general counsel. Before her general-counsel post at Dean Witter, Ms. Edwards had been senior vice president of Sears Consumer Financial Corp., now known as NOVUS Credit Services Inc. Before Dean Witter, Ms. Edwards spent fifteen years with Sears, where she held several management positions in consumer credit.

James M. Allwin, president and chief operating officer of Morgan Stanley Institutional Investment Management: Mr. Allwin joined Morgan Stanley in 1976, became a vice president in 1981, a principal in 1983, and a managing director in 1985. Before his current post, Mr. Allwin had worked in corporate finance and mergers-and-acquisitions, and had run the real-estate business.

Barton M. Biggs, chairman of Morgan Stanley Asset Management: Mr. Biggs founded Morgan Stanley Asset Management in 1975. He joined Morgan as a partner in 1973 after eight years as a managing partner of a hedge fund. He began Morgan's research department, and was U.S. and global research chief. In 1996, he was voted the top global strategist in a poll taken by *Institutional Investor* magazine.

Thomas R. Butler, president and chief operating officer of Discover Card: A former Sears executive, Mr. Butler has held a number of senior posts at Discover, and earlier at NOVUS Services. In 1995, he was appointed to a three-year term as a member of the Federal Reserve Board's Consumer Advisory Council.

Ronald T. Carman, senior vice president and associate general counsel: Mr. Carman has been with Dean Witter's law department since 1984, and associate general counsel since 1994. Mr. Carman previously had been branch chief at the Securities and Exchange Commission's New York regional office.

Walid A. Chammah, global head of debt capital markets services: Mr. Chammah joined Morgan in 1993 as a managing director responsible for U.S. debt capital market services. He was promoted to his current post in 1996. Previously Mr. Chammah was a managing director at CS First Boston, overseeing its U.S. taxable bond capital markets and structured financial groups.

Frederick Peter Churchouse, director and strategist for non-Japan Asia Equity Research: Mr. Churchouse joined Morgan in 1988 in stock research, and left the firm in 1991 to join Salomon Brothers. He rejoined Morgan in 1992 and was elected managing director in 1994.

Mayree C. Clark, global head of stock research: Ms. Clark is a managing director who assumed her current position in 1994. Previously her duties included working with Morgan's chairman, president and operating committee on matters relating to firm policy and administration.

Richard M. DeMartini, president and chief operating officer of Dean Witter Capital: Mr. DeMartini, one of a handful of key decision makers at Dean Witter, received about $3 million in cash and restricted stock in 1996, according to the firm's proxy document. Before his current post, he had been president and chief operating officer of the consumer-banking division, where he was responsible for Discover Card services, Sears Consumer Financial Corp., Sears Mortgage Corp. and Sears Savings Bank.

Kenneth M. deRegt, head of worldwide fixed income: Mr. deRegt assumed his current position in 1997. Among his previous positions at Morgan were head of bond trading and risk management, and manager of the firm's U.S. and international bond trading, based in London.

Robert J. Dwyer, executive vice president, national sales director, Dean Witter Reynolds & Co.: Mr. Dwyer is responsible for directing the sales activities and administration of the branch-office system, overseeing four-hundred offices and more than 9,300 brokers. He joined the firm in 1980 as a branch manager in Dean Witter's Buffalo office. He later was head of the syndicate department, associate national sales director and director of the taxable bond division.

Bruce Fiedorek, vice chairman of Morgan Stanley: Mr. Fiedorek is responsible for some of the firm's most senior client relationships. He joined the firm in 1976 in corporate finance, and worked his way up to global head of M&A and restructuring in 1990; he assumed his current post in 1997.

Charles A. Fiumefreddo, chairman and chief executive officer of Dean Witter InterCapital Inc.: Mr. Fiumefreddo is Dean Witter's senior asset-management executive, overseeing the firm's InterCapital group of mutual funds. He also is an executive vice president and director of Dean Witter Reynolds. In 1969, Mr. Fiumefreddo joined InterCapital, then a unit of Standard & Poor's Corp., as vice president and treasurer. He was appointed president and chief executive in 1974, the position he held when Dean Witter bought InterCapital in 1977.

Spencer C. Fleischer, head of investment banking for non-Japan Asia: Mr. Fleischer joined Morgan Stanley in 1979 in corporate finance; in 1982, he spent a year as executive assistant to Morgan's president. After working in various Morgan offices, Mr. Fleischer assumed his current post in 1990.

James F. Higgins, president and chief operating officer of Dean Witter Financial: Mr. Higgins, one of Dean Witter's top executives, is responsible for the branch-office system, the marketing, sales and trading of all stock, futures, options and taxable bond products. Previously, Mr. Higgins had been president and COO of Dean Witter Capital Markets, then the firm's retail-sales organization. Mr. Higgins received a 1996 paycheck of about $3 million cash and restricted stock, according to the firm's proxy material.

Peter F. Karches, president and chief operating officer of Morgan Stanley & Co.: Mr. Karches has steadily worked his way up Morgan Stanley since joining the firm in 1976. He became a vice president in 1981, a principal in 1983, and a managing director in 1985. He also was named a member of Morgan's management committee in 1987. Among his other senior posts was a stint as manager of mortgage-backed securities sales and trading, and national sales manager for all U.S. bond products. In 1992, he was named director of the firm's worldwide bond division.

Richard L. Kauffman, global head of stock capital markets: Mr. Kauffman replaced James Gantsoudes, a veteran Morgan Stanley executive, who passed away in 1997. In his current post, Mr. Kauffman is responsible for valuing, structuring and executing new stock issues for international and domestic companies. He is a member of the firm's commitment committee, its investments committee and the investment-banking division strategy committee. He joined Morgan Stanley in 1993 from First Boston.

William Kourakos, head of global high-yield capital markets: Mr. Kourakos, a managing director, works closely on bond transactions involving non-investment grade and emerging markets issues. Before joining Morgan in 1986, he worked at Irving Trust Co.

Elaine La Roche, managing director: Ms. La Roche manages the firm's Chinese joint banking venture with China International Corp. She also is the point person in New York for the firm's business activities in India. One of Wall Street's most senior female executives, Ms. La Roche has held a variety of management posts at Morgan Stanley. She has worked in institutional stock, corporate finance, bond capital markets, and the fixed-income division both in New York and London. Ms. La Roche was named head of public finance in 1988.

William M. Lewis Jr., co-head of mergers, acquisitions and restructuring: Mr. Lewis also is president and chief operating officer of the Morgan Stanley Real Estate Funds. He joined Morgan in 1978, became a vice president in 1987, a principal in 1988, and a managing director in 1990. Mr. Lewis's clients have included, among many others, the Rockefeller Family Trust Committee, Sara Lee Corp., Union Carbide Corp. and Weyerhauser Co.

Elizabeth Lynch, head of office of development: Ms. Lynch is a managing director at Morgan who ironically was an analyst at Dean Witter early in her career. She joined Morgan in 1984 as an associate, was elected to vice president in 1988, principal in 1992, and managing director in 1996. Ms. Lynch spent nine years in the investment-banking division, including five years in corporate finance and four years in real estate.

Terry Meguid, head of worldwide corporate-finance department: Before his current post, Mr. Meguid was a managing director in Morgan's mergers, acquisitions and restructuring department. He joined Morgan as an analyst in 1978, rejoined the firm's investment-banking division following a break for business school in 1982, became a vice president in 1987, principal in 1989 and a managing director in 1991.

Mitchell M. Merin, president and chief strategic officer of Dean Witter InterCapital Inc.: Mr. Merin had been Dean Witter's chief administrative officer before assuming his current post in April 1997. He previously had held several senior positions at Dean Witter, including director of taxable bond and futures, responsible for the management of all trading, institutional sales and product administration functions.

Stephen R. Miller, chairman and chief operating officer of Discover Brokerage Direct: Mr. Miller has spent his entire career with Dean Witter, beginning as a sales trainee in the firm's Los Angeles office in 1965. He has held a variety of senior positions, including senior executive vice president and director of the firm's Pacific region, and briefly as president of Dean Witter Reynolds and chairman and CEO of its individual financial-services division.

Stephan F. Newhouse, vice chairman and deputy head of the securities businesses: Mr. Newhouse joined Morgan in 1979, and held management positions in private placements, high-yield new issues and emerging-markets new issues.

Vikram S. Pandit, head of stock division: Before joining Morgan's international stock division, Mr. Pandit had headed the firm's U.S. stock new-issue business. He previously had been a professor at Indiana University and Columbia University.

Gary W. Parr, cohead of mergers, acquisitions and restructuring: Mr. Parr, a managing director, has long been involved in providing advice to insurance companies worldwide. Among the transactions he has been involved in include the Travelers/Primerica merger, and the Farmers Group/BAT acquisition. Mr. Parr previously had been copresident of Wasserstein Perella & Co.

Ralph L. Pellecchio, general counsel of Morgan Stanley & Co.: Mr. Pellecchio replaced Jonathan Clark, who resigned as general counsel in November 1997 after being passed over for the combined firm's top legal post. Mr. Pellecchio, who previously was head of the legal department's advisory section, reports to Christine Edwards, Morgan Stanley, Dean Witter's chief legal officer. Mr. Pellecchio played a key role in managing the legal issues associated with completing the firm's 1997 merger.

Joseph R. Perella, investment-banking chief: One of Wall Street's preeminent deal makers, Mr. Perella joined Morgan as a managing director in 1993, after being aggressively sought by several investment banks. He was named head of investment banking in 1997. Mr. Perella made a name for himself at First Boston, where he founded the firm's M&A group and managed it for fifteen years. He left First Boston in 1988 and was cofounder of Wasserstein Perella, acting as chairman until he left the firm in late 1993. He has extensive investment-banking experience in Europe, Latin America and Japan.

Thierry Porte, president of Morgan Stanley Japan: Mr. Porte, a managing director, also is head of capital markets and the corporate-coverage group and head of bond capital markets for the firm's Asia Pacific region. Mr. Porte joined the firm in 1979 as an analyst in the corporate-finance department, and has held management positions in Tokyo and London.

Don G. Powell, chairman of Van Kampen American Capital Inc.: Mr. Powell previously was president and chief executive officer, overseeing more than 1,300 employees at Van Kampen American Capital Inc., the fund firm bought by Morgan. Before being named as CEO of Van Kampen, he served as chairman and CEO of American Capital Management & Research Inc.

Richard F. Powers III, executive vice president and marketing chief at Dean Witter: Mr. Powers spent his entire career on Wall Street working for Dean Witter, holding a wide range of management positions.

Stephen S. Roach, chief economist: Mr. Roach, a managing director, oversees the firm's team of economists in New York, London, Paris, Tokyo and

Hong Kong. Before joining Morgan Stanley in 1982, he was a vice president at Morgan Guaranty Trust Co.

V. Eric Roach, chairman and chief executive officer of Lombard Brokerage Inc.: Mr. Roach founded Lombard in 1992 in San Francisco. Before launching the discount broker, Mr. Roach worked at various securities firms in Southern California, rising from branch manager to vice president. Dean Witter bought Lombard in late 1996.

Jeffrey H. Salzman, head of private-client services: Mr. Salzman, a managing director, has responsibility for Morgan's private bank and asset management for well-heeled individual clients worldwide. Before joining Morgan in 1977, Mr. Salzman worked at Merrill.

Robert M. Santora, head of Dean Witter Reynolds's bond businesses: Mr. Santora is responsible for Dean Witter's bond trading, sales and marketing activities. He previously had overseen the firm's taxable bond group.

Robert M. Scanlan, president and chief operating officer of Dean Witter InterCapital: Mr. Scanlan is a senior executive in Dean Witter's mutual-fund operation; among his posts, he is executive vice president and director of Dean Witter Trust Co.

John H. Schaefer, director of planning: Mr. Schaefer joined Dean Witter in 1987 to manage East Coast investment banking. Before his current post, he had been director of Dean Witter's corporate-finance operations for six years.

Robert G. Scott, chief financial officer of Morgan Stanley, Dean Witter: Mr. Scott assumed his current post in 1997. He previously had held a variety of senior-level banking posts at Morgan, including head of worldwide investment banking.

Robert B. Schulthorpe, executive vice president and stock chief for Dean Witter Financial: Mr. Schulthorpe is responsible for research, branch stock sales and marketing, institutional stock sales and listed block trading, among other things. He began his career at Dean Witter in 1965 as a broker, and held a variety of retail-brokerage posts before assuming his current position in 1990.

Mark A. Seigel, head of worldwide debt syndicate: Mr. Seigel, a managing director, is responsible for Morgan's global bond syndicate activities and has had vast experience in pricing a wide variety of public offerings in the U.S. and worldwide.

Neal Shear, head of worldwide commodity trading: Mr. Shear, a managing director, oversees trading in, among other things, precious metals, energy and soft commodities. He joined Morgan in 1982, and previously had worked at Citicorp and J. Aron & Co.

Monroe R. Sonnenborn, general counsel, litigation and regulatory affairs at Morgan Stanley & Co.: Mr. Sonnenborn previously was a managing director in the firm's legal and compliance department; he was promoted to his current post in December 1997. He reports to Ralph Pellecchio, Morgan Stanley's general counsel. "Monty's experience is a tremendous asset to the firm," said Christine Edwards, Morgan Stanley, Dean Witter's chief legal officer.

John J. Studzinski, head of investment banking in Europe: Mr. Studzinski joined Morgan Stanley in 1980 and has held a variety of investment-banking posts in M&A, stock financing, and a broad range of restructuring projects.

John S. Wadsworth Jr., chairman of Morgan Stanley Asia Ltd. and Morgan Stanley India: In addition to Mr. Wadsworth's responsibilities in non-Japan Asia, he has policy and strategic oversight for Morgan's business in Japan. He previously had held a number of posts in the firm's U.S. investment-banking division.

Sir David Walker, executive chairman of European operations: Mr. Walker joined Morgan in 1994 as executive chairman of Morgan Stanley International. He previously had been deputy chairman at Lloyd's Bank, and chairman of the Securities and Investments Board, the British authority that regulates the securities markets.

J. Steven Ward, head of global technology and operations: Before his current position, Mr. Ward was head of investment banking for Morgan's European operations. He previously had been cohead of Morgan Stanley Europe. Before joining Morgan in 1983, he worked for many years at Merrill Lynch & Co.

Marna C. Whittington, chief operating officer of Morgan Stanley Asset Management and Miller Anderson & Sherrerd: Ms. Whittington joined Miller Anderson in 1992 and became a partner in 1994. She previously had been executive vice president of the University of Pennsylvania.

Samuel H. Wolcott III, executive vice president of Dean Witter Reynolds: Mr. Wolcott's career with Dean Witter began when his former employer, J. Barth & Co., was acquired by Dean Witter in 1970. His other posts included manager of West Coast institutional sales and syndicate manager.

In the Beginning . . .

By Wall Street standards, the newly combined firms have had a sedate history. Morgan Stanley & Co. was created in 1935 to continue the investment-banking business of J. P. Morgan & Co. Harold Stanley was a senior partner at J. P. Morgan. This followed the Glass-Steagall Act, which separated commercial banking from the investment-banking business. Morgan Stanley's name has remained throughout the years. The firm qualified for membership on the New York Stock Exchange in 1941.

In 1952, it comanaged the issue of $50 million in bonds for the International Bank for Reconstruction and Development. Morgan Stanley in 1964 created the first computer model for financial analysis. Twelve years later, the firm moved to midtown Manhattan from Wall Street, one of the first major securities firms to do so.

Dean Witter & Co. was formed in 1924 in San Francisco by Dean, Jean and Guy Witter. The firm kept its name through a series of mergers. (Duisenberg, Wichman & Co. in 1929; William Cavalier & Co. in 1940; Lieb, Keyston & Co. in 1941; Harris Hall & Co. in 1953; Laurence Marks & Co. in 1959; J. Barth & Co. in 1970; Laird, Bissell & Meed in 1973; and Standard & Poor's Inter-Capital Inc. in 1977.) Dean Witter & Co. went public in 1972. Its name was changed to Dean Witter Reynolds & Co. after buying Reynolds Securities International Inc. in 1978. After being spun off by Sears, Roebuck & Co. to shareholders in 1993, the firm became Dean Witter, Discover & Co.

Then came the 1997 merger, and a clunky new name: Morgan Stanley, Dean Witter, Discover & Co. Few on Wall Street expected such a mouthful to live on for long; indeed, it's risky business to bank on the second name in a merger remaining forever. "If a name gets unwieldy, or less than positive things are associated with it, one of them eventually will disappear," said Richard Lipstein, managing director of Solomon-Page Group Ltd., a Wall Street consulting firm.

"Culture is everything on Wall Street, and we have a simple rule of thumb for such combinations: the more names in the merged company's title, the lower the chance of the merger succeeding," quipped *Gimme Credit*, the Chicago market newsletter. "And Morgan Stanley, Dean Witter, Discover is a mouthful."

Executives at the new firm conceded the new name was awkward. "It is a mouthful," said Morgan Stanley's Mr. Duff. "I haven't counted the number of syllables, but it's more than a couple." But Mr. Duff vowed that the Dean Witter name won't be driven to Wall Street's big graveyard of long-lost names. "Brand names will be more important in the next ten years than they have in the past," Mr. Duff said. That didn't stop the firm from dropping the Discover name in 1998. An internal memo referred to "the obvious need to shorten our corporate name and to increase its memorability among individual investors."

Robert E. Wood II, executive vice president for marketing and advertising for Discover Card Services: Mr. Wood assumed his current post in 1994. He is responsible for all Discover Card brand marketing and advertising functions.

Byron Wien, U.S. investment strategist: Mr. Wien joined Morgan as an adviser in 1985, and was elected managing director later that year. One of Wall Street's most well-known strategists, he has made a name for himself with solid market calls, though he incorrectly predicted a major swoon in stocks in the fall of 1996, and later revised his view.

SALOMON SMITH BARNEY HOLDINGS INC.

"TAKING A WALK ON THE WEILL SIDE"

Sculpting a Financial-Services Juggernaut

For years, Sanford I. Weill pined for the day when he could cobble together a Wall Street firm that would top giant Merrill Lynch & Co. That day may be here. In a move that stunned Wall Street, Mr. Weill's Travelers Group Inc., along with its Smith Barney Inc. brokerage unit, in September 1997 announced plans to buy the parent of Salomon Brothers Inc., the biggest-swinging trading firm on the Street, in a stock swap initially valued at about $9 billion. In one bold swoop, the new giant—Salomon Smith Barney Holdings Inc.—eclipsed Merrill and the recently married Morgan Stanley, Dean Witter Discover & Co. in market capitalization. And by other measures, Salomon Smith Barney is snapping at Merrill's heels: The combined firm would have been ranked No. 2 in bond underwriting in 1996 and No. 1 in United States stock research, as measured by *Institutional Investor* magazine.

"Sandy Weill has had ambitions to be out in front of Merrill Lynch for most of his life—and now he has a crack at doing that," said Roy Smith, a New York University professor and a limited partner at Goldman, Sachs & Co.

But the deal also saddles Mr. Weill with big risks. Known for gobbling up distressed Wall Street firms on the cheap, Mr. Weill bought Salomon in the seventh year of the long bull market. Salomon, long known as Wall Street's most daring trading firm, has lost big chunks of money in a hurry. Indeed, Salomon had pretax losses of as much as $300 million in its global investment-banking and stock departments for the twelve-month period preceding the September 1997 merger announcement, people familiar with the matter say. As part of that, Salomon's stock group accumulated losses of $100 million from a risk-arbitrage position in the then-pending merger of British Telecommunications PLC and MCI Communications Corp.

Salomon also had a loss of about $60 million in October 1997, which largely stemmed from Salomon's stock derivatives-trading business. Salomon lost as much as $50 million in stock-derivatives trading during the week of October 27, people familiar with the firm said. But analysts said the $60 million loss for the entire firm indicated that its trading losses may have been greater since other parts of Salomon's business were presumably profitable in the same period. The losses prompted Smith Barney chief executive officer James Dimon to arrive unannounced at Salomon to quiz Salomon Brothers stock chief Arthur Hyde about the matter, the people said.

In the wake of the losses, Salomon started scaling back its risk positions in customer stock trading. Salomon shuttered its stock risk-arbitrage trading in its New York customer business, and cut its risk positions in stock derivatives by two-thirds. "This is inevitable given that Travelers is trying to integrate a firm [Salomon] that has a well-developed principal-trading culture and retro-fit it into a global customer business," said Peter Davis, a partner at Booz Allen & Hamilton Inc.

In the short run, there could be cultural clashes between daring Salomon traders and the more conservative Smith Barney mentality. When the deal was announced, Salomon executives said that the acquisition would likely result in job losses for at least fifteen hundred bankers, traders, analysts and back-office workers, to yield cost savings of about $500 million. Salomon bore the brunt of the cuts, particularly in overlapping areas such as stock, research and trade processing. Among the first casualties was Jonathan Sandelman, the thirty-nine-year-old head of Salomon's global stock-derivatives group, who was dismissed days after the merger announcement in the wake of losses in his group. A Salomon official said at the time that Mr. Sandelman's departure was "not the result of losses" but was "made as a result of the new management team in equities." And at least 500 Salomon employees will be laid off when Salomon's trade processing center in Tampa, Florida, is closed in April 1998.

Some Salomon analysts quickly bore the brunt of the fallout from the merger. Among the Salomon research analysts who left their posts to Smith Barney counterparts were those covering banking, industrial goods, semiconductors, mortgage, construction and insurance industries, as well as David Schulman, Salomon's high-profile, and often bearish, strategist.

In 1997, the combined Salomon Smith Barney had net income of $1.65 billion, down from $1.76 billion in 1996. And some on Wall Street are skeptical that the combined firms will win more business, despite Mr. Weill's penchant for cutting costs. "Travelers is a company that has prided itself on having a predictability to their earnings. Salomon's earnings are anything but predictable," said Sallie Krawcheck, an analyst at Sanford C. Bernstein & Co.

Still, some on Wall Street praised Mr. Weill for making yet another smart deal—his trademark. Travelers bought Salomon for about two times book value, far below that of other recent brokerage mergers. And he didn't have to put up any of the firm's money, just its stock. Mr. Weill "is the ultimate opportunist—

his currency is Travelers stock, not cash," said Michael Holland, a former Salomon money-management executive who heads Holland & Co. Between 1998 and the time of the deal, Travelers stock had soared an astounding 1,189 percent, more than four times that of the broader market averages.

The blockbuster deal highlights Mr. Weill's grand dream of creating the world's largest financial-services firm. It also underscores the swiftly changing sands of Wall Street, which is undergoing its biggest consolidation ever. The plan, people on Wall Street say, is for Mr. Weill to try to control Salomon's riskier businesses and attempt to beef up its international cachet and investment-banking prowess. (There were immediate dividends: Salomon Smith Barney was selected as a financial adviser to South Korea's government amid that country's financial crisis in late 1997, and the firm stood a chance of helping to underwrite any bond issues to ease the debt crisis hammering South Korea's government.) And with merger mania sweeping Wall Street this year, he knew "we'd have to do something real soon—or miss it on this go-around," said a senior Smith Barney executive.

But eclipsing Merrill will be no easy task. Despite a powerful brokerage force of 10,300 catering to individual investors—the nation's second largest, behind Merrill's approximately 13,700—Smith Barney has three big problem areas: nearly no international presence, a weak bond business and a relatively feeble investment bank catering to institutions. Salomon helps provide all three. "In one fell swoop, Smith Barney will have more equity capital than Merrill Lynch," the sixty-four-year-old Mr. Weill crowed the day of the merger announcement. "That makes me happy."

Of course, it took years for Merrill to put together its strong dual franchises in brokerage and investment banking. Only one large firm, Merrill, "has ever successfully combined a major institutional investment-banking business and a major retail securities business under one roof over a long period of time," said Raphael Soifer, an analyst at Brown Brothers Harriman & Co. "For Merrill, this happy state of affairs did not come easily, but took more than twenty years to evolve, accompanied by no small amount of Sturm und Drang during that time."

Sure, the Salomon deal will give the merged firm a shot at joining the so-called bulge bracket that dominates the securities industry, said David Komansky, Merrill chairman and chief executive. But he said the firm won't be there from day one. "What it does is put them in the position to build the capability to compete with the bulge bracket," Mr. Komansky said. "I wouldn't say at this point in time they're there. It's a long way between the starting line and the finish line."

Though Mr. Weill is known for buying distressed companies in bad markets, he faced a big gamble if he waited for a market tumble to make an acquisition. Earlier in 1997, Morgan Stanley merged with Dean Witter, Discover & Co.

to leapfrog ahead of Smith Barney as a Wall Street powerhouse. The betting inside Smith Barney was that the bull market could last a while longer. And Smith Barney executives expressed concern that another big merger—say, between Chase Manhattan Corp. and Merrill—could relegate the firm to being a second-tier player.

Unlike other brokerage-firm mergers in 1997, particularly that of Morgan Stanley and Dean Witter, the Smith Barney–Salomon deal was driven by how much Mr. Weill can cut costs. That's nothing new for him: After buying Shearson Lehman Brothers Inc.'s brokerage operations in 1993, the newly merged firm slashed fifteen hundred jobs. Over the years, Mr. Weill has cut out perks ranging from newspaper subscriptions to employee benefits in a drive to pare expenses to the bone.

Mr. Weill said Salomon Brothers chief executive Deryck Maughan initiated the merger discussions with a call in mid-August, with the two meeting during the last two weeks of August. ("Deryck said 'Please,' and I said 'OK,' " Mr. Weill gloated to analysts.) On the Thursday before Labor Day, Mr. Weill spoke to Warren Buffett—Salomon's biggest shareholder and former chairman—"about how he would feel about something like this, and he was very encouraging." On the Sunday after Labor Day, instead of going to the U.S. Open tennis finals, Messrs. Weill and Maughan went up to a house near the Westchester County, New York, airport that Travelers uses as a retreat and worked all day on the deal. Mr. Weill said they wanted to "get to the rating agencies before" taking the deal to the company's boards. "I think it was the smoothest coming-together of a big company that I've ever been involved in," said Mr. Weill. He said the talks went "really fast."

But before doing the deal, Mr. Weill needed to be convinced that he could swallow Salomon's risky trading area. Mr. Weill's concerns were so great that Salomon's then-proprietary trading chief, Shigeru Myojin, was flown in from London during the talks to make a presentation to Mr. Weill about Salomon's risk-arbitrage businesses and to make him more comfortable about the firm's risk profile and the positions it puts on.

Mr. Weill is expected to try to rein in Salomon's risky trading, but not eliminate it. "Obviously, Sandy thought this through—they're not going to take out that element of Salomon's profit, or they wouldn't make money," said Richard Barrett, former Salomon investment-banking chief, now heading UBS Securities' financial-institutions investment banking. "To some degree, Smith Barney's retail side will provide a stable core to offset the wild swings" from Salomon's trading, Mr. Barrett said. Mr. Weill took pains to reassure analysts about the volatility of Salomon's proprietary trading. "If you're a financial services company and you have better than $6 billion of pretax profits, you can afford to make a mistake every now and then," Mr. Weill told analysts around the time of the merger. "If you look at Salomon's earnings over time, except for one blip in 1994, they have been very steady." As for his initial apprehension, Mr. Weill said: "I think it's fair to say before we knew anything, we were very nervous and went from being nervous to appreciating what they do."

In some ways, Salomon was a fallback for Mr. Weill. Mr. Weill had long expressed an interest in Goldman Sachs, one of Wall Street's premier investment banks. But Goldman senior executives wouldn't bite, people familiar with the situation say. Meanwhile, Mr. Weill made an informal overture to Bankers Trust New York Corp., other people familiar with the situation say. But the overture didn't go very far, allowing Bankers Trust to issue a statement saying that the two hadn't held talks. Mr. Weill declined to comment on Bankers Trust. In addition, Travelers had expressed interest in J. P. Morgan & Co.

Smith Barney and Salomon couldn't be more dissimilar. Smith Barney caters primarily to individual investors. At the time of the merger, it boasted $156 billion of assets under management, making it one of the largest fund concerns among brokerage firms, behind Merrill and Dean Witter, making it one of the largest fund concerns among brokerage firms. The firm has come a long way since 1988, when it lacked clout, focus—and profits. The $1 billion Shearson purchase made the firm an instant brokerage giant. Its return-on-equity has consistently exceeded that of many brokerage rivals, showing how size and tough cost control can succeed on Wall Street. In the two years before the merger, the firm slashed its fixed operating costs by more than $100 million.

Smith Barney also has strong stock-trading operations and clout in municipal bonds. It remains the top market maker in small stocks; on average, the firm accounts for between 10 percent and 15 percent of the daily volume in the Nasdaq Stock Market. But the firm's efforts to build up investment banking had been frustrated. Smith Barney ranked No. 10 among Wall Street underwriters in 1996, the same as in 1995. The combined Salomon Smith Barney vaulted to No. 2 in the underwriting race for 1997, with a 12.9 percent market share.

By contrast, Salomon has earned a reputation as a smart and aggressive bond-trading house. Its specialty is proprietary trading—trading for the house account, using the firm's own money. Salomon's bond-arbitrage group generated a whopping pretax profit of more than $750 million in 1996, according to people familiar with the firm. Salomon has tried to diversify its earnings, but it hasn't come easily. Sales and trading, mostly in bonds, represented more than three-quarters of Salomon's 1996 revenue—and nearly all its profit. Before the merger, the firm ranked No. 2 in investment-grade debt—its bread and butter—as well as fifth in junk bonds and sixth in new-stock issues. Salomon's mortgage-backed bond department, after suffering debilitating losses in 1994, has rebounded strongly.

Salomon never fully recovered from a crippling 1991 bond scandal, in which the firm disclosed having made a series of improper bids at several United States Treasury note auctions. After nearly imploding in the aftermath of the scandal, Salomon suffered mass defections, which crimped the firm's earnings power. The low point came in 1994, when Salomon had a pretax loss of $831 million. In a major miscue, its mortgage group held $10 billion of bonds—with some positions three years old—that it couldn't adequately value or easily peddle. The firm also had to take charges totaling $175 million after taxes to clean up nearly ten years of botched bookkeeping on its trading desks. Even in 1996, a record year for Wall Street's securities firms, Salomon had to restate its profits after selling its money-losing Basis Petroleum oil-refining unit to Valero Energy Corp. The sale resulted in an after-tax loss of $290 million, slashing Salomon's reported 1996 profits by nearly one-third, to $617 million. This put Salomon's profit far below its rivals, including Merrill, Smith Barney, Morgan Stanley, Dean Witter and Goldman Sachs.

Mr. Maughan, for his part, freely concedes that the Treasury scandal—surfacing as it did at the beginning of the biggest bull market ever—cost the firm untold amounts of lost business that never could be regained.

In the months before the Smith Barney merger, Salomon scrambled to design a "new" firm with a broader emphasis on investment banking. One means was by looking for novel ways to distribute its stock offerings. In an unusual move, Salomon forged an alliance in 1997 with mutual-fund giant Fidelity Investments that allows Fidelity's brokerage arm to market Salomon stock offerings. Under the three-year deal, Salomon will allocate at least 10 percent of any stock offering it lead-manages to Fidelity Brokerage Services Inc.

Salomon is betting on using the Fidelity link as a calling card when it visits corporate-finance clients. And it may well prove to have been a smart move. But the Fidelity alliance means Salomon won't have the ability to control all the investors who buy its new issues. This could be a concern to corporate clients: They typically like to know that their stock is placed in strong hands—investors who won't quickly "flip," or sell back, the shares in the market.

Salomon has made strides in some areas. Before the merger it did business in twenty-three countries, compared with thirteen five years ago and five a decade ago. Yet it still lacked the punch to reach any major global aspirations without hooking up with a merger partner, according to a 1997 report by Moody's Investors Service Inc. The Dun & Bradstreet Corp. credit-rating concern said firms such as Salomon also are taking more risk to generate returns in some new businesses.

Mr. Maughan has said Salomon revels in a "risk-accepting culture" that sets it apart from the rest of the Street. In the past, Mr. Maughan has brushed aside suggestions that Salomon needed to hook up with a merger partner to succeed. Sitting in his office in 1997, next to a pillow with the slogan "Don't Confuse Brains With a Bull Market," Mr. Maughan boasted that Salomon already traded with 3,500 clients and traded $250 billion in securities a day. The day of the merger, Mr. Maughan, in a talk to employees over the firm's "squawk box," pointed out: "This provides us with the scale so that we can compete with Merrill and Morgan."

Yet Salomon remains held back by a simple fact: The firm still lives and dies primarily by trading. This has left it far more vulnerable to declining markets or trading missteps. And powerful traders have resisted efforts to rein in their pay even as the firm's costs have mounted in recent years. In 1995, for instance, a radical pay plan launched to scale back the firm's sky-high paychecks backfired, triggering dozens of defections in its customer operations and a fractured culture.

Despite some recent efforts to cut compensation costs, Salomon still doles out some of the fattest paychecks on Wall Street to its trading stars. Andrew Fisher, a trader of mortgage-backed bonds, retired in 1997 from Salomon at age thirty-nine after receiving a 1996 bonus of $25 million. And Salomon had the highest reported pay package on the Street in 1996, when it paid Mr. Myojin $31 million for the year.

This isn't the first time Mr. Weill has tried to buy an investment-banking presence. In 1993, he made an embarrassing gaffe by overpaying about two dozen former Morgan Stanley investment bankers—including former Morgan Stanley president Robert Greenhill—who didn't bring in much business. Nearly all the hires have since left.

The Morgan Stanley hires showed the cultural clashes that could crop up. On several plane trips in 1994, ex–Morgan Stanley bankers sat in first class as Smith Barney bankers fumed in coach. (The Morgan hires, accustomed to flying first class, didn't know Smith Barney's policy typically forbids such perks, Smith Barney executives said.) The gap between the Morgan and Smith Barney cultures was so wide that when one senior Morgan banker, Robert Lessin, arrived at the firm in 1993, he said: "I was trained not even to know how to spell" Smith Barney. Thus, some on Wall Street aren't betting the Salomon marriage will work out much better.

Though Mr. Weill hasn't had luck with investment bankers, he has learned from the experience, some Wall Street executives say. Gerard Smith, a former Salomon banker now at UBS Securities, said the deal stands the best chance of succeeding if Mr. Weill lets "Salomon be Salomon and graft[s] onto it the important pieces of Smith Barney."

Meanwhile, don't bet on this being Mr. Weill's last acquisition. Travelers is getting "some strong Asian and United Kingdom capability" by acquiring Salomon but is adding only "marginal investment-banking capability" in the United States, said a Wall Street investment banker. Mr. Weill still must build upon the Salomon deal for even more United States investment-banking and global clout.

Still, the transaction also will give Travelers a larger market capitalization. "So they have more reach to do bigger deals," the banker said. "On balance, this is an improvement" over where Smith Barney stood, he said. "And if anybody has a chance of pulling it off, it's Sandy—but it won't be easy."

Sharing Power at the Top;
Easing Out the Boss's Daughter

One of the more striking aspects of the Salomon Smith Barney pact was a power-sharing arrangement at the top. Mr. Weill appointed co–chief executives to run the merged firm: Jamie Dimon, Travelers president and Smith Barney chairman, and Mr. Maughan, Salomon Brothers' CEO. Though Mr. Dimon is a longtime Weill confidant, Mr. Maughan could wind up with the higher billing partly because the merged firm could need his leadership to keep Salomon's money-making bond traders happy. The arrangement is particularly ticklish for Mr. Dimon because his relationship with Mr. Weill recently became strained after Jessica Bibliowicz, Mr. Weill's daughter, quit Smith Barney in June following repeated clashes with Mr. Dimon.

Messrs. Dimon and Maughan say they are committed to working together as co-chiefs. But some Smith Barney and Salomon insiders and Wall Street investment bankers are skeptical that the dual-head structure will survive, particularly once Travelers has fully digested the Salomon purchase. "There are now two very senior people that Sandy can turn to," said William Benedetto, who heads Benedetto, Gartland & Greene Inc., an investment-banking boutique. "That's why I think it's an unstable organizational structure and, at some point, Sandy is going to choose one or the other."

For his part, Mr. Weill brushes aside suggestions that the arrangement is "unstable. Jamie and Deryck have the intellect and personalities to get along fine and be a perfect team." Still, some insiders and analysts say if a horse race between the two executives picks up steam, Mr. Maughan has a surprisingly good shot at winding up as the top banana—assuming, of course, that the businesses he runs are humming. "Jamie and Deryck are both good guys, but there is one major distinction: One of them was there when Jessica Bibliowicz left," said Mr. Holland, the former Salomon executive.

The fallout from the Bibliowicz matter appeared to have surfaced even before the merger. In August, Mr. Weill named Thomas Jones, a pension-fund executive, to run the firm's asset-management group, taking away a major responsibility from Mr. Dimon. In naming Mr. Jones a Travelers vice chairman and head of asset management, Mr. Weill took control of the operation from Mr. Dimon and set it up as a stand-alone unit reporting directly to the Travelers chief. Some on Wall Street viewed the change in responsibilities as an expression of Mr. Weill's displeasure that Mr. Dimon couldn't work with Ms. Bibliowicz. Mr. Weill brushed aside such suggestions. "If I wanted to retaliate, I would really retaliate," Mr. Weill said. "I don't think there is anything to retaliate for. My daughter wanted to do her own thing and she is very happy doing her own thing."

Smith Barney's Backbone:
The Brokerage Business

The basic brokerage business typically isn't very lucrative for Wall Street firms. But it has been very good to Smith Barney. The firm's profit margins soared to more than 15 percent in 1996; anything over 10 percent is considered heroic. Smith Barney brokers are a productive lot, averaging annual commissions in 1997 of a lofty $428,000. One reason is many of the firm's brokers serve small to mid-size institutions, in addition to individual investors.

Each broker at the firm manages about $55 million in assets—exceeding the assets of the nation's average bank branch. One incentive: Smith Barney has raised the bar for its brokers to earn bonuses. In recent years, the firm began requiring Smith Barney's brokers to attract an average of 33 percent more in customer assets for the firm and an average of 29 percent more in trading commissions to earn "asset-gathering" bonuses in addition to their regular commission pay.

These bonuses, which can't be cashed in for five years, are "golden hand-cuffs" tying the broker to the firm. They are aimed at, among other things, persuading brokers to bolster their client base in Smith Barney's Financial Management Account, the firm's cash-management account that investors often use to park idle cash not in stocks, bonds or mutual funds.

Clients with FMA Accounts—which also include credit-card and check-writing privileges—are less likely to leave the firm if the broker bolts to a rival, some analysts say. "Brokerage firms feel that binds the client closer to the firm, and makes the account harder to move," said Mark Elzweig, who heads a New York brokerage-recruiting firm that bears his name. "The trend is capturing assets—that's the name of the game right now." Robert Connor, a former senior vice president at Smith Barney, said such bonuses represent a small fraction of brokers' overall pay. Besides, he added, it makes sense to raise the asset bar because, in an environment such as the recent bull market in stocks and bonds, "you can just sit there and watch" assets grow.

Meanwhile, Smith Barney executives brushed off studies showing that full-service brokerage firms have lost about 25 percent of the individual-investor market to discount brokers, mutual-fund companies and other specialized vendors in recent years. "Some of these [investors] have never seen a real down market," said Steven Black, Salomon Smith Barney's global stock chief. "In the next big crack in the market, I'm not so sure the tide won't turn." He expects clients to return to full-service firms such as Smith Barney that can offer "some advice and [trade] execution."

On the trading side, Salomon Smith Barney was stung, along with twenty-nine other brokerage firms, in a December 1997 settlement of an investor class-action case alleging price-fixing in the Nasdaq Stock Market. The firm agreed, without admitting wrongdoing, to pay about $70 million to settle allegations that the dealers unfairly kept prices, and profits, in Nasdaq stocks unduly high between 1989 and 1994.

Selling No-Load Funds:
If You Can't Beat 'Em, Join 'Em

Smith Barney in 1996 became the first brokerage firm to have it both ways: selling no-load mutual funds in addition to the load funds that are every brokerage firm's bread and butter. The firm began by adding four hundred no-load funds—the haven for do-it-yourself investors who want to pinch pennies—from twenty-eight fund families to the panoply of funds it already offers. It was Wall Street's equivalent of dining with the enemy. Brokers at firms such as Smith Barney have long put dinner on the table by imposing an up-front sales charge, or load, on every mutual fund they sell. But times are a-changing: Broker-sold funds have been losing market share to no-loads, and Smith Barney felt driven to go with the tide.

Brokers who steer clients into no-loads won't go hungry, however: They get annual fees. While investors don't pay sales loads to buy the funds, they pay an annual fee of up to 1.5 percent to participate in the program, about standard among such mutual-fund supermarkets. Smith Barney is betting that with the explosion in the size of the mutual-fund industry, it can keep old clients and lure new ones by offering more services to investors who have come to expect lower costs.

But by moving into the no-load segment, Smith Barney also is taking a calculated risk. The firm already offers 2,300 mutual-fund choices, through both proprietary (in-house) funds and outside funds it offers for a load fee. By adding the no-load group to the equation, it is wagering that it won't compete against itself to a damaging extent. "We want to do what is right for our clients," Mr. Dimon said. "If one product cannibalizes another, so be it."

Smith Barney also rolled out a high-powered weapon in its fight with financial advisers. In late 1996, the firm unveiled a "fee-based" program called AssetOne, aimed at investors who want to pay a flat annual rate for investment management rather than commissions on individual transactions. The move was similar to a program earlier launched by rival Merrill Lynch.

Under this program, investors with at least $100,000 to invest can get investment advice and management of stocks, bonds and no-load mutual funds for a flat fee. The fee varies according to how much money they hand over to Smith Barney and how actively they want to manage it. Investors with $100,000 who want to make only twelve trades a year pay $1,500 annually, or 1.5 percent; those making more trades pay a steeper fee. The package is cheaper than many brokerage-house "wrap" accounts—the one-fee accounts launched in the mid-1980s as Wall Street began trying to reduce its dependence on trading commissions. Fees for those can run as steep as 3 percent a year.

Seeking a Stronger Investment-Banking Toehold

Since the departure of Mr. Greenhill in early 1996, Smith Barney has made a bid to climb up the underwriting rankings. But it had been slow going: The firm ranked No. 10 among Wall Street underwriters in 1996, the same as in 1995, though it moved up to No. 5 in underwriting fees from No. 6. Yet Smith Barney was unable to crack the vaunted No. 1 spot in any of the fourteen underwriting categories covered by Securities Data Co.

Of the twenty-five largest stock deals of 1996, Smith Barney lead-managed just one, and that was the $886 million stock offering of Travelers/Aetna Property—Smith Barney's parent. There has been some progress in market share: Smith Barney's share of new municipal issues rose to 10 percent in 1996, from 8 percent the year earlier; its share of new stock issues rose to 7.5 percent, from 6.7 percent in the year before.

It was a different story in 1997. The combined Salomon Smith Barney was ranked a lofty No. 2 in the rankings of Wall Street underwriters in 1997, helping to bring to market $167 billion of new stock and bond issues for a 12.9 percent market share. The firm snagged the lead spot in underwriting mortgage bonds in 1997 (overtaking Lehman Brothers), and captured the top spot in new municipal-bond issues, with an 11.7 percent share of the market, Securities Data said. The overall underwriting rankings of the combined company were helped by Salomon, which managed the $642.5 million stock deal of YPF Sociedad Anonima and the $504 million stock offering by Clear Channel Communications.

The combined firm's 1997 showing landed it among the leaders in most underwriting categories. In addition to placing second in money raised overall, Salomon Smith Barney also was second in proceeds from bond offerings, fourth in stock offerings, seventh in initial public stock offerings and fourth in disclosed fees. "The biggest difference in fees is big M&A deals," said Salomon Smith Barney's Mr. Black. "That's where you get paid. We, at Smith Barney, did a huge number of M&A deals but they were not huge deals. Now, we'll be in there fighting for every large transaction there is."

Smith Barney dropped the ball on a few big deals in the Greenhill era. The most notable: miscalculating how much of a $1.9 billion RJR Nabisco Holdings Inc. preferred-stock deal it could sell in 1994. Instead of the $750 million it promised, Smith Barney sold only $250 million of the high-profile issue.

Smith Barney executives said the firm's banking effort has become more focused. "We began looking at the process of taking a company public as a product, not an event," said Stephen Stonefield, then a Smith Barney managing director.

As part of this focus, Smith Barney expanded its expertise from passively advising clients on strategic issues to taking a more active role. Take Union Pacific Corp.'s 1995 spin-off of its oil-and-gas unit. Smith Barney mobilized its energy group, led by Robert Jeffe, whose connections to the oil industry ran deep. Group members used the expertise of Smith Barney's homegrown bankers and the connections of the Morgan Stanley expatriates, who had had a relationship with Union Pacific while at their old firm. As a new company seeking its independence, Union Pacific Resources Group Inc. wasn't wedded to using its parent's traditional investment bankers, CS First Boston Inc. And Mr. Weill also called on his old friend, Union Pacific Chairman Drew Lewis. The result: Smith Barney snagged the lead-manager role on the coveted initial public stock offering, which spun off 15 percent of the unit and raised $890 million.

There have been pockets of strength, particularly in health care. Led by specialist Ben Lorello, Smith Barney was involved in 209 health-care transactions in 1996 and 1997 alone. In one 1997 advertisement, Smith Barney featured Mr. Lorello, with the text crowing: "On his office credenza, Ben Lorello is building a wall of Lucite blocks representing the transactions he's worked on during his 12 years as head of Smith Barney's health care group."

But there have been some blunders. The firm was forced to pull out of a six-million-share stock offering for DeBartolo Realty Corp. in 1995 after the firm violated a rule barring underwriters from trading a company's stock forty-eight hours before the offering. The matter was particularly sensitive for Smith Barney, the co-manager on the offering—rival Morgan Stanley was the deal's lead manager. People at Smith Barney said the firm had to pull out of the deal at the last minute when it discovered that some of its traders had traded the stock on the morning of the day it was to be priced. Since Smith Barney had committed to selling the stock to its retail investors, it was forced to buy DeBartolo shares in the secondary market after the stock was freed to trade.

As a mergers adviser, Smith Barney fell to No. 11 in 1996 from No. 8 a year earlier—and was absent in the many blockbuster deals of the year. Yet the combined Salomon Smith Barney placed fifth in the 1997 merger race, advising U.S. companies on $191.8 billion in announced merger or acquisition deals, for a 20.9 percent of the market share.

Salomon's banking effort, particularly abroad, will help. Yet even in one of the biggest underwriting and mergers environments ever, Salomon's investment-banking group was barely profitable. One reason is that Salomon is making investments to build up its banking group. The other is that its banking rankings are highest in lower-margin areas, such as asset-backed securities; the firm's rankings in the more lucrative stock and mergers-and-acquisitions league tables are far lower.

Lost business stemming from the Treasury scandal clearly set back the firm. Droves of banking defections also have hurt Salomon amid the firm's failed efforts to revamp its pay system. Returns aren't about to turn around in

Trading Traumas

Buffett Saved Salomon In '91, They Say, but It Needs Some Aid Again

His Team Misjudged Bonds And Is Driving Talent Away With Its Pay Plan

Separate and Unequal Staffs

By Michael Siconolfi
And Anita Raghavan
Staff Reporters of The Wall Street Journal

NEW YORK—Warren Buffett's vision of Salomon Brothers was crystallized for some executives in a homespun way at a 1994 board meeting of parent Salomon Inc.

Charles Munger, Mr. Buffett's close associate and a director, likened Salomon's two trading arms to a "gambling casino with a restaurant out front." The casino—the group doing proprietary trading for the house—"is the thing we really want because it makes a lot of money," he told directors, according to participants. "And we're happy to have the restaurant"—customer businesses such as stock and bond trading and investment banking—"as long as it doesn't cost too much."

Mr. Munger explains today that all he meant was that the two parts "are symbiotic." But now, the "restaurant" part of Salomon is in deep disarray, and its woes are threatening the stability of the entire Salomon operation.

In the midst of a disastrous 1994 in which Salomon lost $831 million before taxes, the firm, with Mr. Buffett's backing and influence, launched a radical new pay plan that has triggered dozens of defections in its customer operations. Yesterday came another one: Andrew Barrett, Salomon's European stock chief. More departures are expected.

The result is that the firm's flagship Salomon Brothers unit is stumbling, more unsteady now than at any other time since the depths of its 1991 Treasury-bond scandal, when it nearly collapsed before Mr. Buffett launched an intense rescue effort. Because of its losses, Salomon may face a debt downgrade that could boost its annual funding costs by as much as $50 million. In Wall Street's toughest operating environment in years, Salomon's situation is especially difficult.

All this has disenchanted some shareholders. Salomon's stock is down about 30% in the past 12 months. The firm "suffers from a pattern of shooting itself in the foot," laments James Gipson, portfolio manager of the $300 million Clipper Fund of Beverly Hills, Calif. Clipper has cut its Salomon holdings but still owns about 2% of the firm's stock.

The biggest shareholder, of course, is Berkshire Hathaway Inc., the Omaha, Neb., company of which Mr. Buffett owns 40.3%. Some Salomon executives speculate that Mr. Buffett will eventually push Salomon to sell its customer businesses and keep proprietary trading operations, or even sell its 21% Salomon holding. Mr. Buffett declines to comment. Mr. Munger says: "You're talking about very remote speculation."

But after a Salomon Brothers executive-committee meeting earlier this year, Deryck Maughan, the man Mr. Buffett installed as chief executive after the bond scandal, told an associate, "Either we make some money or get the firm ready for sale," according to a person familiar with the meeting. Mr. Maughan declines to comment. Salomon spokesman Robert Baker says, "Deryck has not discussed the sale of the firm with the executive committee; however, he has stated strongly that earnings must improve."

Why is Salomon, once Wall Street's most feared trading power, now facing such tumult?

One reason is that, while rivals like Merrill Lynch & Co. and Morgan Stanley Group Inc. have broadened business lines, Salomon still lives and dies primarily by trading. This has left it far more vulnerable to declining markets or trading missteps. Powerful traders have resisted efforts to rein in their pay even as the firm's costs have mounted. The controversial pay plan is partly an effort to trim such costs.

Salomon Chairman Robert Denham says that he and Mr. Maughan "have not run the firm with the idea that we only make money from proprietary trading. We think each [part] is a good business, and we think each exists better with the other."

But when it comes to managing Salomon, both men face handicaps. Mr. Denham, who like Mr. Maughan was a Buffett choice for his post, never ran an investment bank before; he is a veteran corporate lawyer. And Mr. Maughan never was a trader—a disadvantage at a rough-and-tumble trading firm known for its bawdy antics depicted in the Michael Lewis book "Liar's Poker." Mr. Denham says he doesn't think Salomon Brothers "has to be run by a trader to make effective use of trading talent and effectively manage trading."

The Salomon story underscores the difficulties even the savviest outsiders have in trying to manage Wall Street firms. Mr. Buffett has been patient, but no one expects him to allow Salomon to keep hemorrhaging red ink; the firm's customer business had a 1994 pretax loss of $636 million. But more important, the recent defections suggest that he badly misjudged the impact the firm's strict new pay plan would have on Salomon's morale.

In a telling passage in Berkshire Hathaway's latest annual report, Mr. Buffett spelled out his pay philosophy. Describing how he pays the chief of a Berkshire-owned company that makes, among other things, vacuum cleaners, he said: "In setting compensation, we like to hold out the promise of large carrots, but make sure their delivery is tied directly to results in the area that a manager controls."

But what works for widget companies on Main Street often fails on Wall Street, where traders can contribute so heavily to the bottom line that they often take home more than the chairman.

Under the plan launched in October, managing directors in Salomon's client-driven businesses will suffer an average cut in their fixed pay of 65%. They can earn back that much and more if the

client-driven business has an after-tax return on allocated equity of as much as 10%. But few are counting on achieving that goal. Salomon concedes in its annual report that the firm faces a "difficult" operating environment this year. And traders in an array of customer businesses such as equities complain that restrictions on how much they can have at stake make it even harder to generate high returns.

Moreover, the customer traders can't count on the value of their individual contributions to company profit for the size of their paycheck; the new plan is tied to the overall performance of a wide array of Salomon's divisions, from government-bond and mortgage-securities trading to equities and investment banking. Typically, Wall Street firms pay traders and others from a bonus pool based more narrowly on the performance of the individual employees, their specific divisions and the firm as a whole.

Short Run and Long

Salomon defends the new pay plan. In the annual report, Mr. Maughan says it "demands a radical shift in our culture" and "could hurt earnings in the short run. On the other hand, if we are not willing now to accept the responsibility for raising the returns of our business, when will we?" (Mr. Denham says he and Mr. Maughan crafted the controversial plan.)

The flap over pay came at a particularly sensitive time. Just as Salomon launched the plan last fall, traders learned that Stephen Posford, the London trading chief, had negotiated a 1994 pay package of $20 million even though his European operation had losses of $450 million. Only months earlier, Salomon unveiled a performance-based compensation formula for Mr. Maughan that gave him the chance to earn $25 million a year.

Further, Mr. Posford, Dennis Keegan, Salomon's powerful New York trading head, and Shigeru Myojin, who was Tokyo trading chief, had privately worked out a pact where they divided among them nearly $100 million of the bond-arbitrage group's 1994 bonus pool, people close to the firm say. "We felt it was important for each of the three to have a stake in what the other was doing," Mr. Denham says.

Meanwhile, Salomon's proprietary traders—who historically have received the firm's fattest pay packages—won't suffer nearly as badly as their customer counterparts. Their pay plan calls for a chunk of their pay to be set aside by the firm. If they continue to perform well, that money eventually will be paid out. But, in an unusual twist, if they stumble and lose money for the firm, Salomon can keep the funds it withheld. Nevertheless, the basic pay structure for proprietary traders won't be reduced and their pay will be based on their own group's performance instead of the broader performance standards for the customer businesses.

The split in pay has exacerbated a caste system that has left customer traders feeling disenfranchised. "It's difficult to be told you're going to earn $400,000 when across the aisle, [proprietary] traders are making tens of millions of dollars," a Salomon executive says.

Salomon long has earned the bulk of its profit from proprietary trading, but now some analysts wonder if the firm can re-create its earlier proprietary-trading profits. This is partly because the core of the proprietary trading group defected earlier to a trading boutique launched by John Meriwether, who had been pressured to resign at Salomon in the wake of the 1991 Treasury-bond scandal.

So loathsome is the new customer pay plan inside Salomon that it has triggered more than two dozen defections since October. Among them: utilities investment banker Ronald Calise and equity syndicate chief Robert Nau. The defections came as a handful of Salomon's most senior and respected executives also jumped ship, including investment-banking chief Richard Barrett. Messrs. Nau and Barrett and investment banker Gerard Smith are close to joining Union Bank of Switzerland's securities unit, Wall Street executives say. Faced with growing discontent, Salomon this week added $20 million to the 1995 bonus pool for its customer businesses. But this may be too little, too late, some analysts say.

The widespread rejection of the Buf-fett-influenced pay plan marks a turning point in Mr. Buffett's relationship with the firm. Since 1991, when he stepped in as interim chairman, he had been widely credited with saving a reeling Salomon after its admission of exceeding Treasury-auction bidding limits and of making unauthorized bids in customers' names.

The plain-spoken Nebraskan placated Washington regulators, took over the reins of Salomon and slashed its swollen asset base and pay levels. Messrs. Buffett and Denham negotiated the firm's $290 million settlement with the government in 1992.

Mr. Buffett's involvement in Salomon had started in October 1987, when the firm struggled to avoid the unsolicited attentions of investor Ronald O. Perelman. Berkshire Hathaway bought $700 million of Salomon convertible preferred stock paying a 9% annual dividend and convertible into common at $38 a share. Mr. Buffett hasn't converted those shares, but he may soon convert or redeem part of his preferred holdings: Salomon is scheduled to redeem 140,000 of the preferred annually, starting Oct. 31. The stock closed yesterday at $34.75 on the New York Stock Exchange.

Though Mr. Buffett gave up Salomon's chairmanship in 1992, he keeps a close eye on the firm. Besides him, four of the nine directors are Buffett associates or appointees. And he is chairman of the board's executive committee.

Early this year, Mr. Buffett peppered senior Salomon executives with probing questions in a series of conference calls as the firm grappled with a bookeeping blunder, insiders say. Salomon has set plans to take charges totaling $175 million after taxes to clean up nearly 10 years of botched bookkeeping on trading desks.

What has surprised analysts is that Salomon seemingly wasn't minding the store during the 1994 bond-market collapse. In a major miscue, its mortgage group held a whopping $10 billion of bonds—with some positions three years old—that it couldn't adequately value or easily peddle. In Salomon's annual report, Mr. Denham conceded the oversight: "Management of inventory and trading risks was weak in a few specific business units contributing to significant losses in those units."

Possibly under pressure from Mr. Buffett to turn around the firm, Mr. Maughan has started taking what some Salomon executives consider rash steps. In February, he walked into an executive-committee meeting and presented a plan to shut down the highly valued brokerage operation. Mr. Maughan "never [previously] talked to anyone about eliminating" it, a participant at the meeting says. Mr. Denham counters that "Deryck wasn't under any pressure to turn the firm around other than that self-generated pressure—and there's plenty of that."

Mr. Maughan was hit by a firestorm of controversy over the decision, partly because the brokerage operations weren't a big drain on Salomon's expenses. The group—which catered mainly to wealthy families and individuals—was shuttered in February "to concentrate our resources on our core advisory, underwriting and trading businesses," Salomon says. Mr. Baker says that its future had been reviewed with "relevant members of the executive committee" three times before being discussed by the full committee in early January, and that "Deryck took the decision to shut [it] himself based on the information from these meetings."

Some Salomon executives also criticize Mr. Maughan for continuing to aggressively build up the firm's overseas presence as its European operations have sunk deeply in the red. Even with Salomon's 1994 pretax losses of $450 million in its London operations, the firm continues to expand abroad.

There have been other mishaps. A $400 million investment fund called "Sizzle" that sought to mimic Salomon's proprietary-trading strategy sank 15% in 1994, angering institutional clients. The fund was supposed to make complex trades based on price discrepancies among various fixed-income, currency and futures markets, but Solomon executives say it also took directional bets on interest rates and the dollar. Mr. Baker says, "There were a broad range of trading strategies. Taking directional bets on interest rates and currencies was not the strategy."

Heralded last year as a major Salomon entry into asset management, the fund now is sometimes derisively referred to internally as "Fizzle."

And Mr. Maughan's vision of creating a global investment bank was set back recently when Salomon had losses of more than $50 million in the fledgling Russian stock market, traders say.

Meantime, world-wide operations were so hamstrung by trading mishaps that the firm now is looking to sharply slash costs. It has to take in some $1.5 billion a year before it can turn a profit, Salomon executives say. To cut costs, the firm recently banned first class flights and hotel stays at the Ritz; now, employees must fly coach and lodge at the Inter-Continental instead.

As for Mr. Buffett, his folksy letter to shareholders in the latest annual report from Berkshire Hathaway doesn't even mention its Wall Street investment. "He thinks about these things," an associate says. "He's distancing himself."

Not so, counters Mr. Munger. "I wouldn't read anything into that at all," he says, adding that Mr. Buffett frequently varies the investments he discusses in shareholder letters. "It's crazy to go through the Berkshire report reading tea leaves."

April 21, 1995

any big way soon because of Salomon's push to ramp up the unit, including hiring high-priced bankers in areas such as health care and technology. Yet Mr. Maughan said the banking group has turned around from several years ago. When he was brought over from Japan to run the banking division in 1990, Mr. Maughan said, it had more than $100 million in annual losses. "The bank today has viable profits, is respected—that's a key word—and has position in the U.S.," Mr. Maughan said.

Salomon's banking group caused some industry tremors in 1996, when it underwrote Berkshire Hathaway's $574 million offer of Class B shares for a skinny underwriting fee of $7.8 million—or about 1.5 percent of proceeds. That's far less than the average fee to sell an add-on stock offering, which runs nearly 6 percent of proceeds, according to Securities Data Co. Even Berkshire's chairman, Warren Buffett, chirped about the slim fees on the investment company's deal. At Berkshire's 1996 annual meeting, Mr. Buffett noted that the underwriting spread, or percentage of the issue paid to the underwriter, for these "Baby Berkshire" shares would be less than half that on the spin-off of Lucent Technologies Inc. from AT&T Corp. Some weren't surprised by the small-fry fees because of Mr. Buffett's close ties to Salomon: After all, Mr. Buffett is widely credited with saving Salomon following its Treasury scandal and at the time was the firm's single biggest stockholder, with an 18.7 percent stake.

There have been some banking coups. These included advising Orange County in its bankruptcy proceedings and advising Northrop Grumman Corp. on its acquisition of the defense-electronics business of Westinghouse Electric. But 1996 also was notable for its banking disappointments. Salomon was shut out of the lucrative underwriting of Lucent—the $3 billion AT&T spinoff and among the biggest United States initial public stock offerings ever. Some Salomon insiders blamed the snub on the firm's star telecommunications analyst, Jack Grubman, who has helped the firm win many underwriting assignments in recent years. Just a week before the bankers on the Lucent deal were unveiled, Mr. Grubman was quoted in *The Wall Street Journal* saying AT&T's repeated restructuring charges "raise the question, have they really earned any money?" He added that he believed such jumbo charges should be subtracted from AT&T's earnings over a longer period that would more resemble the time frame in which the losses were actually incurred. "Wall Street investors are getting the wool pulled over their eyes. They don't realize the whole earnings are a fake." Mr. Grubman is unrepentant. (Mr. Grubman had the last laugh; the star telecom analyst took home a pay package valued at more than $7 million in 1997, double the $3.5 million he earned in 1996.) On the merger side, Salomon lost out when it advised Northrop Grumman on a failed bid for the sale of General Motors Corp.'s Hughes Electronics defense operations.

Salomon got a big piece of one of the most high-profile takeover fights of 1997. The firm advised WorldCom, the upstart that knocked off British Telecommunications to buy MCI Communications, earning Salomon $33 million in fees. The windfall helped ease the pain of the $100 million in trading losses Salomon suffered when the value of MCI's then-existing deal with BT was revised downward. Moreover, the firm's sometimes-maligned banking group got to boast a big part in the largest-ever U.S. takeover.

Salomon also advised Northrop Grumman Corp. in its $11.8 billion acquisition by Lockheed Martin Corp. And Salomon helped advise General Motors Corp.'s Hughes Electronics defense business in its $9.5 billion acquisition by Raytheon Co.

Less than two weeks after the Smith Barney/Salomon merger was announced, Smith Barney's beleaguered banking team took pains to be noticed. In an unusual full-page newspaper ad, Smith Barney trumpeted its investment bank with the shadow of a fiery orchestra leader behind a straightlaced banker and the words: "Creative fire. Behind every deal lies an idea. At Smith Barney, orchestrating deals from conception to close is what we do best."

During the past several years, banking has accounted for 20 percent of Salomon's net revenue—and just 5 percent of pretax income. Mr. Maughan said Salomon is "investing internationally" to build its banking prowess, and that its global operations as a result have been unprofitable. "It takes time" to build big profits, Mr. Maughan said. He quickly added: "We have a global trading platform—it makes sense to leverage that with the investment bank."

International: Seeking to Put Smith Barney on the Map

For years, Smith Barney desperately sought an international partner. In 1995 came a golden opportunity: Barings PLC. Hearing that the venerable British merchant bank was set to collapse after big trading losses, Messrs. Weill, Dimon and Greenhill sprang into action, flying to London to negotiate with Barings' chairman, Peter Baring. Smith Barney bid £155 million—then about $250 million—for the firm's Barings Securities unit, people familiar with the matter said.

This wasn't a shock: Mr. Weill has a long history of buying troubled firms at bargain prices. But before the bid was considered, Dutch concern Internationale Nederlanden Groep NV bought nearly all the assets of the collapsed merchant bank. Smith Barney executives aren't ashamed. In the past few years, with Smith Barney absorbing Shearson and building investment banking, "it would have been very difficult to do anything at all" internationally, Mr. Black said. "Barings was a fire sale."

In early 1997, the firm entered into a pact with a British financial-services firm to buttress its clout in Europe. Under the agreement, analysts at Smith Barney made their research on United States companies available electronically to counterparts at BZW, the securities unit of Britain's Barclays Bank PLC. In turn, analysts at the London firm shared research on European stocks with Smith Barney. The deal was aimed at helping Smith Barney compete with brokerage firms, such as Merrill, that can offer clients in-house research on companies in the United States, Europe, Asia and Latin America. Smith Barney also hired a team of twenty-one people from the European stock-research teams at Dillon Read Securities, covering Belgium, France, Germany and Spain.

But Smith Barney is betting that Salomon will provide it with much more clout outside the United States. Salomon's strength was evident in July 1997, when it sold $989 million in stock of Argentine oil and gas producer YPF SA in a "block," or bulk, trade. The transaction was agreed to on a Tuesday evening, a price determined the following morning, and all the stock was sold to clients in the United States, Europe and Argentina before the markets in New York opened. Such block trades have become a popular way for companies or major shareholders to sell large blocks of stock quickly.

In recent years, Salomon has tried to use such bulk trades to climb the ranks of stock underwriters. Salomon has bought and resold billions of dollars of clients' stock in dozens of so-called equity takedowns. These transactions— which allow corporate clients to skip the time-consuming steps in a standard underwriting—are essentially block trades. Salomon typically commits to buy stock at a certain price from a company after the market closes, then seeks to redistribute the same shares to its investment clients before the market opens the next day. Until the stock is resold, Salomon has its own capital at risk.

The strategy was born of necessity for Salomon, which doesn't have as many cozy investment-banking relationships with corporate clients as some other large rivals. But it carries the risk that if Salomon can't resell the stock to investors, it could wind up stuck with the shares and the prospect of having its capital tied up for days. Through it all, Salomon has upset some competitors because it has undercut the old-line banking relationship some Wall Street firms had cultivated with corporate clients. "The long-standing banking relationships that Goldman and Morgan Stanley carry have given them an unusual franchise and oligopoly," said Mr. Holland, the former Salomon executive who now runs his own investment firm. "To break into that oligopoly, the only thing that Salomon can compete with is capital and muscle."

Salomon Brothers' Bond-Trading Muscle

Salomon has earned its stripes on Wall Street trading bonds. Bond sales and trading accounted for nearly 60 percent of the firm's net revenue in the first half of the 1990s, and more than 100 percent of its pretax income (because of losses in other businesses), according to some estimates. One reason is juicy margins of more than 30 percent in this risky business. Salomon's bond-arbitrage group—which uses complicated mathematical formulas to make long-term bets around the globe involving the relationships of various securities and currencies—typically puts on just several big arbitrage trades.

The bulk of Salomon's profits still come from trading for the house account. Charles Munger, Mr. Buffett's close associate and a director, once likened Salomon's two trading arms to a "gambling casino with a restaurant out front." The casino—the group doing proprietary trading for the house—"is the thing we really want because it makes a lot of money," Mr. Munger told directors. "And we're happy to have the restaurant"—customer businesses such as stock and bond trading and investment banking—"as long as it doesn't cost too much."

Indeed, Salomon's stock business for clients has posted losses in recent years. Total stock sales and trading accounted for about one-fifth of net revenue in recent years—but less than 5 percent of pretax income. In the latter part of 1996, trading stocks, both for itself and for customers, bedeviled Salomon. Revenue from stock sales and trading plunged 55 percent, for instance, in the fourth quarter of 1996 from a year earlier, partly from continuing losses on the firm's proprietary trading of stocks, which was concentrated in the weak Japanese stock market. "We have a very profitable business in the States and we are making investments overseas," Mr. Maughan said at the time. Though the stock side of Salomon's proprietary-trading group is in the black, it isn't profitable enough to push the returns for the entire equities operation above industry levels, analysts say.

Salomon was a big player in one of the biggest trends of 1997: super-block trades. In this tactic, gone are the roadshows and lengthy meetings with prospective investors. Instead, underwriters like Salomon simply buy entire blocks of stock from the seller at a fixed price, then spend the next twenty-four hours putting together a group of buyers. During five days in July 1997 alone, Salomon sold a total of more than $1.6 billion of shares for YPF Sociedad Anonima, AES Corp., Viacom Inc. and Excel Realty Trust Inc.

In a newspaper advertisement, Salomon relished in the spurt of clout that it routinely boasted in the 1980s: "Working around the clock. Four diverse clients with one thing in common. The need for solutions. Salomon Brothers solved the needs of these clients by executing four overnight equity block trades in just five days."

Meanwhile, Smith Barney, along with Merrill and other Nasdaq powerhouses, saw trading margins squeezed in the wake of new trading rules on the Nasdaq Stock Market. As a result, Smith Barney slashed the number of small stocks it makes markets in to 1,100 in 1997 from 1,200 the year before.

Commodities: Taking the Refining out of Oil

Salomon's Basis Petroleum oil-refining unit has been a disaster, as persistently narrow refining margins triggered losses. After years of losses, Salomon finally sold Basis in 1997 for about $485 million in cash and stock. The sale capped an unprofitable foray into oil refining in which Salomon bought three refineries for about $120 million between 1985 and 1988 as part of a bid to boost its Phibro Inc. commodity-trading business. But since 1990, the last big year for Basis, refining has largely been a drag on Salomon's profits, contributing pretax losses of $369 million between 1991 and 1996.

Like many refiners, Basis Petroleum has suffered in recent years because the rise in oil prices has not been accompanied by a corresponding rise in the price of refined products such as gasoline, jet fuel and heating oil. As a result, refiners have not been able to pass higher raw-materials costs along to customers. This sale "allows us to focus our energy and resources on things that we are better at than refining," said Robert Denham, Salomon Inc.'s former chairman.

Meantime, Phibro laid off 20 percent of its workforce in 1996 as inflation remained subdued. Phibro dismissed eighty of its four hundred employees as the firm retrenched from such commodity markets as coal, coke and fertilizer. The cutbacks came as several Wall Street firms, including Merrill and Goldman, had pared commodity desks amid pinched trading volume and profit. A Phibro executive said the high-overhead coke, coal and fertilizer businesses had been losing money in recent years. "We don't think these are core to our business and they have not contributed anything to our bottom line," the executive said.

Instead, Phibro is focusing on trading oil and some other selected commodities, all while trying to use less capital. Bonuses had been cut in recent years: Compensation as a percentage of earnings before taxes and bonuses was 40 percent in 1996, down sharply from the 52 percent of a year earlier. Mr. Denham summed up the firm's commodity-trading strategy in its 1995 annual report: "Our objective for Phibro is to make some money during the frequent periods when commodities markets are unexciting and to make significant money in the occasional periods when commodities markets are hot."

The trouble for Salomon is that the last time commodities markets were smoking—and when Phibro generated fat earnings—was back in 1990.

Harassment Hassles

Smith Barney in late 1997 settled perhaps its most pressing legal issue: a highly public sexual-harassment suit. In the case, three women initially alleged that Nicholas Cuneo, a former Smith Barney branch manager, built a room in the basement of the Garden City, New York, branch that he named the "boom-boom room," which was decorated in fraternity-house style, complete with a toilet bowl hanging from the ceiling. This is where, the women alleged, some female brokers were disparaged by male colleagues.

Mr. Cuneo declined to comment. Smith Barney called allegations of systemic bias "absurd." A spokeswoman said: "Any complaint received is acted upon immediately; it is investigated thoroughly, promptly and, we hope, fairly." After an investigation into the Garden City matter, Smith Barney executives said, Mr. Cuneo was placed on a leave of absence and later left the firm.

The original case triggered a flurry of media stories, particularly in New York's tabloid newspapers. Then came more bad news: An amended complaint named twenty more women who alleged they were victims of discrimination, bringing the case back into the news. The case caught the public's attention because it alleged institutional sexual harassment. Smith Barney in November 1997 settled the notorious case by, among other things, agreeing to spend $15 million over four years on programs to recruit and promote women within its ranks. Specifically, Smith Barney agreed to boost the female representation in its training classes for brokers to 33 percent and for investment bankers to 25 percent in three years. Another goal of the settlement is for Smith Barney to increase the number of women managing its branches by at least 110 percent in three years, up from fifteen now.

The settlement certified as a class as many as 20,000 women who worked for Smith Barney since May 1993. Each of those women who wants to file a claim of sexual discrimination or sexual harassment has the option of accepting a settlement offer from the firm or taking her case to a private mediation system that Smith Barney will fund. If mediation doesn't produce an accord, the women can pursue their claims in a special arbitration forum to be created by the settlement and funded by Smith Barney. Meeting all the accord's goals would make Smith Barney a leader in the hiring of women in the securities industry, where women long have been poorly represented in the ranks of brokers. At Merrill, for instance, 15 percent of the firm's brokers are women.

Another high-profile case that surfaced in 1996 was filed against the firm by a broker at Scott & Stringfellow Inc., a small Richmond, Virginia, brokerage firm. Thomas Inman contended in an arbitration case that he had developed a unique and complex financial product that Smith Barney used to rescue what had been a failed bid by Viacom Inc. to win control of giant Paramount Communications Inc. in 1994. Smith Barney denied the allegations, and said any similarities between Mr. Inman's work and the Viacom bid were "superficial." Smith Barney ultimately prevailed, though the case brought up a tantalizing question: Can you copyright an idea on Wall Street?

Research

By the beginning of 1997, David Shulman's recurrent bearishness when it came to the long-lived bull market for stocks was looking embarassingly wrong. And by the end of the year, the four-year veteran of Salomon Brothers found himself looking for new employment in the wake of Wall Street's latest brokerage firm megamerger of Salomon with Smith Barney. Instead of being run by a lonely bear, the merged firm's strategy department will be run by one of Wall Street's most congenial bulls, A. Marshall Acuff.

While a number of Salomon's research analysts made the jump to the merged firm, including Ann Knight, now director of global research integration, and James Crandell, a former director of Salomon's research effort who now heads Latin American research for Salomon Smith Barney, the new company's strategy effort looks much like the old Smith Barney Group.

At the helm is Mr. Acuff, a veteran of the still-youthful discipline of investment strategy. For him, the name of the game is finding the right themes to play in the stock market.

"The markets are overloaded with information, information about earnings, about interest rates, about all kinds of economic developments," he said. "It's not that those aren't important, but it's the kind of context they're in that is most important when deciding what stocks to buy."

The search for well-capitalized companies that are poised to outperform the market as a whole is one that Mr. Acuff had gradually evolved ever since his boss at Smith Barney told him back in 1969 that henceforward, he'd be called a "strategist."

"I wasn't too sure what that meant at the time, no one really knew," he acknowledged. "It was a process of deduction, figuring out that doing well in investing isn't just a question of being in the market, but of picking the right stocks."

Few of Mr. Acuff's contemporaries remain in the investment business: most quit the field during or shortly after the prolonged bear market that buffeted stocks for much of the 1970s. But Mr. Acuff hung on, convinced it was possible to make money in both bull and bear markets by playing themes.

Most recently, Mr. Acuff argued investors should follow a "Feed the World" theme, focusing on the need to improve crop yields to feed the world's growing population. Investing in stocks of fertilizer and seed companies, he argued, would help them reap rich rewards. Other themes he has advocated over the past year include the "Graying of America," "Outsourcing" and "Global Growers," the latter a group with strong product cycles and dominant market share positions.

"Marshall's been one of the guys who identified the trend to buying big stocks, and has pushed it forward," said one large institutional client. "He's rarely controversial, but he often adds value to us around the margins."

Mr. Acuff and his team of strategists are respected on Wall Street, but their views seldom rock financial markets. In part, that's because of the focus of their work, which is resolutely long-term in nature: Mr. Acuff's recommendations don't change overnight and the relaxed, amiable strategist isn't given to extravagant or controversial predictions on the direction of the overall market.

That doesn't mean he hasn't made some timely investment calls, however. Late in 1996, he argued that the market would continue to reward large stocks with above-average price to earnings multiples, and that the seasonal "December effect" would fail to materialize. Often, his investment advice on particular stocks is contained within his ruminations on a particular segment of the market: his bullish stance on stocks with dependable earnings growth, clients say, implicitly translates into a more cautious attitude toward aggressive growth stocks like the technology sector. While by the end of 1997, the always-volatile technology sector was battered by investors fleeing disappointing earnings projections, some investors still felt Mr. Acuff had been too cautious by not recommending the group more aggressively on its way up.

"If there's a fault with this group, it's that they're too cautious," said one investor. William Helman, who determines recommended asset allocation for Salomon Smith Barney, "has been overly cautious in not anticipating the potential for the sharp decline in interest rates or the pace of earnings growth."

Still, Mr. Acuff's clients praise his ability to decipher for Salomon Smith Barney's diverse clientele the implications of issues such as the rising dollar. Most recently, those were tested by the stock market meltdowns in Asia, and he spent a week traveling the region. He concluded that the turmoil in Asia will lead to sluggish growth in the U.S. market as well as overseas, but that more cash might flow to U.S. markets, now viewed as "safe havens" by most Asian investors.

Mr. Shulman, who early in 1998 joined a hedge fund, doesn't regret his bearishness. In his final report for Salomon Bros., he reiterated his concerns about lofty stock market valuations.

"I'm the new kid on the block, but I'm still going to call them as I see them," said Mr. Shulman, an intense, focused man with little small talk. "And I've got the scars on my back to prove it."

Those institutional investors who follow Mr. Shulman's work say it doesn't matter that he's more wrong than most in the last year or two. "I'm paid to make that kind of judgement," argues one investor, who hopes to see Mr. Shulman resurface shortly in a strategist's role. Instead, they looked to his curmudgeonly comments for help in testing their own hypotheses about the market's direction, and to see if they're missing any signals. Part of the problem, his defenders argue, is that portfolio managers under pressure to find places to put the cash in their portfolios want to hear ideas, not worries about the market's direction.

Ideas will be readily available from Salomon Smith Barney's merged research team. The new firm's head of research, John Hoffman, a Smith Barney alumnus, has been able to cherry-pick the cream of Salomon's analysts, including Leanne Baker, a well-known gold and metals analyst, retailing analyst Jeffrey Feiner and Julius Maldutis, transportation analyst. Investors around the country heaved a sigh of relief when Eric Sorensen, Salomon's head of quantitative strategy, widely praised for his coverage of the issues surrounding corporate stock options, was handed the same post at Salomon Smith Barney. Some of those picked for the new team, however, didn't stick around long: shortly after being named to the merged research effort as analyst responsible for multinational banks, Diane Glossman opted to jump ship for Lehman Brothers.

The new team also includes a number of veteran Smith Barney all-star analysts, including Ronald Frank, a top stock-picker in the life and health insurance industry and Keith Mullins, the widely praised head of emerging growth stock analysis, an area in which Smith Barney has been building a solid reputation.

"The new group won't be flashy, but very, very solid," said one large institutional investor. "There's a belief out here that these guys will fight to get and keep the best analysts, although only time will tell."

The Outsider

Did Smith Barney Cheat a Stockbroker To Clinch a Merger?

Mr. Inman Claims Firm Stole His Finance Ideas to Save Viacom-Paramount Deal

'Enough Juice for Everybody'

BY MICHAEL SICONOLFI

Staff Reporter of THE WALL STREET JOURNAL

RICHMOND, Va.—In the movie "Working Girl," actress Melanie Griffith gets the last laugh after exposing an investment banker who stole her idea for a corporate acquisition.

Thomas Inman is trying to achieve the same result in real life. He is a broker at Scott & Stringfellow Inc., a sleepy securities firm in this former Confederate capital. Mr. Inman claims he developed a unique and complex financial product that Smith Barney Inc., the nation's second-largest brokerage firm, then used to rescue what had been a failed bid by Viacom Inc. to win control of giant Paramount Communications Inc. in 1994.

Nonsense, says Smith Barney, which advised Viacom—and pocketed fees of nearly $30 million in what has been one of the longest and most heated takeover battles of the 1990s. The Travelers Group unit says any similarities between Mr. Inman's work and the Viacom bid were "superficial."

Clinching Mergers

Mr. Inman's claim, originally filed as a lawsuit in Richmond federal court, is now in arbitration. The legal claim shines a light on the low-down jostling that sometimes breaks out over high-minded intellectual property. It also underscores the difficulty of "copyrighting"

the expression of an idea on Wall Street. In Hollywood, writers long have accused studios of stealing screenplays. On Wall Street, such squabbles promise to surface more as investment banks increasingly scramble to develop hybrid securities as a creative way of clinching merger deals or offsetting risk. The problem in claiming original corporate-finance products: They often grow out of other products already in the marketplace.

"There are very few truly original ideas in our business," contends Robert G. Scott, world-wide investment-banking chief at Morgan Stanley Group Inc. "About all of them are evolutionary—not revolutionary."

The result: "It's common to roll over" individuals who come to big Wall Street firms with capital-markets ideas, says veteran Wall Street investment banker Michael Madden. "Intellectual capital is something you can't put a fence around" in the brokerage business, he says. Because of this, "usually these folks protect themselves" legally so they aren't "left out in the cold."

Idea With Promise

That is what Mr. Inman believed he did. In October 1993 he signed a contract with Smith Barney and presented a 139-page, two-volume book detailing a financial product he had dreamed up. An unusual combination of securities, the product would allow a corporation to treat as debt for tax purposes an instrument having a variable payment with an inverse relationship to the issuer's stock price. In a confidentiality pact, Smith Barney agreed to promptly tell Mr. Inman if the firm "has independently developed or is independently developing similar financial products."

Smith Barney never did that. Instead, Mr. Inman says, Smith Barney derivatives executives told him the idea had promise. In a Nov. 4, 1993, phone call, Mr. Inman said Vincent Cirulli, then a Smith Barney vice president of bond derivatives, gushed: "There's enough juice in this for everybody."

In a Jan. 4, 1994, internal memo to Bruce Fox, a Smith Barney managing director, Mr. Cirulli pulled no punches. According to the memo, filed in Richmond federal court, Mr. Inman "personally owns the intellectual property to this product." The memo adds that Smith Barney executives "need to decide whether we want to commit to" using Mr. Inman's work. In a phone call that day, Mr. Inman says, Mr. Cirulli told him just three issues remained unresolved: Mr. Inman's compensation; the involvement, if any, of Scott & Stringfellow; and who would act as outside tax counsel. Mr. Cirulli, who now works at Deutsche Morgan Grenfell, didn't return calls for comment. Smith Barney argues that Mr. Cirulli had no input into the Viacom deal. Mr. Fox wasn't involved in the Viacom deal and declined to comment for this article.

High-Priced Crew

What is indisputable is that Smith Barney badly needed its client to win the Paramount fight. Long known as a brokerage giant catering to individual investors, Smith Barney had just hired a crew of high-priced investment bankers in a bid to build a banking dynamo. Indeed, the Viacom/Paramount deal created a big splash for Smith Barney and earned it immediate recognition, plus those hefty fees. The Viacom deal helped "legitimize the [mergers] product coming out of this firm," said Conrad Bringsjord, Smith Barney's co-mergers chief and an architect of the Viacom deal.

The clash pits one of Wall Street's savviest firms with someone who never will be mistaken for Gordon Gekko, the slick financier in the movie "Wall Street." A short, balding man with a genteel Virginia manner, the 42-year-old Mr. Inman says he chose the brokerage business partly to help overcome shyness: "Cold calling was extremely difficult for me." An interview for an investment-banking position at Kidder, Peabody Group Inc. was a bust. "I was intimidated by New York—still am," Mr. Inman says. "I'm a Southern boy." Finally, he landed a job as a broker catering to individual investors in Richmond at Wheat First Butcher Singer.

In 1989, he joined Scott & Stringfellow in Richmond, which seems much farther away than the 352 miles from Smith Barney's headquarters near New York's World Trade Center. Nestled a block from the federal courthouse—which once housed part of the Confederate States of America's Treasury Building—Scott & Stringfellow's edifice includes quaint Old English lettering and a Dow Jones Industrial Average sign with price changes that aren't real-time, but updated periodically throughout the day.

Fingering through the bound volume he submitted to Smith Barney, Mr. Inman recalls the nearly three years he spent staying up late in his den crunching numbers and tapping data into his Macintosh computer. "This was sweat equity," he says. "I am not a wealthy man." He is frank about his motivation for cranking out the project: to make money and "advance my career."

His paycheck never would be confused with that of an investment banker. Last year, Mr. Inman took home roughly $50,000 in brokerage commissions. (By contrast, Michael Levitt, a senior Smith Barney banker on the Viacom deal who has now left the firm, received 1994 pay of nearly $5 million.)

Meantime, Mr. Inman's case seems to have gotten personal. He bristled when Smith Barney, in response to his claim, said his product wasn't novel because of "the prior existence of the components in the public domain." Extending that logic, he said, his then six-year-old son, "who knows the notes of the musical scale, should be able to compose a sonata." In a letter to one of Mr. Inman's lawyers, Smith Barney Deputy General Counsel Joan Guggenheimer said: "Mr. Inman's musical analogy is cute, but completely off target and, to the extent he analogizes Smith Barney to a six-year-old child, rather insulting."

The claim, says Mr. Bringsjord, the Smith Barney co-mergers chief, is "an affront to the truly original financial instruments created in the transaction."

Mr. Inman's product contained complex hybrid securities—two call warrants, a debenture, and a contingent note—that basically would provide investors with protection against a downturn in an issuer's stock price. (Mr. Inman made the proposal without a specific issuer or transaction in mind.)

As Mr. Cirulli and other Smith Barney executives considered Mr. Inman's proposal, the firm was in the midst of advising Viacom on its four-month battle with QVC Network Inc. to buy Paramount. On Jan. 12, 1994, Paramount's board rejected Viacom's latest bid—which in addition to cash contained only Viacom common and preferred stock.

During the next few weeks, Viacom made a new bid—one that included hybrid securities absent from its previous proposals, including a debenture, a contingent note and two different call warrants. "The four components of" the winning Viacom bid "directly correspond to securities in and reflect the unique structure of Inman's" product, according to Mr. Inman's federal-court complaint.

Smith Barney's Ms. Guggenheimer, in a letter filed in federal court, conceded "certain superficial similarities" between Mr. Inman's product and that used by Smith Barney in the Viacom bid. But Ms. Guggenheimer said "those responsible for designing the Viacom bid had never seen Mr. Inman's materials."

Mr. Inman disputes that, saying that one Smith Barney derivatives executive, Douglas Hiscano, was familiar with his work and had bragged to Mr. Inman about having designed one part of the Viacom bid. But Ms. Guggenheimer plays down Mr. Hiscano's role in the deal, saying it was limited to pricing portions of the proposal. She adds that Mr. Hiscano "never studied" Mr. Inman's work. Mr. Hiscano, now a managing director at Bear Stearns Cos., declined to comment.

Smith Barney bankers on the deal say they considered using the securities in the Viacom bid well before they were presented by Mr. Inman. And they argue that Mr. Inman's package, which was partly an attempt to create a tax-deductible instrument, never factored into the Viacom bid.

In the letter filed in federal court, Ms. Guggenheimer said the similarities between Mr. Inman's work and the Viacom bid "were attributable to the reliance of both on components already in use in the investment community." She said one integral part of the Viacom package—the use of warrants—originated not with Smith Barney but with the "well-known and highly regarded CEO of another investment-banking firm, who was pro-

viding independent financial advice to Viacom."

The mystery man? Alan "Ace" Greenberg, chairman of Bear Stearns. In an interview, Mr. Greenberg said, yes, he pushed the warrants idea on the Viacom deal because they provided some protection against a decline in the value of Viacom's stock. Meantime, Mr. Greenberg said it is "ridiculous" for anyone to stake a claim on an idea on Wall Street.

For instance, Mr. Greenberg brags about creating the "Dutch auction tender offer"—in which a company permits holders to tender their shares at a price of their own choosing, up to a level set by the company—in a 1981 deal. "I wish I could have copyrighted it," he says. "Maybe if this guy wins, I'll sue everybody who has used the Dutch auction" since.

For its part, Mr. Inman's claim is based not on the originality of any one of the securities used in his product but rather on the "uniqueness of their combination and the resulting economic benefits."

In the end, legal specialists say the spat could hinge on the contract between Mr. Inman and Smith Barney. The pact, agreed to three months before Viacom's victorious bid, barred Smith Barney from using Mr. Inman's work without his consent and contemplated the "mutual commercial exploitation" of the product by Mr. Inman and the firm. The claim, which alleges breach of contract and a violation of the Virginia trade-secrets act, has been transferred to an arbitration panel of the New York Stock Exchange, and seeks damages that weren't specified.

There haven't been many similar cases on Wall Street, says Kenneth Plevan, head of intellectual-property practice at Skadden, Arps, Slate, Meagher & Flom, a New York law firm that isn't involved in the case. The Inman-Smith Barney spat probably isn't clear-cut because hybrid securities are difficult to understand, unlike a typical case involving alleged theft of, say, the script to "NYPD Blue." Adds Mr. Plevan: "If they stole his idea and got value from it, they should pay him."

August 8, 1996

Salomon Name Snatches Lead Billing

It was a Wall Street oddity: The acquired firm wound up with the lead billing in a big brokerage-house merger.

Among the curiosities of the merged firm is its name: Salomon Smith Barney Holdings Inc. The fact that Salomon grabbed the top spot was striking because the names of acquired firms often take second place in Street deals, before eventually being trashed forever.

But in this case, the order makes sense, Wall Street executives said. Mr. Weill, Travelers chairman, is looking to leverage the international cachet of Salomon, which was sorely missing at Smith Barney. "The Salomon name is more useful to Sandy in growing the business worldwide," said Mr. Holland, the former Salomon executive who now heads his own money-management firm. Salomon is an established name among the big institutions of the world, particularly in Asia—a weak spot for Smith Barney. "In talking to central bankers in Hong Kong, to have the Salomon name come first is an advantage," Mr. Holland said.

But some Street specialists say that could change in time. "Salomon is the better-recognized international name than Smith Barney, but it's transitory," said Jay Higgins, a former Salomon vice chairman who now also manages money. In a few years, "if Sandy doesn't like it, he'll change it."

Salomon Smith Barney's People

Sanford I. Weill, chairman and chief executive, Travelers Group: Mr. Weill has no formal title at Salomon Smith Barney. But make no mistake about it: He helps oversee the brokerage firm's vast operations, and few major decisions are made without his OK. Indeed, it was Mr. Weill who orchestrated the merger on Smith Barney's end.

Mr. Weill delights in recounting his humble upbringing. Prominent in his office is a huge picture of the yellow three-family house where he grew up. But the Weill family was far from poor; though Mr. Weill's father was a Polish immigrant, he made enough money as a dressmaker to send Sandy to Peekskill Military Academy and to Cornell University.

Nothing in his career was handed to him, Mr. Weill said. He once recalled how in his early days on Wall Street in the 1950s he supported his wife, Joan, and their first child, Marc, on $150 a month. After graduating from Cornell, he peddled business directories. He started as a runner for Bear Sterns Cos. and later became a stockbroker.

He can be tough on managers. At a 1992 meeting of Smith Barney's top brokers, executives were reporting on the firm's fortunes. After then–Smith

Barney chairman Frank Zarb presented record earnings, Mr. Weill gibed: "That's not bad, Frank. Just keep going and you'll be here for another year." Though the remark was playful, those who knew Mr. Weill said at the time that it carried some truth.

They were right. Mr. Zarb—who had been tapped to run the new Smith Barney Shearson—was replaced when Mr. Weill hired Mr. Greenhill in June 1993. He left Smith Barney later that year. (Mr. Zarb is now chairman of the NASD.)

Jamie Dimon, cochairman, Salomon Smith Barney: After graduating near the top of his class at Harvard Business School, Mr. Dimon followed Mr. Weill from American Express to a small office where he helped plot Mr. Weill's next takeover, the 1986 acquisition of Commercial Credit Co., a consumer lender.

Some compare the close relationship between the two men with one Mr. Weill previously had forged with former Shearson chairman Peter Cohen, who like Mr. Dimon was in his twenties when he became Mr. Weill's confidant and numbers cruncher. Mr. Dimon has deep connections to Smith Barney; his father and grandfather were longtime brokers at Smith Barney or its predecessor firms.

He was named chairman and chief executive at Smith Barney in 1996. Before assuming that post, Mr. Dimon was the firm's chief operating officer and chief administrative officer. He graduated from Tufts University and has an MBA from Harvard.

Mr. Dimon knows inside out the consumer-finance, insurance and retail-brokerage businesses that have turned Travelers into a U.S. financial jugger-naut. He is a proven commodity, helping to generate big profits at Smith Barney in recent years. So, what

Dimon, Jamie
Cochairman-Salomon
Smith Barney

is the likely outcome of the horse-race with Mr. Maughan for the ultimate top spot at the newly merged firm? Says veteran investment banker William Benedetto: "I think Jamie is going to persevere in this thing. He is a very talented person and he has a long history working with Sandy."

Deryck Maughan, cochairman, Salomon Smith Barney: Mr. Maughan rose to the top of Salomon Brothers in 1991 with lightning speed: He replaced Mr. Gutfreund in the early days of the Treasury scandal, soon after returning to New York from running Salomon's Tokyo office. The courtly, British-born Mr. Maughan has never been mistaken for the brash, cigar-chomping New Yorkers, including Mr. Gutfreund, who previously had run Salomon before being forced out in the wake of the scandal.

Initially portrayed by Salomon officials as "Mr. Integrity" and the "Savior from the East," Mr. Maughan was widely credited with building Salomon's Japanese business into a major force. While in Tokyo, Mr. Maughan was at the center of several controversial issues, such as the active use of computer-aided program trading in the Japanese stock market by United States securities firms. But he tried to avoid public confrontation. Traders in Tokyo cited his hands-on management style.

Running Salomon has been bumpier. Mr. Maughan has been widely criticized for, among other things, putting into place a controversial pay plan that cut the pay of traders and bankers in Salomon's client businesses. The move led to dozens of defections and an uproar that looked for a time as if it would cost Mr. Maughan his job. Some Salomon

Maughan, Deryck
Cochairman-Salomon
Smith Barney

executives criticized Mr. Maughan for continuing to aggressively build up the firm's overseas presence even when its European operations sank deeply into the red a few years back. And he was hit with a firestorm of controversy over his apparently rash decision to eliminate Salomon's brokerage operations. Through it all, Mr. Maughan defends his record. "I took over a company with the stock at $18; now it's at $60," he said in early 1997. He said he isn't concerned if people believe he was ruthless in trying to turn around Salomon. "We're highly competitive," Mr. Maughan said.

Eduardo Mestre, cohead of investment banking, vice chairman, and member of operating committee: Before taking up his new post, Mr. Mestre was cohead of Salomon's investment-banking group (with Eric Fast); he also was a member of Salomon's five-member operating committee, which set and implemented business strategy and plans for Salomon's stock, bond and banking businesses. Mr. Mestre also sat on the firm's management board, which met monthly to consider firm-wide issues. Mr. Mestre made his mark representing clients in the communications, technology, aerospace, defense, media and power industries; these include AT&T, GTE, BellCanada, WorldCom and Frontier. Previously, he headed the firm's mergers unit, among other banking posts.

Eric Fast, cohead of investment banking and member of management committee: Mr. Fast, along with Mr. Mestre, formerly ran Salomon's worldwide investment banking business and sat on the firm's management board. Within the investment bank, Mr. Fast had day-to-day responsibility for all United States corporate-finance activities, as well as oversight of all European banking activities. Among his advisory assignments was the PacTel/Air Touch breakup. Mr. Fast formerly held a variety of investment-banking roles at the firm, including cohead of Salomon's United States corporate-finance department. Before joining Salomon in 1984, he was treasurer at Macmillan Inc.

William Mills II, cohead of investment banking and member of management committee: Before his current post, Mr. Mills was a Smith Barney vice chairman and cohead of investment banking (with James Boshart). Mr. Mills also had been given formal control of the banking group, where as chief operating officer he had much of the practical day-to-day responsibility of running the banking operations. Before the banking posts, Mr. Mills had formed and headed the firm's debt-origination and securitization group. He previously had been cohead of the financial-institutions group. Before joining Smith Barney in 1982, he had been a vice president at Standard & Poor's Corp.

Ronald Freeman, cohead of investment banking and head of European investment banking: Mr. Freeman previously was Salomon's cohead of global investment banking, based in London. He worked at Salomon between 1973 and 1991 as head of the projects finance, oil and gas and cohead of the mergers-and-acquisitions group. Mr. Freeman was at the European Bank for Reconstruction and Development before rejoining Salomon in 1997.

Steven Black, head of global equities and tax-exempt securities, vice chairman, and member of operating committee: Before his current post, Mr. Black was Smith Barney chief operating officer. That move, made in 1996, followed a long career at Smith Barney: He joined in 1974 as a trainee and spent the next fifteen years in the municipal-bond department, becoming manager of the group in 1988.

Mr. Black was named deputy head of capital markets in 1990, becoming head of the division a year later. He was elected vice chairman in 1993.

Robert DiFazio, cohead of equities and member of management committee: Before his current post, Mr. DiFazio, a managing director, was responsible for retail and institutional equity sales and trading at Smith Barney; he held that post since 1992. Since joining Smith Barney in 1982, he has had a variety of positions within the stock-trading department, from listed equity position trader to manager of the listed block desk.

Arthur D. Hyde III, cohead of equities and member of management committee: Mr. Hyde was a Salomon managing director and headed the firm's stock department and earlier its United States corporate bond department. He joined Salomon in 1982 on the corporate-bond desk, was named managing director in 1989 and assumed his last Salomon post in 1994.

Thomas Maheras, head of global fixed income, vice chairman and member of operating committee: Mr. Maheras was head of Salomon's fixed income operations and a member of the firm's operating committee and management board. Previously, he had been head of mortgage trading and head of the high-yield trading group with responsibility for junk-bond trading activities both for clients and for the firm's proprietary account. He joined Salomon as an associate in 1984, rising to vice president in corporate-bond trading three years later. He was named a managing director in 1992.

Peter Hirsch, member of management committee: Mr. Hirsch oversees Salomon's United States government, finance and derivatives business. In early 1997, he was appointed to the firm's management board and fixed-income operating committee. Mr. Hirsch joined Salomon in 1985 on the futures-execution desk, becoming a backup bond trader in 1987 and the head zero-coupon trader a year later. He has held a variety of other bond-related positions at the firm.

Costas Kaplanis, cohead of global arbitrage, head of London arbitrage and member of the management committee: Mr. Kaplanis previously headed Salomon's arbitrage group in London and was a member of the European management committee and Salomon Brothers Inc.'s management board. He joined Salomon as a trainee in 1985. A year later, he transferred to London and was appointed a vice president in 1988. He was promoted to managing director in 1992.

Robert Stavis, cohead of global arbitrage, head of New York arbitrage and member of the management committee: Mr. Stavis previously had headed Salomon's New York proprietary-trading operations and sat on Salomon's management board and global risk-management committee, as well as the internal control and compliance task force. His department, which included research and trading groups, was active in United States Treasury, mortgage, high-yield and derivatives markets, and in trading emerging-markets securities around the world. He joined Salomon in 1984 as an analyst of bond portfolios. After becoming manager of the group providing derivatives research, he left Salomon to launch a trading firm called Davco Associates. He rejoined Salomon as an interest-rate swap trader in 1989. Since 1990, he has been involved in arbitrage trading for Salomon's account.

Jay Mandelbaum, head of sales and marketing, private client division and member of the operating committee: Mr. Mandlebaum was executive vice president, retail marketing and client services, at Smith Barney. Before that, he had been vice president, corporate development at Primerica Corp. He joined Primerica from McKinsey & Co., the consulting firm, where he had been a senior engagement manager.

W. Thomas Matthews, head of national sales, private client division and member of the management committee: Mr. Matthews was formerly executive vice president, director of national sales at Smith Barney. He joined the firm in 1975 and got his last Smith Barney post in 1994. He began his career at Merrill as a broker. During his tenure at Smith Barney, he has been a producing branch manager and regional director.

Paul Underwood, deputy head of retail and member of the management committee: Mr. Underwood previously was senior executive vice president in Smith Barney's retail-sales division. That post involved oversight of Smith Barney's branch system. Previously he had been senior officer of the national sales division and director of marketing.

James Boshart, head of transition team, vice chairman, and member of operating committee: Mr. Boshart, formerly cohead of Smith Barney's investment-banking group (with William Mills), quickly rose through the ranks at Smith Barney since joining in 1990 as manager of its public-finance department. Before that he had been president of the Stamford Co., an investment-banking boutique. The boyish-looking Mr. Boshart previously had a long career at Lehman Brothers, where he most recently had been chief administrative officer.

Peter Middleton, CEO of European operations and member of the management committee: Mr. Middleton previously was chief executive of Salomon Brothers' European operations, the head of the firm's European management committee and a member of the management board at Salomon Brothers Inc. He joined Salomon in 1995 from Lloyd's of London, where he was chief executive officer.

Toshiharu Kojima, CEO of Japanese operations and member of the management committee: Mr. Kojima previously headed Salomon's Japanese operations, and was chief executive officer and member of the Tokyo management committee of Salomon Brothers Asia Ltd. His responsibilities included the businesses of Salomon in Japan and fixed-income sales in the Asia-Pacific region. Mr. Kojima also was a member of the management board and fixed-income operating committee of Salomon Brothers Inc. He joined Salomon in 1983 after ten years at Nomura Securities Co.

Robert Morse, chief executive officer of Asia-Pacific operations and member of the management committee: Mr. Morse previously held the same post for Salomon, and was a member of Salomon's management board, responsible for the firm's investment banking, stock, bond and other operations conducted from ten offices in the Asia-Pacific region. He formerly was head of Salomon's global natural-resources group in investment banking. He joined Salomon in 1985 as a vice president and was appointed director in 1989 and managing director in 1992.

Robert Druskin, chief administrative officer and member of the management committee: Mr. Druskin managed Smith Barney's asset-management and futures divisions. He formerly had been chief administrative officer. Before joining Smith Barney in 1991, he had been senior executive vice president and chief financial officer at Shearson Lehman Brothers Inc. Mr. Druskin joined Shearson Hammill, a predecessor firm, in 1969 and served in various financial posts before becoming chief financial officer in 1986.

Robert H. Mundheim, general counsel and member of the management committee: Mr. Mundheim previously was an executive vice president and general counsel at Salomon, as well as a member of the firm's management board. Before joining Salomon in 1992, he was cochairman of the New York law firm of Fried, Frank, Harris, Shriver & Jacobson and University Professor of Law and Finance at the University of Pennsylvania Law School, where he had taught since 1965. He was dean at that institution for seven years. Mr. Mundheim also has been general counsel of the United States Treasury Department, special counsel to the SEC, and vice chairman, governor-at-large and a member of the executive committee of the NASD.

Charles Scharf, chief financial officer and member of the management committee: Before his new post, Mr. Scharf was Smith Barney's chief financial officer. He joined Travelers Group in 1987 as assistant to the CFO and in 1990 became vice president, financial planning, at Smith Barney. In 1992, he joined Commercial Credit as a vice president and returned to Smith Barney in 1993 as senior vice president, financial planning.

Heidi Miller, head of risk management and member of the management committee: Ms. Miller also is chief financial officer of Smith Barney parent Travelers Group. She joined Travelers in 1992 as an assistant to Mr. Dimon and subsequently assumed a number of key finance-related roles, including responsibility for credit and risk management at Smith Barney.

William Heinzerling, head of retail fixed-income, securities lending/short-term securities: Mr. Heinzerling previously coheaded Smith Barney's taxable bond group. Before that post, he had held a variety of different jobs in fixed income. He joined Smith Barney in 1984 from Lehman Brothers.

Steven Bowman, head of U.S. fixed income sales and global fixed income research division: Mr. Bowman previously coheaded Smith Barney's taxable fixed-income division, responsible for trading, sales and bond origination. Before that post, he had been manager of a number of the firm's bond businesses, including sales, corporate debt, high-yield, preferred stock and emerging markets and debt syndicate.

Denise Kelly, cohead of the United States government-bond unit: Ms. Kelly joined Salomon Brothers in 1982 as a salesperson in the firm's foreign central- and commercial-bank group; she became a manager of the commercial-bank unit in 1986. Before her new post, Ms. Kelly was Salomon's worldwide government-products manager.

Charles Parkhurst, cohead of United States government-bond unit: Mr. Parkhurst previously was a Salomon Brothers managing director and trader of zero-coupon government bonds. He joined the firm in its bond-portfolio analysis group in 1985 and later moved to the hedge-management group before joining Salomon's government-trading operations in 1989.

Mark Tsesarsky, cohead of United States mortgage unit: Mr. Tsesarsky formerly headed Salomon's pass-through and ARMs desk of mortgage trading. He joined Salomon as a summer intern in 1985 and was appointed managing director in 1996.

Jeff Perlowitz, cohead of asset back mortgage unit: Mr. Perlowitz previously was a Salomon Brothers managing director in the bond group, responsible for the worldwide distribution of the firm's mortgage-backed securities products. Mr. Perlowitz joined Salomon in 1980 and was a salesman in San Francisco and New York; he was named a Salomon managing director in 1995.

John Hoffmann, director of global equity research: Mr. Hoffman previously was global-research chief at Smith Barney. He joined the firm in 1964 and assumed the research post in 1995. He also served as cochairman of the firm's investment-policy coordinating committee. Mr. Hoffmann began his career as an analyst and served in a variety of management posts in both corporate finance and research.

Ann Knight, director of global-research integration: Ms. Knight previously was a Salomon managing director and head of its global equity research group. She joined Salomon in 1997 from PaineWebber Group Inc., where she had been research chief since 1994 and the No. 1–ranked auto analyst for seven years. Before PaineWebber, Ms. Knight worked at, among other firms, Smith Barney Inc.

In the Beginning . . .

Smith Barney's roots date back more than a century. The firm's predecessors were two Philadelphia companies: Chas. D. Barney & Co., founded in 1873 by a son-in-law of the financier Jay Cooke, and Edward B. Smith & Co., founded in 1892. Both catered to well-heeled clients. They merged in 1937 to form Smith, Barney & Co. With the acqusition of Harris, Upham & Co. in 1976, the firm gained significant clout with smaller investors. It became known as Smith Barney, Harris Upham & Co.

Then came the 1993 Shearson merger, and a new name: Smith Barney Shearson Inc. In most brokerage mergers, the bigger firm gets top billing. But beleaguered Shearson had been in the red in the early 1990s. In 1992, it had a loss of $116 million even as others in the securities industry—including Smith Barney—enjoyed record profits. Shearson's 1990 loss of $966 million set a record for the brokerage business.

As board members of Smith Barney's parent batted around possibilities for a new name, Gerald R. Ford, of all people, made his mark. Mr. Weill asked the nation's thirty-eighth president—an honorary director of Smith Barney's parent and a former Shearson director—for his opinion. Mr. Ford said Smith Barney Shearson "sounded right."

That was enough to sway Mr. Weill. He said he sought out Mr. Ford's advice because he had "a feel for both names."

Smith Barney Shearson was the eighth name change for Shearson since its birth in 1902 as Shearson Hammill & Co. under Ed Shearson, a Canadian brokerage executive. But the new combination was the first in which Shearson hadn't had top billing. And that annoyed some Shearson brokers, who complained to Joseph Plumeri, then Shearson's brokerage chief.

Mr. Plumeri tried to soothe the brokers' bruised egos in a conference call the day the merger was announced. He too would have preferred Shearson Smith Barney, he said, but "this whole name thing is overblown." Mr. Plumeri encouraged brokers to look at the bright side. He predicted Smith Barney Shearson would thrive—and reporters "will take 'beleaguered' off our name."

A year later, the brokerage firm went one step further: It shelved the Shearson name altogether. It seems Shearson had lost its cachet following its 1990s losses. "With all the baggage, people will be just as happy that it's gone," Theodore Krebsbach, Shearson's former litigation chief, said at the time. He turned out to be right.

Salomon Brothers had similarly humble roots. In January 1910, Arthur, Herbert and Percy Salomon, along with a clerk, formed the firm to continue their father's money-brokerage business. Three months later, it merged with Martin Hutzler & Co., partly in a bid to obtain more capital, and became Salomon Brothers & Hutzler. In 1970, the Hutzler name was dropped, and the firm reverted to Salomon Brothers. After a 1981 merger with Phibro Corp., a big oil trader once known as Philipp Brothers, the firm was changed to Phibro-Salomon. By 1986, Salomon's chief, John Gutfreund, had wrested control of the firm, which was renamed Salomon Inc. In the 1990s, the firm's Salomon Brothers investment-banking arm and Phibro oil-trading division operated under the Salomon Inc. roof.

Kevin J. McCaffrey, deputy director of research: Mr. McCaffrey, a managing director, joined the research department in late 1995; previously, he was responsible for Smith Barney's New York institutional stock sales in the firm's capital-markets division. He joined Smith Barney from CS First Boston.

Jeffrey Waters, associate director of U.S. research and global product manager: Mr. Waters was a managing director and global equity research product manager at Salomon. He joined Salomon in 1986, where he was an institutional equity salesman and manager of the institutional sales force before joining research as product manager. He previously was a commercial bank lending officer at Hartford National Bank and Chemical Bank.

Mark Loehr, director of primary product: Mr. Loehr previously was cohead of Smith Barney's equity capital-markets services group. He had been promoted to that post after heading worldwide equity institutional sales. He began his career at Smith Barney in 1978 in the listed block-trading group. In 1984, he joined CS First Boston Inc. and spent ten years there in a variety of senior management posts in the listed stock and stock-syndicate units.

James Crandell, director of Latin America research: Mr. Crandell previously was a Salomon managing director and director of its U.S. equity research group. He also has run global equity research. His work as an oil service and offshore-drilling stock analyst has earned him a place on *Institutional Investor* magazine's "All America Research Team" for ten years, five of them as No. 1. Before joining Salomon in 1981, Mr. Crandell was an investment analyst with Connecticut Mutual Life and Standard & Poor's Corp.

Albert D. Richards, director of European research: Mr. Richards previously was a Salomon managing director and head of its European equity research in London. Before that post, he had spent eight years with CS First Boston as, among other things, director of sector research for European stocks and European chemical analyst.

Michael Carr, member of investment-banking management committee: Mr. Carr is cohead of global mergers-and-acquisitions at Salomon Smith Barney, and earlier had been head of industrial M&A for the firm, where he worked on a variety of transactions involving industrial companies for twelve years. Mr. Carr joined Salomon in 1985.

Michael Eck, member of the investment-banking management committee and cohead of the consumer group: Mr. Eck, a managing director, was cohead of the retail investment-banking group at Smith Barney. Before joining Smith Barney in 1993, he was director of the retail investment banking group at CS First Boston.

David Jarvis, member of the investment-banking management committee: Mr. Jarvis previously was Salomon's European investment-banking chief. He joined Salomon in 1986 from Norwest Corp. He established Salomon's European financial institutions group in 1986, and also was in charge of its investment-banking activities in Spain and Portugal.

Michael Klein, member of the investment-banking management committee and head of the financial entrepreneurs group and cohead of acquisition finance: Mr. Klein, a managing director, was head of the financial entrepreneurs' group at Smith Barney and cohead of acquisition finance. The financial entrepreneurs group provides stock and bond financing and mergers-and-acquisition advice, primarily to leveraged-buyout firms and their portfolio companies. Before Smith Barney, he had worked for nine years at Salomon Brothers.

Christopher Lawrence, member of the investment-banking management committee: Mr. Lawrence heads, among other things, the technology and large capitalization coverage groups within Salomon's investment-banking department. In that position, he had senior coverage responsibility for a select number of Salomon's largest industrial clients. He advised General Motors on the restructuring of Hughes Electronics. He joined Salomon in 1981 and has held a variety of positions at Salomon and its parent, including a stint as John Gutfreund's chief of staff from 1987 to 1989.

Benjamin Lorello, member of the investment-banking management committee: Mr. Lorello, a managing director, is the founder and head of Smith Barney's health-care investment-banking group. A veteran investment banker, Mr. Lorello worked at Shearson Lehman Brothers before joining Smith Barney in 1985.

Edward Miller, member of the investment-banking management committee: Mr. Miller, a managing director, most recently led the general industrial group in Smith Barney's investment-banking division. Since joining Smith Barney in 1968, he has held a variety of banking posts, including heading the firm's international operations from 1980 to 1991.

Hans Morris, member of the investment-banking management committee: Mr. Morris, a managing director, headed Smith Barney's financial-institutions group. Mr. Morris joined Smith Barney in 1980, and has held a variety of positions in the firm's public finance and mortgage and asset finance areas.

Louis Susman, member of the investment-banking management committee: Mr. Susman was a vice chairman of investment banking and a managing director at Salomon in charge of Midwest investment banking, among other things. Before joining Salomon in 1989, he was a senior partner at the law firm of Thompson & Mitchell, focusing mainly on mergers-and-acquisitions and merchant banking.

Frank D. Yeary, member of the investment-banking management committee: Mr. Yeary, a managing director, headed the communications investment banking unit, covering the media, telecom, leisure and education industries. Mr. Yeary joined Salomon in 1990 and began his career at Lehman Brothers Kuhn Loeb in 1984.

PART TWO

THE RETAIL BROKERS

PaineWebber Inc.

•

Prudential Securities Inc.

PAINEWEBBER INC.

AFTER KIDDER: NEEDING A NICHE

Gaining Kidder, But Not Much Ground

PaineWebber Inc.'s stunted investment-banking clout on Wall Street was crystallized a few years back when it was snubbed by a small Quincy, Illinois, tire-and-wheel maker.

Titan Wheel International Inc. went public in May 1993, tapping PaineWebber to help sell $40.5 million of common stock. PaineWebber again was selected later that year to help Titan raise capital. But in 1995, Titan (now Titan International) shut PaineWebber out of another stock deal after the broker's machine-tools analyst bolted for rival Schroder Wertheim & Co., which snagged the underwriting mandate.

On paper, PaineWebber Group Inc.'s December 1994 purchase of ailing Kidder, Peabody & Co. vaulted the brokerage firm toward the upper ranks of the securities business. By snaring some of Kidder's top investment bankers in the deal, PaineWebber hoped to boost its business catering to institutional clients. In practice, however, the firm hasn't yet gained much ground against its biggest brokerage-firm rivals—and still struggles to make a name for itself on Wall Street.

The experience shows that acquisitions can't always buy megaprofits on Wall Street. Even after Kidder, PaineWebber's investment-banking group remains a Wall Street weakling. Miscues at its asset-management group have kept a lid on growth in coveted fee income. The firm isn't a clear market leader in any major business. It all adds up to a firm needing to carve a niche to call its own.

It's not that the nation's fourth-largest brokerage firm has entirely missed the party from the big bull market in stocks and bonds. It earned $415.4 million in 1997, a record, its fifth in seven years amid heavy trading by individual investors, the firm's bread-and-butter clients. But the 1997 results don't come close to matching the $1.9 billion at Merrill Lynch & Co., the $1.65 billion at Salomon Smith Barney Holdings Inc. or the $2.59 billion at the combined Morgan Stanley, Dean Witter, Discover & Co.

Despite adding Kidder, PaineWebber has been an underwriting flop. In 1994, PaineWebber was ranked No. 6 in stock underwriters on Wall Street, with a 5.2 percent market share. In 1996 and 1997, the firm didn't even crack the top ten; it ranked a lowly eleventh, with a slim 2.4 percent share of the market, according to Securities Data Co. More significant, PaineWebber hasn't been able to keep pace with the strategic moves of competitors. Merrill has dramatically broadened its international business. (PaineWebber has none to speak of.) Smith Barney has boosted its return-on-equity to among the highest in the business. (PaineWebber's return-on-equity, though solid, lags behind it.) And Dean Witter trumped all others when it agreed to merge with blue-chip investment bank Morgan Stanley, making the combined operation by some measures the largest securities firm on Wall Street.

Indeed, PaineWebber is among a handful of U.S. securities firms that will be forced to make acquisitions or merge if they are to become significant players in the global arena, according to a March 1997 report by Moody's Investors Service Inc. "The outlook for both institutional and retail businesses points to an industry that faces continued consolidation," the Dun & Bradstreet Corp. credit-rating concern said. And with the announcement of a $25 billion merger of Union Bank of Switzerland and Swiss Bank Corp. in December 1997, the odds are better than ever that the newly created bank giant might make a play for a major U.S. securities firm such as PaineWebber, analysts said.

PaineWebber executives dispute the notion that their firm is squeezed by the brokerage behemoths. PaineWebber generated 21 percent of Merrill's earnings a decade ago—and 22 percent in 1997, noted PaineWebber Chairman and Chief Executive Donald Marron. "We've built a firm with very good earnings power," he said. PaineWebber oversees $297.1 billion of client assets; that's "substantial clout." And accelerated investing by individual investors, he added, "gives our distribution base a stronger position."

Nevertheless, PaineWebber has stumbled in managing assets for individual clients. Its Mitchell Hutchins Asset Management unit manages just $48.9 billion in assets, far behind the asset-management subsidiaries of rivals Merrill, Salomon Smith Barney, and Morgan Stanley, Dean Witter. Managing such assets generates steady fees, even in down markets. MHAM has been roiled in past years by poor performance, coupled with heavy turnover among executives and portfolio managers, leading *Institutional Investor* magazine to quip that MHAM should be pronounced "Mayhem." It's not surprising, then, that PaineWebber brokers have shied away from pushing the firm's internal funds.

Now, PaineWebber executives predict the firm's assets under management will grow to $80 billion by the year 2000. Some on Wall Street say that goal could best be met through an acquisition; the firm is actively looking to buy a money-management firm. With the stock market at lofty heights, "it's absolutely the worst time to buy anything," Mr. Marron argued. "But it's not a bad time to be looking."

Through the years, PaineWebber has had a penchant for lurching into highly publicized new ventures, then pulling out. After PaineWebber bought Kidder in 1994, the firm made a big move to upgrade its investment-banking effort, luring Kidder veteran Michael Madden to run the banking group. In a sign of his importance to the firm, Mr. Madden was given the title of vice chairman, the No. 3 ranking. Soon the firm decided it couldn't afford the buildup, and pulled back. Mr. Madden then left the firm—and PaineWebber sharply slashed its investment-banking group.

Some of PaineWebber's strategic forays and retreats have been poorly timed. In early 1993, PaineWebber left the arbitrage business, only to find itself facing a boom in takeover-stock trading a year later. And in 1994, PaineWebber hired several of Kidder's mortgage-backed bond traders at fat guaranteed pay packages even as the market for these mortgage securities dried up. Shortly after the move, PaineWebber scaled back the mortgage effort and absorbed the group into the firm's real-estate operation under Steven Baum, a Kidder veteran.

PaineWebber *has* made strides in recent years. Its purchase of Kidder has made it a stronger, larger firm with a more diverse asset base. Its nearly $300 billion in client assets is more than double that in 1994. Despite some turmoil, its research team remains highly ranked. And PaineWebber executives believe the firm still can thrive. This is because, as Mr. Marron has preached, the 1990s is the decade of the individual investor. He bases this view on the fact that baby boomers—concerned they won't have sufficient resources to retire, fund their children's education or care for elderly parents—now need more than ever before to turn to brokers for financial advice. With 6,250 "investment executives," PaineWebber clearly is positioned to snare a chunk of that business.

"Changing demographics, the aging of the baby-boom generation and the shift from defined-benefit to defined-contribution plans will continue to drive growth in our individual and institutional businesses," Mr. Marron said, "Those individuals are going to want advice on how to invest their money—it's their future. That's what's driving the bus."

PaineWebber probably would have been more successful had it been able to hire all the Kidder stars it originally sought. Kidder's junk-bond team, led by Thomas Bernard, initially indicated that it would move to PaineWebber. After PaineWebber's existing junk-bond traders were told of the expected move— and began looking for other jobs on the Street—Mr. Bernard pulled back and decided not to join the firm. (He and most of his team landed at rival Lehman Brothers Holdings Inc.)

PaineWebber hired Mark Sutton, Kidder's brokerage chief and a former PaineWebber manager, partly in a bid to stem defections of Kidder brokers. Yet a handful of brokerage rivals snatched some high-producing Kidder brokers before PaineWebber closed on the Kidder purchase. Merrill, for one, snapped up Kidder's top-producing broker, David Moyne, along with a team of four other brokers. Mr. Moyne generated 1993 gross commissions of about $6 million, Kidder brokers said; his team had commissions totaling as much as $9 million.

And PaineWebber sued two rivals, Donaldson, Lufkin & Jenrette Securities Corp. and Dean Witter, accusing them of raiding Kidder by paying its brokers exorbitant bonuses to derail the planned Kidder acquisition. DLJ had hired three Kidder brokers, two of whom each generated $1 million in annual commissions. Dean Witter had hired six top Kidder brokers and said publicly it hoped to hire many more. DLJ and Dean Witter "are orchestrating an attack on an announced deal," PaineWebber's Mr. Grano complained at the time.

In 1995, PaineWebber withdrew the suit. But the firm won the war. Rivals' poaching of Kidder brokers dried to a trickle after the suit, which sought $10 million in punitive damages. PaineWebber ultimately hired about 85 percent of Kidder's brokers in completing the $670 million transaction. "PaineWebber came out a winner because the suit might have dampened other firms looking to hire brokers," said Wall Street analyst Perrin Long. For his part, Mr. Grano said "we didn't do this for a tactical message to the Street. We were trying to protect the assets we were purchasing."

The victory, and the Kidder purchase, nevertheless didn't translate into immediate impact. This never was more apparent than in 1995 when, in an unusual bid to boost trading profit, PaineWebber invested about $125 million of its capital with a high-profile investment fund. The investment—with Long-Term Capital Management Corp., a hedge fund run by former Salomon Brothers Inc. executive John Meriwether—was viewed by some on Wall Street as an admission by PaineWebber that it lacked expertise in some segments of the bond market. It was highly unusual for a Wall Street firm, whose reputation is often linked to its trading prowess, to use an outside source to invest its own money.

PaineWebber executives fumed over the disclosure, which they had sought to keep secret. But there aren't any red faces anymore. The Meriwether move was one of PaineWebber's best trades ever, with returns of more than 40 percent in 1995 and 1996 alone. Mr. Marron, still stung by the media exposure of the Meriwether trade, refuses to say anything about it, except: "It's been a good investment."

The Kidder purchase, meantime, triggered cultural frictions from the start. In a controversial move, PaineWebber passed on hiring some of Kidder's top talent, including stock chief Tom Ryan and research chief Ted Johnson. When some PaineWebber executives pushed for these hires, Mr. Marron put his foot down. "We've got too many Kidder people in key positions—we don't want them to take over the firm," Mr. Marron said, according to an associate.

The culture clash in investment banking came to a head in early 1995. Paul Guenther, then PaineWebber president, told the Kidder banking recruits the

Bond Epic

How Kidder, a Tiger In April, Found Itself The Prey by December

Scandal, Lax Management, Rising Interest Rates Sealed Company's Doom

The V-Man Takes a Bow

BY MICHAEL SICONOLFI
Staff Reporter of THE WALL STREET JOURNAL

NEW YORK—This spring, Kidder, Peabody & Co. was considered one of the tigers of Wall Street, snaring seemingly miraculous bond-trading profits.

These days, however, the onetime Wall Street powerhouse more closely resembles Animal House in the throes of disbanding. Kidder traders pass the day thinking up pranks and rap songs; some while away the time playing video games—Mortal Kombat and Microsoft Golf are the favorites. Others have repeatedly played a recording of Frank Sinatra singing "My Way" ("And now the end is near, and so I face the final curtain . . .") on the firm's sound system. One recent day, Michael Vranos—Kidder's former mortgage-bond chief and a former Mr. Teen Connecticut—stripped to the waist and performed muscle poses to catcalls from the idled trading floor.

It will still be a few weeks before Kidder pays out all of its bonuses and severance, leading to a 1994 net loss of about $1 billion. But in one of the most dizzying implosions in Wall Street history, the 129-year-old investment bank officially ceased business this month after parent General Electric Co. sold most of the firm's assets to PaineWebber Group Inc. for stock valued at $670 million.

Kidder's demise was the result of a double whammy: a costly bond-trading scandal last April that has focused on Joseph Jett, a onetime star bond trader, and eventually entangled Edward Cerullo, a former top Kidder executive, in the resulting broad civil investigation; and the collapse of Kidder's risky strategy to dominate the market for mortgage-backed bonds. Kidder might have survived either crisis alone. But the combined effect was to focus intense scrutiny on the company at precisely the wrong moment. Add top management unversed in the ways of Wall Street and unable to oversee its own business, and the result was deadly.

"The top of the firm didn't understand the business," says Abram Claude Jr., managing director of investment-banking business at Russell Reynolds Associates Inc., an executive-search firm. "Someone ought to have smelled" the budding Jett scandal, Mr. Claude says, echoing a widely held view on Wall Street.

The speed of the Kidder collapse eclipses even the spectacular fall of Drexel Burnham Lambert Inc., which survived for more than three years amid a junk bond scandal before it crumbled in 1990. A mere six months after the Jett scandal surfaced, Kidder was auctioned off. About 2,250 Kidder employees have lost jobs amidst the brokerage industry's worst slump in years. Despite the Kidder hit, GE says it expects a year of record profits.

While much has been written about the Kidder case, few details have emerged before now about what happened inside the firm just before the scandal broke and in the months since then. Here is some of that story, based on extensive interviews with former senior Kidder traders and executives and a report stemming from an investigation by an outside law firm for Kidder that largely hasn't been publicized. None of the former Kidder traders or executives would comment publicly because the entire Jett matter currently is being investigated by the U.S. attorney's office in Manhattan, the Securities and Exchange Commission and the New York Stock Exchange. Both Mr. Cerullo and Mr. Jett have previously denied any wrongdoing.

There is at least one irony: Kidder took a tremendous beating on some $350 million in phony profits allegedly concocted by Mr. Jett to mask losses and boost his bonus. The firm had to take a $210 million net charge. But Kidder managed, with a bit of good luck, to liquidate Mr. Jett's valid bond portfolio—valued in the billions—for an $8 million profit. Some had predicted losses in the tens of millions of dollars on that portfolio as well.

For many Kidder traders, the first scent of trouble came in mid-March, weeks before news of the Jett scandal broke. Kidder auditors began roaming the firm's sprawling trading floor in lower Manhattan. David Bernstein, Mr. Cerullo's aide, spent hours burrowed in his glass-enclosed office adjoining the trading floor, riffling through thick stacks of trading records. When asked, Mr. Bernstein said the activity was simply a "routine audit," traders say.

It was far more than that. Mr. Bernstein and his boss were suspicious of Mr. Jett's bulging profits, which totaled $66 million in January and February alone—more than double Mr. Jett's reported profits for all of 1992. On March 21, Mr. Bernstein confronted Mr. Jett after the trader returned from a business trip to London, asking him to explain his trading activity in detail.

It was only when Mr. Bernstein pored over Mr. Jett's ledger at home the following weekend that he detected a possible "distortion" totaling as much as $300 million in Mr. Jett's government-bond book. On March 28, Mr. Bernstein called Mr. Cerullo, who had flown off on a Colorado family vacation, with that news.

Mr. Jett traded so-called government strips, which are created by splitting the interest and principal portions of bonds into separately traded issues. Mr. Jett had entered into "forward" contracts that essentially involved the exchange at a later date of strips for bonds. But instead of settling these forward contracts when they came due, Mr. Jett apparently rolled over these trades, taking fictitious profits, Kidder now feared. Thus, Mr. Jett purportedly circumvented the firm's accounting system, which normally eliminated any false profit or loss by the time such trades settled.

In reponse to intense questioning, Mr. Jett told Kidder executives that his trading positions were part of a hedging strategy and that they stemmed from the firm's effort to slash its assets. In a taped conversation with Kidder's chief financial officer on April 1, Mr. Jett disputed that his trading created any bogus profits.

But it was an ominous sign when Mr. Cerullo aborted his trip to fly back to New York. "Cerullo never canceled vacations," says a colleague.

What followed were two weeks of frantic activity, as teams of Kidder operations and accounting staff tried to reconstruct Mr. Jett's trading records and quantify the loss. On Friday, April 15 Kidder analytics expert Michael Benatar, after logging 20-hour days for two weeks, estimated the Jett hit at $350 million.

Then came the hard part. The next morning, Mr. Cerullo phoned Melvin Mullin, Kidder's derivatives chief, at his Long Island home. "I need you in the office," Mr. Cerullo said, adding that Mr. Jett would soon be fired. "We need help liquidating his positions."

It was Saturday, so the trading floor was eerily quiet but for a flurry of activity in the adjoining office of risk manager Barry Feiner. Draped on his desk was a two-foot-long computer printout of Mr. Jett's holdings of government securities. The sheet listed more than 75 bond positions, 30 of which were valued at more than $100 million each. The bonds' combined market value was an astounding $15 billion, traders say. (GE says Mr. Jett's actual trading positions were no more than $9.5 billion; the discrepancy may involve futures positions also held by Mr. Jett.)

Mr. Mullin's task: Quietly dump the positions to avoid big losses. Dubbed simply "the Liquidation Plan," the maneuver would be ticklish. Many of Mr. Jett's huge bond positions—including both "long" and "short" market bets—weren't hedged, putting Kidder at risk. What's more, Kidder executives knew if rival traders figured out the firm's specific plans and trading positions, they might force Kidder to sell positions at disadvantageous prices.

Mr. Mullin—who had hired Mr. Jett and ran the government-bond desk before him—told Mr. Feiner to brace for losses of $25 million over a few weeks. "We would have been squeezed if anybody knew our positions," a Kidder trader who sold some of Mr. Jett's bonds says.

But Kidder got a break. On Monday—the day after the scandal was disclosed and Mr. Jett was officially fired—bond prices plummeted. This triggered big gains in Mr. Jett's short positions, which were bets that the market would fall. Kidder quickly closed those trades, and locked in a tidy profit of $12 million. "It was luck," a Kidder trader who sold the securities says. "We were short a ton of bonds and covered them right away."

Instead of a few weeks, the liquidation took more than two months as the bond market gyrated. With a multibillion-dollar position, "when the market moves even just a little bit, it's a big swing in value," says another Kidder trader who sold some of the securities. "Nobody was used to trading such a large book."

Messrs. Mullin and Cerullo declined to comment. Mr. Feiner couldn't be reached.

The scandal and its aftermath sent shock waves through GE's Fairfield, Conn., headquarters. Several times a day, GE audit executive Vidya Chauhan called Mr. Mullin, who sat in Mr. Jett's chair on the trading floor, according to Kidder traders. "What have we sold so far?" he would ask. (A GE official says Mr. Chauhan never made such calls, noting that, as part of the outside law firm's investigation of Kidder, he wasn't supposed to discuss with traders the sale of the positions.)

However it got the information, GE created multicolor charts for periodic meetings updating the liquidation's progress, Kidder traders say. The pressure was intense; a colleague says Mr. Mullin confided that the period "was hell." When all of Mr. Jett's positions finally were sold, however, Kidder logged an $8 million profit instead of a $25 million disaster.

But by then cracks had begun to tear apart Kidder's senior ranks. Just a week after the scandal surfaced, Kidder managers gathered in a cramped cottage abutting a Victorian mansion in Greenwich, Conn. There, James Mullin, a senior Kidder bond executive (unrelated to

Melvin Mullin), lashed out at Mr. Cerullo, who was the firm's fixed-income chief. His complaint: Mr. Cerullo's slack supervision of Mr. Jett and other traders. "You don't even bother to come out of your office to go onto the trading floor," James Mullin seethed, according to participants.

Mr. Cerullo shot back. "I had nothing to do with it—I can't watch the guy every second of the day."

But Mr. Mullin persisted. "Ed, it's because of the way you operate," he said. Kidder Chairman Michael Carpenter finally stepped in, gently chastising Mr. Mullin for not being "constructive," people at the meeting say.

Soon other embarrassments emerged. In late April, Kidder fired another trader, Neil Margolin, for allegedly hiding $11 million in losses on a bond-derivatives transaction. Two months later, Kidder fired Peter Bryant, an options trader in London who the firm alleged had hid losses totaling $6 million on a dozen options trades. Both traders denied wrongdoing, but the cases raised broader questions about Kidder supervision.

Meantime, losses in other areas began deepening amid the bond-market slump. Through June, Kidder's syndicate desk, which priced and managed bond underwritings, had lost about $30 million before taxes.

But Kidder's most severe financial strain stemmed from its huge portfolio of mortgage-backed bonds, securities created by pooling home mortgages. Kidder's mortgage group had generated more than two-thirds of Kidder's profit for the prior three years.

When the market for these bonds shriveled in the wake of this year's sharp rise in interest rates, Kidder faced a big problem: Its massive mortgage inventory—by far Wall Street's heftiest—became costly for the firm to own. That was because with interest rates rising and bond prices falling, each bond the firm held lost value. In the bull market of the prior three years, Kidder had made money simply by holding a big bond inventory, which had surged in value.

For Kidder, it was a frustrating predicament. The firm's mountain-size mortgage portfolio—a whopping $16 billion early this year—further paralyzed prices, closing the window for bringing new mortgage issues to market. In July, Kidder lead-managed just one new mortgage deal, helping to raise $500 million—down from 15 mortgage deals and $7.07 billion raised by Kidder in July 1993. Kidder's bread-and-butter mortgage-bond group had a pretax loss of more than $50 million in July 1994 alone, and about $150 million for the year, Kidder traders say.

In a bid to calm market fears, Kidder in May cited a review by KPMG Peat Marwick saying the accounting concern approved the way the firm valued its portfolio. But the mortgage-market meltdown later forced Kidder to write down the value of its existing mortgage holdings. The group's losses deepened as the firm slashed its mortgage inventory to $4 billion before hiring an outside firm last month to liquidate the portfolio.

Even Mr. Vranos—Kidder's powerful mortgage-bond chief, who was dubbed the "V-Man" by colleagues and a "hero" by GE Chairman John Welch—couldn't drum up more business. Between April and June, Kidder received capital infusions of $550 million, including $200 million from GE. The pressure was rising.

New management couldn't turn the firm's fortunes around. In June, Mr. Welch ousted Mr. Carpenter; in July, Mr. Cerullo was pressured to resign. Though Mr. Carpenter's replacements—top Welch lieutenants Dennis Dammerman and Denis Nayden—moved fast to restructure Kidder, they had no more experience on Wall Street than Mr. Carpenter. The GE saviors soon discovered problems were worse than imagined.

To set strategy, Messrs. Dammerman and Nayden called a series of September meetings at GE's conference center in Crotonville, N.Y. The question: Which business units Kidder could justify keeping? On the first day, Mr. Nayden blew up when Kidder's new co-chiefs of fixed-income—Steven Baum and William Watt—couldn't answer a question about how they quantified risk in various bond businesses. Both men, though longtime Kidder employees, had been brought in to jointly head the bond group in July and pleaded ignorance. "What do you mean?" bellowed Mr. Nayden in the big amphitheater, his arms flailing. "I can't believe that." Mr. Baum declined comment on the incident; Mr. Watt couldn't be reached for comment.

Mr. Nayden soon alienated veteran Kidder executives. At another Crotonville strategy session, Mr. Nayden decided to lop off Kidder's energy-futures business in Houston because it wasn't a core operation. When Mr. Baum noted that Charles Hornsby, who headed the group, had just celebrated his 10-year anniversary at the firm, Mr. Nayden had a swift response, participants say: "So what?"

Soon a frustrated Mr. Nayden appeared to grow paranoid over press leaks. In late September, Mr. Nayden burst into Kidder's 19th-floor conference room at Hanover Square in New York, where Kidder's management committee was convening. Waving a news story about the Crotonville conferences that had cited unattributed Kidder sources, a red-faced Mr. Nayden barked: "Tell me how this is happening."

Michael Madden, Kidder's No. 3 executive, raised his hand; he suggested the leak hadn't originated with Kidder's management group, participants said. Finally, Thomas Ryan, Kidder's equities chief, suggested the matter be settled by a lie-detector test.

"I already thought of that," Mr. Nayden snapped, according to people at the meeting. "It's not legal." (Messrs. Nayden, Madden and Ryan declined to comment.)

After Kidder's monthly financial results began appearing in the press—before the numbers were reported to the regulators or any outsiders—some Kidder executives even considered "setting a trap, where they would give different sets of profit numbers to different executives to identify the leaker, according to people who were briefed on the plan. (The trap was never set.)

Meanwhile, Kidder's financial squeeze became severe. New business had slowed to a standstill. Losses piled up, with pretax deficits of some $30 million in both August and September. After declaring publicly in June that they wouldn't sell Kidder, the two Kidder chiefs now huddled to mull their alternatives as Kidder's losses topped $400 million, before taxes, for the year.

Among the options was selling Kidder

outright, which led to discussions with PaineWebber and Equitable Cos.' Donaldson, Lufkin & Jenrette Securities Corp. unit, Wall Street executives say. Kidder also considered finding a European partner to take 25% or 50% of the business in a joint venture, and began talks with Dresdner Bank AG and Natwest Securities Corp., a unit of National Westminster Bank of the U.K., the executives say.

Messrs. Dammerman and Nayden also considered having Kidder executives raise $50 million of equity and take parts of the firm private in a leveraged buyout, the executives say. This option was feasible because Kidder senior executives already had $50 million in a deferred-compensation plan that could be used for the LBO.

If GE couldn't shed its ailing brokerage unit, the conglomerate would have had to inject an additional $500 million or so to shore it up in a rescue plan that had no guarantee of succeeding, Kidder executives say.

That wasn't necessary. Within weeks, a deal with PaineWebber was struck. But there soon were hitches. Some top Kidder brokers jumped ship. Kidder's junk-bond team, led by Thomas Bernard, initially indicated that it would move to PaineWebber. After PaineWebber's existing junk-bond traders were told of the expected move—and began looking for other jobs on the Street—Mr. Bernard pulled back and decided not to join the firm. (Yesterday Mr. Bernard and most of his team joined Lehman Brothers Holdings Inc.)

By early this month, the deal was firmly back on track. Within weeks, PaineWebber hired more than 300 key Kidder employees in sales, trading, research and investment banking. On Dec. 16, the transaction closed, a month ahead of schedule. Already, some former Kidder kingpins have resurfaced. Mr. Carpenter landed at Travelers Group's life-insurance unit; Mr. Vranos is close to launching a hedge fund in a joint venture with the Ziff family's investment firm.

Through it all, Kidder and Mr. Jett remain locked in a nasty legal spat. Kidder has alleged in an arbitration claim that Mr. Jett created the $350 million in bogus profits to mask losses of about $85 million over a 2^{1}/$_{2}$-year period. Kidder also froze Mr. Jett's assets of about $5 million from a Kidder money-management account. Mr. Jett has denied the allegations; he asserts in a counterclaim that his superiors at Kidder knew about and directed his trading.

Mr. Jett has told federal prosecutors that Kidder used him as a scapegoat to deflect scrutiny of its mortgage-bond woes, according to people familiar with the investigation into his activities.

These days, the wind-down of Kidder is accompanied by much gallows humor. As the investment-banking concern crumbled, a former Kidder mortgage structurer even became something of a Wall Street rap star. Michael Osinski's "Requiem Rap at Kidder P Blow" recently made the rounds on the Street. Among the verses:

Big Boss and Joe went skiing in the snow;

He said, Joe, what you're doing, don't wanna know;

But, keep on doing it, doing it though,

'Cause I am the Main Man at Kidder P Blow.

. . . Then one month Kidder P took a double blow;

Joe's profits were phony, the Man said so;

And the Fed jacked rates so the economdy'd slow;

April was the cruelest month at Kidder P Blow.

. . . GE aimed all the blame at Ed Cerullo

He was the man who'd let the boys go.

To Joe and the V-Man he never said no.

'Twas the worst of times at Kidder P Blow.

December 29, 1994

---

firm had "finally put some A-players on the field," an associate said. Mr. Guenther's talk infuriated veteran PaineWebber banker Robert Pangia. He stormed into Mr. Guenther's office, screaming at the slight to the firm's longtime bankers. The Kidder recruits derisively referred to these veteran PaineWebber bankers as "Friends of Bob." (Mr. Pangia was replaced as investment banking chief a year later.)

Some newly arrived Kidder bankers were embarrassed by PaineWebber's shoddy digs. The carpet was threadbare and stained on the firm's thirteenth-floor banking reception area; a small torn spot was taped. The conference rooms were similarly shabby. When an executive at Harvard Industries Inc. sat in a conference-room chair, the arm fell off. The firm finally paid about $200,000 to fix the banking floor, according to a former PaineWebber executive. Mr. Marron—dubbed "The Don" for his domineering style—oversaw every detail, including picking the artwork and approving the fabric for the chairs.

On the brokerage front, veteran PaineWebber brokers were angered when the firm wrested lucrative investment accounts from top PaineWebber brokers and gave them to Kidder newcomers. Even the firm's highly regarded research group had its snits. There were defections of a handful of key analysts in recent years. And in a misstep, PaineWebber alienated several of its veteran analysts by making public the lofty pay package granted to a star recruit, Jerome Brimeyer, a top pharmaceutical analyst on *Institutional Investor* magazine's All-America Research Team. The pay disclosure came in a 1995 lawsuit after Mr. Brimeyer bolted for Lehman. In the suit—in which PaineWebber attempted to bar Mr. Brimeyer from working at Lehman—PaineWebber revealed that it promised Mr. Brimeyer a 1995 pay package of at least $1 million. This included a $50,000 signing bonus, $200,000 salary and a minimum bonus of $750,000, according to papers filed in a New York state court by PaineWebber.

PaineWebber said Mr. Brimeyer violated his contract with the firm, which included a clause barring him from accepting "employment with any business" that is "in competition with the business of PaineWebber." In a settlement, PaineWebber agreed for $175,000 to drop the suit against Mr. Brimeyer.

The pay spat grew so sensitive that one health-care analyst refused for a time to speak with Ann Knight, his boss and the the firm's research chief. Amid the furor, Ms. Knight put out weekly memos chiding employees for keeping "offensive items," such as cardboard storage boxes, on the floor or under desks. It seems that Ms. Knight sparked Mr. Brimeyer's departure in the first place. In an affidavit filed in his suit, Mr. Brimeyer said he soured on PaineWebber when he was asked to "evaluate the stock of a small pharmaceutical company called Ivax (Corp.), primarily a generic company with which I was not familiar." Traders say Ms. Knight specifically asked Mr. Brimeyer to start research coverage of Ivax. The stock—which PaineWebber helped underwrite and heavily sold to its individual clients—was reeling and needed to be covered. Mr. Brimeyer declined to elaborate in his affidavit.

PaineWebber "sold Ivax fairly aggressively through the retail system," a person familiar with the matter says. The person says PaineWebber "had done substantial corporate-finance work" for Ivax and that the stock "hadn't done well" and Ms. Knight, along with PaineWebber investment bankers, pressed

Mr. Brimeyer to pick up coverage. Hogwash, said Ms. Knight. She said any decision to cover specific companies was Mr. Brimeyer's. "We would never force an analyst to pick up coverage" of any stock, added Ms. Knight, who moved to Salomon Brothers in 1997 and is now at Salomon Smith Barney.

In an affidavit, Ms. Knight said the analyst was irreplaceable. "To locate another analyst, even one whose services are less valuable than Brimeyer's, will be difficult because the demand is greater than the supply of capable research analysts in the pharmaceuticals industry."

PaineWebber eventually found a replacement for Mr. Brimeyer, of course. More broadly, however, the firm still hasn't seemed to find its niche. A year after the Kidder merger, a PaineWebber executive said: "Now the question is, what do you do at our size. Where do you go from here?" In 1997, PaineWebber executives didn't have a solid answer.

Neither does Wall Street.

Looking for a Mate While Avoiding Big Hits

PaineWebber faces a peculiar quandary: To secure its place on the Street, it must either buy another firm or be gobbled up itself. Brokerage executives say potential suitors include foreign banks looking for a brokerage toehold in the United States (like Germany's Deutsche Bank AG), or big domestic investment banks seeking distribution clout among individual investors (like Credit Suisse First Boston). These scenarios would at least ensure that PaineWebber's brokerage operations would remain intact.

Indeed, PaineWebber has been among the oft-mentioned candidates for a takeover on Wall Street. In an ironic twist, the day before the giant Morgan Stanley/Dean Witter merger was announced in February 1997, the hottest rumor among investors was that Morgan Stanley would buy PaineWebber. Only a month earlier, *Business Week* magazine said BankAmerica Corp. had talked with PaineWebber over a possible acquisition or merger. This report prompted an unusual public denial by Mr. Marron. He said he has "had no conversations with the chairman of BankAmerica regarding a possible acquisition of PaineWebber by BankAmerica or a merger of the two firms." An incredulous Mr. Marron told associates he had never even met the BankAmerica chairman.

In fact, the most probable course for PaineWebber is an acquisition of another firm before it is snatched up itself. In a February 1997 talk with the firm's executives, Mr. Marron said PaineWebber has $1 billion in excess capital, and that the firm was talking with a small group of money managers. Mr. Marron also told executives the firm was interested in several regional brokerage firms with asset-management capabilities. "We are ourselves actively looking for acquisitions," Mr. Marron said at the time. "We believe a strong, independent firm is very good for our clients and employees." To head off serious suitors, though, could require PaineWebber to make a major purchase of as much as $1 billion, some investment bankers say. This isn't at all a certainty; Mr. Marron suggests that PaineWebber wouldn't part with all its excess capital.

In August 1997 PaineWebber said it would buy back six million shares of its stock from General Electric Co. for $219 million, dampening speculation that PaineWebber would be gobbled up in Wall Street's takeover wave. Many analysts considered PaineWebber a likely target for a commercial bank seeking a presence in the securities business. But the stock sale suggested to some that GE doesn't see a buyout on the horizon. "The stock's reaction reflects the implication that a sale is not imminently pending," Joan Solotar, an analyst at Donaldson, Lufkin & Jenrette Inc., said at the time. PaineWebber's shares fell more than $2 a share the day the announcement was made.

What's clear is that PaineWebber made great strides in 1997. It sustained a healthy level of profits, and came through the stock-market slide in October with flying colors. It was a major test all along Wall Street: Many brokers and traders hadn't experienced the 1987 crash, and it wasn't clear how they would react. On Bloody Monday, Mr. Grano walked around the firm's trading floor amid the continuing decline. "Everything is going to be fine," Mr. Grano, a former Green Beret, told his troops. "We're going to ride this out."

To show his confidence on late Monday, Mr. Grano even bought two stocks, including an Argentine utility issue, after the Big Board halted trading for the first time. A few days later, Mr. Grano beamed that the positions had made money.

But before the market turned Tuesday, there was concern about how clients would act. Mark Sutton, PaineWebber's brokerage chief, went on the "squawk box" to remind his brokers about the "lessons of eighty-seven." Among other things, Mr. Sutton told his troops to call their clients so that if the market continued its free-fall they wouldn't feel they had been ignored. It wasn't entirely new news: PaineWebber's brokerage force only recently had received a brochure entitled: "Managing Volatile Markets."

Like many other firms, PaineWebber jumped on the market break to turn it into a positive. For years, as the bull market raged, major full-service brokerage firms had watched in frustration as no-frill discounters and no-load mutual funds ate into their market share. Now was a chance to strike back.

PaineWebber's course? Taking out a series of advertisements with a picture of a man's hands behind his back, fingers crossed. The message: "Is your investment plan driven by uncertainty? Or fueled by a philosophy?" PaineWebber then argued that its brokers build investment philosophies for clients to ride out market bumps "so that, while the market will always have its uncertainties, your approach to investing won't."

The solid 1997 made it two consecutive years that PaineWebber completed without any big charges, write-offs or other catastrophes. In 1995, PaineWebber took pretax charges of $230 million to settle claims over improper sales of limited partnerships. In 1994, the firm paid out some $268 million to repay investors for losses and buy back sinking mortgage bonds from its Short-Term U.S. Government Income Fund.

Propped by strong markets and heavy trading activity, PaineWebber reported record net income in 1997 of $415.4 million, for a 22.4 percent return on equity.

But there were potholes along the way. PaineWebber's small-stock group was hit by a double-whammy in late 1997. The firm was one of 30 Nasdaq dealers to settle a highly visible class-action case alleging price fixing in the Nasdaq Stock Market. PaineWebber in December 1997 agreed to pay $50 million without admitting wrongdoing to resolve its part of the case, which was filed by investors in a New York federal court. In all, the Nasdaq dealers agreed to pay a total of $910 million to settle allegations that they conspired to keep the trading "spreads" between the buy and sell price of 1,659 Nasdaq stocks unduly wide.

At the same time, PaineWebber announced it was reorganizing its over-the-counter, or Nasdaq, trading operations under new coheads, William Heenan and Patrick Davis, with PaineWebber's president, Mr. Grano, citing "the significant challenges faced by over-the-counter firms in the changing competitive and regulatory environment." The reorganization came as the SEC prepared civil charges against dozens of traders in its own investigation of alleged price manipulation in the past on Nasdaq, according to people familiar with the SEC probe.

PaineWebber officials declined to say whether the changes were connected to the SEC's investigation. But after announcing the changes, Mr. Grano told Bloomberg News that "hundreds of (Nasdaq) traders on the Street, including ours, are under some sort of inquiry." People familiar with the inquiry say only several dozen are likely to face charges. Mr. Grano added in the same interview: "Because of the inquiries, because of the changes in economics, the old ways weren't appropriate." A firm spokesman said at the time that Mr. Grano was quoted accurately.

Meanwhile, regulatory records revealed that in 1995, PaineWebber paid a total of about $3.5 million to several celebrities, including comedian Jackie Mason and singer Joan Jett, to offset losses in their brokerage accounts. The settlements came as the New York Stock Exchange investigated allegations that the celebrities' former PaineWebber broker, Armando Ruiz, engaged in unauthorized trading that resulted in client losses of more than $3 million, people close to the investigation said.

In an unusual twist, PaineWebber made the payments to Mr. Ruiz's clients before any complaints were formally lodged. The firm quickly went through Mr. Ruiz's client list and offered to make full restitution to many investors, the people said. "It was the most honorable resolution of any dispute I've been involved in," said David Robbins, a lawyer in New York for Ms. Jett, Mr. Mason and his wife, Jyll Rosenfeld, and some other former Ruiz clients.

Yet the woes didn't end there. After Mr. Ruiz was fired, some of his client accounts were passed along to Reuben Taub, a top PaineWebber broker who himself was ousted in January 1996 after he allegedly exceeded trading limits for his wife's account. Mr. Taub, who disputed the allegation, long had been one of PaineWebber's top brokers. For several years, he was a member of the firm's Chairman's Club, reserved for brokers generating annual commissions of more than $1 million.

"There's been a cooperative effort on the parts of the major firms" and the Securities and Exchange Commission on weeding out potential problem brokers, said William Fitzpatrick, consultant for litigation matters at the Securities Industry Association, Wall Street's major trade group. Mr. Fitzpatrick summed up the reason. Doing this helps Street firms "protect their rear end."

PaineWebber in October 1997 set a new executive committee to further integrate the firm's businesses. Besides Messrs. Marron and Grano, the new committee included Steven Baum, global bond chief, who also was named director of capital markets. That meant investment banking, global stocks and transaction services, and global bond and research reported to Mr. Baum. Another committee member was Regina Dolan, the firm's chief financial officer, who also assumed the additional duties of chief administrative officer from Ronald Schwartz, who planned to retire in April 1998. Finance, corporate services and human resources now report to Ms. Dolan. The other members of the new committee were Mark Sutton, brokerage chief, and Robert Silver, director of operations, service and systems.

High Broker Production, High Arbitration Payouts

In 1988, PaineWebber's brokerage force was the least productive of any major Wall Street firm, and lost money. Now, its army of 6,250 brokers is among the most productive of Wall Street's retail-brokerage houses, averaging $372,000 in annual commissions. And in recent years, the brokerage division has generated about half the firm's annual income. The firm's share of the retail-brokerage business has jumped to about 13 percent from 8 percent several years back.

Mr. Marron said in October 1997 that PaineWebber increased its broker-training program substantially, and plans to train another 1,200 brokers in 1998, up from 625 in 1997. Though his firm continues to search for an investment-management or securities firm partner, Mr. Marron argued that it isn't absolutely necessary for PaineWebber to grow. "The issue isn't size, it's momentum," Mr. Marron said. "And right now I'm pretty happy with our momentum."

In the past few years, PaineWebber's recurring fee income per broker has about doubled, to $112,000. And its bid to control more assets is ahead of schedule. The firm has far exceeded its plan to have $180 billion in assets under control by the end of 1996. "Our goal is to be in touch with the affluent investor, who has at least hundreds of thousands of dollars of assets or more," Mr. Marron says. One way is through overseeing $21.4 billion in "wrap" accounts—the one-fee accounts that Wall Street has been pushing to reduce its dependence on trading commissions—second only to Smith Barney.

But this shift away from trading commissions hasn't yet helped the firm's relatively poor arbitration record. PaineWebber ranked worst among big brokerage firms in disputes with clients, according to a survey of arbitration awards between May 1989 and June 1995 by the *Securities Arbitration Commentator*, a newsletter. PaineWebber clients won 61 percent of the cases they filed against the firm, and had the highest average award ($145,100). Meantime, PaineWebber had the highest arbitration cost per broker ($7,000), according to the survey. (Overall, brokerage clients won 51 percent of their cases, with an average award of $81,000.) PaineWebber played down the 1996 study, saying, "These results are attributable to three large awards early on in the study period and don't clearly reflect the current environment at PaineWebber."

Arbitration awards against the firm have rolled in more slowly. In May 1996, a National Association of Securities Dealers arbitration panel ordered the firm to pay $2.2 million to Frank Regas, a prominent Tennessee restaurateur whose family business was sold to the Chili's restaurant chain. It was an unusually beefy award, but this wasn't an ordinary case. Mr. Regas alleged that PaineWebber negligently wired more than $5 million from his account over three years, acting on forged and altered letters of authorization from his accountant without confirming their authenticity. Instead of sending monthly account statements to Mr. Regas, PaineWebber sent them to the accountant—even though he held neither a power of attorney nor was signatory for the account, according to Mr. Regas. PaineWebber disagreed. It said Mr. Regas "repeatedly authorized PaineWebber in writing to take instruction from his accountant."

In one case, PaineWebber started a legal wrangle with three breakaway brokers in a small Texas town and wound up shooting itself in the foot. In the case, involving Wall Street's practice of "raiding" brokers from other firms, a NASD arbitration panel ordered PaineWebber in 1997 to pay $1.4 million in damages for the way it allegedly treated the three brokers after they left to start a competing business. The award included $1 million in punitive damages against PaineWebber, an unusually large amount in securities arbitration. PaineWebber said it was "surprised and extremely disappointed with the panel's decision. It is not consistent in any way with the facts of the matter."

Asset-Management Woes; Now Offering "No-Loads"

PaineWebber has tripped up in trying to build its money-management operations. The firm's Achilles' heel: its Mitchell Hutchins Asset Management unit. What has held down the unit's progress? Heavy turnover and poor performance that began in a big way a few years back, when the firm was roiled by a messy defection of executives and portfolio managers.

Within a few days in the spring of 1993, more than a dozen executives, managers and others quit Mitchell Hutchins; three top executives defected to the U.S. unit of Kleinwort Benson Group PLC, the London-based investment bank. PaineWebber sued the former officials, accusing them of stealing client lists; the firm said in a New York state-court suit that the "mass defection was all part of a prearranged scheme to disrupt [Mitchell Hutchins's] business and to pirate its client base." Then came another embarrassment. Barely a month later, PaineWebber suddenly settled the suit, acknowledging that "it had discovered no evidence" that the officials solicited clients or stole firm property while employed at PaineWebber.

Mitchell Hutchins's woes had just begun. It managed the PaineWebber Short-Term U.S. Government Income Fund, which was pummeled in the 1994 mortgage-bond meltdown. In the largest bailout ever of a mutual fund, Paine-Webber paid about $268 million to reimburse investors and buy back volatile mortgage bonds from the fund. Later, PaineWebber yanked Mitchell Hutchins from managing the fund. In its place, PaineWebber hired Pimco Advisors L.P., a big bond-management firm, to manage the battered fund. The annual cost? about $1.5 million.

Even after the Kidder purchase, the asset-management unit lost several key bond managers to rival Cowen & Co. In a one-year period through mid-1996, Mitchell Hutchins had a dizzying turnover of nearly 100 percent among managing directors in its institutional-stock business alone. Clients fled. Only in 1996 did Mitchell Hutchins stabilize. And this only after PaineWebber brought in a respected manager, Margo Alexander, to run the unit. "We revamped the investment side," said Mr. Grano, noting that the firm's lackluster performance has improved a bit. "Now we're revamping the marketing side."

But the damage had been done. Mitchell Hutchins funds "lost credibility" among PaineWebber brokers, said Mr. Grano. Thus, the percentage of proprietary mutual funds sold by PaineWebber—the most lucrative for the firm—slumped to a skimpy 5 percent in 1995, down from 50 percent a few years earlier. The split between proprietary and outside fund sales at most brokerage firms is 50–50. PaineWebber says the percentage of proprietary funds sold by its brokers now has inched above 10 percent. "We couldn't close the credibility gap until we had adequate performance," Mr. Grano said. "Brokers frankly were doubting Thomases—show me, show me—they're very Missourian."

The SEC in 1997 accused Mitchell Hutchins of fraud in connection with the marketing of its Short-Term U.S. Government-Income Fund. Though the fund was marketed as relatively conservative, with slightly higher risk than money-market funds and certificates of deposit, the SEC said a Mitchell Hutchins portfolio manager began investing in certain derivatives securities in 1993. The SEC said Mitchell Hutchins didn't adequately supervise the portfolio manager and monitor the fund's investments. The PaineWebber unit settled the charges without admitting or denying the charges, agreed not to violate securities laws in the future and hired an independent consultant to review the firm's policies. The SEC also fined Mitchell Hutchins $500,000.

In 1997, Mr. Grano predicted that the unit's assets under management will jump to $80 billion by 2000. One way the firm hopes to do it is by raising the Mitchell Hutchins asset targets that branch managers must hit to achieve various pay goals. The other possible route: an acquisition of a money manager. "We need to have a bigger share of asset flow," according to Mr. Marron.

In the meantime, PaineWebber in January 1998 joined the mad scramble to offer brokerage customers no-load mutual funds. These funds, which don't carry a sales charge, are part of a fund "supermarket" that gives investors a broad choice of mutual funds and fund families. (PaineWebber offers 200 no-load funds from twenty-one fund families.) Like other brokers' supermarkets, PaineWebber's offers both load and no-load funds to clients. Load funds typically carry a 4 to 5 percent sales charge. In this case, the normal sales charge is eliminated because the brokerage firms put high minimums into the funds and in turn charge customers annual "wrap" fees for a broker's help.

"Ultimately, it doesn't matter whether a fund starts out as load or no-load," said Brendan Boyle, PaineWebber's director of fund marketing. "People are willing to pay for advice, and that's what this program is designed to give them."

PaineWebber has made strides in the asset-management arena. In newspaper advertisements, the firm trumpeted a *Smart Money* magazine survey that ranked PaineWebber number one in both the quality and quantity of the mutual funds they offered investors. "With its 'open shop' approach to offering a wide variety of mutual funds, PaineWebber topped the chart with the most sizable stable of funds (2,597) and 276 funds that were top quartile performers over the past five years," the ad boasted.

Investment Banking and International: Lagging

Perhaps the biggest disappointment of the Kidder acquisition was Paine-Webber's inability to bulk up its investment-banking arm. In the months before the Kidder deal, PaineWebber ranked fourteenth among Wall Street's underwriters, according to Securities Data. There were big aspirations, particularly in select banking areas such as transportation, natural resources and health care. The strategy was to use the banking business as a "feeder" into the brokerage system to generate new stock and bond offerings to sell to individual clients. "The grand plan was to take the great leap forward," said Mr. Madden, who was hired from Kidder in late 1994 to lead the banking effort before he left in 1995.

Three months into the next year, however, Mr. Marron decided the firm couldn't afford the big build-up. The banking group had lost about $12 million in the first quarter, executives say—below the projected budget of breaking even for the year. So Mr. Marron quickly decided to scale back the business, laying off bankers, and the group still lags behind its peers.

Thus PaineWebber revamped its strategy. The firm has halved the number of industry areas its investment-banking department focused on, to six. The highly touted transportation group was one area that was combined with other areas to form the "industrial group." "We were spread out over too many industry groups," Mr. Grano said. "We're better off if the business is more focused."

Meanwhile, PaineWebber decided that the international realm was too costly and dominated by too many bigger players. So the firm has pulled back in that area too; it now fancies itself as a national firm with little global reach. In 1995, it shifted its then-international chief, Brian Barefoot, to director of "reengineering." A successor wasn't named. To offer its clients global views, PaineWebber has agreed to pacts with Britain's Barings PLC and Union Bank of Switzerland; for a fee, PaineWebber distributes UBS's European research and Barings's emerging-markets research to its U.S. clients.

"We view our business as primarily domestic," said Mr. Grano. He added that U.S. growth in individual-investor activity could last for twenty years, and saw no reason PaineWebber should do battle with the Deutsche Banks of the world. Said Mr. Grano, "What makes us think we can hurt them on their shore?"

Municipal Strength—and Woes

One of PaineWebber's few areas of institutional strength is municipal bonds. The firm tied for No. 2 among Wall Street's municipal-bond underwriters, with a 10.2 percent market share in 1997, up from fourth in 1996. That's the good news. The bad news is that municipal bonds aren't among the more lucrative areas of the underwriting arena. The average muni-deal generates a fee of about 1 percent of assets, compared with about 7 percent for an initial public stock offering, Securities Data says. Thus, even with its muni strength, PaineWebber still lacks clout in other areas of the fixed-income universe, such as corporate bonds and high-yield "junk" bonds. The firm's fixed-income group has generated just about 15 percent of the firm's annual profit, Wall Street executives say.

And the news on the muni front hasn't been all peaches. In 1996 Paine-Webber became the first big Wall Street firm to violate new regulatory rules restricting political contributions by muni-bond executives. The firm voluntarily banned itself from doing such business for two years in Nashville, Tennessee, after one of its brokers made a campaign contribution to a local political candidate.

It was the most high-profile fallout from a 1994 rule seeking to stamp out "pay-to-play" practices in the business. The rule restricts brokerage firms' muni-bond executives from making campaign contributions to state and local officials as a way of winning muni-bond business. Under the rule, issued by the Municipal Securities Rulemaking Board, firms generally can't do muni business with an issuer "within two years after" making a contribution.

The move was particularly sensitive for PaineWebber and the MSRB because the firm's managing director of municipal operations, Terry Atkinson, sat on the MSRB board. PaineWebber said at the time that it remains "fully committed to complying" with the rule. But the move cost the firm business. Muni executives said PaineWebber will be shut out of more than $200 million in underwriting business; it wasn't clear how much the firm will lose in fees.

PaineWebber also is one of a handful of major securities firms involved in a sweeping SEC investigation of "yield-burning" abuses in the $1.3 trillion muni-bond market. The probe concerns Wall Street's role in the sale of complex bond deals known as advanced refundings, where municipalities hired Street firms to replace their old, outstanding debt with newer, less costly securities.

To complete the deals, PaineWebber and other Wall Street firms created escrow accounts, composed of Treasury bonds. The SEC's enforcement staff is examining if some of Wall Street's biggest firms, including PaineWebber, charged municipalities inflated prices for the Treasury bonds by artificially lowering, or "burning" down, the yield on those securities. (A bond's yield moves in the opposite direction of its price.)

The Wall Street firms have denied wrongdoing; in late 1997, PaineWebber declined to comment on the probe. Yet the yield-burning issue remains an enforcement priority at the SEC.

Research: The Demographical Bull

Just don't tell Edward Kerschner that his firm is anything less than cutting edge.

As he bounded onto the stage at the Grand Ballroom of New York's Waldorf Astoria Hotel on a rainy June afternoon in 1997, the ebullient Mr. Kerschner, the firm's chief market strategist, had the impact of a whole team of cheerleaders on the five hundred or so clients and brokers crowding the room. He waved his arms, he thumped his fist on the podium, he made quips about everything from the behavior of teenage children to brokerage house expenses. By the time he finished his presentation, arguing that demographic factors mean the bull market has years to run, the cheering audience was in the palm of his hand.

That's exactly the kind of reaction PaineWebber's senior managers hoped to elicit—and one that they hope will spill over from the individual investors attending the conference on the impact of demographics on stock market investing to institutional clientele. Already, those pension fund investors say they've noticed a broadening in the kind of research and strategy reports they're receiving. Although PaineWebber is known more for its U.S. research effort, Mr. Kerschner produced a widely read survey of the impact on European Union of the election victories by left-wing parties in Britain and France in the spring of 1997.

But while Mr. Kerschner's blend of high-profile conference performances and his quantitative studies of stock market trends command a following, the same hasn't been as true for the firm's research department. To be sure, in the 1996 *Wall Street Journal* all-star analyst review, PaineWebber boasted twenty all-stars, putting it in seventh place. But that still left the firm trailing rivals like Dean Witter, Morgan Stanley and even Oppenheimer Inc. To fix that, in April 1997 PaineWebber hired Michael Culp, Prudential's former head of research, to revamp the division, after Ann Knight left PaineWebber for a similar role at Salomon Brothers. As of the 1997 report, it had slid to twelfth place, with only fifteen all-stars.

Mr. Culp's arrival unleashed a full-scale raid by PaineWebber on Prudential, as it proceeded to bring on board two of the latter's top oil analysts, two electric utility analysts and a senior banking analyst. The goal, people in the firm say, is to put together a research team that can compete effectively with the 800-pound gorillas of the investment research world such as Merrill Lynch and the newly-merged Morgan Stanley, Dean Witter, serving not just the firm's retail clientele but also institutions.

In that battle, Mr. Kerschner is likely to emerge as a key weapon, institutional money managers say. He's a strong believer in working closely with the firm's analysts, arguing that PaineWebber's job is to provide clients with "areas of agreement, not areas of disagreement where the clients have to serve as referees." His populist approach when dealing with individual investors (he even fields brokers' questions via cellular phone in the middle of lunch meetings), hasn't meant any loss of influence among the pension fund managers, even though some of the latter are still prone to view PaineWebber's research product as "too much of an effort to find a good story to tell and not enough real ideas."

Mr. Kerschner, one of several strategists to launch their market-watching careers at Cowen & Co., sees his job as at least partly gazing into crystal balls in an effort to determine the future.

"We try to see where there's a change coming, and get in to play the stocks that will benefit as that change occurs," he said. For instance, in mid-1997, he began moving out of stocks he had bought heavily early in the 1990s in the expectation that corporate restructuring at a wide range of industries would lead to fatter bottom lines. By the time he's sold the last of those stocks at the end of 1997, he'll be fully invested in companies he expects to benefit from what he's dubbed "Demogrowthics," or spending on products linked to the age of a consumer. For instance, he likes Revlon because of its appeal to young women, who are the biggest consumers of cosmetics. Equally, he likes companies with strong brand appeal to teenagers, or health-care firms with products aimed at a demographic group he's dubbed the "senior seniors."

"Institutional clients want provocative new ideas; they don't want us to call

the market," he said. "That's not much different really from what we give to
the retail market. The brokers need a reason they can give to clients for buying
certain stocks. But the story really stays the same, even though the presentation may be a bit different for the two groups."

Despite his flamboyant personality, Mr. Kerschner is one of the lower-
profile strategists on Wall Street. His colleague, Mary Farrell, known for her
ability to track small stocks, is usually the firm's spokesperson on broad market
issues as well, even though it's Mr. Kerschner who sets asset allocation policy
and fills the role of chief investment officer.

Still, he's well-known among institutional clients for a handful of savvy
calls. Ironically, he described his best call as also one of his worst: Early in the
summer of 1987, worried about the rising values of stocks at a time when bond
yields were also climbing, he issued an interoffice memo suggesting it might be
a good time to bail out of stocks in favor of bonds.

"That went out in May," he recalled. "I watched in pain as stock prices rose
in June, July, August. That one day in October was probably the happiest of my
life. My worst calls, I think, have just been being early, which as everyone
knows, is just the same as being wrong."

Mr. Kerschner said that calls like this may attract attention from clients,
but that on an ongoing basis, it's more useful to provide them with specific investment themes such as the "Demogrowthics" ideas than it is to encourage
them to try to time the market. "There's too much of a short-term fixation on
the market," he snapped. "If you buy and hold something for a year, the odds
are very, very good that if you pick the right stock you'll beat the market for
that year. But if you sell it the first month it disappoints you, you'll give up
some of that outperformance. Patience, patience, patience—don't chase instant
gratification or you'll be doomed to disappointment."

Clamoring to Clean Up Its Legal Act

When PaineWebber hired Theodore Levine as its general counsel in 1993, he
said the firm wanted "to have the best legal and compliance system on Wall
Street." He soon found out how challenging that would be. Besides its poor
record in arbitration cases with investors, PaineWebber has had its share of
high-profile legal flaps.

In June 1994, the firm, in an extraordinary move, injected $33 million of its
money as part of a $268 million bailout of a floundering government-bond fund.
The payment, which covered losses from questionable mortgage bonds, "re-
moves all doubt that any one of our shareholders were damaged," a Paine-
Webber executive said at the time.

The firm wasn't required to make the repayment. And PaineWebber
stressed that it didn't intend to pay investors in the future simply for market

drops. But, the executive said, "We want to take the high moral ground." The move nevertheless wasn't totally altruistic. It was part of an agreement to settle class-action litigation brought by some of the fund's investors over the portfolio's poor performance. It was all part of changes launched by Mr. Levine that included establishing a dispute-resolution system to settle tough cases early.

In 1996, PaineWebber faced another big legal test. The firm agreed to pay $250 million—including a total of $45 million toward a restitution fund and civil penalty—to settle an SEC civil administrative complaint and related class-action claims that some of its brokers misled investors in selling hundreds of millions of dollars in limited partnerships.

The SEC alleged that PaineWebber's sales and marketing materials for four partnerships, including Geodyne oil and Pegasus aircraft, overstated the benefits and understated the risks of these investments and characterized them as suitable for conservative investors. The deal brought the total cost of PaineWebber's partnership woes to $332.5 million, some of which already had been paid out.

Though that paled in comparison to the $2 billion paid out by Prudential Securities Inc. to settle civil and criminal charges of widespread fraud in connection with partnership sales, it was far higher than what PaineWebber had expected to pay less than a year earlier. In a statement, Mr. Marron was contrite. "We accept our full share of responsibility for the situation."

PaineWebber's People

Donald B. Marron, chairman and chief executive officer: Mr. Marron, a member of PaineWebber Inc.'s executive committee, is one of Wall Street's most veteran executives, beginning his career in 1951 at New York Trust Co. In 1959, he formed his own investment-banking firm, which merged seven years later with Mitchell Hutchins & Co. Mr. Marron was named executive vice president, then president, at the age of thirty-four. During the 1960s boom in institutional research, he cofounded Data Resources Inc. When Mitchell Hutchins merged with PaineWebber in 1977, Mr. Marron became PaineWebber president.

Marron, Donald
CEO & Chairman-
PaineWebber

Mr. Marron is credited with rescuing PaineWebber from a trade-processing crisis in 1980, and was named chief executive. A year later, he was elected chairman. In that role, Mr. Marron led a firm that rode the bull market that began in 1982, but never adequately built the firm's investment-banking group. PaineWebber missed the 1980s bonanza in mergers, merchant banking and underwriting.

Outside of Wall Street, Mr. Marron has made a name for himself collecting art. The firm's contemporary-art collection was ranked as one of the top three in the world in 1993 by a Harvard Business School survey. Acquired with company funds and valued at roughly $25 million a few years back, the 650-piece collection includes giant multicolored aluminum sculptures by Frank Stella, and other abstract or hard-edged works by Jasper Johns, Willem de Kooning and David Smith. He is vice chairman of New York's prestigious Museum of Modern Art.

Joseph J. Grano Jr., president: Mr. Grano, a member of PaineWebber Inc.'s executive committee, is among the strongest executives recruited by PaineWebber in recent years. After a five-year stint as a captain in the U.S. Army's Green Berets, Mr. Grano joined Merrill in 1972 as a broker. In 1978, he became Merrill's youngest vice president, at age thirty. In 1987, he was named the industry's best retail-marketing executive in a survey conducted by *Investment Dealers' Digest* magazine.

He joined PaineWebber in 1988 to head the firm's brokerage operations, rose to the president's post in 1994, and is widely viewed as heir apparent. Mr. Grano has helped the firm make strides in the basic brokerage group; he turned around an operation that was losing money when he joined it, to one that generates about half the firm's annual revenues.

Mr. Grano is former chairman of the NASD, and has been in the forefront of several positive shifts in the brokerage business, including paying brokers the same for selling proprietary versus non-proprietary products.

Steven P. Baum, director, capital markets: Mr. Baum, a member of Paine-Webber Inc.'s executive committee, previously was director of the firm's global-bond and commercial real-estate division. His new role encompasses oversight for those areas, plus investment banking, global equity and transaction services, and research. Mr. Baum has been in the mortgage-bond business since 1979. He began his career at Salomon Brothers Inc., where he served four years as head of the loan-trading desk, and two years as analyst for the Bond Portfolio Analysis Group. Mr. Baum made a name for himself at Kidder Peabody; at various times, he oversaw whole-loan trading, managed the commercial and real-estate securitization group, and coheaded the firm's bond department. He was one of the high-profile Kidder hires after PaineWebber's 1994 acquisition of the troubled firm.

Regina A. Dolan, chief administrative and financial officer: The blunt-talking Ms. Dolan, a member of PaineWebber Inc.'s executive committee, joined PaineWebber in 1992 as senior vice president and director of finance and controls. She assumed her current post in 1994. Ms. Dolan began her career in 1975 at Ernst & Young; in 1986, she was named partner.

Robert H. Silver, director, operations, service and systems: Mr. Silver, a member of PaineWebber Inc.'s executive committee, oversees the development of the firm's technological capabilities. In a decade-long tenure at PaineWebber, he has served as director of retail products and marketing, retail branch offices, and finance and controls. Before PaineWebber, Mr. Silver spent five years in financial services at Merrill.

Mark B. Sutton, director, brokerage operations: Mr. Sutton is a member of PaineWebber Inc.'s executive committee. His position as director of the private-client group at PaineWebber is a homecoming of sorts. A protégé of Mr. Grano's, Mr. Sutton was a PaineWebber branch manager and a Mitchell Hutchins managing director before being lured to Kidder with much fanfare in 1992.

Mr. Sutton began his career in 1978 with Merrill Lynch in Arkansas, after graduating from the University of Arkansas, where he was captain of the baseball team. In 1980, he moved to Rotan Mosle Inc., a regional brokerage firm in Houston that PaineWebber acquired in 1983. Before joining PaineWebber, Mr. Sutton also worked briefly at Cowen & Co.

Mr. Sutton is highly regarded on Wall Street. "Sutton's just a terrific guy—a very intense, hard-driving, smart Texan," said former Kidder executive Michael Keehner when Kidder hired him. "He certainly understands how to run a brokerage operation."

Margo N. Alexander, president and CEO, Mitchell Hutchins: One of Wall Street's most senior female executives, Ms. Alexander is a Harvard Business School graduate with more than twenty-five years of Street experience. She began her career in 1970 with Arthur Young and was a securities analyst with Standard & Poor/InterCapital from 1971 to 1973. Ms. Alexander initially joined Michell Hutchins, before it was bought by PaineWebber, as an analyst covering the retail industry.

At PaineWebber, she was named research chief in 1982. She took over the firm's institutional-stock operations in 1988 along with Charlie Milligan. When she coheaded PaineWebber's capital-markets group with Mr. Milligan in the early 1990s, irreverent traders at the firm's New York offices nicknamed their efforts, "The Charlie and Margo Show." Ms. Alexander has said general management skills are her strong suit. She assumed her current post in early 1995, with a big challenge that she has met: to turn around a flailing asset-management group beset by management turmoil and poor performance.

Terry L. Atkinson, managing director and director, municipal-securities group: Mr. Atkinson was appointed to his current post in 1989. He joined PaineWebber in 1987 and previously had been at Salomon Brothers. He began his career in 1975 in institutional sales at Shearson Hayden Stone.

Brian M. Barefoot, director, investment banking: The veteran Mr. Barefoot started his Wall Street career in 1967 at Merrill. He held several positions there, including director of merchant banking, director of the global broker-dealer division, director of institutional services and head of global institutional sales. Mr. Barefoot joined PaineWebber in 1994 as president of PaineWebber International. When that group was scaled back, he became director, engineering, amid a firm reorganization. He was named to the investment-banking post in 1996, replacing Robert Pangia.

Michael Culp, director of research: Mr. Culp joined PaineWebber in 1997 from Prudential Securities, where he had been director of global research. Mr. Culp, who had been involved in Wall Street research for twenty-four years when he joined the firm, replaced Ann Knight, who left for Salomon, now Salomon Smith Barney Holdings. Mr. Culp was *Institutional Investor* magazine's top-ranked analyst in the restaurant and lodging sector between 1983 and 1986. Before Prudential, he was an analyst at E.F. Hutton and began his career at Standard & Poor's Corp.

Theodore A. Levine, general counsel, PaineWebber Group Inc.: Once the No. 2 executive in the SEC's enforcement division, Mr. Levine joined Paine-Webber in 1993. Since then, he has made strides in slowly cutting the firm's investor caseload. Among his big changes: establishing a way to settle tough disputes early, and placing the legal department in charge of the employee group that handles sales-practice complaints. In the past, the complaint staff had consulted with lawyers only on an ad hoc basis. Mr. Levine also boosted the firm's staff of lawyers, and established a confidential hot line to the legal department for employees who seek to report suspicious activity.

The loquacious Mr. Levine has had a varied career. After leaving his post at the SEC as associate chief of enforcement in 1984, he spent nearly a decade as a partner at the elite Washington law firm Wilmer, Cutler & Pickering. His clients included nearly all of the biggest brokerage houses—though not PaineWebber—as well as infamous arbitrager Ivan Boesky.

James P. Mac Gilvray, director, global equities and transaction services: Mr. Mac Gilvray has held management positions with specialists and brokerage firms on the New York Stock Exchange and the American Stock Exchange. He joined Paine,Webber, Jackson & Curtis, a predecessor firm, in 1973, and has held several management positions in PaineWebber's stock sales, trading and stock-exchange floor business. He was named to his current post in 1995.

Scott G. Abbey, chief information officer: Mr. Abbey, an executive vice president, was appointed to his current post when he joined PaineWebber in 1996. He previously had worked at Morgan Stanley in various positions, including chief information officer and head of worldwide operations.

Mark D. Altman, managing director and associate director, research: Mr. Altman was named to this post in 1994. He joined PaineWebber in 1983 as a research analyst, a position he previously had held at Merrill and U.S. Trust Co. of New York.

Brad Anderson, portfolio manager, Mitchell Hutchins: Mr. Anderson, a managing director, was appointed to his current position when he joined Mitchell Hutchins in 1975. He previously had been a senior portfolio manager with Hornblower Asset Management.

William M. Bain, director, reengineering: Mr. Bain, a senior vice president, was named to his current post when he joined PaineWebber in 1995. He previously had been vice president of reengineering at Bankers Trust.

Kirkham Barnaby, managing director and chief investment officer, quantitative services, Mitchell Hutchins Asset Management Inc.: Mr. Barnaby has spent eleven years with Mitchell Hutchins Asset Management, having also served as a senior vice president, responsible for quantitative management and asset allocation models. In addition to his chief investment officer duties, he currently serves as portfolio manager of PaineWebber Tactical Allocation Fund and determines the allocations for PaineWebber Balanced Fund.

Robert S. Basso, president, Correspondent Service Corp.: Mr. Basso joined PaineWebber as a managing director in 1990. He was named president of Correspondent Services, a PaineWebber unit, when it was formed in 1991.

Paul Becker, managing director and portfolio manager, Mitchell Hutchins: Mr. Becker joined Mitchell Hutchins in 1978 from Wall, Paterson, McGrew & Richards. He previously was with Baker, Weeks & Co. and Waddell & Reed.

Gerald A. Blitstein, managing director, product development: Mr. Blitstein was appointed to his current post in the global stock division in 1997. He joined PaineWebber's M&A group in 1987, was named a first vice president in 1993, and later was assistant to the chairman.

Brendan D. Boyle, director, sales and marketing of Mitchell Hutchins: Mr. Boyle was appointed to his current post when he joined Mitchell Hutchins in 1996. He previously had been executive vice president and director of sales and marketing at Prudential Mutual Funds, and director of sales and marketing for Smith Barney's mutual funds and unit trusts.

Robert W. Brokaw III, managing director and head of corporate finance, investment banking: Mr. Brokaw joined PaineWebber in 1997 from Robert

Brokaw, LLC, an independent investment banking concern. He is also an adjunct professor of finance at the New York University Leonard N. Stern School of Business. Mr. Brokaw also worked in investment banking at Merrill Lynch for twenty-two years, where he was a managing director and corporate finance specialist.

Donald C. Cacciapaglia, managing director and chief operating officer, investment banking: Mr. Cacciapaglia was appointed to his current post when he joined PaineWebber in 1996. He previously had been COO of short- and intermediate-term trading at CS First Boston. He earlier had held several positions at Merrill, including COO and senior managing director of investment banking.

Brian P. Carey, senior vice president and director, human resources: Mr. Carey rejoined PaineWebber in 1996 in his current post. He had been a partner at Buck Consultants and a director of compensation and benefits at Chase Manhattan Bank after an earlier stint at PaineWebber as director of compensation and benefits between 1986 and 1989.

Arthur D. Cashin, managing director and director, floor operations/ New York Stock Exchange: Mr. Cashin joined PaineWebber in 1980 as an institutional-floor broker and was named to his current post in 1984. Before PaineWebber, he worked at P.R. Herzig & Co. He began his career at Thomson McKinnon in 1959.

J. Scott Coburn, managing director and cohead, equity capital markets: Mr. Coburn was appointed to his current post when he joined PaineWebber in 1996. He previously had been managing director of equity capital-markets services for Smith Barney.

F. Daniel Corkery, deputy general counsel: Mr. Corkery, a senior vice president, joined PaineWebber in 1984 as a vice president and assistant general counsel; he assumed his current post in 1995. Mr. Corkery previously had worked for the Securities and Exchange Commission as a lawyer in its Boston regional office.

John Coughlin, managing director and national sales manager, institutional-sales trading: Mr. Coughlin was appointed to his current post in 1989. He joined the firm as a stock trader in 1980; he previously had been a trader at First Manhattan Co. and Eastman Dillon Securities.

Roger J. Curylo, director, global credit: Mr. Curylo joined PaineWebber in 1991 as vice president and manager of the institutional-credit group. He assumed his current position in 1994, after being compliance chief at the firm. Previously, Mr. Curylo was credit director at Wertheim Schroder.

Patrick O. Davis, senior vice president and cohead, over-the-counter trading, global equity division: Mr. Davis joined PaineWebber in 1997. He previously had served five years as vice president and manager of over-the-counter trading at Salomon Brothers. He has served on the issues committee and quality of markets committee for the Security Traders Association of New York.

Anthony DiIorio, executive vice president, controller, finance: Mr. DiIorio was appointed to his current position when he joined PaineWebber in 1995. From 1994 to 1995 he was senior vice president and chief financial officer of the capital markets group at NationsBank. Before that, he spent five years as an executive vice president and controller at Goldman, Sachs & Co. and seven years with LeBoeuf, Lamb Green and MacRay as a managing director. In 1977 he joined Dime Bank Corp. as executive vice president and chief financial officer. He began his career with KPMG Peat Marwick in 1968.

William J. Evans, portfolio manager, Mitchell Hutchins: Mr. Evans, a managing director, assumed his current post when he joined Mitchell Hutchins in 1976. He earlier had been a portfolio manager at Lehman Brothers and Merrill, among other firms.

Terrence E. Fancher, managing director and cohead, real-estate investment-banking group: Mr. Fancher was appointed to his current post when he joined PaineWebber through the acquisition of Kidder in 1994 where he had been a managing director and director of real-estate investment banking.

Miguel A. Ferrer, president and chief executive officer, PaineWebber Inc. of Puerto Rico; chairman, PaineWebber Latin America: Mr. Ferrer joined PaineWebber's Puerto Rican operations in 1980. Before PaineWebber, he had been a branch manager and partner with Blyth Eastman Dillon and Merrill Lynch.

Kevin W. Finn, senior vice president and chief administrative officer, Global Prime Brokerage and Stock Loan: Mr. Finn joined PaineWebber in

1984 and was appointed to his current post in 1997. Before PaineWebber, he was an audit manager at Coopers & Lybrand.

Diane Frimmel, executive vice president and director of operations: Ms. Frimmel joined PaineWebber's finance division in 1979, and served in a variety of posts before being named director of operations in 1994 and executive vice president in 1997.

Maury N. Harris, managing director and chief economist: Mr. Harris joined PaineWebber in 1980. He previously had been chief of the financial markets' research division at the Federal Reserve Bank of New York.

William P. Heenan, managing director, cohead of OTC trading and head of principal trading: Mr. Heenan joined PaineWebber in 1995 as a senior vice president and senior trader in the firm's global stock division; he was named to his current post in 1997. He previously had been a senior vice president and senior trader at Kidder and vice president and senior trader at Lehman Brothers.

C. Wolcott Henry, managing director and portfolio manager, Mitchell Hutchins: Mr. Henry was appointed to this post in 1988. He joined Mitchell Hutchins in 1965 as a partner. When the firm was acquired by PaineWebber in 1978, he became a vice president at Mitchell Hutchins Asset Managment.

Reginald Hollinger, managing director, head of telecommunications industry group, investment banking: Mr. Hollinger joined PaineWebber in 1997 from Morgan Stanley, where he was a principal in the corporate finance department, focusing exclusively on the telecommunications sector. Before that, he worked with Chemical Bank's leveraged buyout group.

Walter S. Hulse, managing director and cohead, integrated energy group, investment banking: Mr. Hulse was appointed to this post in 1997. He joined the firm's utility-finance division in 1986 and later was named managing director of bond capital markets.

Graham T. Hunt, chairman and chief executive of Financial Counselors: Mr. Hunt, a managing director, in 1989 was appointed to this post at Financial Counselors, a Mitchell Hutchins unit. He previously had worked at, among other firms, Kidder Peabody.

Richard L. Intrator, managing director and group head of media and entertainment, investment banking: Mr. Intrator joined the firm in 1997, having previously been chairman and chief executive officer of the Josara Cos., a merchant bank serving traditional and new media enterprises. From 1992 through 1995 he directed the media, entertainment and communications practice of the Lodestar Group/LSG Advisors in New York, a division of Société Générale Securities Corp. From 1986 to 1992 he served as senior vice president in the media and entertainment investment banking group of Kidder, Peabody and Co.

Herbert F. Janick III, general counsel: Mr. Janick, a senior vice president, joined PaineWebber in 1993 as a senior associate general counsel of Paine-Webber's brokerage group; he was named deputy general counsel in 1994 and general counsel of PaineWebber Inc. a year later. He previously held a variety of posts at the SEC's enforcement division, including assistant director.

Oscar J. Junquera, managing director and group head, financial-institutions group, investment banking: Mr. Junquera was appointed to this post in 1991. He joined PaineWebber in 1980.

Robert L. Karem, senior vice president and director, quality and service, operations, service and systems: Mr. Karem was appointed to his current position in 1994. He joined PaineWebber in 1978 and served as the firm's New Orleans branch manager and a New York branch manager.

Brendan H. Kennedy, managing director, floor operations/Chicago Board Options Exchange: Mr. Kennedy was appointed to his current post in 1983. He joined PaineWebber in 1978 and previously had been a floor broker at Blyth Eastman Dillon.

Edward M. Kerschner, managing director and chairman, investment policy committee, research: Mr. Kerschner was appointed to this post in 1982, when he joined the firm as an investment strategist from Cowen & Co. Mr. Kerschner has been recognized by *Institutional Investor* magazine with positions on its All-America Research Team for both portfolio strategy and quantitative analysis.

Isaac B. Krim, senior vice president and director, risk management: Mr. Krim was appointed to his current post in 1994 when he joined the firm from Prudential Securities, where he had been a senior vice president and risk manager.

Frank A. Lenti, executive vice president and director, taxes: Mr. Lenti joined PaineWebber as senior vice president and director of taxes in 1990 and was promoted to executive vice president in 1997. He previously had been with Drexel.

Kevin S. McCarthy, managing director and cohead, integrated energy group, investment banking: Mr. McCarthy joined PaineWebber in 1997. He was previously a managing director in the global energy and power group at Smith Barney and head of the energy group at Dean Witter. Mr. McCarthy has been involved in energy investment banking since 1984.

Dennis L. McCauley, managing director and chief investment officer, fixed income, Mitchell Hutchins: Mr. McCauley was appointed to his current post when he joined Mitchell Hutchins in 1994. He previously had spent thirty years with International Business Machines Corp. in several positions, including director of bond investments.

Joel J. McKoan, managing director and director, emerging markets, corporate bond and high yield trading: Mr. McKoan was appointed to his current post in 1997. He joined PaineWebber in 1994 through the acquisition of Kidder as managing director and director of global sales. At Kidder, Mr. McKoan, known as "JJ," had served as head of national bond sales and a senior bond salesman.

Joseph L. Morea, managing director and cohead, equity capital markets: Mr. Morea was named to this post when he joined PaineWebber in 1996 from Smith Barney. He previously had been with Merrill, Coopers & Lybrand and Commodity Exchange Inc.

Charles H. Nobs, senior vice president and director, corporate services: Mr. Nobs was appointed to his current post in 1997. He joined PaineWebber from a management-consulting firm he founded in 1994. He previously had been a managing director at Bankers Trust Co.

William J. Nolan III, treasurer: Mr. Nolan, an executive vice president, was appointed to his current post in 1997. He joined PaineWebber in 1984 as managing director for money-market trading and the commercial-paper dealership, a position he previously had held at Becker-Paribas.

Dhananjay Pai, cohead, principal transactions: Mr. Pai joined Paine-Webber in 1990 and was named to his current post in 1993. He previously had been a vice president of corporate finance at Drexel Burnham Lambert Inc.

Stelios Papadopoulous, managing director and group head, health care, investment banking: Dr. Papadopoulous joined PaineWebber in 1987 and was appointed to his current post in 1990. He previously had been at Drexel and Donaldson, Lufkin & Jenrette.

Dongwook Park, managing director, stock trading: Mr. Park was named to his current post in the global stock division in 1995; he is responsible for the risk management of listed, derivatives, international and convertible securities trading units. He joined PaineWebber in 1978, and previously had been a portfolio manager at Irving Trust Co.

Robert A. Pellicone, managing director, floor operations/American and Philadelphia Stock Exchanges: Mr. Pellicone was named to this post in 1990. He previously had been a vice president in the capital-markets division of Blyth Eastman Dillon and the floor manager at the American Stock Exchange for Dean Witter.

Donna C. Peterman, director, corporate communications: Ms. Peterman joined PaineWebber in 1996. She previously had been at Hill and Knowlton U.S.A., a public relations firm, and director of corporate communications at Dean Witter Financial Services Group.

Joseph A. Piscina, managing director and head, asset trading and finance: Mr. Piscina assumed his current post in 1996. He joined PaineWebber through the firm's acquisition of Kidder in 1994. Before Kidder, he had been head of residential whole loan trading and a senior trader at Deutsche Bank's mortgage-backed securities department.

David M. Reed, managing director and group head, mergers and acquisitions: Mr. Reed has been in this post since 1994. He joined PaineWebber in 1986 as a vice president in the mergers group. He previously had been a vice president in the investment-banking department of Citicorp.

Michael G. Ricciardi, managing director and head, global fixed-income sales: Mr. Ricciardi assumed his current position when he joined PaineWebber in 1997. He had been a managing director at Citicorp, and previously had worked in a variety of sales positions at Kidder, Merrill, Salomon and Chase Manhattan Bank.

Charles W. Santoro, vice chairman and head, industrial and financial buyers group, investment banking: Mr. Santoro was appointed to this post when he joined PaineWebber in 1995. He previously had held numerous positions at Smith Barney. Before Smith Barney, Mr. Santoro had been at Morgan Stanley in its mergers-and-acquisitions group in New York and London.

Victoria Schonfeld, general counsel at Mitchell Hutchins Asset Management: Ms. Schonfeld assumed her current position when she joined Mitchell Hutchins in 1994. She previously had been a partner at the New York law office of Arnold & Porter.

In the Beginning . . .

In 1880, William Paine and Wallace Webber opened a brokerage office on Congress Street in Boston, just a few doors up the street from another brokerage office opened a year earlier by Charles Cabot Jackson and Laurence Curtis. On July 1, 1942—the day the two firms merged to form Paine, Webber, Jackson & Curtis—total trading on the New York Stock Exchange was 206,800 shares, the lowest daily volume for any day but one since 1918.

The firm moved its headquarters to Broadway in New York twenty-one years later, and issued its shares to the public in 1972. Meantime, the firm went on an acquisition binge that transformed it into a national brokerage house with some research and investment-banking clout: Abbott, Proctor & Paine (1970); Mitchum, Jones & Templeton (1973); Mitchell Hutchins Inc. (1977); Blyth, Eastman Dillon & Co. (1979); and Rotan Mosle Inc. (1983).

After PaineWebber bought reeling Kidder in 1994, it considered keeping the 129-year-old Kidder name, one of Wall Street's longest-running. Some executives pushed for keeping Kidder. For instance, Kidder still was respected in Europe, where it was "Paine-Who?"

In the end, Kidder didn't make the cut. After a six-week "global study" of its individual and institutional clients, PaineWebber decided to make Kidder Peabody a Wall Street footnote. Said a PaineWebber official at the time: "We want to behave as one company, with one voice and one name."

■

Hercules Segalas, managing director, consumer products, investment banking: Mr. Segalas was appointed to this post when he joined PaineWebber in 1988. He previously had been at Drexel Burnham Lambert; before Wall Street he held a variety of positions in manufacturing and engineering at Procter & Gamble Co.

Dennis Senneseth, portfolio manager, Mitchell Hutchins: Mr. Senneseth, a managing director, joined Mitchell Hutchins in his current post in 1983. He earlier had been chief investment officer at First Trust Co., St. Paul.

Ramesh Singh, managing director and head, mortgage backed securities, global fixed income and commercial real estate: Mr. Singh was appointed to his current position in 1995. Mr. Singh joined PaineWebber in 1994 through the firm's acquisition of Kidder Peabody as a senior vice president in derivative trading and new issue CMOs, a position he had held since 1992. He began his career with Kidder as a mortgaged back trading analyst in 1989.

J. Richard Sipes, executive vice president and director, products and trading: Mr. Sipes was appointed director of products and trading in 1995. He joined PaineWebber in 1978 from Merrill.

John A. Taylor, managing director, commercial real estate, global fixed income and commercial real estate: Mr. Taylor joined PaineWebber in 1994 through the firm's acquisition of Kidder Peabody, where he served as managing director in their real estate group since 1989. He had originally joined Kidder in 1985 as a mortgage products salesman, with an emphasis on commercial and residential whole loans. Before that, he had practiced law with Richards & O'Neal in New York from 1983 to 1985.

Mark A. Tincher, chief investment officer, stocks, Mitchell Hutchins: Mr. Tincher assumed his current post when he joined Mitchell Hutchins in 1995. Before then, he had been a vice president and senior portfolio manager at Chase Manhattan Bank.

Robert E. Weeden, managing director and head, high-yield origination, investment banking: Mr. Weeden was appointed to his current post when he joined PaineWebber in 1996. He previously had been at Dillon, Read & Co., Kidder, L.F. Rothschild & Co. and Merrill.

James W. White, chief operating officer, international sales: Mr. White, a senior vice president, was appointed to his current post in 1996. Since joining PaineWebber in 1988, he has held a variety of positions, including chief administrative officer for the global derivatives, foreign exchange and Asian divisions.

Peter L. Zurkow, managing director, principal transactions group: Mr. Zurkow joined PaineWebber in 1992 as managing director of high-yield trading, and has held his current position since 1997. He previously had been a portfolio manager and analyst in the risk-arbitrage department at Wertheim Schroder.

PRUDENTIAL SECURITIES INC.

EMERGING FROM SCANDAL'S DEPTHS

The Worst Is Over—But What Next?

Thanksgiving 1996 had special meaning for Prudential Securities Inc.: The day before the holiday, criminal prosecutors closed an investigation of current and former executives at the brokerage firm over improper limited-partnership sales. No charges were brought.

But the damage was done. The Prudential Insurance Co. of America unit already had paid about $2 billion in legal costs after selling partnerships by misleading investors about their risks and returns. Yes, Prudential executives escaped blame. But the firm was tagged with directing Wall Street's biggest small-investor fraud.

The scandal couldn't have come at a worse time. The damage to Prudential's franchise wiped out any chance of maximizing one of the most massive bull markets ever seen. Some Wall Street firms earned more in 1995 and 1996 than they had in some prior decades. "We missed the party," lamented Hardwick Simmons, Prudential Securities Inc.'s president and chief executive officer.

Even in 1997, a record year for Wall Street, Prudential Securities managed net income of just about $200 million—one-tenth that of rival Merrill Lynch & Co. And this was a year when Prudential had long since emerged from the worst of its partnership scandal and boasted its second-best results ever.

It all goes to show how difficult it is for a retail brokerage firm catering to individuals to recover from a prolonged crisis of confidence. All scandal-ridden firms facing intense public scrutiny will suffer through lost business and personnel. But unlike other firms fighting to get past scandals, such as Salomon Brothers Inc. in the early 1990s, Prudential Securities has lost a core of individual investors who vow never to return.

Loretta Rupert is one of them. A retiree who bought the partnerships as an equivalent to safe certificates of deposit, Ms. Rupert said she was lured by the marketing clout of the Rock—Prudential's famous logo that resembles the Rock of Gibraltar. "I grew up with the Pru—to me it was the greatest insurance company," the Cape Coral, Florida, widow said. After losing nearly all of her $90,000 savings in soured Prudential Securities partnerships, Ms. Rupert said she shudders to see the Prudential Rock on television. "Something turns inside of me when I see it."

Prudential Securities executives vow that the blunders are over. "We are determined not to repeat those mistakes," Mr. Simmons said in early 1997. "Our clients' interests are absolutely, positively number one."

Number two should probably be a broader corporate focus. Unlike Merrill, Prudential hasn't had much success in plunging into many areas outside of retail brokerage. This will make it difficult to ride through any prolonged market downturns. Though Prudential is looking to build its once-gutted investment-banking unit, its bread-and-butter brokerage business isn't all that profitable in anything but the most ebullient markets.

The bottom line: Prudential Securities could be doomed to be merely a marginal player among big securities firms, Wall Street executives say.

Until recently, there has been little of the hoped-for synergy with Prudential Insurance,which has had its own share of problems. Indeed, the alliance has been held up as an example of the difficulty of having a deep-pocketed parent outside the brokerage business buying a presence on Wall Street. Prudential Insurance has poured more than $2 billion into its securities unit since buying it in 1981 for $381 million. Since 1981, Prudential Securities has made payments to the parent of about $1 billion and generated a relatively meager profit, people familiar with the firm say.

For several years in the mid-1990s, the big insurer bristled at Prudential Securities, believing the brokerage unit's woes were soiling the Pru's pristine reputation. But now the tables have turned: Prudential Insurance has been roiled by a scandal of its own, involving massive deception by its agents in excessive sales of insurance policies, and Prudential Securities in 1996 became the big money-maker in the Prudential empire. "We're the shining light on the hill now," Mr. Simmons chuckled. "They need us nearly as much as we need them."

Not surprisingly, the parent's view of its once-wayward child has changed considerably. Several years ago, then-Prudential Insurance Chairman Robert Winters tried unsuccessfully to sell the securities unit. And Prudential Insurance went out of its way to distance itself from the broker's problems.

Now, ties between the two firms have strengthened. This can be seen in a series of advertisements rolled out in 1997 reflecting a "One Prudential" mantra. The ads, created partly by a coterie of executives Prudential Securities hired from mutual-fund giant Fidelity Investments, include a prominent mention of the Prudential name and logo, but some don't clearly spell out either the parent or the brokerage unit.

There is more palpable evidence. For years, Prudential Insurance paid J. P.

Morgan & Co. to act as custodian for its $60 billion of general account assets. In 1996, the parent gave that mandate for the first time to Prudential Securities, saving the Pru $17 million in annual fees. And Prudential stopped requiring the brokerage unit in 1996 to pay a dividend that had represented 40 percent of its earnings. "They are funding us by allowing us to use all of our earnings to build our capital," said Mr. Simmons.

Prudential Securities can use all the help it can get. The firm's widely publicized partnership problems in the 1980s stemmed from—what else is new on Wall Street?—intense pressure to produce profits. Fast.

When Prudential Insurance bought Bache Group Inc. in 1981, the brokerage firm's sales force was the least productive of Wall Street's top firms. The mandate for George Ball, the newly hired chief executive of what was then called Prudential-Bache Securities Inc.: Get the brokers to sell more.

The partnership push came as Prudential-Bache suffered steep losses in the early 1980s and became the butt of jokes at Prudential Insurance. At a 1984 retirement party for a colleague, Mr. Ball was presented with a statue of a mother suckling a child. The mother represented Prudential Insurance, and the infant was supposed to be Pru-Bache. "Shed the statue," Mr. Ball later wrote in a memo to brokers and managers. "Losses suck." The missive was just one of more than eleven thousand quirky memos Mr. Ball wrote to the firm's employees before resigning under pressure in early 1991.

In the meantime, Pru-Bache brokers went on a selling binge. The firm sold about $8 billion of partnerships to 340,000 investors in the 1980s. The partnerships—which invested in wide-ranging ventures including real estate, energy, horses and aircraft—were lucrative for the firm. It received 15 percent of partnership proceeds from commissions, acquisition and finder's fees, plus "organization and offering costs"; these covered, among other things, such brokers' sales incentives as trips to Spain, Hawaii, Switzerland, Paris, London and Germany's Octoberfest. But the deals were anything but lucrative for investors. Many lost much of their original investment as the partnerships' values plunged amid sinking markets and tax-law changes.

Yet it was the way the partnerships were sold, not just their dismal performance, that ultimately soiled the firm. Pru-Bache brokers routinely misstated the risks and rewards of the partnerships in what appeared to be a systemic problem. Brokers were advised in sales scripts how to persuade various investor "types" to buy partnerships. In selling to "friendlies," a 1987 sales script told brokers to "stress safety and guarantees. Give your personal assurances." The partnerships were anything but safe or guaranteed.

Another script advised brokers to "avoid getting bogged down in facts and details—move quickly." The firm later said the sales sheets were "wrong" and not "representative of our sales-practice policy."

The government disagreed and nearly brought down the firm. The Securities and Exchange Commission and state securities regulators struck first. In October

1993, the SEC and the states accused the firm of widespread civil fraud by making "false and misleading statements" to investors in selling them the partnerships.

Prudential neither admitted nor denied the allegations. But the firm agreed to set aside $330 million to go into a restitution fund for defrauded investors who had partnership losses stemming from Prudential misconduct. And in a unique twist, the firm agreed that the claims fund wouldn't have any ceiling. Thus, Prudential's liability was open-ended—a huge gamble.

The firm rolled snake eyes. The legal tab from settling claims arising from the partnership mess eventually hit $2 billion. That was more than triple what Prudential executives initially predicted. Part of that steeper legal bill stemmed from a criminal case filed by the Manhattan U.S. attorney's office in October 1994. The good news for the firm: It dodged what could have been a deadly bullet, and avoided a potentially crippling criminal indictment. The bad news: Prudential agreed to be put on probation for three years, admit criminal wrongdoing for the first time, and pay an additional $330 million into the original restitution fund.

The separate criminal investigation of individuals, including several former high-ranking Prudential executives, raised the specter of further bad publicity and lost business. But the U.S. attorney's office closed the probe without comment in November 1996. By then, Prudential had lost brokers, business and prestige. In 1994 alone, more than one thousand of Prudential's six thousand brokers bolted for rival firms.

The company's reputation wasn't helped when a $35 million advertising campaign bombed after a featured broker was sued by an elderly priest. (The broker since left; the case was settled for an undisclosed amount in April 1996.) Then the company fired its top broker-trainee of 1993 for alleged insubordination and dismissed a high-ranking mortgage trader who narrated an in-house training film for allegedly misleading brokers on the prices of esoteric bonds.

Even now, hurdles abound. The firm must slash its costs and boost its broker productivity, which has been hurt by turnover stemming from the partnership scandal. In 1996, Prudential Securities' pretax operating margins "were about half those of the best firms in our industry although our return on equity was almost their equal," the January 1997 memo said. "We must improve here."

Ditto on the firm's overall standards. Even Mr. Simmons conceded that "we're not an organization committed to excellence, only to market standards." Early in 1997, he challenged his employees to improve their public speaking, to "thoroughly understand" the advice they're giving clients, and to work more on weekends. "Simple but profound, high standards are the difference between good organizations and great ones, and our standards aren't high enough," Mr. Simmons said. "We must challenge ourselves more."

One challenge is to prevent clients from seeking financial advice elsewhere. Half the firm's customers buy only a single product from Prudential, according to the January 1997 memo; just 17 percent of the households that buy Pru products use its cash-management account. "Too many of our clients (70 percent) fund a retirement plan somewhere else, too few know of and use the advantages of" the firm's on-line brokerage-account system, the memo says.

"We are making strides here but we must make them quicker if we're to become our clients' 'prime broker': a 'single basket for all my investments' relationship that technology encourages," said Mr. Simmons. *"To become our clients' primary financial advisor is our most important quest."*

Meantime, Prudential searches for a corporate identity. Mr. Simmon's vision? A firm that is perceived both as a technological leader and one that is intertwined with its well-known parent. This dual personality, a combination of computer savvy and apple-pie roots, will bolster Prudential's leverage on the Street, he believes. "We're on the threshold of developing a corporate personality, a personality that in concert with that of The Prudential will define us in the marketplace," Mr. Simmons said in January 1997. Noting that personalities are difficult to alter once established, he added: "We'd be smart to examine ours before the cement hardens."

Some on Wall Street wonder if it already has.

Better Profits, New Broker Leadership

Prudential, in 1996 and 1997, has enjoyed stability after a tumultuous period when it seemed that the firm got more bad headlines than the rest of Wall Street combined. A booming stock market, with record trading volume at both the Big Board and Nasdaq, helped level the ship. In 1997, Prudential had revenue of $3.78 billion, up from $3.5 billion in 1996. The money flowed evenly from among the firm's brokerage, asset management and "capital-markets" business, which includes trading for customers' accounts and investment banking.

Like some other big full-service firms, Prudential sought to take advantage of the October 1997 stock-market rumble to tout its differences with barebones discount brokerage firms. During that month's two most volatile days, there were widespread complaints by investors that they weren't able to get through to Charles Schwab Corp., E*Trade Securities and other discount firms to trade on-line.

So in a full-page newspaper advertisement, Prudential blared: "Here's What 'Full Service' Meant to Prudential Securities Clients Last Week"; the ad boasted that Prudential's clients "received personalized advice" by calling on a broker "who understood their situation." The result, the ad said: "Our clients felt more confident trading person-to-person."

And when stock mutual-fund investors began shifting some of their cash into bond funds, Prudential tried to jump on the trend. In newspaper ads, the firm cited its array of bond funds with superior performance, including its high-yield, municipal-bond, diversified-bond and global total-return funds. Again, the emphasis was on the difference with discount firms and no-load mutual funds, where investors make their own choices (and pay less). Said the Prudential ad: "Discover the difference professional advice can make."

But the firm's net income of about $200 million, though up from $160 million a year earlier, lagged behind big rivals that also catered to individual investors. In 1997, Merrill earned $1.9 billion, Salomon Smith Barney Holdings earned $1.65 billion, Morgan Stanley, Dean Witter, Discover & Co. earned $2.59 billion, and PaineWebber Inc. earned $415.4 million.

One of the problems is that Prudential still is saddled with the costs of defending its franchise a few years back. In an eighteen-month period ending March 1995, it cost Prudential $100 million just to recruit brokers to replace defectors, though that number was shaved to $24 million in 1996 and less in 1997. Some replacement brokers with experience haven't come cheap. In a few cases in 1994 Prudential paid up-front bonuses as high as 70 percent of annual production, according to headhunters. Other Wall Street firms typically limit such payments to 50 percent. Prudential said at the time that it had no choice but to pay for brokers.

And the new brokers have shied away from pushing Prudential's internal mutual funds. This has cost Prudential needed profit, since the firm earns a steady stream of revenue on assets it manages. In the early 1990s, the ratio of these so-called proprietary funds to external funds was 65 to 35 percent. That slumped to as low as 25 to 75 percent in 1996, though it has crept back to 27 to 73 percent in 1997. Prudential is banking that a big influx of broker trainees since 1996 will cut costs—and change the culture. "Brokers hired from everywhere else have established ties to other fund groups," Mr. Simmons said. "Gradually, what we'll see is a growing acceptance."

Prudential overhauled its brokerage operations after the fallout from its limited-partnership scandal lifted. In 1997, the firm named New York regional director James Price as head of its mammoth brokerage network. Prudential also restructured the management of its brokerage operation, creating a new layer of three divisional directors to oversee sixteen regions. The firm boosted the number of its regional directors from eight to sixteen.

The changes came as regulators increasingly hold brokerage-firm managers responsible for the missteps of firms' brokers. Mr. Simmons said at the time that the changes will allow the firm's regional directors to spend more time in branch offices. Each regional director will oversee fifteen to eighteen branches. The brokerage chief job previously had been shared on an interim basis by Michael Madigan and William McCormick. After the shift, Mr. Madigan left the firm "to pursue other opportunities" and Mr. McCormick stayed on as chief administrative officer for the firm's brokerage operations.

The change was the second shift in the management of Prudential's brokerage operations in slightly more than a year. Messrs. Madigan and McCormick had been named interim heads in late 1996 after longtime Prudential executive George Murray retired.

The firm is showing signs of broadening its business. It is pumping up its feeble investment-banking effort, thanks partly to business from parent Pru. The brokerage firm was tapped in 1996 to advise its parent on the disposition of $7 billion of equity real estate. And Prudential Securities also has "merged our pension plan assets with theirs, begun a major new inter-Prudential insurance sales effort and (is) considering a joint merchant-banking facility," according to a 1997 internal memorandum to employees.

The biggest public spat of the past few years was the firm's dealings with the collapsed Foundation for New Era Philanthropy and that scandal's aftermath. New Era collected millions of dollars from nonprofit groups with the promise that their funds would be doubled by wealthy, anonymous donors. Scores of philanthropists and donors, including many from Wall Street, also gave New Era money, hoping to double their charitable contributions. But the donors didn't exist, and federal authorities say New Era was a Ponzi scheme, in which early participants are paid off with the proceeds of later ones.

Prudential, which held much of New Era's liquid assets, wasn't accused of wrongdoing by regulators. But the firm was sued by the bankruptcy trustee and about three dozen charities. The trustee's suit alone sought a return of $160 million in funds that the brokerage firm had either lent New Era or held for it. The trustee claimed that Prudential had overlooked obvious signs that the charity was fraudulent out of desire to earn commissions and interest. Prudential settled the lawsuits in November 1996 by paying $18 million. Prudential had called the lawsuits groundless, but spokesman Charles Perkins said the brokerage firm agreed to settle because "clearly, we were headed toward lengthy litigation that served no one. . . . We made the settlement knowing that it would go to important, nonprofit organizations." As part of the settlement, Prudential dropped a claim it filed against thirty-nine charities and nonprofit groups.

Prudential got some more good news on the investigative front in June 1997. That's when the SEC dropped its remaining probes of former Prudential Securities employees and their possible roles in one of the biggest financial scandals of the 1980s. The SEC had been investigating five former senior employees who worked at Prudential's New York headquarters and the role they played in the sale of $8 billion in limited partnerships from 1980 to 1990.

The decision to drop the cases underscored the impact on the SEC's enforcement program of a five-year statute of limitations established by a federal court in 1996. The decision effectively barred the commission from seeking penalties against the former Prudential employees. The commission retained the option of bringing proceedings seeking cease-and-desist orders, which the SEC believes aren't subject to the same five-year rule. But such orders would have been of little significance because none of the people still worked for Prudential and most no longer work in the insurance or securities industries, according to people familiar with the investigation.

But that didn't mean that Prudential escaped the glare of federal regulators. The enforcement division of the Commodity Futures Trading Commission in 1997 charged Prudential Securities with failing to adequately supervise a former employee charged with cheating investors in orange-juice futures contracts. The CFTC specifically alleged in its civil complaint that the former broker fraudulently allocated trades between customer accounts and his own personal futures accounts. On at least twenty-eight different trading days, the CFTC said, the former Prudential broker traded for both accounts and gave customers less profitable prices.

Prudential maintained that it took appropriate steps in investigating the broker. Indeed, the firm said it informed the CFTC that a company investigation had begun into the broker's trading. "The trading pattern appeared to be irregular, so we immediately looked at an internal review," a Prudential spokesman said. The broker resigned before the completion of the review, the spokesman said, which found inconclusive results.

Prudential also couldn't escape being tagged for a piece of a big industry-wide settlement of a class-action lawsuit alleging price-fixing on the Nasdaq Stock Market. In December 1997, Prudential agreed—without admitting wrongdoing—to pay $40 million to settle its part in the case. The suit was filed by investors in a New York federal court, alleging that thirty dealers rigged prices of small stocks between 1989 and 1994. In all, the thirty dealers agreed to pay a total of $910 million to settle the case.

Stopping Broker Defections

Prudential's brokerage force of 6,473 has undergone nothing short of a major facelift in recent years. In the first quarter of 1994, turnover among the brokerage army totaled an astounding 30 percent; in the eighteen-month period ending March 1995, the firm lost half its brokers who had between six and ten years' experience. Lost, too, were nearly twenty members of its Chairman's Council, an elite corps of the top 105 or so brokers. Rivals pounced: PaineWebber alone gained $31 million in net annual production from brokers hired from Pru in an eight-month period in 1994.

A killer defector was superbroker Richard Gadbois III. He ran a five-person group that specialized in selling restricted stock for company executives before bolting to Merrill. Mr. Gadbois earned gross annual commission at Prudential of more than $3 million and helped win a big chunk of Prudential's investment-banking business.

After recruiting reams of brokers from rivals to replace those who left, Prudential now has turned to training novices in-house. In 1997, the firm trained 1,037 new brokers, who Prudential calls "financial advisors." Fully 40 percent of its brokers now are trained internally. And that percentage will rise, Prudential executives say. "We want to create character, and a culture," according to Mr. Simmons.

Thanks to the roaring market, the average annual production of Prudential's brokers jumped in 1997 to $335,000 from $255,000 three years earlier. And the firm hopes that the increased tie with the Pru will further bolster business. Prudential's brokerage force contributed about one-third of the firm's profit in 1996. It's a volume business. And with trading records being smashed on the nation's stock exchanges, "brokerage is a good business," said Mr. Simmons. He added that despite all the problems at the insurer and brokerage unit, "our name is Pru. It's a wonderful calling card."

But there have been some bumps in hiring newcomers. In 1996, the New York Stock Exchange censured Prudential and fined the firm $125,000 for letting telemarketers solicit customers without adequate supervision. In a disciplinary case, the Big Board said Prudential allowed telemarketers in a downtown Manhattan office to make unsolicited "cold calls" to potential customers and offer coming securities issues, although they weren't registered brokers. The telemarketers also used scripts with aggressive sales pitches—remember the partnerships?—that Prudential says it didn't approve.

Some of the brokers improperly offered cash incentives to the telemarketers who worked for them to open new accounts. On one occasion, a cold-caller falsely identified himself as the broker he worked for. Prudential had hired the telemarketers to make unsolicited calls in a joint partnership with three of its brokers. Prudential—consenting to the disciplinary action without admitting or denying guilt—said it closed the office in question in 1994. The firm said the telemarketers no longer work there. "We regret the problems cited by the stock exchange," Prudential said. Noting that most of the infractions occurred a few years back, it added: "We have taken numerous steps to improve our policies and procedures in those areas."

In another bid to bolster assets, in 1995 Prudential bought twenty thousand brokerage accounts of small-fry investors from Lehman Brothers Inc. for $1 million. The deal called for Lehman accounts with assets of $25,000 or less to be transferred to Prudential. Typically, such large account transfers occur only when Wall Street firms are sold, go out of business or jettison their brokerage operations. The unusual agreement was a clear sign that Prudential, then with 2.3 million customer accounts, was scrambling to offset the loss of brokers and accounts. (Lehman didn't want the accounts because the firm wanted to focus on more wealthy clients.)

Meantime, Prudential is banking on snaring new business in cyberspace. Officials say they're seeking to combine advice with technology; Mr. Simmons boasts about 150,000 accounts that "talk to us and look at their accounts nightly on-line." Prudential brokers are required to take twelve hours of computer training. And the firm launched its "Architect" computerized financial planner that it doles out to clients for free.

In a 1997 interview, Mr. Simmons said, "We want to speak to all those [who are] technically literate, but who want advice—those clients in the middle."

Securities Firms Set Pact Making Funds Portable

Accord of Prudential Unit, PaineWebber Group Is Big News for Investors

BY MICHAEL SICONOLFI
Staff Reporter of THE WALL STREET JOURNAL

PALM DESERT, Calif.—Two big brokerage firms, breaking rank with rivals, have struck an unusual accord to make their proprietary in-house mutual funds portable.

The agreement between Prudential Securities Inc. and PaineWebber Group Inc. will allow clients who transfer from one firm to the other to now take their mutual-fund shares with them, according to brokerage executives gathering at an industry conference here.

The accord, set to be announced today, is big news for investors. Most big brokerage houses don't have selling agreements with other securities firms. The practical effect for investors looking to switch such fund accounts to competing ones: They are forced to stay with their old firm, or liquidate the old account—often paying costly exit fees.

"This provides our clients with flexibility—and empowers them to make the best decision," says Charles Perkins, a Prudential spokesman who confirmed the agreement. "It's not done anywhere else." Adds Joseph Grano, PaineWebber

president: "Why should you create indentured servitude?"

The move promises to please federal regulators. At the behest of the Securities and Exchange Commission, brokerage firms in recent months have attempted to reduce the conflicts of interest between brokers and clients. Several big firms have cut out the practice of paying more to brokers to sell their firms' proprietary products, including mutual funds. And some firms have slashed higher payouts and, to a lesser degree, upfront money for new broker recruits.

But brokerage firms have long shackled investors in proprietary mutual funds, primarily because of competition. That's because if a broker bolts from his firm, he won't easily be able to take his clients with him. Though the firm loses the broker, it keeps the assets—and firms make most of their money in funds from management fees that are based on the size of those assets.

Securities firms justify the practice. They say the trade-processing costs of transferring such funds to other firms are too high. They also note that a receiving firm often won't want to pick up a new account because of commissions that would have to be paid to the broker over time from the original fund purchase.

The new move was strongly backed by Prudential Securities President Hardwick Simmons, brokerage executives said. Indeed, the **Prudential Insurance Co. of America** unit sought out many firms to sign up with, but found a taker initially only in PaineWebber. The agreement is likely to go into effect around April 1.

Won't this make the two firms more vulnerable to lose clients when their brokers jump ship? Says Prudential's Mr. Perkins: "It also makes it easier to bring in clients when we recruit a broker."

March 18, 1996

Putting "Portability" in Proprietary Mutual Funds

On the money-management front, Prudential Securities in 1996 found itself in the unusual position of being complimented publicly by federal regulators for an action it took involving investors.

The scene: the plush Marriott International in sunny Palm Desert, California. SEC Chairman Arthur Levitt—in the middle of a speech excoriating brokerage firms for their lax oversight of bad brokers—praised a new agreement struck between Prudential and PaineWebber.

The unusual accord allowed clients who transfer from one firm to the other to take their mutual-fund shares with them. That was a big deal for investors: Most big brokerage houses don't have selling agreements with other securities firms. That means that investors looking to switch such fund accounts to competing firms are often forced to pay costly exit fees. As a result, investors often elect to stay put, even if they aren't happy with the services and performance they are receiving.

The move was strongly backed by Mr. Simmons. Prudential had sought out many firms to sign up with; it found a taker only in PaineWebber. But wouldn't this make the two firms more vulnerable to lose clients when their brokers jumped ship? Prudential's Mr. Perkins said at the time: "It also makes it easier to bring in clients when we recruit a broker."

A few months later, Prudential extended the portability pact unilaterally to all other securities firms. The move reflected Prudential's frustration that other rivals hadn't followed suit. Of course, Prudential had less to lose than some competitors. At Prudential, these so-called proprietary funds at the time represented just 24 percent of all funds sold by its brokers. This percentage since has risen to more than one-third, but remains far less than the 50–50 split at many rivals, and the historic 75–25 ratio favoring proprietary funds at Dean Witter.

Prudential is a big asset-management player, with $80 billion in mutual funds under management. Eventually, other firms adapted similar pacts, including Smith Barney. With all the criticism that Prudential has faced in recent years about abuses against clients, the irony here is that Prudential actually changed the way Wall Street does business—to the benefit of small investors.

"This is probably a win-win," said Cella Quinn, a former Smith Barney broker who now runs her own investment firm in Omaha, Nebraska. This is because even if clients switch to another firm, they no longer are forced to sell their Prudential mutual funds, allowing Prudential to continue to receive annual fees for managing the fund portfolios. She said, "Prudential wins because it continues to get the management fee from the fund, and the clients win because they have more flexibility."

Traditionally, Prudential's mutual funds have followed the "value-investing" strategy. This approach typically entails seeking companies whose prices have been beaten down. But Prudential executives, seeking to capitalize on soaring stock prices, said they want to add racier funds looking for high-flying growth companies. One constant in the mix is the $4.77 billion Prudential Utility Fund, the nation's largest and one of the most successful funds focusing on utility companies. In 1997, the Prudential Utility Fund had an annual return—price change plus dividends—of 27.77 percent, beating the 26.01 percent gain in the

Lipper Utility Funds Average. A 1997 ad boasted that the fund ranked No. 1 over five years out of twenty-two utility funds, according to Lipper Analytical Services Inc.

In prominent type, the ad said the utility fund seeks to "capitalize on advancing technology as well as political and regulatory trends." Though a stellar performer, the fund isn't without risks. In smaller type, the ad noted that investing in just one industry "increases vulnerability to any single economic, political or regulatory development in the industry."

Some investors must have read the fine print. During the first eleven months of 1997, $439.5 million flowed out of the Prudential Utility Fund, despite its solid performance. Overall, investors pulled out a net $656 million from funds managed by Prudential Investments, the parent's asset-management arm, according to Financial Research Corp. That was more than any other mutual-fund operation with its own brokerage-firm sales force. Indeed, Prudential acknowledged that its U.S. mutual funds ended 1997 with their fourth consecutive year of net redemptions.

Brian Storms, Prudential's mutual-funds chief, contended that Prudential's ups and downs aren't much different from the fortunes of other fund firms. "In the past, we weren't getting our share—and now we are, both good and bad," Mr. Storms said. But some analysts had a different view. "What you've seen at Prudential is somewhat of a breakdown in confidence among some of its brokers," said Louis Harvey, president of financial-research firm Dalbar Inc. "In the absence of confidence in the institution, what you have is no new sales coming in."

Seeking the "Middle Market" in Investment Banking

The size and role of Prudential's investment-banking group has lurched back and forth over the years. In the mid-1980s the group went from about sixty investment bankers to four hundred in a failed bid by Mr. Ball to build a major banking department. It never made an annual profit and in a major retrenchment in 1990, Prudential slashed the number of its bankers to seventy-five, took a charge of $220 million, and lowered its sights. The goal: to create a "boutique" to come up with products to feed the brokerage force. It still didn't make an annual profit.

Prudential believes it finally has found the formula. It is building an investment-banking group to cater to the "middle-market"—companies too small for most major investment banks to bother with. Its focus won't be broad; rather, it centers on real estate, energy and asset-backed securities transactions. Consider Cali Realty Corp., one of the nation's fastest growing real-estate investment trusts, or REITs. The brokerage firm was the lead manager on Cali's initial public stock offering and on four add-on offerings totaling $1.15 billion in proceeds. Then the capper: Prudential snared the advisory role in Cali's agreement to purchase Robert Martin Co., a real-estate concern, for $265 million in cash and stock.

And guess what? The investment bank finally made a profit in 1996. It wasn't much to write home about on Wall Street—about $30 million—but Prudential will take it.

Prudential's strategy isn't to take a run at the "bulge bracket," the nation's largest, most prestigious, and most profitable investment banks. Rather, it quietly is aiming to pick off firms such as BT Alex. Brown, which have thrived by helping to bring midsize companies to the stock market. It hopes to be able to bring along companies "up the S&P scale"—those that grow and have their credit ratings upgraded by Standard & Poor's Corp.

Still, investment banking isn't core. And Prudential faces competition from regional banks seeking toeholds in the securities business, such as First Union Corp. "With a few exceptions, we're not a 'top of mind' investment bank," Mr. Simmons notes. He said in the January 1997 memo that the firm "won substantial praise from many of our issuing clients for achieving the 'programmed credit upgrades' we'd promised." But to achieve the firm's goal of being the No. 1 "middle-market equity provider," the memo said, "we must align ourselves much more closely with The Pru, increase our new-business effort and achieve even better coordination between research and banking."

With the heightened competition, anything short of that could spell failure.

Buying an Overseas Brokerage Presence

Prudential has formed one of the larger international operations of the major retail-brokerage houses, though it still falls way short of industry leader Merrill.

Like Merrill, Prudential has grown through purchases. But rather than entire companies, Prudential has chosen to buy international chunks from other firms. In late 1997, Prudential bought Lehman's brokerage divisions in Asia and London. The divisions employed about twenty employees in London and fifty people in Singapore and Hong Kong. In late 1995, it made a major leap on the Continent by buying six key European branches from Lehman. The branches it bought—in Madrid, Paris, Frankfurt, Hamburg, Brussels and Geneva—employed fifty brokers and sixty-six support personnel. Unlike Merrill's overseas push, Prudential bought only the brokerage, or "private client" operation; Lehman kept its investment-banking and sales and trading personnel. "The purchase of these offices enables us to further expand our presence in key centers of international finance," Laurence Norton Jr., Prudential's then-international chief, said at the time.

But make no mistake. Prudential's global operations still lack clout. The firm employs just 1,046 of its 17,661 employees overseas; in 1996, the profit from its international operations totaled less than $10 million, though profits far exceeded that in 1997. But at least the firm is trying. Mr. Simmons says the firm is making a particular push into Latin America and Asia; Prudential has opened offices in São Paulo, Brazil, and Santiago, Chile, and for the first time posted research analysts in Asia in 1996. And in 1995 Prudential added staff in China at a time when other U.S. investment banks scaled back. Yet one of its smartest moves has been a strategic retreat: Prudential pulled out of Japan before the carnage in the market in the past couple of years. The firm radically slashed its operations in Japan in 1995, giving up its seat on the Tokyo Stock Exchange and sharply reducing its staff in Tokyo. Mr. Simmons said at the time that the firm "can't add value in Tokyo."

Meantime, Prudential professes not to be worried about Merrill dominating the brokerage business overseas. "Even Merrill, with its scope, has barely scratched the surface," Mr. Simmons said. In Europe particularly, he added, "there's a whole new class of younger, entrepreneurial, high-tech client without ties to the old banks."

Now if Prudential could only get to more of them.

Toughing It Out on the Legal Front

Prudential has pursued a controversial legal strategy throughout the decade that some on Wall Street say backfired badly.

Instead of quickly settling big partnership and other investor and employee cases, as rivals Merrill and Dean Witter did, Prudential decided to aggressively fight many of them in arbitration and in court. The tactic, spearheaded by Loren Schechter, Prudential's former general counsel, clearly failed. In addition to the $2 billion in legal costs from the partnership mess, Prudential consistently has ranked among the worst firms in how it fares in arbitration overall, according to *Securities Arbitration Commentor*, a newsletter. Mr. Schechter didn't fare much better. Prudential stripped him of his general-counsel post in late 1993 amid a widening investigation of the firm; he quietly resigned from the firm in 1995.

But the firm's legal problems didn't end there. In late 1995, a disparate group of former Prudential brokers accused the firm of putting derogatory information in their termination notices as retribution for assisting clients in disputes against Prudential. Indeed, some former Prudential brokers claimed the firm changed their employment records dozens of times over several years by adding customer complaints that never formally named them.

"Prudential (employed) a plan of selectively amending employees' records," said Fritz Collett, a former Prudential broker who contended the firm included in his record a legal claim filed by a client who never named Mr. Collett in the complaint. "Their objective is to punish or threaten to punish employees to keep them from helping investors damaged by their fraud." Prudential adamantly denied wrongdoing. "We have a very careful process to individually evaluate these situations, and it's monitored both by persons here at the firm outside of those business areas and by the NASD," said Charles Perkins, the firm's spokesman.

But the bitterness remained. Sandra Simpson, a former Prudential broker in Michigan, had her termination notice amended by a claim filed by—of all people—her parents Earl and Alice Lyons. The Lyonses had no complaint about the way their daughter handled the account; David Jarvis, Ms. Simpson's lawyer, says they filed the claim against Prudential only. The Lyons's case against Prudential eventually was settled for $57,846, yet the notation of the claim remains on Ms. Simpson's regulatory record.

Going Beyond Retail Research

While Prudential's research effort, with a few exceptions, continues to struggle, reflecting the difficulty the firm has had broadening its activities beyond the world of retail brokerage, its strategy team commands the attention of many top U.S. institutional investors.

Heading that group is Greg Smith, one of Wall Street's deans of investment strategy. Mr. Smith, a self-confessed stock bull for most of his career, jumped into Wall Street thirty years ago when an unexpected medical exemption from the draft left him unemployed. The quiet, soft-spoken Mr. Smith joined Prudential in 1982 from E. F. Hutton & Co. (a predecessor firm to Smith Barney) and has watched in amazement and some trepidation at the way the world of investing has changed.

"Very often, a research department had only one stock quote machine and news terminal," he said in early 1997. "Now every number's a crucial number, the market has become obsessed with information, and we all feel compelled to use it somehow. This is a lot of noise and should be ignored."

While Mr. Smith may be rattled by the volume of information he's receiving, it hasn't seemed to hamper his performance. His asset allocation model has been one of the top performers over the last decade, according to *The Wall Street Journal*'s quarterly review of strategists. And the themes he's chosen to raise as issues for investors to ponder has won him the kind of following among institutional investors that's rare for a strategist at an investment dealer that's geared toward serving retail clients.

The soft-spoken Mr. Smith remains one of the biggest—if not the most vocal—optimists among his peers, boosting his stock allocation to 70 percent during the first quarter of 1997, at a time when other major Wall Street strategists were paring their exposure to stocks. At the same time, he cut his bond exposure to zero from 35 percent, while raising his cash to 30 percent, the largest position of any strategist surveyed by *The Wall Street Journal*. But in recent years following his advice has paid off handsomely for clients, particularly after he spent the early months of 1996 slashing his 50 percent exposure to bonds to 10 percent in favor of stocks.

While Mr. Smith has long been a stock market bull, during the summer of 1997 he made an unusual change in his proposed asset allocation, suggesting to his clients that they put as much as 25% of their portfolios into real estate investment trusts. He expected these investments to grow in popularity as investors continue to hunt for high-yielding products, and as the real estate industry undergoes a shift in ownership.

Going back to the early 1990s, Mr. Smith was one of a handful of strategists arguing that structural changes meant that corporate earnings would rebound far more rapidly than normal in a traditional business cycle. Although some of his calls were too bullish, his peers were too bearish. More recently, he was among the first to urge investors to concentrate on large, multinational companies that he believes will continue to outperform their smaller counterparts around the world. He's highlighted—early—ideas such as the absence of pricing power in the economy, which he believes will make rising wage costs more of a problem for the profit margins of smaller companies than an inflation problem for the stock market as a whole. In mid-March of 1997, he cautioned investors not to be too rattled by any Federal Reserve decision to raise interest rates at their March 24 meeting. In about the four-week time frame he cited, stock prices had retrieved virtually all of their large losses from the post-rate increase sell-off.

The role of most vocal bull on Wall Street would have to be reserved for his colleague Ralph Acampora, Prudential's technical market analyst, who joined the firm in 1990. Back in June 1995 the flamboyant Mr. Acampora called for the blue-chip indicator to hit 7,000—the first analyst to do so—as part of a sixty-two-page research effort citing statistics and trends. When the benchmark was reached, at least temporarily, in mid-February of 1997, the event was celebrated with a press release, media conference call with Mr. Acampora and a series of full-page newspaper ads taken out by Prudential to fete their new guru.

By late 1997, however, Mr. Acampora had begun to mix his ebullient optimism with a dose of caution. He said he was already preparing a report suggesting to investors a number of different ways to cut their exposure to stocks, and thus their market risk, ready for release sometime during the first quarter of 1998, if the stock market continued to climb as he expected. "All good things must come to an end," he said, adding he expected the bull market to turn into a bear market lasting between six and eighteen months sometime in 1998, after the Dow hits the 10,000 point level as he has repeatedly forecast.

"He's not immodest in his confidence, or unambitious in his calls," says one institutional client. "He's the retail face of Prudential's strategy effort."

While Mr. Acampora believes this will lead to broader leadership, Mr. Smith is sticking to his guns, arguing that the big blue-chips that have led the stock market higher will continue to be the biggest winners for investors. The biggest beneficiaries for the foreseeable future, regardless of temporary shifts in interest rates and foreign exchange upheavals, will be companies that look outside their home country for a big chunk of their profits.

Rounding out the strategy group are Melissa Brown, whose quantitative studies on earnings and stock valuations are keenly followed, thanks in part to her bluntness in criticizing the market's obsession with earnings "surprises" and the growing trend of companies to "manage" analysts' expectations and thus the degree of surprise. Despite the lackluster performance by small stocks until late in the summer of 1997, Claudia Mott, the small-stock strategist, has won kudos from many retail brokers for her tips on how to invest in the increasingly risky initial public offering market. Although she's been fighting for an ear among institutional investors, given Mr. Smith's aversion to smaller stocks, she still heads a four-person research and strategy effort, reflecting the firm's retail orientation.

While Prudential's investment strategy may be mandatory reading for many institutional clients, that's not the case with its research. The department is still viewed as geared largely to the firm's retail clientele, and has struggled to make an impact. Its team ranked only seventeenth of the forty departments surveyed by *The Wall Street Journal*'s annual all-star analyst team in 1996, beaten by newcomers like J. P. Morgan & Co., and regional firms such as A. G. Edwards. (But in 1997, it rose in the standings, to rank eleventh.) The only analysts to make the list were the specialty retailing and computer hardware analysts, who earned a place in the standings for their skill at estimating earnings rather than picking stocks.

But there are flashes of light in the research department. One of these is J. Clarence Morrison, who has made eight appearances on the all-star survey for his skill in picking stocks and estimating earnings for precious metals, steel and other nonferrous metals companies. Reflecting the clout he's earned in years of covering the sector, his January 1997 call that aluminum companies are on the comeback trail triggered a flurry of buying—and left the group on the list of stocks to watch for many investors.

The research department was hit by the departure of Michael Culp for PaineWebber in April 1997, declaring bluntly and publicly that he saw that firm's research department as "stronger and more respected" than Prudential's. Mr. Culp was a fifteen-year veteran at Prudential. His successor is Michael Shea, director of institutional sales, a move interpreted by both outsiders and insiders as an effort to win for research the same respect now accorded the strategists.

Prudential's People

Hardwick Simmons, president and chief executive officer: When Mr. Simmons joined Prudential as CEO in 1991, he knew there were problems at the beleaguered brokerage firm. He just didn't know how deep they were.

He tried to move quickly to clean shop, and forced out many protégés of his predecessor, Mr. Ball. One of his first major actions was to fire Richard Sichenzio as president of the firm's vast brokerage operations. In his place, Mr. Simmons appointed George Murray, a former colleague at Shearson who had given Mr. Simmons his first job as a management trainee on Wall Street.

Simmons, Hardwick
President & CEO-
Prudential Securities Inc.

Still, partnership problems that took place before he joined the firm overwhelmed him. At first, senior executives assured him the partnership problem would cost no more than $50 million. That number soon ballooned. The biggest miscalculation came in 1994, a year after Prudential had agreed to put $330 million into a restitution fund for investors. Under a settlement with the SEC, Prudential's liability was open-ended, depending on how many claims were brought. For months, Mr. Simmons said the $330 million would cover investor claims. Then disaster struck. Days before Memorial Day, John Murray, Prudential's chief of corporate risk management, came to an inescapable realization as he reviewed investor claims: "It's not going to be enough."

The problem was a huge misjudgment on interest payments. Prudential had expected to pay out interest costs in only one-third of the claims; it ended up paying interest in nearly every case. In a humiliating move, Prudential in July 1994 was forced to set aside an extra $305 million. Employees were furious. Some groused that their annual bonuses, which are based partly on the firm's overall profit, would be slashed.

"I wasn't lying. I may have been stupid," Mr. Simmons later said. "I had to eat crow, but I genuinely believed" the $330 million would suffice. Prudential ended up paying $2 billion in legal costs from its soured partnerships.

Mr. Simmons also was criticized for continuing to back Mr. Schechter as legal strategist, and for hiring Woody Knight as chief of corporate strategy. Both Messrs. Schechter and Knight at times infuriated state regulators who were investigating the firm. Mr. Simmons was blamed for taking so long to push out Mr. Schechter; it was only after Mr. Schechter himself became ensnared in the government's investigation in December 1993 that Mr. Simmons accepted his resignation as general counsel. (Mr. Schechter, along with other current and former Prudential executives, never were formally charged with any wrong-doing. Mr. Knight, whose brusque manner at times upset both Prudential executives and regulators, left Prudential in 1995; he now is out of the securities business.)

Mr. Simmons has a long brokerage career, dating to 1966, when he left Harvard Business School with an MBA to become a broker at Hayden Stone, a predecessor firm of Shearson Lehman. In 1968, he was named vice president in charge of Shearson Lehman's data-processing and communications division; in 1970 he became manager of Shearson's Boston office. Mr. Simmons was appointed chief of Shearson's northern region in 1972, and soon was named national sales manager. He was tapped to become president of Shearson's brokerage operations in 1983.

Mr. Simmons likes to joke about the former Shearson clique that now dominates Wall Street. He said that Arthur Levitt, the former Shearson executive who now heads the SEC and a social acquaintance, occasionally calls him for advice on brokerage matters. Among other Shearson colleagues to hold high-level positions on Wall Street these days are Frank Zarb, appointed chairman of the NASD, and Sanford Weill, CEO of Salomon Smith Barney parent, Travelers Corp.

Lee B. Spencer Jr., executive vice president and general counsel: Mr. Spencer, a former SEC official, was a controversial choice to replace Mr. Schechter as general counsel in early 1994. Initially, his appointment was a stopgap measure for Prudential, which wanted to act quickly to bring in an outside executive not involved in its limited-partnership mess; Mr. Spencer since has grown into the job.

Yet Mr. Spencer's SEC experience largely centered on the public-offering area, not the regulatory arena for brokerage firms. In his seven years at the SEC, Mr. Spencer had stints as director of the agency's division of corporate finance and chief counsel for its investment-management division. Before joining Prudential, Mr. Spencer was a partner in the New York office of Gibson, Dunn & Crutcher, a law firm.

When he was appointed to the Prudential post, Mr. Spencer said one of the firm's goals is "fairness to customers and former customers, and carefully listening to customer concerns." His predecessor, Mr. Schechter, had been blamed by some plaintiffs' lawyers for hardball tactics taken by Prudential in handling many arbitration and court cases involving the partnerships.

And under Mr. Spencer's watch, Prudential at least hasn't been involved in any other investor scandals. Among his roles at Prudential is overseeing the law and compliance departments. He also is a member of the operating committee, the Prudential Securities Group board, and the operating council.

Leland B. Paton, chief administrative officer: Mr. Paton, a twenty-nine-year Bache veteran, is a member of Prudential Securities' operating committee, board and operating council. Mr. Paton joined Bache Group in 1969 as vice president and institutional stock salesman. He was named manager of national institutional stock sales in 1975; in 1979, he was elected a Bache director. In 1985, he was named president of international and commodities groups. In 1986, he was named president of capital markets. He assumed his present position in 1997.

Vincent Pica, president and group head, capital-finance group: The group he oversees includes the firm's equity, investment-banking and high-yield bond groups. Mr. Pica is a member of Prudential Securities' operating committee, board and operating council. Before his current post, Mr. Pica headed the firm's mortgage- and asset-backed capital group, overseeing the area's trading, sales, research and other functions.

A. Laurence Norton Jr., executive vice president, president of futures and international divisions: Mr. Norton is a member of the Prudential Securities' operating committee, board and operating council. Internationally, he oversees Prudential Bache International Bank. Mr. Norton joined the firm in 1991, after nineteen years at Shearson Lehman Brothers Inc.

Alan D. Hogan, director, global-risk management: Mr. Hogan also is a member of Prudential Securities' operating committee, board and operating council. The global-risk management group includes corporate security, law, compliance and internal audit. Before joining Prudential, Mr. Hogan was a manager at Arthur Andersen & Co., the big accounting firm.

Martin Pfinsgraff, president, capital markets group: Mr. Pfinsgraff oversees Prudential's bond, equity and corporate finance businesses. Previously, he was vice president and treasurer of Prudential Insurance. Most recently he was executive vice president and chief financial officer of Prudential Securities.

Richard Rippe, senior vice president, chief economist: Mr. Rippe joined the firm in 1991 after nineteen years at Dean Witter Reynolds and its predecessor firms. Before Dean Witter, he taught business economics at Columbia University's Graduate School of Business.

Greg A. Smith, chief investment strategist: Mr. Smith has consistently been ranked among the top three strategists on *Institutional Investor* magazine's All-America Research Team in portfolio strategy since 1983. In addition to Mr. Smith's role as chief investment strategist, he also manages a hedge fund. Before coming to Prudential, Mr. Smith was an executive vice president, chief strategist and research chief at E. F. Hutton & Co., where he was in charge of institutional sales and marketing.

Ralph Acampora, first vice president and managing director of technical analysis: Mr. Acampora has more than thirty years' experience in modern-day "technical analysis," which follows quantitative, rather than fundamental, measures in gauging the market's direction. He has gained respect as his extremely bullish predictions in recent years have panned out.

Claudia E. Mott, first vice president, managing director of small-cap research: Ms. Mott provides quantitative research to small- and mid-capitalization investment communities in the form of stock valuation and earnings surprise models. She is well known for her work on various benchmarks used to measure small- and mid-cap performance.

Melissa R. Brown, first vice president, managing director of quantitative research: Ms. Brown joined Prudential in 1982, and has held various positions in the quantitative-research and investment-strategy departments. Her primary function now is to research, develop and deliver stock-valuation analysis and ratings.

William H. Anderson, executive vice president and chief information officer: Mr. Anderson is responsible for the firm's information systems and communications group. Before joining Prudential in 1984, he had been a group information systems director at IBM.

Martin J. Brophy, senior vice president, head of listed stock block trading: Mr. Brophy is responsible for all equity listed-block trading, listed-sales trading, floor services, convertible securities, institutional options and special-situations trading. A member of Prudential's operating council, Mr. Brophy previously had been a vice president at Union Bank of Switzerland.

Jeff Theodorou, head of taxable fixed income trading: Mr. Theodorou is a member of the firm's operating council and is a member of the PSA Executive Committee on MBS Securities. He joined Prudential Securities in 1980. He spent the first five years at the firm in the government trading area, then joined the mortgage group in 1986. His current responsibilities include running the various mortgage pass-through, Remic, whole loan, asset-backed and commercial trading and government trading groups. The retail group trading operation also reports to Mr. Theodorou.

Kenneth P. Crowley, senior vice president: Mr. Crowley is a member of the firm's operating council. He is a manager of the international operating, securities lending and Wexford correspondence clearing. Before his current post, Mr. Crowley managed the capital-markets operations department. He previously had been a manager at Lehman Brothers Inc.

Thomas M. Farley, executive vice president, divisional officer of the northern division: Mr. Farley is responsible for the supervision of the retail-branch offices in Maine, New Hampshire, Massachusetts, Rhode Island, Connecticut, New York, New Jersey, Ohio, Michigan, Illinois, Minnesota, Indiana and Wisconsin. This includes the supervision of all sales, administrative and compliance activities. He also is a member of the firm's operating council. Before his current position, Mr. Farley was the regional director of the mid-Atlantic region. Before joining Prudential, Mr. Farley was a vice president at Merrill.

Richard Franchella, national sales manager: Mr. Franchella oversees the day-to-day operations of the national sales desk and coordinates the marketing and sales efforts for all product units. He joined Prudential Securities in March 1997. Before joining the firm, Mr. Franchella spent fourteen years in various retail positions. He began his financial services career at Merrill Lynch and then went on to PaineWebber.

William Horan, senior vice president, chief financial officer: Mr. Horan directs the treasury, controller's, tax, financial analysis and planning and credit activities of Prudential Securities in the United States and internationally. Mr. Horan most recently served as controller of Prudential Securities, a position he had held since 1995. Previously, he served as treasurer from 1985.

Gerald Kuschuk, senior vice president and head of the executive services and strategies group: Mr. Kuschuk also is a member of the firm's operating council. He joined Bache in 1969 and held a variety of positions in the options, futures and equity products before his current post.

Richard F. Lynch, senior vice president, manager of Nasdaq domestic and international trading: Mr. Lynch also is a member of the firm's operating council. He joined the firm as senior vice president in the stock group in 1989, when Prudential acquired the individual-investor assets of Thomson McKinnon Securities. Before the purchase, Mr. Lynch, a twenty-five-year Thomson veteran, had been executive vice president of capital markets.

Gerald P. McBride, executive vice president, head of the tax-exempt division: Mr. McBride has about twenty-five years of experience in the municipal industry. In 1985, he became the manager of the newly formed tax-exempt division, which incorporated the municipal and public-finance departments. In 1991, the unit investment trust department was added to the division.

William G. McCormick, executive vice president, executive director of sales and administration: Mr. McCormick oversees the firm's nearly three hundred branches, as part of being named to cohead the firm's brokerage opera-

In the Beginning . . .

The firm now known as Prudential Securities has its roots in the Bache family, which emigrated to the United States from Germany in the 1870s. Jules Bache, grandson of an officer who fought under Napoleon, took over Leopold Cahn & Co., a brokerage operation launched by his uncle. He renamed it J. S. Bache & Co. in 1892. In 1914, his nephew Harold joined the firm and after Jules died in 1944, the firm was renamed Bache & Co. The firm was a mutual-fund pioneer, and was the first to explore investments in Japan following World War II.

In the 1950s and '60s, Bache vied with Merrill Lynch as one of the nation's largest brokerage firms catering to individual investors. It made a series of acquisitions of Halsey, Stuart & Co. (1973), and Shields Model Roland (1977)—that led to clout in research and utility finance, and more basic brokerage capacity. Eventually, the firm was named Bache Halsey Stuart Shields Inc., a name that was then shortened at the holding company level to Bache Group Inc.

Giant Prudential Insurance Co. of America bought Bache in 1981, and changed its name the following year to Prudential-Bache Securities Inc. The firm bolstered its brokerage capabilities in 1989 by acquiring more than 150 offices and accounts from Thomson McKinnon Securities Inc.

But the Bache name had become a drag. It was ditched in 1991 in a bid to tie it more to Prudential Insurance at a time of internal turmoil. That's ironic. In the past few years, it was Prudential Insurance that was roiled by a scandal in which its agents were accused of widespread fraud selling insurance policies.

tions in 1996. He joined the firm in 1979 as branch manager of the Bay Colony, Florida, office. In 1982, he became manager of the Miami branch; in 1988, he was promoted to southern regional director.

John R. Mueller, executive vice president, director of human resources: Mr. Mueller is responsible for, among other areas, compensation, human resources, information systems, benefits, staffing, employee relations, training and international human resources.

Thomas J. Owens, executive vice president, western division director: Mr. Owens is responsible for 65 retail branches that employ about 1,694 brokers and 825 administrative and support staff. He joined the firm as a broker in 1974, and held a variety of managerial posts in the brokerage operations.

Charles H. Perkins, senior vice president, director of public relations: Mr. Perkins is responsible for the firm's external and internal corporate communications; he is Prudential's chief spokesman. He has had a relatively easy run; most of the partnership woes, which seemed to dog Prudential daily in the media, occurred before Mr. Perkins joined the firm in 1994. He previously had been an executive vice president at Robinson Lake Sawyer Miller, a public-relations firm.

Carol E. Robbins, senior vice president, director of marketing: Ms. Robbins is responsible for leading the marketing activities of the firm. She and her team are developing integrated strategies that will strengthen the company's ability to address the complex and changing marketplace. Ms. Robbins was previously with R.R. Donnelley & Sons' financial division where she was vice president of marketing and product development.

David M. Pierce, executive vice president and southern divisional officer: Mr. Pierce oversees the southern division, which consists of eighty-three offices in sixteen states. He is responsible for managing risk, developing revenue and controlling costs. Mr. Pierce is on the firm's operating council. He has been with Prudential Securities since 1987, most recently as senior vice president and regional director of the Midwest region.

James D. Price, president, consumer market group: Mr. Price also is a member of the firm's operating committee and operating council. Most recently, he was senior vice president and metropolitan regional director for the firm, overseeing a region of 22 retail branch offices and 730 brokers, located in Manhattan, Long Island, Westchester and northern New Jersey. He joined Prudential in 1992; earlier, he had been at E.F. Hutton and Shearson Lehman Hutton.

Paul V. Scura, managing director, head of investment banking: Mr. Scura also is a member of the firm's operating council, and sits on the business review committee, the firm's investment-banking screening group. Since joining the firm in 1986, Mr. Scura has held various investment-banking positions, including in mergers-and-acquisitions, restructuring and reorganization, private finance, high-yield finance and international investment banking.

Michael J. Shea, senior vice president, director of equity research: Mr. Shea is a member of the firm's operating council. In his current position, he supervises the firm's research analysis and is a member of the company's capital finance management committee. Previously, he was the firm's director of institutional equity sales since 1993, having joined the firm sixteen years ago.

Anand K. Bhattacharya, senior vice president, taxable fixed income: Mr. Bhattacharya is a member of the firm's operating council. He is the director of fixed income research and securitization. Previously, Mr. Bhattacharya was with Security Pacific Merchant Bank as a vice president.

Christopher Shipp, senior vice president, director of training and professional development: Mr. Shipp is responsible for all education and development programs for the firm's consumer-markets division, including U.S.

branches, the international and futures divisions, asset-management services and marketing and administration.

J. M. Taylor, executive vice president, director of the stock group: Mr. Taylor oversees the trading of stocks and stock derivatives, both listed and over-the-counter; institutional stock sales and trading; and all stock and options exchange activities. He is a member of the firm's operating council. Before joining Prudential in 1982, he had been with E. F. Hutton.

David Weild IV, managing director, capital finance group: Mr. Weild oversees the West Coast, high tech, health care, private equity & equity products and Israel investment banking efforts. In addition, he oversees technology for the investment bank. He is a member of the business review committee and operating council. Previously, Mr. Weild held a variety of positions, including head of corporate finance and head of the global equity transactions group.

Stanley F. Witkowski, director of strategic client initiatives: Mr. Witkowski is also responsible for the sales and marketing efforts for all mutual funds and annuities. He is a member of the firm's operating council and sits on the new products review committee. He is in charge of directing the firm's commitment to technology.

PART THREE

THE TRADING POWERHOUSES

Bear Stearns Cos.

•

Lehman Brothers Inc.

BEAR STEARNS COS.

BIDDING TO BRANCH OUT BEYOND TRADING

Talented Outcasts: The Contrarian Bent

Wall Street snickered when Bear Stearns Cos. hired Howard Rubin, a trader fired by Merrill Lynch & Co. in 1987 after being blamed for a $377 million bond loss. But the Bear's laughing now: Mr. Rubin's group has generated a big chunk of the firm's mortgage-bond trading profit in recent years, and has helped propel Bear to a 28 percent return on equity, among the best on Wall Street. In the process, Mr. Rubin has often pocketed paychecks of more than $5 million a year.

"Howie's our superstar," boasted James Cayne, Bear's cigar-chomping president and chief executive. "He's here at night, on the weekends. Our compensation discussions are over in seven seconds. He had a problem" at Merrill—but not at Bear.

The controversial hire neatly sums up Bear Stearns's contrarian bent. Bear long has thrived by hiring those shunned by others on Wall Street, attracting talented outcasts. Bear also loves to hire people who left their firms in pursuit of more clout. Besides Mr. Rubin, they include Donald Mullen, former junk-bond salesman at Drexel Burnham Lambert Inc.; and bankers Denis Bovin, from Salomon Inc., and Michael Urfirer, from Credit Suisse First Boston Corp.

In the process, Wall Street's quintessential trading culture now is making a big bet on an entirely different business: investment banking. The broadening effort stands as the clearest mandate of Mr. Cayne since he took over the CEO post from Alan Greenberg in 1993. (Mr. Greenberg, still chairman, remains one of Bear's biggest producers.)

The face of Bear's banking effort began to shift when the firm hired Mr. Bovin, a senior investment banker from Salomon Inc., a few years back. Mr. Bovin then pressed Mr. Cayne to hire Mr. Urfirer, a banker specializing in defense companies. At their first meeting, Mr. Urfirer brought along the chief financial officer of Martin Marietta Corp.—and the next day Bear was hired to advise Marietta in its bid for Grumman Corp. Though rival Northrop Corp. ultimately won the bidding for Grumman, it was Bear's first big-league assignment in the defense business.

Bear in recent years became a leader in defense-related mergers-and-acquisitions work. In April 1995, Bear even represented both the acquirer and the target in Raytheon Corp.'s $2.3 billion acquisition of E-Systems Inc., thanks to Mr. Bovin's and Mr. Urfirer's respective ties to Raytheon and E-Systems.

Meanwhile, some of Bear's banking clients have put the firm in ticklish situations. A few years back, Bear backed away from a decision to informally advise Wall Street raider Kirk Kerkorian, a Bear banking client, in his hostile bid to buy Chrysler Corp. It turned out that Chrysler, another Bear banking client, sent a letter to Bear's Mr. Greenberg complaining about the investment bank's proposed role. Mr. Greenberg called Chrysler Chairman Robert Eaton to tell him Bear was ditching Mr. Kerkorian in the deal. Bear's move doomed Mr. Kerkorian's bid, which he dropped in 1995.

And Bear's broader client roster includes firms and individuals others wouldn't touch. The firm traded with Ivan Boesky amid rumors of his insider trading in the 1980s; Mr. Boesky later was convicted in the government's massive insider-trading investigation. (Bear never was accused of any wrongdoing.) Bear's "clearing," or trade-processing, division, which generates as much as one-third of the firm's business, processed trades for, among others, penny stock firms widely considered the underbelly of Wall Street. These include several firms kicked out of the securities business amid allegations of sales abuses, such as Stratton Oakmont Inc., Sterling Foster & Co. and Rooney, Pace Inc.

This roster of clients led to regulatory scrutiny that has dogged Bear for much of 1997. Federal and state authorities are investigating Bear's clearing operation, looking at whether Bear Stearns has any legal liability for the allegedly fraudulent activities of some of those brokerage customers, particularly the defunct A. R. Baron & Co., a small brokerage house accused by a New York state grand jury of defrauding investors of $75 million. Bear Stearns has denied wrongdoing in its clearing operations, which are the nation's largest.

The investigators suggested they mean business. The Manhattan district attorney's office, in a bid to quiz Bear Stearns personnel in the investigation, tracked down the firm's executives in places such as their bridge clubs. The aggressiveness of John Moscow, the assistant U.S. attorney handling the case, led some Bear Stearns executives to privately call him "Mad Dog."

Indeed, tensions boiled over at one meeting in the Manhattan office of District Attorney Robert Morgenthau in May 1997. The purpose of the meeting—held with officials of the SEC, the district attorney's office and Bear Stearns—was to warn the big Wall Street trading firm that the probes shouldn't be taken lightly, according to participants. At one point, William McLucas, the SEC's enforcement chief, expressed his displeasure that Bear officials hadn't provided trade-processing documents to the agency that the firm already had handed over to the district attorney's office, the participants said.

Regulators also warned Bear Stearns at the meeting of the seriousness of destroying documents, according to a person at the meeting. The warning came as a Bear Stearns employee alleged that a firm executive told him to destroy documents sought by federal and state authorities investigating the role of Bear Stearns in processing trades for A. R. Baron, people familiar with the matter said. Mr. McLucas declined to comment, as did the district attorney's office. Bear Stearns said it has launched an internal investigation into the matter, adding: "If we discover any relevant information, we'll turn it over to the authorities promptly."

Bear's hiring strategy doesn't always work out. In 1997, the firm eased out trader Kyriacous Papious, whom it hired from National Westminster Bank PLC after the trader allegedly mispriced options. After NatWest announced a charge for losses allegedly triggered by Mr. Papious, Bear executives grilled him: Are you innocent? When Mr. Papious declined to answer, on the advice of his counsel, he was urged to resign, people familiar with the matter say. The move reflected the sentiment of Bear's Mr. Greenberg: "The definition of a good trader is a guy who takes losses. The definition of an ex-trader is one who tries to cover up a loss."

Which goes to show that while Bear will give trading outcasts second chances, the firm has little tolerance for surprises. In 1993, when the firm alleged that Michael Sidoti, an eight-year veteran and talented trader, mismarked an options position by $200,000 and tried to cover it up, he was fired on the spot. Mr. Greenberg said at the time: "There's no appeal, no nothing." Get caught, he said, and "you're out, O-U-T." Mr. Cayne, for his part, said Bear's hires don't always work out, but contends that "we're right ninety percent of the time."

A look at Bear's strategy shows how. The firm gives many of its traders and others wide freedom—then scrutinizes their every move. Each Monday at 4:10 P.M., traders and investment bankers who put the firm's capital at risk gather for a "cold-sweat" risk-committee meeting to declare big trading positions and why they hold them. In addition, in-house spies, called "ferrets," patrol the trading floors, investigating unusually priced or risky trades.

The firm's hiring strategy also breeds loyalty. Bear historically has had among the lowest turnover on Wall Street. When Deutsche Bank's U.S. securities unit was aggressively poaching scores of bankers and traders from Wall Street firms in 1996, David Komansky, then-president of Merrill Lynch & Co., had lunch with Bear's Mr. Cayne. Merrill had lost nearly seventy of its employees to Deutsche's hiring campaign.

"How many did you lose?" Mr. Komansky asked Mr. Cayne.

"None," Mr. Cayne replied.

"Come on," Mr. Komansky plied.

"Zero," insisted Mr. Cayne.

Indeed, Bear boasts a trader, John Slade, who has worked more than sixty years trading stocks and bonds at the firm—an unheard-of feat on job-hopping Wall Street. Mr. Slade says he will never forget that Bear gave him a shot at the American Dream in 1936, the day after he arrived in the United States from his native Germany.

Bear's stance on employees reflects its contrarian bent. After largely avoiding the junk-bond business in the go-go 1980s, Bear now is a significant junk-bond player; in 1997, it underwrote more than $6 billion, or 5.9 percent of new junk-bond issues brought to market, according to Securities Data Co. Bear also was among the first on Wall Street to plunge successfully into trading Latin American bank loans. Unlike CS First Boston and the former Shearson Lehman Brothers Inc., Bear sidestepped the 1980s pitfall of "temporary" bridge loans to corporate clients and, instead, made more mundane loans. Now, Bear has outstanding a near-record $43.8 billion in margin loans to investors, and its clients represent 32 percent of the short-selling activity on the New York Stock Exchange.

Bear's risk controls have helped shield it from the wild earnings zigzags of some Wall Street trading rivals. The ferrets are chief among Bear's risk police. These spies, who have sported such nicknames as "Snoop" (Kenneth Cowin) and "the Hawk" (Kenneth Edlow), even scrutinize senior executives' brokerage accounts. When William Montgoris, then Bear's chief financial officer, deposited a check from another Bear executive into his brokerage account several years back, Mr. Cowin immediately asked Mr. Montgoris to explain it. (The Bear executive was repaying a loan from Mr. Montgoris.)

At Bear's weekly "cold-sweat" meetings, Messrs. Greenberg, Cayne and others grill Bear traders on their holdings. Mr. Greenberg is fanatical about having static or losing positions sold. Quickly. The firm prints an "aged-position report" that shows "stale" trades not sold within ninety days. Mr. Greenberg once recalled that his father, a clothing retailer, often told him: "If something isn't moving, sell it today because tomorrow it will be worth less."

The firm has a simple credo on costs: The easiest way to make money is to cut expenses. In a legendary memo, Mr. Greenberg exhorted employees to save paper clips rather than buy new ones. He saves electricity costs by compulsively shutting off computers not in use, and he turns out the lights when he leaves his office, whether it is to go home at night or simply to stroll to the trading floor. At a junk-bond conference in 1993 at the Waldorf-Astoria, some Bear executives wanted Aretha Franklin to sing. But she was too expensive for Bear's taste; the firm went with the Temptations.

Executives are fined for tolerating fiscal fat. Treasurer Michael Minikes once was docked $2,000 for allowing two investment bankers to fly to London on the Concorde. The firm won't pay first-class fares, except to Asia or to join

Mentor of Chairman Of Bear Stearns Still Sticks Around

* * *

John Slade Earns His Keep After 60 Years on the Job; A Trader Who Likes IBM

By Michael Siconolfi
Staff Reporter of The Wall Street Journal

NEW YORK—You don't get to be a Wall Street marathon man by taking a cab to work.

John H. Slade, 87 years old, should know. Mr. Slade briskly walks the 23 blocks to his Bear, Stearns & Co. office in half an hour flat (it's downhill). On the way he stops to peep at the market newswire at Fidelity Investments.

Mr. Slade has reached a milestone in the brokerage business: 60 years trading stocks and bonds at one firm—a feat much like Cal Ripken's consecutive-games played for the Baltimore Orioles. Mr. Slade revels in his loyalty to the Bear Stearns Cos. unit, where he went to work at the age of 27 in 1936, the day after arriving in the U.S. from Germany.

"If Bear Stearns told him, 'Pack up, you're too old,' it would be the end of him—he just loves it," says his 48-year-old daughter, Barbara Bolsterli, visiting from Switzerland.

Rising through the ranks to senior managing director, Mr. Slade still trades four days a week at Bear Stearns (his wife insisted he pull back a few years ago). "He trades like a kid—he watches the tape—he doesn't miss a trade," marvels Michael Tarnopol, a Bear Stearns executive vice president.

Mr. Slade loves to remind visitors that he was a mentor to Bear Stearns's Chairman Alan "Ace" Greenberg nearly 50 years ago. Mr. Greenberg, himself 68, was so grateful he promised to work with him as long as he lived. Last month, Mr. Greenberg playfully confronted Mr. Slade, saying, "John, I made a terrible mistake—I never thought that you would live that long."

Mr. Slade started humbly at $15 a week as Hans Schlesinger. (A Jew who had fled Hitler, he changed his name because of anti-German sentiment in the 1940s.) Last year, he earned about $225,000. His apartment overlooking Park Avenue is lined with Picassos, Miros and Chagalls.

Blanket Gratitude

And he still has a sense of humor. When colleagues toasted his tenure at a recent reception, Mr. Slade marched to the podium, smiled broadly and announced in his German accent: "Thank you very much for whatever you said."

Mr. Slade's career has had its embarrassing moments. In 1980, comments he made to a Wall Street Journal reporter caused a huge stir. Asked to classify foreigners according to their investing savvy, Mr. Slade ranked the British best, the Germans second and the Swiss the "worst." The story, picked up in Swiss papers, raised such a ruckus that Union Bank of Switzerland officials at first refused to see him when he flew over to apologize.

And Mr. Slade no longer has the swell office digs he once had. Last year, Bear Stearns handed over his office overlooking Park Avenue to Richard Sachs, a new recruit and one of Wall Street's top-producing brokers. Now, Mr. Slade sits at a long row of desks along with other traders and shares a small private office with a colleague. Having a power office is "not as important as [it is] when you are young," Mr. Slade observes.

But he can't resist getting in a dig. Showing a visitor Mr. Sachs's office, Mr. Slade says: It used to look "much nicer."

It didn't take long for him to advance from his first job here as "runner"—running trade tickets around the exchange floor. The 5-foot-11 Mr. Slade says he was promoted to clerk after dancing with the wives of four Bear Stearns partners at the firm's 1936 holiday party. "I was young, and quite good-looking," he says.

Familiar Names

He began drumming up commissions in the late 1930s by meeting boats in New

York harbor that carried German refugees. He scanned passenger lists. "I was able to make contact with those individuals whose names were familiar to me and who might, hopefully, have money in Swiss accounts," Mr. Slade recalls. In a few years, he says, he had about 20 clients and became the firm's foreign-bond trader.

Mr. Slade made a lot of friends for Bear Stearns. Mr. Slade began inviting trainees from banks throughout the world to do short stints at the firm. "Those people grew up to run the major institutions of the world, and they never forgot the fact that they trained at Bear Stearns," says Vice Chairman E. John Rosenwald Jr. "This was simple, but it was brilliant."

In 1940, Mr. Slade made his biggest killing—then nearly quit. As a foreign-bond trader, he had offered bonds overnight without owning them and made sure buyers had the money to pay for them in New York banks, then covered his "short" position. He made one such transaction, involving a Norwegian bank's bonds, on April 10, 1940—the day Norway was invaded by Germany. Covering his position, Mr. Slade had a profit of $80,000.

But that wasn't seen as a triumph. Mr. Slade also held a small position in another Norwegian bank and had a loss in those bonds of $400. His boss laced into him for the loss. "I couldn't take it," Mr. Slade says. He was about to resign when another Bear Stearns executive offered him a post in risk arbitrage.

Physical Fitness

Mr. Slade stays healthy with a strict regimen. He regularly wakes at 5:45 and hops onto his exercise bike for 25 minutes as he catches up on the business news of the day. Then there is a quick five-minute workout before he walks to work.

He is never late—and expects others not to be. Checking his watch, he nods with approval when a visitor arrives right on time for two different appointments. His daughter, Mrs. Bolsterli, predicted how a noon lunch would go in the Bear Stearns' dining room. "The longest lunch is going to last is 1 p.m.," she says. "Then he'll say he has to go back to work." She was right. Says Mr. Slade with a chuckle: "I'm very disciplined. Typical German."

If Mr. Slade's big love is the stockmarket, his longest fling has been with International Business Machines Corp. In July 1982, he urged his clients to put 70% of their cash into IBM, and made a killing.

Then Mr. Slade got the Big Blues: When IBM hit $175^7/_8$ in 1987, Mr. Slade bought 50,000 shares on margin—that is, with borrowed money—and rode the stock down to $58^1/_2$ in 1992. How much did he lose? "I don't want to think of it," he says, shuddering as he puts down his fork.

Cold and Hot

He vowed never to touch IBM again and urged his wife, Marianne, to do the same. But he got IBM fever all over again a few years ago after a management overhaul, and he bought 50,000 shares, which has increased in value manyfold.

So where are the markets headed now? Nowhere but north, he says. His advice: Buy on market dips.

He practices what he preaches. On a recent volatile market day, he strode into the office. "How much are we down?" he barked for a market update before taking off his overcoat. 108. "IBM"? Down $2^1/_2$. After quietly calling his wife, he bought call options on IBM shares—bets that the stock would rise. "The stock is very cheap," he said, surveying his personal IBM stockholdings in a black-bound file book.

That day the Dow Jones Industrial Average closed down 88 points. "Yes." Mr. Slade says with a chuckle, "but IBM closed up $1^5/_8$."

April 19, 1996

clients flying first class. Bear hasn't any corporate jets, limousines or corporate apartments. And Mr. Greenberg personally heads the effort to weed out abuses; the bulk of the more than one hundred memos he has written in the past twenty years are about controlling costs.

Stephen Cunningham, a former Bear investment banker, returned in 1993 with Mr. Greenberg to New York from a trip to Mexico and called his secretary to arrange for cars to pick them up at Kennedy Airport. When he told Mr. Greenberg he had ordered the cars, Mr. Greenberg responded, "Why? Are the yellow cabs on strike?"

In fiscal 1997, Bear's compensation expenses represented just 49 percent of net revenue; anything below 50 percent is viewed as heroic on Wall Street. And Bear doesn't pay big up-front bonuses or issue stock options. But its big producers often are among the highest paid on the Street. In one of the biggest-ever bonus bonanzas, Bear gave its top five executives fiscal 1996 paychecks totaling $81.3 million. Three Bear executives—Mr. Cayne, Mr. Greenberg and Executive Vice President Warren Spector—got record pay packages of $19 million or more each for the year. To put that in perspective, consider that the $81.3 million for Bear's top five players easily topped the $58 million then paid to the twelve-man basketball squad of the Chicago Bulls, the highest-paid team in the National Basketball Association. Which goes to show, perhaps, that even in the 1990s record-setting stock market, the Bears sometimes beat the Bulls.

In 1997, Bear paid a total of $87 million to its top five executives—and *that* handily beat the New York Yankees—the best-paid hitters in pinstripes with a 1997 payroll of $66 million. Of course, Mr. Greenberg could argue that his gang had a better year; the 1997 Yanks didn't even make it back to the World Series. Meanwhile, Bear's profit jumped 25 percent to a record $613 million in the fiscal year ended June 30, 1997. Among those who earned more than $20 million for the year: Messrs. Cayne, Greenberg and Spector.

The big paychecks didn't come without controversy. A few years back a compensation guru included Mr. Greenberg, then Bear's chief executive, in a list of "the most overpaid chief executives in America." (Top Bear executives are paid an annual salary of $200,000; the rest is a bonus tied to the firm's profit.) And for the first time in recent memory, Bear executives took some heat for their compensation packages at the firm's October 1996 annual meeting. It was then that Mr. Greenberg offered up an unusual defense of Bear's pay formula, comparing the firm to yet another pro-sports team.

"I know there's a floor" to the pay formula for the firm's senior executives, one shareholder said. "But where's the ceiling?"

"Do you know how much Shaquille O'Neal makes?" Mr. Greenberg retorted, referring to the Los Angeles Lakers star center. "And the Lakers don't make any money."

(Actually, the Lakers had operating income of $6.2 million for the fiscal 1994–95 season, according to *Financial World* magazine; and Mr. O'Neal is paid $120 million over seven years.)

Mr. Greenberg, in a later interview, said he continued the conversation with the shareholders after the meeting and that they eventually left "very, very satisfied."

A postscript: The Lakers' Mr. O'Neal was injured for much of the 1996–7 season, and his firm was eliminated in the second-round of the playoffs; Bear's five executives led the firm to yet another year of record results.

Bear's controversial ways extend further. In 1993, the firm staffed its Park Avenue headquarters with models, seductively clad in short skirts, to escort visitors to meetings. After some women executives complained, Bear clothed the models, dubbed "Geisha girls" because senior executives hatched the idea after a trip to Asia, more conservatively. Now, Mr. Cayne drops his cigar ashes in, among other things, an ashtray of the Women's Financial Club of New York.

Bear exhibits little of the bureacracy that plagues other investment banks. There are no detailed job descriptions, territorial boundaries or organizational charts. The way to rise within the firm is simple: Make money. "They want 'mailmen' because mailmen deliver," said Chuck Ramsey, a former Bear senior managing director.

Despite tight controls, Bear typically gives green employees big responsibilities. A few years back, Mr. Cayne recruited a young salesman in Los Angeles, Donald Tang, who had no Wall Street experience, but shared a love for bridge. Now, Mr. Tang is president of Bear Stearns Asia Ltd. and branch manager of Bear's Hong Kong office. "He took the heat, that he was one of 'Jimmy's pets,' " Mr. Cayne commented. "Now, everyone thinks he's terrific."

Another Bear employee who worked up the firm's ladder, Daniel D'Amato, son of Senator Alfonse D'Amato, has drawn some media criticism. In 1997 the *New York Observer* newspaper tweaked Bear for giving money to Senator D'Amato, hiring Daniel as a broker—and then winning an advisory mandate to help New York State in its takeover of Long Island Lighting Co.

Bear executives brush aside any suggestions of influence-peddling. They defend Daniel D'Amato as a successful broker who pulled himself up from the ranks of $5-an-hour cold-callers. "He does everything by the book," Mr. Cayne said. "He never opens a [brokerage] account that his father has anything" to do with. In 1997, Mr. Cayne bragged that Mr. D'Amato "is a million-dollar producer and a credit to the firm."

It was a typical Bear success story.

Growing Profit; Stunted Tax Dodge

Bear continues to muster the bulk of its pretax income from core bond-trading and clearing businesses. Bear had net income of $321.8 million for the six months ended December 31, 1997. Its fiscal second quarter was the tenth consecutive quarter that Bear posted return-on-equity of more than 20 percent; in the six months ended December 1997, Bear's ROE was 22 percent.

Bear let the big securities-industry mergers of 1997 pass it by. The firm's executives brushed aside rumors involving Bear, including that it would buy a regional or midsized brokerage firm.

"You won't see us buy PaineWebber or anybody for distribution," a senior Bear executive said. But the executive added that Bear would consider acquiring a money-management firm. "We could buy someone for managing assets," the executive said. Trouble is, asset managers are selling for steep multiples in a bull market for mutual funds and other packaged products.

A few years back, Bear scrambled to make up for a number of defections and lost business in its mortgage-bond group, following the industry-wide debacle in that market in 1994. The firm in particular has beefed up its asset-backed securities group, hiring a team from CS First Boston. Its new asset-backed clients include American Express, AT&T, Chase Manhattan, First Chicago and Sears Roebuck, all of whom have done credit-card transactions underwritten by Bear. Its market share for new asset-backed securities rose to 6.5 percent in 1997 from 5 percent a year earlier. Meanwhile, Bear's credit-card market share jumped to 9.2 percent from 3.7 percent in the same time.

Bear continued to make big money in 1997. And the firm made it through the October 1997 market mess extremely well. There even were bright spots on Bloody Monday: Bear Stearns made money on a small short position—betting on a price decline—on a Brazilian sovereign debt issue that plunged, a senior executive said.

There nevertheless were some hiccups. Some trading positions were marked down between 20 percent and 25 percent on Bloody Monday, a senior executive said. And with the market action so fast and furious, there were squabbles with clients. One Bear Stearns client refused to pay for a buying position totaling about $1 million for Oxford Health Plans Inc., a high-flying managed-care company that plunged $42.875 in Nasdaq Stock Market trading Monday, the executive said. The Bear Stearns broker, believing she had discretion in the trading account, had apparently tried to pick the bottom in Oxford unsuccessfully, the executive said. When the client found out, he was indignant, and reneged on the trade, the executive said. After a brief investigation, Bear Stearns decided to eat the loss, which totaled $120,000.

But Bear suffered a blow in early 1997 when the government moved to shut down a controversial method that Bear had aggressively used for companies to sidestep taxes. The product, "step-down" preferred stock, was sold to tax-exempt investors such as pension funds. Bear sold more than $7 billion of these deals, which had buyers and sellers jointly create a real-estate investment trust, each contributing, say, $100 million. Through the REIT, buyers would get inflated dividends that, because of the buyer's tax status, would be tax-free. After paying the oversized dividends for ten years, the seller would "buy out" the buyer's share of the investment for a nominal amount, liquidate the REIT and distribute the remaining $200 million in assets to the seller.

Such a liquidation was tax-free under tax law. But the Treasury objected. The real deal was that the seller was selling preferred stock and not paying taxes on $100 million of income. The Internal Revenue Service issued a notice saying it would draft regulations declaring such deals taxable; the Treasury said its ruling will apply retroactively to all sales in 1997.

So the damage was done. Bear was by far the most aggressive underwriter of the stock, which was issued by blue-chip companies ranging from Walt Disney Co. to Union Carbide Corp. The deals generated $60 million to $70 million in net fees for Bear's bond capital-markets group, equaling its entire bookings for the previous fiscal year. Bear officials were irate over the ruling. "Treasury's proposal creates needless disruption and uncertainty for investors by retroactively changing the law," said Bear's Mr. Spector. "It's as though the speed limit were lowered to forty miles per hour today and everyone got tickets for going fifty-five yesterday."

Bear returned about $40 million in underwriting fees and could repay a total of $100 million if enough clients give up. Eight months after the Treasury announcement that it would treat all step-down-preferred deals as taxable—including the more than $10 billion worth of transactions already done—such clients as Disney and PepsiCo threw in the towel and canceled step-down-preferred offerings. Nevertheless, most of Bear's deals remain outstanding and the firm said it "eagerly" awaits publication of official Treasury rules and will decide then whether to take the Treasury to court.

Trading: Calculated Risks

Messrs. Cayne and Greenberg, both accomplished bridge players, urge their traders and others to take calculated risks. But unlike many other Wall Street firms, Bear swallows trading losses as a part of doing business. If you haven't taken losses recently, Mr. Greenberg tells traders, you haven't been taking enough risk. When Bobby Steinberg, cohead of risk arbitrage, had a $50 million loss on the day of the October 1987 stock-market crash, Mr. Greenberg urged him to keep his cool. "I was shell-shocked—there didn't seem to be any end in sight—but Ace told me if there were deals with great opportunity, to be a buyer."

Indeed, Mr. Greenberg broke the tension on Black Monday by getting up from his chair on the trading floor, pretending to swing a golf club and loudly announcing he was taking the next day off—even though he doesn't play golf and came in the following day. Despite a $96 million loss in the crash, he said, "I wanted to show that there was no panic at Bear Stearns."

In building its strength in bond trading, Bear has cobbled together a particularly strong franchise in the market for mortgage-backed securities. But unlike Salomon and other trading firms, Bear doesn't take much proprietary risk;

that is, trading for the house account. Bear takes proprietary positions only in small selected markets, such as risk arbitrage, bankruptcy trading and the Japanese convertible-warrant market. "This has allowed it to earn returns that we estimate are in line with those of the industry without taking on a great deal of proprietary risk . . . and without yet having a strong presence in derivatives," according to a report by Sanford C. Bernstein & Co.

Bear in 1996 scored a big bond coup by arranging a private placement of more than $1 billion of Brazilian debt owned by the Dart family. After approaching Goldman and Salomon, the Darts turned to Bear, which had an arbitrage-trading relationship with the secretive family. Bear ended up doing the deal, and pocketed $20 million in commissions.

Over the past several years, bond sales and trading have accounted for an average of one-quarter of Bear's net revenue and more than 40 percent of pre-tax income, Bernstein estimates. Bear's stock business has been far less lucrative, accounting for less than one-quarter of net revenue and about 5 percent of pretax profit. One reason is its lack of a big stock-derivatives business, which generates higher margins than other stock areas.

Bear, like other big Nasdaq players, has been squeezed a bit by new trading rules on the sprawling small-stock market. In 1997, Bear Stearns made markets in 390 small stocks, down from the 440 it traded a year earlier. The profit-margin squeeze began in January 1997, when the Securities and Exchange Commission imposed sweeping new rules that for the first time allowed some orders from investors to help set prices if they are better than market makers' quoted prices. The rules also forced market makers to publicly display their best prices on Nasdaq's public trading system, not just on private systems like Instinet. Meanwhile, Nasdaq and other exchanges now allow stocks to be quoted in increments of $1/16$ of a point—or 6.25 cents—rather than the previous minimum for most stocks at $1/8$ of a point, or 12.5 cents. The lower the trading increments, traders say, the lower the spreads and profits margins per trade.

Bear also played a part in a mega price-fixing case involving Nasdaq dealers. In December 1997, Bear agreed to pay $40 million to settle, without admitting wrongdoing, a class-action case filed against the firm and twenty-nine other dealers alleging that they conspired to keep the trading "spreads" between the buy and sell prices of Nasdaq stocks overly wide between 1989 and 1994. (The thirty firms agreed to pay a total of $910 million to settle the case, filed in a New York federal court.)

Forging into the Investment-Banking Majors

Bear's banking effort wasn't taken seriously on the Street until a few years ago. It had an early coup with a $102 million initial public stock offering for EK Chor

China Motorcycle; a red motorcycle still stands in Mr. Cayne's office as a trophy from the deal.

Rather than trying to build the banking business willy-nilly, Bear has focused on cobbling together teams aimed at business niches, such as media, telecommunications and retail. Bear got its first big break in the merger wars when investment-banking chief Alan Schwartz served as co-adviser on Viacom Inc.'s bruising $9.6 billion takeover battle for Paramount Communications Inc., which closed in 1994.

Then the firm became a star in defense. Messrs. Bovin and Urfirer in particular have emerged in recent years with Wall Street's hottest hands in defense-industry acquisitions. Just a few years back, "it was kind of, 'Bear who?' " said John Montague, vice president of financial strategies for Lockheed Martin Corp., which became the nation's largest defense-and-aerospace company in 1995 after a Bear-assisted merger. Mr. Montague added at the time: "Now, I think Bear Stearns has carved out a niche as a leading investment bank in the area of defense consolidation." One reason is the connections Bear executives have with industry. Mr. Bovin, for instance, has forged close ties with top military and civilian defense officials.

Still, Bear's broader banking effort has a long way to go. In 1997, Bear ranked No. 8 among Wall Street stock and bond underwriters, with a market share of 4.4 percent. Over the past several years, Bear's banking business has accounted for about 20 percent of net revenues and more than 30 percent of pretax profit. Though Bear hasn't snatched a bigger slice of the stock-underwriting market, "it has among the highest investment banking margins in the industry," according to Sanford C. Bernstein & Co. This stems partly from Bear's historically strong position in mortgage-backed bonds and an improving share in junk-bond transactions. Bernstein added that, "It is also due to the company's famous attention to expense control in what has generally been a relatively expense-lax business."

There were several banking coups in 1997. Bear helped advise HFS Inc. in an $11.3 billion merger with CUC International Inc., and Raytheon Co. in its purchases of General Motors Corp.'s Hughes Electronics defense business ($9.5 billion) and Texas Instruments Inc.'s defense business ($2.95 billion.)

Bear has had its share of banking disappointments. The firm lost out in the bidding war for Joseph Perella, a Wall Street merger star who had split up with his longtime partner, Bruce Wasserstein. Archrival Morgan Stanley—a firm Bear officials derisively refer to as "Stanley Morgan"—eventually hired Mr. Perella, who in 1997 became Morgan's investment-banking chief.

Power(ful) Brokers

Despite its trading roots, Bear long has had a penchant for brokerage catering to wealthy investors, reflecting Mr. Cayne's initiation at the firm peddling stocks and bonds to big-hitting investors in Chicago. Though Bear's small brokerage business has accounted for an average of about 12 percent of the firm's net revenue in recent years, it hasn't made money, analysts say. But that's not a pressing problem for Bear: The firm's strategy for its brokerage operations partly is to use them for valuable introductions that could lead to investment-banking and trade-processing businesses.

Bear's 513 brokers are among Wall Street's most productive, averaging $735,000 in annual commissions. Bear brokers who generate more than $400,000 in annual commissions typically get to keep 50 percent of that—even as some rivals have cut the percentage of commissions their brokers keep. Bear has no such plans. "The second we cut it, we lose their confidence that we won't cut it again," Mr. Cayne says. On an RJR Nabisco underwriting led by Merrill a few years back, Bear's brokers actually outsold Merrill's far bigger salesforce, because Bear was booking far bigger orders. "Our distribution capabilities are the best on the Street," boasts Mr. Cayne.

Bear's brokerage effort received a boost when the firm bested several rivals in a high-stakes sweepstakes for Richard Sachs and Gary Budlow, Wall Street's most productive brokerage team, who serve some of the world's wealthiest families. In the past few years, Messrs. Sachs and Budlow have generated about $20 million in annual commissions, making them among the biggest brokerage producers ever, according to Wall Street executives. Mr. Sachs was nominated to Bear's board after just fifteen months, more quickly than any new hire, and was given a prized office next to Mr. Greenberg, Bear's chairman.

Because of the duo's client list, which includes some fifty of the world's wealthiest families, they were promised up-front bonuses of as much as $9 million by other firms. Still, they chose Bear, even though the firm refuses to pay up-front bonuses. "The money thrown at us was incredible, but that's not what has ever driven our business or relationships," Mr. Sachs said. "We chose 'the Bear' for its very strong client-driven culture."

Messrs. Sachs and Budlow have fit in well because, like the firm, they avoid hanging on to losing positions for long. "When there's a loss, it's boom, out, gone," said E. Craig Coats, a senior Prudential Securities Inc. executive and a Sachs/Budlow client. Another client is Bear's CEO, Mr. Cayne. Mr. Sachs "fights for the last one-sixteenth for his customers," Mr. Cayne marvels. Just like Bear.

Trade-Clearing: Threatened by Probe, Regulation

Bear has long had a thriving clearing business. It processes trades for 2,274 customers, up from 725 in 1987, making it the nation's largest clearing firm. Bear handles 12 percent of the New York Stock Exchange volume; it even processes a chunk of trades for a major rival brokerage firm, Lehman Brothers Holdings Inc.

Bear Stearns Takes Stand On Clearing

Firm Says Regulation Could Hurt Industry

BY MICHAEL SICONOLFI

Staff Reporter of THE WALL STREET JOURNAL

NEW YORK—Bear Stearns Cos., facing regulatory scrutiny of its trade-processing business, is fighting back to protect one of its most lucrative franchises.

James Cayne, Bear Stearns's chief executive officer, in a letter to New York Stock Exchange Chairman Richard Grasso, warned that any regulatory or other proposals to hold "clearing" firms responsible for the activities of the smaller firms that hire them to process trades would likely squeeze big Wall Street brokerage houses and trigger some to "abandon their clearing business outright."

The move comes as the Securities and Exchange Commission and the Manhattan district attorney's office investigate the role of Bear Stearns, the nation's largest clearing firm, in processing trades for defunct A.R. Baron & Co., a small brokerage house accused by the district attorney's office of defrauding investors of $75 million.

The state grand jury empaneled in the district attorney's case is considering, among other things, recommending changing state law to hold clearing firms more liable for the sales practices of the smaller brokers that hire them to process trades, people familiar with the matter say. Currently, regulations don't hold clearing firms responsible for the activities of such securities firms.

Manhattan District Attorney Robert Morgenthau declined to comment on the investigation.

At issue is one of the more profitable parts of Wall Street. Small securities firms, called "introducing brokers," hire powerhouses such as Bear Stearns to execute trades, maintain client records, send out trade confirmations and monthly statements, and settle the smaller firms' transactions. Bear Stearns handles 12% of the volume on the New York Stock Exchange; its clearing business represents about 25% of the firm's profit.

The Big Board, for its part, earlier this month proposed rules that would place a greater obligation on clearing firms to keep tabs on what their clearing clients are doing. Among those proposals was a requirement for clearing firms to forward to regulators any complaints they receive from clients of introducing brokers.

But the Bear Stearns letter says more can be done to overhaul the business without harming clearing firms. Among the firm's proposals: requiring introducing brokers to immediately notify clearing firms of regulatory inquiries or investigations—and giving clearing firms the right to end agreements based on the results of such probes. The letter also proposed that clients of introducing brokers receive documents—"in plain English"—noting that their brokerage accounts are managed and controlled solely by the introducing broker, not the clearing firm.

Moreover, the letter warns against holding clearing firms liable for any investor abuses by introducing brokers. "Clearing brokers do not—and cannot—have any meaningful access to or control over introducing brokers, or their principals and employees, their customers, records or system," Mr. Cayne wrote. "Moreover, the difficulty in enforcing any such programs undoubtedly would expose clearing brokers to the risk of claims for substantial liability (even if unfounded) arising out of the introducing broker's deliberate or inadvertent misconduct, and attendant potential legal fees, far outweighing the compensation they receive for the clearing services they provide." The Big Board declined to comment on the letter, as did Bear Stearns.

Already, Bear Stearns has stopped doing business with several introducing brokers amid the investigation, the firm's executives said. And if stricter rules were imposed on clearing-firm liability, Bear Stearns executives said, the firm likely would abandon processing trades for introducing brokers, and clear transactions only for bigger institutional players such as arbitragers and market makers.

September 26, 1997

But, as is typical with Bear, there have been controversial clients. When other firms shunned John Mulheren Jr., who was charged in the 1980s insider-trading scandal, Bear continued to clear trades for him. (A federal appeals court eventually exonerated Mr. Mulheren.) "We felt comfortable with him," said Richard Harriton, Bear's clearing chief. "There was no reason legally not to do business with him."

But the highly publicized clearing investigations have pinched Bear—and Mr. Harriton—more recently, and potentially threaten one of its most profitable businesses. In the wake of the probes, clearing firms including Bear have stopped processing trades for some less-than-stellar clients. The investigations, among other things, are scrutinizing the activities of Mr. Harriton, and were expanded to cover the behavior of Matthew Harriton, his son. As part of the wide-ranging probe, investigators are examining the younger Mr. Harriton's participation in several small public companies in conjunction with Randolph K. Pace, whom regulators suspended for alleged stock manipulation in 1988 from association with any NASD member for two years. The investigators are looking into whether Mr. Pace and associates granted business favors, such as the opportunity to buy bargain-priced stock, to the younger Mr. Harriton as part of an effort to get Bear Stearns, through the elder Mr. Harriton, to clear trades by two brokerage firms that have been charged by authorities with misconduct, according to an individual familiar with the inquiry.

Matthew Harriton declined to be interviewed by *The Wall Street Journal*. The elder Mr. Harriton referred questions to a Bear Stearns public-relations office. A Bear Stearns spokeswoman said: "After a thorough internal investigation Bear Stearns has concluded unequivocally that there is absolutely no evidence of any improprieties on the part of Mr. [Richard] Harriton or Bear Stearns in the operations of its correspondent-clearing department. We will continue to cooperate with the authorities until all these types of unsubstantiated allegations from anonymous sources of improper conduct are proven baseless."

The probes already have led to new clearing rules proposed by the New York Stock Exchange that would place a greater obligation on clearing firms to keep tabs on what their clearing clients are doing. Among the proposals was a requirement for clearing firms to forward to regulators any complaints they receive from clients of introducing brokers. In fact, Bear's Mr. Cayne, in a letter to the Big Board's chief, warned that any regulatory or other proposals to hold clearing firms more responsible for the activities of their clearing clients would likely squeeze big Wall Street brokerage firms and trigger some to abandon the business altogether.

Challenging Conventional Wisdom

Elizabeth Mackay is not a believer in efficient markets. In fact, she argues, the stock market "stands the efficient market theory on its head."

That may sound like an unusual approach for one of Wall Street's investment pundits, but Ms. Mackay didn't rise to the level of head of investment strategy at a freewheeling firm like Bear Stearns without challenging conventional wisdom. In fact, her willingness to do so dates back to her first job when, as a college graduate with a degree in psychology, she called an options-trading firm to ask if they had any openings. Asked if she had any background in options, she replied confidently that she did—then before going in for an interview spent a day calling all her friends for briefings on how the financial instruments worked.

She landed the job, and rapidly moved into the even more complex world of technical market analysis as a member of the Merrill Lynch team headed by Robert Farrell, taking evening courses at the New York Institute of Finance. But the opportunity to head an investment strategy division lured her to Brown Brothers Harriman, where she also managed a pool of investment capital for the firm.

"That really taught me to pay attention to what a money manager needs in the way of information from a strategist," she said. "And at a time when the market's been seen as being basically a one-way street for so long, that's been a big help."

While less high-profile than some of her competitors, Ms. Mackay has a solid track record in her five years at Bear Stearns. Throughout 1995 and 1996 she remained a steadfast bull, although she voiced caution as the market approached 6000 that further gains might prove less sustainable. So far, her views of a "more normal" market environment in 1998 seem to have been borne out by reality.

Clients say what distinguishes her from other strategists isn't her accuracy in forecasting the direction of the market as a whole, but the fact that she catches things others will miss. Cases in point, they say, include her 1996 analysis that higher energy prices weren't just a flash in the pan. Energy costs were likely to remain above-average thanks to a surge in demand from emerging economies in Southeast Asia and elsewhere, she concluded, and indeed prices have stayed significantly higher than their averages earlier in the decade.

Ms. Mackay says Bear Stearns's "free-flowing" corporate structure means she has a lot of contact with analysts in the research department as she formulates her investment strategy approach. "I think that's perhaps more the case here than in many other firms," she says.

Reflecting Bear Stearns's market niche in corporate underwriting, that research department's strengths are largely in the areas of health care, media and technology stocks. Flexibility is the name of the game; often, analysts who cover a sector that's temporarily quiet or in the doldrums will pick up coverage of related businesses. That's what Linda Leiberman (ranked a *Wall Street Journal* all-star stock picker in 1996) did when she added coverage of packaging firms and other companies whose businesses had some links to the paper and forest products companies she followed. When the aerospace industry went through its own slump, Stephen Binder, another all-star on *The Wall Street Journal*'s list, added environmental services companies to his coverage. Most recently one of the banking analysts decided to start tracking the growth in companies specializing in lending to sub-prime borrowers for the purchase of new homes or cars. Michael Diana identified the shift in lending patterns because of his coverage of the banks, and became one of the first analysts to monitor the fledgling business. Still, the firm ranked only fifteenth in the 1997 *Wall St. Journal* all-star survey, with thirteen analysts of note.

In addition to its stock research department, Bear Stearns has a team of veteran corporate bond researchers on staff, with nine analysts covering so-called junk bonds and still more tracking investment-grade debt. The average experience is fifteen years in credit research and analysis, unusually high for a sector which only began to expand significantly in the 1980s. Again, the focus within the department has been on areas where the firm has investment banking expertise, such as media. Clients also note the corporate bond research division has been particularly quick to track the complex developments in the rapidly-deregulating world of electric utilities.

Proxy Battle

Bear's most contentious legal battle in recent years involved a suit it filed against D. F. King & Co., a major proxy-solicitation firm. In a highly public spat, Bear accused a King employee of stealing confidential data by calling up the brokerage firm and impersonating a Bear worker. The activities were embarrassing for Bear because they suggested that the firm couldn't keep coveted trading records of its clients under wraps. (In a confidential accord reached in 1997, D. F. King paid about $1.5 million to Bear, settling the case, according to a person familiar with the matter.)

In 1996, federal regulators grilled a Bear broker in an investigation of yet another controversial ex-Bear client. The Securities and Exchange Commission launched an investigation into whether Eddie Antar secretly sold $5.6 million of Crazy Eddie Inc. stock in the name of an Israeli charity through a brokerage account at Bear, as part of a continuing investigation of Mr. Antar, the controversial founder of the failed electronics chain.

Trading Secrets

Bear Stearns Is Aghast To Find Data Leaking To a Proxy Solicitor

---

Squabble Shows How Agent Of D.F. King Snooped To Learn Stocks' Owners

---

Hockey Tickets for a Clerk

By MICHAEL SICONOLFI
Staff Reporter of THE WALL STREET JOURNAL

NEW YORK—A lawyer at Bear Stearns Cos. was jolted early last month by a mysterious caller with an ominous message: "D.F. King is at it again."

Scribbling furiously in his 11th-floor office, General Counsel Mark Lehman was horrified to hear that Bear Stearns was doing a lax job of guarding its clients' privacy. The tipster said confidential data on client names and stockholdings were being leaked to D.F. King & Co., a proxy-solicitation firm that is in the business of ferreting out the identities of publicity-shy shareholders and tracking their trades.

Worse, the leaks seemed to be coming straight from a Bear Stearns clerk, in return for freebies such as liquor and choice hockey seats. Yet discretion is supposed to be the very soul of a securities firm, especially at Bear Stearns with its many powerful clients who trade stocks of companies that are takeover candidates.

Barely a month would pass before Thomas Cronin, a D.F. King vice president, was fired. The 39-year-old Mr. Cronin freely concedes that he plied the Bear Stearns clerk with gifts. But he says in an interview that the proxy-solicitation business "has always been done this way." He adds: "I was hired to do this. I was doing what was expected of me."

Although that point is in dispute, the affair sheds considerable light on the dark corner of Wall Street known as proxy solicitation, a business that began a half-century ago to tally the votes of shareholders absent from annual meetings but has evolved well beyond that to digging up hard-to-find data about stockholdings. Closely held D.F. King is one of the top proxy firms.

Somehow Bear Stearns, a major securities firm that prides itself on its controls, can't seem to stop employees from occasionally leaking sensitive information. For the second time in five years, it is suing D.F. King in New York state court over such a leak. The latest suit names Mr. Cronin in addition to D.F. King.

In it, Bear Stearns portrays its clerk as an unwitting dupe who was misled when Mr. Cronin telephoned pretending to be a Bear Stearns employee in another office. Balderdash, says Mr. Cronin, adding that he has been friends for years with the clerk, Donald Cush, and never hid his identity.

The spat illustrates the natural tension between brokerage houses and proxy firms, whose sophisticated sleuthing services often are vital to those companies seeking to discover who is holding their stock. Such corporate clients may, for instance, want to reach shareholders to try to persuade them to vote a certain way. But many shareholders' stock is held in a "street name." This means a brokerage house is the owner of record and must handle all solicitations.

Nuggets about ownership can be gleaned from public filings. But sometimes it is crucial to move faster, and this is where information gathering can get sticky for a proxy solicitor.

'Secret Arrangement'

"You have to go to either the brokerage firm or the bank" to press for data, says a former executive of rival proxy-solicitor Georgeson & Co. "That is a problem," because some clients don't want their names known while they accumulate a position lest others pile in, driving up the price. Financial firms have a fiduciary duty to clients to keep their confidential trading positions secret, lawyers say.

It isn't my problem, contends Mr. Cronin, who sees the job as a cross between detective and reporter. "You talk to people; they can tell you, 'Take a walk,'" he says. "If they tell you information, that's their problem."

Now the two firms are at war, and they don't agree on what happened. The Bear Stearns lawsuit alleges fraud, citing the alleged impersonation that fooled the clerk. But a D.F. King news release contends that the clerk and the proxy solicitor knew each other and had a "secret arrangement" unknown to King.

The proxy firm denies any culpability, saying it neither knew of nor sanctioned Mr. Cronin's actions. The case is particularly awkward for the firm because it paid about $1 million to settle an unrelated suit by Bear Stearns in 1991; that complaint also alleged that data had been pilfered by someone impersonating a Bear Stearns employee.

Bear Stearns takes extensive measures to guard against rogue traders. For example, it has in-house spies known as "ferrets" who patrol the trading floors looking for overly risky trades. It offers cash payments to employees who turn in errant colleagues. It has employees sign a pact saying: "To disseminate information is to STEAL. You wouldn't take someone else's money. DON'T TALK ABOUT HIS TRANSACTIONS." Yet a brokerage house must give even low-level employees instant access to records. And occasionally, people do talk.

The tipster who called Bear Stearns's general counsel last month knew several chillingly precise details about two D.F. King clients: Aviall Inc., a Dallas transportation-equipment concern, and Medford Savings Bank in Massachusetts. The caller said the proxy firm had been able to learn data about investors in both companies at a time last February when it was important because investor groups had acquired or controlled blocks of each stock. D.F. King would have wanted to know the identities of these stockholders and their positions.

The extent of the tipster's knowledge enraged Bear Stearns. After a brief internal probe, Chief Executive Officer James Cayne phoned the proxy firm's CEO, John Gavin, and vowed to make D.F. King "feel so much pain that [it]

won't ever do this again," according to an affidavit Mr. Gavin filed last week.

Bear Stearns says its in-house computer trail confirms that the data on Aviall and Medford shareholders had been looked at by Mr. Cush, who declines to comment. But Bear Stearns executives say the clerk told them he thought Mr. Cronin was an employee at Bear Stearns's "uptown" office who needed help in "accessing customer information" in the two stocks. Bear Stearns says it ordered Mr. Cush to take a polygraph test and he passed it.

Bear Stearns executives can't explain why Mr. Cush, an 11-year veteran, never checked to confirm that Mr. Cronin worked at the firm. The clerk said in an affidavit that Mr. Cronin gave him tickets to "seven or eight" New York Islanders hockey games, liquor at Christmas and $400 to send his son's roller-hockey team to California to play in the junior Olympics. The clerk's affidavit also said he had known Mr. Cronin for about two years, believing the whole time that he worked at Bear Stearns.

A sturdy 6 feet 4 inches, with curly brown hair, a mustache and a New York accent, Mr. Cush is "rough around the edges," a colleague says. He has been earning about $50,000 a year in Bear Stearns's stock-record department. That site is in Brooklyn, light years away from the company's luxurious headquarters on Manhattan's Park Avenue. Bear Stearns says Mr. Cush hadn't any reason to visit headquarters and get to know the people working there.

All this is beside the point to Mr. Cronin. He maintains that the clerk frequently called him at his office, where secretaries answer the phone "D.F. King." Mr. Cronin adds that Mr. Cush also sometimes met him down the street from D.F. King's 77 Water Street headquarters in lower Manhattan to pick up sports tickets.

Liquor and Tickets

Mr. Cronin says the relationship dated from the mid-1980s, when Mr. Cronin worked for another proxy firm. He adds that he has received information about Bear Stearns clients from Mr. Cush "many dozens" of times over the years. "He was the only guy I ever talked to there when I needed information," Mr. Cronin says. "He would give me whatever I asked for."

Mr. Cush sometimes requested freebies, particularly hockey and football tickets, Mr. Cronin says. He also tells of giving Mr. Cush gift certificates to liquor stores. Mr. Cronin says he once gave Mr. Cush tickets to an Islanders hockey playoffs game where Mr. Cush sat in a skybox with, among others, Mr. Cronin and his boss at D.F. King, Thomas Kies.

Mr. Kies declines to comment, but according to D.F. King he did speak to the firm's co-general counsel, Peter Harkins. Mr. Harkins says Mr. Kies told him he was introduced to those in the skybox only on a "first-name" basis, there were "eight, 10 or 12" people there and he didn't know Mr. Cush was among them.

Mr. Cronin counters that Mr. Kies "knew I talked to" Mr. Cush. "He knew I dealt with him. He knew the information we were getting." Through D.F. King, Mr. Kies denies this. (Mr. Kies initially was suspended, but was recently reinstated at King.) Either way, there was no strict quid pro quo at work, Mr. Cronin maintains. Tickets "were not given in exchange for giving me information," he says; rather, the give-and-take was part of the "good will" of an informal relationship with sources. "It's done this way all over, not just with him."

An affidavit Mr. Cronin's lawyer, William Ford, filed this week, says D.F. King's "senior management, indeed virtually every employee of D.F. King, was not only aware, but made use, of information Cronin received from Bear Stearns and other like securities houses"—an assertion that D.F. King denies. Says the proxy firm's Mr. Harkins: "The guy who did that would like you to believe that's how it's done. It's not true. And he knows it."

Mr. Cronin says D.F. King had an annual budget of $25,000 for tickets to games at Yankee and Shea stadiums, Madison Square Garden and elsewhere. "Everyone takes what they feel they need," he says. D.F. King executives won't comment on the budget, other than to say it included the cost of tickets and other entertainment expenses. They allege that Mr. Cronin falsified expense reports and made off-premises calls to avoid disclosing that he gave tickets to Mr. Cush.

Mr. Cronin doesn't deny doing so, but says D.F. King employees frequently asked him to obtain trading data from Bear Stearns. He says he made outside calls and inaccurate expense reports to avoid detection by Bear Stearns—not by his bosses.

Founded in 1942, D.F. King has more than 500 clients, including AT&T Corp. and McDonald's Corp. Its stock-watch department has 146 clients and generates about 5.3% of the firm's revenue. The firm doesn't disclose earnings, but the business can be lucrative: King's top 10 account-executive partners received 1995 pay packages of about $300,000 each, according to a person who was briefed on the matter. A D.F. King executive disputes that number, but won't elaborate. Mr. Cronin, as a manager and No. 2 executive in the stock-watch department, received a pay package of salary and bonus of $110,000 last year, he says.

When Bear Stearns filed suit, D.F. King responded that the trading and shareholder information it collects for clients "is obtained from legitimate sources and used to improve communications between issuers and stockholders."

A Crucial Phone Call

Inside D.F. King, the allegations came to a head 10 days before Bear Stearns served its suit. At about 11 A.M. on Nov. 5, Mr. Cush, the Bear Stearns clerk, called Mr. Cronin, and Bear Stearns taped the call in an apparent bid to confirm Mr. Cronin's identity before suing him, a person familiar with the matter says.

"Tom, I'm under a lot of pressure," Mr. Cronin says Mr. Cush told him. "I hear from people here you work for a proxy-solicitation firm," he says Mr. Cush continued, adding that he needed "some answers." Mr. Cronin says that, incredulous, he immediately told Mr. Kies about the phone call. He describes his boss's response as: "You've got to be kidding me." D.F. King contends Mr. Cronin never told Mr. Kies about the call.

When Mr. Cronin came back from lunch, he says, there was a pink message slip on his desk referring to Mr. Cush, saying "Don wants to meet you at the corner of Wall and Water at 5 P.M." Mr. Cronin decided not to go. Bear Stearns says it has no knowledge of such a call.

Mr. Cronin then was summoned into a meeting by two senior King executives, Mr. Harkins and the other co-general counsel, Walter Denby. Sitting in Mr. Denby's corner office at King's headquarters, Mr. Cronin was grilled about his relationship with Bear Stearns. During the meeting, Mr. Harkins says, Mr. Cronin told the two executives he contacted Bear Stearns out of "stupidity" but maintained that Mr. Kies was aware of his Bear connection.

Three days later, Mr. Cronin says, Messrs. Harkins and Denby called him into the office and asked him to sign an affidavit that he says painted him as a "scapegoat." Mr. Cronin, on the advice of his counsel, the New York firm of Ford Marrin Esposito Witmeyer & Gleser, refused to sign. Mr. Cronin says the affidavit put the blame for the entire affair at his doorstep: D.F. King executives say it accurately reflected what Mr. Cronin told them.

Meantime, Mr. Cronin agreed to take a polygraph test, partly in a bid to avoid litigation with Bear Stearns. His lie-detector appointment was set for the following Friday, Nov. 15. He never took the test; Bear Stearns filed suit that day.

So, who is the mysterious tipster? Some people familiar with the matter think it was a person who talked to Michael Gallagher, an employee who left D.F. King in June. Mr. Gallagher had a dispute with D.F. King over his severance package, Mr. Cronin says.

At D.F. King, Mr. Gallagher was an analyst on the Aviall account, Mr. Cronin adds. He says Mr. Gallagher was the person who asked him to obtain Bear Stearns's trading data on the stock in the first place.

Mr. Gallagher, who now works in the compliance department at Smith Barney Inc., says: "Your information is erroneous to some degree." He declines to comment further.

December 19, 1996

At issue were nearly 500,000 shares of Crazy Eddie stock Mr. Antar said he contributed to the American Friends of Kiryat Sanz Laniado Hospital. Records at Bear show that the Crazy Eddie shares were transferred to three accounts at Bank Leumi Trust Co. of New York. But there were two small problems: The American Friends say they never received such a contribution from Mr. Antar, and none of the three account numbers correspond to any account numbers ever maintained at Bank Leumi. Regulators want to know whether the stock sale was a "sham transaction by which Antar was able to sell $5.6 million worth of Crazy Eddie stock without paying taxes on his capital gains and getting a charitable deduction for the basis value of the stock," a person close to the case said.

In early 1997, Bear received a favorable court opinion in a widely watched case against another former controversial client, Askin Capital Management Inc., a $600 million hedge fund that was wiped out when interest rates soared in 1994. A federal judge in New York ruled that investors could proceed with a claim of aiding and abetting fraud against Bear and two other securities firms, but the judge dismissed several other claims of racketeering, breach of fiduciary duty, negligent misrepresentation, and unjust enrichment, among other things. The case is pending.

Bear's People

James E. Cayne, president and chief executive officer: Mr. Cayne also is chairman of the firm's management and compensation committee, which sets Bear's daily strategy. With an ever-present cigar, the tough-talking Mr. Cayne personifies Bear's aggressive style of doing business. After joining Bear in 1969 as a salesman in New York, Mr. Cayne quickly rose through the ranks and became president in 1988. He was named CEO in 1993.

Cayne, James
CEO-Bear Stearns

Mr. Cayne shares Mr. Greenberg's love of bridge; they frequently can be found after hours playing at New York's Regency Whist Club. Mr. Cayne has won nearly every major bridge championship in recent years. A few years back, Mr. Cayne (aware that it was neither acceptable nor possible to go into China solely for the sake of doing business) used his talents at the bridge table to garner an invitation to play bridge with key Chinese officials and dignitaries—which led to investment-banking business there, and the opening of Bear offices in Shanghai and Beijing. This led *Institutional Investor* magazine in 1993 to quip that when Mr. Cayne played bridge with China's leaders, "he gave new meaning to bridge finance."

Alan C. Greenberg, chairman: Mr. Greenberg also is a chairman of the firm's executive committee. After joining Bear in 1949, he made partner in 1958 and became chief executive officer of the partnership in 1978. When Bear went public in 1985, Mr. Greenberg became its chairman and chief executive.

Though Mr. Greenberg gave up his CEO post in 1993, he continues to most reflect Bear's cultural personality. Mr. Greenberg is known as much for his voluminous memos and expertise outside Wall Street as his trading acumen. His admirers include the legendary investor Warren Buffett. Mr. Greenberg "does almost everything better than I do—bridge, magic tricks, dog training, arbitrage—all the important things in life," Mr. Buffett marveled.

Mr. Greenberg's memos, spoken through a fictional character Haimchinkel Malintz Anaynikal, are part of Wall Street lore, particularly one exhorting Bear Stearns employees to save paper clips. Mr. Anaynikal "is my kind of guy—cheap, smart, opinionated," Mr. Buffett said. "I just wish I'd met him earlier in life, when, in the foolishness of my youth, I used to discard paper clips. But it's never too late, and I now slavishly follow and preach his principles."

A typical memo from 1995 is short, sweet and to the point. "The media has been having a field day with the problems at Daiwa Bank. Quoting from Newsweek, 'It wasn't that the Daiwa dummies lost $1.1 billion; it is that they lied about it and dissed the Fed. It doesn't pay to get too arrogant.' This was not the first time nor will it be the last that we have seen what arrogance can lead to. This danger has been pointed out many times to all of us by Haimchinkel Malintz Anaynikal; it should be brought to the attention of our associates on a regular basis. Our job is to look out for arrogance and stomp on it every time we see its ugly head rearing up."

Warren J. Spector, executive vice president and head of fixed-income: Mr. Spector is widely viewed as Mr. Cayne's heir apparent. Besides his all-important role as head of the 1,440-member bond group, Mr. Spector is a member of the firm's executive and management and compensation committees. His bond role includes overseeing the firm's sales, trading and research, as well as related investment-banking securities, plus preferred stock. Mr. Spector also pioneered the firm's derivatives business. Mr. Spector joined Bear in 1983 in the government-bond department, and has spent his entire career at the firm.

Alan D. Schwartz, executive vice president and head of investment banking: Mr. Schwartz also is a senior managing director and member of the firm's executive and management and compensation committees. He joined Bear in 1976 as institutional sales manager in the firm's Dallas office; in 1979, he was named director of research, general partner and portfolio strategist. He assumed his current post in 1985 and became a senior managing director when the firm went public that year.

Mark E. Lehman, executive vice president and general counsel: Mr. Lehman also is a member of the firm's executive and operations committees. As chief counsel, he oversees Bear's legal and compliance departments. Mr. Lehman joined Bear in 1979 as an associate director of legal and compliance. He was made a limited partner in 1983 and general partner in 1985. Following the firm's incorporation that year, Mr. Lehman became general counsel and senior managing director in 1986. Before joining Bear, he had been a litigation lawyer at Merrill. He is a member of the Securities Industry Association's legal and compliance division and also is on the SIA's board of directors.

Kay Booth, senior managing director and head of stock research: Ms. Booth has responsibility for sixty-five analysts worldwide. She joined Bear in 1987 after working in the asset-management group at Shearson Lehman Brothers Inc.

Denis A. Bovin, senior managing director and vice chairman of investment banking: Mr. Bovin is a member of the management team that directs all of the firm's worldwide investment-banking operations, and has direct responsibility for a wide variety of the firm's key U.S. and international banking clients. Before joining Bear, Mr. Bovin spent more than twenty years at Salomon. In 1985, *Institutional Investor* magazine selected him as one of the nation's twelve outstanding investment bankers under age forty. In 1995, he was awarded the Defense Department's Medal for Distinguished Public Service, the highest honor that can be conferred on a civilian, for his "dedication and commitment to the men and women of the U.S. Armed Forces" and for his "vital and lasting contributions" to the Defense Department.

Peter D. Cherasia, senior managing director and head of financial analytics and structured transactions: Mr. Cherasia is responsible for the creation, structuring and issuance of all derivative bond products, including collateralized mortgage obligations and asset-backed bonds. He also serves as president of Bear Stearns Spain, Bear Stearns Belgium and Bear Stearns Philippines, among other posts. Before joining the firm in 1985, he was a senior software specialist for Digital Equipment Corp.

Barry J. Cohen, senior managing director and head of risk arbitrage: Before joining Bear, Mr. Cohen was a risk arbitrager at First Boston and a mergers-and-acquisitions lawyer at Davis Polk & Wardwell, a New York law firm.

Victor A. Cohn, senior managing director and head of stock capital markets: Mr. Cohn joined Bear in 1996 from UBS Securities, where he was a managing director, cohead of investment banking and head of that firm's capital-markets group. Previously, he had been head of global stock capital markets and syndicate at Salomon.

Wendy L. deMonchaux, senior managing director and head of global derivatives and bond-finance department: Ms. deMonchaux joined Bear in 1993 and founded Bear's derivatives group. She boasts a varied career in derivatives products, at First National Bank of Chicago, Drexel and Banque Indozuez.

David H. Glaser, senior managing director and cohead of domestic investment banking: Mr. Glaser is a generalist mergers banker involved in all types of M&A transactions. He is chairman of the firm's corporate finance operating committee and chairman of the firm's equity subcommittee. Mr. Glaser also is a member of the firm's principal activities subcommittee, the firm's commitment and valuation committees. Before joining Bear in 1985, he was an associate at the law firm of Skadden, Arps, Slate, Meagher & Flom, specializing in M&A.

Richard Harriton, president and chief operating officer of the firm's clearing subsidiary: Mr. Harriton is a member of Bear's operations, management and compensation, institutional credit and internal audit committees. Mr. Harriton serves on the American Stock Exchange's member firm advisory committee and the Big Board's competitive position advisory board. Before joining Bear in 1979, he was president of First Wall Street Settlement Corp., the former administrative and clearing arm of Loeb Rhoades.

Ronald M. Hersch, senior managing director and head of futures: Mr. Hersch joined Bear in 1992 after a long career as a trader at, among other firms, Loeb Rhoades, Hornblower & Co., where he established a metals trading department.

William Mitchell Jennings, senior managing director and global sales manager of international stock division: Mr. Jennings joined Bear in 1969 as a trainee. He became a limited partner in 1977 and general partner in 1981. He was promoted to senior managing director in 1985.

Daniel Keating, senior managing director and head of municipal operations: Mr. Keating is responsible for municipal sales, trading and underwriting, and is head of Bear's public-finance department. He joined the firm in 1975 as a municipal underwriter and was made senior managing director in 1985.

Mark Kurland, senior managing director and head of asset management: Mr. Kurland also is chief investment officer and equities chief at the firm's asset-management unit. He joined Bear in 1991 as director of global research. Previously, he had been cohead of institutional stock and research chief at Mabon, Nugent & Co.

Bruce M. Lisman, senior managing director and head of global stock group: Mr. Lisman also is a senior managing director and member of the firm's management and compensation committee. He joined Bear in 1984 as research chief; in 1987, he assumed his current post, which includes the sales, trading and research departments.

Anthony J. Magro, senior managing director and head of mergers and acquisitions: Mr. Magro also is a member of Bear's valuation committee. Before joining the firm in 1992, he was an M&A banker at Kidder, Peabody & Co. and Dillon Read.

Jeffrey A. Mayer, senior managing director and head of mortgage-backed department: Mr. Mayer joined Bear in 1989 as a senior mortgage trader on the CMO desk. Before Bear, he had been senior mortgage trader at Merrill.

Gary McLoughlin, senior managing director, government-bond department: Mr. McLoughlin joined Bear in 1993 as a member of the firm's government-bond group. Before then, he was a trader at First Boston and Merrill.

Michael Minikes, treasurer: Mr. Minikes also is a senior managing director and member of the firm's operations committee. Mr. Minikes, who joined Bear in 1978, also is credited with having helped build Bear's extensive clearing network and with bringing the firm into the banking business.

William J. Montgoris, chief operating officer: Mr. Montgoris also is a senior managing director overseeing the accounting, benefits, communications, corporate communications, financial reporting, information services, marketing, office services, personnel, purchasing, recruiting and travel departments. He also is on Bear's operations and management and compensation committees. Before joining Bear in 1979, Mr. Montgoris was CFO at Blyth Eastman Dillon, and previously had managed the audit staff at Coopers & Lybrand. He serves on the board of St. John's University.

Donald R. Mullen Jr., senior managing director and head of high-yield and bankruptcy, high-grade corporate bond and emerging-markets debt departments: Mr. Mullen joined Bear in 1991 from Salomon. He is credited with bolstering Bear's junk-bond and bankruptcy business. Previously, Mr. Mullen had been a vice president at Drexel and First Boston.

Craig M. Overlander, senior managing director: Mr. Overlander heads Bear's global bond institutional sales group, supervising more than two hundred employees. He has been a member of the firm's bond sales group since joining Bear in 1982.

Aldo Parcesepe, senior managing director and head of OTC department: Mr. Parcesepe has more than thirty years' experience in the trading of small stocks. He joined Bear in 1979 and was promoted to senior managing director in 1988. Before Bear, he was an OTC trader at Allen & Co. He serves on the Securities Industry Association's trading committee.

Lewis A. Sachs, senior managing director and head of global capital markets: Mr. Sachs joined Bear in 1985 and is on the firm's board. As head of capital markets, Mr. Sachs oversees all U.S. and international bond-financing activities. He also serves on the executive committee of the Public Securities Association's corporate-bond division.

Daniel Scotto, senior managing director and director of corporate bond research: Mr. Scotto oversees the firm's credit analysts covering a variety of

In the Beginning . . .

Bear dates back to 1923, when it was formed as a small partnership that focused on stock trading. Ten years later, the legendary Salim "Cy" Lewis joined the firm from Salomon Brothers and transformed it into an institutional-bond player. Even in its early days, the firm was contrarian and opportunistic. Bear entered the arbitrage business in 1940 because Mr. Lewis had an instinct that something was about to happen in railroads. Mr. Lewis deduced that New York City was about to "take over" the IRT and BMT lines. In exchange for their stock, shareholders were to receive unwanted New York City bonds. Anticipating an opportunity, Mr. Lewis first bought both IRT and BMT stock and made a market in New York City bonds that later soared in value, reaping the firm big profits. Bear eventually moved aggressively into trading large blocks of stock, becoming an industry powerhouse.

But Mr. Lewis tended to hold onto every stock he bought. This led to a famous confrontation with Mr. Greenberg in the early 1960s. Mr. Greenberg told the intimidating Mr. Lewis he believed it was bad business practice to refuse to take a loss. Mr. Lewis listened, and relented. "That confrontation marked a turning point both in the career of Alan Greenberg and the future of Bear Stearns," according to a case study of the firm prepared in 1993 by Dialectics Inc.

In 1985, Bear became one of the industry's first publicly traded firms, with its shares listed on the New York Stock Exchange. In 1988 the firm moved its headquarters out of the Wall Street area to midtown Manhattan on Park Avenue.

The firm long has prized making rapid-fire decisions. But this sense of urgency has spread beyond Bear's trading floor. Delays and dawdling are unacceptable. Meetings are expected to start on time and end quickly. Even the festivities honoring Mr. Greenberg's forty years with the firm were over in fourteen minutes. Phone calls are expected to be returned within ten minutes, if possible. "When a phone rings, it should be answered promptly—if you keep a client waiting, they will and probably should call our competition," Mr. Greenberg said in a 1991 memo.

■

companies and industries. For several years, he has been an *Institutional Investor* All-America First Team analyst. Before joining Bear in 1994, he was with Donaldson, Lufkin & Jenrette Securities and L.F. Rothschild.

David M. Solomon, senior managing director and cohead of domestic investment banking: Mr. Solomon serves on the firm's commitment committee. Before joining Bear in 1991, he worked at Salomon and Drexel Burnham Lambert Inc. in various junk-bond posts.

Robert M. Steinberg, senior managing director and cohead of risk arbitrage: Mr. Steinberg also is chairman of Bear's institutional credit committee and is a member of the firm's management and compensation committee. He joined the firm in the risk-arbitrage department in 1971, became a general partner in 1977, and was made a senior managing director in 1985.

Jeffrey Urwin, senior managing director and head of international investment banking, excluding Asia: Mr. Urwin joined Bear in 1996 as a member of the firm's investment-banking group. Before Bear, he worked at Lehman Brothers and Midland Bank PLC in London.

Eli Wachtel, senior managing director, international stock trading and strategic structured transactions: Mr. Wachtel joined Bear in 1983 as a member of both the international-stock trading and strategic-structured transactions groups. Previously, he had been general partner at Bedford Partners.

LEHMAN BROTHERS INC.

REACHING TO RECAPTURE ITS FORMER GLORY

Independent, but with Limited Clout

When Moody's Investors Service Inc. gave Lehman Brothers Inc. an upbeat credit-rating review in February 1995, Lehman's trading floor erupted in cheers. Lehman officials reveled in a raucous celebration that night at Manhattan's swank Hudson River Club. There were high-fives all around, and with good reason: In affirming the ratings on Lehman's debt, the credit-rating concern was saying to the world that Lehman was a top-notch Wall Street player.

But the partying didn't last long. In a rare turnabout a month later, Moody's stunned Lehman by abruptly downgrading the firm's debt ratings. Why the about-face? Moody's said the brokerage business, which then was in a slump, wouldn't recover as quickly as it had believed. "This operating environment may lead Lehman to take additional risks to generate adequate returns," Moody's said. The move made it more expensive for Lehman to borrow funds for its daily operations. It wasn't only a financial blow; Moody's move suggested that Lehman wasn't quite ready for prime time on Wall Street. Moody's rated Lehman's debt Baa-1, lower than rivals Morgan Stanley, Dean Witter (A-1), Merrill Lynch (Aa-3) and Bear Stearns and Salomon Smith Barney (A-2).

"Symbolically, I didn't like it at all," said Richard Fuld, Lehman's chairman and chief executive officer. "It was another stake in the ground that we had to get over."

In late 1997, Lehman received a bit of a boost when IBCA, a European-based ratings concern, raised the firm's short-term ratings after solid progress in Lehman's efforts to increase earnings and cut costs. But that isn't likely to happen at Moody's anytime soon. Though Moody's credits Lehman with turning to higher-margin businesses and cutting costs, "the firm is still challenged," said Moody's analyst Haig Nargesian, in late 1997. "It's largely fixed income, though they're making some very interesting progress on the equity side."

Despite an impressive pedigree, Lehman Brothers remains a second-tier player on Wall Street with limited clout. Its 1997 net income of $647 million, a Lehman record, still was less than half the income of competitors such as Merrill Lynch & Co, and Morgan Stanley, Dean Witter and Salomon Smith Barney. Long a force in bonds, Lehman must beef up its presence in stock trading and stock underwriting, and build more stable sources of income to fall back on in bad times. And Lehman continues to absorb expenses that most firms of its size avoid. For instance, it pays rival Bear Stearns Cos. more than $20 million a year for the task of processing Lehman's own trades.

And data from a table prepared for a budget meeting in early 1997 showed an amazing fifteen business lines that Lehman budgeted to show a loss in 1997. As important, the table disclosed that a mere seven businesses accounted for nearly three-quarters of Lehman's net income. Lehman declined to comment.

All this has made it difficult for Lehman to regain some of its former grandeur. Once widely respected on Wall Street, Lehman Brothers Kuhn Loeb Inc. was so focused on client service that "if your phone rang three times you'd get your hand chopped off," T. Christopher Pettit, the late Lehman veteran, once recalled. But the venerable Wall Street investment bank, founded in 1850, was bought by American Express in 1984 after a bitter internal fight for control between the securities firm's traders and investment bankers. After the American Express union foundered, Lehman was spun off in 1994 only to suffer lagging returns amid thin management and relatively heavy turnover.

The issue for Lehman now is whether it can realize its ambitions to rise beyond being just a niche player on the Street. Lehman's Mr. Fuld likes to explain how the firm seeks to expand by scrawling two lists on a piece of paper—Lehman clients on the left and Lehman products on the right. Then he drew boxes in between, representing new clients and products the firm needs to grow. "My job is to fill in as many boxes in the middle [as I can]," Mr. Fuld said. Mr. Fuld brushed aside suggestions that Lehman can't compete with the likes of Wall Street's preeminent investment banks such as Goldman, Sachs & Co. and Morgan Stanley. Though Mr. Fuld conceded Lehman "can't be all things to all people," he said the firm must compete on many fronts to succeed. "At the end of the day, clients don't want one (firm) for Asia, one for Europe and one for equities," he said.

Lehman has started to show some signs of progress. In 1997, the firm's mergers-and-acquisitions group completed 120 U.S. deals totaling $135 billion, for a nearly 15 percent market share. In 1996 Lehman was involved in forty-two cross-border merger deals, and in twenty-eight transactions valued at more than $1 billion each. Among the blue-chip companies the firm advised that year were General Motors Corp., BankAmerica Corp. and Loral Corp. Lehman also advised Hoechst AG, one of the world's largest producers of chemicals and drugs, on a series of acquisitions and other deals.

In the past few years, Lehman has cut its compensation to about 51 percent of net revenue, down from 55 percent in 1992. Its return-on-equity has risen amid frenzied activity in the stock and bond markets. Lehman's net revenue per employee surged to an average $488,000 in 1997 from $304,000 in 1994. And in the past few years, the firm has cut more than $250 million of costs from its expense base and has slashed its bloated head count to 7,600 from 9,400.

A big part of the expense cuts came when Lehman asked many "high-ticket" employees with paychecks of between $300,000 and $500,000 a year to leave. Few areas at the firm were spared the ax. In a 1994 memo, Lehman said it had spent $12 million a year on company cabs—including more than $1.2 million for "waiting time" and more than $1.3 million for using car-phone services.

"Quite frankly, as a Firm, we are a disaster when it comes to car service," according to the memo, written by Robert Genirs, then a managing director referred to internally as Lehman's "cost-control czar." Mr. Genirs also complained in the memo about seeing corporate limousines "lined up in droves" in front of Lehman's downtown Manhattan headquarters well before 8 P.M., which is when employees were allowed to start using the car service.

The firm also slashed the number of outside law firms it used to handle its litigation docket, and it began to order pencils from a single vendor, as opposed to several stationery outlets. Among other signs of the times around Lehman were notices tacked up around the office exhorting employees not to spend money the way they used to. The notices read: "Don't Just Accept It! Rethinkit!"

The cost-cutting effort didn't come without controversy. Even as Lehman slashed jobs and perks, it was busy throwing money at other areas. The firm courted some internal controversy by renting out Giants Stadium at a cost of nearly $200,000 so its bond salesforce could throw footballs with New York Giants players and have field-goal kicking contests. When Lehman was spun off from American Express in 1994, the firm held a party for every New York employee of the firm, hastily arranged in the posh rotunda of Manhattan's World Financial Center. The cost: tens of thousands of dollars. The firm also has spent heavily to take its bond group to the Museum of Natural History.

The big question now is how to raise Lehman's revenue line. Though the firm's bond and investment-banking divisions have thrived, Lehman's stock and asset-management divisions have suffered. Between 1993 and 1996, for instance, Lehman's stock sales and trading group had pretax losses totaling more than $1 billion, according to Sanford C. Bernstein & Co.

A bigger problem is that Lehman lacks the ability to generate big profits in all markets. The simple reason: It has no recurring streams of fee income. Rivals Merrill and Bear grind out profits in all market cycles, for instance, because of their huge asset-management and trade-processing divisions, respectively. Lehman has neither. Indeed, since the sale of the firm's Shearson brokerage and asset-management division to Primerica Corp. in 1993, Lehman has been left with a puny presence in the lucrative money-management area.

Lehman's asset-management group had pretax losses every year between 1993 and 1996.

Meantime, analysts wonder whether the firm's newfound independence will last long. For the past few years, investors have marked Lehman as among the Wall Street firms most vulnerable to being gobbled up by a big financial institution. Indeed, several foreign firms, including Union Bank of Switzerland and Dresdner Bank, have looked at Lehman's books and passed. In 1995 and 1996, Lehman quietly has explored the possibility of merging with Donaldson, Lufkin & Jenrette Securities Corp. and Salomon Brothers Inc. The informal overtures went nowhere. The pressure to merge only has risen with 1997's megamergers creating Morgan Stanley, Dean Witter, Discover & Co., Salomon Smith Barney Holdings Inc. and the union between Alex. Brown Inc. and Bankers Trust New York Corp. For now, Lehman executives profess to be happy with the firm's independence. In early 1997, they predicted that there wouldn't likely be any deals on the table any time soon.

Still, Lehman continued to be the subject of rumored takeover speculation throughout 1997. At various times, the talk was that Lehman would be acquired by Chase Manhattan Corp., Union Bank of Switzerland, BankAmerica Corp. NationsBank Corp., J. P. Morgan or Deutsche Bank AG, among others. But Lehman officials are adamant: The firm wants to remain single; repeat: single.

Perhaps until the right mate comes along.

Better Returns, but a Regulatory Stumble

After several years of subpar returns, Lehman finally put up solid profit numbers in 1996 and 1997. The firm posted net income of $416 million in 1996 and $647 million in 1997, and its return on equity jumped to 14 and 17 percent, respectively, in 1996 and 1997, thanks partly to the raging bull market. The robust results stemmed from across the board strength in its trading, stock and bond underwriting, and merger-advisory businesses. The record 1997 profit came despite losses of about $70 million trading in Asian markets in the fourth quarter, according to a person familiar with the situation.

One of Lehman's most high-profile trading gains in 1997 was selling its investment in Manhattan's One Times Square building, where the New Year's Eve ball has been dropped for nearly a century. Just two years after buying the international landmark for $27 million—and being criticized for overpaying—Lehman sold the property for some $110 million. The transaction underscored Lehman's strength in the real-estate business, including the mortgage-backed securities, collateralized mortgage bonds, and real estate investment trusts.

The firm's 12 percent growth in net revenue in 1996 nevertheless trailed the growth of more than 35 percent for rivals Goldman and Salomon, notes Standard & Poor's Corp. And "pretax returns on equity of 28% or more (again, except for Lehman) reflect the sweet spot of the cycle," S&P noted in a 1997 article on securities firms. The question is how Lehman will fare in a down market.

Yet Lehman did show some positive momentum. The firm has made strides in keeping payroll costs under control; Lehman's compensation accrual of 50.7 percent of net revenues for the past eleven quarters kept it on par with that of competitors. The firm kept non-personnel expenses to below 26 percent of net revenue, which is at or below some rivals; this was accomplished partly by slashing these costs by more than $250 million. The result: a reduction in Lehman's break-even point, since fixed costs now account for less than half the firm's net revenues.

Lehman took an $84 million pretax charge in 1996 to jettison or slash some of its less productive businesses. These included energy trading and its metals operations in the United States, Europe and Asia; and the consolidation of its foreign-exchange, municipal-bond, Asian bond and brokerage businesses. The 1996 charge freed Lehman up to make investments in areas that it believes offer the highest margins: investment banking, stock, high yield bond, derivatives and merchant-banking activities.

Meantime, the National Association of Securities Dealers tagged one of Lehman's lower-margin businesses with a high-profile sanction. The NASD in 1997 censured and fined Lehman and Smith Barney $250,000 each and ordered the two firms to pay a total of more than $5.6 million in refunds to investors who were overcharged when they redeemed nonproprietary mutual funds from the firms. More than 15,700 accounts were affected by the improper practice of charging commissions when none were allowed, the NASD said.

"This case underscores the need for customers to inspect their trading confirmations closely, and to report any suspected problems immediately," said Mary Schapiro, president of the NASD's regulatory arm. Lehman and Smith Barney agreed to the settlement without admitting or denying the NASD's findings.

Lehman suffered a bigger embarrassment on the local level. In 1997, Martin Harding, a managing director and cohead of the firm's asset-backed securities group, pleaded guilty in a Manhattan state court to tax fraud and agreed to pay New York City $220,000 in back taxes and penalties. As a result of the plea, New York City reviewed whether or not to hire Lehman to lead-manage a securitization of delinquent property taxes, a New York finance commissioner said. The deal involved packaging into bonds expected cash flows from the collection of unpaid property taxes. (Lehman ultimately was awarded the mandate.) Mr. Harding declined to comment at the time. In the end, it worked out for Lehman: The firm priced the deal in the summer of 1997, and it "sold well," a spokesman said.

Lehman also was among the firms hardest hit in the settlement announced in late 1997 requiring thirty Nasdaq dealers to pay a total of $910 million to investors to end a high-profile class-action suit. Lehman agreed, without admitting wrongdoing, to pay about $80 million to settle the matter, filed in a New York federal court, alleging that the firms colluded to keep "spreads"—or the difference between a dealer's selling price and buying price—in Nasdaq stocks unfairly wide from May 1989 to May 1994.

Moreover, a federal judge in December 1997 accused Lehman of having "played ostrich" in executing highly suspicious options trades for accused insider trader Emanuel Pinez in Centennial Technologies Inc. stock in February of that year. At the time of the rebuke, Mr. Pinez, the former chief executive of Centennial, was in jail awaiting trial on charges of insider trading and issuing fraudulent financial statements. U.S. District Judge Patti B. Saris in Boston said Lehman "had actual knowledge, which upon reasonable inquiry, would have clearly revealed Pinez's violation of the securities laws."

The comments came as Judge Saris granted an SEC motion to freeze Mr. Pinez's assets. The freeze denied Lehman access to $4.7 million of what the SEC maintains are "illicit profits" from insider trading. Lehman asserted a claim to the money as repayment for margin loans it had made to Mr. Pinez. Attorneys for Lehman in Boston declined to comment. Juan Marcelino, district commissioner of the SEC's Boston office, said the judge's statements "are very significant. The court made it clear that brokerage firms can't turn a blind eye to the suspicious activities of its clients and expect to profit from such activities."

Investment Banking:
Growing Prowess and Profits

Lehman's investment-banking group bolstered its presence in 1996 and 1997. Lehman advised U.S. companies on $135.95 billion in announced mergers or acquisitions, for a 14.8 percent market share—a fifth-place ranking on Wall Street. Over the past several years, investment banking has generated about 21 percent of the firm's net revenue, and about 45 percent of pretax profit along with healthy pretax margins of about 30 percent, according to Sanford C. Bernstein. In 1997, Lehman was an adviser to MCI Communications Corp. in its planned $37 billion merger with WorldCom Inc., to US West's $16.1 billion spin-off of its cable business US West Media Group to shareholders, and to Lockheed Martin Corp. in its planned $11.8 billion purchase of Northrop Grumman Corp. In 1996, Lehman boasted some big M&A coups, including advising Loral Corp. on its $12 billion sale to Lockheed Martin Corp. and the simultaneous spin-off of Loral Space & Communications Ltd. to Loral shareholders.

Still, Lehman's Mr. Fuld is looking for more of what he calls "8 A.M. calls" for its banking services. The way Mr. Fuld sees it, clients that call Lehman that early have awakened with a problem and want the firm to solve it; if the firm gets a call at noon, clients already have thought of a solution and simply want the firm to execute it. Translation: far less challenge, and a much smaller fee.

Mr. Fuld broadened the firm's banking base in 1997, increasing staffing by 14 percent, or one hundred professionals, and expanding Lehman's push to call on "middle-market" clients that aren't among the Fortune 500. Among the areas the firm is beefing up are its financial institutions, natural resources/utilities and industrial/consumer banking segments. While Lehman still doesn't have the client depth of, say, Goldman or Morgan, "we have made some serious headway," Mr. Fuld says.

In 1996, for instance, Lehman lead-managed the largest commercial mortgage-backed securities deal ever: a $1.9 billion securitization for the Confederation Life Insurance Co., an insolvent Canadian insurance company. As part of the deal, Lehman sold $1.6 billion in investment-grade bonds placed with nearly one hundred clients—several times the typical investor base for a mortgage deal. Mr. Fuld won the deal for Lehman with typical brashness. In a face-to-face meeting to get the business, Mr. Fuld was challenged by Victor Palmieri, who was assigned the role of disposing the ailing insurer's assets. After predicting to Mr. Palmieri that the deal was just the first of a series of public issues by Confederated, Mr. Fuld said he told him: "If I blow this one, you can laugh at me. . . . But I don't care about this one—I'm going for the next one. Give me a shot to do it." Lehman won the mandate to manage the deal, and later was retained as financial adviser for the insurer's investment portfolio, as well as to design and execute a reinvestment program for the proceeds of the mortgage-backed bond deal. Later, Lehman's M&A group also was retained to advise on the possible sale of Confederation's related businesses.

Lehman played a major role in one of 1997's biggest stock sales in Latin America in a year. The firm helped lead a group of global coordinators underwriting a $1.07 billion international stock offering for Uniao de Bancos Brasileiros SA and its holding company, Unibanco Holdings SA. Despite deals such as these, Lehman still isn't recognized as a leading player in stock-related businesses. Indeed, Lehman executives privately have bristled as other firms, such as Donaldson, Lufkin & Jenrette Inc., BT Alex. Brown, Salomon Smith Barney Holdings Inc., NationsBanc Montgomery Securities were described variously in the media in 1997 as "top IPO houses," "major equity underwriters" and "stock powerhouses." At the same time, Lehman's stock activities have been dubbed "embryonic," "lagging," and even "second-rate."

Lehman spokesman William Ahearn noted in 1997 that the firm ranked higher in managing stock issues and IPOs, ahead of "a number of top IPO houses, major equity underwriters, and stock powerhouses, such as J. P. Morgan, DLJ, Alex. Brown, Montgomery Securities and Furman Selz." True, Lehman's bond rankings exceed those in stocks. But, Mr. Ahearn argued, "it should be apparent from the numbers that those rankings don't reflect a *weakness* in equities, but rather a significant *strength* in debt."

Mergers-advisory work, another high-margin core business, heated up for Lehman in 1997. Among many other deals, Lehman advised CalEnergy Co. in its $3.3 billion offer for New York State Electric & Gas Corp. Lehman also was involved in two other large transactions in the summer of 1997: The firm is representing Pennzoil Co. in its defense of Union Pacific Resources Group's $6.4 billion unsolicited offer. And Lehman advised Tandem Computers on its sale to Compaq Computer, valued at about $3 billion.

Lehman has had success turning its banking relationships into merchant-banking investments, where the firm pools its capital with others to invest. For instance, Lehman put up $60 million in partnership with Loral, a longtime banking client, to invest in a new business consisting of ten former Loral divisions. In Lehman's 1989 merchant banking fund, ten of the thirteen investments made were sourced through existing investment-banking clients, and generated an annual return of 39 percent. What's clear is that merchant banking has been lucrative for the firm; it generated more than $400 million in net revenues between 1993 and 1996.

Lehman in September 1997 closed on a $2 billion merchant-banking fund. Of this amount, Lehman invested about $650 million of its own cash. In a speech at New York's Metropolitan Club, Steven Berger, then Lehman's merchant-banking chief, described how the fund-raising process evolved over a year. "We held over five hundred meetings with domestic and international institutions, corporations, individuals and their representatives. We were faced with the pleasant predicament of being oversubscribed and the awkward task of turning certain investors away," Mr. Berger said. The fund, which originally sought to raise $1.5 billion, has a five-year life.

Merchant banking is one of Lehman's four "core" firm-wide product areas; the firm has been in the business since the mid-1980s. The firm's first institutional merchant-banking fund, Lehman Brothers Merchant Banking Portfolio Partnership L.P., closed in 1989 with $1.3 billion in commitments from thirty-four investors in the United States, Europe and Asia/Pacific. The 1989 fund "has had an excellent investment performance with annual rates of return just under forty percent," Mr. Berger said in September 1997.

Lehman is one of several big investment banks with mega-funds of this sort. Goldman, Sachs & Co. and Morgan Stanley, Dean Witter Discover & Co., among others, have had a strong presence in the merchant-banking game. And Credit Suisse First Boston has rejoined the merchant-banking business after soured loans nearly crippled the firm in 1989 and 1990.

There has been controversy. On the final trading day in 1996, Lehman priced an unusual last-minute asset-backed securities deal that vaulted the firm above leader Merrill Lynch & Co. in asset-backed underwriting for the year that had some rivals crying foul. Competitors accused Lehman of pricing the $2.08 billion deal—that "resecuritized" bonds by repackaging already publicly traded asset-backed securities—just to win the asset-backed underwriting race.

"The truth of the matter is that everybody has done similar deals," Lehman's Mr. Fuld argued. He said Lehman had no remorse, despite the controversy: "It is fair."

Meaty Bond Trading but Scraps for Stocks

Lehman's bond business clearly is the firm's engine. Bond sales and trading have accounted for just over half Lehman's earnings over the past several years, and pretax margins have approached 30 percent, according to Sanford C. Bernstein. These margins would have been higher had Lehman not been so late to the lucrative business for bond derivatives. Mr. Fuld said the firm didn't have the infrastructure to develop a big derivatives operation in the past years, but added: "It's a huge part of the business today." He put revenues from derivatives trading at more than $700 million across the firm, and said it "better get well over $1 billion."

Unlike Salomon Brothers, Lehman doesn't generate much income from proprietary bets for the house account. Proprietary trading for the most part is like a "flip of the coin," which Mr. Fuld said he would rather do in Las Vegas. "We don't really play that game." Rather, Lehman tries to snare fees trading huge amounts of government and corporate bonds, among other instruments, for clients. "We're a customer-flow house," Mr. Fuld said.

Proprietary trading accounted for just 14 percent of net revenue in 1996 and 1997, 9 percent in 1995 and 6 percent in 1994. Now, Lehman wants to "selectively enhance" this risky trading strategy "by upgrading staff," according to an internal document. And it's not as if Lehman doesn't put its own cash at risk. A few years back, Lehman made a killing of more than $100 million when it used its capital to buy a bundle of battered real-estate loans at a steep discount to par value from Westinghouse Electric Corp., then securitized and resold the loans at a fat profit. When Mr. Fuld presented the plan to the firm's board, he said he initially promised a 22 percent return on capital, and was asked: Can you really do that? His response: If I do only that, "you should shoot me." Thinking of the deal, Mr. Fuld in 1997 sat back in his chair, and said: "It was one of the greatest trades we ever made."

The big disappointment for Lehman has been its slack stock operations. Its stock sales and trading business has generated about 22 percent of net revenues during the past few years, but has lost a significant amount of money, according to Sanford C. Bernstein. To help turn around the business, Mr. Fuld appointed three of his best executives—Joseph Gregory, Michael McKeever and Stephen Lessing—to run the equity group. "I took my three best guys, and said: 'Figure it out and set it straight. You're the guys I trust.' " Mr. Fuld said the move showed Lehman was "serious" about becoming a player in the stock business. Analysts watching Lehman predicted in 1996 that the new infrastructure and management will significantly reduce losses, but probably won't produce profits, stemming from projections of slow growth industry-wide.

Lehman's stock business has had some success. In 1996, Lehman beat out rivals to sell a $620 million block of shares in France's state-oil company as part of the government's privatization. After winning the bid late on a Tuesday night, Lehman (in partnership with Credit Lyonnais) placed the securities with investors all over the world within twelve hours. "The record-sized trade . . . underscores the Firm's market making, execution, and distribution capabilities," Lehman crowed in an internal memo.

And in 1997, Lehman was a player in a trading trend that picked up steam in the bull market: so-called blind bids. That's when Wall Street program traders commit their firms' capital—sometimes as much as $1 billion—to buy huge baskets of various stocks from big fund managers on a few hours' notice—and the traders don't even know what stocks they're getting. For Wall Street traders, the deals offered a new way to profit on market fluctuations. The trend has been fueled by growing competition among traders as well as increasingly sophisticated trading technology.

These blind bids to both buy and sell massive portfolios have surged in popularity as many fund managers, under pressure to keep pace with market indexes, seek ways to maximize their profit on trades. Because funds trade such big chunks of stocks, they can run the risk of pushing up prices when they buy and sending them lower when they sell. The blind-bid transactions allow managers to get a guaranteed price for their stocks, eliminating at least some market risk.

Concerns among fund managers about market risk while completing trades have risen as stock prices have become more volatile throughout 1997, said Ravi Singh, head of Lehman's global portfolio trading. "The clients see a big benefit to getting [a trade] done entirely in one day, and the only way is to have a broker bid on the basket and promise the close."

Here's how one blind bid worked for Lehman in 1997. At about 2 P.M. one day, Lehman's program desk received a ten-page facsimile from a money manager wanting to sell several hundred stocks valued at about $500 million from an index portfolio at the same time it wanted to buy less than a hundred stocks also valued at about $500 million for an active portfolio. The money manager didn't name the stocks, but he did describe how closely the two baskets tracked the Standard & Poor's 500 index, how liquid the stocks were, which industry groups they belonged to, and the market capitalization of each company's stock. Lehman traders analyzed the fax for about twenty minutes before submitting a blind bid of less than ten cents a share as the upfront charge.

Shortly after the 4 P.M. close of the stock market that day, Lehman learned it had won the trade, and the manager relayed the names of the stocks. Lehman traders set to work analyzing the stocks, to see how much of the trade it could match from internal inventory, whether it could use the stocks to generate or complement other trading business, and how much of the position it would like to get rid of immediately. Meanwhile, the actual transactions were completed in London and thus never appeared on the "tape" of regular U.S. stock-exchange transactions. Over the next week, Lehman program and block traders executed the trades necessary to eliminate most of the unwanted risk taken on with the position. (The risk, of course, is that the stocks the broker has bought from the money manager will drop in price before the broker can resell them.)

Asset-Management and Brokerage Disappointment

Lehman has missed the boat on Wall Street's big push toward gathering assets from small investors. The firm largely left the retail-brokerage and asset-management business with the sale of its Shearson brokerage division in 1993. The result hasn't been pretty: Lehman's brokerage and asset-management business lost money between 1993 and 1996, analysts said.

The firm's strategy is to aim for only the most well-heeled investors, and give others the boot. In an unusual move, Lehman in 1995 sold twenty thousand brokerage accounts with assets of $25,000 or less to rival Prudential for $1 million. Such large account transfers typically occur only when Wall Street firms are sold, go out of business or jettison their brokerage operations. "You don't make enough money for us, so we don't want you anymore—that's what Lehman is saying," said David Robbins, a securities lawyer and former arbitration chief at the American Stock Exchange. The move showed that Lehman "isn't making enough money off these clients."

Lehman suffered a blow in 1996 when Robert Lunn, the chief of brokerage and asset-management group, abruptly resigned after briefly bolstering the firm's presence. Mr. Lunn, a former executive at Morgan Stanley and member of Lehman's operating committee, had recruited a handful of big-producing brokers from Morgan Stanley, Goldman, First Boston and Salomon. Under Mr. Lunn, brokers' annual average production surged to about $800,000 from $470,000, and the unit's revenue rose more than 15 percent. "A lot of people came to Lehman because of Bob—he was *the* selling point . . ." one brokerage consultant said.

In the meantime, Mr. Fuld complained that Lehman's brokerage operations were losing money even though the firm had 480 brokers averaging $700,000 in annual commissions. So between mid-1995 and the end of 1996, Mr. Fuld got rid of 150 brokers who each were generating more than $500,000 in annual production because they were putting their interests before those of the firm. Now, Lehman's 250 brokers catering to private investors and midsized institutions average annual production of more than $2 million, thanks partly to the reassignment of seven hundred midsized corporate accounts from the firm's equity

Lehman Bros. Keeps Well-Heeled Clients; Others Get the Boot

* * *

With a Few Weeks' Notice, 20,000 Brokerage Accounts Sold to Rival Prudential

BY MICHAEL SICONOLFI
Staff Reporter of THE WALL STREET JOURNAL

NEW YORK—Lehman Brothers Inc., with just a few weeks' notice, is sending its small-fry clients to another pan.

Lehman, seeking to court only the most well-heeled individual investors, sold 20,000 brokerage accounts to rival Prudential Securities Inc. Terms of the unusual deal weren't disclosed. But the **Prudential Insurance Co. of America** unit paid $1 million for the accounts, people familiar with the transaction said. The move leaves Lehman with about 35,000 brokerage accounts, analysts say.

The deal calls for Lehman accounts with assets of $25,000 or less to be transferred to Prudential. Typically, such large account transfers occur only when Wall Street firms are sold, go out of business or jettison their brokerage operations.

"You don't make enough money for us, so we don't want you anymore—that's what Lehman is saying," says David Robbins, a securities lawyer and former arbitration chief at the American Stock Exchange. The move is an insult to small Lehman clients, Mr. Robbins says, and shows that Lehman "isn't making enough money off these clients."

The move is part of a broader push by the **Lehman Brothers Holdings** Inc. unit to upgrade its retail-brokerage division. Lehman largely has left the retail-brokerage business since the sale of its Shearson brokerage division two years ago. As part of its upgrading effort, Lehman has set a minimum of $1 million for new brokerage accounts; previously, there were no formal account-size minimums.

"We're not geared to service [smaller investors], and they're really better served elsewhere," says Robert Lunn, chief of Lehman's brokerage division. Many of Lehman's brokerage clients now are executives with more than $2 million to invest. "Of course, if the chairman's son" wants to open an account with far less cash, "we'll accommodate that," Mr. Lunn adds.

Prudential, for its part, has been scrambling to offset the loss of brokers and accounts during the past few years amid the fallout from its limited-partnership scandal. Prudential has lost many high-producing brokers and is expected to eventually pay a total of at least $1.5 billion to settle its partnership claims.

Prudential, the fifth-largest brokerage firm, with 6,000 brokers, has 2.3 million customer accounts. "We believe that our core strategy of developing well-informed relationships with individual investors will make this a smooth transition," says George Murray, president of Prudential Securities' consumer-markets group.

In a letter to clients dated yesterday, Lehman says the transfer will occur Sept. 22 "unless we receive written instructions from you directing an alternative disposition of your account prior to Sept. 8." The move was first disclosed in Wall Street Letter, a trade publication.

August 22, 1995

sales force (which sells stocks to institutional clients) to Lehman brokers. The result is that Lehman brokers now account for an average of about 15 percent of distribution of the firm's stock offerings, according to an internal document. And the unit finally has shown a modest profit. "We were close [to making money] in '96, and we're in the black today, although not a lot," Mr. Fuld said in mid-1997.

International: Growth, but Not Without Stumbles

Lehman has made strides in its international operations; it now boasts thirty-seven offices in twenty-three countries. Nearly 30 percent of its revenues in the mid-1990s have come from Europe and the Middle East; 12 percent of its revenues stemmed from its Asia Pacific operations. Lehman's international group now generates more than 40 percent of the firm's business, more than double that of several years ago. Between 1994 and 1996, Lehman generated more than $1 billion of revenues that "resulted from relationships with international clients and customers," the firm said.

The firm wants to further bolster its global activities because it fits into its broader emphasis on high-margin business lines. "In selected activities in certain markets, the spreads are big, it's a good business," Mr. Fuld said. "Money is being made there." In 1996, the firm scored a coup by lead-managing a $1.14 billion IPO for Compania Anonima Nacional Telefonos de Venezuela, that nation's primary telecommunications-services company.

Lehman boosted its staff in Asia. In June 1997, it hired eleven executives in Asia, including Credit Suisse First Boston's chief representative in Beijing, as part of a global push to boost businesses with high profit margins.

But there have been bumps, highlighting the risks in doing big global deals. Lehman was one of several Wall Street firms that sued Citic Shanghai Co., a Chinese government-owned investment firm, for failing in 1994 to meet margin calls amid rising losses mainly related to copper-futures trading. Margin calls require investors to immediately put up more cash and collateral to offset losses in their accounts. Four employees of Citic Shanghai subsequently were arrested, including the president and two traders.

The dispute underscored the concern among U.S. brokerage firms about the apparent propensity of some Chinese clients to walk away from trading losses. A few years ago, more than thirty foreign financial institutions urged Chinese authorities to help them recover some $600 million in loans paid to Chinese state industries. The urging worked, at least in the Citic case. In a symbolic victory for Lehman and the Street, in 1995 Citic settled its dispute, paying Lehman roughly $7 million to cover 100 percent of Citic's losses that were incurred trading copper futures on the London Metals Exchange. Lehman was diplomatic in a statement after the settlement. The firm said Citic remained an "extremely valued" client and praised Citic for what it called the "expeditious and highly professional manner" in which it resolved the dispute.

That wasn't Lehman's only squabble with Chinese clients, by a long shot. Lehman also filed legal claims against two Chinese trading firms for allegedly failing to repay loans totaling nearly $100 million from soured foreign-exchange and swap transactions. Those separate suits were filed in a New York federal court against Minmetals International Non-Ferrous Metals Trading Co. and China International United Petroleum Chemicals Co., or Unipec. The Unipec case was settled; the Minmetals action is pending.

Research

Lehman Brothers is struggling to emerge from the upheaval of the late 1980s and early 1990s that finally left it an independent entity in 1994. And within the ranks of its strategy and research operations, Jeffrey Applegate is pushing his way to the forefront of Wall Street strategists.

After working for one of Lehman's many predecessor firms, Mr. Applegate rejoined the investment dealer in the fall of 1995 from a post as chief strategist of what was then known as CS First Boston. Since that time, he's rapidly won a following among institutional investors, and has led *The Wall Street Journal*'s quarterly survey of strategists since the second quarter of 1996.

"I really begin my analysis of markets with economic policy," he said. "You need to go back and look at what has happened to markets at similar points in history when we've had secular disinflation. I think policy is the major driver of markets."

In fact, clients will find Mr. Applegate's fascination with policy, honed during a dozen years working for Wall Street firms as a Washington analyst, reflected in his investment newsletters. During the first half of 1997, his focus remained intensively on the Federal Reserve, measuring the likelihood of rising interest rates and evaluating the fallout on stock market, drawing comfort from the fact that the Fed traditionally hasn't acted preemptively.

Still, Mr. Applegate was one of the first strategists to trim his exposure to stocks in late 1996, cutting his recommended allocation to 65 percent from 70 percent. That call was partly a consequence of the surge in stock prices, which had left stocks relatively expensive compared to bonds, but also partly due to his anxiety about the fallout of a Fed interest rate increase.

But Lehman's new strategist wasn't always that canny. While he cut stock market exposure in early 1987 in his early days in New York as a strategist for E. F. Hutton, he responded to better-than-expected earnings that July by switching back again. The market peaked in August and plunged in October, leaving Mr. Applegate with a lasting respect for valuations.

"When you think prices are out of whack, you listen to your gut and follow through," he said in 1997. "I like to think that now I'm forty-seven, I won't get tricked like that again."

Still, Mr. Applegate is convinced that the current business cycle of the 1990s is far from typical. That's a view he's formed by tracking the impact of fiscal and monetary policy on everything from industrial production to consumption. Working closely with Lehman's chief economist, Steve Slifer, he has recommended stocks of companies that produce the capital goods on which companies are spending money, including technology. "This has been an unusual business cycle, and we could only be in the middle innings of the game," he said. "The way we've restructured global trade, and ended the cold war, means we're in a completely different world." The result, he said, is a focus on large multinational stocks that he believes will benefit most from global economic growth.

Mr. Applegate is one of several new recruits to Lehman betting that the firm has the ability to make itself into one of the top five players in all aspects of the stock market, from corporate finance to trading and research. "That's why I came back," he said.

So far, the firm remains better known for its trading skills than its ability to generate a large quantity of informed research. In *The Wall Street Journal*'s 1996 all-star analysts' survey, Lehman ranked thirteenth in the all-star survey, with twelve analysts on the all-star list, none of whom were top-ranked that year. By 1997, it had slid further, to twenty-first, with only nine all-stars.

But moves are afoot to boost exposure. Raids on Salomon, Merrill Lynch and Credit Suisse First Boston have brought top analysts in specialty finance, technology and energy to Lehman, and the firm plans to continue the hiring binge. It has also picked up some talent from Salomon Brothers Inc.

"Our stock operations haven't enjoyed the success that the debt side has," acknowledged Joe Amado, managing director in charge of U.S. equity research. "So there's a big push on. For Lehman to succeed, it needs to enhance this business and research is a part of that."

As Joe Gregory was brought over from running Lehman's bond operations to take charge of boosting the flagging equity dealings, Mr. Amado followed suit, relinquishing his role as head of high yield bond research to take the stock research job.

"It's not as though it was a disaster, especially given all the changes that Lehman's been through and the fact that the firm's had to completely change its approach to stock research as it's gone through all these stages of existence," he said.

Lehman's People

Richard S. Fuld Jr., chairman and chief executive officer: Mr. Fuld joined Lehman in 1969 and worked his way up the ranks. In 1974 he was asked to run the REIT desk, and his first question was, "What's a REIT?" (real-estate investment trust). Mr. Fuld attended the New York Institute of Finance and found out, then went to graduate school at night, receiving his MBA from New York University after a thesis on REIT financing. Mr. Fuld's blunt ways have earned him the nickname of "Gorilla"; he keeps a stuffed gorilla in his office.

Mr. Fuld is a hands-on boss; he still signs off on big trades and negotiates deals for the firm. Colleagues marvel at his knack for winning, both at bond trading and outside Wall Street. One Lehman partner once told an associate, "If Dick Fuld were in front of you on line to buy a lottery ticket, hand him your $2 because that bastard is going to win."

Mr. Fuld was elected chief executive officer in late 1993, and became chairman in April 1994 when Lehman went public. He has been a Lehman director since 1984, and previously had been president and chief operating officer. At Shearson Lehman Brothers, a predecessor firm, Mr. Fuld was president and co-chief executive officer. He currently is a board member of the New York Stock Exchange.

Fuld, Richard
CEO-Lehman Bros.

John L. Cecil, chief administrative officer: Mr. Cecil is a managing director and a member of Lehman's operating committee. He joined the firm from McKinsey & Co., the big consulting firm, where he was a director. On the big-picture side, Mr. Cecil oversaw the reduction of Lehman's expense base by well over $300 million in the years after it became a public company. He also is known to get involved in the nitty-gritty of Lehman's affairs; a couple of years back, he rejected a proposed Lehman annual report because the document's blue color was too similar to the report prepared by rival Morgan Stanley, colleagues recall. (The Lehman annual ultimately was printed with a green cover.)

Thomas Russo, chief legal officer: Mr. Russo is a managing director and member of Lehman's corporate-management committee. He wears a variety of hats at the firm, including head of its corporate-advisory division with responsibilities for legal, compliance, internal audit, corporate communications, investor and government relations. Before joining Lehman in 1993, Mr. Russo was a corporate partner at Cadwalader, Wickersham & Taft, a law firm where his practice covered financial markets and general corporate practice. A member of the American Bar Association, Mr. Russo serves on the executive council of its futures-regulation committee and advisory committee. He also is on the board of trustees of the Futures Industry Institute. He has appeared several times in the *National Law Journal* listing of "100 Most Influential Lawyers in America."

Joseph M. Gregory, cohead of global equities division: Mr. Gregory is a managing director and member of Lehman's operating committee. He joined the firm in 1974 as a commercial-paper trader. In the 1980s he held a variety of management positions, including head of mortgage-backed securities, matched book, and money market/commercial paper groups. Mr. Gregory was named cohead of the firm's fixed income group in 1991 and a managing director in 1992. He was named to his current post in 1996; he is in charge of the firm's overall stock business.

Jeremiah Callaghan, chief of operations and technology: Mr. Callaghan is a managing director and member of the firm's operating committee. Before joining Lehman, he held various senior posts in the securities-processing and operations groups of what is now First Data Corp. and Shearson Lehman Brothers. Previously, Mr. Callaghan was a senior managing director at Bear Stearns as well as a member of its management and operations committees.

Stephen M. Lessing, cohead of global equity and fixed income division: Mr. Lessing is a managing director and member of Lehman's operating committee. He joined the firm in 1980 in money-market/government sales. He has held a variety of senior posts in money markets and national sales and was named cohead of fixed income in 1991. In 1996, Mr. Lessing assumed responsibility for global capital-markets sales and research and the private-client business, which focuses on high net-worth investors.

C. Daniel Tyree, chairman and CEO of Lehman Brothers Asia: Mr. Tyree is responsible for Lehman's Asia Pacific region businesses, including the firm's offices in Tokyo, Hong Kong and Singapore. Also a member of Lehman's operating committee, he assumed his current post in 1995. Before then, Mr. Tyree was chairman and chief executive of Lehman's European operations. Before joining Lehman in 1992, he was a managing director at Salomon Brothers and head of its high-yield business.

Bruce R. Lakefield, chairman and CEO of Lehman Brothers Europe: Mr. Lakefield is responsible for Lehman's activities in Europe and the Middle East. He also is a member of Lehman's operating committee. He joined Lehman in 1974 and held various positions in the firm's bond operations. Before joining Lehman, he was a corporate-bond trader at Smith Barney, where he graduated from the firm's MBA program.

Charles B. Hintz, chief financial officer: Mr. Hintz is a managing director and a member of Lehman's operating committee. He is responsible for, among other things, the firm's financial planning control, treasury and creditor and ratings-agency relations. Before joining Lehman, he was a managing director and treasurer at Morgan Stanley.

Bradley H. Jack, cohead of global investment banking/fixed-income division: Mr. Jack is a managing director and member of the firm's operating committee. He is in charge of fixed income origination, and cohead of investment banking, responsible for leveraged finance, Asian investment banking, and certain industry groups. He joined the firm in 1984 as an associate in the fixed-income division, and previously had been at Bank of America.

Michael F. McKeever, cohead of global investment banking/equity division: Mr. McKeever is a managing director and member of the firm's operating committee. He is responsible for stock origination and cohead of investment banking, responsible for the firm's activities with clients in global industry groups and for U.S. offices. He joined the firm in 1979 from First National Bank of Chicago.

Alan H. Washkowitz, head of merchant banking: Mr. Washkowitz replaced Steven Berger in January 1998; before adding this post, he was senior fund manager and a principal of the firm's merchant-banking group, overseeing Lehman Brothers Fund I. He joined Kuhn Loeb & Co. in 1968 and became a general partner in 1976. When Lehman acquired Kuhn Loeb in 1978, Mr. Washkowitz was named a managing director.

Jeffrey Vanderbeek, cohead of fixed income division: Mr. Vanderbeek is a managing director and member of Lehman's operating committee. He joined Lehman in 1984, and has held several senior positions in the firm's bond group. He assumed his current responsibilities in 1996. He is in charge of Lehman's overall bond business. Before joining Lehman, Mr. Vanderbeek worked at Donaldson, Lufkin & Jenrette Securities Corp.

Maryanne Rasmussen, head of human resources and administration: Ms. Rasmussen has responsibility for employee relations, benefits and compensation, among other things. She also is a managing director and member of Lehman's operating committee. Before her current post, Ms. Rasmussen was executive vice president and chief quality officer for the Shearson Lehman Brothers division of Lehman's predecessor firm.

Edward M. Feigeles, head of private-client services: Mr. Feigeles is a managing director who runs Lehman's group catering to high-net-worth individuals. Before joining Lehman, Mr. Feigeles was managing director and head of private-client services at Morgan Stanley.

Jeffrey M. Applegate, chief investment officer and strategist: Mr. Applegate is currently responsible for assisting the firm's institutional customers with U.S. asset allocation and portfolio strategy. He also is chairman of Lehman's investment policy committee. Before joining Lehman, Mr. Applegate had worked at Smith Barney, E. F. Hutton and First Boston.

Stuart J. Francis, group head of global investment banking: Mr. Francis is a managing director responsible for West Coast investment banking and the global technology group. Located in San Francisco, Mr. Francis also is a member of Lehman's investment-banking operating and management committees. He joined Lehman in 1991 after fourteen years with Smith Barney.

Frederick Frank, vice chairman and director: Mr. Frank is a Lehman vice chairman and director. He is responsible for Lehman's global health-care banking group. Before joining Lehman as a partner in 1969, Mr. Frank was cohead of research at Smith Barney.

Jeremy Isaacs, head of stock operations in Europe and global head of stock derivatives: Mr. Isaacs, based in London, joined Lehman in 1996 from a senior management position at Goldman Sachs, where he gained experience in stock derivatives and structured products. He previously worked at Kleinwort Benson and Smith New Court.

Raymond C. Mikulich, head of real-estate and mortgage-industries group: Mr. Mikulich is a managing director who joined Lehman in 1982. He is responsible for Lehman's banking activities with real-estate concerns globally. He assumed his current post in 1990. Before joining Lehman, Mr. Mikulich worked at LaSalle Bank in Chicago.

Carolyn Moses, director of global stock research: Ms. Moses is a managing director who started her career at Lehman in 1988 as the European stock strategist. In 1990, she became director of European stock research and later head of global stock research. She currently is responsible for about 250 research staff members in New York, San Francisco, Washington, DC, London, Hong Kong and Tokyo.

Michael J. O'Hanlon, head of financial-services group: Mr. O'Hanlon is a managing director and sits on the finance committee of Lehman's operating committee. He is responsible for Lehman's banking activities with financial services organizations. He started his career at E. F. Hutton, and became head of mortgage finance at Lehman in 1988. Before his current post, Mr. O'Hanlon was cohead of the real estate and mortgage industries group.

Robert D. Redmond, managing director and head of the financial sponsors group and cohead of the leveraged-finance group: Before joining Lehman, Mr. Redmond was a managing director at Kidder Peabody, where he was head of private placements and high yield capital markets, as well as a member of the firm's underwriting and commitment committees. Previously, he worked at Prudential Securities and Chase Manhattan Bank.

In the Beginning . . .

Lehman Brothers has among the oldest roots of any major investment bank. In 1844, Henry Lehman came to America from Rimpar, Germany, and set up a small shop in Montgomery, Alabama, selling groceries, dry goods and utensils to farmers. Six years later, two younger brothers, Emanuel and Mayer, joined Henry and launched a commodities firm named Lehman Brothers. The Lehmans sold basic goods to local planters and often settled accounts in bales of cotton instead of cash. Then the brothers resold the cotton in bulk, often making a profit on both ends of the transaction.

To understand how long the Lehman Brothers name has been around, the Lehman bank is on record as buying at least one slave, a fourteen-year-old black woman named Martha, for $900 in 1854. In 1858, the firm opened its first New York office and, four years later, formed an affiliated company, Lehman, Durr & Co., with cotton merchant John Wesley Durr. In 1870, Lehman Brothers spearheaded the formation of the New York Cotton Exchange, the first experiment in commodity-futures trading. About seventeen years later, Lehman Brothers bought its first New York Stock Exchange seat and became famous as one of the Street's most aggressive investment banks.

Early in this century, the alliance of Lehman Brothers and Goldman Sachs dominated Wall Street's new-issue market. From 1906 to 1924, the two houses comanaged a then-astounding 114 securities issues, beginning with the first public stock offering by Sears, Roebuck & Co. At the height of its influence after World War II, Lehman was growing faster than any other investment bank. Lehman was admired for its "integrity, philosophy, aggressiveness and, above all, for its methods," wrote Joseph Wechsberg in his book *The Merchant Bankers*.

Lehman merged with Kuhn Loeb & Co. in 1977 and changed its name to Lehman Brothers Kuhn Loeb Inc. In the early 1980s, a civil war between Lehman's investment bankers and its traders led to the 1984 sale of the firm to American Express Co.'s Shearson American Express unit for about $360 million. The brokerage firm was dubbed Shearson Lehman/American Express Inc. During the next several years, the firm was renamed Shearson Lehman Brothers/American Express Co, and then Shearson Lehman Hutton/American Express Co.

In 1990, American Express launched a reorganization that combined the firm's investment-banking and trading divisions under the Lehman Brothers name. (The firm's stock-brokerage and money-management business retained the Shearson name until American Express sold this division to Primerica Corp.—now Travelers—in 1993.) In 1994, American Express spun off Lehman Brothers to the public, as the firm flew solo in the stock market for the first time in its 144-year history.

■

Gregory E. Sacco, head of global equity capital markets: Mr. Sacco is a managing director and a member of the firm's investment-banking management committee and equity executive committee. He joined Lehman in 1967, and has held a variety of positions at the firm in corporate finance, institutional sales and research.

Jeffrey L. Weiss, cohead of global fixed income syndicate: Mr. Weiss is a senior vice president who joined Lehman in 1983. Before his current post, he was a senior corporate bond trader as well as head of U.S. bond syndicate business.

Steven B. Wolitzer, head of global mergers and acquisitions: Mr. Wolitzer is a managing director who joined Kuhn Loeb, a predecessor firm, in 1977. He was one of the founding members of the M&A group at Lehman Brothers Kuhn Loeb Inc., and was named cohead of M&A in 1989.

Paul Zoidis, cohead of telecommunications and media group: Mr. Zoidis is a managing director who joined Lehman in 1988 after spending seven years at E. F. Hutton. Hc has been involved with several big M&A transactions, including MCI's proposed $37 billion merger with WorldCom, US West's $10.8 billion acquisition of Continental Cablevision and the $13.5 billion merger of US West's and Airtouch Communications' U.S. cellular business.

Brian R. Zipp, head of emerging markets business: Mr. Zipp is a managing director and serves on Lehman's fixed-income operating committee. He joined Lehman in 1982 as a Treasury-bond trader dealing with Treasury bills and strips. He also has worked in a variety of mortgage-backed trading positions. Before joining Lehman, he served as the international economist for the Treasury Department and previously worked at the State Department.

PART FOUR

THE INVESTMENT BANKS

Goldman, Sachs & Co.

•

Credit Suisse First Boston Corp.

GOLDMAN, SACHS & CO.

STILL PRIVATE, STILL PROFITABLE

Whither the Partnership?

I t was a burning topic at Goldman, Sachs & Co.'s annual partners' retreat in 1996 at the Doral Arrowwood conference center in Rye Brook, New York. Should Goldman, Wall Street's last major private partnership, issue its own shares to the public for the first time in its 127-year history?

For months, Goldman's 172 partners had been bitterly divided. The debate was heightened after the firm's zigzagging profit and partner defections depleted some of its capital in 1994. Some veteran partners said a public offering would beef up the firm's capital and insulate it from rocky times. These veteran partners also would pocket big bucks from a public sale.

But Goldman's younger partners were dead set against it. For them, the issue came down, once again, to money. If the firm went public, they would have dibs on relatively paltry amounts of the stock of the new publicly traded company. On the first day of the retreat, there was widespread opposition to the idea. The next day the matter was settled, without a vote, when Goldman suddenly decided to scrap a tutorial on the issue of compensation in a public company. In a tersely worded memorandum distributed to general partners, Goldman's senior partner and vice chairman said, "After careful review and thoughtful discussion, the partners once again enthusiastically decided that the firm should remain a private partnership."

For Goldman, some things never change. The white-shoe investment bank remains private even amid internal discussions of a public sale that have persisted for years. (At the 1996 retreat, one senior partner amused colleagues by trotting out a potential offering plan from 1968.) And the firm continues to consistently churn out stellar profits. After a rare disappointing performance in 1994, Goldman has rebounded. In 1997, the firm posted its best year ever, earning $3 billion in pretax profit for the fiscal year ended November, despite a sharp decline in autumn caused by turmoil in Asian financial markets.

Goldman's internal battle over a public sale is sure to smolder for some time. The continuing concern of the younger partners is that the "older partners, by having a large amount of capital, may get a disproportionate share of the equity," said John Gutfreund, who headed Salomon Brothers Inc. in 1981 when it became public as a result of its sale to Phibro Corp. The clout of Goldman's younger partners is surprisingly strong; more than half of the firm's partners were named to the coveted post since 1992.

But Goldman's senior partner, Jon Corzine, is seen within the firm as a proponent of a public sale. And the betting on Wall Street is that Goldman eventually will join its rivals and tap the public market for a capital injection. Indeed, some Goldman partners expect Mr. Corzine to again raise the going-public issue within a year or so. "He isn't going to jam it down the partners' throats; like anyone in that kind of position, he wants to keep his job," said one partner. "But he won't give up on the idea."

Goldman's predicament illustrates the difficulties that can arise when a private partnership expands rapidly. A little more than a decade ago, most Wall Street securities firms were private. But in the 1980s, Bear Stearns Cos., Morgan Stanley Group Inc. and Salomon Brothers Inc. went public, caving in to pressure for capital to support their growing trading businesses. Something had to give. "You don't have to go back that many years when Goldman was less than one thousand people with seventy-five partners," said Tom Saunders, a partner at the investment firm of Saunders Karp & Co., who played an important role in taking Morgan Stanley public more than a decade ago. "That works. But when you get to an eight-thousand-person firm with about two hundred partners owning the equity, that doesn't work." (Goldman had 10,600 employees at year-end 1997.)

With $6 billion of capital at its disposal—up from $5.3 billion in 1996—Goldman, Sachs competes effectively with big rivals Merrill and the newly created Morgan Stanley, Dean Witter, Discover & Co. Meanwhile, Goldman changed its corporate structure in 1996 to limit individual partners' exposure in the event of a legal or financial catastrophe. The move was significant in the wake of the firm's struggle over whether to go public. In a private partnership, members assume the full liability of other partners; with a limited-liability status, their personal assets are shielded by law.

One way Goldman could go public is through a merger. Indeed, Goldman partners weighed the going-public move in 1995, when Goldman senior partner Jon Corzine held talks with then-Salomon Inc. Chairman Robert Denham and Salomon Brothers Inc. Chief Executive Deryck Maughan about merging the two firms and becoming public in the process, people familiar with the talks said. The talks were purely explanatory, and went nowhere. But they showed that taking itself public may not be the only route open to Goldman should it decide that it wants to become a public company.

For Goldman, a merger would offer several advantages, analysts said;

these include being able to sidestep the costly, cumbersome effort of restructuring a private partnership and preparing it to go public. Goldman also could avoid incurring the typical underwriting discount involved in an initial sale of stock. "Would something like a merger be more palatable?" asked a banker familiar with the talks. "I think yes. The younger partners would have a significant equity position because they would get equity rather than cash."

"The most preferred way is to do a straightforward public offering, but I don't see any particular reason to go public other than to capture current high market value," Mr. Corzine said. "For me, going public would have to be for the right strategic reasons."

Some Goldman partners still shudder when they think back to 1994, when the partnership showed serious signs of strain. So many partners had left Goldman that year that at the annual partners' dinner, Mr. Corzine did away with a tradition. Instead of personally thanking each departing partner for his service, he just asked for a round of applause honoring them all. In the two months after senior partner Stephen Friedman abruptly retired following four years in the top job, two dozen partners bolted the firm in quick succession. The Friedman resignation was the meteor that threw the partnership off course, and it had reverberations. One of biggest blows in 1994 was the resignation of Mark Winkelman, the partner who turned Goldman's commodities and foreign-exchange business into a big profit center for the firm. Mr. Winkelman left after being passed over for one of Goldman's top jobs in the musical chairs that followed Mr. Friedman's departure.

Goldman also has faced external battles. Deutsche Morgan Grenfell, in a bid to bulk up, went on a hiring spree, hiring scores of Wall Street investment bankers and traders—and Goldman was among those hardest hit. In an eighteen-month period in 1995 and 1996, the investment-banking arm of Deutsche Bank AG hired fifty midlevel vice presidents and analysts from Goldman, as well as Paul Spillane Jr., who headed the nondollar bond desk, and Ageiji Nakai, a trader of Japanese government bonds. "It was extremely aggressive in 1996. 1995—their hiring moved from the bond area to equities, to research and finally operations," Mr. Corzine said.

In a bid to stem the tide of defections, Goldman created a new class of "junior" partners. In doing so, Goldman used a new title—"partner-managing director"—as a carrot offered to employees it wanted to keep. The firm expects most of the managing directors eventually will be named partners, though "making MD" won't be a guarantee to partnership status. In October 1996, Goldman named thirty-eight new partner-managing directors, boosting the partnership class at the time to a record 199 partners.

Becoming a Goldman partner is Wall Street's equivalent of being annointed a prince. Every two years, Goldman picks a small number of chosen ones from among its hundreds of young executives. The promotion might seem like a somewhat dubious prize. Goldman partners toil notoriously long hours. The firm is known as a fraternal but tough place to work and it has had a poor record of promoting women and blacks, though in recent years it has appointed more women and minority partners than before. (Mr. Corzine said in 1997 he wasn't "satisfied with where we are, by any stretch of the imagination," adding that one measure he'll judge his tenure at Goldman's helm will be by the progress Goldman makes in hiring and promoting minorities and women.) On the other hand, partners typically retire as multimillionaires after only a decade or so. Winners are set for life. And while losers don't exactly get a one-way ticket to Palookaville, they're often devastated. Some lock themselves in their offices for hours. Others miss days of work. They console themselves with their paychecks—in 1997, even the most junior partner's share approached $4 million—and dreams of better luck next time.

With Goldman's record profits, the partnerships are bigger trophies than ever. Besides an annual draw of about $150,000, partners share in those profits. In good years, that share starts at several million dollars and up. But it's harder to decide who gets the prize. In the old days, Goldman was small enough that anyone who joined the firm, worked hard and did well had maybe a fifty-fifty chance of becoming partner. But Goldman now has thousands of employees, and despite a ballooning in the number of partners in the past decade, the competition has grown ever more fierce.

Some young employees just can't wait. David Eifrig, a top futures salesman, bolted Goldman several years back after he saw his path blocked. He said he knew he couldn't beat out two managers in his department with far more experience than his four years. "I was looking at eight years out," Mr. Eifrig said. "It didn't make sense."

Exactly what goes on behind the scenes of the competition is a closely held secret. But it starts with a winnowing down of the worldwide workforce to a list of several dozen serious candidates. After a complicated procedure involving written nominations, a cross-examination of candidates' qualifications and an eleventh-hour "town meeting" of all partners, Goldman names the select members of its exclusive club.

Some on Wall Street say Goldman is looking for automatons willing to give up their entire lives for the firm. "They brainwash you," said Mr. Eifrig. Claimed a former trader who never made partner, "They want you to think, feel and dream about the place. They want your life." Not so, Goldman says. The firm says it simply looks for what it calls "culture carriers," people willing to fit into Goldman's rich tradition.

But there's no denying that partner candidates face enormous pressure to conform to Goldman's conservative style. Many on Wall Street favor flashy Armani suits and French cuffs; Goldman partners take pride in rolled-up sleeves. At Goldman, the hot tempers and irreverent sense of humor seen frequently at other Wall Street firms are taboo. Several years back, a Goldman partner was talking with one talented candidate about his abilities, pointing out that the firm boasted several top athletes and a chess champion. The candidate shot back, "I can pick up girls in singles bars." The Goldman executive wasn't amused. "I'd like you to change your sense of humor," he responded. The candidate ultimately left Goldman and launched his own firm.

Goldman secretaries joke about seeing young executives who suddenly cut their hair shorter and start wearing white shirts instead of blue. They call these employees "pithy"—Partner In Training. Some traders who once screamed to celebrate big trades start toning down. "You're not supposed to show feelings," said Mr. Eifrig, the departed salesman. "You don't want to ruin anything."

Nor does Goldman. In the past, the firm rarely devoted much effort to traditional media advertisements. But the firm isn't depending on word of mouth anymore. In a 1997 round of Goldman newspaper ads, the firm trumpeted its asset-management arm. "After 128 years in finance, we know a good investment when we see one," the ads said. Typical Goldman. Understated and oh-so-refined.

Though Goldman has largely steered clear of scandal, it did get nicked in the growing investigations into influence-peddling in the market for government financial services. Goldman was fined $3,500 by the state of Massachusetts in 1997 for illegally buying dinner and theater tickets for two state officials, including one who had helped pick Goldman to manage $100 million in state pension funds in 1991. In an agreement with the Massachusetts State Ethics Commission, Goldman admitted, among other things, that it violated state law in 1992 when a vice president at the firm provided Steven Kaseta, then the state's deputy treasurer, with tickets to *Man of La Mancha* and dinner at Boston's Locke-Ober restaurant. Mr. Kaseta was a member of the selection committee that recommended awarding Goldman the contract to manage the pension funds. Goldman, in a statement, said it "cooperated fully" with the ethics committee and stressed that the commission found no evidence that the gifts were intended to influence the officials. "We are pleased to put the matter behind us," Goldman added.

One thing is clear. Goldman doesn't feel pressure to make big acquisitions or cater to individual investors like some rivals. The firm already holds a leading position in underwriting new stocks in the United States and abroad, noted Goldman's Mr. Paulson. So even after the 1997 mega-deals creating Morgan Stanley, Dean Witter, Discover & Co. and Salomon Smith Barney Holdings Inc., he said: "We are highly disciplined about which businesses we pursue and which clients we serve. We could get much bigger real easy. But our primary goal is to get *better*, as opposed to simply getting *bigger* as a goal in and of itself." Though Goldman isn't number one in every category, Mr. Paulson said its trading revenue is "well above that of our primary competitors," adding: "We are a global powerhouse in the trading, as well as the underwriting and advisory areas. With over 14,000 people and assets in excess of $200 billion and our global network, we are hardly a small firm."

Mr. Corzine compared Goldman to Tiffany, adding: "There will be room in the marketplace for a wholesaler, operating in the institutional high-net worth markets."

A New "Class" of Partner and New Vice Chairmen

Goldman's coveted partnership roster ballooned to 199 in 1996 with the addition of thirty-eight new partner-managing directors. (There were 190 partners at year-end 1997.) But the real news in 1996's partnership announcements was the election of "extended" managing directors. The creation of this new extended class, the biggest change in the partnership's structure since the firm's founding, was designed to stem defections and give Goldman's top management greater flexibility should the investment bank decide to go public someday.

But there was fallout. A number of young executives who didn't make the grade bolted the firm, faulting, among other things, not being promoted to MD. Among them were Christopher Hogg, a preferred-stock vice president, and Brian Maier, who headed Goldman's hospitality and gaming group. They both departed for rival Merrill. The cult of Goldman, however, still had too much pull for Mr. Hogg, who was a hot property for helping to create a popular type of preferred security called "monthly income preferred stock," or MIPs. He returned to Goldman just three weeks after he left, saying he "missed" Goldman.

In return, Mr. Hogg was given expanded responsibilities. The firm placed him in charge of new products, with seven subordinates, one more than before he left. Merrill had given Mr. Hogg the more prestigious title of managing director and a pay package that compensation experts pegged at more than $1 million a year. (He declined to divulge what Goldman offered to lure him back as a vice president.)

In 1997, Goldman appointed 126 new managing directors, bringing the total to 406. Those appointed became extended partners, meaning they don't hold an equity stake in the private partnership as full partners do, but instead take part in a profit-sharing pool. Mr. Corzine shrugged off any disatisfaction with the junior-partner status. "The partnership broadly supported it," he said.

In the meantime, an increasing number of the firm's veterans have stepped down to make room for new partners. In 1996, David Silfen and Willard J. "Mike" Overlock Jr., the firm's fifty-year-old co-chiefs of stock and investment banking, respectively, retired. It was Mr. Silfen who, along with his fellow co-head Roy Zuckerberg, merged sales, trading and arbitrage into the firm's stock division in 1990. Mr. Overlock, who engineered Goldman's explosive growth in mergers in the past decade, was one of Wall Street's most highly paid bankers; he was granted a 1995 pay package of more than $10 million before taxes, people familiar with the matter said. But unlike Mr. Silfen, who will retain some ties to the firm, Mr. Overlock made a clean break. He chose to completely leave the firm just months after he was dropped from its influential executive committee as part of a broader overhaul at Goldman.

Goldman actually lost one partner who was lured with a pay deal exhorbitant even by Wall Street standards. Michael Fascitelli, a Goldman real-estate banker, left the firm in late 1996 to become president of Vornado Realty Trust, a New Jersey real-estate investment trust. The hook: a compensation package that could be worth nearly $50 million. The pay package consisted of $25 million in deferred compensation and stock options that could be valued at about $24 million. "This is one of the ten biggest (stock) options grants ever, on par with what Michael Eisner got at Disney," marveled Alan Johnson, a New York compensation consultant. At Goldman, where Mr. Fascitelli was a partner in charge of the firm's real-estate banking practice, he had earned more than $5 million a year, according to people familiar with the firm's pay levels.

Change swept Goldman's senior-executive suites, too. In 1997, Henry Paulson Jr. was named president, and Roy Zuckerberg and Robert Hurst were appointed vice chairmen. Mr. Paulson, who had been vice chairman and chief operating officer, continued as COO with his new title. "The title of President is more appropriate for Hank's position in light of our recent move to a limited liability structure," according to an internal memo. Meantime, Mr. Zuckerberg continued to head the firm's stock division, and Mr. Hurst remained in his role overseeing investment banking. In their new roles, Messrs. Zuckerberg and Hurst are working to win more business from corporate clients. Goldman has a roster of blue-chip clients including Ford Motor Co., Chase Manhattan Corp. and Sears, Roebuck & Co.

The move was a bid to keep the profits rolling in. Goldman earned a whopping $3 billion before taxes in its fiscal year ended November, 1997. The single biggest contributor to Goldman's profit for the year was its investment-banking business, said John Thain, Goldman's chief financial officer. Investment banking, including underwriting and advising on mergers and acquisitions, accounted for nearly 40 percent of Goldman's revenue.

Investment Banking Growth

Goldman's investment-banking remains the soul of the firm. In 1997, the firm was ranked the nation's No. 4 underwriter, according to Securities Data Co., and raked in $1.18 billion in fees for lead-managing U.S. stocks and bonds. Goldman's impressive showing stemmed largely from its clout in helping bring to market lucrative stock transactions. Among Goldman's biggest underwriting mandates in 1997 were managing the $1.49 billion stock offering of Safeway Inc.—the second largest underwriting of a U.S. company for the year—as well as the $1.1 billion Santa Fe International IPO.

The firm's biggest coup in 1996 was its role in the mammoth offering of shares of Deutsche Telekom AG, Germany's national telephone monopoly. This deal alone produced a total of $40.1 million in disclosed fees, Securities Data said.

But the Deutsche Telekom deal wasn't without controversy. Goldman, one of the three global coordinators for the $10 billion IPO, angered the phone company's executives by arguing that the proposed sale price was too rich for international investors. Joachim Kroeske, Deutsche Telekom's finance chief, had argued for two years that he wanted his company's offering to be priced at thirty marks, then about $20 a share. Like Goldman, the other lead banks in its underwriting group, Deutsche Bank AG and Dresdner Bank AG, also raised questions about the thirty-mark figure. But Goldman's arguments, delivered during a September 30, 1996, meeting that lasted several hours, apparently struck a nerve.

Soon after the spat, Goldman failed to make the short list of potential underwriters for the public offering of the Hungarian phone company, which was partly owned by Deutsche Telekom, in what may have been retaliation for angering the German giant. Deutsche Telekom denied that Goldman's opinion on pricing influenced its decision to exclude the investment bank from the offering for Matav Rt., and argued that it excluded Goldman only because it likes to rotate its bankers. "There is no fight with Goldman Sachs," a spokesman said. Meanwhile, Goldman insisted it maintains a good relationship with Deutsche Telekom. Said a Goldman spokesman, "We've been working with them successfully for six years."

Goldman played a more easygoing role in another high-profile IPO: Ralph Lauren Corp.'s $767 million initial public stock offering in 1997. Goldman, selected lead manager of the deal, received more than just $33.6 million in underwriting fees, thanks to a 28 percent stake Goldman had bought in the famous fashion house. The proceeds of the offering were largely used to pay down notes and other borrowings to Mr. Lauren, Goldman and banks, according to a regulatory filing. Among the borrowings were a $7 million loan Goldman made to the company. In addition, as a result of the offering, the company doled out $82.5 million in "undistributed earnings" to Mr. Lauren and Goldman. The offering capped a string of handsome dividends to Mr. Lauren and Goldman in recent years. During the three-year period before the offering, Goldman received distributions of $39.8 million.

In another big-name investment, Goldman in 1997 helped bring AMF Corp. public in an initial public stock offering after buying the nation's biggest bowling-center operator for about $1 billion a year earlier. The firm's profit: about $600 million. The 1996 purchase represented the largest new investment ever made by a Goldman merchant-banking fund, in this case, GS Capital Partners II. Like many Wall Street securities firms, Goldman is investing in such far-flung businesses as fashion and bowling because the firm believes it can reap fat returns by deploying its capital in these areas.

Indeed, the deal to buy privately held AMF underscored how merchant banking—a business that requires Wall Street firms to put up their own capital to buy companies or stakes in them—has formed a big chunk of profits for investment banks, particularly Goldman. One of the reasons principal investing is so attractive to Wall Street investment banks is that it helps smooth out profits, especially in years when returns from bread-and-butter securities businesses such as trading and investment banking are low. When Goldman's earnings slumped 80 percent to $508 million in fiscal 1994, merchant-banking gains helped "offset poor results in some other areas," according to a report by Moody's Investors Service Inc.

But there have been less-than-stellar deals. China Telecom Ltd., which launched a $4.25 billion stock offering through Goldman, slipped in price in the days after the offering, as Goldman couldn't maintain the customary post-offering effort to support the Chinese company's share price amid a steep market decline in Asia. The deal nevertheless underscored Goldman's teamwork approach, with thirty people in three different cities over four departments involved.

On the bond side, in September 1997 Goldman helped underwrite a $4 billion offering of new thirty-year global bonds issued by Venezuela—more than double the projected amount—in what underwriters said was the largest global-bond deal ever. Said Chip Seelig, a Goldman managing director: "It was unbelievable."

Meanwhile, Goldman also has carved out a stake in the international banking arena. In 1996, Japan's giant Sumitomo Bank Ltd. asked Goldman to underwrite sales of new preferred stock to help the financial institution to raise money to replenish coffers depleted by problem write-offs. Indeed, Goldman generated about half its total revenue in 1997 from international operations, compared with about 35 percent in 1996, and about 25 percent in the early 1990s, Goldman officials said. Closer to home, Goldman also made waves by quietly launching an underwriting of a $136 million bond issue for embattled Orange County, California. The 1997 deal, which marked Orange County's first financing since it emerged from its 1994 bankruptcy filing, was unusual in that Goldman bought the bonds from the county and held on to them for a week before formally completing the transaction. Some analysts suggested that Goldman kept the deal quiet because of possible adverse publicity; "This is, after all, Orange County," said one. Goldman, for its part, said it merely followed orders from the county. "The county asked the underwriters to underwrite the issue, and the underwriters agreed," Michael McCarthy, a managing director in Goldman's municipal-bond department, said at the time.

That's not to say that Goldman escaped the legal wrangle over Orange County's bankruptcy. The county's transportation authority sued Goldman in 1997 in a Santa Ana, California, state court, alleging that Goldman failed to warn the authority about the risks in Orange County's ill-fated investment fund. Other than the county itself, the transportation authority suffered the largest financial losses of any investor in the pool. The suit claims the authority relied on Goldman as its "advisers in financial matters" and that Goldman possessed "a unique understanding of plaintiffs' particular needs in connection with the investment of plaintiffs' funds, including acceptable degrees of risk." Goldman countered that the firm "was not responsible for any losses" sustained by the transportation authority. Goldman "performed underwriting services for the Transportation Authority and in no way acted as the investment adviser for the proceeds."

Controversial Merger Role

Goldman's M&A group thrived in 1997 amid the boom in corporate mergers, generating "well more" than $500 million in revenue for the year, a Goldman official said. Goldman was ranked No. 2 among merger advisers in 1997, advising U.S. companies on $236.85 billion of mergers or acquisitions, for a 25.8% market share. The firm helped advise Ford Motor Co. in its $17.6 billion spinoff of Associates First Capital Corp. to shareholders, and NationsBank Corp. in its $14.8 billion acquisition of Barnett Banks, among many others. Goldman has among the most elite investment-banking corps on the Street, and often works more effectively than most of its rivals because of a highly prized teamwork approach stemming from its partnership structure.

The firm long has prided itself on being so loyal to blue-chip corporate clients that the firm makes a point of never managing a hostile tender offer. The firm has been revered in some quarters for often defending those clients against hostile bids. Its telephone directories said, "Our clients' interests always come first."

But Wall Street was taken aback in late 1996 when Goldman advised Newmont Mining Co. on an unsolicited $2 billion "bear hug" takeover bid for Santa Fe Pacific Gold Corp.—a company that only two years earlier had been brought public by none other than Goldman. The move was the latest example on Wall Street of what some consider a fraying of long-term loyalty of securities firms toward their blue-chip clients. "Goldman has always been cleaner than Caesar's wife, and so I am sure some people are raising their eyebrows at this," said Samuel Hayes, professor of investment banking at Harvard University.

In Goldman's defense, it must be said that Santa Fe had solicited bids a few months earlier from both Newmont and Homestake Mining Co. on a friendly basis. Newmont apparently launched its bear hug to make sure its bid received due consideration. A Goldman spokesman said, "Anyone who is in the market knows that Goldman Sachs has been, is, and will continue to be a client-driven firm."

But some merger specialists said Goldman's role in the Santa Fe Pacific deal appeared to represent a looser approach to client conflicts. "I think Goldman has been changing," said Morris Mendelson, professor emeritus of finance at the University of Pennsylvania's Wharton School. "They are less hostile to hostile takeovers" today.

Goldman's official policy is that it will never act as a "dealer-manager" on a tender offer for a target's shares unless the target is in favor of the deal. In practice, this actually leaves the firm some leeway to advise clients on unsolicited bids as long as it brings in another firm to run the former tender offer. Still, defense is Goldman's game. The firm, which typically ranks among the busiest mergers advisers, has a thriving "anti-raid" practice defending companies against unsolicited bids, and chalked up some big victories in recent years against clients' unwanted suitors.

It's a rare day that Goldman has advised on unsolicited bids. Goldman advised both Ford Motor Co. on an unsolicited, unwelcome bid for Jaguar PLC in 1989, and B.A.T Industries PLC in its hostile takeover of Farmers Group Inc. in 1988. In the Newmont case, some specialists said Goldman's move represented a practical business decision. Goldman recognized that "once Santa Fe was put into play, they will offer no prospect as a client in the future," said Harvard's Mr. Hayes. "The prospect of future business is not with Santa Fe, it's with Newmont."

Meantime, Goldman and other investment banks could face some potholes stemming from a proposed rule by the Financial Accounting Standards Board that would either restrict or end "pooling of interests," the most popular method companies use to account for big stock mergers. The result could be a chilling effect on merger activity in the United States. The FASB, the chief rule-making body that sets U.S. accounting standards for public companies, said in April 1997 that it may amend or abolish the popular pooling rule, which lets merging companies add together the book value of their assets and liabilities to avoid big hits against earnings after they combine. Current mergers wouldn't be affected because any changes wouldn't take effect until 1999 at the earliest. Still, some Wall Street specialists fear there may be fallout. "If the limits pass, it would not only slow down record M&A activity, but a third of all mergers may get torpedoed," predicted Robert Willens, a managing director at Lehman Brothers Inc.

A Big and Powerful Trader

Goldman is widely known as a pure investment-banking powerhouse. But in some periods, the firm makes the bulk of its money from trading and making markets in stocks, bonds, currencies and other products. The firm's commodities unit, J. Aron, long has been a trading force.

In early 1997, Goldman made one of the Street's savviest fixed-income trades by spinning the bond-market roulette wheel one Friday morning and coming up big. Minutes before the 8:30 A.M. EST release of a hotly anticipated monthly employment report, some traders, including Goldman, were snapping up bonds and other securities, apparently on a hunch the data wouldn't reveal any alarming inflation news.

The bet paid off. Goldman alone was said to have bought $500 million of bond contracts for customers around 8:28 A.M. Two minutes later—after the Labor Department said January payrolls rose only slightly more than expected—the price jumped. Estimated paper profits to Goldman clients: $3.5 million. A Goldman trader acknowledged that the firm was a big buyer before the data release, but wouldn't confirm the transaction's size. "We were talking at 8:28 about how crazy these people were for trading," said Anthony Crescenzi, a bond-market strategist at Miller, Tabak Hirsch & Co.

The get-rich-quick success had some apparently jealous rival dealers speculating that maybe the firm knew something the rest of the world didn't. Not from the Labor Department, said Bureau of Labor Statistics Commissioner Katharine Abraham, who dismissed speculation about possible leaks at a news conference. Instead, most Wall Street observers took the less sinister view that investors who hit the jackpot simply enjoyed the benefit of an old-fashioned educated guess.

Goldman has made a splash in stock trades, too. The firm has been a leader of a new stock-market trend, "off-board" trading. These are trades in which big blocks of U.S. stock change hands in foreign markets in risky transactions that seldom appear on trading records. Wall Street traders said Goldman pocketed a cool $1 million fee, for instance, in early 1997 when the firm handled a 19.9 million-share trade of RJR Nabisco Holdings Corp. made by investor Carl Icahn. Mr. Icahn sold the RJR stake to Goldman for more than $730 million; Goldman bought the stock outside the United States after the markets there closed and resold it before the markets reopened the next day. Neither the original sale nor resale showed up on the "tape," the record of regular trades in New York Stock Exchange-listed stocks.

Heightened demand for off-board block trades is being driven by professional investors with sizable stakes in companies and by big institutional investors such as mutual funds that deal in multimillion-dollar stock positions. Said Robert Steel, Goldman's co-chief operating officer of stocks: "With the market so volatile, people are willing to accept a discount to be out as quickly as possible."

In fact, Goldman has usurped Salomon Brothers as the king of giant headline-making trades on Wall Street. It was Goldman, for instance, that handled a four-million share sale of Walt Disney Co. shares by Chairman and Chief Executive Michael Eisner in late 1997. Goldman also handled in 1997 the giant block sales of the stock of British Petroleum ($2 billion) and US Airways Group ($506 million). Although Salomon made a bid on the BP stock, Goldman's trading desk won the right to buy the stock from the sellers and resell it, mainly to institutional investors.

In the case of BP, Goldman outbid competitors for $2 billion of stock from Kuwaiti investors that Goldman then resold overnight to customers around the globe for a gain of more than $15 million. The block of 170 million BP shares—one of the largest single blocks ever to be traded—was bought by Goldman on a Wednesday afternoon at 710.5 pence ($11.59) for each ordinary share of BP. Goldman then lined up 500 institutional and individual buyers in the United States, Europe and Asia, reselling the stock to them at a price of 716 pence ($11.70).

How risky was the transaction? Goldman officials were told they had an hour to decide if they wanted to risk $2 billion of capital—or nearly 40 percent of the capital of the firm's partners—and bid for the stock. Such an underwriting can be extremely dangerous. If stock markets were to tank, the underwriter could wind up stuck with a big block of stock as buyers disappear.

Some competitors say Goldman's aggressive block-trade bidding is a sign that the firm is trying to "buy" investment-banking business by getting into the good graces of customers who might throw future stock and bond underwriting its way. But Goldman officials dismiss any notion that the firm has shifted its focus or decided to devote more of its balance sheet to block trading. As evidence, they point to Securities Data Co.'s ranking of Goldman as the top underwriter of stocks during 1997.

Indeed, in taking a lead on such block trades, Goldman is merely reasserting dominion over a field pioneered in the 1960s by its late chairman, Gus Levy, and continued in the 1970s and 1980s under former chief stock trader Robert Mnuchin, says Roy Smith, a former Goldman partner who teaches at New York University's business school.

"This has been a part of our strategy for a long, long time," said Roy Zuckerberg, who oversees Goldman's stock operations. "This firm has always had a certain risk mentality and a dedication to using our balance sheet to help our customers."

Goldman understands the risks. Indeed, the firm lost $100 million in a BP underwriting when the market tanked in 1987. "I hate to say it, but almost inevitably we will lose money from time to time in the trading area," Mr. Corzine said. But because Goldman has "been there, done that, and gone on," the firm holds an edge over many competitors in dealing with block trades, he added.

Meanwhile, Goldman was among the thirty trading firms nicked in a December 1997 settlement to resolve a class-action case filed over pricing practices in the Nasdaq Stock Market. Goldman agreed to pay $75 million (out of a total of $910 million for the thirty firms) to settle investor allegations that the firms conspired from 1989 to 1994 to keep the trading "spreads" between the buy and sell price of 1,659 Nasdaq stocks overly wide. (As part of the settlement, Goldman didn't admit wrongdoing.)

Real-Estate Ruckus; Looking East for Profit

Goldman is one of the Street's most active real-estate players. And Goldman partner Daniel Neidich is perhaps the most aggressive buyer of real estate in the 1990s, clashing with rival investors in a handful of high-profile negotiations in the past few years. Mr. Neidich has usually won. But he has come under fire for hard-charging tactics in a 1996 battle for control of Rockefeller Center Properties Inc. and elsewhere, reflecting the potential pitfalls of a new breed of aggressive Goldman investment bankers.

Among the Goldman clients that have criticized Mr. Neidich are investor Sam Zell and the California Public Employees Retirement System, or Calpers— both losers in showdowns with Mr. Neidich. Some clients have been offended that Mr. Neidich acted as principal—buying properties for Goldman and clients—rather than merely acting as an agent. Mr. Zell, referring to Goldman's penchant for being an agent and competitor, said he has told Goldman executives, "You can't dance at both weddings."

During Mr. Neidich's tenure on the board of Rockefeller Center Properties, for instance, he alienated some fellow board members by breezing into meetings flanked by an entourage of Goldman associates and advisers, leaving some directors wondering whether he was more concerned with the future of the company or with Goldman's $225 million investment in it. Mr. Neidich has said he recused himself from board discussions in which his firm's investment posed a conflict, and eventually resigned from the board altogether.

Mr. Neidich offered no apologies for his style. "In negotiations where we hold the stronger hand, we have an obligation to our investors" to maximize the value of our position, he said. "We think we are more fair-minded and treat people better than we see other people being treated."

Clients aren't so sure. Calpers, one of the nation's largest retirement funds, joined forces in 1995 with Fidelity Investments, the nation's largest mutual-fund company, and a handful of other Goldman clients to protest the role of Goldman's real-estate fund in the restructuring of Cadillac Fairview Inc., a large Canadian real-estate developer. As a holder of senior debt, Mr. Neidich forced through a restructuring plan unfavorable to unsecured debtholders, including Calpers and Fidelity. Calpers temporarily stopped doing business with Goldman, and Fidelity and two other clients reduced their trading with the firm. "Why should we be doing business with someone when they're using the fees to hire the best lawyers to fight us on other business?" asked Sheryl Pressler, Calpers's chief investment officer.

Goldman's Mr. Paulson, then-vice chairman, played down the potential for conflicts at the time. "We've invested over $2 billion in equity to acquire over $7 billion in assets," he said in 1996. "This amounts to over seventy investments involving over 2,500 assets. It is significant that only a couple of these investments have generated any criticism."

In 1997, Goldman also dived into the commercial-mortgage securitization business with the sale of a $980 million pool of loans backed by prestigious office buildings and shopping centers around the nation. Goldman's offering represented the first time the firm made several large loans with the intent of packaging them for sale as publicly traded bonds. Goldman plans to offer two pools each year of similar size, under what it dubs its "Grande Loan" program.

One of the places Goldman is looking for profits in 1998 is in Japan. The firm, on the prowl for real-estate investments held by struggling Japanese investment banks, is looking to buy nonperforming loans with a total face value of as much as $3.8 billion, a person familiar with the firm said. Japanese banks, hurt by a long slide in property values, hold more than $200 billion in nonperforming loans, the country's Finance Ministry has reported. Goldman is among the investment banks looking for properties with mortgages that can be bought at a discount and resold, possibly through the securitization of bundles of mortgages. Though bonds backed by pools of mortgages and other assets are a hot commodity on Wall Street, such securitizations in Japan are relatively rare. A Goldman spokesman in New York declined to comment.

Goldman has completed two purchases of loans from Japanese banks. Its Goldman Sachs Realty Japan unit in 1997 bought about $100 million of loans from a lending affiliate of Bank of Tokyo-Mitsubishi Ltd. Earlier in 1997, Goldman was a buyer in a sale of $310 million in bad loans by Sumitomo Bank Ltd.

Buying an Asset-Management Presence

Goldman, scrambling to make up lost ground to key rivals, has bought several money-management firms in the past couple of years. But there have been no mega purchases that immediately would vault Goldman to the ranks of the nation's top asset managers.

In 1996, Goldman bought CIN Management Ltd., a British pension-fund manager with more than $20 billion of assets; Liberty Investment Management, a Tampa, Florida, firm that manages about $5 billion in stock investments for institutions and wealthy individuals; and Commodities Corp., which manages $1.8 billion and invests in a broad range of commodities and futures markets. With the purchases, Goldman has $134 billion under management. Though that's double the level managed by the firm in 1996, it still falls far short of competitors such as Merrill, Morgan Stanley, Dean Witter and Salomon Smith Barney.

Wall Street firms have been rushing to buy asset-management businesses in a bid to even out their volatile trading businesses with recurring fee income.

Goldman's purchases fit with the firm's public posture on the importance of a large asset-management business. The firm has said, in a well-publicized study, that U.S. fund groups running less than $10 billion were unlikely to survive. The Goldman study said money managers would need as much as $150 billion to prosper. Before the recent purchases, most of Goldman's assets were in low-yielding money-market accounts.

Goldman had been slow to expand its asset-management operations because it had hunted for bargains in an industry where prices have been driven up by the long bull market and the battle for market share on the Street. That tack stands in contrast to the strategy used by Morgan Stanley, which has spent huge sums acquiring fund companies with individual-investor distribution networks.

Goldman said its headcount in asset management has tripled over the past couple of years, and revenues doubled throughout most of 1997. Mr. Paulson said Goldman already has world-class capabilities, top tier performance, "is adding new products" and already is a leader in asset management in some markets, particularly Japan. "We're not showing large profits" in asset management, Mr. Paulson said, "but we're growing revenues rapidly and plowing most of them back" to build the business. "We believe it makes more sense for us to grow this business organically rather than through a large acquisition." In October 1997, Mr. Corzine predicted that "in five years, we will be one of the preeminent money-management firms."

Meanwhile, Goldman hasn't been above snatching top talent from competitors. In 1996, the firm hired Robert Beckwitt, a pioneering portfolio manager at Fidelity Investments, in a bid to beef up its asset-management team. Mr. Beckwitt joined Goldman as a vice president in the firm's asset-management division, and as cohead of emerging-markets equities, focusing on Latin America, Eastern Europe and Africa. At Fidelity, Mr. Beckwitt's forays into Latin American markets, after initial success, stumbled badly in 1994, and the executive's wings were clipped. Mr. Beckwitt defended his record at Fidelity, saying he had just one bad year in seven.

Goldman officials defended hiring Mr. Beckwitt. "We think he has tremendous investment experience and, over a long period of time, delivered tremendous investment performance," said John McNulty, cohead of Goldman Sachs Asset Management. Still, Mr. Beckwitt joined Goldman at a lower level than another former Fidelity executive. In 1993, Goldman hired away Sharmin Mossavar-Rahmani from Fidelity, making her a partner as part of her appointment.

Goldman has a highly productive brokerage force of more than 750. But the firm suffered a loss in 1997 when three of its brokers quit, walking out with $750 million in client assets. The three—Michael Horowitz, Mark Fife and Gregg Hymowitz—set up EnTrust Capital Inc., an investment firm focusing on managing assets for wealthy individuals and families. The trio had earned a reputation at Goldman as successful money managers, racking up average annual returns of 30.8 percent for the six years ended December 31, 1996. The departures came just after Goldman lost four high-net-worth brokers in its Los Angeles office to rival Merrill. Some of the brokers said they quit Goldman because of a recent push by the firm to make its brokers focus on gathering assets and channeling them into Goldman products.

"We love picking stocks, we love dealing with client assets, we just don't want to be an asset gatherer for a major institutional firm," said Mr. Hymowitz. Goldman, for its part, said there is no move toward making its brokers asset-gatherers. "To the contrary, we are moving toward a fee-based management system," a Goldman spokesman said. A Goldman executive added that the firm has a lot less turnover than retail-brokerage firms.

Goldman in 1997 also lost two top European stock managers, Roderick Jack and Marcel Jongen, who left the firm to launch a private hedge fund. From the beginning of May 1994 through the end of May 1997, the Goldman Sachs European Small-Cap Portfolio run by Messrs. Jack and Jongen had an average annual return of 27.4 percent in U.S. dollar terms, more than 10 percentage points better than the 15.6 percent average for offshore European small-cap funds over the same period, according to Lipper Analytical Services Inc.

The Princess of Wall Street

There are influential market strategists—and then there's Abby Joseph Cohen. Since joining Goldman Sachs & Co. in 1990 as the firm's U.S. equity market strategist, Ms. Cohen has become a virtual celebrity among investors on Main Street, even though they are a far cry from the institutional clientele to whom her firm caters.

Her accuracy in forecasting the remarkable bull market of the last few years, and her unshaken conviction that the market's fundamentals remain intact even in the midst of upheavals throughout 1997, have won her one of the biggest followings seen among those institutional clients in nearly a decade. Even a rumor that her optimism might be faltering has proved enough to rock stock prices over the last year. In November 1996, in what came to be known as "Abby Cohen Day," the Dow Jones Industrial Average tumbled fifty-five points on chatter that she was about to cut her recommended allocation to stocks. After she held an impromptu conference call to deny the reports, the market bounced back. When she boosted her stock allocation during the October 1997 market debacle, traders attributed the rapid rebound in part to her declaration of confidence. In the wake of events like this, her name popped up on a list of the hottest fads of the spring of 1997 in *Vanity Fair* magazine, right below that of Carolyn Bessette Kennedy.

"Other people use the term 'guru,' but I never do," Ms. Cohen insisted. "I'm an analyst, a fundamental analyst."

In fact, Ms. Cohen's analytical skills are highly technical in nature. With an academic background in economics, she was an enthusiastic user of new analytical tools, including computer models, during her eight years at mutual fund manager T. Rowe Price and her subsequent seven-year tenure at now-defunct Drexel Burnham Lambert. While her fascination with data and models remains, she deliberately downplays the jargon associated with this quantitative approach to markets in her comments to clients.

"Statistics and econometrics have produced some very good investment ideas for clients, but I don't want the writing I do to be laden down with them," she said. For instance, while her analysis of the stock market's likely reaction to an interest-rate increase by Federal Reserve policymakers last spring was driven by quantitative analysis, in her report she described the rate increase as a "flu shot" that would make investors temporarily queasy, but leave the stock market as a whole in better health and more resistant to stray germs. The current market environment as a whole she describes as the "Silly Putty expansion"—something that stretches almost endlessly, like the children's toy of the same name.

Ms. Cohen's early call that a new kind of bull market was emerging was a result of her interest in statistics. Studying the industrial production reports for the summer of 1990, she noted that technology-related spending was growing at double-digit rates, a dramatically higher level than spending in the overall economy. After further study, she concluded—correctly—that U.S. companies were restructuring and cutting costs in a way that could lead to a surge in both profitability and stock prices. She found further support for this theory in otherwise-overlooked employment statistics in 1992 and 1993, noting a surge in laid-off employees finding part-time work or describing themselves as self-employed. This, she concluded, meant that they were recognizing that the structural changes to the companies and industries in which they had worked were permanent—and that they were successfully adapting to a new type of economy.

Still, Ms. Cohen hasn't been infallible. A call that small stocks were about to rebound late in 1996 proved flawed, something she readily admits, although by late summer 1997, when small stocks began consistently outperforming their larger counterparts, the call was looking more prescient.

Consistency is a key ingredient of the approach to investment strategy and research for Ms. Cohen and Goldman as a whole. The firm's institutional clientele—the financial markets. She hasn't changed her recommended portfolio mix since May 1995, noting that Goldman's institutional clients prefer to stick with long-term trends rather than make quick shifts between sectors or specific stocks, and look to the firm's researchers and strategists for guidance on broad issues rather than buy or sell recommendations.

"The kind of consistency we strive for is a broad enough one that allows us to present our industry and market positions within the context of a given market outlook, without putting us in a straitjacket so we can't discuss other alternatives," said Steven Einhorn, Ms. Cohen's predecessor as U.S. strategist, who now heads global investment research at Goldman and cochairs the investment policy committee with her. "But I don't think it's a good idea to be delivering wildly inconsistent messages."

In some cases, the cue comes from the analysts themselves, as in the technology stock meltdown during the spring of 1997. Goldman technology analysts found few reasons for anxiety in the fundamentals of most of the stocks they cover, a view that found expression in Ms. Cohen's calm reaction to the sell-off and her assurances that the technology sector didn't appear to be overvalued.

"We don't let the market dictate our view. This is our hallmark," said Mr. Einhorn. "We've also tried not to let history determine our view if we think secular changes are under way, as in the case of our opinion that the current economic expansion has a different character than those that preceded it, which would make it longer-lived, less inflationary and more profit-generating."

Both Mr. Einhorn and Ms. Cohen have watched as both investment strategy and research departments have soared in importance over the last decade, a fact Mr. Einhorn attributes to the proliferation of mutual funds, all with managers looking for help in the constant quest for outperformance. Every year in the last ten, he says, Goldman's research department has increased in size by more than the firm's average headcount. Today, the firm has 220 analysts following 2,000 stocks worldwide, based in eleven countries and regions, up from 130 analysts covering 1,250 companies five years ago. That aggressive hiring seems to be yielding dividends. In the 1996 *Wall Street Journal* all-star research analyst survey, Goldman ranked third, with twenty-one all-stars, including Richard Simon, who tracks entertainment stocks, Marc Cohen, their tobacco analyst, and Amy Gassman, a veteran metals analyst. In 1997, the firm was ranked second, with thirty all-star analysts. More than half of the companies Goldman tracks are non-U.S. firms, and more than half of its research staff are based abroad.

"The importance of research is ever-increasing because the world of investments has become more complex, and investors are in need of more expertise," Mr. Einhorn says. To cope with the rapid growth, Goldman has made heavy investments in new technologies that will allow it to deliver research products via the Internet or allow investors to input new data into Goldman's models for quick updates. It's also publishing an internal electronic newspaper that facilitates communication among the various parts of its research department.

Unique to Goldman Sachs's research effort in the last five years is its growing focus on commodities, an area long shunned by a large portion of its institutional clientele. The firm recommends investors hold up to 5 percent of their assets in its proprietary Goldman Sachs Commodity Index. That went a long way in 1996 when the GSCI rocketed 33.9 percent higher thanks to strong oil prices and a bull market in grains. The research effort, headed by a former economist with the Federal Reserve Bank of Chicago, Steve Strongin, includes a high-profile annual commodities investment conference and is aimed at supporting Goldman's efforts to market a wide range of high-margin investment vehicles linked to commodity prices. Despite the heavy investments made in this area, it remains to be seen whether institutional investors will accept commodities as a core part of their portfolios and investment strategy.

Goldman's People

Corzine, Jon
Chairman and CEO
Goldman Sachs

Jon Corzine, chairman and chief executive officer: Mr. Corzine was appointed to his post in 1994. The easygoing Mr. Corzine, one of the few top executives on Wall Street to sport a beard, previously had been Goldman's cohead of fixed-income. Among his earlier positions was partner in charge of government, mortgage and money-markets trading within the firm's bond group. He joined the firm in 1975, became a vice president in 1977 and a partner in 1980. Before joining Goldman, Mr. Corzine had worked at Bancohio Corp. and Continental Illinois National Bank.

Henry Paulson Jr., president: Mr. Paulson was named president and chief operating officer in 1996. He previously had been vice chairman and COO. Before that Mr. Paulson was cohead of investment banking, and became a partner in 1982. Before joining Goldman in 1974, Mr. Paulson was a member of the White House Domestic Council serving as staff assistant to President Nixon in 1972 and 1973.

Roy Zuckerberg, vice chairman: Mr. Zuckerberg is also a member of the executive committee and head of Goldman's stock division. He joined the firm in 1967 in securities sales and was made a partner in 1977. Mr. Zuckerberg is chairman of the executive committee of the Goldman, Sachs & Co. Bank in Zurich. He serves on the firm's partnership committee and research users committee.

Robert Hurst, vice chairman: Mr. Hurst is head of investment banking and a member of the firm's executive committee. Mr. Hurst became a member of the management committee and cohead of investment banking in 1990. He joined the firm from Merrill Lynch and became a partner in 1980.

John Thain, chief financial officer: Mr. Thain also is a member of Goldman's executive, operating, finance and risk committees, as well as a managing director and chief financial officer of Goldman, Sachs & Co. He joined Goldman in 1979 and became a partner in 1988.

John Thornton, executive committee: Mr. Thornton is responsible for Goldman's Asian operations. He also has primary responsibility for certain key Goldman clients in Europe, where he was based for more than a dozen years. Mr. Thornton became a partner and a managing director of Goldman Sachs International in 1988. He joined the firm in 1980.

Paul Achleitner, cohead, Frankfurt office: Mr. Achleitner became a partner in 1994. An Austrian citizen, he jointly heads Goldman's investment-banking division in the German-speaking region. Before joining the firm in 1988, he worked at Bain & Co. as a project manager.

Andrew Alper, cohead of financial-institutions group: Mr. Alper joined Goldman in 1981 and became a partner in 1990. He joined the investment-banking's financial-institutions group in 1990 after nine years covering industrial companies, primarily in the Midwest.

Peter Barker, head of investment banking, West Coast: Mr. Barker became a partner in 1982. He is resident manager of Goldman's Los Angeles office. Between 1971 and 1977, Mr. Barker was in the firm's global-finance department in New York.

Milton Berlinski, investment banking: Mr. Berlinski leads the asset-management business for the firm's financial-institutions group in New York and became a managing director in 1996. He also is actively involved in bank, commercial/consumer finance, and insurance mergers and acquisitions.

Lloyd Blankfein, cohead, bond, currency and commodities division: Mr. Blankfein became a partner in 1988 and serves on a variety of Goldman's committees; these include the operating, risk, diversity, recruiting and training committees. He joined Goldman in 1982.

William Buckley, equities: Mr. Buckley was named head of private-client services in 1990, the same year he became a partner. Previously, he was co-resident manager of Goldman's Boston office.

Mary Ann Casati, cohead of the retail-industry focus group in corporate finance: Ms. Casati joined the firm in 1982 in investment banking and became a managing director in 1996.

Zachariah Cobrinik, cohead of equities in Tokyo: Mr. Cobrinik has held a variety of stock-related posts, including trading in equity derivatives and index options. He became a managing director in 1996.

Abby Joseph Cohen, investment research: Ms. Cohen is cochair of the firm's investment-policy committee and a member of the stock-selection committee. Before joining Goldman in 1990, she was a vice president at Drexel Burnham Lambert Inc.

Carlos Cordeiro, bond, currency and commodities division: Mr. Cordeiro is jointly responsible for Goldman's bond capital-markets activities in Europe. He joined the firm in 1990 from Credit Suisse First Boston, and became a partner in 1992.

Henry Cornell, investment banking: Mr. Cornell is head of Goldman's principal-investment and real-estate principal investment areas in the Asia-Pacific region, a position he has held since 1992. He became a partner in 1994.

E. Gerald Corrigan, executive administration: Mr. Corrigan is cochairman of the firm's risk committee and of the global compliance and control committee. He became a managing director in 1996. Before joining Goldman in 1993, he held a variety of posts at the Federal Reserve System, most recently as president and CEO of the Federal Reserve Bank of New York.

Claudio Costamagna, investment banking: Mr. Costamagna heads the Italian market effort for Goldman's investment-banking division in London. He became a managing director in 1996.

John Curtin Jr., chief executive, Goldman Sachs Canada: Before his current post, Mr. Curtin was cohead of global money markets and chairman of Goldman Sachs Money Markets L.P. He joined the firm in 1976 and was made a partner in 1988.

Timothy Dattels, investment banking: Mr. Dattels became a managing director and head of investment banking services for Asian countries other than Japan in 1996.

Gavyn Davies, investment research: Mr. Davies is chief international economist and cohead of investment research in London. He joined the firm in 1986 and was made a partner in 1988.

Robert Delaney Jr., investment banking: Mr. Delaney is head of the leverage-finance group in corporate finance. He joined Goldman in 1986 and became head of the high-yield group in corporate finance in 1991. He became a partner in 1994.

Joseph Della Rosa, comanager of Nasdaq department: Mr. Della Rosa has held his current post since 1991. He joined the firm as a trader in 1983 and became a partner in 1994. Mr. Della Rosa serves on Goldman's global compliance and controls committee.

Eric Dobkin, equities: Mr. Dobkin has been head of global equity capital markets since 1985. He joined Goldman in 1967 in institutional sales and became a partner in 1982. He serves on Goldman's operating committee and commitments committee.

John O. Downing, equities: Mr. Downing, a member of stock capital markets, previously was head of European stock capital markets. He joined Goldman in 1982 and was made a partner in 1992 and a managing director in 1996.

Connie Duckworth, fixed income, currency and commodity division: Ms. Duckworth was made a partner and became manager of Goldman's fixed-income division in Chicago in 1990. She is on the firmwide compensation committee, and serves as an adviser to the diversity committee.

William Dudley, investment research: Mr. Dudley is head of U.S. economic research in New York. He joined the firm in 1986 and became a managing director in 1996.

Dexter Earle, equities: Mr. Earle is cohead of Goldman's stock derivatives department. He joined Goldman in 1981 and became a partner in 1988.

Glenn P. Earle, new markets: Mr. Earle leads a cross-divisional effort focusing on developing Goldman's business in the new markets of Central and Eastern Europe, the Middle East and Africa. He joined Goldman in 1987 and became a managing director in 1996.

Herbert Ehlers, asset management: Mr. Ehlers joined Goldman in 1997 and made a managing director when the firm bought Liberty Investment Management. Mr. Ehlers was cofounder, CEO and chief investment officer of Liberty and its predecessor, Eagle Asset Management.

Steven Einhorn, global investment research: Mr. Einhorn is partner-in-charge of the global investment research department and cochairman of Goldman's investment policy committee. He joined the firm in 1977 and became a partner in 1986.

Guy Erb, vice chairman, Mexican operations: Mr. Erb has held a variety of senior posts at Goldman Sachs Mexico Casa de Bolsa S.A. de C.V. since 1990.

J. Michael Evans, equities: Mr. Evans is head of European equity capital markets in London. He joined Goldman in 1993 from Salomon Brothers Inc., and became a partner in 1994.

W. Mark Evans, executive administration: Mr. Evans became chairman of Goldman Sachs (Asia) L.L.C. in 1994. He joined the firm in 1984 and became a partner in 1992.

Lawton W. Fitt, equities: Ms. Fitt has worked in stock capital markets since 1989; previously, she had worked in corporate finance. She joined the firm in 1979, became a partner in 1994 and a managing director in 1996.

J. Christopher Flowers, investment banking: Mr. Flowers became cohead of the financial-institutions group in 1994. He joined the firm in 1979 and became a partner in 1988.

David Ford, asset management: Mr. Ford is cohead of Goldman Sachs Asset Management. He joined the firm in 1970 and became a partner in 1986.

Richard Friedman, principal-investment area: Mr. Friedman is head of Goldman's principal-investment area. He joined the firm in 1981 and became a partner in 1990.

C. Douglas Fuge, operation, technology and finance: Mr. Fuge is the firm's controller; he joined Goldman in 1984.

Fredric Garonzik, cohead, fixed income: Before his current post, Mr. Garonzik was head of debt capital markets in London, and has held a variety of bond posts.

Gary Gensler, head of operations, technology and finance in Asia: Mr. Gensler joined the firm in 1979 and became a partner in 1988.

Peter Gerhard, fixed income, currency and commodities division: Mr. Gerhard is the firm's chief dealer in foreign exchange, a position he has held since 1992. He became a partner in 1994.

Nomi P. Ghez, food analyst in investment research: Ms. Ghez became a partner in 1994 and a managing director in 1996. She joined Goldman in 1982.

Alan R. Gillespie, investment banking, London: Mr. Gillespie is in Goldman's investment banking services department with specific responsibility for corporate and financial services clients in the U.K. and Ireland. He became a partner in 1990 and a managing director in 1996.

Jeffrey Goldenberg, equities: Mr. Goldenberg became head of private client services in New York in 1996. He joined Goldman in 1981 and became a managing director in 1996.

Jacob Goldfield, fixed income, currency and commodities division: Mr. Goldfield is a member of Goldman's bond derivatives group. He joined the firm in 1985 as a bond-option trader and was made a partner in 1990.

Richard Hayden, investment banking: Mr. Hayden is head of Goldman's European investment-banking division. He joined the firm in 1969 and became a partner in 1980.

Walter Haydock, equities: Mr. Haydock is chief administrative officer of Goldman's equities division. He joined the firm in 1979 and became a partner in 1994.

Thomas Healey, pension services group: Mr. Healey became head of pension services in 1990. He joined the firm in 1985 to create real-estate capital markets. He was made a partner in 1988.

Sylvain Hefes, investment banking: Mr. Hefes has responsibility for Goldman's banking activities in France and Belgium. He joined the firm in 1989 and became a partner in the M&A group in 1992.

Steven Heller, investment banking: Mr. Heller heads Goldman's M&A department. He joined the firm in 1982 and became a partner in 1990.

David Henle, equities: Mr. Henle was named cohead of global private client services in 1992. He became a partner in 1994.

Robert Higgins, investment banking: Mr. Higgins coheads the investment-banking services department in the United States for the Americas group. He became a partner in 1988.

Hideo Ishihara, chairman of Japanese operations: Mr. Ishihara became head of Goldman Sachs (Japan) Ltd. in 1994, when he joined the firm as a partner.

Reuben Jeffrey, investment banking: Mr. Jeffrey is head of the European financial-institutions group. He joined the firm in 1983 and became a partner in 1992.

Stefan Jentzsch, investment banking: Mr. Jentzsch is a member of the advisory group in Frankfurt and served as the lead relationship and execution banker on the Deutsche Telekom IPO. He joined the firm in 1987 and became a managing director in 1996.

Daniel Jick, equities: Mr. Jick has served as head of Goldman's equities group in Boston since 1993. He joined the firm in 1981 and became a managing director in 1996.

Suzanne Nora Johnson, investment banking: Ms. Johnson coheads Goldman's health-care activities. She joined the firm in 1985 and became a partner in 1992.

Ann Kaplan, fixed income, currency and commodities division: Ms. Kaplan is partner-in-charge of municipal finance. She is cochairman of Goldman's diversity committee, and became a partner in 1990.

Robert Kaplan, investment banking: Mr. Kaplan became cohead of the Americas corporate-finance department in 1995. He previously held senior banking posts in Goldman's Tokyo office, and became a partner in 1990.

Robert Katz, general counsel: Mr. Katz also is co-general counsel of Goldman's parent, sharing senior responsibility for the firm's legal advice and representation, and for management of Goldman's legal unit. Mr. Katz also is a member of the partnership committee, the global compliance and control committee and the diversity committee. Before joining the firm and becoming a partner in 1988, Mr. Katz was a partner at Sullivan & Cromwell.

Kevin Kelly, fixed income, currency and commodities division: Mr. Kelly is head of Goldman's corporate-bond department. He joined the firm in 1985 and became a partner in 1994.

Kevin Kennedy, investment banking: Mr. Kennedy became head of the Americas group in 1994. He joined the firm in 1974 and became a partner in 1984.

James Kiernan Jr., president, Canadian operations: Mr. Kiernan has been head of Goldman Sachs Canada since 1998, after serving a stint in the United Kingdom and the United States.

Peter Kiernan, investment banking: Mr. Kiernan has been cohead of the communications, media and entertainment group since 1992. He joined the firm in 1984 and became a partner in 1990.

John Kleinert, fixed income, currency and commodities division: Mr. Kleinert is in charge of municipal-bond trading, sales and underwriting. He joined the firm as a bond trader in 1982 and became a partner in 1994.

Bradford C. Koenig, head of high-technology group, investment banking: Before his current post, Mr. Koenig worked in investment banking in New York. He joined Goldman in 1984 and became a managing director in 1996.

Darell Krasnoff, equities: Mr. Krasnoff is cohead of Goldman's stock division with oversight responsibility for private-client services. He joined the firm in 1981 and became a managing director in 1996.

Bruce Larson, personnel: Mr. Larson became director of global personnel in 1996. He joined the firm in 1987 and became a managing director in 1996.

David Leuschen, investment banking: Mr. Leuschen is cohead of the energy and power group in the investment-banking division. He joined the firm in 1977, became a partner in 1986 and a managing director in 1996.

Gwen R. Libstag, investment banking: Ms. Libstag joined the merger department in 1983 and became a managing director in 1996.

Lawrence Linden, operations, technology and finance: Mr. Linden is responsible for Goldman's global operations. He joined the firm and became a partner in 1992 after serving as McKinsey & Co.'s principal consultant to Goldman. He became a managing director in 1996.

Robert Litterman, operations, technology and finance: Mr. Litterman is in charge of firmwide risk management. He joined the firm in 1986.

Robert Litzenberger, fixed income, currency and commodities division: Mr. Litzenberger is head of derivatives research and of the quantitative modeling group in New York. He joined the firm in 1995 and became a managing director in 1996.

Jonathan Lopatin, fixed income, currency and commodities division: Mr. Lopatin is the global manager of foreign-exchange sales. He joined the firm in 1984 and became a partner in 1994.

Jun Makihara, equities: Mr. Makihara is cohead of the stock division in Tokyo. He joined the firm in 1981 and became a partner in 1992.

Peter Mallinson, equities: Mr. Mallinson became head of the stock division for Southeast Asia in 1993 and a partner in 1994.

Eff Martin, investment banking: Mr. Martin directs Goldman's investment-banking activities in Northern California and the Pacific Northwest. He joined the firm in 1983 and became a partner in 1988.

Oki Matsumoto, fixed income, currency and commodities division: Mr. Matsumoto is a partner in Goldman's bond, currency and commodities unit in Tokyo.

Charles Mayer Jr., fixed income, currency and commodities division: Mr. Mayer is head of money-market sales, trading and origination. He joined the firm in 1987 and was made a partner in 1988.

Thomas Mayer, investment research: Mr. Mayer became a managing director and cohead of European economic research in 1996.

Michael McCarthy, fixed income, currency and commodities division: Mr. McCarthy became partner-in-charge of the municipal-bond department in 1994 after four years as head of municipal finance. He joined the firm in 1977.

John McNulty, asset management: Mr. McNulty is cohead of Goldman's asset-management division and a member of the firm's operating committee. Previously, he had been partner-in-charge of the firm's special investments group in stock capital markets.

Eric M. Mindich, manager of the stock arbitrage department: Mr. Mindich joined Goldman in 1988 in the stock arbitrage department, became a partner in 1994 and a managing director in 1996.

Steven Mnuchin, fixed income, currency and commodities division: Mr. Mnuchin is head of Goldman's mortgage-securities department. He joined the firm in 1985 and became a partner in 1994.

Masanori Mochida, investment banking: Mr. Mochida is cohead of investment banking in Tokyo. He joined the firm in 1985 and became a partner in 1992.

Thomas Montag, fixed income, currency and commodities division: Mr. Montag is manager of derivatives marketing and trading in London. He joined the firm in 1985 and became a partner in 1994.

Michael Mortara, fixed income, currency and commodities division: Mr. Mortara is cohead of Goldman's fixed income, currency and commodities division. He previously was head of mortgage securities. He joined Goldman and became a partner in 1987 after a high-profile stint at Salomon Brothers, where he was cohead of that firm's mortgage, corporate and short-term trading areas. He became a managing director in 1996.

Sharmin Mossavar-Rahmani, chief investment officer for bond assets in the asset-management division: Ms. Mossavar-Rahmani joined the firm as a partner in 1993 and became a managing director in 1996. Before Goldman, she worked at Fidelity and Lehman.

Edward A. Mule, cohead of the distressed and special situations financial instruments business in high yield: Before joining Goldman's high-yield area in 1995, Mr. Mule worked in executive administration and mergers and acquisitions. He joined the firm in 1984, became a partner in 1994 and was made a managing director in 1996.

Philip Murphy, investment banking: In 1997, Mr. Murphy was appointed president and managing director of Goldman Sachs (Asia) L.L.C. He joined Goldman in 1982 and became a partner in 1992.

Gaetano Muzio, fixed income, currency and commodities division: Mr. Muzio became the managing director resident fixed-income sales manager of the San Francisco office in 1995. He joined Goldman in 1977.

Avi M. Nash, securities analyst, U.S. chemical industry: Mr. Nash, who became a managing director in 1996, also coheads the firm's global chemical research effort. He has been highly ranked in *Institutional Investor* and Reuters surveys of research analysts.

Daniel Neidich, investment banking: Mr. Neidich is head of Goldman's real-estate principal-investment area; he previously had been head of the firm's real-estate unit. Known as Goldman's "Rottweiler" because of his aggressive deal-making ways, Mr. Neidich was made a partner in 1984 after joining Goldman in 1978.

Robin Neustein, executive administration: Ms. Neustein is Goldman's chief of staff, serving as adviser to the chairman and the vice chairman and overseeing the executive office. She joined Goldman in 1982 and became a partner in 1990.

Terence O'Neill, global investment research: Mr. O'Neill joined the firm in 1995 as a managing director and chief currency economist.

Timothy J. O'Neill, fixed income, currency and commodities division: Mr. O'Neill joined Goldman in 1985 and was made a partner in 1990. He became a managing director in 1996.

Robert O'Shea, fixed income, currency and commodities division: Mr. O'Shea is head of bank-loan syndication sales and trading. He joined the firm in 1990 to start Goldman's bank-loan business and became a partner in 1994, and a managing director in 1996.

Terence M. O'Toole, principal investment area: Mr. O'Toole joined the principal investment area when it was launched in 1991. He joined the firm in 1983, made partner in 1992 and became a managing director in 1996.

Gregory Palm, legal: Mr. Palm is co-general counsel of Goldman's international operations, co-general counsel of Goldman's parent, and cohead of the firm's worldwide legal department. He is cochairman of the global compliance and control committee, joining the firm and becoming a partner in 1992.

Scott Pinkus, fixed income, currency and commodities division: Mr. Pinkus is partner-in-charge of the bond-research department. Mr. Pinkus joined the firm in 1986 after stints at Morgan Stanley and Merrill; he became a partner in 1990.

Stephen D. Quinn, investment banking: Mr. Quinn is with the corporate finance department of the firm's Americas group. He joined Goldman in 1981, became a partner in 1990 and a managing director in 1996.

Arthur J. Reimers III, cohead of the healthcare department in investment banking: Mr. Reimers previously had been cohead of the investment banking advisory group in Europe, as well as cohead of European mergers and acquisitions. He became a partner in 1990 and a managing director in 1996.

Simon Robertson, president of European operations: Mr. Robertson, former chairman of Dresdner Kleinwort Benson, joined Goldman as a managing director and president of Goldman Sachs Europe Ltd. on September 1, 1997. Mr. Robertson, a mergers-and-acquisitions specialist, develops client relationships and is also involved in setting the firm's global investment-banking strategy.

J. David Rogers, equities: Mr. Rogers oversees stock-derivatives, capital commitment and risk management. Before joining Goldman in 1982, he had been a financial analyst at Mobil Oil Corp.; he became a partner in 1992.

John Rogers, corporate affairs: Mr. Rogers is a vice president and director of corporate affairs. Before joining Goldman, he served in a variety of administration posts, including undersecretary of state for management at the U.S. State Department.

Jack L. Salzman, U.S. director of research marketing and product development: Before his current post, Mr. Salzman was a senior analyst and associate director of research. He became a partner in 1994 and a managing director in 1996.

P. Sheridan Schechner, investment banking: Mr. Schechner is responsible for leadership of the commercial-mortgage joint venture with the firm's bond division. He became a managing director in 1996.

Mark Schwartz, president, Japanese operations: Mr. Schwartz in 1997 was appointed president of Goldman Sachs (Japan) Ltd.; previously, he had been head of global capital markets. He joined the firm in 1979 and became a partner in 1988.

Charles Seelig Jr., fixed income, currency and commodities division: Mr. Seelig is head of the bond emerging-debt markets group. He joined Goldman in 1984 and became a partner in 1992.

Steven Shafran, investment banking: Mr. Shafran is cohead of Goldman's principal-investment area in the Asia-Pacific region, a post he has held since 1993. He became a managing director in 1996.

Richard G. Sherlund, computer software industry analyst: Mr. Sherlund has held this position since joining Goldman in 1982. He became a partner in 1994 and a managing director in 1996.

Howard A. Silverstein, investment banking: Mr. Silverstein is in the financial institutions group and specializes in advisory, financing and merger assignments for insurance companies and other nonbank financial institutions. He joined the firm in 1972, became a partner in 1980 and a managing director in 1996.

Daniel Stanton, equities: Mr. Stanton is the manager of global securities services and is president of Goldman's trust company. He joined the firm in 1981 and became a partner in 1994.

Robert Steel, equities: Mr. Steel is co-chief operating officer of the stock division and a member of the operating committee. He joined the firm in 1976 and became a partner in 1988.

Robert Stellato, equities: Mr. Stellato is cohead of Nasdaq product in New York. He joined the firm in 1974 and became a managing director in 1996.

Peter Sutherland, chairman, Goldman Sachs International: Mr. Sutherland also is a member of the operating committee. Before his current post, Mr. Sutherland was an international adviser to the firm and director-general of the World Trade Organization.

Mark Tercek, investment banking: Mr. Tercek became head of Goldman's real-estate department in 1996. He previously had been head of the transportation group, and had worked for Goldman's investment-banking group in Tokyo. He joined the firm in 1984 and became a managing director in 1996.

Leslie Tortora, operations, technology and finance: Ms. Tortora manages Goldman's global information technology department. She joined the firm in 1984 and became a partner in 1992.

Thomas E. Tuft, co-chief operating officer and cohead of stock capital markets: Mr. Tuft joined the firm in 1976 as a vice president in New York institutional sales and moved to stock capital markets in 1985. He became a partner in 1986 and a managing director in 1996.

David Viniar, operations, technology and finance: Mr. Viniar is Goldman's cohead of finance, responsible for controllers and treasurers worldwide. He joined the firm in 1980 and became a partner in 1992.

Patrick Ward, equities: Mr. Ward is head of Goldman's stock division in London. He earlier had been head of the firm's Tokyo stock operations. Mr. Ward joined the firm in 1980 and became a partner in 1990.

Peter Weinberg, investment banking: Mr. Weinberg is head of global communications, media and technology and also head of the leveraged-buyout group. He joined the firm as a vice president in 1988 and became a partner in 1992.

Jeffrey Weingarten, asset management: Mr. Weingarten is Goldman's global strategist. He joined the firm in 1977 and was made a partner in 1990.

George Wellde Jr., fixed income, currency and commodities division: Mr. Wellde is manager of Goldman's bond business in Tokyo and also the Tokyo branch manager. He joined the firm in 1979 and became a partner in 1992.

Peter Wheeler, investment banking: Mr. Wheeler is a senior banker in Hong Kong who has helped expand Goldman's presence throughout Asia. He joined the firm in 1985 and became a partner in 1994.

In the Beginning . . .

Belying its highbrow reputation, Goldman had modest beginnings. Marcus Goldman, making the rounds of local businesses, began hawking commercial paper on the streets of New York in 1869. "He purchased the promissory notes of their customers, providing an alternative to bank credit, which was expensive and in short supply," Goldman said in a 1993 review celebrating its 125th anniversary. "He stuffed the notes in the headband of his hat for safekeeping and, at midday, sold them to New York's commercial banks." Goldman formed a partnership with Samuel Sachs in 1882. Unlike most other Wall Street firms, the firm's name has remained the same throughout the years.

The firm joined the New York Stock Exchange in 1896. Beginning in the late nineteenth century, the firm began establishing a regional network of offices in the United States that included Chicago. One early client from the 1880s was Sears, Roebuck & Co.; Goldman led Sears's initial public stock offering in 1906. Goldman soon became a pioneer in underwriting IPOs, and remains among the leaders in this lucrative field. After difficulties during the Great Depression, Goldman regained its momentum by the end of World War II under the direction of Sidney Weinberg, who ultimately sat on the boards of forty corporations and was known as "Mr. Wall Street."

Goldman was among the first Wall Street firms to successfully tap the growing role of institutions in the securities markets. Led by Gus Levy, head of the firm's securities-trading business, Goldman pioneered buying and selling large blocks of stock. (Much later, applying financial techniques used in the securities markets, J. Aron, acquired in 1981, became a leader in currency and commodity markets worldwide.)

In 1956, Goldman helped to orchestrate the $657 million IPO of Ford Motor Co.—the largest common-stock offering to that time. The Ford offering advertisement—a "tombstone" in Wall Street parlance—lived up to its name. Most of the more than seven hundred securities firms in the selling syndicate no longer exist. The Ford relationship was so close that Goldman's senior partners drove only Ford cars, and its bankers, for fear of offending Ford, refused to even call on the auto maker's rivals, General Motors Corp. and Chrysler Corp. For years, Ford awarded virtually all its considerable investment-banking business to Goldman.

But that didn't help Goldman in 1997, when it lost out to J. P. Morgan & Co., which advised Ford on the $1.7 billion sale of its Budget Rent-A-Car division and lead-managed a $460 million IPO of Ford's Hertz Corp. unit, the nation's largest rental-car company. Though Goldman still does a considerable amount of underwriting for Ford—indeed, Goldman advised Ford in its $17.6 billion spinoff of Associates First Capital Corp. to shareholders in 1997—the snub was particularly stinging because of the long relationship with the auto maker.

Gary Williams, equities: Mr. Williams is responsible for Goldman's stock-trading unit in London. He previously was manager of the global-convertibles desk, which he continues to advise. He joined the firm in 1980 and became a partner in 1994.

Jon Winkelried, fixed income, currency and commodities division: Mr. Winkelried is responsible for all of Goldman's corporate-bond business. This includes investment-grade corporate bonds, high-yield bonds, bank-debt trading and preferred stock. He joined the firm in 1981 and became a partner in 1990.

Steven Wisch, equities: Mr. Wisch became head of stock capital markets in Hong Kong in 1994 and a managing director in 1996.

Richard Witten, fixed income, currency and commodities division: Mr. Witten is cohead of capital markets in New York. He previously had been head of J. Aron Marketing and was responsible for recruiting and hiring for the J. Aron division, and earlier had been J. Aron general counsel. He joined the firm in 1981 and became a partner in 1990.

Jaime Yordan, investment banking: Mr. Yordan heads the Latin America group within the Americas group. He joined the firm in 1990 and became a partner in 1992.

Michael Zamkow, fixed income, currency and commodities division: Mr. Zamkow was named European bond sales manager in 1996. He became a partner in 1994.

Gregory Zehner, fixed income, currency and commodities division: Mr. Zehner has been head of emerging market trading since 1995. He joined the firm in 1987 and became a managing director in 1996.

Joseph Zimmel, investment banking: Mr. Zimmel is cohead of the communications, media and entertainment group in the investment-banking division. He joined the firm in 1979 and became a partner in 1988.

Barry Zubrow, operations, technology and finance: Mr. Zubrow is head of the credit department, which is responsible for managing the firm's global credit exposures. Mr. Zubrow joined the firm in 1980 and became a partner in 1988.

Mark Zurack, equities: Mr. Zurack is cohead of global stock derivatives research, the department in which he has worked since 1986. He joined the firm in 1983 and became a partner in 1994.

CREDIT SUISSE FIRST BOSTON CORP.

SEARCHING FOR SWISS PRECISION

Yet Another Makeover

I t was a bold bet. In a sweeping 1996 revamping by Switzerland's CS Holding AG, the financial-services giant melded its First Boston U.S. investment bank and Credit Suisse commercial bank. First Boston was merged into a new unit—Credit Suisse First Boston Corp.—dealing in securities, derivatives, advisory and wholesale commercial banking.

But there were quick hiccups. The new unit's combined annual net income initially was estimated at $1.2 billion. Then staffers believed it could be closer to $700 million. But they still weren't sure. Finally, First Boston's investment bankers were advised not to tell prospective clients about the new unit's profitability at all until it was straightened out. It turned out that the initial estimate was a "back of the envelope" guesstimate. And the numbers kept changing because of discussions over which Credit Suisse unit got what businesses, and at what cost.

"The original discrepancy came from where we cut the baby in the inter-company trading area—there was shifting from this pocket to that pocket," said Credit Suisse First Boston chairman and chief executive Allen Wheat. The real number for the newly combined unit, Mr. Wheat said in mid-1997: "The best guess is that it's somewhere around $900 million."

First Boston still seeks that Swiss precision that would vault the firm back to its days as one of Wall Street's most preeminent securities firms. After scores of defections, First Boston's Swiss parent has grabbed more control of the investment bank's destiny—and promises better returns ahead. Maybe borrowing the Credit Suisse name will help. Indeed, behind the shift is the perception that the Swiss name lends stability to one of Wall Street's most volatile franchises.

"The deep pockets of Credit Suisse now are being played up as the ten-foot-tall giant standing behind the firm," said Samuel Hayes, professor of investment banking at Harvard Business School.

The move followed several makeovers of the firm in recent years. At one point, First Boston was broken up into three major units, covering the United States, Europe and Asia. But that organizational structure allowed its U.S. and European units to compete for the same underwriting and merger assignments; this triggered internal rivalries. A few years back, that grid was chucked in a reorganization that enabled First Boston to operate along product lines instead of geography. This helped the firm cut costs by eliminating triplicate bureaucracies in all three markets.

For several years, the biggest drag on First Boston's performance was its lack of capital, which was cut slightly by CS Holding's buyout of the firm in 1988, and far more substantially by losses from soured bridge loans. And though First Boston became a powerhouse in mergers, mortgage trading and Eurobonds in the 1980s, it didn't invest heavily in areas that now are spewing out profits for other firms, including money management and foreign stocks and bonds. "The old CS First Boston had a miserable portfolio of business. Everything was highly correlated. Nothing was a reoccuring cash business and all of them were correlated," CEO Allen Wheat said in a speech to First Boston executives after the 1996 reorganization. He said that won't be a problem with the new Credit Suisse First Boston.

Still, the 1996 revamping took some on Wall Street by surprise. Because of First Boston's uneven results, some analysts had expected CS Holding to shed First Boston entirely. CS Holding was forced to bail out the investment bank in 1990 after troubles over its $1.1 billion high-risk "bridge-loan" portfolio nearly sank the firm. CS Holding made a $300 million capital infusion into First Boston as part of an $800 million recapitalization that saved the firm from collapsing. And in 1994, CS Holding made an additional equity-capital infusion of about $400 million into the investment bank.

"It's always been very clear the Swiss like control," said William Mayer, a former First Boston chief executive. The new reorganization, and new name with Credit Suisse's top billing, underscores that First Boston "is under their total grip."

There's no denying that the newly combined Credit Suisse First Boston unit will help by creating a stronger international investment-banking franchise. It has about $7.2 billion in equity capital and about 11,000 employees worldwide. Before the new combination, First Boston had about $1.7 billion in equity capital and 5,400 employees, making it the most thinly capitalized of the top-tier Wall Street powerhouses. "The size and financial strength" of the new Credit Suisse First Boston "compares favorably to our competitors," the firm said in an internal March 1997 memo. "Our equity capital exceeds all our special bracket competitors (with the exception of the merged Morgan Stanley, Dean Witter) and our revenues and profits also reinforce our 'global special bracket' positioning and are clearly ahead of other European competitors."

Then there's First Boston's increased clout with its Swiss parent. In the 1990s before the merger, CS Holding had about a 65 percent ownership interest in CS First Boston. The investment bank "and its prima donnas" were blamed for anything that went wrong, Mr. Wheat said. Also, the investment bank's earnings represented a relatively small percentage of the parent's results. With the restructuring, the newly combined corporate and investment banking firm was renamed Credit Suisse First Boston, became 100% owned by Credit Suisse Group, and had the largest block of the parent's capital, so, Mr. Wheat said: "There's instant respect for our people and our business."

But challenges abound. First Boston didn't get many high-margin businesses from Credit Suisse in the marriage; some analysts don't expect the union to generate much in the way of beefier profit margins. Though the Swiss trading group the firm inherited is solid, the new wholesale-banking operation generates measly returns, and takes up a huge chunk of the firm's capital. ("It breaks your heart," said Mr. Wheat. "You see returns that are great, great, great—then two percent" for the lending business.) Moreover, the newly combined firm now has so much capital that it will be difficult to muster a high return-on-equity, the premier gauge of Wall Street profitability. First Boston executives have predicted that the firm will hit a 15 percent ROE by 1998. Fat chance, say some Wall Street executives.

"Despite 1996 R.O.E.'s exceeding 20% in some of our business areas, new Credit Suisse First Boston as a whole had an R.O.E. for 1996 under our target rate of at least 15% across business cycles and we would like to be able to earn at a still higher rate in favorable market conditions such as those at present," according to the internal memo. "We need to progress towards the target through a mixture of focused investment and growth plans financed by determined cost cutting and resource allocation."

Among the areas that were cut are the firm's Cairo operations (thirty-three employees); its Luxembourg branch (about forty employees); and 180 bankers in Switzerland that handled a total of five hundred accounts. The uncoordinated and low-tech approach to corporate lending and balance-sheet usage in the wholesale banking area, in particular, frustrated First Boston officials. Mr. Wheat said, "It didn't make any sense in today's market and at today's spreads."

Though First Boston's profits have rebounded amid the roaring bull market of the past couple of years, its returns in the 1990s have lagged behind most of its rivals. And defections have rocked the firm during the past several years. The culprit always seemed to be the same: bonuses.

After bonuses were paid out in February 1996, more than fifty high-level traders, investment bankers and salesmen quit the firm amid complaints that their pay fell below their expectations. The resignations included the firm's highly regarded global and U.S. bond chiefs. To keep traders at the firm, First Boston was forced to dole out guaranteed pay packages of as much as $2.5 million apiece.

The lightning rod for the newer pay problems was Mr. Wheat, now First Boston's chief executive. One reason was that Mr. Wheat received a pay package of about $8 million even as others at the firm were getting their bonuses pared. At a 1996 meeting with 140 traders and salesmen in First Boston's mortgage and asset-backed group, Mr. Wheat was blamed for botching the latest bonus payouts. For instance, though First Boston's mortgage and asset-backed group had losses of $68 million in 1995, traders had been assured they would be paid well.

Mr. Wheat conceded at the time that bonus expectations in the bond area were mismanaged. "We probably—and I am not blaming anybody but me—made some mistakes," Mr. Wheat said. "I should have been more aware of what (employees) were feeling or what they were told."

The pay issue reached almost bizarre proportions. In early 1996, First Boston filed a suit in a New York federal court charging an unknown prankster or pranksters with libeling the firm by sending out confidential salary data by E-mail. The suit sought damages of at least $1 million against "FBCbuster" and "FBCbuster2," the screen names of an America Online subscriber or subscribers who posted the E-mails to hundreds of First Boston employees, according to the suit. (The firm believes it discovered the prankster, who no longer works there; no charges were filed against the individual.)

In 1996, First Boston made up for the pay woes with wildly generous pay packages. The firm paid out a whopping $2.6 billion of about $5.3 billion in revenue for compensation. About fifty people in the firm's bond group received 1996 bonuses of $1 million and higher, partly because a year earlier the firm had been forced to issue pay guarantees under generous formulas. There were so many bond professionals with such pay formulas that those without them were dubbed "Toowoafs"—which stood for The Only Ones Without A Formula. Among the 1996 pay winners: Andrew Stone, First Boston's mortgage and asset-backed securities chief, who received a pay package of about $30 million, Wall Street executives said (though CSFB wouldn't confirm it). "We probably overpaid in a couple of areas—an aggregate across the firm by $50 million to $75 million," Mr. Wheat said. "The problem was that we probably underpaid the year before." The firm has "refined" its compensation system and created higher hurdles for employees to reach to receive the generous pay packages of 1996. Said Mr. Wheat, "It's a high-class problem."

Meantime, CS Holding is betting that the new reorganization will prevent the types of intramural tensions that once rocked the firm. A few years back, Hans-Joerg Rudloff, then-powerful head of First Boston's European operations, ruffled feathers in the firm's U.S. group when after yet another reorganization, he publicly called Credit Suisse a "well-oiled machine," but added, "Our cousins in New York need a little more attention." A startled Mr. Hennessy, then First Boston's chief executive, complained to Mr. Rudloff in a phone call from his office, "Hans-Joerg, I would have put it differently."

And CS Holding Chairman Rainer Gut seems to be hoping that the new plan will improve not only performance, but the firm's appearance in the press. Mr. Gut once felt slighted by *Institutional Investor* magazine because of a negative cover story, in which he was pictured dabbing his eye, as if he were crying, according to a former First Boston executive. Mr. Gut was so infuriated he yanked the firm's advertisements from the magazine for awhile, the executive said.

Pulling ads clearly isn't in Credit Suisse First Boston's game plan now. In 1997 the new firm bombarded financial newspapers and magazines with a new advertising campaign that included bright red, white and blue messages such as: "Eliminate Boundaries," "Break Barriers," "Erase Preconceptions," "Defy Categories," "Obliterate Obstacles" and "Reject Limitations." Good copy. The proof will be in the pudding.

Buying BZW on the Cheap; an IPO Link with Schwab

Credit Suisse First Boston, capitalizing on a weak rival, had a major coup in late 1997: buying the European stock and investment-banking businesses of Barclays PLC's BZW unit for just $170.5 million. The price was far below expectations; indeed, it was significantly less than the operations' declared book value, or assets minus liabilities. "Barclays doesn't look very good on this one," said John Leonard, a banking analyst at Salomon Brothers Inc. in London. "This is clearly a case where the seller was more anxious than the buyer."

The move will help boost two main business lines that are important to Credit Suisse First Boston's global strategy. About 960 BZW workers are expected to move to Credit Suisse First Boston, which has more than 11,000 employees in more than 50 offices in more than 30 countries. Included will be BZW's stock capital markets, research, sales and trading, corporate-finance and mergers-and-acquisitions operations. "The addition of BZW will give us a third home market in the U.K.," said Mr. Wheat. "We now [will] have a home market in the U.S., Switzerland and the U.K. This acquisition will not only enhance our presence in Europe and the U.K., but it will also help us serve our clients around the world."

Credit Suisse First Boston will take a charge of about $170.5 million to cover integration costs. The acquisition is expected to be completed in early 1998. The company said the expenditure will be partly offset by efficiencies from combining the businesses.

The result: a stock-trading force in Europe. Said Brady Dougan, head of the firm's stock operations: "We're convinced that CSFB's top franchise in Eastern Europe, BZW's leading franchise in the U.K., and the strength of our combined Continental business, gives us the platform to become the top equity firm in Europe."

Moreover, Credit Suisse First Boston took a bold step to broaden its core business to institutions in 1997. The firm was one of three investment banks to join the rush to sell stock to small investors by arranging to distribute shares of stocks they underwrite to customers of Charles Schwab Corp., the leading discount brokerage firm. First Boston hopes the two-year linkup with Schwab will make it more competitive with Merrill Lynch & Co. and other full-service securities firms. First Boston is joining with Schwab "so we can be as competitive as we possibly can against the big retail wire houses," said Ernesto Cruz, the firm's managing director of U.S. stock underwriting.

First Boston will treat Schwab as a "silent co-manager" of stock issues it leads, Mr. Cruz said, giving his firm as much stock to sell in some deals as it would allocate to a top-rank Wall Street brokerage house. First Boston ranked fourth in 1997 among IPO underwriters, according to Securities Data Co. Initially, First Boston and the other investment banks will cut Schwab in on IPOs and other stock offerings based on how much demand they expect from individual investors. Eventually, however, Schwab hopes to expand the arrangements to include bonds and, possibly, other products such as options and futures.

Meanwhile, First Boston got nicked on the legal front. In early 1998, the firm became the first on Wall Street to be charged by the Securities and Exchange Commission for financing activities in Orange County, California, before its 1994 bankruptcy. In a civil settlement, the firm agreed to pay $800,000 to resolve SEC claims that it negligently "misrepresented and omitted material facts" from the offering statement covering more than $110 million of Orange County pension-obligation bonds in the fall of 1994. First Boston didn't admit or deny the allegations. The county filed for bankruptcy-law protection after losses of more than $1.7 billion when a bet on risky derivatives went sour. The First Boston settlement is expected to increase pressure on other firms that remain under SEC investigation for their involvement with Orange County, according to government and Wall Street officials.

Investment Banking: Staying Near the Top

A new generation of hungry young investment bankers has catapulted First Boston to among the leaders of the mergers business, nearly a decade after Bruce Wasserstein and Joseph Perella abruptly bolted the firm, taking many investment bankers and clients with them. Staffed mostly by the generation who cut their teeth in the go-go 1980s, First Boston has surprised some on Wall Street. In 1997, it was ranked seventh in announced U.S. M&A transactions with a 12.4 percent market share, up from 1994, when it had an 11 percent market share, according to Securities Data Co.

The banking group's 1997 performance included an impressive list of M&A transactions valued at more than $1 billion. The firm scored big in 1997 by helping advise CoreStates Financial Corp. in its planned $17.1 billion acquisition by

First Union Corp., Raytheon Co. in its $9.5 billion purchase of General Motors Corp.'s Hughes Electronics defense business, and US Bancorp in its $8.9 billion acquisition by First Bank Systems Inc. In all, the firm advised U.S. companies on $113.68 billion of mergers or acquisitions.

On the underwriting side, the firm helped bring to market two huge transactions: the $10 billion initial public stock offering of Telestra, the Australian telecommunications giant, and the $1.04 billion stock offering for Matav, the Hungarian telecom company (in which Credit Suisse First Boston shared the management mandate with Merrill Lynch). In 1997, Credit Suisse First Boston ranked No. 7 among Wall Street underwriters, helping bring to market $67.7 billion of new U.S. stocks and bonds, according to Securities Data Co.

One of the firm's chief deal makers in the 1990s was Brian Finn, cohead of mergers, who resigned in 1997. Traveling by limousine to a Seagram Co. board meeting in 1995, Edgar Bronfman Jr., the distiller's chief executive officer, turned to Mr. Finn and asked his age. Mr. Finn was about to appear before the Seagram board as the company's financial adviser to discuss the planned $5.7 billion acquisition of 80 percent of MCA Inc. from Matsushita Electric Industrial Corp. "Thirty-four," replied Mr. Finn, though a receding hairline and a slight paunch made him look somewhat older. Mr. Bronfman's swift response: "Don't tell the board."

First Boston was stung by the departure of Mr. Finn, who joined Clayton, Dubilier & Rice, a New York buyout firm. Though Mr. Finn was a "very, very special talent," Mr. Wheat said the firm has plenty of depth in its banking area. Indeed, Mr. Finn's replacement, Gordon Rich, had previously been the firm's cohead of mergers.

In March 1997, the firm boasted its busiest week ever, advising on five megadeals each exceeding $5 billion—a total for the week of more than $40 billion. It was an impressive lineup: Credit Suisse First Boston advised German-based Thyssen AG in a rare hostile acquisition offer from another German company, Fried. Krupp AG Hoesch-Krupp; U.S. Bancorp in its acquisition by First Bank System Inc.; H. F. Ahmanson & Co. in its raised offer for Great Western Financial; Tyco International Ltd. in its acquisition of ADT Ltd.; and Texaco Inc. in a joint venture with Shell Oil Co. to combine some refining operations. Credit Suisse First Boston crowed that the flurry of advisory activity demonstrated "our strengths in executing complicated strategic transactions— from hostile offers to takeover defenses—across the globe."

Of course, First Boston's mergers group has had its share of knocks. Its European brethren missed out on the then-biggest-ever corporate transaction, the $30 billion-plus merger of Sandoz Ltd. with longtime CSFB client Ciba-Geigy Ltd. The firm was noticeably absent in some of the major megadeals of 1996. And First Boston's underwriting arena hasn't escaped some embarrassments. BJ Services Co., a Houston provider of oil-pressure pumping services, dumped First Boston, which had managed its $135 million initial public stock offering in 1990. For a $291 million stock sale in July 1996, BJ Services picked rival Merrill—which had picked off the energy-service banking team from First Boston.

Still, the overall success of the firm's investment-banking group is impressive given the turmoil the firm has faced in recent years over bonuses. Credit Suisse First Boston's ability to sustain waves of departures of key executives and weather the drought of the early 1990s underscores a fact of life on Wall Street: Killing an investment-banking franchise is hard to do. This is because many clients are reluctant to throw away years of relationships, whether it's with bankers or their firm. And many clients want and need the services of a full-service investment bank.

In the meantime, the firm bought a 25 percent stake in San Francisco's Volpe Brown Whelan & Co. in a bid to raise the ante in the lucrative and fast-growing area of technology and health-care banking, which Volpe specializes in. Terms of the joint venture weren't disclosed, but analysts valued the stake at $25 million. The alliance also involved the creation of a $100 million merchant-banking fund with Credit Suisse as lead investor. While Volpe isn't a big player in the mergers business, the bet First Boston is making is that some of Volpe's clients will want M&A advice in the next few years. Said First Boston's Mr. Finn at the time, "The more bets we make, the more likely it is that we will have winning bets."

Taking the Lead in "Off-Board" Trades

Credit Suisse First Boston is in the vanguard of a growing business in "off-board" trades in which huge blocks of U.S.-listed stocks change hands in foreign markets, in risky transactions that seldom appear on trading records. In 1997, Ronald Perelman sold about $400 million in New York Stock Exchange-listed American depositary receipts in News Corp. to First Boston. The sale was transacted in Canada late on a Friday night, and First Boston and its affiliates sold most of the shares the following Monday morning on the Big Board and in Australia.

Off-board trades such as these have become a popular way to sell huge blocks of stock with minimal risk to the seller. But some regulators say such trades detract from the stock market's transparency, or the ability of investors to see all trades, and would like to bring that trading back to the stock exchanges.

Mike Clark, First Boston's managing director of stock trading, said customers typically prefer to trade on the exchange because it proves the investor received a market price. But if it's a big sale that has to be sold piecemeal, the first piece might alert other sellers, who then drive the stock down. "After the market is closed, you don't have the interference from the wrong type of audience," Mr. Clark says.

First Boston's activity in this area helped vault the firm's stock operations into the black in 1996 after several years in the red. First Boston officials credit the turnaround to better management and discipline. It may seem basic, but the firm now trades stocks of companies and products it provides research in. "Before, there was not sufficient overlap," Mr. Wheat said. "It was crazy, just random," he said.

But it's First Boston's bond group that is the meat of the firm. The fixed-income group generates about 45 percent of the firm's revenue. The most consistent driver in the trading group's success is its derivatives unit, which totals about 30 percent of the firm's income. "Year in and year out, it makes at least $300 million after taxes," boasts Mr. Wheat, who founded the derivatives group several years back.

Perhaps the most telling reflection of how well First Boston's bond group fared in 1996 was in the paychecks of some senior fixed-income executives. Mr. Stone, head of mortgages and asset-backed securities, had a 1996 pay package of about $30 million, after his group generated hefty profits of more than $250 million, Wall Street executives said. "Stone's group did a fabulous job," Mr. Wheat said. "They made more money than anyone had expected." Mr. Stone has made big bets financing deals in New York City, Southern California and Florida, traders said. The firm has given Mr. Stone a significant chunk of the firm's capital to play with, and, more recently, leeway to trade internationally. "There's more risk, no question," Mr. Wheat said. "But I haven't seen Andy to be a crazy guy—he has a prudent approach to weighing risk/reward."

There have been trading embarrassments. First Boston investigated how a London-based stock-options trader allegedly lost $10 million through unauthorized options trading on the Financial Times-Stock Exchange 100 index, people familiar with the firm said. The trader, Philip Penner, was fired in July 1997 in connection with the losses, a First Boston spokeswoman said. The firm contacted the Securities and Futures Authority, Britain's top securities regulator, about the losses after they were discovered and is cooperating with the investigation by the SFA, the people familiar with the firm said.

The SFA is examining if the buildup in Mr. Penner's trading position, which once amounted to hundreds of millions of British pounds, went undetected because of a failure in Credit Suisse First Boston's internal controls. Mr. Penner failed to liquidate the options position when he was told to do so a few months before his ouster, the people said, and may have actually increased it.

And First Boston faced criticism on Wall Street in 1997 over a trading report it issued recommending the sale of four Nasdaq stocks. The report, entitled "The Year 2000 Bubble"—a reference to the potential for widespread computer failures at the turn of the century—was issued in June 1997 by Credit Suisse's proprietary stock group, which trades for the firm's own account. Known within First Boston as "trading notes," the report recommended that clients sell four stocks, Viasoft Inc., Data Dimensions Inc., Zitel Corp. and SEEC Inc.

But in a surprising turnabout the following day, First Boston issued a new version of the trading notes that hit clients with one new and important disclosure: First Boston held short positions—or had sold borrowed shares in hopes of buying them back at a lower price—in two of the stocks cited in the report, Data Dimensions and Viasoft. And the new report, unlike the first one, didn't explicitly recommend that clients sell the four stocks.

First Boston said in a statement that the trading notes "were not a product of the firm's standard operating procedures, and should not have been circulated in their original form." A First Boston spokesman added that the firm's compliance officials investigated the matter and determined that there was no evidence that the short positions were covered by buying shares at lower prices. The firm also found that no profit was made on the positions. But that didn't satisfy Bob Holmes, managing partner of Chicago hedge fund Gilford Partners. "Obviously, this is an attempt to get themselves out of hot water," said Mr. Holmes, whose fund had long positions—or bullish bets—on a couple of stocks that First Boston slammed in its report.

In December 1997, meanwhile, First Boston agreed to pay $40 million for its share of an industry-wide settlement of a class-action complaint alleging improper pricing on the Nasdaq Stock Market. The suit, filed in a New York federal court, alleged that thirty Nasdaq dealers improperly fixed prices on Nasdaq stocks between 1989 and 1994. (First Boston didn't admit any wrongdoing, as part of the settlement.)

Mutiny Over Compensation

First Boston was one of several Wall Street firms in recent years to jettison its municipal-bond operations amid pinched profits in the business. First Boston's move came as part of a broader restructuring in 1995 that led to the departure of about one thousand employees to save about $300 million a year. In shutting the muni area, First Boston let go a total of about 110 professionals.

"There's no strategic relevance" to the business, Mr. Wheat said at the time, "where, frankly, we tend to take our eye off the ball." The firm's muni-bond unit had "very little overlap" with First Boston's other businesses "and nobody really watches it," Mr. Wheat added.

But the sudden muni shuttering was even more traumatic for those let go because First Boston gave them more bad news: They weren't getting any 1994 bonuses. On Wall Street, bankers and traders depend on bonuses for the bulk of their annual pay; they feel entitled to at least a portion of their annual bonuses for the time they worked, even when they leave voluntarily.

First Boston's rare move sparked broad-based litigation that raised a big question in the wake of its muni-bond layoffs: Are Wall Street securities firms obligated to pay bonuses to investment bankers they fire? A high-profile arbitration claim filed in 1995 jointly by about 40 First Boston bankers fired by the firm (many of whom worked in the muni department) sought $20 million. The bankers' beef: They say they were paid no 1994 bonuses even though they worked the entire year and made money for the company. In 1997, First Boston quietly paid a total of about $6 million to settle the claims, people familiar with the matter said. Credit Suisse First Boston declined to comment.

Investment bankers don't often spark sympathy when they howl about skimpy pay, natch. "But bonuses are integral—it's the reason why you do it," said veteran investment banker M. William Benedetto. "You can get a great bonus or a lousy bonus," depending on individual and firmwide performance and profit. "You never get no bonus," Mr. Benedetto said. "I find that rather shocking."

This is because bonuses at investment banks, unlike most businesses, constitute nearly all an executive's yearly paycheck, sometimes totaling hundreds of thousands or even millions of dollars. The First Boston claimants, for instance, received annual bonuses in 1992 and 1993 ranging as high as $950,000, according to papers filed with arbitrators. In the past, securities firms traditionally have paid annual bonuses to bankers who worked the entire year. In their claim, the First Boston bankers also said the firm never paid them a promised severance package.

For its part, First Boston said it takes the view that bonuses are purely discretionary. In a statement, the firm added, "We believe our severance policies are fair and consistent with general industry practice." First Boston's overall bonus pool in 1994 was down more than 40 percent from 1993 amid a 25 percent profit plunge.

The firm's muni-securities division generated net income of $18.8 million on revenue of $73 million in 1994, "despite the fact that transaction volume decreased by as much as fifty percent from the prior year," said Jeffrey Liddle of Liddle & Robinson, the New York law firm that filed the claim. At the same time, some First Boston bankers in its mortgage-backed securities unit were paid bonuses, despite a loss of about $40 million at their unit, Wall Street traders said.

Restructuring Research

The restructuring efforts that have characterized Credit Suisse First Boston for 1996 and 1997 have been particularly evident in the firm's research and strategy operations.

The post of strategist was left vacant for more than a year, following the 1995 departure of Jeffrey Applegate for Lehman Brothers. That particular departure wasn't related to the bonus spat, but as top managers struggled to rebuild other areas of the firm affected by the defections, research and strategy suffered from benign neglect. "We just didn't hear an awful lot from them in most parts of the market," said one money manager. Other institutional investors say it will take time for these groups to regain the audience lost during the early stages of one of the headiest bull markets seen this century.

Not that the company isn't trying. In the first six months of 1997, the roster of U.S. stock research analysts grew nearly 25 percent, as the firm added to its health-care research efforts, strengthened its well-known energy research group, and initiated new areas of coverage. Meanwhile, Christine Callies marked her first anniversary as chief strategist in May 1997.

While the company has been forking over big bucks in pay packages to retain key trading and investment banking personnel, that largesse hasn't spread to the research and strategy operations. Ms. Callies, a former geological engineer, is a relative newcomer to the ranks of Wall Street strategists, and remains low-profile in comparison to many of her competitors. She's also doing double or triple duty: While research powerhouses like Merrill Lynch or Goldman Sachs have teams of strategists to ponder quantitative, technical or sectoral issues, Ms. Callies flies solo. Over the next year, she says she hopes one of her new recruits to the world of strategy will be ready to take on some of that load, but for now, she said, "I don't make any pretense of trying to compete on the breadth of research."

A similar approach is seen in the research department, where Alfred Jackson, head of global equity research, said he's tried to avoid the increasingly prevalent bidding wars in rebuilding the roster of analysts.

"There is a culture of 'growing' people in-house, which we're going to continue," he said. "Also, you can find some very capable people out there if you look in less conventional places." These, he said, include the "buy" side of Wall Street, among institutional investors, or in teams of research analysts. In such teams, he says, the number two analyst often is less caught up in marketing the research product, and can devote more time "to doing some very capable and often quite original research."

Among the most recent additions to the firm's research team are a second biotechnology analyst, two analysts covering the market for medical devices, and a pharmaceutical analyst, as CSFB tries to expand its presence in health-care research. Other new hires included an additional exploration and production analyst for the firm's energy research group, and two people to cover the new area of outsourcing—companies that have sprung up to cater to corporate America's itch to contract out work ranging from catering to data processing. Rather than hiring big names from outside to boost the technology research team, Mr. Jackson plans to let "a couple of young guys that we have grow into it."

The remaining challenge for both Ms. Callies and the rebuilt research team is to grab the attention of clients inundated with investment ideas not only from the big Wall Street firms but a myriad of boutique research firms.

"My goal here is to try to give some help on the actual money management problems that our clients deal with on a day-to-day basis," Ms. Callies said.

"Debating whether the market is ten percent above or below fair value isn't the way the battle is fought in the trenches every day. I'd like to take strategy along a more practical path than has sometimes been followed in the last twenty years or so."

That's a legacy of Ms. Callies's background as a fundamental, bottom-up analyst. After her first career as an exploration geologist in the U.S. Southwest went belly-up when commodity prices nosedived in the early 1980s, Ms. Callies jumped into the investment world, convincing Dean Witter Reynolds that her skill in managing her own portfolio meant she would be able to help other investors master the market. After eight years at Dean Witter as a general market analyst, she jumped to Cowen & Co., where she began her transformation into a market strategist, joining Brown Brothers Harriman in that role in 1993.

"I probably write a lot more about stocks than most of the other people out there," she says. "Whether the price-to-book ratio is appropriate or not doesn't tell anybody how to survive until the end of the quarter, and that's my job."

So far, Ms. Callies's approach hasn't produced the kind of daring—but successful—calls that create strong followings among clients. Moreover, her cautious approach to stocks throughout the rocky first half of 1997, when the market soared, then erased its gains only to rebound, may have been prudent but didn't pay off for those who followed her advice. Still, some readers praise her careful evaluations of market sectors as well researched and offering interesting insights.

The research department has had more success in distinguishing itself from the pack. Mr. Jackson credits a new approach, dubbed "value-based analysis," for some of their successes, which included a buy recommendation on Compaq Computer months before the stock set new fifty-two-week highs.

"Compaq had adopted a lot of new value-based tools to run its business, that were boosting cash generation and returns," he says. "Looking for things like this helps you figure out where change is taking place on the margin that could show up in higher stock prices and multiples. You need to look at where value is being created . . . This is something that isn't a me-too approach to research, that will serve us well."

The company is also expanding its international research presence. In addition to covering Latin America from its New York office, CSFB has analysts in Russia and several Eastern European nations, as well as more conventional financial centers such as Zurich and London. Another thirty analysts track Asian companies from Hong Kong, Singapore and Seoul, as well as a new office in Mumbai, India. The international side of the business is expected to grow more rapidly than domestic research, Mr. Jackson said.

In *The Wall Street Journal*'s 1996 all-star analysts survey, Credit Suisse First Boston ranked eighth with eighteen of its team making the list of those most skilled at estimating earnings and picking stocks. It climbed to sixth place in 1997, with twenty-two all-star analysts.

Credit Suisse First Boston's People

Allen Wheat, chairman, chief executive and president: Since he was appointed president in 1993, Mr. Wheat has shaken things up, moving CSFB toward higher-margin businesses and more proprietary trading. Mr. Wheat joined the firm in 1990 as president and chief operating officer of the firm's Pacific operations. That year he founded Credit Suisse Financial Products in London and made a name for himself as chief executive officer of the lucrative provider of derivative and risk-management products. A joint venture between Credit Suisse and First Boston, CSFP represented the first separate derivatives and risk management division in the industry.

Wheat, Allen
Chairman,
CEO & President-
Credit Suisse
First Boston

In 1992, Mr. Wheat was named vice chairman of the firm's London-based fixed income trading and sales and foreign exchange. In 1993, he became president and chief operating officer of CS First Boston and succeeded John Hennessy on the CS Holding executive board. He assumed the posts of chief executive officer and chairman of the executive board of Credit Suisse First Boston in January 1998 from Hans-Ulrich Docrig who was named vice chairman of the executive board of Credit Suisse Group and chief risk officer of the Group.

Born in New Mexico, the son of a career military officer, Mr. Wheat was known even in college for his talent at turning a profit. As an undergraduate economics major at the University of Pennsylvania, he and a friend started a typewriting and copying service for students. But instead of paying the student workers in cash, Mr. Wheat offered them compensation of a different sort: a chance to use a high-tech Selectric typewriter to type their papers.

Before joining First Boston, he worked at Bankers Trust, where he assembled an elite team of swap traders. Several of them, including Brady Dougan, Chris Goekjian and Marc Hotimsky, followed Mr. Wheat to Credit Suisse First Boston where they now head up key business units.

Christopher Goekjian, president and chief executive, Credit Suisse Financial Products: A member of Mr. Wheat's team from Bankers Trust, Mr. Goekjian joined First Boston in London in 1990 as a founding member and trading chief for Credit Suisse Financial Products, the firm's derivatives-trading arm. In 1992, Mr. Goekjian took on additional responsibilities as head of European bond business for First Boston; he held that post until becoming president and CEO of CSFP in

1995. Mr. Goekjian is a member of the executive board of Credit Suisse First Boston. At Bankers Trust he worked in swaps, options, structured products and stock-derivatives trading in New York, Tokyo and London.

Oswald J. Gruebel, head of global trading: Mr. Gruebel is a managing director and member of the executive board of both Credit Suisse First Boston and Credit Suisse Group. Mr. Gruebel joined White Weld Securities, a predecessor firm, in 1970; eight years later, he became chief executive officer. Mr. Gruebel joined the group executive board of Financiere Credit Suisse-First Boston in 1985, where he was responsible for all trading within CSFB and its sister companies in Asia and Europe. In 1988, Mr. Gruebel became a member of the group executive committee of CS First Boston Inc. and deputy chairman of CSFB Ltd. In 1991, he became a member of Credit Suisse's executive board, where he was in charge of stocks, bonds, global foreign exchange, money market and asset/liability management.

Stephen Hester, chief financial officer: Mr. Hester also is a member of Credit Suisse First Boston's executive board. Before assuming his current post, Mr. Hester was managing director and cohead of European investment banking. He joined the firm in 1982, and served as personal assistant to the firm's then-chairman. He also has held a variety of senior investment-banking posts in London, becoming cohead of European M&A in 1991 and cohead of European investment banking in 1993.

Charles G. Ward III, head of global corporate and investment banking: Mr. Ward is also a member of Credit Suisse First Boston's operating committee and executive board. He joined the firm in 1979, and has been involved in all aspects of financial advisory and external capital raising for the firm's clients, with an emphasis on M&A. Before his current post, Mr. Ward was cohead of M&A and the media and telecom group, and previously had been president of Wasserstein Perella & Co. for six years. Among the transactions Mr. Ward has been involved with in recent years: the purchase of McDonnell Douglas by Boeing, the purchase of Lotus Development by IBM and the sale of Borden to Kohlberg Kravis Roberts.

John Hennessy, chairman of the private equity group at Credit Suisse First Boston: Before the 1996 reorganization, Mr. Hennessy was First Boston's most visible leader, serving as chairman of the executive board and chief executive officer for seven years. A square-jawed man who calls himself "a tough Irish kid from Boston"—Mr. Hennessy decorated his office with a plaque quoting a favorite verse that begins: "People don't want to be managed. They want to be led." He was one of the architects of the 1978 First Boston-Credit Suisse original alliance.

Walter Berchtold, head of securities trading and sales: Mr. Berchtold is a managing director who began his career in 1982 as a junior dealer in the precious-metal options department of the firm's futures unit. He has held a variety of futures-related positions, and assumed responsibility for Credit Suisse's derivatives department in 1991. Before his current post, his other duties included head of stock and stock derivatives activities and head of securities trading and sales.

Benjamin Bloomstone, stock-product manager and institutional stock sales chief in Boston: Mr. Bloomstone is a managing director and is responsible for institutional stock sales in the firm's Boston office. Before joining the firm in 1989, he was a principal at Sanford C. Bernstein & Co.; he began his career as a certified public accountant at Price Waterhouse.

Richard Bott, senior banker and head of global industry groups: Mr. Bott is a managing director; he joined the firm in 1972. He has broad experience with industrial, transportation and energy companies, as well as in project finance. In recent years, Mr. Bott has been actively involved in a number of large equity transactions, including Chrysler's $2 billion offering and Tenneco's $1 billion issue. He also has participated in many big M&A deals, including Union Pacific Corp.'s $5.4 billion acquisition of Southern Pacific and Crown Cork & Seal's $5.2 billion purchase of CarnaudMetalbox.

John Brydson, head of global risk arbitrage in New York: Mr. Brydson is a managing director responsible for proprietary trading of all risk arbitrage and other similar event-driven opportunities, such as restructurings, asset sales and spin-offs. Before joining the firm in 1995, Mr. Brydson was a managing director at Lehman Brothers, with joint responsibility for proprietary trading in risk arbitrage.

Philippe Buhannic, head of global bond, foreign exchange, commodities, listed derivatives: Mr. Buhannic is a managing director who joined the firm in 1995. He previously had been chief executive officer of Fimat U.S.A. and deputy chief financial officer of Credit Commercial de France.

Paul Calello, cohead of global trading for Credit Suisse Financial Products: Mr. Calello is a managing director who has worked for the firm's derivatives subsidiary in Tokyo, London and, currently, New York. His duties include managing CSFP's North American subsidiaries, North American bond, global stock and commodity derivatives. Mr. Calello is a member of CSFP's management committee of the executive board as well as a member of Credit Suisse First Boston's operating committee. Before joining CSFP at its inception in 1990, Mr. Calello worked at Bankers Trust.

Christopher Carter, head of global stock capital markets and European investment banking: Mr. Carter is a managing director who also shares responsibility for European stocks with Brady Dougan. He is a member of the firm's operating committee and chairman of the European investment banking management committee and the European stock executive committee. Mr. Carter joined Credit Suisse First Boston in 1987.

James Clark, stock analyst: Mr. Clark is a managing director who covers international and U.S. integrated oil companies and independent refining companies. He joined the firm in 1984 as a member of the investment-banking department, holding positions in the financial institutions and generalist groups. Mr. Clark joined the stock-research group in 1989, and has been covering the major oil companies since.

Michael Clark, head of U.S. stock trading: Mr. Clark is a managing director who joined the firm in 1991. Before First Boston, he was a senior convertible trader at Drexel Burnham Lambert Inc. Mr. Clark previously had worked at Salomon Brothers Inc. and was a commodities trader and member of the Commodity Exchange.

John Conlin, head of European stock research in London: Mr. Conlin is a managing director who joined the firm in 1983. He has held various positions in Cleveland, New York, Los Angeles, and San Francisco. Before moving to London, Mr. Conlin was the U.S. institutional sales manager and product manager in New York.

Ernesto Cruz, head of stock capital markets in the Americas: Mr. Cruz is a managing director involved with new offerings in media, telecommunications, leveraged buyouts, retail, apparel and consumer products, among other sectors. He chairs the firm's equity valuation and sponsorship committees for new issues. He joined the firm in 1985, and previously had worked for Lehman Brothers.

David A. DeNunzio, chief executive officer of the private stock division: Mr. DeNunzio is responsible for all the private-equity activities of the Credit Suisse Group globally. This group includes more than fifty people in four offices worldwide. Mr. DeNunzio has held a variety of senior banking posts at First Boston. Before joining the firm in 1989, he was a senior vice president at Kidder, Peabody & Co.

Jack J. DiMaio, head of global credit trading: Mr. DiMaio is a managing director who joined the firm in 1989. After completing the firm's sales and trading program, he joined the credit research group. In 1990, he joined the corporate bond trading desk where he was appointed head trader in 1995, and then department head a year later. At the end of 1997, he was appointed head of global credit trading.

Brady Dougan, head of global stock department: Mr. Dougan is a managing director and member of both the Credit Suisse First Boston executive board and operating committee. Since joining the firm in 1990, Mr. Dougan built Credit Suisse Financial Products' business in the Pacific, was cohead of Credit Suisse First Boston's global bond capital markets group and cohead of CSFP's marketing effort in the Americas. Before joining the firm, Mr. Dougan was a managing director at Bankers Trust.

Marcus Everard, head of European and non-Japan Pacific marketing for Credit Suisse Financial Products (CSFP): Mr. Everard joined Credit Suisse First Boston in 1982, and assumed full responsibility for the swaps and financial arbitrage group in 1986. He was named an executive director of the firm in 1988. In 1990, upon the creation of Credit Suisse Financial Products he assumed cohead of European marketing responsible for CSFP's business with the corporate and financial institutions sector. In 1993, he assumed an additional role within CS First Boston as cohead of global bond capital markets. In early 1995, Mr. Everard relinquished his Credit Suisse First Boston role in debt capital markets to assume sole responsibility for CSFP's marketing in Europe and non-Japan Pacific.

H. Andrew Fisher, managing director: Mr. Fisher manages the origination and execution of stock transactions for all Asian countries outside of Japan. In the past several years, Mr. Fisher has been responsible for many stock offerings, including Tata Engineering and Locomotive, Macronix International and Samsung Corp. He joined the firm in 1982.

Craig Foster, head of global government-bond operations for the Americas: Mr. Foster is a managing director and member of the firm's executive committee and the global fixed income management committee. Before joining the firm in 1992, Mr. Foster held several senior positions at Morgan Stanley.

Stephen Greene, global general counsel: Mr. Greene is a managing director who formerly was general counsel at CSFP. Mr. Greene joined CSFP in 1990 and was responsible for organizing, building and managing its legal department. Before joining the firm, he had worked at the law firm of Cadwalader, Wickersham & Taft.

Alfred Gremli, managing director: Mr. Gremli is responsible for global coverage of financial institutions, correspondent banking and trade finance, as well as corporate and investment banking for the Middle East and Africa. Before his current post, Mr. Gremli held several positions at Credit Suisse.

C. P. Greuter, head of stock capital markets international in Zurich: Mr. Greuter is a managing director responsible for origination, production and delivery of stock-linked transactions in the Swiss capital market mainly for Asian borrowers. He began his career in 1981 with Credit Suisse.

Geoffrey Hall, head of Atlanta office: Mr. Hall is a managing director who coordinates the firm's activities in the Southeast region. He joined the firm's Atlanta office when it first opened in 1976, and previously had worked at Merrill Lynch.

Paul R. Hofer, cohead of corporate banking and structured finance for Europe and Asia: Mr. Hofer is a managing director who joined the firm in 1977. Previously he had worked at Union Bank of Switzerland.

Richard Holbrooke, vice chairman: Mr. Holbrooke is responsible for developing the investment-banking business in Asia and assisting in U.S. and European new-business development. Before his current post, Mr. Holbrooke was Assistant Secretary of State for European and Canadian Affairs, and was credited with leading the Bosnian negotiations to a successful completion. Previously, he had been U.S. Ambassador to Germany and a managing director at Lehman.

Marc Hotimsky, global head of fixed income: Mr. Hotimsky is a managing director and member of the firm's operating committee and the extended executive board. Before joining the firm in 1992, he worked at Bankers Trust in derivatives. At First Boston, Mr. Hotimsky has helped expand its emerging markets and foreign-exchange sales and trading activities.

Andrew Ipkendanz, global head of emerging bond markets: Mr. Ipkendanz is a managing director who joined the firm in 1993. Previously, he worked at Macquarie Bank in Australia, responsible for sales and trading in foreign exchange cash and structured-derivatives products.

Alfred Jackson, global stock-research chief: Mr. Jackson is a managing director who joined the firm in 1980 as a food analyst. He ranked No. 1 for four years consecutively on the *Institutional Investor* Team as a food analyst. He became stock-research chief in 1985. During the next five years, the firm's research group consistently held one of the top three positions in the *Institutional Investor* All-America Research Team. Since 1990, he has held a variety of senior sales and research posts. Before joining the firm, Mr. Jackson was a food-industry analyst at Pershing & Co. and Merrill.

Giles Keating, head of global fixed income and economics research: Mr. Keating, who is a managing director, is the firm's chief economist and manages a team of some 170 bond research and economics professionals worldwide. Before joining the firm in 1986, Mr. Keating was a Research Fellow at the London Business School.

Steven Koch, cohead of mergers and acquisitions: Mr. Koch is a managing director who joined the firm in 1985. He became cohead of the global mergers and acquisitions group in 1993. He has advised clients in a wide variety of industries, with particular expertise in takeover defense, the food and consumer products industries and heavy industry.

James Leigh-Pemberton, head of European stock capital markets and syndication: Mr. Leigh-Pemberton is a managing director who was a director at S. G. Warburg Securities before working at the firm.

Robert Levitt, group head of Western region and cohead of technology group: Mr. Levitt is a managing director and has held a variety of senior posts in the firm's investment-banking department. He played a critical role in establishing the firm's market position in both the Dallas and Houston offices. His clients have included Lockheed Martin Corp., Western Atlas, Hewlett Packard, Litton Industries and Hughes Electronics.

Scott Lindsay, cohead of global mergers and acquisitions: Mr. Lindsay is a managing director. He joined the M&A group in 1982 and became cohead of the global mergers and acquisitions group in 1993. He has worked with clients in a wide variety of industries and has headed both takeover defense and cross-border M&A. Mr. Lindsay was an economist before joining the firm and has experience in academia, consulting and government.

Bruce Ling, global head of acquisition and syndicated finance: Mr. Ling is a managing director who joined the firm in 1994 from BT Securities, where he oversaw the bank's noninvestment grade loan syndication. Before the Bankers Trust unit, Mr. Ling worked at GE Capital Corp. and Citicorp Securities Inc.

Robin Macdonald, managing director: Dr. Macdonald is responsible for trading and risk management of the European stock product, which includes both Western and Central Europe and Russia. Before Credit Suisse First Boston, Dr. Macdonald worked for ten years at Goldman Sachs.

Christopher Martin, head of operations and technology: Mr. Martin is a managing director and member of the firm's operating committee. He also is head of administration for CSFP and a member of CSFP's management committee. Before joining the firm in 1986, Mr. Martin was financial controller at E. F. Hutton & Co. in London.

Michael Martin, cohead of global financial-institutions group: Mr. Martin is a managing director, focusing primarily on the firm's worldwide M&A practice for financial institutions. Mr. Martin joined First Boston in 1987, and has worked exclusively on bank, finance company, thrift and insurance-company transactions. Previously, he practiced law at Wachtell, Lipton, Rosen & Katz, where he specialized in M&A.

David Matlin, head of special situations and workouts group: Mr. Matlin is a managing director who manages the firm's proprietary trading activity in distressed securities. Before joining First Boston in 1994, Mr. Matlin was a partner at Merrion Group LP, a boutique securities firm he founded in 1991.

Michael J. Mauboussin, stock product manager: Mr. Mauboussin is a managing director and the product manager for the firm's value-based research effort. Mr. Mauboussin has been repeatedly named to *Institutional Investor*'s All-America research team in the food category.

John McAvoy, manager of global convertible securities sales and trading: Mr. McAvoy is a managing director who joined the firm in 1991 after seven years at Lehman, where he co-managed convertible sales and trading. He has managed U.S. convertible sales and trading at Credit Suisse First Boston since 1991. In 1997, he also assumed responsibility for managing the U.S. equity-linked capital markets group.

Ken Miller, vice chairman: Before joining Credit Suisse First Boston in 1994, Mr. Miller was president and CEO of the Lodestar Group, a merchant bank he founded in 1988. He previously held senior posts at Merrill Lynch and earlier had been an investment banker at Lehman. Before coming to Wall Street in 1976, he founded and ran a venture-capital company that invests in African American and other minority businesses. He is a member of the board of directors of Viacom Inc.

Neil Moskowitz, chief operating officer of the stock division: Mr. Moskowitz is a managing director and oversees all administrative and technology functions that directly support the firm's stock division. He also oversees the global stock finance and prime-brokerage business. Before joining the firm, he held several management posts at Goldman.

David Mulford, vice chairman: Mr. Mulford is also a member of the firm's executive board and chairman of Credit Suisse First Boston (Europe) Ltd. Before joining the firm, he was undersecretary and assistant secretary of the U.S.

Treasury for International Affairs for Presidents Reagan and Bush. Previously, he was senior adviser to the Saudi Arabian Monetary Agency.

Robert Murley, head of Americas region and Chicago office: Mr. Murley is a managing director and member of the firm's global operating committee and the management committee of the investment-banking department. Among his other roles, Mr. Murley serves as an account officer, handling many of the firm's largest corporate-finance clients. He joined the firm in 1975.

Stefano Natella, head of Latin America research: Mr. Natella is a managing director and also the firm's Latin America stock strategist. He joined the firm in 1989, and earlier had worked at McKinsey & Co.

Alasdair Norton, comanager of stock derivatives: Mr. Norton is a managing director and head of the stock capital markets group in Asia. He joined the firm in 1986, and held posts at CSFP.

Robert O'Brien, chief credit risk officer: Mr. O'Brien is a managing director and head of the global credit and loan management unit with responsibility for credit policy/risk management, loan structuring and loan portfolio management. Before his current assignment, he was head of global corporate banking and structure finance and held positions as region head for North America and head of leveraged lending. Before joining the firm in 1994, he held several senior posts at Bankers Trust and Chase.

Thomas F. X. O'Mara, head of convertible trading, customer trading and proprietary arbitrage: Mr. O'Mara is a managing director who joined the firm in 1991 as a senior convertible trader; he later became the manager for customer convertible trading. Previously he worked at Lehman.

Adebayo Ogunlesi, head of global project finance group: Mr. Ogunlesi is a managing director who joined the firm in 1983. He has advised clients on transactions and financings on every continent in a broad range of industries, including oil and natural gas, petrochemicals, power generation, airlines, mining, natural resources, infrastructure and consumer products.

Susumu Omori, Tokyo branch manager: Mr. Omori is a managing director and also Pacific regional bond sales manager. He was a founding member of the firm's Tokyo bond department. Before joining the firm in 1990, he was a bond executive at Nomura.

J. Craig Oxman, global cohead of technology group: Mr. Oxman is a managing director responsible for the firm's overall technology M&A activities. Before joining the firm in 1983, he was a consultant at McKinsey & Co.

Mark Patterson, head of leveraged-finance group and global investment-grade mortgage and asset-backed securities business: Mr. Patterson is a managing director and serves on the firm's operating committee, the fixed income management committee, the investment-banking management committee, and the investment committee that approves the firm's principal investments and merchant-banking activities. He joined First Boston in 1994 from BT Securities Corp.

Jonathan Plutzik, cohead of global financial institutions group: Mr. Plutzik is a managing director with primary responsibility for the firm's insurance practice. He joined the firm in 1978.

Gordon Rich, cohead of mergers-and-acquisitions: Mr. Rich replaced Brian Finn in this role in 1997; previously, he had specialized in M&A for large industrial companies such as AT&T, Revlon, New World Communications, USA Networks, Marvel Entertainment and W. R. Grace. Before joining the firm, he was a lawyer with Skadden, Arps, Slate, Meagher & Flom.

John Romanelli, cohead of U.S. bond capital markets group: Mr. Romanelli is a managing director who since 1990 has been responsible for managing the liability management and financing needs of clients. He joined the firm in 1986, and has worked in mortgage finance and investment banking, where he managed the firm's relationships with the U.S. federal agencies.

Paul Scheufele, manager of liability-management department; comanager of short-term U.S. Treasury group: Mr. Scheufele is a managing director who joined the firm in 1992 in trading. He previously worked for Paribas Ltd., Citibank Securities Markets and Arthur Young & Co. He is vice chairman of the funding division of the Bond Market Trade Association.

Neal M. Soss, senior advisor and chief U.S. economist: Dr. Soss is a managing director who joined the firm in 1984; he previously had been with the Federal Reserve Bank of New York.

Andrew Stone, head of principal-transactions group: Mr. Stone is a managing director and one of Wall Street's best-known traders. At First Boston, he is responsible for trading, structuring, originating and securitizing real estate, mortgage and other asset-backed securities, among other things. In 1997, Mr. Stone founded the principal transactions group's European division, making the entity global. His group thrived in 1996, earning Mr. Stone a pay package of about $30 million, Wall Street executives said. Before joining First Boston, he headed Daiwa Securities' mortgage, asset-backed and real-estate operations. Previously, he had been at Prudential Securities Inc., and at Salomon Brothers, he helped pioneer the creation of

In the Beginning . . .

First Boston's genesis ironically stemmed from the Glass-Steagall Act, the Depression-era law that separated investment and commercial banking. In the wake of the new law, First of Boston was formed by combining the securities affiliate of the First National Bank of Boston with key personnel from Chase Harris Forbes Corp., an affiliate of Chase National Bank. The result: the first publicly held investment bank in the United States.

In 1946, Mellon Securities merged with the newly named First Boston, increasing First Boston's capital and client base. First Boston soon blossomed into a major underwriting force on Wall Street. It helped to bring to market securities for top-flight firms in corporate America such as Alcoa Corp. and Gulf Oil Corp. First Boston carved out a niche as a dealer in securities traded off the exchange in the so-called third market. The firm also was aggressive in underwriting bond issues for foreign companies in New York. First Boston's underwriting expertise was such that it helped bring to market several securities-firm rivals, including the IPOs of Donaldson, Lufkin & Jenrette, Merrill Lynch and Reynolds Securities Inc. (which ultimately became part of Dean Witter, now Morgan Stanley, Dean Witter, Discover & Co.)

First Boston and Credit Suisse, an old-line Swiss banking powerhouse, in 1978 entered into a cross-shareholding agreement, resulting in joint ownership of White Weld & Co.'s former London subsidiary, now Credit Suisse First Boston. The firm, a leader in the European credit markets, pioneered the use of adjustable-rate preferred stock issues and so-called CMOs, or collateralized mortgage obligations, in the 1980s.

In 1988, First Boston and CSFB merged, in what was ballyhooed as the first "truly global" investment bank. The new holding company, CS First Boston, went private, and Credit Suisse (later CS Holding) bought a 44.5 percent interest in the firm. In 1990, CS Holding lifted its First Boston stake to more than 60 percent, becoming the first foreign firm to take majority ownership of a major U.S. investment bank. As part of the 1996 reorganization, CS Holding bought the remaining 31.3 percent of the firm from institutional holders and First Boston executives, who got shares in the new parent company. CS Holding changed its name to Credit Suisse Group, forming four separate units, one of which is Credit Suisse First Boston.

many new mortgage products and was among a group of traders that established Salomon as a powerful force in the mortgage market in the 1980s.

Stephen Stonefield, chairman of Pacific Region: Mr. Stonefield is a managing director and member of the firm's executive board. Before joining First Boston in 1996, he was a managing director at Smith Barney, and earlier, with Morgan Stanley.

Michael Tarrant, cohead of European mergers and acquisitions: Mr. Tarrant is a managing director who joined the firm in 1997. Previously, he served in various positions at Deutsche Morgan Grenfell (DMG) in New York, most recently as head of mergers and acquisitions.

Andrew R. Taussig, head of retail, apparel and textile investment-banking group: Mr. Taussig is a managing director who joined the firm in 1983 from Willkie, Farr & Gallagher, where he was a corporate lawyer.

Scott Ulm, head of global asset and mortgage finance: Mr. Ulm is a managing director who is responsible for the firm's structured finance activities. He has held positions in the U.S. Senate staff, law firms and a commercial bank before joining First Boston in 1986.

Philip Vasan, global head of foreign exchange: Mr. Vasan is a managing director who joined the firm in 1992. Previously he worked at Citibank, heading foreign exchange options for the U.S.

Franz von Meyenburg, deputy chairman of Credit Suisse First Boston (Europe) Ltd.: Mr. von Meyenburg is a managing director who before his current post was a member of Credit Suisse's executive board.

David Walker, cohead of corporate and investment banking in Asia: Mr. Walker is a managing director and also chairman of the firm's subsidiaries in Hong Kong, branch manager of its Hong Kong branch, and a member of the firm's global management committee. Before joining First Boston in 1990, he was a managing director at Bankers Trust.

John Walsh, cohead of global bond capital markets: Mr. Walsh is a managing director responsible for underwriting activities related to high grade, high yield and emerging market bonds. Before his current post, Mr. Walsh was cohead of international bond capital markets and international corporate trading based in London. He joined the firm in 1989 from Prudential Securities in London and began his career at Bank of America.

George Weiksner, senior advisor: Mr. Weiksner is a managing director who works with a variety of clients in the investment-banking global corporate finance group. He began his career in the firm's investment-banking department in 1970.

Jonathan Wilmot, chief global strategist: Mr. Wilmot is a managing director whose work focuses on major secular and cyclical themes in the world economy. He also heads the firm's European bond research group.

John Wylie, head of Australian corporate and investment banking: Mr. Wylie is a managing director who joined the firm in 1987 in the M&A group. Before First Boston, Mr. Wylie worked at Britain's Hill Samuel & Co.

Simon de Zoete, deputy chairman of Credit Suisse First Boston, Europe:
Mr. de Zoete joined Credit Suisse First Boston (Europe) with the firm's acquisition of BZW's UK and Continental European mergers and acquisitions, corporate finance advisory, and equity capital markets businesses on December 31, 1997. His responsibilities include working to develop the firm's stock capital markets as well as the UK corporate brokering business for CSFB. He held a number of stock-related positions throughout his career, most recently as chairman of BZW's equities division for the past three years.

PART FIVE

THE BANKS

J. P. Morgan & Co.

•

Bankers Trust New York Corp.

J. P. MORGAN & CO.

BECOMING THE CLIENT'S FIRST CALL

Transforming a Culture

Not long after becoming chief executive of J. P. Morgan & Co. in late 1994, Douglas "Sandy" Warner paid a visit to the Chicago office of financier Sam Zell. On its face, the meeting was not terribly unusual for the head of a bank that, since its inception in 1838, has prided itself on the strength of its client relationships. "Clients have always been central to Morgan's strategy, a mark of the firm's character," Mr. Warner stressed in a memo to employees just three months after taking the helm. "Our challenge is to reinforce this emphasis."

But Mr. Zell was no ordinary J. P. Morgan client. Feisty, sharp-tongued and Jewish, he didn't fit the WASPy, reserved mold of the white-shoe firm that was one of the original lenders to blue-chip corporations like General Electric and AT&T. Hanging up the telephone as Mr. Warner walked into his office, Mr. Zell—known among associates as "Grave-Dancer" for his style of vulture-investing—noted that he'd just been chatting with a J. P. Morgan banker. "He thinks he's hot-s— for making me a $50 million loan," Mr. Zell intoned mockingly.

Startled at first, it was Mr. Warner who had the last laugh. When Mr. Zell's Manufactured Home Corp. made a hostile bid for rival Chateau Properties, it used J. P. Morgan as its adviser. And on other deals, too, Mr. Zell, who previously had done most of his considerable investment-banking business with Merrill Lynch and Goldman Sachs, began throwing much of his work to Morgan. "They have done an extraordinarily competent job of helping us with our investment-banking work," Mr. Zell explained. Of Mr. Warner, he added, "Sandy and I have developed a comfortable relationship. We understand each other very well."

If it highlights the undiminished importance of a client-centered attitude at

J. P. Morgan, the episode also says much about the changing nature of the firm's clients—and about the changing nature of Morgan itself. Of course, the firm's unrivaled pedigree as *the* private bank of the nation's elite remains pristine; indeed, with $1 million in liquid assets the unstated, but understood, minimum for opening an account, only the elite are *permitted* to bank at J. P. Morgan. And as the nation's fourth-largest commercial bank, with total assets exceeding $260 billion, Morgan is still a leading institutional lender, ranked as the world's fifth-largest arranger of syndicated loans in 1997.

But in other ways, J. P. Morgan is no longer a commercial bank at all. The firm now derives less than 25 percent of its total revenue from traditional banking businesses such as lending, and the rest from such new lines of business as trading and underwriting that the company began pursuing during the late 1970s. It was then, under the leadership of Lewis Preston, who became the bank's chairman in 1980, that J. P. Morgan made a determined choice to transform itself from a staid commercial bank into a high-flying investment bank à la Morgan Stanley and Goldman Sachs.

At the time, associates say, Mr. Preston had come to the conclusion that commercial banking as it had always been practiced was a dying profession whose historical role of lending and deposit-taking was being gradually replaced by the public markets for stocks and bonds. A dozen or more years before his commercial banking contemporaries, Mr. Preston, a hard-charging ex-Marine, decided that to survive, Morgan needed to adapt, and that to adapt, the firm needed to change radically the way it did business. "We can either change our products or change our clients," Mr. Preston frequently admonished the bank's employees. "We're not going to change our clients."

If Mr. Preston's realization and drive to reform his company came years before other commercial bankers would begin following Morgan's lead, it was also a decision years in the making. Since 1933, when Congress passed the Glass-Steagall Act as a response to the Great Depression and the stock market crash of 1929, Morgan had chafed under the legislation's separation of commercial banking from investment banking. Indeed, it was the passage of Glass-Steagall that prompted several of the bank's partners to resign and set up an independent securities firm, Morgan Stanley & Co., leaving J. P. Morgan to concentrate on the lending business. Stung by the losses, and by the ultimate success of Morgan Stanley, the bank vowed one day to reclaim its investment-banking heritage.

But though Mr. Preston's vision seemed premature in 1980, with Glass-Steagall still firmly in place, it seemed less so by 1987, when the Federal Reserve used a loophole in the law to begin allowing a handful of banks, including J. P. Morgan, to underwrite stocks and bonds on a limited basis. In 1996, with efforts to repeal Glass-Steagall picking up steam, the Fed loosened those restrictions even further, allowing the banks to derive up to a quarter of the reve nue in their securities affiliates from stock and bond underwriting, up from 10 percent previously. By that point, J. P. Morgan was already far ahead of most of its commercial banking rivals, having become the only commercial bank to join the "bulge bracket" of the world's top six underwriters, and well on its way toward its ultimate goal: to combine the best attributes of commercial, investment, and merchant banking, and become the "first call" of clients in need of complex financial services.

Still, Mr. Preston's goal of changing Morgan's products without changing its clients or its culture has ultimately proved unattainable. Though traders in the pits of the Chicago Board of Trade still use the hand-symbol of tightening their neckties to refer to J. P. Morgan—mocking the firm's stiff, straight-laced style—the shift in product lines that began in the late seventies has actually been accompanied by a dramatic transformation in the bank's culture. With trading making up a growing part of the firm's revenue, and profitability tied more closely than ever to the volatile stock and bond markets, J. P. Morgan has become as risk-taking a firm as any on Wall Street. And in trying to win business away from other investment banks, J. P. Morgan bankers are no less aggressive, and frequently more so, than their counterparts at Morgan Stanley or Merrill Lynch.

Then, too, businesses such as mergers-and-acquisitions and stock underwriting cater to an entirely different type of customer than traditional corporate lending. Though a key part of the bank's plan has been to convert its longstanding lending ties into investment-banking relationships, J. P. Morgan can no longer rely solely on the stable of established corporate clients that have used its lending business in the past. Rather, in bringing to market the stock of fledgling companies, the bank now finds itself, more often than not, working for less patrician firms such as United Auto Group, a new- and used-car dealer, and Engineering Animation Inc., an Ames, Iowa, concern specializing in three-dimensional animation for various manufacturing industries. In pursuing its capital markets businesses around the world, Morgan is developing a diverse client list that no longer has the distinctly American flavor it once had; since 1995, more than half of its revenue has had its origins outside the United States. And in advising on hostile acquisitions, such as Mr. Zell's run at Chateau Properties—an operator of trailer parks—the bank is involving itself in the kind of work its blueblood founders might have considered downright ungentlemanly.

Inside the firm, the change of attitude has been more subtle. At some level, J. P. Morgan has remained true to its commercial-banking roots: the firm remains reluctant to pay outsized Wall Street-type compensations, emphasizes teamwork instead of the star system that prevails at many investment banks, and prefers to grow from within, training its own employees, rather than hiring from its competitors. But in other ways, the J. P. Morgan of today is a very different place from the Morgan of its founders' day, or even that of a dozen years ago. For one thing, the firm once known, like many banks, for its job security, no longer offers the kind of lifelong employment guarantees it once did. Twice in recent years, once in 1989 and again in 1995, the bank laid off hundreds of employees as part of a wide-ranging effort to cut costs and become more efficient.

Meanwhile, as Morgan has become more of a meritocracy, the makeup of its senior management has also changed. While many of its top executives are still white, male, American-born, and Ivy League-educated, the firm's leadership now includes several women and is made up of citizens from six countries. "We are a completely passport-blind company," said Ramon de Oliveira, the bank's Franco-Argentine, Sorbonne-educated head of asset management. "It's not a bunch of Americans who take the train in from Greenwich and play golf together."

For his part, Mr. Warner downplayed the changes in the bank's culture and its clients. "Sure it's changed some, but I would not highlight that as one of the most important things to have happened here in the last fifteen years," he said. "We are seeking to adapt to a very different business proposition than we used to have, but we're doing it without altering one iota our commitment to principles of integrity and objectivity. The soul of the place is not what's changing." Of Mr. Zell, he added, "That is exactly our kind of client, given the new businesses we're in. Pre-1988, we had no business calling Sam Zell, not because he wasn't fun to do business with, but because we'd have been wasting his time. Forget about what's fun. If we're going to sit and have a productive discussion, you've got to have something to talk about."

With its makeover now nearly complete, J. P. Morgan is beginning to see the results of its efforts. Profit soared through the first three quarters of 1997, aided by a sizzling stock market and a booming year for mergers and acquisitions. But the good fortune ended in the fourth quarter as the bank was badly buffeted by turmoil in Asian markets that caused it to lose money on swaps contracts there, as well as by lower income from stock derivatives and bond trading in developed markets. For the year, Morgan's net income slipped 7 percent, to $1.5 billion. Still, at a time when other banks were struggling to raise their revenue, Morgan's total revenue rose 5 percent, to $7.2 billion, boosted by a 22 percent increase in investment-banking revenue and a 16 percent increase in investment management revenue. More than half of that revenue came from businesses which, just a half dozen years earlier, contributed little or nothing to the firm's bottom line. In a report to the company's stockholders written in early 1996, Mr. Warner wrote, "The impact of investments made over the past decade is visible. . . . The vital strategic task of our recent history—transformation into a firm that integrates investment, commercial, and merchant banking globally—is essentially complete. We now have the challenge of realizing the potential inherent in the new J. P. Morgan."

A Trading and M&A Powerhouse

By 1997, Sandy Warner, who took over as chairman of J. P. Morgan in late 1994, was able to point to the bank's makeover as the principal reason for its strong earnings and revenue growth. Two factors in particular contributed to the results: a red-hot stock market kept trading revenue strong, while a continued boom in merger-and-acquisition activity allowed the bank to demonstrate its recently honed prowess in that area as well. Of course, Morgan's profitability was as subject to a market downturn as at any time in its history, as became evident in the fourth quarter. Still, even as other commercial banks struggled to raise their revenue by a few percentage points—resorting to mergers with one another when all else failed, and cutting expenses mercilessly to squeeze out profits—Morgan recorded healthy increases almost effortlessly through the first three quarters of the year. And even as other banks got caught in escalating wars for talent, bidding on each other's star dealmakers as though they were NBA all-stars, Morgan stayed largely on the sidelines, its bankers focused on the gradual, relentless pursuit of the firm's goals.

The firm made a big mark in 1997 in the M&A arena, where it served as an adviser on some of the year's blockbuster transactions. The firm ended the year as the nation's eighth-ranked M&A house, up from sixteenth a decade earlier. All told, Morgan advised on deals worth more than $92 billion in 1997, far outstripping the next-most-active commercial bank, Chase Manhattan Corp., which advised on deals worth $37 billion.

Nevertheless, several areas of the firm's performance in 1997 reflected the fact that its transformation was not yet entirely complete. First, though Morgan's overall underwriting operation was both successful and profitable—with revenue rocketing up 38 percent, to $486 million—it was carried by the bank's underwriting of corporate bonds, a natural offshoot of its institutional lending business. Morgan's young stock underwriting operation, by contrast, while making huge progress leading initial public offerings and co-managing common stock offers, was unable to break into the ranks of the top-ranked common stock lead-managers, such as Goldman Sachs, Merrill Lynch, and Morgan Stanley.

Second, though Morgan is not known on Wall Street for particularly generous pay packages, and though it refuses to woo stars from other firms with promises of big bucks, the firm nonetheless experienced a 12 percent jump in expenses in 1997, as staff levels grew and individual bonuses soared in step with the bank's overall returns. In addition, the firm's continued investments in developing its new lines of business outweighed its concerted efforts at cost control.

Third, though a booming market helped push Morgan's stock to record highs in 1997, the bank still trailed its peers among commercial banks and investment banks by a considerable margin. For the year, Morgan's stock rose an impressive 16 percent. But stocks of securities firms soared 81 percent, and money-center banks saw their shares surge 32 percent. Analysts blamed the bank's sluggish stock price on a variety of factors, among them that investors remained uncertain of what Morgan's transformation was really all about, and that to the degree they were aware of the shift, they were worried about the risky nature of the bank's trading activities. Then, too, there was the market's lingering skepticism that Morgan could pull off its makeover and succeed in its ambitious plans of competing with the nation's leading investment banks.

In response to those kinds of lackluster results, Mr. Warner began in 1996 to make a big public splash about the "new" J. P. Morgan. He started in the spring, hosting an elegant dinner for analysts at the bank's Wall Street head-quarters, followed by a cross-country road show for investors. Such meetings, commonplace at other companies, were never common at J. P. Morgan. Analysts invited to the New York dinner said it was the first such event they could remember in two dozen years.

They left impressed, as much by what Mr. Warner had to say as by the filet mignon he said it over. For the first time, the bank's chairman publicly acknowledged that he was unhappy with the performance of its stock, which he said reflected the big investment Morgan had been making, over fifteen years, in new lines of business that had not yet had an opportunity to become profitable. But he said he expected those new businesses—particularly stock underwriting—to pay off in a big way in the relatively near future. And he said he expected the new J. P. Morgan to be less interest-rate sensitive than the old one was, as it became less dependent on lending, and more driven by reliable, fee-based businesses such as advising on mergers and acquisitions. Over the long term, Mr. Warner said Morgan was aiming for a return on equity of between 15 and 20 percent or more. The company came close to that target in 1996, turning in a return-on-equity of 14.9 percent, though it slipped back to 13.4 percent by the end of 1997.

Not content with an occasional dinner to get the word out, Mr. Warner decided to launch a major print advertising campaign. The $8 million campaign—featuring full-page ads in *The Wall Street Journal*, *The New York Times*, and *The Economist*, among others—centered around the slogan "Morgan means more," and was designed to reinforce public awareness of the bank's transformation.

But Morgan officials felt it was also important to remind people of the bank's heritage. Hence, then-head of equities Ramon de Oliveira, facing ribbing on Wall Street from competitors who chuckled over Morgan's claim that it was the "fastest-growing equity house" on Wall Street, sent the bank's public relations staff scurrying to the Pierpont Morgan library to find original documents relating to the initial public stock offering of U.S. Steel, underwritten by Morgan more than sixty years earlier, before the Glass-Steagall Act. A photograph of those documents promptly began appearing in the bank's ads.

Meanwhile, Morgan did receive some good news on the Glass-Steagall front in 1996. After the latest in a series of attempts to repeal the law outright and achieve comprehensive reform of the financial-services industry died on Capitol Hill, the Federal Reserve responded by raising the cap on banks' Section 20 underwriting operations to 25 percent, from 10 percent. The move meant nothing for the vast majority of banks, which did not have Section 20 privileges. Even for those banks with underwriting operations, the Fed's action meant little, since most of those operations were still a long way from hitting the 10 percent mark. But for J. P. Morgan, Bankers Trust, and a handful of foreign banks that were beginning to bump up against the cap, the move translated into significant extra breathing room. Though Morgan officials vowed to continue their fight for the complete repeal of Glass-Steagall and a leveling of the financial-services playing field, in practice, the Federal Reserve's action diminished the urgency for Glass-Steagall reform.

The Original Private Bank

If there is a business that is synonymous with J. P. Morgan, it is private banking. Today, most commercial and investment banks offer money-management services for high-net-worth individuals, but that is a relatively new development. The business was mastered by Morgan decades ago. Ironically, though, as other banks increasingly emulate Morgan, offering the privileges of private banking to their wealthiest clients, Morgan is increasingly moving downscale, opening up the rarified world of its private bank to more and more investors.

A few years ago, the bank's advertising targeted customers with $5 million to invest. Today, Morgan bankers regret the move, because the ads left people with the impression that Morgan would turn away customers with less than $5 million, though that wasn't the case. The ads prompted many investors with $500,000 or $1 million to turn to other banks to manage their money—and by the time their fortunes grew to $5 million, they weren't about to switch to the bank that, they thought, had turned its nose up at them before. More recently, Morgan has sought to let investors know that it will accept their business as long as they have $1 million in investable assets—and in some cases, it will accept customers with less. The idea is to target customers who have the potential to earn considerable fortunes, even if they haven't amassed those fortunes yet.

But Morgan has also taken a giant—and once unthinkable—step of targeting average investors in addition to its traditional, wealthy clientele. In July 1997, it announced its acquisition of a 45 percent stake in American Century Cos., the Kansas City, Missouri, mutual-fund company, for about $900 million. The deal pairs blue-blood Morgan with a middle-American firm known for its no-load mutual funds. It indicates Morgan's recognition of the fact that while wealthy investors control a lot of money, average investors, taken together, control a great deal more.

Morgan officials touted the deal as a perfect match, pairing their expertise in private banking and defined-benefit pension plans with American Century's strong presence in defined-contribution profit-sharing accounts, in which individual employees can choose to distribute their assets among a variety of mutual funds. Going into the deal, Morgan had just a handful of mutual funds, with just $30 billion in assets spread among them; American Century, by contrast, had seventy mutual funds, with $60 billion in assets.

But for all the benefits of the transaction, analysts point to several risks—not least of them how well buttoned-down Morgan will mesh with the more relaxed, Midwestern culture of American Century. Another concern: that by opening its elite money-management operation to the masses—Morgan now allows investors to buy into its mutual funds with just $2,500, down from $25,000 before the deal—the bank could end up demystifying and devaluing its carefully honed image.

In addition to the private-banking and mutual fund operations, Morgan's institutional money-management operation is sizable, providing a reliable, annuity-like stream of profit. Among its long-term clients: the giant General Motors pension fund. All told, Morgan manages $250 billion for institutional and individual clients. In 1997, the money-management business contributed $279 million to Morgan's bottom line, a 12 percent increase from the year earlier.

Morgan left the lucrative domestic securities processing business in 1995, prompting criticism from some analysts, who like the business as a steady source of fee income. Nevertheless, the bank is still under contract in Europe to operate the Euroclear system, which offers securities settlement and clearing services, and which Morgan developed a quarter century ago.

Back to the Future in Underwriting

A major focus of Morgan's energy—and its money—in recent years has been in building an equity business from scratch. And with more than 1,100 professionals, up from about two hundred just six years ago, the equity business is the fastest-growing division in the firm. Yet, despite making significant inroads in the area in a relatively short amount of time, the bank faces formidable obstacles in the form of Merrill Lynch, Morgan Stanley and Goldman Sachs, the business's entrenched leaders, who together control over 40 percent of the market for all stock issues, including initial public stock offerings, according to Securities Data Co. For Morgan, the result has been a laborious and humbling effort to convince longtime lending clients to trust the bank with their underwriting work, and to reach out to new clients who, in some recent instances, haven't even been aware that the bank is in the equity business.

True to form, Morgan has resisted the temptation to scoop up an existing securities firm and with it, an instant underwriting presence. Rather, a key strategy of the bank's underwriting effort has been to leverage its strength as a lender into strength as an underwriter. The firm has shot up the closely-watched league tables for bond underwriting, a natural fit for its core lending business. Morgan ranked sixth among underwriters of all forms of debt in 1997, with a market share of 8.2 percent, up from eleventh place, with a market share of 2.4 percent just four years earlier, according to Securities Data Co. Excluding mortgage- and asset-backed debt, where the firm's lack of a broad retail consumer base puts it at a disadvantage relative to bigger commercial banks, Morgan's performance is even better. The firm ranked fifth in 1997—behind Merrill Lynch and Goldman Sachs, but well ahead of Morgan Stanley or any commercial banks—with a market share of 11.3 percent, up from ninth place, with a market share of 2.8 percent five years earlier.

But breaking into the ranks of the busiest stock underwriters has proved more of a challenge. Morgan has had considerable success among the ranks of underwriting comanagers, ranking ninth in 1997, with a market share of 12.6 percent, up from thirty-third place, with a 1.8 percent market share in 1991. More coveted—and profitable—lead-managed roles, however, have materialized at a far slower pace. In 1997, Morgan commanded less than 3 percent of lead-manager assignments, and ranked tenth in the market. Still, the bank did lead-manage three of the largest initial public offerings of 1997, including offerings for CIT Group and Security Capital Corp. helping boost its rank to fifth among lead managers of IPOs for the year.

Nevertheless, in a business where it takes lead-manager assignments to get lead-manager assignments, J. P. Morgan has only a handful of sizable lead-managed offerings to show for itself. In 1996, for the first time, the bank managed a public stock offering worth more than $1 billion—but not for an American client. Even longtime clients who are willing to throw the bank a bone once in a while, in the form of a comanager role on a stock offering, are generally unwilling to take the risk of letting Morgan lead-manage an offering, when they can achieve predictable results with a market leader such as Goldman Sachs or Merrill Lynch.

Thus, for example, when Ford Motor Co. decided to spin off its Associates First Capital division to the public in 1996—on the advice of J. P. Morgan—it chose Goldman Sachs to lead the underwriting. "J. P. Morgan did the groundwork, [but] we try to recognize who's the best at each particular transaction," explained John Devine, Ford's chief financial officer. "Goldman in my view, and in the Street's view, is the leader on the Street for public offerings."

Bank officials, while acknowledging that the loss of the lead role on the Associates deal was a "bitter pill," said the overall lag between co-managed and lead-managed offerings doesn't bother them, since they are convinced the former will eventually translate into the latter. "You want to be at the head of the table, but the first step to get to the head of the table is getting invited to the

Hertz IPO Is the Latest Coup for J.P. Morgan

BY STEPHEN E. FRANK AND
ANITA RAGHAVAN
Staff Reporters of THE WALL STREET JOURNAL

When Ford Motor Co. names J.P. Morgan lead underwriter for the initial public stock offering of Hertz Corp. as early as this week, it will be a sweet victory for J.P. Morgan.

And it will be a bitter pill for Goldman, Sachs & Co., the auto maker's longtime Wall Street investment bank.

A decade ago, when Goldman advised Ford on its purchase of Hertz, J.P. Morgan had to beg for the chance to help out on the transaction. The big New York commercial bank wasn't even allowed, under federal law, to underwrite stocks in the U.S., and its merger practice was virtually nonexistent. Goldman, meanwhile, had helped take Ford public 40 years ago. Its senior partners drove only Ford cars, and its bankers, for fear of offending Ford, refused to even call on the auto maker's rivals, General Motors Corp. and Chrysler Corp. For years, Ford awarded virtually all its considerable investment-banking business to Goldman.

The tables have turned. The Hertz offering, on which J.P. Morgan won't comment, caps a tremendous year for the commercial bank (which shares a history but is no longer connected with the Wall Street securities firm Morgan Stanley Group Inc.). Just last month, J.P. Morgan advised Ford on the $1.7 billion sale of its Budget Rent-A-Car division. And in 1996, it was lead adviser to Ford on a series of merger-and-acquisition assignments valued at $6.4 billion, according to Securities Data Co. During the same period, Goldman's M&A team advised Ford on just one transaction—the sale of its life-insurance division, in a deal valued at $172.5 million.

J.P. Morgan's snaring of one of Goldman's most prized clients is a coup in its nearly two-decades-long transformation from stodgy lender to highflying investment bank. "If you're going to win in this business, you're not going to win picking up dime-store accounts," says Barrett Petty, the Morgan banker responsible for managing the Ford account.

It also points to the mercurial nature of investment-banking relationships on Wall Street. No longer content to rely on a single bank, corporations are playing the field, pitting investment banks against each other in the quest for the best advice.

"We wanted to go to the dance with Goldman Sachs, but we wanted to dance with other people," says Bill Blood, recently retired treasurer of Ford's Financial Services Group.

Ford and Goldman officials insist they are still close. Goldman partner John L. Thornton last year joined Ford's board of directors. And Goldman still does a considerable amount of underwriting for the auto maker, including leading last year's $1.94 billion initial public stock offering of Associates First Capital Corp. Goldman also just completed a $1.25 billion global bond offering for Ford Motor Credit Co.

"We have a long historical relationship with Goldman, and they're very important to us," says John M. Devine, Ford's chief financial officer.

"A business relationship, like any relationship, is best judged by its durability," a spokesman for Goldman says. "By this standard, Goldman Sachs's relationship with the Ford Motor Co. remains strong and very special."

While J.P. Morgan's investment-banking efforts are only now beginning to bear fruit, they started in the late 1970s, under the leadership of Lewis Preston, who became the bank's chairman in 1980. Anticipating the erosion of Depression-era laws separating commercial and investment banking—laws that had caused the bank to lose its investment-banking privileges in 1933, resulting in Morgan Stanley as a separate company—Mr. Preston dispatched a cadre of J.P. Morgan bankers, including Mr. Petty, to gain experience overseas, where regulations were less strict. "The whole culture of this place was to recover its birthright," says Mr. Petty.

In 1983, Mr. Preston summoned Mr. Petty back to the U.S. for a key assignment, heading up Morgan's Midwest operations and persuading Ford—one of its biggest lending clients—to throw Morgan some of its investment-banking work. Such efforts were critical to J.P. Morgan: If the bank couldn't convince its best clients to trust it with more of their business, it could hardly expect others to do so.

In the early days, J.P. Morgan had to fight for scraps. Indeed, so scornful were Ford executives of the bank's push into investment banking that a senior Ford official asked a J.P. Morgan banker: "If you guys decide to go into advertising, do we have to give you our advertising business too?"

Morgan got its first investment-banking assignment from Ford—advising the auto maker on the sale of its Philco electronics business in Brazil—because Goldman didn't have an office there. "We could've used somebody operating from New York or London, but we gave them a chance," says Ford Treasurer Malcolm S. Macdonald. "It was small potatoes." Though the mandate for the deal was awarded in mid-1980s, the $100 million sale ultimately closed in 1989.

In 1987, the auto maker tossed Morgan a bigger fish: to offer advice on the financing of the Hertz acquisition, valued at $1.3 billion. "We had had good experiences with them in other areas and knew that they had some excellent people, so we thought, why not see what they had to say?" recalls David McCammon, Ford's recently retired vice president for finance. "They were anxious to participate, and you always get good work from people who are anxious to participate."

Technically, the job was simply to help arrange financing. But J.P. Morgan saw it as a chance to take Goldman by surprise and upstage the investment bank.

In mid-1987, a series of meetings and telephone conference calls culminated in a tense confrontation at Ford's Dearborn, Mich., headquarters. As senior executives from the auto maker looked on, teams of bankers from Morgan and Goldman faced off over how to finance the acquisition.

According to people familiar with the situation, Goldman, led by partner Gary Rose, outlined several options, ultimately recommending an $800 million junk-bond offering—which Goldman would underwrite—with Morgan setting up a temporary multibank loan until the bonds could be sold. But Morgan had a proposal of its own: Scrap the junk bonds and use bank loans exclusively. Since Ford didn't want to keep the debt on its balance sheet, Morgan suggested a complicated holding company structure that would allow Ford to obtain the best possible interest rates, without having to guarantee the loan.

Savings to Ford: at least $75 million over the life of the loan, in addition to tax benefits. Cost to Goldman: millions of dollars in lost junk-bond financing fees.

Ford jumped at the Morgan proposal. "It was a better way to go," recalls Mr. McCammon. "It seemed pretty clear-cut."

Goldman officials play down the significance of the Hertz discussions, saying that several options were debated and Goldman agreed bank financing was the best choice. But at one point during the talks, according to people familiar with the conversation, then-Ford treasurer Stanley Seneker told Mr. Petty: "We think you beat the pants off Goldman." Mr. Seneker says he doesn't recall making the statement, though he concedes "somebody else might have said it."

After Hertz, Ford began to take Morgan more seriously. In 1990, when Ford toyed with acquiring archrival Chrysler, it turned to Morgan—not Goldman—to take a preliminary look at the numbers, though the talks, initiated by a group of Chrysler executives, never got very far.

By the late 1980s, there were other signs that the Goldman-Ford relationship was fraying. Some Goldman partners began to question the bank's single-minded devotion to Ford, charging that it prevented the firm from snaring lucrative business from other auto makers. And at Ford, the 1989 purchase of British luxury-car maker Jaguar PLC became a lightning rod for criticism. People close to Goldman say Ford's finance team blamed Goldman for the decision to pay nearly $2.4 billion for Jaguar, even though these

Loyal . . . to a Point: Ford and Goldman

Despite a long relationship, including Goldman Sachs's help in taking the auto maker public in 1956, Ford has favored J.P. Morgan in recent merger-and-acquisition assignments.

DEAL	LEAD ADVISER	DATE	DEAL VALUE (BILLIONS)
Purchase of Hertz	Goldman Sachs	1987	$1.30
Purchase of BDM International	Goldman Sachs	1988	0.45
Sale of Hertz Penske Truck Leasing	Goldman Sachs	1988	0.11
Sale of stake in Park Ridge	Goldman Sachs	1988	0.10
Purchase of Jaguar PLC	Goldman Sachs	1989	2.39
Sale of Philco electronics division	J.P. Morgan	1989	0.10
Sale of Ford Aerospace	Goldman Sachs	1990	1.99
Sale of Ford Dealer Computer Services	J.P. Morgan	1992	0.10
Sale of First Nationwide Bank	J.P. Morgan	1994	1.10
Sale of Ford Life Insurance	Goldman Sachs	1996	0.17
Purchase of stake in Mazda Motor	J.P. Morgan	1996	0.48
Sale of USL Capital division (in several parts)	J.P. Morgan	1996	5.93
Sale of Budget Rent-A-Car	J.P. Morgan	1997	1.68

Source: Securities Data Co.

people say Goldman told Ford the price was too steep. A Ford spokesman denies it assigned any blame to Goldman.

Soon, the Goldman-Ford relationship was under assault from all sides. At First Boston Corp. (now known as Credit Suisse First Boston), investment bankers decided to target Goldman's prized client. First Boston's stepped-up efforts won it a role representing Ford in its 1987 purchase of U.S. Leasing International Inc.

For Morgan, Ford's 1992 decision to sell First Nationwide Bank, an ailing California thrift, proved pivotal. The auto maker asked J.P. Morgan to take the lead role, with Goldman relegated to the second-tier status of co-adviser. Over the next three years, Morgan banker Joe Walker shuttled frequently between New York and San Francisco, where he and Mr. Devine, then chief executive of First Nationwide, worked closely to clean up the bank's troubled loan portfolio, before selling First Nationwide to an investor group for $1.1 billion.

The following year, Ford named Mr. Devine its chief financial officer, a move widely viewed as a big boost to the Ford-Morgan relationship. Indeed, since Mr. Devine has been in charge, virtually all of Ford's merger-and-acquisition business has gone to Morgan. Meanwhile, the camaraderie between Morgan bankers and Ford finance officials has grown. In the summers of 1993 and 1994, Messrs. Petty and Walker joined Mr. Macdonald and other Ford officials for overnight trout and salmon fishing trips to Michigan's Leelanau peninsula.

"I certainly wouldn't want to show a preference," says Mr. Macdonald. Still, he concedes, since Morgan has entered investment banking, "its relationship with Ford has flourished."

February 26, 1997

dinner party," said James E. "Jess" Staley, the bank's head of equity syndicate and capital markets. Mr. Staley and other J. P. Morgan officials point to the bank's comanager role on AT&T's 1996 spinoff of Lucent Technologics, at the time the largest initial public stock offering ever, as well as its comanager role on the Associates spin-off, then the second-largest new issue, as evidence that the bank was getting invited to a growing number of dinner parties.

What's more, in 1997 Ford finally did trust J. P. Morgan to lead the $500 million initial public stock offering of 20 percent of Hertz Corp.—a big blow to the automaker's longtime investment bank, Goldman Sachs—demonstrating that J. P. Morgan's star in the business of stock underwriting might yet be rising. Morgan officials saw Hertz as a turning point. "League tables are a lagging indicator," said Mr. de Oliveira. "The fact that they gave us a deal like [Hertz] is a breakthrough," he said, adding that he intended to "use Hertz for the next one," by using the bank's performance on the assignment as a marketing tool for other clients. "We have now built the capacity and have proven that we can execute," he said. "The next challenge, to take that to the next level, is a marketing challenge with new and existing customers."

A Meteoric Rise in M&A

Unquestionably the biggest success of J. P. Morgan's transformation has been its meteoric rise as an adviser on mergers and acquisitions. In 1981, when that process was in its infancy, J. P. Morgan advised on four transactions, with a total value of $2.6 billion. By early 1997, when the bank ranked, for the first time, among the nation's top six merger advisers, J. P. Morgan had completed nearly three times as many deals, with a total value more than five times as great, in just the month of January. (By year end, Morgan had fallen back to eighth place, with about 10 percent of the M&A advisory market.)

J. P. Morgan's growth as an M&A adviser has been fueled in large part by the bank's existing client relationships, developed over decades as one of the country's preeminent lending institutions. In 1996, for example, the bank advised Ford on the sale of its USL Capital subsidiary. The multibillion dollar transaction was the culmination of Morgan's concerted effort, over a decade, to transform Ford from a lending client exclusively, which the automaker had been since the 1940s, into a client that turned to Morgan as its "first-call" for a wide variety of needs. USL was a particular bonanza for Morgan not just because the bank won the assignment over Goldman Sachs, but also because of the deal's large size and unusual complexity. Rather than recommend a single, clean sale of the entire division, Morgan suggested a multistep sale of various parts of the division. The process, which took most of the year, nevertheless turned out to be hugely profitable for Ford.

In addition, Morgan's M&A department has been helped by the unprecedented increase in consolidation activity in the early to mid-1990s. Recent big deals that are a product of that consolidation include the 1995 merger of pharmaceutical giants Ciba-Geigy and Sandoz, in which Morgan advised Sandoz, and the 1996 aerospace megamerger of Boeing and McDonnell Douglas, where Morgan beat out M&A king Merrill Lynch for a spot advising McDonnell Douglas.

In 1997, Morgan helped advise CoreStates Financial Corp. on its $16.3 billion sale to First Union Corp., as well as Barnett Banks Inc. on its $13.8 billion sale to NationsBank Corp. In addition, Morgan served as lead adviser to Ford on the $18 billion spinoff of its 81 percent stake in Associates First Capital Corp.

Trying to Sustain a Trading Bonanza

Trading is a business of booms and busts, and the first three quarters of 1997 were boom-time for J. P. Morgan. Though it slipped a bit from the record level of 1996, the bank's combined revenue from trading and interest income associated with trading was $2.6 billion—36 percent of the company's total revenue for the year. But trading hasn't always been kind to Morgan, as the fourth quarter demonstrated, with a 33 percent plunge in trading income over the previous year. In 1994, volatile securities markets contributed to a 23 percent decline in the bank's profits.

Mr. Warner has told analysts that he aims to reduce the bank's reliance on proprietary activities—trading and investing for the firm's own account—in an effort to reduce cyclicality in the firm's earnings. Still, proprietary trading and stock investments, which made up 18 percent of J. P. Morgan's total revenue in 1997, contributed 49 percent of its pre-tax profits. In 1996, proprietary trading and gains on the firm's own stock investments accounted for 17 percent of J. P. Morgan's revenue, and just over 43 percent of its pre-tax income.

Indeed, Morgan can't wean itself from trading too much. As the bank builds its underwriting presence, it must necessarily build its presence in the secondary markets as well. In 1997, Morgan ranked sixteenth in listed stock-trading volume, according to data compiled by AutEx, a unit of Thompson Financial Services; seven years earlier, the bank didn't even rank among the top fifty secondary traders.

Strength in Europe and Emerging Markets

Now that regulatory barriers are no longer in its way, Morgan is focused on building its U.S. client roster, even as its rivals in the United States focus increasingly on building their operations abroad. Still, by virtue of its English origins, and the subsequent limitations it faced as a U.S. commercial bank, Morgan's business today remains lopsided in nature—with its strength in foreign markets equaling or exceeding its strength at home, particularly in investment-banking. All told, Morgan now has operations in more than thirty countries. Since 1995, more than half of the bank's revenue has come from operations outside the United States, mostly in Europe and Latin America. And success, for Morgan's leaders, is measured in global terms. "The bulge bracket is a U.S. concept, and is increasingly irrelevant," said Mr. Warner. In the not-too-distant future, he adds, competition for clients' business is going to be a contest between "twenty or twenty-five aspirants" from all over the world.

The bank's diversification has on occasion hurt as much as it has helped, as the 1997 fourth quarter's losses in Asia demonstrate. In 1994, losses in Europe contributed to a net loss of $111 million in Morgan's proprietary trading portfolio. But the following year, strength in Asian markets contributed to revenue of $184 million in the same portfolio.

In Europe, where more than 40 percent of its assets are based, the bank ranks as one of the continent's top mergers-and-acquisitions advisers. In securities trading, Morgan ranks as the top futures broker on the London International Financial Futures Exchange. What's more, the bank developed the Euroclear system, the dominant system of securities transaction settlement and clearance in Europe. Though Morgan still operates the system, under a long-term contract, the bank was forced to sell Euroclear to a consortium of member institutions because regulators viewed its ownership as monopolistic and fraught with potential conflicts. In fixed-income, Morgan's business is about equally divided between Europe and North America, unlike most other U.S. banks, which are heavily focused on the U.S. bond market. In lending, a 1995 mandate from Siemens AG made Morgan the first non-German bank to lead a loan syndication for a German company.

Morgan also has a long and proud record in Latin America, where it boasts a top ranking in mergers-and-acquisitions work and corporate finance. In 1997, for example, the bank arranged and joint-lead-managed a $3 billion debt exchange for the Republic of Brazil, which ranked as the largest unsecured non-investment grade issue by an emerging markets sovereign until that date. Also in 1997, Morgan lead-managed a 500 million peso bond offering for the Republic of Argentina that ranked as the country's first long-term, ten-year Argentine peso-denominated bond.

Morgan has a smaller presence throughout Asia, though during the Asian financial crisis that began in late 1997, the bank played a key role in organizing an international, private-sector bailout of the South Korean financial sector. Morgan has just started building its operations in Australia, where its principal U.S.-based competition is Bankers Trust, long a local market leader in money management, and pension-fund management in particular.

Indeed, pension-fund management is one area of potential growth for Morgan overseas. Convinced that the market for managing defined contribution plans in the United States is already far too competitive, the bank has aspirations of growing this fee-based business elsewhere. In Europe, for example, where Morgan has a strong presence, the pension-fund business is still in its infancy, offering the bank a vast market of potential growth.

Another possibility for foreign expansion: insurance. To be sure, Morgan has no interest in selling insurance, and insurance underwriting remains illegal for commercial banks in the United States. But Mr. Warner said he is confident that banks will be allowed to enter the business of insurance underwriting in the not-too-distant future. At that point, he said, Morgan could set up offshore underwriting and reinsurance businesses in Bermuda, where it has already counseled insurance giants like Marsh & McLennan.

Building a Research Team

When Douglas Cliggott arrived at J. P. Morgan in August 1996, he found himself at the center of an experiment: the creation, from scratch, of a research and investment strategy team.

Mr. Cliggott is one of the few members of the new team to come from outside the bank's ranks. Joining Morgan from Merrill Lynch, where he worked closely with veteran strategist Chuck Clough, Mr. Cliggott was lured by the prospect of building and putting his mark on the kind of research effort he believed Morgan's senior management would throw its weight behind.

The bank still has a long way to go before it will be able to offer the range of investment advice available from the other major Wall Street players. Compared to a research behemoth like Merrill, with its eight-hundred-strong research team, J. P. Morgan currently boasts no more than 130 analysts and still has some significant holes in its coverage. For instance, the firm has yet to hire or name an analyst to cover Intel and Microsoft, the two key stocks in the technology industry and the Standard & Poor's 500-stock index. Nor were large oil companies covered throughout 1996, even as crude prices rocketed to levels not seen in nearly a decade.

But many of these gaps will be covered as the bank continues to expand its research presence over the next year or two. It is adding companies to its coverage list at a rapid clip; with six hundred firms now covered, about twenty-five more are added each quarter. In doing so, it's taking a decidedly Morgan-esque approach: turning former credit-risk analysts for its commercial bank into stock analysts for its investment bank. The bank generally has resisted the temptation to dangle fat paychecks in front of rainmaking analysts from other firms.

Already, the approach seems to be yielding dividends. In 1996, the first year the bank's analysts were included in *The Wall Street Journal*'s all-star report, twelve made the list, more than firms like Lehman Brothers or Prudential Securities could boast. In 1997, twenty analysts were all-stars.

Even with the coverage gaps, Morgan's effort to convert existing client ties into new types of relationships is paying off. The bank wants to offer its research as an integral part of its other financial services, in the hope that not only will research support its investment banking operations and asset management division but also that these operations will in turn have spin-off benefits for research. Already, given its relatively small size, the bank's research department has a surprisingly strong presence outside the United States: It covers companies in thirty different countries and thirty-seven of its analysts are based outside the United States, something the bank's officials like to emphasize.

Among the bank's assets is Mr. Cliggott himself. Although he didn't publish his first strategy report until late December 1996 (a decidedly unprescient call for "more yawns than thrills" in the stock market in 1997), his straightforward snapshots of market trends have quickly become important reading for many institutions. Among the reasons: an early warning to investors to scale back their holdings of technology stocks, and reduce their exposure to the market generally just prior to the rocky ride in the spring of 1997.

Still, Mr. Cliggott and his expanding team have an important hurdle to surmount in their quest to be counted among Wall Street's research elite, one that will be common to any bank as it forges into the world of underwriting. It's at least in part one of perception; many of the group's would-be clients are investment managers who also compete with J. P. Morgan for business. "It's hard to see how we could look at their research completely objectively when we still see them as a competitor," said an investment official at a rival New York bank.

A Blemish to Morgan's Pristine Image

One possible cost of Morgan's increasingly aggressive and high-flying culture became evident in late 1996, when the firm was reprimanded by federal and state banking regulators for lax management and controls in its base-metals business, following a six-month investigation of the bank's business relationship with Sumitomo Corp., the Japanese trading firm. Morgan was one of at least four U.S. banks that did considerable business with Sumitomo, which lost $2.6 billion on rogue trading by its head copper trader. In particular, Morgan loaned at least $400 million to Sumitomo, structuring the loan as a complex derivatives transaction, which apparently allowed the Sumitomo trader, Yasuo Hamanaka, to account for the money as copper trading profits, rather than bank loans.

Though Chase Manhattan Corp. loaned Sumitomo even more money—as much as $500 million, according to people familiar with the bank—Morgan was the only bank disciplined for its behavior, making the joint action by the Federal Reserve Bank of New York and the New York State banking department even more embarrassing. The regulators demanded that Morgan's chairman, Mr. Warner, sign the reprimand, called a memorandum of understanding, which committed the bank to a period of tight supervision of its base-metals business. Though the memorandum was essentially little more than a slap on the wrist, the move was the first time in recent memory that Morgan had been disciplined, and Mr. Warner and other top Morgan executives were said to be outraged at the severity of the action.

According to people familiar with the bank, the regulators were troubled by the extent of Morgan's relationship with Sumitomo, which was much deeper than the relationship of the other banks, and included an extensive business trading copper options. Indeed, one of the ways Morgan apparently financed Sumitomo was by purchasing massive quantities of copper put options from the trading house—essentially a bet that the price of copper would decline—even as Sumitomo was hoarding enough of the metal to ensure that its price remained high. Regulators were partly concerned that the volume of the put options Morgan bought from Sumitomo was so great that the bank could not possibly have hedged its position adequately to guard against big swings in the metal's price, according to people familiar with the bank. In addition, these people say, regulators were troubled by the degree to which the credit risk in Morgan's base-metals business was concentrated in Sumitomo, which one person familiar with the bank says was its biggest base-metals client "by a factor of ten."

Morgan ended up dramatically scaling back its money-losing base-metals business, shuttering the division's main operation in London and dismissing several of its employees. For its part, the bank insisted the change was "a business decision not required by any regulatory action."

But Morgan did face regulatory action in another case, almost exactly a year later, when it was fined by the London Stock Exchange in connection with an incident in which two traders were found to have engaged in market manipulation.

On November 28, 1997, the day after Thanksgiving, the two traders sold shares of a number of stocks, including those of Glaxo Wellcome PLC and Smith-Kline Beecham, as part of a successful attempt to knock down the FTSE 100 index by 38 points in the last minutes of trading. The two traders, who were quickly fired after the incident came to light, were responsible for managing option contracts and had a position linked to the FTSE 100 index, people familiar with the matter said.

Like the problems in the base-metals business, the London Stock Exchange episode laid bare the potential pitfalls that accompany Morgan's new culture and its chosen role as an aggressive player in the rough and tumble world of investment banking.

Morgan's People

Douglas A. "Sandy" Warner III, chairman and chief executive officer: Mr. Warner succeeded Dennis Weatherstone as chairman and chief executive in 1994. A lifelong Morgan banker, he joined the firm shortly after graduating from Yale College and steadily rose through its ranks, ultimately replacing Mr. Weatherstone as head of Morgan's London office, and then as head of the entire bank.

Warner, Douglas "Sandy"
Chairman-J. P. Morgan

Mr. Warner has made raising the bank's public profile a priority, engaging in more frequent meetings with analysts and investors and flashier advertising. Partly, this is because he wants to raise the value of Morgan's stock, which while a strong performer, is far from a high-flyer. He also wants to broaden the bank's customer base and make it more accessible, though he is conscious of the risk of devaluing Morgan's blue-blood image and bristles at the suggestion that he is trying to have the bank cater to "average investors."

"The goal today is to deliver as much of our private-banking capability to as many people who value that business as we can," he said. "There's nothing average about it." At the same time, he notes, the firm's advertisements of several years ago, which addressed themselves to "individuals with at least $5 million in investable assets," were "stand-offish and negative." "We want to do business," he said. And he takes the firm's client focus seriously, frequently jetting around the country to meet with current and prospective customers of the bank.

In his personal life, though, Mr. Warner shuns the limelight, preferring to vacation with his family at his home in northern Michigan, where he spent summers as a child, than to frequent the trendy spots preferred by many of his investment-banking brethren, or the elite vacation communities of the northeast.

Roberto G. Mendoza, vice-chairman: Mr. Mendoza joined Morgan's London office upon graduating from Yale College in 1967, leaving five years later to pursue a master's degree from Harvard Business School. He rejoined the firm in 1975, in New York, working in international corporate finance, and then in capital markets. He became part of the fledgling mergers and acquisitions group in 1985, helping build that operation to its current prominence, before being named vice chairman in 1990.

Michael E. Patterson, vice-chairman: Mr. Patterson is a former Supreme Court clerk and longtime corporate lawyer who joined Morgan as its general counsel in 1987. A graduate of Harvard College and Columbia Law School, who serves as a Columbia trustee, he was named the bank's chief administrative officer in 1994, and was elected vice chairman in 1995.

Walter A. Gubert, vice-chairman and global head of investment banking: A native of Italy who trained as a lawyer at the University of Florence, Mr. Gubert has been based in London continuously since 1987. Since joining the firm as a chemical analyst in Paris in 1973, he has worked, at various times, as a senior executive in each of the bank's four major lines of business: corporate finance, mergers-and-acquisitions, securities and treasury. To wit: In 1977, he became head of the bank's treasury management advisory group in London; in 1981, he moved to New York to head Morgan's U.S. capital markets business; in 1987, he returned to London to head the firm's European and Asian securities business; in 1989, he succeeded Mr. Warner as head of J. P. Morgan in London, with responsibility for European mergers-and-acquisitions. In 1991, he took over all invest-ment-banking operations in Europe, the Middle East and Africa, becoming head of global investment banking in late 1997, and a vice-chairman in 1998.

Thomas B. Ketchum, chief administrative officer: Prior to his latest appoint-ment, which was announced in late 1997, Mr. Ketchum had been responsible for Morgan's clients relationships and investment-banking business in the United States, Canada and Latin America since 1995. He joined the bank in 1973, one year after graduating from Yale College, and, after completing the bank's training program, began working in New York with clients in the oil and gas industry. In 1979, Mr. Ketchum moved to London, where he ran the firm's business with energy companies in Europe, the Middle East and Africa. In 1984, he moved to Hong Kong, becoming head of that office the following year, and head of the Asian business, excluding Japan, in 1986. In 1987, Mr. Ketchum moved to Brussels, where he took charge of Euroclear's day-to-day operations, before being asked to head a firmwide cost restructuring project in 1991. Later that year, he was named head of corporate finance in the Americas. In his new role, Mr. Ketchum will again focus on trying to cut costs and improve productivity.

Peter L. Woicke, senior executive for the Asia-Pacific region: A native of Germany who graduated with a degree in business administration from the University of Saarbruecken, Mr. Woicke has followed one of the more interest-ing career paths at J. P. Morgan. After joining the bank's Frankfurt office in 1969, he was transferred to a Morgan affiliate bank in Beirut, Lebanon, in 1973. From there, Mr. Woicke moved to London in 1976, where he focused on the pe-troleum sector, becoming head of the petroleum department in 1978. He moved to Brazil to head an affiliate bank in Rio de Janeiro in 1982, becoming Morgan's country manager in 1984. In 1987, his eighteenth year at the bank, Mr. Woicke was assigned for the first time to the New York office, as head of the securities industry department. The following year he was named to head Morgan's secu-rities processing business, and was promoted to head J. P. Morgan Securities Inc. in 1989. In 1990, he took on additional responsibility for Morgan's Latin American business, and was named head of global technology and operations in 1991. In 1992, he became cohead of global markets, before taking charge of the client business in Asia and the Pacific in 1995.

Joseph P. MacHale, senior executive for Europe, the Middle East and Africa: An Oxford University graduate and former Price Waterhouse consul-tant, Mr. MacHale is responsible for overseeing Morgan's business in a wide swath of territory. He joined the bank's London office in 1979, working in its fledgling mergers-and-acquisitions group, and was transferred to New York in 1984 to work in the international financial management group, which arranged capital markets transactions for clients. He returned to London in 1986 to head the eurobond underwriting business, and later the international capital markets group. In 1989, he was named head of U.S. capital markets, responsible for structuring, syndicating and distributing debt securities, before being named head of global credit, responsible for worldwide credit exposure, in 1993. He was named to his current post in late 1997.

Ramon de Oliveira, head of asset management: Mr. de Oliveira was named to head Morgan's combined asset-management business for individuals and institutions in May of 1997. In that role, he is expected to beef up the firm's $250 billion in assets under management, through such arrangements as Morgan's joint-venture with American Century. Prior to his new job, Mr. de Oliveira oversaw 1,100 professionals in Morgan's developing stock-underwriting business, which he labeled the fastest-growing sector of the firm, as well as the "fastest-growing equity house on Wall Street." A detail-oriented manager, he keeps in his office a framed copy of a print-advertisement for the stock operation that he helped design, and that he boasts has been acclaimed by clients and envied by competitors. Though reputed to be a tough boss, Mr. de Oliveira also has a healthy sense of humor and believes in the power of cheerleading and motivational leadership. After a reporter questioned his claims about Morgan's rapid growth in equities, Mr. de Oliveira shot out an e-mail message to the firm apprising employees of the pending article and noting that, regardless of what it suggested, he was proud of their efforts. A native of Argentina and a French citizen, Mr. de Oliveira graduated from the Sorbonne in 1976 and joined Morgan the following year, in Paris, after noticing an advertisement for the bank. He started out "carrying envelopes," he says, before going through Morgan's training program in New York in 1978. He stayed in New York until 1980, working in the research department, before moving to the corporate finance office in London, where he specialized in the oil and gas sector. In 1985, Mr. de Oliveira joined the eurobond syndicate department, and in 1987 was named head of the department's equity syndicate operation. In 1989, he returned to New York to become head of high-yield securities, and was named head of global equities in 1992, and chairman of the asset management division in 1997.

Peter D. Hancock, head of global fixed income and credit: Mr. Hancock oversees the firm's giant fixed-income operation, which includes making markets in U.S. and foreign government securities, emerging market debt, and derivatives. In contrast to other Wall Street firms, Mr. Hancock says Morgan's fixed-income business is about equally split between Europe and North America. In addition, he says it is heavily focused on swaps. He views the firm's three biggest competitors in fixed income as Merrill Lynch, Salomon Brothers and Goldman Sachs. Considered a rising star at Morgan, Mr. Hancock, who is English, joined J. P. Morgan in 1980, after graduating from Oxford University. He worked initially in corporate finance, specializing in the petroleum business, and joined the eurobond syndicate desk in 1984. In 1986, he became manager of the multi-currency asset and liability desk in New York, and in 1987, became manager of swap and interest-rate derivative trading. He was named head of the New York swaps group in 1989, head of global swaps in 1990, and cohead of foreign exchange, equity and commodity derivatives in 1991. He became head of global fixed income in 1995, adding oversight of credit—responsible for managing the bank's worldwide credit exposures—in 1997.

Nicholas S. Rohatyn, head of emerging markets, foreign exchange, and commodities: Mr. Rohatyn is another of Morgan's fast-rising stars. The Brown University graduate joined Morgan's capital markets group in 1982, and was transferred to its Tokyo swaps desk in 1984. In 1988, he was named to head the bank's emerging markets division, then known as developing country asset trading, and was named to his current post in 1995. He is currently cochairman of the Emerging Markets Traders Association, which he has chaired since it was founded in 1990. A dual French-U.S. citizen, Mr. Rohatyn is the son of Felix Rohatyn, the widely known former head of Lazard Frères & Co.

Ernest Stern, senior relationship manager in emerging markets: Mr. Stern, who joined Morgan in March 1995, is a former senior official of the World Bank and has played a lead role organizing international bailouts of distressed economies around the world. Regarded as something of a senior statesman at Morgan, Mr. Stern, who reports directly to Mr. Warner, is in charge of client relationships in Latin America, Asia, Eastern Europe and the former Soviet Union. During the Asian economic crisis that began in late 1997, Mr. Stern played a key role in helping put together a private sector plan to rescue the South Korean financial system.

Pilar Conde, cohead of proprietary positioning: Ms. Conde, a native of Spain who studied law and economics, joined the bank in 1979 as assistant treasurer of its Madrid office, and became head of its foreign investment portfolio in New York in 1985. In 1989 she took over the foreign exchange forward desk and foreign currency asset and liability management, before being named to her current post in 1991.

Michael R. Corey, cohead of proprietary positioning: Mr. Corey joined Morgan in 1970 in Operations Research, after stints at Stauffer Chemical Co. and Mobil Oil Corp., and as an instructor at the Polytechnic Institute of Brooklyn, where he earned a doctorate in 1969. He was appointed to the investment portfolio unit in 1975, becoming its head six years later. He was named treasurer of Morgan Guaranty Trust Co. in 1991, and of the parent company in 1993, before assuming his current post.

In the Beginning . . .

The proud heritage and tightly knit culture of J. P. Morgan & Co. has its origins in the strong, continuous leadership provided by the Morgan family. During the firm's first century, it was dominated by just three men, all of them Morgans: Junius S. Morgan, an American who settled in London during the early part of the nineteenth century; his son J. Pierpont Morgan, who set up the family's American operations; and Pierpont's son, J. Pierpont "Jack" Morgan Jr., who ran the firm from 1913 until 1943.

Though no Morgan has played an active role in the firm's day-to-day operations since 1943, the Morgan legacy still prevails. All members of the bank's staff are coached in the company's history. And to this day, Morgan employees feel a sense of pride—competitors might call it arrogance—about their firm's heritage that is unmatched on Wall Street. It isn't uncommon to find staffers throughout the bank with several books about its history prominently displayed on their desks.

J. Pierpont Morgan was just twenty-three years old in 1860 when he settled in New York and founded the merchant-banking firm that bears his name. But the firm's origins actually precede that date by more than two decades, when Mr. Morgan's father, Junius S. Morgan, became a partner in a British merchant bank, George Peabody & Co., founded in London in 1838. Separately incorporated and divided by an ocean, the firms were nonetheless tightly bound from the start through the leadership of Junius Morgan, the de facto head of both banks, and later through Pierpont Morgan. The firms offered corporate lending and advisory services, as well as stock underwriting and trading, and specialized in assisting companies doing business on both sides of the Atlantic.

Mr. Peabody died in 1864 and the British bank took the Morgan name. In 1871, J. P. Morgan merged with Drexel & Co., a Philadelphia investment bank, and briefly adopted the name Drexel Morgan. The company reverted to the Morgan name in 1895. Meanwhile, Junius Morgan died in 1890 and the British bank was renamed Morgan Grenfell & Co. two decades later to reflect the contributions of E. C. Grenfell, who had joined the firm in 1900.

Morgan was severely hobbled by the Glass-Steagall Act of 1933, which left it unable to conduct the type of investment-banking business that had helped it flourish. The firm responded by spinning off its investment-banking business into a new company, headed by several of Morgan's most senior partners, including Harold Stanley and Harry Morgan, Jack's younger brother. At the time, the move was viewed as only temporary, a means to pacify lawmakers, but certainly not with the intent of permanently exiting the investment-banking business.

(continued on next page)

Luc Bomans, head of Euroclear: A native of Belgium, Mr. Bomans worked at Unilever before joining Morgan's Euroclear division in 1978. He has risen steadily through the division's ranks, and is credited with developing the system's settlement and custody services. He became manager of Euroclear in 1994.

Stephen G. Thieke, head of corporate risk management and research: Mr. Thieke is responsible for developing policies and procedures for assessing and controlling market and credit risk across Morgan's various businesses. A former executive vice president of the Federal Reserve Bank of New York who chaired its financial policy council, Mr. Thieke joined Morgan in 1989.

The departure of Mr. Stanley left the ownership of the firm in the hands of just three partners: Jack Morgan, who would lead the company for another decade, Charles Steele, who died in 1940, and Thomas Lamont, one of the founders of Bankers Trust who also became a chairman of J. P. Morgan. The concentration of ownership, and the loss of a big chunk of its business, prompted fears that the bank's capital base would erode. In addition, the firm's partnership structure legally prevented it from entering the trust business, a lucrative and growing field. These twin factors led to Morgan's decision to go public in 1940.

Public ownership only temporarily eased Morgan's cash crunch. Forced to compete against other commercial banks whose large base of retail deposits fueled their lending growth, Morgan, which had never catered to the average customer, realized it was in a losing position. The situation worsened during the 1950s, when a series of sizable mergers brought together wholesale and retail banks, creating a new cadre of fierce competitors. Morgan responded in 1959, merging with Guaranty Trust Co., another big wholesale bank, to form the Morgan Guaranty Trust Co., today the principal subsidiary of J. P. Morgan & Co.

If Morgan managed to survive and even prosper as a narrowly focused commercial bank in the half century following Glass-Steagall, it never gave up on its dream of returning to its investment-banking roots. That dream was the central concern of Mr. Preston, a lifelong Morgan banker and former head of its London operation who became the bank's chairman and chief executive in 1980. Presciently, Mr. Preston foresaw a time when corporations would learn that they could increasingly fund their operations more cheaply and flexibly without bank loans, by issuing stock, or their own debt, directly to the public, and the public would realize that they could achieve higher returns on their investments by placing their savings in the public markets, rather than in their bank accounts. He organized and oversaw a dramatic change in the bank's business practices—a shift back to its investment-banking roots—beginning in Europe, where laws governing what Morgan might do were less restrictive than they were at home.

In 1990, Dennis Weatherstone, a lifelong Morgan banker who started as a bookkeeper in Morgan's London office, succeeded Mr. Preston as the bank's chairman. Merely by becoming chairman, Mr. Weatherstone, the British-born son of blue-collar parents, was completing the cultural transformation Mr. Preston had started. Yet it was also fitting that it was Mr. Weatherstone, who personally embodied the bank's British heritage, who oversaw the final phases of the bank's redevelopment of the businesses that were its roots.

Clayton S. Rose, head of global equities: Mr. Rose joined Morgan in 1981, serving stints in banking and corporate finance, as well as in the London office, trading fixed income and option instruments and managing various trading groups. He returned to New York in 1988, playing an integral role under Mr. de Oliveira in the development of the equity business, before being named to succeed Mr. de Oliveira as head of that business in 1997.

Joseph A. Walker, cohead of global mergers and acquisitions: Mr. Walker, who joined Morgan in 1979 and was assigned to the financial advisory group in 1980, joined the New York M&A group in 1988 and three years later become head of the unit specializing in corporate restructurings. He was appointed head of the basic industries M&A unit in 1992, and named to his current post in 1994.

Klaus Diederichs, cohead of global mergers and acquisitions: Mr. Diederichs, who is a member of Morgan's European Management Committee, has managed a wide range of corporate finance and mergers-and-acquisitions transactions for clients in France, Germany, Italy and the United Kingdom.

Nicholas B. Paumgarten, head of U.S. mergers and acquisitions: Mr. Paumgarten, an alumnus of Dillon Read and First Boston, joined Morgan as cohead of the financial institutions group in 1988. He now heads Morgan's U.S. M&A department, as well as its Media Group, and is chairman of the Corsair Partnership.

Sarah Elizabeth Nash, managing director, investment banking: A member of the investment banking management team, Ms. Nash is responsible for client and regional issues in North America. A graduate of Vassar College, she was a marketing representative at IBM Corp. before joining J. P. Morgan in 1976, where she worked for a decade in various corporate finance functions in Chicago and New York. In 1987, she became a managing director in leveraged finance, and since 1990, she has been actively involved in client development and investment banking management.

Michael Enthoven, chairman of planned sponsors group: A Dutch citizen, Mr. Enthoven was named to his current post in early 1997 in what was intended to be a temporary assignment pending his recovery from a serious illness. His responsibilities include focusing on strategy and improved productivity. He had previously served as head of technology and operations since 1993, and before that as cohead of the bank's global markets group since 1991, responsible for its swaps, equities and commodities businesses worldwide. Since joining Morgan in Amsterdam in 1976, he has worked in Morgan's London-based eurobond underwriting group, as executive director responsible for client coverage in Northern Europe, as head of private finance in New York, and as chief executive of J. P. Morgan Securities Ltd. in London and cohead of corporate finance in Europe.

John A. Mayer Jr., chief financial officer: Mr. Mayer, who goes by his nickname, "Tony," assumed his current post in 1995, after serving as head of global corporate finance for five years. He joined the bank in 1965, became head of project finance in London in 1974, and head of its London-based securities subsidiary in 1979. He returned to New York in 1986 as head of the funding services unit in corporate finance, became a senior member of the firm's mergers and acquisitions team the following year, and head of global corporate finance in 1990.

David H. Sidwell, controller: Mr. Sidwell joined Morgan in 1984, following nine years with Coopers and Lybrand. A graduate of Cambridge University, he is a member of the Emerging Issues Task Force of the Financial Accounting Standards Board.

Rachel F. Robbins, general counsel: Ms. Robbins, who began her legal career as an associate at the law firm of Milbank, Tweed, Hadley & McCloy, joined Morgan's legal department in 1980, becoming general counsel of J. P. Morgan Securities Inc. in 1986, and general counsel of the parent company in 1996.

James E. Staley, head of equity syndicate and equity capital markets: Mr. Staley, who joined J. P. Morgan in 1979, worked in Morgan's Latin American department from 1980 until 1989, including an eight-year stint in Brazil. In 1989 he became head of convertible debt, sales and trading, and was named head of equity sales and trading in 1990. He is currently head of equity syndicate and equity capital markets.

S. Luke Ellis, global head of equity derivatives: Mr. Ellis heads a group which includes 130 front-office professionals in sales, trading and research for listed and over-the-counter equity derivatives as well as convertibles and equity financing in London, New York, Hong Kong and Tokyo. He also heads equity proprietary trading and sits on Morgan's European Management Committee.

T. Timothy Ryan Jr., head of investor client management group: Mr. Ryan, who also heads the financial institutions, government institutions and real estate groups for the Americas, joined Morgan in 1993, after serving as director of the Office of Thrift Supervision. While at the OTS, he was a principal manager of the savings and loan cleanup.

Edward J. "Ned" Kelly III, head of financial institutions group: Mr. Kelly, who joined Morgan as its general counsel in 1994, is in large part responsible for Morgan's rapid growth in financial institutions mergers and acquisitions, as well as for its Latin American investment-banking effort. He was the lead negotiator in the bank's acquisition of a 45 percent stake in American Century Cos. in 1997. A former clerk for Supreme Court Justice William J. Brennan Jr., he worked as a lawyer in New York before joining Morgan, where he became head of the financial institutions group within two years.

Frederic A. "Rick" Escherich, head of analysis policy group: Mr. Escherich, who joined Morgan as an auto and airline industry analyst in 1978, has headed the analysis policy group within the firm's mergers-and-acquisitions department since 1993.

James M. "Jamie" Grant, managing director in investment banking: Mr. Grant, who joined Morgan in its London office in 1980, is responsible for key corporate finance clients in Ohio and Pennsylvania.

Barrett R. Petty, managing director in investment banking: Mr. Petty, who joined Morgan in 1966, and served as general manager of the Saudi International Bank from 1979 to 1983, is responsible for major client relationships in the central United States.

Michael C. Lobdell, managing director in investment-banking: Mr. Lobdell heads the group that provides investment banking services to private investment companies, leveraged acquisition partnerships and related financial firms. He joined Morgan in 1979.

Jon H. Zehner, head of real estate investment banking: Mr. Zehner joined Morgan in 1981, and was assigned to its real estate department in 1982. He headed the bank's European real estate investment banking operation in 1993 and 1994, before assuming his current post, based in New York.

Benjamin Meuli, chief executive, J. P. Morgan Life Assurance Ltd.: Mr. Meuli joined Morgan in 1978 in its London office and became head of its European Capital Markets group before assuming his current responsibilities in 1995.

Brian F. Watson, president of J. P. Morgan Capital Corp.: Mr. Watson heads Morgan's proprietary private investment arm, which has 100 investments worldwide with an estimated book value approaching $1 billion. He joined Morgan in 1986.

Mark C. Brickell, head of derivatives strategies group: Mr. Brickell, who joined Morgan in 1976 in its international banking group, joined the treasurer's division as head of the commercial lending liaison unit in 1983, and the swap group in 1986. He now heads the derivatives strategies group and is a director of the International Swaps & Derivatives Association, which he chaired from 1988 until 1992.

Robert J. Hugin, head of spread product fixed income: Mr. Hugin heads the unit that includes Morgan's new issue and secondary market trading activities, North American and Latin American Capital Markets Groups and Swaps marketing. He was previously head of the fixed income syndicate department.

William L. Cobb, vice chairman of asset management services: Mr. Cobb joined Morgan's equity research department as an analyst in 1971, and became a portfolio manager, focusing on international clients, in 1974. After various other positions, he became vice chairman of J. P. Morgan Investment Management and regional head of the firm's business in North America, before assuming his current post.

Preben Prebensen, chairman of London Management Committee: Mr. Prebensen is responsible for J. P. Morgan's investment banking clients in the U.K., Scandinavia, Holland and South Africa. He was named chairman of the London Management Committee in 1994.

J. Roderick "Rod" B. Peacock, cohead of European mergers and acquisitions: Mr. Peacock's responsibilities include advising corporate clients in corporate strategy and acquisitions and divestitures in the United Kingdom, Scandinavia and continental Europe, and developing and structuring investments between Europe, the Americas and Japan. He joined Morgan in 1974.

Jacques Aigrain, head of J. P. Morgan Paris: Mr Aigrain, who has a PhD in economics from the Sorbonne, was named head of J. P. Morgan's Paris office in 1996, and is also in charge of the firm's Pharmaceutical and Healthcare advisory practice in Europe. He joined the bank in 1981 in the international banking area, before switching to mergers and acquisitions.

Enrico M. Bombieri, general manager, Milan office: Mr. Bombieri, who heads J. P. Morgan's corporate finance and private banking operation in Italy, is a graduate of Lausanne University in Switzerland, and joined J. P. Morgan in 1989. He is also a member of the firm's European Management Committee.

Nick Draper, head of U.K. advisory team: Mr. Draper is responsible for financial advisory work in the United Kingdom. He joined the bank in London in 1981.

Georges van Erck, managing director: Mr. van Erck is a senior banker in Morgan's Paris office, having served stints for the firm in New York, Frankfurt and London. He joined Morgan in 1974.

Anthony J. Best, head of European Emerging Markets Sales Trading and Research (EMSTaR): Mr. Best heads the European operation responsible for the distribution and trading of debt instruments and foreign exchange in major emerging economies, including in Latin America, southeast Asia, and eastern Europe.

William T. Winters, head of European fixed income, capital markets and swaps group: Mr. Winters, who is based in London, joined Morgan's petroleum department in 1983, before switching over to the marketing of interest rate and currency swaps and commodity hedging products in 1988. He became head of the bank's global commodity derivatives group in 1990, before assuming his current post in 1993.

Ferrell P. McClean, cohead of natural resources, power and project advisory group: Ms. McClean is responsible for project finance and investment banking work in the energy, utility, mining and natural resource industries. A graduate of Radcliffe College, she joined Morgan as a trainee in 1969, and has held various positions in the financial advisory and mergers and acquisitions groups.

Eduardo F. Cepeda, general manager, Mexico office and head of investment banking for Northern Latin America: Mr. Cepeda is responsible for various J. P. Morgan subsidiaries in Mexico and is in charge of the firm's business in Colombia, Venezuela, Peru, Ecuador, Central America and the Caribbean.

Susana de la Puente, country manager, Peru: Ms. de la Puente, who was ranked among the Top Ten Women in Finance by *Euromoney* in 1997, is responsible for investment banking operations in Ecuador, the Caribbean and Central America. She is also in charge of Morgan's business in Peru.

Alfredo D. Gutierrez, chairman of Brazil Management Committee and head of investment banking for southern Latin America: Mr. Gutierrez, who is based in Brazil, worked at the World Bank before joining J. P. Morgan in 1983. He is head of Morgan's investment banking group for Mercosul.

Guido Mosca, global head of external debt trading and risk management, EMSTaR: Mr. Mosca, who joined Morgan in its Buenos Aires office in 1980, is head of external debt trading and risk management for the emerging markets sales, trading and research unit.

Timothy Purcell, cohead of Latin American investment banking and equity capital markets: Mr. Purcell joined Morgan's mergers-and-acquisitions group in 1986, specializing in Latin American mergers-and-acquisitions. In 1993, he moved to Santiago to start up J. P. Morgan Chile.

Carlos M. Hernandez, cohead of Latin American investment banking and equity capital markets: Mr. Hernandez joined Morgan in 1986, and has worked on an array of mergers, acquisitions, divestitures, privatizations and equity offerings across Latin America.

Ronald H. Menaker, head of corporate services: Mr. Menaker, who joined Morgan in 1966 in its custody department, was transferred to its systems and data processing division in 1975, and became head of the administration department in 1980. He assumed his current responsibilities—which include facilities, procurement, mailing, health, restaurant, security, payroll, and records management—in 1990.

Laura W. Dillon, head of corporate communication: Ms. Dillon, a former writer and editor at *Institutional Investor* magazine, joined Morgan's corporate communications department in 1980, and became assistant to the chairman and chief executive officer five year later. She assumed her current role in 1990, which includes overseeing press relations, advertising, and internal communication.

Herbert J. Hefke, head of human resources: Mr. Hefke joined Morgan as a trainee in operations in 1970, and was transferred to the personnel department two years later, rising steadily through the bank's human resources department, before assuming his current post in 1987.

BANKERS TRUST NEW YORK CORP.

A TURNAROUND IN PROGRESS

Developing a New Model

What a difference eighteen months make.

In October 1995, when the Board of Directors of the Bankers Trust New York Corp. appointed Frank N. Newman, the bank's newly hired president, to the additional posts of chairman and chief executive, the bank was at an all-time low. Once a stodgy commercial lender, Bankers Trust had been transformed during the 1980s into an aggressive trading house—and one of the most profitable firms on Wall Street—that flourished in the cowboy culture fostered by Mr. Newman's predecessor, Charles Sanford. At Mr. Sanford's behest, the bank had become the undisputed master of a single product, the derivative, a complex instrument of financial risk-management that exploded in popularity during the late 1980s and early 1990s, fueling Bankers Trust's stratospheric earnings. Then, almost overnight, the company saw its profitability and reputation evaporate in late 1994, as client after client began accusing it of misleading them in its sales and trading of derivatives. The bank, the nation's seventh-largest, was hit with a series of high-profile lawsuits, as well as disciplinary action by regulators. Its top talent began leaving en masse.

By the time Mr. Sanford was forced to resign in 1995, the ability of Bankers Trust to survive as an independent corporation was very much in doubt. As customers left in droves and derivatives revenue dried up, the bank suffered hundreds of millions of dollars in trading losses, its stock was pummeled, and its credit ratings lowered. The company's net income plunged, from over $1 billion in 1993 to just $215 million two years later, sending its return on equity plummeting from 26 percent to 4 percent over the same period. Ultimately, the firm responded by laying off 10 percent of its staff and revamping its top management. Still, as of the end of 1995, many on Wall Street were speculating that

Bankers Trust was as likely to be taken over by a rival, or even go under, as it was to recover.

Flash forward eighteen months: after tripling during 1996, Bankers Trust's profit increases again during the first quarter of 1997, to $169 million, 25 percent higher than the year-earlier quarter. Its return on equity is 14.3 percent, up from 11.9 percent a year before, and well over three times what it was when Mr. Newman was hired. In addition, the bank announces a major coup, agreeing to pay $2.7 billion to buy Baltimore-based Alex. Brown Inc., one of the nation's oldest and best-regarded securities firms. The move, part of Mr. Newman's effort to turn Bankers Trust into a full-service investment bank, is expected to vault the company from a standing start into the big leagues of stock underwriting, ranking among the top securities firms in the nation.

What's more, the acquisition is the second in a year for Mr. Newman, who within six months of taking the bank's helm announced the acquisition of Wolfensohn & Co., one of Wall Street's most venerable merger boutiques. Though Wolfensohn is much smaller than Alex. Brown Inc.—the entire company cost about $200 million—that acquisition quickly established Bankers Trust as a force in the business of mergers and acquisitions. Just as important, it resulted in Wolfensohn's senior partner, former Federal Reserve Chairman Paul Volcker, joining Bankers Trust's board of directors. The move was seen as a turning point for the troubled bank, since the highly esteemed Mr. Volcker brought with him instant credibility and an impeccable reputation, even as Wolfensohn brought a stable of high-quality corporate clients.

Impressive as Mr. Newman's accomplishments so far appear—he has, after all, restored the bank's beleagured reputation, breathed new life into its businesses and reduced the likelihood that the bank itself will be taken over anytime soon—the toughest part of his turnaround effort remains ahead. The model he has pursued, growing into a full-service investment bank through the acquisition of existing boutiques, has rarely been attempted on such a large scale, or so rapidly. Still unanswered is the critical question of whether Mr. Newman can integrate his acquisitions into the rest of the firm, thereby turning the bank into a cohesive whole, rather than simply a collection of independently operating entities. Given the vast cultural differences that exist between the three companies, that is no mean task.

Already, there have been problems. Within the new firm, Wolfensohn employees are regarded as separate from the rest of the bank, reporting through their own chain of command directly to Mr. Newman. Other Bankers Trust executives routinely refer in conversation to "the Wolfensohn guys," as distinct from the rest of Bankers Trust. On several occasions, Wolfensohn bankers have clashed with their Bankers Trust counterparts over the responsibility for shared client accounts.

What's more, after Mr. Newman introduced a new compensation plan to tie employees' pay closer to the bank's long-term performance, rather than to short-term gains, the employees' loud grousing was the talk of Wall Street. "Some people were upset, and some have left," conceded vice chairman George Vojta. Of course, not everyone was complaining. James E. "Ted" Virtue, a former junk-bond specialist at Drexel Burnham Lambert who joined Bankers Trust when Drexel collapsed, earned close to $12 million in 1996 as the bank's head of global corporate finance. And Mr. Newman himself earned nearly $9 million—not including $1.1 million in refunded relocation expenses—in his first full year at the bank.

Then again, if Mr. Newman is successful, it won't be the first time Bankers Trust has turned around its culture on a dime. Founded shortly after the turn of the century, Bankers Trust was created for the sole purpose of helping other banks maintain their relationships with clients. At the time, banks were legally barred from managing their clients' money, and so were losing their best clients' business to trusts—companies that offered higher rates of return on deposits because they invested the assets in stocks and bonds, while also offering many of the same lending services as banks. The banks' answer was Bankers Trust: a trust company formed to manage money for the clients of referring banks, but which would make no attempt to steal those clients from the banks.

Among Bankers Trust's founders were the best-regarded bankers of the day from the bluest of the blue-blood firms, including J. P. Morgan & Co. and Kidder Peabody & Co. The firm's focus, from its inception, was the long-term appreciation of its clients' wealth, and hence, its own long-term relationship with clients. That focus stayed with Bankers Trust, even through a series of dramatic changes in its business strategy, such as when it became a wholesale commercial bank in 1917, a retail bank in 1951, and a trading house in the late 1970s.

But the focus was essentially abandoned during the late 1980s, after Mr. Sanford became the firm's chairman in 1987. A protégé of Bankers Trust chief executive Alfred Brittain III who rose through Bankers Trust's ranks and was widely revered as a brilliant strategic thinker, Mr. Sanford nonetheless presided over Bankers Trust's near-collapse by de-emphasizing client relationships and pinning the firm's profitability almost exclusively to derivatives, which he firmly believed were the future of financial risk management. "Charlie thought [derivatives] were the be-all and end-all," a former colleague recalled. In making them a mainstay of Bankers Trust's business, his idea was that the bank would become such a recognized expert at the creation, sales and trading of the arcane instruments that long-term client relationships wouldn't matter. In short, clients would have little choice *but* to do business with Bankers Trust. "He walks around the trading floor and asks, 'Have you made any money today?' not 'Have you built any relationships?' " said a former Bankers Trust executive speaking shortly before Mr. Sanford was forced to resign.

By late 1994, when eight major clients filed lawsuits accusing Bankers Trust of defrauding them in the sales and trading of derivatives, the bank had metamorphosed from a prestigious, blue-blood firm known for developing innovative solutions, to a scrappy, profit-driven company that had little regard for its clients' interests, and often disdained them. To many of its customers and competitors, the firm's name itself seemed an oxymoron.

Enter Mr. Newman. A highly regarded former undersecretary of the Treasury, dubbed "Mr. Credibility" by some colleagues, Mr. Newman cut his teeth in banking on the West Coast, first at Wells Fargo & Co. and later at Bank-America, where as chief financial officer during the early 1990s, he helped rescue the bank from near insolvency, staving off at least one hostile takeover offer in the process. Described by colleagues as a secretive man who enjoys the perks of high office, Mr. Newman's closest confidant at Bankers Trust is chief financial officer Richard H. Daniel, who worked closely with him both at Wells Fargo and BankAmerica, before following him to Washington, where Mr. Daniel worked at Freddie Mac while Mr. Newman was at the Treasury. Mr. Daniel, who joined Mr. Newman at Bankers Trust in 1996, has helped reign in Bankers Trust's freewheeling culture by putting together comprehensive daily reports of the bank's risk profile, together with highly detailed monthly reports of its profitability.

Ultimately, however, responsibility for the turnaround's success—or its failure—falls squarely on Mr. Newman's shoulders. His goal is to reposition Bankers Trust as an institution built on long-term relationships, not individual transactions, and to make Bankers Trust the client-centered company it once was. "Our principal commitment will be to serve our clients faithfully, with the highest standards of professionalism," Mr. Newman said upon being named to the company's top job. A simple pledge for most institutions, the words carried unusual significance at the new Bankers Trust.

Back from the Brink

Mr. Newman's first objective upon becoming chairman was to end the last of Bankers Trust's messy public spats with its clients: a $200 million lawsuit filed by Procter & Gamble, the big Cincinatti-based consumer-products company. Bankers Trust had already settled the rest of the cases out of court, agreeing to pay millions of dollars in fines and absorb tens of millions of dollars of its customers' trading losses without admitting or denying guilt. The Procter & Gamble case was particularly difficult, however, partly because Procter & Gamble had lost more money on derivatives trades than any of the bank's other customers, and partly because the firm had obtained damaging evidence of Bankers Trust's illicit intent.

The bank was particularly embarrassed when Procter & Gamble produced transcripts of tape-recorded conversations between Bankers Trust salespeople and P&G officials to back up the claim that the bank had misled P&G about the value and risks of its derivatives positions, thus violating federal securities laws, and engaging in civil racketeering. In one example, a Bankers Trust salesman responded to another employee's question about how the salesman had obtained a derivative customer's confidence: "Funny business, you know? Lure people into that calm and then just totally f— 'em." Eventually, the dispute was only settled when Mr. Newman himself stepped in, meeting secretly with Procter & Gamble chief John Pepper and offering to absorb as much as $150 million of P&G's derivatives-related losses.

Even with the lawsuits behind it, however, Bankers Trust faced another major hurdle: the report of an independent counsel hired as part of a settlement with federal regulators to investigate the company's risk-management operations. The report, issued in July 1996 following an eighteen-month investigation, proved scathing, sharply criticizing the bank's former management for the firm's lax internal controls. Specifically, the report said the bank didn't have enough senior managers in the derivatives area, and placed too much emphasis on profitability at the expense of compliance and control. It said several of the bank's bookrunners, staffers responsible for managing the bank's side of derivatives contracts, regularly misled customers about the potential risks of those transactions.

"In short, BT's derivatives business was not well managed or controlled in certain important respects and certain individuals exploited these weaknesses for their own purposes," the report said.

Though it stopped short of recommending punitive actions against the bank, noting that the institution itself didn't set out to defraud its customers, the report did recommend disciplinary actions against nine former employees and one current employee, managing director Ari Bergman. The report, which described some of those employees as "venal" and others as ill-prepared for their jobs, was also highly critical of Mr. Sanford, former president Eugene Shanks, former chief financial officer Timothy Yates, and two former senior managers of the derivatives business, Brian Walsh and Yves de Balmann. Of those, only Mr. de Balmann is still employed by the bank, as cohead of its global investment-banking division.

Bankers Trust had already responded to many of the report's findings even before it was publicly released, in part by firing several employees, and by shaking up the management of the derivatives and investment-management businesses. Afterward, Mr. Newman concentrated on damage control and image repair.

He began in the spring, by taking out full-page newspaper ads touting the "professionalism" of the bank's culture. A glossy brochure distributed to clients and carrying the slogan, "Architects of Value," emphasized the bank's new attitude by proclaiming its "singular commitment" to clients through "long-term, mutually productive relationships." Then, emboldened by the company's improving financial performance, in May 1996 Mr. Newman agreed to buy Wolfensohn & Co.

The acquisition was applauded by analysts as an important step in diversifying Bankers Trust's capabilities beyond the derivatives business. And, though the firm's founder and chief rainmaker, James Wolfensohn, was no longer part of it, having left to head the World Bank, its senior partner, Paul Volcker, was expected to help Mr. Newman rebuild the client-relationships that had been damaged during the Sanford years. Wolfensohn "does a tremendous amount for Bankers Trust's image in the marketplace," said Judah Kraushaar, an analyst with Merrill Lynch. Moreover, the deal, which closed in the third quarter of 1996, appeared to start paying off immediately. By early November, Bankers Trust, which in 1995 acted as an adviser on just $1.58 billion worth of M&A transactions, was advising Britain's Invesco PLC on its $1.6 billion acquisition of Houston-based AIM Management Group Inc.

The Wolfensohn team hadn't even started moving into their new quarters in Bankers Trust Plaza when Mr. Newman announced his next move: the acquisition of Alex. Brown Inc. for a pricey $2.7 billion. The move marked the first time since Glass-Steagall that an institution with commercial-banking roots acquired a securities firm. What's more, the venerable Alex. Brown, one of the country's oldest stock underwriters, was applauded by analysts as a perfect fit for Bankers Trust, whose attempt at building its own stock-underwriting operation was floundering. Indeed, Mr. Newman, who had been pitching Alex. Brown chairman A. B. "Buzzy" Krongard on the idea of an acquisition for several months, went to great lengths to make the deal work. In addition to paying a steep premium for Alex. Brown, and awarding hundreds of millions of dollars' worth of stock options to its senior executives in an effort to keep them from leaving, Mr. Newman allowed the firm to retain its Baltimore offices and to keep its name. He made Mr. Krongard a vice chairman of Bankers Trust, and named Alex. Brown president Mayo A. Shattuck cohead of global investment-banking.

The acquisition is expected to vault Bankers Trust, already a force in debt underwriting, into the top tier of the nation's stock underwriters, where Alex. Brown ranked sixth in 1996 in underwriting initial public offerings of stock. In so doing, the move essentially rounds out Bankers Trust's strengths as a full-service investment bank. With its newly acquired mergers-and-acquisitions and stock underwriting teams complementing its existing expertise in lending and the underwriting of high-yield debt, Bankers Trust now has the ability to fund fledgling firms from their inception through all the stages of their development.

The Wolfensohn and Alex. Brown acquisitions appear, for the time being, to have diminished the speculation that Bankers Trust may itself be a takeover candidate. Indeed, even before those purchases, the company had made notable financial progress in its first full year under Mr. Newman's leadership, with its profit nearly tripling, to $766 million, and its return-on-equity increasing more than threefold, to 14.5 percent. In 1997, profit increased still further, to $866 million, for a return of equity of 15.6 percent. The strong performance of the company's investment-banking operation made up the bulk of that improvement, but Bankers Trust also displayed the virtues of its international diversification, with operations in Australia, Latin America, and Asia contributing a full 49 percent of the company's earnings.

The company also had a solid trading year in 1997, earning $190 million on revenue of $1.1 billion, buoyed by the same strong markets that helped other Wall Street firms. During the year, Bankers Trust also displayed particular strength in leading multibank loans to leveraged companies, a business in which it has long been a market leader, and where it ranked second through the first three quarters of the year, as well as in underwriting high-yield bonds, ranking eighth in the United States. And the company continued to show strength in its securities-processing operation, a scale-driven business where it ranks fourth in the world in assets under administration, which delivered earnings of $117 million for the year.

In general, Mr. Newman emphasized a desire to grow fee-driven businesses such as securities processing and mergers-and-acquisitions advisory services, which currently account for about 40 percent of total revenue. Those businesses, desirable because they provide a steady, annuity-like source of income and because they do not require the type of long-term capital reserves needed to sustain the lending business, nevertheless require heavy up-front investments that some analysts worried could impair Bankers Trust's earnings in 1998. In particular, several analysts spoke of the need for a sizable investment in updated technology for the securities-processing business, which was expected to offset any short-term revenue increases in that area.

Meanwhile, 1997 saw mixed results in two core lines of business, risk management and investment management. Risk management, which includes derivatives, remained in the red for the year, losing $12 million, slightly worse than its $11 million loss in 1996, and a far cry from the heady days of 1994, when it earned a profit of $163 million. Investment management, by contrast, which is now spread between the private client services and global institutional services units, contributed to profits of $197 million in those areas, up sharply from $135 million in 1996. Goldman Sachs analyst Robert Albertson said profit from both "could and should go up" in 1998.

Revamping Investment Management

Bankers Trust was founded as a money-management organization, and investment management—including private banking for high-net-worth individuals and general money-management for institutional investors—remains a core part of the company's business. With offices from Los Angeles to the Cayman Islands to Hong Kong, Bankers Trust now has $318 billion in assets under management, most of it for institutional investors. The number includes $277 billion in the United States, $28 billion in Australia, and $13 billion in Japan. For the year, Bankers Trust ranked among the top five managers of investments in the United States (measured by asset size), and among the top three managers of stock index funds. In Australia, the bank is the largest manager of mutual funds and the largest manager of institutional pension-fund assets. In Japan, it was the third U.S.-based firm to receive approval to distribute mutual funds.

The bank's requirements are strict: Only customers with at least $5 million of investable assets are accepted. For these clients, Bankers Trust provides a broad spectrum of services, from tax and estate planning, to real estate management, to help navigating the exclusive, secretive world of Swiss banking. In keeping with an evolving emphasis on banking by computer, the private bank even offers its clients on-line access to their accounts, complete with information on the risks and rewards of their investments.

The bank is not shy about its expertise, boasting in brochures that it can help clients "minimize estate taxes," or structure trusts that allow clients to control the distribution of their money across generations, even if the recipients of that wealth are "unprepared to manage substantial assets." In addition, private-banking clients have access to products and services normally reserved for Bankers Trust's institutional customers, including research reports compiled by the bank's stock-market analysts, derivatives products created by its risk-management division, and mutual funds not available to the general public.

For most of those funds, Bankers Trust has traditionally adopted a passive investment style, offering a variety of indexed funds that seek to match, rather than outperform, various market indices. As opposed to active management, a high-cost business with wider margins but also requiring a heavy research commitment, indexing is a low-margin, scale-driven business, requiring just a few computers and little in the way of actual personnel.

Despite its lower initial cost and the bank's relative success at attracting investor dollars, the indexing approach hasn't proved hugely profitable for Bankers Trust. Indeed, investment management worldwide remains an underperformer, even by the bank's own standards. Mr. Newman said in the firm's 1997 annual report that the division remains short of its "full earnings potential."

As a result, Bankers Trust in 1996 launched a major overhaul of the investment-management business, centering around a streamlining and repackaging of its mutual-fund business. Heading the effort: Ian Martin, head of Bankers Trust Australia, a highly profitable part of the bank's investment-management operation that ranks as one of Australia's leading pension and investment managers. In Australia, Bankers Trust is both an active and a passive manager of funds, and Mr. Martin's most significant move to date has been to launch a push into active fund management worldwide. In addition, the Alex. Brown acquisition represents a big step forward in the bank's investment-management expertise, bringing with it a sizable, highly regarded team of stock research analysts, and its stable of high-net-worth clients.

Still, the bank has also faced setbacks in its effort to develop a presence in actively managed funds, such as the defection of star money manager Mary

Lisanti to Strong Funds in 1996. And while it is well known among institutional investors, the bank has no retail presence to speak of, and its name means little to average individual investors—a big drawback when trying to market mutual funds. What's more, the bank's commitment to the business of active management may be open to question. Consider: in 1997, Bankers Trust sold its processing business for 401(k)-style defined contribution plans. To be sure, the business, with $33 billion in assets under administration, was unprofitable because without a range of actively managed funds to sell to 401(k) clients, Bankers Trust was left to handle the low-margin administration work involved in selling other firms' mutual funds. Nevertheless, were Bankers Trust to develop a presence of its own in actively managed funds, the processing business could presumably have made money.

Indeed, aside from the 401(k) processing business, securities processing generally has been highly profitable for Bankers Trust, delivering a reliable, annuity-like stream of revenue. The bank is a leader in the area, ranking as the fourth-largest custodian in the world, with close to $2 trillion in assets under administration. Assets under administration and client-processing revenue are expected to grow significantly in the near-term as the industry consolidates. But it appears that continuing investments in the requisite technology upgrades needed to accommodate that growth and stay competitive with market leaders will largely offset any revenue increases.

An Underwriting Powerhouse, Overnight

The Alex. Brown acquisition, which has catapaulted Bankers Trust to a leading position among stock underwriters, was born in part of the frustration Bankers Trust experienced in its efforts to grow an underwriting operation from scratch. Much like J. P. Morgan, Bankers Trust sought to leverage its way into the underwriting business by first applying its expertise at lending to the markets for corporate debt. The effort met with some success, notably in the market for high-yield, or junk, bonds. A consistent leader in arranging multi-bank loans to highly leveraged companies, Bankers Trust is now also one of the top-ranked underwriters of junk bonds, the type of debt highly leveraged companies issue.

The bank counts several sizable junk-bond offerings among its recent successes, including two 1996 issues worth $100 million or more for which the bank was the sole manager, one for Specialty Paperboard and one for Spinnaker Industries Inc. In addition the bank led a $100 million issue for MOL, the Hungarian oil company, and a $150 million issue for Royal Oak Mines, one of only a few such issues in the gold-mining industry. On a $250 million junk-bond issue for Tracor Corp., a defense contractor, in early 1997, Bankers Trust obtained the narrowest spread ever for a single-B rated junk-bond issue.

In other areas, however, the bank's attempts to break into the highly competitive underwriting market proved substantially more difficult. In 1996, Bankers Trust ranked a distant twenty-second among underwriters of investment-grade corporate debt, barely improved from its twenty-fourth place showing three years earlier, according to Securities Data Co. Among issuers of all types of debt, it didn't even rank among the top twenty-five.

The bank's progress in underwriting stock issues was even slower. Bankers Trust acted as lead or comanager on twenty-seven public stock offerings in the United States in 1996, up from fifteen in 1995, and just four in 1994. Again, however, the bank failed to break into the ranks of the top twenty-five stock underwriters, lagging behind much smaller firms such as J. C. Bradford and Robert W. Baird. Bankers Trust's difficulty in gaining an underwriting foothold can be blamed as much on the bank itself as on the competitive nature of the underwriting industry. Indeed, the bank's own explanation is that it didn't want to develop an investment-grade underwriting presence, because that business, while just as capital- and personnel-intensive as underwriting for leveraged companies, is less remunerative. Moreover, bank officials said, Bankers Trust's recipe for growth in underwriting is representative of the bank's overall approach to investment-banking, which calls for focusing on certain key industries in which the bank can be a leader, rather than jumping head-first into the market as a whole.

Now, however, Bankers Trust officials say that as the bank's leveraged clients move up the credit-quality spectrum, the bank will follow them. "The strategy is to take our leveraged-finance business and move up a tier, and then move up another tier, to broaden our scope with a series of incremental steps," said Alex Mason, the bank's head of U.S. corporate finance. The Alex. Brown acquisition will allow the firm to do just that, by complementing Alex. Brown's strength in initial public offerings with Bankers Trust's strength in underwriting high-yield debt.

Moreover, Bankers Trust officials say, now that the firm has the full breadth of capabilities investment-grade clients require, including a highly competent mergers-and-acquisitions team, underwriting business from new investment-grade clients will also follow. "The platform in 1997 is dramatically different than it was a decade ago, when we were pulling away from the investment-grade market," Mr. Mason said.

Nevertheless, the company faces considerable hurdles in coming so late to the game, not least that it missed out on the booming stock market of the mid-1990s, which saw an explosion in the number of initial and secondary public offerings, and presented rivals such as J. P. Morgan a golden opportunity to rise in the underwriting league tables. If the stock market cools off in coming years, as is widely expected, making back the money Bankers Trust paid for Alex. Brown may prove more difficult than Mr. Newman expected.

Buying a Presence in M&A

Bankers Trust began building its strategic advisory business during the late 1970s, under the leadership of Alfred Brittain. Initially, it grew faster in the business than J. P. Morgan, ranking as the twelfth-busiest adviser on mergers-and-acquisitions by 1987, having arranged deals worth nearly $7 billion. But Bankers Trust largely abandoned its M&A strategy during the Sanford years. By 1995, at a time when M&A activity was soaring, Bankers Trust's total deal volume was well under $2 billion. J. P. Morgan, by contrast, is today a top-ranked M&A adviser and a significant competitive threat to the top investment banks. Meanwhile, even Chase Manhattan Corp., which as of a few years ago wasn't even considering entering the M&A business, ranked well ahead of Bankers Trust in 1996, participating in deals worth more than $17 billion.

Realizing that the development of an M&A business can take years, Mr. Newman determined to buy his way into the business, coughing up $200 million to buy Wolfensohn & Co. In 1996, Wolfensohn participated in deals worth about $50 billion, according to Securities Data Co. In addition to helping the bank's image through the addition of Wolfensohn's senior partner, Paul Volcker, to Bankers Trust's board of directors, the acquisition gave the bank overnight "access to clients it would take years to penetrate," said Brian Sullivan, president of a New York executive-search firm that has done work for both Bankers Trust and Wolfensohn.

Still, whether the Wolfensohn acquisition will accomplish for Bankers Trust what Mr. Newman hopes remains open to question for several reasons. First, the firm no longer has Mr. Wolfensohn as its chief rainmaker, and though it has continued to rise in the M&A rankings since his departure, some experts speculate that much of that momentum was built during his tenure.

Second, it remains unclear how well Wolfensohn's boutique culture will mesh with that of Bankers Trust, and how long Wolfensohn's lead investment-bankers will want to work as employees of the big bank. Already, Wolfensohn bankers have clashed with their Bankers Trust counterparts over who was responsible for handling certain client relationships. "You can't say there hasn't been an argument or two," concedes Mr. Vojta. In general, he says, the acquisition "has gone extremely well."

Third, notwithstanding Mr. Newman's efforts to remake his company as one that emphasizes client-relationships, the firm's reputation has been damaged, and it is by no means certain that Wolfensohn's clients—or other clients—will want to turn to Bankers Trust for corporate-advisory services, rather than to some other, more established, firm. Finally, as with its stock-underwriting efforts, Bankers Trust is turning its attention to M&A in the midst of a boom in merger activity, rather than in anticipation of such a boom. Whether the unprecedented level of M&A activity will continue, allowing the bank to gain a foothold as a strategic adviser, remains to be seen.

Still, several big deals in 1997 did give cause for hope. Among them: Promus Hotel Corp.'s $4.7 billion merger of equals with Doubletree Corp., in which BT Wolfensohn advised Promus, and E.I. du Pont de Nemours' acquisition of Protein Technologies Inc. for $1.5 billion, and various businesses of Imperial Chemical Industries for $3 billion, in which BT Wolfensohn advised du Pont. The company also advised Lyonnaise des Eaux in its merger with Cie de Suez, the largest merger in French history.

A Smaller, More Profitable Trading Shop

After losing close to $100 million in 1994, and close to $80 million in the first quarter of 1995, mostly as a result of losses in Latin America and declining derivatives revenue, Bankers Trust's trading operation has recovered, turning a profit of $105 million in 1996, on total revenue of $1 billion, and earning $190 million, on revenue of $1.1 billion, in 1997. Still, trading is a volatile business, and the bank's recovery was aided as much by the underlying strength of the market as it was by any institutional factors. Some analysts have suggested that the bank's strong performance is unsustainable, and that trading, which in 1997 accounted for about 18 percent of the bank's revenue, will fall sharply in 1998. Moreover, Bankers Trust's trading revenue continues to lag that of other big commercial and investment banks by a wide margin.

Under Mr. Newman, Bankers Trust's trading operations have been overhauled. The bank has focused recently on beefing up its operation, hiring entire teams of salesmen and traders who were put out of work by the megamerger of Dean Witter, Discover & Co. and Morgan Stanley. Moreover, though derivatives remain a significant driver of the bank's trading business, they are accorded far less emphasis than in previous years. This doesn't mean that the bank's trading activities are any less volatile or risky, however. For example, part of the bank's strategy now involves reducing its directional trading in major markets, and focusing instead on structured and arbitrage trading in less liquid, emerging markets, such as southeast Asia and eastern Europe. In addition, more than 50 percent of the bank's foreign-exchange income stems from new business developed since 1993, the result of increased sales efforts in Asia, eastern Europe and Latin America.

In addition to trading for its clients, Bankers Trust maintains a $1 billion portfolio of private, long-term equity investments that it manages for its own account, through direct investments averaging between $10 million and $25 million, as well as investments in various leveraged buyout funds. In 1995, the sale of part of the bank's stake in Northwest Airlines netted $62 million, helping improve the bank's bottom line in an otherwise disappointing year. Though small relative to the size of the bank's overall trading operations, the proprietary fund has an impressive long-term performance record, racking up average annual returns in the 30 percent-plus range in recent years.

A Force Down Under

Bankers Trust's international presence rivals that of most other U.S. commercial and investment banks. The bank does business in more than fifty-five countries, and derives about half of its revenue outside the United States, a figure that has increased slightly in recent years.

One of the biggest contributors to the bank's international success is its Australian operation, which contributed 12 percent of profit in 1997. One of the first American banks to recognize the potential of Australia, Bankers Trust took advantage of the country's cultural and language similarities to the United States, and the fact that the Australian and American pension systems are comparable, to become one of Australia's leading investment managers, responsible for $28 billion in assets. Its Australian operations are a relatively reliable contributor to the bank's bottom line, contributing a profit of $101 million in 1995, $131 million in 1996 and $103 million in 1997. More recently, competitors such as J. P. Morgan have tried to penetrate the market, representing a potential long-term threat to Bankers Trust's dominance.

In Latin America, which accounted for 12 percent of the bank's net income in 1997, Bankers Trust's presence is strongest in stock and bond trading, but its performance is mixed. Though highly profitable of late—to the tune of $107 million in 1997—the volatile Latin American markets accounted for losses of $120 million in 1995. The bank aims to invest in building its corporate finance and private equity presence in Latin America, objectives evident in its investment-banking venture with a large Brazilian bank, Bank Itau, and its 50 percent stake in Consorcio, Chile's largest life insurance company.

In Europe, where it has twenty-five offices, Bankers Trust has a growing presence in investment banking, specializing in real estate and lending. The bank ranked as the top lead manager for European high-yield debt and the top arranger of leveraged loans in Europe in 1997. But, though strong in fixed income, the bank has had almost no equities activity in England or on the continent. It moved to address that issue in 1997, expanding its European presence in equities through the acquisition of National Westminster Bank PLC's pan-European stock business, a $218 million deal expected to be completed in the second quarter of 1998. The purchase marks a significant international step for Bankers Trust, which will now have NatWest's top-ranked equities analysts, institutional sales and trading and primary-markets-origination businesses.

Bankers Trust also has a relatively small but growing presence in Asia, where it is planning to target the emerging markets in the southeast, including

India, Indonesia, Malaysia and Singapore. The new business comes with risks; Bankers Trust lost $52 million in Asia in 1997, as the economic turmoil there took its toll. In 1996, the bank earned $20 million in Asia. The bank was the third U.S.-based firm to receive approval to distribute mutual funds in Japan, where it now manages $13 billion in assets. In 1997, Bankers Trust sought to boost its presence in Japan still more, striking a novel deal to help clean up the troubled loan and real estate portfolio of Nippon Credit Bank Ltd., one of that country's venerable, but ailing, banks. Though Bankers Trust has pitched the arrangement as one in which it is acting strictly as an adviser to a client, the deal does call for Nippon Credit to hand over most of its foreign client base to Bankers Trust. In addition, the two banks have agreed to swap small equity stakes in each other, a move filled with symbolic significance, that gives Bankers Trust as deep a relationship with a Japanese bank as any foreign company has ever been allowed.

Adding Alex. Brown's Research Clout

One-stop shopping for Bankers Trust clients took a giant step forward with the firm's acquisition of Alex. Brown Inc.

One of the bank's weaknesses in its efforts to build up an investment banking presence had been its patchwork approach to building up a research team to support those banking efforts. Big gaps included such key areas as high technology; Bankers Trust had no analysts tracking Intel and the other Silicon Valley giants whose performance often dictates the course of the broader stock market. While the bank had begun in late 1996 and early 1997 to slowly and painfully fill some of those gaps, the consensus among many institutional money managers was that it was at least a year away from generating the kind of research product that they would find consistently useful.

To be sure, the pre-merger Bankers Trust research team wasn't without its strengths. Among the handful of well-known analysts were Wolfgang Demisch, its aerospace analyst, and the bank as a whole had become well known for its analysis of high-yield debt in sectors where it has traditionally had a strong investment banking presence, such as wireless communications, paging, media, lodging, gaming and real estate.

But prior to announcing the Alex. Brown transaction last spring, the Bankers Trust research team resembled that of J. P. Morgan in its embryonic stages, with both analysts and managers spread thinly across the ground. Seeking to make a virtue of its weaknesses, the bank had concentrated its research effort on smaller to medium-sized stocks, the kind of companies with which Bankers Trust has had most success in developing research ties. But as investors continued to direct their enthusiasm to the largest stocks in the market, this strategy wasn't reaping the kinds of rewards for which the bank had hoped. Moreover, in the fall of 1996 the bank was still hunting for someone to run the research department, a task which had proved difficult. In the interim, research was being headed by Ed Garden, also in charge of the bank's equity syndication and distribution desk. That kind of linkage between the bank's investment banking and research divisions raised eyebrows among some money managers, used to broader lines being drawn between the two. And the bank had indefinitely postponed hiring an investment strategist, waiting until the research output had reached a critical mass.

Much may change with the Alex. Brown acquisition. For one thing, Bankers Trust will be adding more than fifty analysts to its existing roster, bringing the total to sixty-seven. It also acquires managers used to running a research department. Indeed, Alex. Brown's research track record was frequently mentioned by Bankers Trust officials as one of the firm's biggest assets. While not a research powerhouse like Merrill Lynch or Goldman Sachs, Alex. Brown ranked fourteenth in the 1996 *Wall Street Journal* all-star analysts' review, with thirteen top-ranked analysts, including a two-time all-star bank and brokerage analyst, Mark Alpert. That's the same number as Bear Stearns boasted in the same period, and more than firms like Lehman Brothers—and dwarfs the two all-star analysts at BT Securities itself. It maintained the same ranking and relative status in the 1997 survey.

To some extent, however, the nature of the coverage at the two research departments will overlap. Like Bankers Trust, Alex. Brown has specialized in developing investment banking relationships with medium-sized companies with the aim of developing a niche. In some areas, such as lodging and gaming, overlaps will be inevitable. In others, however, Alex. Brown will bring some sorely-needed skills. One of these is the high-technology sector, where Alex. Brown has well-regarded analysts covering not only the major players but smaller firms manufacturing computer chips, or emerging growth companies developing products such as Internet Web search engines. Other areas in which Alex. Brown has built up coverage include companies specializing in such areas as electronic marketing and computer-aided design.

The merger of the two divisions isn't likely to be seamless. For instance, the research departments have been built up in different ways and filled different roles within the organization, making some kind of culture clash likely.

The combined research departments will be overseen by Geralyn Fitzgerald, who retains her responsibility for all global stock and bond research at Bankers Trust. Day-to-day oversight of the stock research is handled by an Alex. Brown veteran, Denis Callaghan.

Bankers Trust's People

Frank N. Newman, chairman, chief executive officer and president: Mr. Newman was hired as Bankers Trust's president in late 1995, while the firm was in the throes of its derivatives crisis. Deputy secretary of the treasury since 1993, Mr. Newman was the former vice chairman and chief financial officer at San Francisco-based BankAmerica Corp., the nation's fifth-largest bank. Before that, he had worked at neighboring Wells Fargo & Co. Within months of joining Bankers Trust, Mr. Newman was named to succeed Charles Sanford as the firm's chairman and chief executive officer.

Dubbed "Mr. Credibility" by his fellow executives, Mr. Newman's chief task has been restoring Bankers Trust's reputation and returning it to financial stability. He has succeeded remarkably quickly at turning the firm around financially, installing several of his former BankAmerica colleagues in senior posts at Bankers Trust to help with the task. He has also overseen a complete overhaul of the troubled derivatives busi-

Newman, Frank
Chairman & CEO-
Bankers Trust NY Corp

ness, de-emphasizing derivatives as the firm's central product. Moreover, he has begun to broaden Bankers Trust's focus from that of a niche firm focusing on highly leveraged clients, to one that conducts business for clients all across the credit spectrum.

According to colleagues, however, the result of Mr. Newman's efforts to turn Bankers Trust into a client-centered firm à la J. P. Morgan has met with mixed results. Executives who worked for Mr. Sanford retain a tremendous degree of loyalty to their former chairman, and argue that the firm never lacked a client focus under his leadership. Rather, they say, it lacked the range of products to serve all clients. Now that those product lines are in place, they say, Bankers Trust's reputation as a client-driven firm will be restored, though they say Mr. Newman's primary task is to act as a cheerleader and promoter of the company's client-focus. "I will give Frank a lot of credit for having changed the rhetoric around clients," said Alex Mason, head of U.S. corporate finance. "The world perceived that we were not client friendly. Frank understood that perception and the need to change it. As an insider, I've always felt we were client friendly, but the perception needed to be changed."

So far, Mr. Newman has been well rewarded for his efforts on the bank's behalf. In his first full-year, he earned nearly $9 million, in addition to more than $1 million in relocation expenses, and the full-time services of a car and driver.

George J. Vojta, vice chairman: Mr. Vojta is one of the few very senior Bankers Trust executives to survive the purge that accompanied and followed Mr. Newman's appointment as chairman. A vice chairman and director since 1992, he oversees management of the private bank, secured lending and securities processing businesses.

A Yale University graduate, Mr. Vojta joined the bank in 1984 from Salomon Brothers, where he had worked as chief financial officer of the Phibro division since 1981. Before that, he spent twenty years at Citicorp, where he rose to the level of executive vice president in charge of the international banking group.

Yves C. de Balmann, vice chairman, cohead of global investment banking and co-chief executive, BT Alex. Brown: Mr. de Balmann is another survivor of the purge of 1995 and 1996, despite his heavy involvement in the derivatives debacle as head of the risk management products and services business, and as one of the executives mentioned critically in the independent counsel's report on what went wrong at the bank. He serves as cohead of investment banking, which includes bank lending, underwriting, sales and trading, mergers-and-acquisitions, private equity investments for the firm's own account, and the capital markets businesses in the United States, Europe and Canada. In addition, as head of risk management, he continues to be the seniormost executive in the derivatives area, and he is also a member of the firmwide operating committee and business council.

A French native who studied at the École Polytechnique in Paris before obtaining a masters of science degree in operations research from Stanford, Mr. de Balmann began his banking career at Citibank in 1973, where he became head of interest-rate and currency risk management in North America, before leaving to join E. F. Hutton & Co., as senior vice president of capital markets. He joined Bankers Trust in 1988 as head of its financial institutions business as well as its mortgage-backed and asset-backed securities businesses, adding the U.S. taxable finance business to his responsibilities a year later. In 1991, he was named head of global finance, and in 1993 he was promoted to cohead of investment banking, based in London.

Mayo Shattuck III, vice chairman, cohead of global investment banking and co-chief executive, BT Alex. Brown: Mr. Shattuck, who joined Bankers Trust following the acquisition of Alex. Brown, continues to serve as co-chief executive of BT Alex. Brown and cohead of investment banking, along with Mr. de Balmann. Prior to the acquisition, he served as president and chief operating officer of Alex. Brown. His primary investment banking experience was in Alex. Brown's technology group, which he ultimately headed at the time the firm brought public Sun Microsystems, Microsoft, Oracle and Silicon Graphics.

A trustee of the Bryn Mawr School and the Gilman School, he is active in various Baltimore civic organizations.

Richard H. Daniel, vice chairman, chief financial officer and controller: A former colleague of Mr. Newman from his days at Wells Fargo and BankAmerica, Mr. Daniel was chief financial officer of Freddie Mac before following Mr. Newman to Bankers Trust in early 1996. A Harvard College and Harvard Business School graduate, Mr. Daniel has instituted a rigorous monthly process of analyzing the bank's profit-and-loss statements, by line of business, in great detail.

Mr. Daniel began his career at Wells Fargo in 1973, where he ultimately became head of mortgage lending. In 1983, he joined Freddie Mac as senior vice president for mortgage-backed securities, before heading back to the West Coast to become director of financial analysis at BankAmerica from 1987 to 1994. He returned to Freddie Mac as chief financial officer in 1994.

Melvin A. Yellin, general counsel: Mr. Yellin joined Bankers Trust's legal department in 1975, becoming deputy general counsel in 1992, chief legal officer in 1995, and general counsel in 1996.

Rodney McLauchlan, executive vice president: A former cohead of investment-banking who was sidelined in Bankers Trust's merger with Alex. Brown, Mr. McLauchlan is a member of Bankers Trust's management committee, and chairs its client committee, as well as its European and Asian advisory boards. Previously, he served as cohead of the bank's operations in Asia, and before that, its operations in Europe and the Middle East.

Jeffrey Goldstein, co-chairman of BT Wolfensohn: Dr. Goldstein, who received a Ph.D. in economics from Yale University, taught economics at Princeton University before joining Wolfensohn & Co. in 1984. He became vice chairman of BT Wolfensohn after Bankers Trust acquired Wolfensohn in 1996, and co-chairman at the start of 1998.

Glen Lewy, co-chairman of BT Wolfensohn: A lawyer who specialized in mergers-and-acquisitions at Debevoise & Plimpton, Mr. Lewy became a partner at Wolfensohn & Co. in 1986, and became vice chairman of BT Wolfensohn after Bankers Trust acquired Wolfensohn in 1996. He was named co-chairman at the start of 1998.

Mary Cirillo, head of client processing services: Ms. Cirillo, former group head of operations and technology for corporate and commercial banking at Citicorp, joined Bankers Trust as head of client processing in June, 1997. A member of the bank's management committee who reports directly to Mr. Newman, she is responsible for the bank's cash management and securities services, corporate trust and agency services, retirement services, global custody, securities lending and portfolio performance measurement and risk analysis.

Timothy S. Rattray, chairman of Bankers Trust Asia: Mr. Rattray has responsibility for all of Bankers Trust's activities in Asia, including merchant banking, securities underwriting, and private banking. A graduate of the University of California and MIT's Sloan School of Management, he joined Bankers Trust's merchant banking group in New York in 1977, responsible for originating, structuring and executing leveraged buyouts. He eventually earned responsibility for the bank's wholesale financial services business in Latin America, Eastern Europe, Africa and the Middle East, before being named to his current post. He is a member of the firm's management committee and its business council.

Robert Ferguson, head of Bankers Trust Australia Ltd.: A native of Australia, Mr. Ferguson joined Bankers Trust Australia in 1972 as a senior portfolio manager, becoming head of corporate finance five years later, head of retail funds management in 1982, and head of the entire Australian operation in 1985.

Philippe Souviron, vice chairman, Bankers Trust International: Mr. Souviron joined Bankers Trust in 1992 as chairman of Bankers Trust (France), after service as deputy president and head of capital markets and investment banking at Credit Lyonnais, where he worked for twenty-seven years. He was named to his current post, which includes responsibility for client coverage and local offices in Europe, in 1995.

Joseph A. Manganello Jr., chief credit officer: Mr. Manganello joined Bankers Trust in 1961, and rose through its retail bank, serving as president of BT Credit Co., which operated its Visa credit-card program, from 1973 to 1976. He became chief credit officer in 1984.

I. David Marshall, chief information officer: A member of Bankers Trust's management committee, Mr. Marshall joined Bankers Trust in 1996 to oversee technology infrastructure and operations in investment banking, sales and trading, and risk management. A onetime Canadian government official who served variously as that country's assistant auditor general, assistant deputy minister of information technology for revenue, and assistant deputy minister of information technology for employment and immigration, Mr. Marshall also served as chief information officer for the Canadian Imperial Bank of Commerce, one of Canada's biggest banks.

J. Edward "Ted" Virtue, head of global corporate finance and president, BT Alex. Brown: Mr. Virtue was among Bankers Trust's highest-paid employees in 1996, earning close to $12 million, most of it bonus. A former junk-bond trader at Drexel Burnham Lambert who worked closely with that firm's notorious junk-bond king, Michael Milken, Mr. Virtue joined Bankers Trust when

Drexel went bankrupt in 1990. A graduate of Middlebury College, the fair-haired Mr. Virtue is a self-described fan of Bankers Trust's brilliant but controversial former chairman, Charles Sanford, who says Mr. Sanford got a "bad rap." The two men remain close friends, and play squash regularly.

Jay Pomrenze, head of Emerging Europe, Middle East & Africa Merchant Bank: An ordained rabbi, Mr. Pomrenze joined Bankers Trust in 1973, working in government securities for eight years before being named trading manager for liability management in 1982. He became head of worldwide foreign exchange activities in 1984, and head of all trading in 1988, before being named to his current post—responsible for all capital markets, local currency trading, finance, direct investment and advisory activities in central and eastern Europe, the Middle East and Africa—in 1997.

Alexander Mason, co-head of corporate finance operating committee: Mr. Mason supervises corporate finance in the United States, with responsibility for high-yield bonds, bank financing, and equity underwriting. He initiated the firm's coverage of the media sector in 1981, and is heavily involved in the firm's activities in media and telecommunications.

Gar Richlin, cohead of corporate finance operating committee: Mr. Richlin, the former head of investment banking at Alex. Brown, serves along with Mr. Mason as cohead of Bankers Trust's corporate finance operating committee, reporting to Mr. Virtue.

Joseph Lafferty, cohead of global equities: Mr. Lafferty, former global head of cash equities at NatWest Markets, joined Bankers Trust as part of the acquisition of NatWest's pan-European equities business, reporting to Mr. Virtue and based in London.

Bruce Brandaleone, cohead of global equities: Along with Mr. Lafferty, Mr. Brandaleone heads Bankers Trust's equities business globally, reporting to Mr. Virtue.

Edmond Warner, head of global equities business strategy: Mr. Warner, who was global head of equities research at NatWest Markets, joined Bankers Trust as part of the NatWest deal and is responsible for the creation of an integrated global equities business, with a particular focus on the establishment of global industry research teams.

Richard A. Marin, head of private banking: Mr. Marin, who joined Bankers Trust in 1976, has served at various times as general manager of BT Futures

Corp., head of emerging markets, head of global derivative products, head of insurance derivatives, head of BT Bank of Canada, and head of retirement services. Currently, he has responsibility for the firm's private bank, which caters to wealthy individuals.

Duncan P. Hennes, head of global sales and trading: A former manager at Arthur Anderson, Mr. Hennes joined Bankers Trust in 1987 and was named to his current post in early 1998. He replaced R. Kelly Doherty, a fast-rising star who was a vice chairman and head of sales and trading when he suddenly announced his decision to take a one-year leave of absence. Previous to his current post, Mr. Hennes served as head of global treasury and funding, responsible for managing Bankers Trust's capital and liquidity, as well as several other businesses within the global markets proprietary group.

Ivan Ritossa, head of global foreign exchange: Mr. Ritossa, who is based in London, was named to his current post in early 1998. Previously he worked in Singapore as head of the bank's regional foreign exchange desk, responsible for Australia, Japan, New Zealand and Singapore. Mr. Ritossa joined Bankers Trust in 1983, working in fixed-income sales and trading and foreign-exchange trading.

Peter E. Lengyel, head of asset-based lending: Mr. Lengyel, who is also a member of the bank's client management committee, joined Bankers Trust in 1979 after working at Chase Manhattan Corp. for fifteen years. His experience includes heading various departments, including fiduciary and securities services, processing and information products, deposit services, national banking, and most recently, the corporations and financial institutions group within the global assets business.

Timothy F. Keaney, head of retirement services: Mr. Keaney runs the group that provides master trust, defined contribution and plan advisory services, and also heads Bankers Trust Co. of California and Bankers Trust Co. of the Southwest, in Houston. Prior to joining Bankers Trust in 1994, he worked in the retirement services division at Mellon Bank for four years.

William Hirschberg, head of North American risk management services: Mr. Hirschberg joined Bankers Trust's capital markets group in 1986, and has had responsibility for the yen interest rate and Nikkei derivatives desks in Tokyo and for insurance derivatives in New York.

Richard M. Gunthel, head of real estate finance: Mr. Gunthel joined Bankers Trust in 1969 and held management responsibilities in its metropolitan

In the Beginning . . .

Bankers Trust began operations in a two-room office in New York's financial district in 1903. Its founders included Henry Pomeroy Davison, then the thirty-five-year-old vice president of a commercial bank who came up with the idea for the firm and became its first chairman; Edmund C. Converse, a bank president who was named Bankers Trust's first president; and eleven other commercial bankers who formed the new firm's first board of directors. Significantly, the board also included representatives of three investment banks, of which only one still exists today: J. P. Morgan & Co.

The idea behind Bankers Trust was quite simple. At the time, New York state law prohibited commercial banks from also managing their clients' money, permitting them only to engage in basic lending and deposit-taking. As a result, banks were steadily losing their best customers—those with substantial assets—to trust companies that could offer clients similar lending services, as well as better returns on their deposits by investing their money in stocks and bonds. Mr. Davison suggested that banks form their own trust company: an independent firm to which they would refer their trust business, but which would not seek to pilfer the rest of their clients' business, as other trusts did. (Though Mr. Davison would preside over Bankers Trust until his death in 1922, he also went to work for J. P. Morgan. There

he was joined by Bankers Trust's first secretary and treasurer, Thomas W. Lamont, who went on to become J. P. Morgan's chairman.)

Bankers Trust quickly flourished, with assets topping $130 million by the end of its first decade. But for all its success, the company faced a major crisis in 1914, with the creation of the Federal Reserve System and the Fed's almost immediate decision to begin allowing banks into the trust business. The move eliminated the very reason for Bankers Trust's being. The company responded by giving up its original charter, the one pledging not to compete with the banks that founded it, and transforming itself into a commercial bank with an exclusively corporate clientele. In 1917, Bankers Trust became a member of the Federal Reserve System. In 1919, it began underwriting stocks. And in 1920, it began moving overseas, opening its first foreign office in Paris, and its second in London, two years later.

By the time the stock market crashed in 1929, Bankers Trust ranked among the nation's largest banks. And again, trouble struck, this time in the form of Congress's response to the Crash: the Glass-Steagall Act of 1933, which forced commercial banks to exit the investment-banking business. Like J. P. Morgan, Bankers Trust was compelled to shutter its highly lucrative stock-underwriting operation.

banking department and its United States department, before assuming his current post in 1983.

Gavin R. Walker, head of investment banking, Bankers Trust Australia Ltd.: A member of the management committee of Bankers Trust Australia, Mr. Walker established the bank's presence in New Zealand in 1986 before assuming his current post. He is also chairman of the Foreign Direct Investment Advisory Board of New Zealand, reporting to that country's prime minister.

The next radical shift for Bankers Trust came after the conclusion of World War II. Unlike J. P. Morgan, which chafed under the restrictions of Glass-Steagall, but which nonetheless stuck to its core businesses of lending and asset management until the late 1970s, Bankers Trust threw itself wholeheartedly into the commercial-banking business. Viewing the returning soldiers and their growing families as a potential gold-mine, the bank's management determined to abandon their exclusive focus on corporate clients and enter the business of retail banking for individuals of average means.

During the 1950s and 1960s, Bankers Trust developed a network of more than two hundred retail branches throughout New York state. It grew rapidly, becoming one of the first banks to offer no-minimum-balance checking accounts, as well as loans for home remodeling, and car or appliance purchases. In 1969, Bankers Trust began issuing credit cards, becoming one of the first members of what later became the Visa bankcard association. Meanwhile, it continued to pursue aggressive growth on the wholesale side, becoming one of the first banks to offer corporate clients unsecured loans, based solely on their expected cash flow.

In the early 1970s, a medley of macroeconomic factors—including stagflation and the New York City fiscal crisis—that caused area real-estate values to plummet, prompted serious problems at Bankers Trust. The firm, which had built up a considerable portfolio of real-estate loans, saw loan payments dry up, and losses mount. By 1978, when then-chief executive Alfred Brittain III decided to abandon the retail-banking business, Bankers Trust was dangerously close to insolvency.

Over the next two years, the bank sold off its retail branch network and its credit-card portfolio and determined to focus on its core wholesale-banking business. By this time, however, Mr. Brittain had reached the conclusion—as had J. P. Morgan's then-chairman, Lewis Preston—that commercial banking was a dying profession, and that to survive, commercial banks would have to reenter the investment-banking business. Confident, along with Mr. Preston, that Glass-Steagall would ultimately crumble, Mr. Brittain pushed Bankers Trust determinedly into businesses open to commercial banks under Glass-Steagall, such as advising clients on mergers-and-acquisitions, and underwriting the private placement of securities.

Initially, Bankers Trust grew faster in the investment-banking business than did J. P. Morgan. By 1987, Bankers Trust was the twelfth-ranked M&A advisor in the country, well behind the leading investment banks, but ahead of J. P. Morgan, which ranked sixteenth. That year, the Fed began allowing a handful of banks, including both Bankers Trust and J. P. Morgan, to underwrite publicly traded stocks and corporate debt. That was also the year that Mr. Brittain stepped down as chairman and chief executive, to be replaced by Charles Sanford, a longtime Bankers Trust employee who was his handpicked successor. Despite his reputation as a brilliant strategist, Mr. Sanford's determination to accelerate the bank's rise in the investment-banking business by concentrating on transactions, rather than clients, backfired badly. "The mistakes had to do with getting overheated," recalled vice chairman George Vojta. "Some of our people did not behave correctly relative to clients. They got caught up in the profit potential of the business."

Ian Martin, head of Bankers Trust Australia investment management: Since late 1995, Mr. Martin has been charged with integrating Bankers Trust's worldwide investment management operation. As part of that task, he faces the daunting challenge of ramping up the bank's commitment to active fund management, rather than the passive management in which he has specialized for many years. Prior to joining BT Australia in 1985, Mr. Martin was chief economist for Citibank in Australia.

Art Penn, head of global fixed income capital markets: Mr. Penn, who joined Bankers Trust from Lehman Brothers, is in charge of the origination and distribution of all fixed income new issues globally. He also runs the high-yield capital markets business for BT Alex. Brown. Before his stint at Lehman Brothers, Mr. Penn worked for a time alongside Michael Milken at Drexel Burnham Lambert.

Kevin Sullivan, head of syndicated lending: Mr. Sullivan heads Bankers Trust's highly acclaimed syndicated lending department, in charge of big, multi-bank loans to companies. The bank has developed a niche in recent years in complicated transactions to highly leveraged companies.

Andrzej K. Rojek, head of global OTC equity derivatives: Mr. Rojek, who joined Bankers Trust in 1991 to start trading and positioning groups in equities and various equity-linked instruments, is now in charge of its global over-the-counter equity derivatives, equity sales and trading and convertibles. A graduate of Warsaw University who has done graduate work at Columbia University, Mr. Rojek previously worked as an international market analyst at Merrill Lynch.

Mark Bieler, head of human resources: Mr. Bieler is the executive vice president responsible for human resources. As head of the compensation and benefits division, he played a key role in developing the stock-based incentive compensation policy that came under heavy fire from within the firm in 1996. A graduate of Franklin and Marshall College who serves as an adjunct professor at New York's prestigious New School for Social Research, Mr. Bieler began his career at Manufacturers Hanover Trust Company, before joining Bankers Trust's human resources department in 1973. He was named head of human resources in 1987.

PART SIX

THE EXCHANGES

The New York Stock Exchange

•

The Nasdaq Stock Market

THE NEW YORK STOCK EXCHANGE

Walking the Narrow Line
Between Business and Public Trust

The New York Stock Exchange, more than any other institution, symbolizes America's capitalist market-driven economy. Yet it has long presented two faces to the world: that of defender of the public interest, and that of defender of its own interest.

In the former role, it is the world's best financial market: the largest, most liquid and most prestigious stock market, and the best-regulated. America has one of the world's highest rates of individual participation in stocks, and the biggest pool of publicly traded equity capital in the world. It owes this to a great extent to the edifice at the corner of Broad and Wall Streets in lower Manhattan. That market deserves a lot of credit for why investors can confidently invest in enterprise and enterprise can cheaply raise capital in America.

But the New York Stock Exchange is also a business. It makes a lot of money for its members—the specialists and brokers who trade stocks—and is constantly on guard against threats to either its stock listings or its trading in its listed stocks. It wants bigger market share, more listings, more prestige. Like any organization, it wants to be the biggest and best at its business.

The New York Stock Exchange and its many loyal supporters see no contradiction between these two roles. From chairman and chief executive officer Richard Grasso down to the floor brokers, they zealously promote the benefits their market brings to investors and listed companies, always invoking the interests of the smallest investor and often criticizing competing systems as bad for that same investor. When they criticize competitors such as the Cincinnati Stock Exchange, they portray its practices as bad for the public investor, not as a source of unwanted competition for trading in its stocks.

But to the Big Board's competitors at the regional stock exchanges, the securities dealers, the Nasdaq and countless other places, and to its overseers in Washington—many of whom are also its greatest admirers—the Big Board's two roles are often in conflict. They say that many times when the NYSE portrays itself as driven by the public interest, it is in fact driven by self-interest.

Nowadays, the Big Board's competitive, business face is more in the forefront than ever before. It's not that it believes any less in protecting the public investor. Indeed, while the staff devoted to running the trading business has shrunk in recent years, the number of staff who watch for malfeasance in its floor trading and among brokers has grown briskly.

But the world has become a much more competitive place. The Big Board faces competition from an increasing number of alternative marketplaces, and it must deal with a more activist Securities and Exchange Commission, which wants to preserve and promote competition between those marketplaces. Thus, acting more like a business and less like the staid, slow-moving public institution of the past is simply essential if the Big Board is to survive and prosper.

Perhaps the starkest example of this shift was the debate in the first half of 1997 over quoting stocks in decimal increments. Congressman Michael Oxley and Securities and Exchange Commissioner Steven Wallman began their push in late 1996 to quote stocks in decimals, arguing it would bring about a narrowing in the bid-ask spread for stocks, thereby saving investors billions of dollars and making stock prices easier to understand in the process.

But there was no groundswell of public support. Mr. Wallman and Mr. Oxley were almost lone advocates, albeit influential ones. So when New York Stock Exchange President William Johnston appeared before Mr. Oxley's comitee on April 16, 1997, it was in the familiar role for a Big Board executive, that of defending the public's interest against misdirected efforts to change how stocks trade.

"Decimalization could result in a significant shift of power away from public customers [to] professional traders, undermining the very basis of our market," he told the committee. "Public investors could lose confidence in the integrity of the market." He went on to tick off a laundry list of reasons why shifting from the two-hundred-year-old system of quoting stocks in fractions of an eighth of a dollar would be bad for the public: increased "front-running," or professional traders having their orders filled ahead of public investors', decreased depth in the size of quoted orders, higher costs for institutional trades, reduced transparency, and illiquidity.

And in case anyone thought the Big Board was resisting the move out of its own self-interest, he pointedly remarked that in the short run, decimalization would probably help the Big Board and "make it difficult for our competitors to survive."

Such a resounding denunciation seemed to end the debate, as far as the New York Stock Exchange was concerned. As on so many other things in the past, it appeared that if Congress or the SEC wanted to get their way, they'd have to force the Big Board.

So it was with some shock to most observers that a mere seven weeks later, the New York Stock Exchange abruptly announced it was going to move to decimals before the year 2000, and as an interim step would cut the stock price increment in half—from an eighth of a dollar, where it had stood since its founding in 1792, to a sixteenth—in a matter of weeks.

What was behind such a breathtaking about-face? Surely it was not just the threat of decimals by fiat—the Big Board had forced the hand of Congress and the SEC before. Nor could it be solely because the American Stock Exchange and Nasdaq Stock Market had already moved to sixteenths (or "teenies," in professional jargon) a few weeks before, and the latter was considering going all the way to decimals; neither traded Big Board stocks.

Certainly, those factors probably played some part. But if any single factor prompted the turnaround, it was the little-publicized move by Bernard L. Madoff Investment Securities, the largest "third-market" broker of Big Board stocks, to begin quoting stocks in sixteenth spreads, and the rumblings, three weeks later, that some regional stock exchanges might follow suit. For the first time, investors would have a significant source of stock quotes at better prices than those available on the New York stock exchanges. For example, a stock bid at \$20 and offered at \$20\frac{1}{8} on the Big Board might now be offered by Madoff's traders at \$20\frac{1}{16}, a better deal for the buyer. That threatened to suck significant order flow in the biggest, most liquid—and, for the New York Stock Exchange community, most lucrative—stocks away from the exchange floor.

Indeed, in explaining the decision after the board meeting where the move was approved, Mr. Johnston said resolutely, "We are not going to sit back and let anyone take our business away from us. We will be competitive in any fraction."

Mr. Grasso said proudly of the move, "If we could lock people's minds at fifteen minutes prior to my board meeting and say, 'Do you really think New York is going to break the fraction?' I think you'd find the majority of people saying no. And you know why? Because they didn't think we were running a business."

One longtime Washington-based watcher of the Big Board said admiringly, "The New York Stock Exchange a year ago wouldn't have had the foresight to say, 'We'll go to decimals.' I will give them credit: Once they saw the handwriting on the wall, they didn't sit there for six weeks pondering their navels; they made a decision to get it done."

(Implementation of decimals has since been postponed until the year 2000 or later to give the financial industry and marketplaces more time to deal with the so-called "millennium bug," which prevents computers from being able to distinguish between the year 1900 and the year 2000.)

Such considerations aside, the NYSE's overcoming of its earlier misgivings about the impact on the investing public in order to protect its business and its move to teenies and decimals symbolize what has come to represent the Big Board of today under Grasso: an obsessively competitive institution ready to defend and expand its turf, at times at the expense of its image as defender of the investing public.

Mr. Grasso denies that the Big Board's more businesslike posture has grown at the expense of the public's interest, even arguing that decimals were necessary to minimize the investor confusion once the eighth fraction was abandoned. The Big Board's path was therefore obvious, he says: "One, you compete by breaking the fraction, but two, you leap over it all by saying you've got to get to decimals because decimals are the only platform of pricing that the consumer will understand."

Yet there remain many, even within the New York Stock Exchange community, who feel the move to narrower increments has been too fast, as evidenced by continuing confusion among market participants working in teenies and occasional overloads of the networks that disseminate stock quote and trade information around the country. The fact that the Big Board moved so quickly in spite of such lingering doubts speaks to the important shift to a more aggressive, businesslike posture taking place there.

There are many reasons for this shift. One is technology. The advent of alternative electronic trading systems, such as Reuters Holdings' Instinet, the Arizona Stock Exchange, the Pacific Exchange's OptiMark, (which received pilot program approval in September 1997, and in which Dow Jones & Co., the publisher of *The Wall Street Journal*, has a financial interest) and perhaps before long the Internet, are providing investors with countless new ways to trade stock other than on the New York Stock Exchange, on a regional exchange or in the third market. Second is the growing clout of institutional investors. Forty-six percent of stock is now held on behalf of the American public by institutions such as pension and mutual funds rather than by individuals, compared to just 27 percent in 1970. Compared to individuals, institutional investors are much more sophisticated in how they trade stocks and more willing to try an alternative such as Instinet in search of a lower cost or faster execution. But perhaps the most important reason for the shift is Mr. Grasso himself.

Leadership from Within:
A Lifer Takes the Reins

The first chairman in the history of the exchange to rise up through the ranks of the staff, the fifty-year-old Mr. Grasso has a deep understanding of all facets of the exchange and an attachment to the organization that has made him its most enthusiastic and formidable promoter on every front. He has thrown himself into every competitive aspect of the Big Board, personally visiting countless listing candidates in the United States and abroad and calling down to the floor when he sees a big block cross the tape to demand if it traded away from the New York Stock Exchange and if so, why. He breathes competition. He challenged champion boxer Roy Jones Jr. to a sparring match at Madison Square Garden in 1996 to raise money for the U.S. Olympic team, and actually trained for the event.

The New York Stock Exchange has in the past been called its own worst enemy. It is made up of so many constituencies—the specialists, the floor brokers, the "upstairs" brokers who trade big blocks of stock from their Wall Street offices, the listed companies, investors and its own staff—that it is virtually impossible to please all of them when the exchange decides to do anything. It leads, the Washington observer says, to paralysis by analysis, a condition that has hurt its competitive position in the past, such as in its failed effort to become a force in derivatives.

Under Mr. Grasso, the Big Board has shown a willingness to plow ahead quickly, despite the misgivings of some of these constituencies, to maintain its competitive edge. That Mr. Grasso had been able to do so without yet running into serious opposition speaks to his considerable political skills.

One test of his ability to negotiate with the constituencies was the introduction last year of a new system for allocating stocks to specialist units. Traditionally, listed companies had no say in what specialist handled their stock; many resented this, because if they felt their stock was getting inadequate attention from its specialist, they could do nothing about it. On their marketing visits, Catherine Kinney, group executive vice president for new listings and client services, and Georges Ugeux, group executive vice president for international and research, found that current and prospective listed companies wanted some say in who their specialist would be and voiced support for a new system. Under the new system, listed companies can choose their specialist out of a pool of candidates put forward by the exchange.

The program sparked some protests. Some specialists feared the move would squeeze out the smaller firms. But the real source of misgivings was that for the first time, specialists would have to market themselves—a fact of life for years for Wall Street investment bankers, mutual-fund managers and virtually everyone else in the financial industry, but an alien notion in their small circle.

"They've never had to get in front of a customer and sell themselves," said Ms. Kinney. "They now find themselves in a very competitive situation with their peers. They have to do some things very differently."

With Mr. Johnston selling it energetically, the plan has gone into place with little overt protest.

Another pitfall could have arisen in 1997 when Goldman Sachs said it wanted to expand its floor operations to accommodate a high-tech "superbooth" packed with the latest trading technology, which would enable it to put sales traders, who deal directly with customers, closer to the action. But the move sparked protests from some floor brokers, especially those who were going to have to find other space for their booth operations so that Goldman could expand its own. Goldman executives began a painstaking process of meeting with every member of the exchange's facilities committee over breakfast to explain what it wanted. Ms. Kinney called up the Goldman executives halfway through the process and said, "We'll take it from here," recalls an executive involved in the process. Additional space was carved out from the existing floor for the displaced brokers, and now arrangements are being made for several other firms to build their own superbooths.

Ms. Kinney said the exchange wanted an important customer to be able to serve its customers better, but the move was also necessary from a competitive standpoint: "Because we're running an auction market, we're trying to be a magnet to as many buyers and sellers as possible in the location, and use as much technology as possible to support the operations."

Decimalization posed potentially serious resistance among the New York Stock Exchange's constituencies. Since the move would narrow the bid-ask spread on stocks, it would to some extent cut into the profit specialists made trading many of their stocks (although the sums involved were not as large as some proponents of decimalization said). It also posed a big challenge to floor brokers and specialists in adapting their trading techniques for smaller increments and in executing orders in smaller pieces over more trades. But before going ahead with the move, Mr. Grasso met with the specialists and floor brokers and laid it out. "We have no choice, we have to do this for competitive reasons," one participant at the meeting recalled him saying. "We've warned these people, here's what we suspect may happen: Some exchanges may disappear, some liquidity may dry up, some limit orders may disappear, professionals might get in front of public investors—we've warned that may happen. But we have to do it to remain competitive."

The floor community accepted the logic, though not without some grumbling. "Some still think it was a terrible mistake, but the majority agree you have to match competitors or lose market share," this person said.

Indeed, Robert Fagenson, head of a specialist firm and a director on the New York Stock Exchange board, told a conference in Chicago in July that the introduction of teenies may have resulted in increased volatility and higher trading costs for some investors. But he is not advocating going back to eighths.

Mr. Grasso owes his influence with the exchange's many constituencies to his lengthy preparation for the job. He was considered for the top job in 1991, when he was president. But the board of directors instead stuck with tradition and made an outsider—William Donaldson, a co-founder of investment bank Donaldson, Lufkin & Jenrette—chairman and CEO. But one insider says it was Mr. Grasso who maintained hands-on control a lot of the time while Mr. Donaldson embarked on high-profile diplomatic forays abroad in search of foreign listings. Mr. Donaldson strongly endorsed him as his successor.

One of Mr. Grasso's first steps upon assuming the chairmanship was to create an executive office of the chairman. It consists of the group executive vice presidents—Edward Kwalwasser, in regulation; Catherine Kinney, in new listings and client services; and Robert Britz, in trading floor and technology. He had swapped the latter two's jobs, putting Ms. Kinney in one of the key spots. In the fall of 1996, he hired Belgian investment banker Georges Ugeux to fill the new position of executive vice president of international and research and concentrate full time on wooing and servicing foreign listings. In June of 1996 he tapped Mr. Johnston, a lifetime Big Board denizen with the specialist firm Labranche & Co., as president, providing him with a critical link to the Big Board's influential floor community. The creation of this group, which meets weekly, reflects Mr. Grasso's style, which is more hands-on than that of his predecessor.

Beneath the group executive vice presidents are executive vice presidents, senior vice presidents and vice presidents, all responsible for one aspect or another of the exchange's operations. Over time, the number of people in operations has been shrinking as automation does away with many clerical jobs, but the number of people in the regulatory, marketing and client-services areas has grown.

The twenty-six-member board of directors (including the chairman and president) is made up of representatives of all of the exchange's constituencies. The board consists of twelve public directors and twelve industry directors. The public directors include at least one from a nonfinancial listed company and one from an institutional investor. Of the industry directors, five come from New York City–area member brokers, two are from regional brokers, three are specialists, one is an independent local broker and one is an independent floor broker. The board also has fourteen advisory committees, such as the Upstairs Traders Advisory Committee and the Legal Advisory Committee. Although the committees are meant to advise the board, in practice they are more important for feeding the opinions of outsider investors, traders and listed companies to exchange management.

Mr. Grasso answers to the board of directors, which in turn answers to the the exchange's membership. As of 1997, the New York Stock Exchange had 1,366 seats, of which 464 are held by specialists, 317 by commission, also called independent and "two-dollar brokers," and the remainder by upstairs or "house" brokers. This breakdown shows that while the floor community—the specialists and two-dollar brokers—is small relative to the investment industry, it makes up more than half the stock exchange membership, which explains its enormous influence.

While in theory Mr. Grasso is answerable to both the board and the membership, in practice both usually defer to the opinions of management, partly because they have so many avenues for influencing that opinion through the exchange's various committees. Mr. Grasso by all accounts wields extraordinary influence compared to his predecessors, because he is an insider and thus knows both the workings of the exchange and virtually everyone in it, but also because he is a persuasive salesman. "He's the most political person I've ever met," says one insider. "You get into a room with him on any issues, be it decimals or whatever, you come in with one opinion and go out with another. He's very good at explaining and articulating what makes sense from an exchange point of view and why it's good for you."

Bull Markets Are Good for Business

Mr. Grasso's tenure has been marked by tremendous prosperity for the New York Stock Exchange. Net income in 1996 climbed to a record $74.4 million, from $44 million in 1994. Trading volume has smashed record after record, and the Big Board's share of that volume has gone up. In 1997 it captured 83.7 percent of the volume in its stocks, a seven-year high, and, more important, captured 74.4 percent of the trades in its stocks, a better than ten-year high. The price of a seat hit a record $1.75 million in December 1997, compared to a low of $250,000 in 1990. The number of listings has climbed to 3,046 in late 1997, including 343 non-U.S. companies.

This success is part good luck, part hard work.

The stunning bull market in stocks is clearly a major reason for the New York Stock Exchange's prosperity. Another is the travails of its principal domestic competitor, the Nasdaq Stock Market, which has just emerged from a grueling investigation by the SEC and Department of Justice over price-fixing and other abuses.

Some of the groundwork for its current prosperity was laid by Mr. Grasso's predecessors, especially his mentor, John Phelan, chairman from 1984 to 1990, who bit the bullet on the need to make massive and costly investments in technology to remain competitive. That mission was made all the more urgent by the stock-market crash of 1987, the ramifications of which preoccupied Mr. Phelan for years. Thanks to that investment, the New York Stock Exchange has achieved most of the operating efficiency, if not the low costs, that would be possible with a fully automated exchange—as almost all auction markets outside the United States now are—while continuing to give an advantage to those brokers who maintain a physical presence on the floor.

So if Mr. Grasso can put more effort into expanding the Big Board's competitive position, it is partly because the stock market is taking care of itself.

But as president and CEO, he has been far from idle. To increase its listings, in early 1995 the Big Board changed its standards so that more new, start-up companies with no income could come to the Big Board—a direct competitive attack on Nasdaq, and to a lesser extent on the American Stock Exchange. The Big Board in 1997 opened an office in Menlo Park, California, to service listed companies out there and pursue Silicon Valley listing candidates from the Nasdaq.

For the first time it allowed listed companies to choose their specialist. And beyond all these initiatives, Mr. Grasso has personally pitched himself into the fight for order flow and listings, trekking out several times to Redmond, Washington, to try to persuade Microsoft to move to the Big Board from Nasdaq (so far unsuccessfully).

Yet in pushing the Big Board's competitive agenda so aggressively, Mr. Grasso has stuck his elbows in a lot of ribs, bringing accusations of throwing his weight around and at times arousing the SEC's concern.

Nothing illustrated this better than the battle between the Nasdaq and the New York Stock Exchange for the listing of Concert, the product of a proposed merger between British Telecom, whose American Depositary Receipts trade on the New York Stock Exchange, and MCI Communications, whose shares have traded on Nasdaq since the company went public.

MCI chairman Bert Roberts for years had been a director of Nasdaq. Indeed, MCI's loyalty to Nasdaq was so strong that Ms. Kinney said her marketing team in previous years had little success even getting a hearing from MCI management, let alone its listing.

Teams from both sides presented lengthy and elaborate marketing shows to both companies.

When the two sides announced their choice of the New York Stock Exchange in April 1997, it was not the quality of the market that MCI chairman Bert Roberts referred to as the deciding factor. He attributed the decision to the Big Board's Rule 500, which then virtually forbid companies from delisting from the Big Board by requiring such a move to be approved by at least two-thirds of the shareholders with no more than 10 percent objecting, an almost impossible threshold. Choosing Nasdaq would have forced BT to meet the Rule 500 requirements in order to delist its ADRs. BT and MCI did not want to complicate the process of winning shareholder approval for the merger with the far more secondary consideration of the listing, Mr. Roberts said. (As BT has been replaced as acquisitor by Nasdaq-listed Worldcom, the issue appears to be moot.)

Mr. Roberts's announcement was a slap in the face to the Big Board, which felt it had won the listing on the merits of its market.

But the ramifications of Mr. Roberts's disappointment went much further. He fired off a letter to the SEC's chairman Mr. Arthur Levitt, complaining of the anticompetitive nature of Rule 500. Mr. Levitt responded with his own letter to Mr. Grasso. Though it diplomatically asked him to review the rule and justify its current existence, people close to Levitt said the message was clear: Scrap the rule or water it down, or else the SEC will do it for you.

Mr. Grasso responded quickly by referring the matter to an external advisory committee and promising to do something about it by year's end. Indeed, the rule was replaced with a much milder version in November. He also emphasized that he personally didn't like the rule: It was bad for competition, it gave Nasdaq a stick with which to batter the New York Stock Exchange, it interfered with marketing efforts, and besides, it was of virtually no significance, anyway; no companies were clamoring to leave, he said.

That strikes Nasdaq sources as disingenuous. As recently as a year earlier, the New York Stock Exchange had been officially saying it had no intention whatsoever of changing the rule. If Mr. Grasso felt as he said, why didn't he act until he got Levitt's letter?

Still, the incident illustrated two critical things about Mr. Grasso: his willingness to use every tool at his disposal to compete, but also his pragmatism and political acumen. Realizing Rule 500 in its original form was indefensible and the SEC would not let it stand, he moved quickly to defuse the issue and, as much as possible, paint it in a positive light for the New York Stock Exchange.

Upstairs, Downstairs: A Shifting Power Base

In everything the New York Stock Exchange does it must be careful of its numerous constituencies. Of these, the most important are the specialists and the broker-dealers, because they dominate the exchange's membership and are the people at the heart of what the exchange does: quote and trade stock. The specialists and floor brokers together make up the floor community. A specialist's responsibility is to ensure price continuity in a stock—that is, ensuring it does not, for example, trade from 21 down to 20 without trading somewhere in between—and to make sure there is a reasonably sized and priced bid for a given seller and offer for a given buyer. For example, if one broker has ten thousand shares to buy and the lowest priced order offered on the book is for five thousand, the specialist will often sell five thousand out of his own inventory to give the client a complete fill. To do this, he must regularly commit his own capital if public orders are insufficient. Floor brokers take public investor orders to the floor, where they try to obtain the best price. Floor brokers work either for the major "upstairs" broker dealers, such as Salomon Smith Barney, Merrill Lynch or Morgan Stanley, Dean Witter, or for themselves (the so-called two-dollar brokers), taking orders from the Wall Street firms or institutional investors.

The major broker-dealers make up the upstairs community, so called because they frequently put up their own capital to buy or sell large blocks of stock for customers away from the floor of the exchange.

It helps to explain the basics of what the exchange does. When an investor wants to buy a stock, he or she phones a broker, who communicates that order to the trading desk. The trader then can choose between two basic avenues to obtain the stock: (1) He or she can transmit the order to his or her firm's brokers on the New York Stock Exchange floor, who will then go to the specialist post for the stock and negotiate with someone else in the "crowd" at the post to buy the stock, a transaction that the specialist then executes; (2) The trader can enter the customer's order directly in the exchange's electronic display book, where any other broker in the country can attempt to fill it, or the specialist can fill it.

Over time, an increasing number of alternatives to these basic avenues for trading stocks listed on the New York Stock Exchange have sprung up. They include the use of the firm's own capital to take the opposite side of the trade, the availability of non-NYSE member dealers, the so-called third-market brokers, who will execute the order and in fact pay for the privilege to do so, the availability of electronic order systems such as Instinet to search for other investors and efforts by firms to match buyers and sellers internally.

It is the availability of these alternatives that has, over time, shifted power from the floor to the upstairs community. It is also due to the changing nature of the stock business, as more individuals entrust their stock decisions to institutional managers.

That means that stock is increasingly transacted as large blocks, often of a hundred thousand shares or more. Such orders are beyond the ability of a specialist to absorb, and thus it falls to the upstairs desk to execute them. Indeed, the capital Goldman Sachs committed in early 1997 to execute a monster $2 billion block trade of British Petroleum stock was about double the capital of the entire specialist community. Specialists have been consolidating, a trend accelerated by the 1987 stock-market crash, and the number of specialist firms has fallen to thirty-five now, from fifty-five in September 1987. Many are now owned by upstairs dealers such as Merrill Lynch and Quick & Reilly.

That said, the floor community is still tremendously influential. One telling example of their power was Mr. Donaldson's plan in 1991 to open the exchange a half hour earlier, at 9 A.M., ostensibly to win back market share from London. Brokers and specialists revolted against the plan because they—especially those who lived on the West Coast—did not want to start trading so early and because they weren't consulted. Mr. Donaldson had to back away, faced with vociferous opposition.

Many of the Big Board's longtime observers believe it is the multiple constituencies, and in particular the influence of the floor, that are to blame for some of its most serious business setbacks. In the early 1980s, the Big Board made a serious attempt to challenge the supremacy of the Chicago futures and options exchanges in the trading of stock derivative products. The effort failed. Its New York Futures Exchange, opened with fanfare in 1979, flopped and was sold to the New York Cotton Exchange in 1993. In options it did only slightly better. Mr. Grasso sold that business to the Chicago Board Options Exchange in 1997. In both cases, people both inside and outside the exchange blamed the inability of the floor community to make markets in the new products that could compete with Chicago's.

"Exchange management is still shackled by a variety of special interests," William Freund, its former chief economist, wrote in *The Wall Street Journal* in

1985. "It is unable to move fast and reach decisions without cumbersome consultations. And the members, especially on the floor, still tend to think of themselves as 'the' exchange owners."

Mr. Freund, who now heads Pace University's center for the study of equity markets, said a lot has changed since then. "This whole attitude of protecting their monopoly turf is gone. The New York Stock Exchange has now become a public institution as opposed to a private club."

Still, change came too late in some respects. The New York Stock Exchange remains a one-product shop: It does virtually nothing but trade stocks. Its bond business long ago ceased to be a significant alternative to the dealer market, and its forays into portfolio trading have been of limited success.

Mr. Grasso regrets these failures, and adds one to the list: the exchange's failure to realize the value of its stock quote and trade data, which is now carried to the world by outside vendors such as Dow Jones Markets, Reuters, Bloomberg and ADP, although they pay the New York and regional exchanges hefty fees for the data.

But he has acted quickly to shore up the New York Stock Exchange's most important franchise, stock trading. In so doing, he has been careful to get the floor on his side first. In that he has been aided by Mr. Johnston, an affable, Santa Claus–like figure who is friends with virtually everyone on the floor. "Bill is a very good politician," says William Lupien, founder of OptiMark and a former partner of Mr. Johnston. "He carries a lot of weight down on the floor and he understands the dynamics of the floor better than anyone who's been in that position."

It's hard to believe that less than ten years ago, many people inside and outside the exchange were questioning the Big Board's long-term viability. Its market share in order flow was steadily ebbing, to the benefit of the regionals and the third market; the Nasdaq was adding new listings furiously, while the Big Board's list was stagnant; and the crash had aroused serious misgivings about its soundness. All that is behind it, and now its greater challenge is maintaining its lead amidst the continued sniping of its competitors and closer scrutiny of the SEC.

Battling for Listings

Not too many years ago, the Big Board's preferred strategy for dealing with the competitive threat from the Nasdaq Stock Market appeared to be to ignore its existence. At some places around its offices, managers still refused to mention the word *Nasdaq*, and products of Nasdaq-traded companies had Post-it notes and masking tape placed over otherwise visible logos.

Under Mr. Grasso and Ms. Kinney, that's changed considerably. Mr. Grasso now talks openly of intending to get every single one of Nasdaq's major stocks to list on the Big Board. In a speech at Pace University, he said the Nasdaq is a fine market for most of its eight thousand companies, but added: "All I hope is to one day penetrate ten percent of those companies, randomly starting in the alphabet at the letter *M*."

It's been a good couple of years on that front. A record ninety-six companies moved from Nasdaq to the New York Stock Exchange in 1996, and in the first ten months of 1997, another ninety-one made the switch, with Gateway 2000 and Republic Industries the most prominent. The exchange has reserved interesting ticker symbols for its hundred top prospects, such as *M* for Microsoft, and late last year opened a West Coast office with about 10 staff members to service clients and call on listing candidates.

Mr. Grasso has personally taken it upon himself to call on executives of prospective candidates, sometimes uninvited, and pitch the Big Board's virtues. "There's a certain message that a prospective client gets when the chief executive of the institution is willing to sit down with that client's board or top management and open himself up to whatever they want to talk about," Mr. Grasso said.

Ms. Kinney related how it took five visits and slide presentations, as well as books of statistical information, over a period of a year before claiming America Online. The exchange has also in recent years enrolled its own listed companies and institutional investors as allies in trying to get more companies to make the move.

(Far less attention is focused on the American Stock Exchange than used to be the case. Only a handful of its stocks would qualify for a New York Stock Exchange listing. In September 1997, the Amex suffered a severe loss of prestige when the New York Times Co. switched to the Big Board.)

Still, the principal reason companies do or don't defect to the Big Board from Nasdaq has to do with prestige or dissatisfaction with how their stocks trade. Initial public offerings and small, less-liquid companies prefer the dealer market because market makers create liquidity when investor interest is lacking, and also often provide research coverage for stocks in which they make a market. But more mature companies have tended to complain of volatile stock prices and wide bid-ask spreads on their stocks on Nasdaq. Some companies also perceive the Big Board as more prestigious.

There are two principal types of stock markets: auction markets and dealer markets. The New York Stock Exchange is principally an auction market while the Nasdaq is principally a dealer market. However, over the years, the two have begun to share more and more characteristics of each other.

Prices in an auction market are determined by one customer's orders meeting another's. If customer A wants to sell 10,000 shares of Exxon at no less than 99 and customer B wants to buy 10,000 shares at no more than 99, then a trade can occur at 99 with both customers satisfied. There is no intervention necessary. If customer A however will sell his shares at no less than 100, then a trade cannot occur: the market will be quoted at 10,000 bid at 99 and 10,000 offered at 100. A third customer, C, can then choose to "hit" the bid at 99 and sell 10,000 shares, or take the offer at 100 and buy 10,000 shares. In none of these transactions is a dealer's intervention necessary; all orders are public customer meeting public customer. For this reason, auction markets are often called "order driven" markets, in that trades occur only when there are orders. The chances of this sort of interaction between public orders are maximized by having all the orders funneled into a centralized location. In the case of the New York Stock Exchange, that's the specialist's post on the exchange floor.

In a dealer market, on the other hand, intermediaries—in the Nasdaq's case, a "market maker"—constantly quote bid and offer prices for stocks with a commitment to buy a minimum amount at their quoted bid and sell a minimum amount at their quoted offer. In the above example, the market maker would quote both 10,000 bid at 99 and 10,000 offered at 100. Because market makers are committed to always posting quotes at which they are willing to buy or sell, dealer markets are often called "quote-driven" markets. In the event a buyer takes his 10,000 shares at 100 and a seller sells him 10,000 at 99, the market maker will earn the "spread" between the two, in this example one dollar, for a $10,000 profit. This spread pays the market maker for his risk. For example, if a seller hits his bid at 99, there is a reasonable risk the stock price will then fall because of a news event, for example to 98. If the market maker can only unload the 10,000 shares he just bought at 99 at the new price of 98, then he has lost $10,000.

Over the years, market scholars note that the New York Stock Exchange has become increasingly dealerized and the Nasdaq auctionized. Neither is any longer a pure example of an auction or dealer market. For example, on the New York Stock Exchange, each stock has its own market maker, called a specialist, who must use his own capital to ensure that trading is orderly; this principally means making sure that spreads are reasonably narrow, that prices move in small steps instead of big gaps, and that all orders are treated fairly. For example, a one dollar spread would generally be considered unacceptably wide for a blue-chip stock like Exxon. If the only orders available were 10,000 bid at 99 and 10,000 offered at 100, the specialist might enter his own bid at 99 7/8 to ensure a tighter, 1/8 market. If three customers were bidding 99 for a total of 10,000 shares bid at 99, and someone was willing to sell only 8,000 at 99, the specialist might also sell 2,000 shares to ensure all bidders were satisfied. Although a specialist cannot represent both the bid and offer at any one time in his own stock, he can nonetheless in normal market conditions expect to earn some profit on the spread by buying at the bid and selling at the offer, which again is compensation for the risk of losses incurred in volatile conditions.

Furthermore, New York Stock Exchange member brokers often act as market makers themselves. A broker can use his or her principal to buy or sell a block of New York Stock Exchange–listed stock. Many non–New York

Stock Exchange member brokers, so called "third market" brokers, also quote prices in listed stocks, although their quotes are usually determined by those then prevailing on the New York Stock Exchange.

The new order handling rules adopted by Nasdaq in 1997 have given it many characteristics of an auction market. The most important change is that market makers must now display customer "limit" orders. For example, if a customer is willing to buy a Nasdaq stock at 99 and the market maker is currently bidding 98 $7/8$ and offering 99 $1/8$, then by displaying the customer order, the market would become 99 bid and 99 $1/8$ offered, with a public customer on one side and a dealer on the other. Previously, it was possible for most market makers to ignore such limit orders, causing customers to be disadvantaged if, for example, they were bidding 99 through one market maker while another market maker instead bought at 98 $7/8$. The Nasdaq also plans to create a central limit order book in which to display as many such limit orders as possible, maximizing the chances for such limit orders to be filled and making it one step closer to an auction market.

There are advantages and drawbacks to both types of market. Prices are generally less volatile in an auction market because they are more determined by natural supply and demand. On big, liquid stocks, spreads are typically quite narrow, reflecting the strong investor interest to buy and sell. However, New York Stock Exchange stocks are often halted because of an imbalance between buyers and sellers as the specialist tries to find a natural level that matches both sides. Such halts can last up to an hour or more in especially trying conditions, which are frustrating for investors anxious to trade or determine the value of their stock. Furthermore, small stocks with little ongoing investor interest suffer from illiquidity and thin trading, and their management often complains they get little attention from their specialists.

In the dealer market, most every stock has multiple market makers, and thus the markets—even for small stocks—are seldom illiquid. Stocks never stop trading because of imbalances, and even small stocks enjoy reasonable liquidity. But because the dealers are essentially trying to determine the natural level of the stock on their own, prices tend to be more volatile as they move their quotes up and down in response to market conditions. And investors commonly wonder if they got the best price for their stock because they traded with a dealer, not another customer.

These relative advantages have blurred over time. Intel, for example, one of the country's largest capitalization companies, has stuck with Nasdaq because it does not believe volatility or spreads would improve on the Big Board and prefers to be able to trade all the time. And the New York Stock Exchange has made efforts to shorten trading halts due to imbalances and to make specialists more responsive to listed companies' concerns.

Outside stocks, most securities trade in a dealer market. The currency and bond markets, which in terms of dollar volume dwarf the stock markets, have been dealer markets for years. But stocks seem to be different. In 1997, for example, the London Stock Exchange went from a dealer to an auction market in its 100 largest stocks.

For several reasons, the Nasdaq is likely to prove to be less easy pickings in the future. For one thing, the changes to Rule 500 will for the first time enable the Nasdaq to raid the Big Board. (Few blue-chip stocks are likely to move; the more likely candidates are thinly traded companies that feel they get inadequate attention from Big Board specialists.) More important, the price-fixing scandal that so damaged the Nasdaq market's reputation and contributed to the flight of companies in the last two years has also resulted in stringent new order-handling rules handed down by the SEC, which could limit many of the traditional complaints of investors and listed companies about Nasdaq. Under the rules, Nasdaq market makers must publish customer limit orders that are better than the price they themselves are quoting, and they must also expose to their customers the prices they obtain from other dealers and electronic networks such as Instinet. The rules have also limited the activity of so-called SOES bandits. These are day traders who used the Nasdaq's Small Order Execution System to automatically execute orders against dealer quotes in fast-moving, news-driven markets. The SOES bandits are commonly blamed for causing volatility and driving companies off the Nasdaq. Finally, because the SEC forced the NASD to split itself into separate regulatory and stock-trading entities, the Nasdaq may be able to better operate like a stock exchange than like a dealer association.

For all the scandal surrounding Nasdaq, it is a far more viable competitor to the Big Board today than it was ten or twenty years ago. Twelve years ago, it was inconceivable that two of the ten largest capitalization companies in the United States would be Nasdaq companies, as they are today.

Taking the Fight Abroad

At the end of a routine marketing trip to India last May, James E. Shapiro, the New York Stock Exchange's managing director for international and research, abruptly changed his schedule. Leaving a colleague to meet Indian government officials in New Delhi, Mr. Shapiro jetted to the southern city of Bangalore to give a pitch to a software company that was believed close to a deal to list American Depositary Receipts on the Nasdaq Stock Market.

It was another salvo in the Big Board's effort to recruit more foreign listings. Mr. Grasso, like his predecessor, wants his legacy to be the transformation of the New York Stock Exchange into a truly global marketplace. No cause gets him as personally excited as the recruitment of foreign listings. And he's had tremendous success in that area. By last year, 338 foreign companies were listed on the Big Board, up from 106 in 1991, including some of the world's best-known companies, such as Deutsche Telekom and Telefonos de Mexico. A figure he likes to repeat is that if just one-third of the foreign companies that qualified to list on the New York Stock Exchange did so, its market capitalization would double.

In the fall of 1996, Georges Ugeux was hired as the new executive vice president in charge of foreign listings. A former president of Kidder Peabody Europe and of the European Investment Fund, a European Union entity, Mr. Ugeux is animated and enthusiastic. He is also having an increasing influence on the Big Board's agenda.

Many major initiatives, from trading hours to decimals to the new specialist allocation policy, are undertaken with an eye toward how they can encourage more foreign companies to list on the New York Stock Exchange. For example, when the Big Board made its dramatic shift to decimals, Mr. Grasso said it would help bring in listings from foreign companies, which without exception trade in decimals in their home markets. The Big Board hopes to trade foreign stocks in any currency and to list foreign ordinary shares, not just ADRs. (Currently, except for Canadian issues, the vast majority of foreign stocks trade as ADRs, which can pose some settlement problems for certain investors.) It also continues to mull the idea of longer opening hours to facilitate trading in foreign stocks, although it has been mulling that at least since the mid-1980s.

Classically, however, the Big Board is accused even in this area of using its monopoly position to further its own interests. This is illustrated by an obscure dispute between it and Thomson Electronics Settlements Group. Thomson complained to the SEC in 1997 that it was being unfairly deprived of business by a rule of the New York Stock Exchange that in essence allowed only the Depositary Trust Co., in which the Big Board is the largest and most influential shareholder, to issue trade confirmations. Thomson wanted that right as well because it piggybacked neatly onto another of its businesses that had become very profitable at home and abroad, called allocation. Allocation involves slicing up single trades into smaller parts for the various accounts a particular institutional manager runs. Thomson ESG president Howard Edelstein called the New York Stock Exchange "arrogant" and said its real reason for keeping the rule was so that DTC could horn in on Thomson's lucrative foreign allocation business—all in a drive to attract more foreign-stock listings. DTC responded that the rule is necessary to ensure adequate safeguards for investors' stock keeping. Late in 1997, the New York Stock Exchange said it was ready to change the rule.

Despite the Big Board's considerable success in attracting foreign listings, its record of attracting trading in those listings has been less impressive. Even though foreign companies now make up 11 percent of the Big Board list, and their total capitalization equaled 25 percent of the worldwide capitalization of the New York Stock Exchange, trading in foreign stocks as a share of total volume has actually recently declined slightly, to 8.7 percent in 1997. Just two of the fifty most actively traded stocks in 1997 were foreign: Telefonos de Mexico and Telebras. For all the hoopla surrounding the listing of Daimler Benz in 1993, in all of 1996 it traded just 7.2 million shares—equal to a couple of days' trading in Compaq Computer or Coca-Cola. Deutsche Telekom averaged about 50,000 shares, but by comparison Gateway 2000, a recent Nasdaq defector, averaged 1 million shares a day.

Mr. Grasso said it's too early to expect trading volume to be commensurate with the number of foreign listings. "We're still in the asset-gathering stage. We have to bring large numbers of non-U.S. companies. The more you bring, the more critical mass is achieved in terms of U.S. investors using the U.S. arena rather than the home-country market." He added, "We're always going to tell issuers it's a long-term investment." Bringing liquidity to the listing "will involve in some way bringing an offering or making an acquisition or making a benefits program to their employees in the U.S."

The key to the success of listing foreign stocks in the United States is U.S. investors' interest in foreign stocks. Foreign investors have a natural preference for dealing in their home market because of differing time zones and currencies. Apart from some, principally Canadian and Latin American issues, this home-country bias has kept the lion's share of trading in foreign stocks on their domestic exchanges. This suggests, for example, that twenty-four-hour trading on U.S. stock markets could yet be a long way off.

That does not bother Mr. Ugeux or Mr. Grasso. They see the New York Stock Exchange as complementary to, not competing with, foreign exchanges. Indeed, the campaign for foreign-stock listings is one whose greatest payoff is probably in the future. The American investing public's appetite for more foreign stocks has been steadily growing for the last decade; in that period the number of foreign-stock mutual funds in the United States has ballooned to more than four hundred from less than fifty.

But these trends suggest that for all the excitement over foreign listings, the most important fight for the Big Board will continue to be, for the foreseeable future, over domestic listings.

Technology

On October 28, 1997, volume on the New York Stock Exchange soared to 1.2 billion shares, for the first time slicing through the one-billion mark and demolishing the old record set the previous day by 75 percent. That day was as striking for what didn't happen as did happen: there were virtually no glitches in the Big Board's order routing, execution or trade processing systems.

It was a reflection of the more than $1 billion the exchange has sunk into systems and capacity, an investment spurred initially by sheer survival considerations and the trauma of the 1987 stock market crash. The investment was not without controversy. In the early 1980s, a delegation of floor specialists had been sent to then Chairman William Batten to tell him that by spending millions to move to electronic trading and boost capacity, he was "wasting members' money building capacity they would never need," recalled William Freund. Then president John Phelan is generally credited with pushing ahead in spite of such criticism.

Many specialists resisted switching from their leather-bound binders for collecting orders to computer terminals. "There were people who felt this was a back-of-the-envelope scheme to automate the floor out of existence," Mr. Grasso said.

Then came Black Monday: October 19, 1987. On the day of the crash, just a quarter of the Big Board's stocks were traded electronically. At the remainder, specialists were deluged with sell orders. Desperate brokers were sending orders to the floor at the rate of more than eighty per minute; the machines that printed order cards for specialists still working with paper could print no more than twelve. Delays stretched out. Volume topped 600 million shares, four times the then average daily volume. One specialist firm became so inundated with paper it could not determine by the next morning if it was solvent. Mr. Grasso, who had tried to help the firm determine its position without success, then helped arrange for a broker dealer to take it over that day, a person present at the time recalled.

The key lesson of the crash was the need to handle sudden surges in volume. Thus, in the early 1990s, the exchange established a capacity goal of five times average daily volume, or in engineers' terms, average message traffic, which necessitated by 1995 establishing a goal of 2 billion shares a day.

The technology investments are not just a matter of good business. They are also part of an effort to demonstrate that a physical trading floor can be just as competitive as a fully automated one, in an age when virtually every country outside the United States has gone the latter route. Mr. Britz, executive vice president of equities, market data and technology, said if efficiency is the only benchmark, fully automated markets have an inherent cost advantage. But technology is a means, not an end, he said. "We have a physically convened market and the burden is on us to wring every last ounce of efficiency out of that market."

The key technology investments are SuperDOT (DOT stands for Designated Order Turnaround system), the first version of which began in 1974, which automatically receives, routs and confirms orders from brokers around the country; the electronic display book, where orders are stored and executed and which began life in the early 1980s; and the specialist position reporting system (SPRS), initiated in 1993, by which specialists can constantly monitor their profit and loss and capital position. Specialists are much more comfortable with technology today than they were ten years ago. Mr. Britz said, "If we went down there and tried to take SPRS away from them, we'd be shot on sight."

The exchange is currently equipping floor brokers with handheld computers for entering their orders. The display and transmission of trade and quote data around the country is handled by the Securities Industry Automation Corp., two-thirds owned by the Big Board and one-third by the American Stock Exchange.

Share volume is not truly indicative of how busy the exchange is; a 100-share trade involves almost as much processing as a 1-million share trade. Thus, usage and capacity is actually measured by the number of electronic messages—buy-and-sell orders and confirmations. On October 28, the peak number of messages being sent across its central nervous system was 274 a second; the actual record was set on a "triple-witching" day in June, when options and futures expired: 285 messages every second, close to the system's peak capacity of 375. The exchange is expanding that limit to 500 not a second too soon.

October 27 and 28, 1997, were an important test of the system improvements made over the previous ten years. Mr. Johnston called Mr. Grasso at the opening on October 27 to inform him that the market was going to plunge. Mr. Grasso at the time was in the middle of a meeting with the exchange's European Advisory Committee in Paris. They stayed in constant touch most of the day.

The next morning, Mr. Grasso caught the Concorde back to New York. While dashing from Kennedy airport terminal to a helicopter, he called Merrill Lynch chairman and Big Board director David Komansky and assured him the exchange was ready to withstand the expected tumult. Mr. Grasso walked onto the exchange floor just before the opening. As the market fell then rebounded, and volume mounted, Mr. Grasso marvelled: "It was a confirming moment."

The Competition for Trading in Big Board Stocks

Trading stock has always been the core business and priority of the New York Stock Exchange. All its other activities—attracting new listings, maintaining regulatory oversight of its members—are aimed at attracting more trading activity to the stock exchange. Since Congress and the SEC broke the NYSE's virtual monopoly on the trading of its own stocks in the late 1970s, the fight for market share in its own stocks has been a guiding concern.

That fight became desperate in the late 1980s as a variety of new competitors sprang up to compete with the Big Board. They included foreign markets, where some Big Board stocks were dually listed, and third-market brokers such as Madoff, who were not New York Stock Exchange members but made markets, much as Nasdaq dealers did, in Big Board stocks. The regional stock exchanges, in Philadelphia, Boston, Chicago, and the Pacific, ate into its market share by competing more aggressively on price (for example, cutting specialist fees), through technological innovation, and by allowing some practices barred on the Big Board, such as allowing its members to pay brokers for their orders, a practice called payment for order flow.

Its market share bottomed out in 1992 at 81.7 percent of trading volume in its stocks and 65.1 percent of trades. Trade market share is important because data fees are shared among the exchanges based on their share of trades, not volume. The New York Stock Exchange has recovered those shares through a marketing campaign to win back order flow, but with an aggressiveness that has ruffled feathers.

One of the most controversial practices that led to the decline in the Big Board's market share was payment for order flow. In this practice, a broker-dealer sends its customer orders to another dealer to be executed and receives in return a payment, such as a penny per share. The second dealer is paying for the order flow in order to earn the spread between the bid and offer prices of a stock. In other words, if a stock is bid at 20 and offered at $20^1/8$, the dealer can earn 12.5 cents by constantly buying at the bid and selling at the offer. Third-market brokers such as Madoff attract their order flow by paying for it. In addition, some regionals, such as the Pacific Exchange, permit their specialists to pay for order flow in order to earn the spread. In response, many broker-dealers established their own specialist units on the Pacific so that they could capture the spread for themselves.

The New York Stock Exchange has repeatedly called for a ban on payment for order flow, arguing that broker-dealers are putting their own interests ahead of their customers'. For example, had the order in the above example been exposed to the floor of the New York Stock Exchange, the customer might have found someone willing to trade at $20^1/16$, a better price for both buyer and seller. Those calls have gone unheeded, so the New York Stock Exchange fought back in other ways. In 1993, it introduced rebates to brokers for trades under 2,100 shares. Then in November 1995, the Big Board won a major victory when Merrill Lynch closed its specialist operation on the Pacific Exchange. Shortly afterward, it entered into a joint marketing agreement with the New York Stock Exchange called NYSE Prime, under which customers receive a notation on their trade tickets telling them how much money they saved by trading on the New York Stock Exchange.

But the way the New York Stock Exchange claims to save investors money is controversial. As part of its effort to compete with payment for order flow, the exchange obtained approval in the early 1990s for its specialists to "stop" stock. Suppose the market for a stock is 20 bid, $20^1/16$ offered, with both prices representing public limit orders—in other words, the bidder won't pay more than 20 and the seller won't accept less than $20^1/16$. An investor sends to the exchange a "market" order to buy—that is, to buy stock at the lowest available price then prevailing. Under the rule change, the specialist could "stop" that order, guarantee a fill at no worse than the lowest offer, $20^1/16$, look for other sellers, and if he or she wishes, sell the stock him- or herself to the investor at 20. Thus, the investor saved $1/16$ per share, by the Big Board's calculation. Not so fast, say others. For example, Erik Sirri, chief economist at the SEC, pointed out that by stopping the stock, the specialist actually hurt the investor whose limit order to sell at $20^{1}/16$ was not filled.

The argument over whether stopping stock represents price improvement can become tremendously arcane and may seem of interest only to market theoreticians. But the issue illustrates how many things the New York Stock Exchange has done to recapture its market share are, at least to its competitors, not necessarily the great favor to the public it claims them to be.

Indeed, the whole issue of what constitutes price improvement is so controversial that the SEC gave NYSE Prime permanent approval only in August 1997, after first pointing out that since the program doesn't tell investors when they've been "price disimproved," the exchange couldn't use the program to evaluate whether it or its member firms were fulfilling their best-execution obligations.

Another practice the New York Stock Exchange has vociferously attacked is called preferencing. Like payment for order flow, preferencing is a popular way for broker-dealers to capture the spread in a stock by internalizing the order instead of taking it to the open market. In 1991, the Cincinnati Stock Exchange, which has no floor and is actually based in Chicago and at the time had a tiny market share, launched a preferencing program under which, if two specialists on the CSE had the same bid or offer, the exchange could divert its order to the specialist of its choice, in practice one that it owns. The CSE specialists are in fact employed by, and sit in the trading rooms of, major broker-dealers and simply pair off the dealer's incoming customer orders, buying at the then-prevailing bid and selling at the offer. In just four years, the CSE's market share shot from 0.7 percent of trades in Big Board stocks to 3.9 percent. Over the New York Stock Exchange's protests, the SEC gave permanent approval to the CSE's program in 1996.

New York Stock Exchange officials did not give up easily. They have lobbied their member dealers who also maintain CSE specialist operations to close them and bring that order flow back to the Big Board. In 1996, Smith Barney closed its profitable specialist operation there, triggering a big drop in market share for the CSE. One participant in the CSE said Smith Barney made the move after Mr. Grasso personally and repeatedly lobbied Sanford Weill, chief executive of Travelers Inc., Smith Barney's parent. "Every time Sandy Weill would be at a function or on the floor Grasso would go up to him and say, have you shut down CSE yet? And he said, nope. And [Smith Barney] finally gave in."

Mr. Grasso said while he has personally urged executives from broker-dealers to bring more of their order flow to the Big Board, Smith Barney's decision was entirely its own.

The fight over preferencing illustrates an unusual dynamic at work around the Big Board today. Its position has become so dominant that the most effective check on its dominance today is the SEC, not any particular exchange. The SEC approved the CSE's preferencing program in large part because it would make the Cincinnati Stock Exchange a more viable competitor to the Big Board. In 1997 it conducted a lengthy study, at Congress's request, of the quality of markets on the regionals and Big Board and concluded that the CSE's record on price improvement was second best, after the New York Stock Exchange's. New York Stock Exchange insiders tartly noted that the SEC had told the CSE four weeks in advance it was about to sample its trading, giving its members plenty of warning if they were interested in improving their record. The SEC replied that all the exchanges got the same notice.

To Regulate or Be Regulated

The average person, whose knowledge of the New York Stock exchange is shaped by images of its bustling trading floor, might be surprised to learn the single largest part of the organization, at least by head count, is the regulatory division, employing more than one-third of the exchange's 1,450 employees.

Besides being the principal market for stocks in the United States, the New York Stock Exchange is also the primary regulator for its member broker-dealers, which are most of the country's largest.

This capacity puts the New York Stock Exchange in the odd role of being both regulator and regulated (by the SEC). That role is shared by most of the country's other "self-regulatory organizations," but it is most important at the New York Stock Exchange simply because that exchange is the largest.

The Big Board sees its role as regulator as absolutely crucial to its role as marketplace and as a business. The willingness of investors to trade there is directly related to their faith in regulatory oversight of the trading that occurs on its floor and among its members.

Regulation has been a growth area. In 1987, according to Mr. Kwalwasser, it employed forty-two people in enforcement, investigating 150 to 200 cases at any one time. Now, 120 people in enforcement are involved in 650 to 850 investigations at any one time. While technology has helped make hundreds of jobs redundant elsewhere in the exchange, it appears to have increased the workload in the regulatory area. Its Stock Watch division monitors every trade and flags anomalies that could signify wrongdoing. Its automated search-and-match system correlates data on 1.5 million professionals with customer information on 75,000 companies to identify individuals who may be connected to suspicious trading. Suspected cases of violations of securities law, such as insider trading, are referred to the SEC.

The division is run by Mr. Kwalwasser, an intense man who came to the

Big Board from the SEC in 1984 and is one of the truest in an institution of true believers.

The issues occupying Mr. Kwalwasser's division run the gamut from routine investigations and disciplines of stockbrokers at its member firms to full-scale investigations of its member broker-dealers. Whenever a member broker-dealer fails, fingers are immediately pointed at regulators to raise the question of why they didn't spot the problem sooner. For example, the New York Stock Exchange has been drawn into the controversy over the behavior of clearing brokers, who operate joint back offices on the part of introducing brokers who don't directly trade on the New York Stock Exchange. In 1996, A. R. Baron, a small introducing broker, failed, and is accused of having defrauded investors of $75 million. Bear, Stearns & Cos. acted as the clearing broker for A. R. Baron and its actions have also come under scrutiny. Jonathan Kord Lagemann, an attorney representing several A. R. Baron customers with claims against Bear Stearns, says the stock exchange helped spawn firms like A. R. Baron when in 1982 it changed its rules to "immunize" clearing brokers from the misdeeds of introducing brokers.

Mr. Kwalwasser's office is also responsible for writing and updating many of the rules that govern the nation's securities markets. An idea of the complexity that goes into this job can be gleaned from the fact that the current New York Stock Exchange constitution and rule book is hundreds of pages long, and many of the rules have separate interpretation manuals running several hundred pages each.

The threat of a conflict of interest, or appearance of conflict, between the New York Stock Exchange's compliance and marketing roles is often close to the surface. New York Stock Exchange members are loath to publicly criticize the institution, and that is partly out of an awareness that it regulates them.

This was illustrated rather starkly last year when, shortly after the SEC's new order-handling rules were implemented, some regional stock exchanges and third-market brokers heard concerns from broker-dealers that the New York Stock Exchange might, in reviewing order-flow routing decisions, pressure them into sending more orders to the New York Stock Exchange. Mr. Madoff said the marketing people and compliance people seemed to arrive uncomfortably close together. He phoned Mr. Grasso, a friend as well as competitor, to complain. Mr. Grasso immediately called the relevant division heads to his office and, with Mr. Madoff on the speakerphone, instructed them that they should not permit the impression to develop that order-routing decisions were being questioned.

That satisfied Mr. Madoff. Not so the regionals, who fired off an angry complaint to the SEC, where head of the division of market regulation Richard Lindsey and head of the office of compliance and inspections Lori Richards sent a letter to the New York Stock Exchange, sternly reminding it that "it is critical that examination and enforcement of [member brokers' best-execution] obligations be conducted in an objective and impartial manner." The uproar irritated New York Stock Exchange officials, who said they never did anything of the sort. A spokesman issued a testy statement saying that the SEC was welcome to take on the responsibility of examining brokers' order-handling procedures. "I don't want there ever to be a moment where in reality or in perception people think we are using our regulatory responsibility to our competitive advantage," said Mr. Grasso. "It doesn't happen. It will never happen."

The incident also illustrates the strange relationship between the New York Stock Exchange and the SEC. There has historically been a creative tension between the two, with both trying to command the moral high ground of having investors' better interest at heart. In recent years, the activist approach of Chairman Arthur Levitt Jr. and Mr. Lindsey has created a number of conflicts between the two.

More recently, the two institutions clashed over the Big Board's circuit breakers, which were implemented after the 1987 crash. As originally written, they would halt trading on all the nation's stock and stock-derivatives exchanges for an hour if the Dow Jones Industrial Average fell 250 points from its previous close, and two hours if it fell 400. But as the market doubled from its late 1980 levels, executives at some broker-dealers began to question why the stock market should close at a level that was a much smaller percentage than it had been when the circuit breakers were introduced. The SEC in the fall of 1995 began raising similar concerns. Mr. Kwalwasser, the point man on the issue, steadfastly insisted that percentages aside, 250 points was still a big, scary number to most investors.

Then came March 1996, when in one tumultuous session the Dow plunged more than 200 points before abruptly bouncing back. It was the closest the circuit breakers had come to being activated, yet few saw the day's swings as the sort of thing that justified closing the nation's securities markets. The SEC finally demanded that the NYSE take some kind of action. With considerable reluctance, the New York Stock Exchange agreed to widen the circuit breakers to their current 350- and 550-point levels, and the halts were shortened to half an hour and one hour, respectively.

Even recently, Mr. Kwalwasser said, "I'm still not sure we did the right thing by changing" them.

Yet again, the exchange's critics argue, it was the Big Board's self-interest, or more precisely the interest of its specialists, that was behind its foot-dragging. Halting trading in a plunging market relieves the specialist of having to buy large amounts of rapidly depreciating stock and enables him or her to match up buy and sell orders without sacrificing the firm's own capital.

But such interpretations can be unfair. For example, when a public outcry over the alleged destabilizing role of program traders developed in the late 1980s, the New York Stock Exchange dragged its feet on limiting their activity, since they represented an important source of business. Eventually, it did indeed impose a 50-point collar on index arbitrage program trading. When the Dow falls more than 50 points from its previous close, program traders arbitraging between stocks and stock index futures can sell a stock only when it is not falling, that is, on an uptick. The reverse is true when the Dow rises more than 50 points. Given that 50 points is not much in percentage terms nowadays, the collar is activated virtually daily now. Yet not only does the Big Board stick by the rule—to the consternation of the Chicago Mercantile Exchange, where the most important stock-index future is traded—but Mr. Kwalwasser said that if he had his way, "I would put it on all the time. Forget about 50 points."

The circuit breakers were triggered for the first time on October 27, 1997, when turmoil in Asian markets spilled over into New York. The first circuit breaker halted trading at 2:35 P.M. when the Dow industrials were down a little over 350 points. Trading resumed at 3:05, and stocks promptly plummeted another 200 points. The market closed for the day at 3:30 with the average down 554.26 points, its biggest ever point drop, and at 7.2 percent, its biggest in percentage terms since October 1987.

While some floor traders at the exchange defended the circuit breakers, arguing they prevented a more severe drop, the vast majority of market participants and independent analysts believe the circuit breakers came on too soon and in fact made matters worse. Once the first halt ended, buyers went on strike while sellers rushed to trade before the market closed for the day, virtually ensuring the second halt would occur. In addition, many investors who generally place orders on the close to square positions, especially in derivatives, were unable to do so, leaving them with unexpected exposures.

The Big Board's response to demands for change was radically different from a year earlier. The next day, Mr. Grasso, acknowledging criticisms of the circuit breakers, promised to review them. Mr. Levitt weighed in shortly afterward with his own call for change. Exchange staff immediately started consulting members and meeting with other stock and derivatives exchanges. By mid-December, a consensus had emerged that new circuit breaker triggers would be established at 10 percent and 20 percent, close to the percentages that the original 250 and 400 point breakers represented in 1988. In February 1998, a 30 percent trigger was added. The percentages will be fixed in point terms of the Dow Jones Industrial Average quarterly. Those changes are expected to take effect in 1998. Meanwhile, other modifications are that the 550-point circuit breaker would halt trading for just half an hour instead of an hour if it is triggered after 2 P.M. EST. Trading, however, wouldn't resume if it is triggered after 3 P.M. In addition, after 3 P.M., the 350-point circuit breaker wouldn't be allowed to trigger, allowing trading to continue uninterrupted until the 550-point threshold was reached.

Despite occasional public clashes, relations between the two organizations are generally good, owing in part to the cordial relations between their two leaders. Mr. Donaldson, by contrast, got into a very public dispute with Mr.

Levitt's predecessor, Richard Breeden, over foreign-stock listings. Mr. Donaldson wanted U.S. accounting standards relaxed for foreign companies listing in the United States, warning that otherwise the Big Board would be relegated to second-class status among world stock exchanges. Unfortunately, to the public it looked like Mr. Donaldson was trying to sacrifice investor interest for the Big Board's own interest. Mr. Breeden stood his ground, and when Daimler Benz eventually listed in 1993, it was with only minor concessions on the accounting issue.

Mr. Grasso and Mr. Levitt have worked to keep their disagreements quiet and civil. Mr. Grasso has continued to press for easier accounting standards for foreign companies, but more quietly. When Mr. Levitt told Mr. Grasso he wanted Rule 500 changed, he also said he wouldn't publicly bash the Big Board over the issue if Mr. Grasso undertook to change the rule himself, according to some people familiar with Mr. Levitt's thinking. Indeed, the first revelations that the New York Stock Exchange would probably scrap the rule that came from Mr. Grasso, not the SEC. Mr. Grasso said there were no conditions on how he went about reviewing the rule. "He asked that we review it. He obviously wanted, if in fact we were going to continue it, a very solid base of rationalization."

The SEC's Mr. Lindsey is now busy working on another proposed regulatory overhaul for the nation's stock exchanges. A concept release of which he is the principal author has proposed a radical redefinition of what a stock exchange is, taking some electronic networks previously regulated like broker-dealers, principally Instinet, and making them into exchanges, fully integrated into the Intermarket Trading System, which links all the existing stock exchanges and enables their members to access the best price on a stock no matter where it's displayed. Among other things, this system would get rid of the last limitations on the trading of Big Board stocks away from the exchange.

The concept release tackles an important issue facing the nation's stock markets in general and the Big Board in particular, which is the likelihood that in the not-too-distant future, investors will want to trade stocks anywhere they want, and not necessarily through an exchange at all, be it regional, New York or electronic. It may be on the Internet.

Mr. Grasso is aware of these challenges. But he believes the merit of the auction market—all buyers and all sellers meeting at one place so that the best price always prevails—has proved itself through countless challenges. And while massive investments in technology will ensure that the market operates efficiently, technology alone cannot supplant the benefits that a market structure gives to investors.

"On the nineteenth of October, 1987, the dealer in IBM had 100 shares to buy, 1.1 million shares for sale at any price, last sale $132 and a fraction," says Mr. Grasso. "If you reduce that discovery to a collision on a network, when the consumer on the institutional end says 1.1 million shares for sale at any price, last sale 132 and a fraction, how will they feel if that buyer says, okay, $10. Suddenly you get a report back, you sold your 1.1 million shares of IBM at 10, down 122 and a fraction. You might say consenting adults. I might say major opportunity for a congressional investigation."

He says a balance must be struck between what people can do with technology and what they should be allowed to do. "Just because you can do [something] technologically or just because there is an offering in the marketplace that might appeal to a consumer, you've got to remember the strength of the U.S. securities markets has been the public's trust and confidence," and that comes from the market structure Congress, the SEC and the stock exchanges have created, he says.

The New York Stock Exchange's People

Richard A. Grasso, chairman and chief executive officer: In June 1995, Richard A. Grasso became chairman and chief executive officer of the New York Stock Exchange, the first staffer to rise through the ranks to that position in the exchange's 206-year history.

Mr. Grasso is widely regarded as having probably the greatest detailed knowledge of the inner workings of the exchange of anyone to head the institution.

As president for seven years before assuming the CEO position, he has had enormous influence over the organization for the last decade. Indeed, since joining the exchange in 1968, he has held top positions in many areas, especially new listings and market data.

Grasso, Richard
Chairman &
President-NYSE

It was John Phelan, his mentor, who made him president in 1988, but the board of directors passed over him in 1990 when choosing Mr. Phelan's successor, former investment banker William Donaldson.

Despite his exceptionally deep technical knowledge of the exchange, Mr. Grasso's most marked contribution to the organization is his flair for marketing. Most of his initiatives reflect his desire to make the New York Stock Exchange a brand "recognized around the world."

For example, NYSE Prime is probably the first program under which a stock exchange has tried to establish brand awareness among retail investors by telling them, through cooperating brokers, how much money they saved by trading on the New York Stock Exchange. He has personally participated in countless joint promotions with member companies, from having a Holstein calf walk onto the trading floor to welcome Gateway 2000 from Nasdaq to driving the Hershey Kissmobile around to celebrate the seventieth anniversary of Hershey's listing.

William R. Johnston, president and chief operating officer: Mr. Johnston was named president of the New York Stock Exchange in June 1996. He is second in command to chairman Richard Grasso. The exchange's new listings and client services, operations, regulation, and general counsel all report to him. Before joining the exchange staff, he had been senior managing partner at LaBranche & Co., a specialist firm. He has been a member of the stock exchange since 1964.

Robert G. Britz, group executive vice president, equities, market data and technology: Mr. Britz is responsible for equity operations, in particular the technology for transmitting and distributing stock price information. He had previously been in charge of new listings and client services.

Catherine R. Kinney, group executive vice president, new listings and client services: Ms. Kinney is in charge of marketing and relations between the exchange and its listed companies and member brokers. She is also responsible for listing new companies in the United States. Previously she has worked in regulation, floor operations and technology.

Edward A. Kwalwasser, group executive vice president, regulation: Mr. Kwalwasser has one of the broadest areas of responsibility in the stock exchange, overseeing regulation of member firms, market surveillance, and relations between the stock exchange and its own regulator, the Securities and Exchange Commission. He joined the New York Stock Exchange in 1984, from the SEC, which he had joined in 1967.

Georges Ugeux, group executive vice president, international and research: Mr. Ugeux's job is the newest addition to Mr. Grasso's inner circle. Mr. Ugeux is principally responsible for attracting new foreign listings, a priority of Mr. Grasso, and maintaining relations with foreign companies. A Belgian national, Mr. Ugeux had several positions in European finance, in both the public and private sectors, before joining the stock exchange in 1996.

Richard A. Edgar, executive vice president, market operations, real estate and facilities: Mr. Edgar runs trading floor operations, post trade services, and market operations support and is responsible for real estate and facilities.

Donald J. Solodar, executive vice president, market structure: Mr. Solodar is responsible for intermarket relations, market data, bonds, administration, recovery planning and security.

Richard P. Bernard, executive vice president and general counsel: Mr. Bernard joined the stock exchange in 1996 and is responsible for legal affairs and the exchange's audit and regulatory quality review functions. He reports directly to Mr. Grasso.

Salvatore Pallante, senior vice president, member firm regulation: Mr. Pallante oversees member firm regulation, administers financial/operational and sales practice programs and develops and administers regulatory policy.

David P. Doherty, senior vice president, enforcement: Mr. Doherty directs the division that investigates and prosecutes violations of the Securities Exchange Act and the exchange's own rules. Before joining the exchange in 1988, he held positions with the Central Intelligence Agency and the SEC.

Keith R. Helsby, senior vice president and chief financial officer: Mr. Helsby is responsible for the financial operations of the exchange.

Robert J. McSweeney, senior vice president, market surveillance: Mr. McSweeney runs the surveillance of trading in listed securities and investigates possible violations of federal securities laws and stock exchange trading rules.

James L. Cochrane, senior vice president and chief economist: Mr. Cochrane is in charge of the exchange's research, acts as chief economist, and is primarily involved with the exchange's activities outside the United States.

Noreen M. Culhane, senior vice president, listings and client service: Ms. Culhane joined the stock exchange from International Business Machines in March 1997 and oversees the exchange's domestic marketing and liaison effort with its listed companies.

Sheila C. Bair, senior vice president, government affairs: Ms. Bair is the stock exchange's chief lobbyist in Washington and runs the exchange's office there, which represents the New York Stock Exchange on legislative and regulatory matters.

Gerald F. Clark, senior vice president, government relations: Mr. Clark is responsible for all New York Stock Exchange government relations activities, including the national office in Washington, DC, the state and local government affairs office in New York City and the international office in Paris.

James E. Buck, senior vice president and secretary: Mr. Buck is responsible for the office of the secretary, hearing board, board advisory committees, arbitration department and membership services.

William A. Bautz, senior vice president and chief technology officer: Mr. Bautz is responsible for the design, development and implementation of the technology necessary to support the New York Stock Exchange's trading systems.

Frank Z. Ashen, senior vice president, human resources: Mr. Ashen oversees compensation and benefits programs, directs operations of security and administration, and is chief labor negotiator.

Robert T. Zito, senior vice president, communications: Mr. Zito is in charge of marketing, media relations, community relations, internal communications, the exchange's market news center, visitors center and broadcast center.

Anne E. Allen, vice president, floor operations: Ms. Allen is responsible for the trading floor's support systems, including market data and switching and order processing systems, telephone and radio paging systems and facilities allocation.

Dennis Covelli, vice president: Mr. Covelli is responsible for the exchange's post-trade systems and trading floor services to the stock exchange's brokers.

Robert A. Marchman, vice president, enforcement: Mr. Marchman manages the department of lawyers that investigates and litigates violations of New York Stock Exchange and SEC rules.

L. Paige Thompson, vice president, domestic listings: Ms. Thompson is responsible for attracting new U.S. and Canadian company listings.

Thomas E. Veit, vice president, client services: Mr. Veit oversees marketing and liaison with the New York Stock Exchange's listed companies.

Regina C. Mysliwiec, vice president, enforcement and sales practices: Ms. Mysliwiec directs the investigation and prosecution of exchange rules and securities laws, in particular major and complex sales-practice cases.

Lois Zarembo, vice president, equity systems: Ms. Zarembo is responsible for planning and developing specialist trading systems and corporate initiatives.

Salvatore Triolo, vice president, regulatory review: Mr. Triolo manages a staff of examiners who ensure that member firms comply with exchange and federal regulations.

William E. Shields, vice president, regulatory review: Mr. Shields manages a staff of examiners who ensure that member firms comply with exchange and federal regulations.

In the Beginning . . .

New York City became the center of finance early in the life of the United States, in large part because it was the country's major port. Federal government bonds and stocks in banks and insurance companies were traded at public auctions, much like cotton and sugar.

In 1792, twenty-four stock brokers and merchants active in trading these securities joined together and agreed to trade with each other rather than at public auction and collect a minimum commission on their stock. This became known as the Buttonwood Agreement, after a tree on Wall Street where the brokers often met to conduct business, and marked the beginning of the New York Stock Exchange.

In 1817, the brokers created the New York Stock & Exchange Board a place to meet regularly at set hours.

The economic expansion of the United States in the mid-1860s fueled the stock business and the growth of rival marketplaces, one of which, the Open Board of Stock Brokers, occasionally exceeded the New York Stock Exchange in volume. In 1863, the exchange got its first permanent home, at 10–12 Broad Street, just south of Wall Street, and shortened its name to the New York Stock Exchange. (The old name lives on in the nickname "Big Board.") In 1869, the New York Stock Exchange merged with its rivals, the Open Board and the Government Bond Department.

At the time, stocks were traded in a call market. At a designated time, the exchange's president or vice president would call out each stock by name, pausing for brokers to submit bids and offers, then move to the next. Because of rising volume, continuous trading replaced the call market in 1871. A trading floor was created, and brokers dealing in particular stocks eventually became specialists, their locations the specialists' posts.

The stock ticker was introduced to the exchange in 1867, enabling rapid transmission of stock prices around the country. (It replaced messengers who ran between the exchange and brokers' offices.)

Fraudulent behavior and stock-market panics were not uncommon. The failure of a major banking house in 1873 triggered a stock-market panic and a depression. In 1907, another stock-market panic was stopped virtually single-handedly by John Pierpont Morgan. But in 1929, similar efforts failed to stop the worst market collapse in history.

Congress, determined to end the abuses believed to have caused the 1929 crash, drastically changed the structure of the markets. It passed the Securities Act of 1933, designed to create a regulated and open securities market, and the Securities Exchange Act of 1934, which created the Securities and Exchange Commission.

These acts ultimately turned the New York Stock Exchange into a more professional, businesslike place. At first the exchange and its members resented the SEC's tough enforcement actions. Richard Whitney, New York Stock Exchange president from 1930 to 1935, had been a leading opponent of the SEC but in 1938 was found to have embezzled his customers' securities and went to jail.

Richard A. Pecheur, vice president, member firm and institutional marketing and sales: Mr. Pecheur oversees the division that works with member and institutional communities to increase trading on the New York Stock Exchange.

Elaine S. Michitsch, vice president, regulatory review: Ms. Michitsch manages a staff of examiners who ensure that member firms comply with exchange and federal regulations.

Under pressure from the SEC, the New York Stock Exchange in 1938 overhauled its governance. It appointed its first full-time president, William McChesney Martin Jr., hired a professional staff and put outsiders on its board of governors.

Stock prices eventually recovered to their pre-crash highs in 1954. By the late 1960s, heavy trading volume was swamping the exchange and its members in paper, necessitating closure of the exchange each Wednesday to clear the backlog. Paperwork-related problems helped put many brokers out of business. This forced the exchange to begin automating the transmission and reporting of stock quotes and trades, and to move to electronic settlement of trades.

Sweeping changes occurred in 1975. The SEC abolished fixed commissions, stripping the exchange of its primary regulatory role and leading to the disappearance of hundreds of brokerage firms, rapid advances in trading technology and sophistication, and a boom in trading. In addition, Congress mandated a National Market System, under which New York Stock Exchange–listed stocks could be traded on any exchange in the country. Its key features were the Consolidated tape which combined all stock trade information into a single stream no matter which exchange it came from, and the Intermarket Trading System, inaugurated in 1978, which enabled a broker or specialist to automatically access a stock quote on any exchange if it was better than that on his own.

The NMS led to a dramatic decline in the Big Board's share of trading in its own stocks. It was one of several serious setbacks over the coming decade. Futures and options on stocks and stock indexes began prospering on Chicago's commodities exchanges in the 1970s. But James Needham, who became the Big Board's first full-time chairman in 1972, declined to follow, saying derivatives would turn the stock exchange into a casino.

William Batten, a former chief of J. C. Penney Co. and New York Stock Exchange chairman from 1976 to 1984, opened the New York Futures Exchange in 1979, and initiated options trading shortly afterward. But the products never attracted significant interest, and both businesses were sold in the 1990s.

At the same time, the Nasdaq Stock Market had become a serious competitor for listings, thanks in part to its perceived technological superiority. Under Mr. Batten and his successor, John Phelan, the stock exchange began a massive investment in technology in the mid-1980s and had transferred about one-quarter of its stocks to electronic order books from paper when the stock market crashed in 1987.

Because of the crash, the Big Board intensified its technology investment and instituted several market safeguards, such as circuit breakers, collars on program trading, and intermarket surveillance agreements, to prevent a recurrence. Those factors plus a more determined competitive response to the encroachments of regional exchanges and third-market brokers have helped the stock exchange win back a lot of the trading it lost in the early 1980s.

Beginning with William Donaldson, chairman from 1991 to 1995, and continuing with current chairman Richard Grasso, the New York Stock Exchange has aggressively courted foreign-stock listings as the prime source of its future growth. In the United States, regulatory investigations of the Nasdaq Stock Market and the marginalization of the American Stock Exchange have enabled the Big Board to reestablish its dominance in domestic listings.

Alain Yves Morvan, senior vice president, international relations: Mr. Morvan coordinates the New York Stock Exchange's activities throughout Europe and with all foreign governments.

Edmund Lukas, vice president, origination—Europe: Mr. Lukas develops foreign stock listings and relationships with foreign investment banks.

Alan Holzer, controller: Mr. Holzer has been controller since 1988, prior to which he was controller at E. F. Hutton.

Raymond J. Hennessy, vice president, member firm regulatory development and services: Mr. Hennessy is responsible for dealer operations/ financial responsibility, and for interpreting and developing the financial responsibility rules of the Securities and Exchange Commission. He also interprets and develops New York Stock Exchange rules.

Arthur O. Harris, vice president, central region, listings and client services: Mr. Harris provides services to listed companies and identifies companies that are priority listing prospects.

Thomas E. Haley, vice president, market data: Mr. Haley manages the exchange's market-data business.

Agnes Gautier, vice president, regulatory, legal and technical support, market surveillance: Ms. Gautier develops and interprets trading floor rules and is responsible for the allocation and specialist performance-evaluation processes.

John P. Foynes, vice president, fixed income market: Mr. Foynes oversees the exchange's bond market.

Santo A. Famularo, vice president, infrastructure and broker support systems: Mr. Famularo plans and develops infrastructure, communication, systems and networks and broker and post-trade systems.

James C. Esposito, vice president, security: Mr. Esposito manages the exchange's security department and serves as the primary liaison with local, state and federal law-enforcement agencies.

Donald G. Dueweke, senior vice president, regulatory and corporate systems: Mr. Dueweke is responsible for developing and maintaining the market surveillance, regulatory, member firm and enforcement systems.

Richard C. Adamonis, vice president, media relations: Mr. Adamonis oversees the exchange's media relations and broadcast-center activities.

James F. Sullivan, treasurer: Mr. Sullivan has been treasurer of the New York Stock Exchange since 1974.

Vincent F. Patten, assistant vice president, listings: Mr. Patten has been assistant vice president, listings, since 1991.

David P. Lambert, senior vice president, government relations: Mr. Lambert has been senior vice president, government relations, since 1988.

THE NASDAQ STOCK MARKET

IN THE THROES OF CHANGE

Successful, but Chastened

The Nasdaq Stock Market's executives love to boast about the technological sophistication of their screen-based trading system. Indeed, for years the market's immodest motto was "The Stock Market for the Next 100 Years." It was a direct taunt to the New York Stock Exchange's seemingly primitive open outcry auction market that has hundreds of traders jostling one another on an expansive trading floor, yelling for attention and littering the floor with a confetti of order confirmations.

Yet there's a problem. All that technology isn't keeping some of the nation's fastest-growing and most successful technology companies from abandoning Nasdaq for the Big Board. In 1997 alone, ninety-one companies gave Nasdaq the boot, including such high-profile tech firms as Gateway 2000 and aggressive nontech companies like Republic Industries, who joined prior defectors like Bay Networks and America Online. Some delisting companies had to move because they were bought by New York Stock Exchange–listed companies. But many others chose to make the move because they were tired of seeing their stock prices soaring and plunging on the Nasdaq system and they wanted the prestige that comes with listing on the Big Board.

According to Ted Waitt, chairman of Gateway 2000, a fast-growing computer direct-marketer with a market capitalization of $4.2 billion, the move to the Big Board "should provide lower transaction costs and result in a more efficient market for the stock."

To be sure, Nasdaq still retains trading in what are arguably some of the most important technology companies on the face of the earth today, including Microsoft and Intel. But the question is, if an exchange known for its affinity to technology can't keep technology companies from abandoning it, what is its future? The question resonated throughout 1996 and 1997, not just because of

defections, but also because of the very public beatings that regulators administered to Nasdaq. Disciplinary actions administered by the Justice Department
and the Securities and Exchange Commission resulted in a major shake-up of
Nasdaq's methods of trading and regulation through its self-regulatory organization, the National Association of Securities Dealers.

Make no mistake, Nasdaq has clearly been a success story. It can brag about
average daily trading volume of 645 million shares a day compared to less than 300
million a few years ago. Some 85 percent of the companies that decided to go public in 1996 listed on Nasdaq (though in most cases, the companies couldn't meet
the New York Stock Exchange's more rigorous listing criteria), adding 655 new
companies to its roster in 1996, totaling $24.11 billion in market capitalization.

But while Nasdaq is attracting record levels of newly public companies, the
number of companies defecting to the Big Board has also risen steadily in recent years. In 1996, a record ninety-six companies defected to the Big Board,
up from sixty-two in 1995, although Nasdaq gained a total of 434 new companies for 1996. Most of the companies that fled cited the Nasdaq's increased
volatility and the higher prestige of the Big Board as their reason for leaving.

The Nasdaq Stock Market: The Club Is Disbanded

In many ways, since their listing criteria are so different, it doesn't make much
difference how many companies list on each of the two major U.S. exchanges.
But one thing is clear: The Nasdaq Stock Market and the company that runs
and regulates it, the National Association of Securities Dealers, are much different bodies now than they were in the heady 1980s when the market was
growing from trading less than 100 million shares a day to its current daily average of more than 600 million shares.

Until a few years ago, the NASD, which runs Nasdaq but also regulates all
securities dealers, in many ways resembled a private club as much as the overseer of a professional market. Officials from the market's most powerful dealer
firms, including Lehman Brothers, Merrill Lynch, PaineWebber and Salomon
Brothers, dominated the governing bodies that shaped the policies of the market, especially the influential trading committee and the board of directors at
the market itself. They also dominated the regional discipline committees and
determined the conditions for small firms to expand their businesses.

Smaller dealers, especially those in the New York region or those engaged in
the practice of day trading on Nasdaq's Small Order Execution System, or SOES,
often found it difficult to start or expand a business. Serious market problems
often elicited, at best, a slow and plodding response from the governing bodies.
Top officials at NASD, including its then-president, Joseph Hardiman, seemed far
more interested in attracting companies to the exploding marketplace than in
chastising Nasdaq dealers for practices that were unfair but commonplace.

That *laissez-faire* approach was one that Nasdaq's regulators came to dearly regret. When Richard Ketchum, a former SEC lawyer who became second in command at the National Association of Securities Dealers, got wind that dealers who set the prices for Nasdaq stocks seemed to be profiting by not fully competing with one another to offer the best prices, he tried gentle persuasion, not swift and serious action, to force a change.

But once the public got wind of the way the prices they were paying were set on Nasdaq, thanks to a 1994 study by two finance professors, the issue became an all-out scandal. Soon, NASD and Nasdaq's failings were laid bare. "The NASD failed to take appropriate action to investigate effectively and to address adequately violations and potential violations of the federal securities laws and NASD's rules," the Securities and Exchange Commission, which governs NASD, would later write in a searing report detailing the failings of the NASD and its dealers. Regulators and the public had decided: NASD's version of self-regulation hadn't worked.

Today's Nasdaq and NASD are frantically trying to keep up with sweeping changes imposed on them as a result of the crescendo of public outrage, an investor lawsuit against thirty-seven of the firms, and two high-level government investigations. Scrambling the most are Nasdaq dealers, who have had to start setting up new baby-sitter-like enforcement procedures after the government concluded that they couldn't be trusted not to fix Nasdaq stock prices to their own advantage. The twenty-four biggest Nasdaq dealers were obliged to begin tape-recording about 3.5 percent of their dealers' calls and review the tapes to make sure the dealers aren't coercing one another to keep their prices in line. They also have agreed to open themselves up to pop inspections by Justice Department or other regulatory officials, and staff their compliance departments with enforcers to oversee potential trading violations.

The NASD also had to go so far as to bar "the use of profane or obscene language" between its members, a rule that was announced in a July 1996 missive. The NASD was quick to explain that it was simply complying with a Federal Trade Commission rule against abusive language, but it felt to many that NASD's new role of baby-sitter was permanently in place.

Still other changes may ensure that the most effective police overseeing the Nasdaq dealers will be the customers who trade on Nasdaq. In 1996, the SEC came down with sweeping new trading rules designed to ensure that Nasdaq traders no longer have free reign over the prices set for Nasdaq stocks. The SEC required that when a dealer's customer is willing to buy or sell at a better price than a Nasdaq dealer is showing, that price has to be displayed in many cases. That deceptively simple change has roiled Nasdaq dealers, who have spent millions of dollars to make technological changes to accommodate the new orders on their systems, even as they saw their profits eroded as more and more of Nasdaq's prices were being set by nondealers.

Meanwhile, in a vivid testament to how quickly things change on Wall Street, some of the once-heralded structural changes that came out of the crackdown on NASD are already coming apart. Beginning in 1996, NASD began operating as a parent company overseeing two separate entities, one the Nasdaq market and the other a regulatory agency, each with its own executives, committees, and boards of directors that are at least 50 percent from outside the securities industry. When such a structure was created, it was deemed the best way to put daylight between the regulatory and market-development roles of NASD.

But a year and a half later, when former Smith Barney executive Frank G. Zarb became the new NASD president and chairman, he quickly determined that the new structure was unwieldy, with various committees and boards coming up with independent policy recommendations without much thought about how much they would cost or otherwise affect the other units. "I have been unhappy in certain instances with the time it has taken us to address certain policy issues and make crisp decisions," said Mr. Zarb. "I want to make sure issues that need to be raised are quickly addressed and we get all the data we need to make those decisions."

The head of the SEC, Arthur Levitt Jr., was supportive of streamlining the NASD system under his old friend Mr. Zarb, who swore the units would retain their independence. But the idea left some of the original architects of the change extremely wary. They feared that the NASD could be setting itself up for a renewal of the old days, when the sympathies of the few in charge at NASD outweighed most other voices for change.

Meanwhile, it is against that backdrop of such wholesale changes that the NASD and Nasdaq have been grappling with their perennial problems: companies defecting to the Big Board in disgust after seeing their daily stock prices swing up and down on Nasdaq; a long-running bull market enticing rogue firms to manipulate the prices of small stocks after luring in complacent investors; and enterprising Internet scam artists posing as enthusiastic stock investors in stock-talk forums, disappearing after making their quick profits.

In 1997, the market's regulators were also still trying to figure out whether to welcome or shun the growing ranks of individuals using SOES to make rapid-fire trades in many Nasdaq stocks for quick profit. These traders, known as SOES bandits, argued that they were legitimately making a living trading Nasdaq stocks and putting their own money at risk. But mainstream dealers, as well as many companies whose stocks were targeted by SOES traders, said such traders are merely opportunists who make the stock prices jump around so much that long-term investors steer clear of SOES-favored stocks.

The future looked to be very different from the past for the market that once dubbed itself "The Stock Market for the Next 100 Years."

Big Changes In Rules Set For Nasdaq

Investors Stand to Get Improved Stock Prices

SMALL STOCK FOCUS

BY DEBORAH LOHSE
Staff Reporter of THE WALL STREET JOURNAL

A week from today the **Nasdaq Stock Market** will be hit with sweeping new rules that are expected to drastically change the way prices are set for Nasdaq stocks, and, regulators hope, improve investors' access to the best prices for Nasdaq stocks.

Wall Street has been working night and day to make their trading systems ready to accommodate the complicated rules, which were designed to give greater prominence to investor "limit orders" to buy or sell stocks at specific prices. The changes, which start taking effect next Monday, will start with the 50 most-liquid Nasdaq stocks, including **Intel**, **Microsoft** and **Cisco Systems**. Smaller stocks will be phased in over several months.

The Securities and Exchange Commission pushed back the starting date to Monday from Jan. 10, a Friday, to give Wall Street the weekend to implement the vast programming changes required to comply with the rules.

The new rules, among the most sweeping changes in Nasdaq's 26-year history, are part of an overhaul in the market in the wake of last year's government settlements over allegedly unfair trading practices.

Nasdaq dealers say the following new rules will have a variety of impacts on the way Nasdaq stocks are traded. (While the rules technically apply to New York Stock Exchange and other exchange-listed stocks also, dealers on those markets already generally incorporate limit orders into their quoted prices.)

• **Dealers must show the investing public if they are holding customer limit orders of at least 100 shares, with a maximum of 10,000 shares or $200,000.**

This means if a customer shows up with an order to buy shares of a stock at $20\frac{1}{8}$, and the dealer had previously quoted a bid price of 20, the customer's limit order will be displayed on Nasdaq's computer workstations for other investors to see. The dealer can either change his own 20 bid to $20\frac{1}{8}$, or send the order to a private system such as Reuters Holdings' Instinet, where for the first time the price will show up on Nasdaq's workstation as an Instinet price.

Because customers will be able to advertise their willingness to buy or sell at prices that might be better than a Nasdaq dealer's price, the price "spreads" on Nasdaq stocks are expected to shrink. Spreads represent the difference between the prices at which dealers offer to buy and sell stocks—and have been profitable for Nasdaq firms.

"You will have hundreds and thousands of potential buyers and sellers competing for the orders through limit orders," predicts Paul Schultz, a professor at Ohio State University who co-authored an influential study that brought government and national attention to spreads on Nasdaq.

• **Dealers must show the public how many shares are available at their customer's limit price.**

If a customer is willing to buy 750 shares of a company at $20\frac{1}{8}$ at a time when market makers are quoting 20, the dealer who took the order must post the fact that his client wants 750 shares at $20\frac{1}{8}$. And if the dealer had been quoting that he would buy 500 shares at $20\frac{1}{8}$, then he must up the number to at least 750 shares.

While seeing precisely how many shares are behind a quote will be a new advantage for many investors, Nasdaq has proposed accompanying changes that, if approved by the SEC, could make it more difficult for the smallest investors to liquidate their holdings quickly in a sudden downdraft. Currently, market makers usually quote prices to buy or sell 1,000 shares, the minimum quote size required by Nasdaq for many stocks. Nasdaq has proposed decreasing that amount to 100 shares.

But some critics say that the 1,000 share minimum is an important reassurance for small investors that they can get an automatic execution of at least that many shares. Profs. Schultz and David Whitcomb, a finance professor at Rutgers University, say that some investors may find in times of market turmoil that if they have an order for more than 100 shares, they won't be able to get the price they want for more than 100 shares.

"If a serious market incident occurs," says Prof. Whitcomb, "then people will be angry as hell because they won't be able to get their trades done just like in 1987," when the market crashed and investors couldn't get their brokers on the phone.

But Nasdaq says there will be a number of options for small investors in such an event. They cite the Small Order Execution System, or SOES, an automatic-execution system that will execute trades of at least 100 shares automatically, as well as the newly publicized limit orders which they say will add liquidity.

• Dealers must show the investing public any better prices they are posting privately.

If a dealer posts on a private system like Instinet that it is willing to pay 10¹/₈ for a certain stock, but posts a price of just 10 on Nasdaq's public system, the dealer must let the investing public know about the 10¹/₈ bid. That can be done by changing the publicly quoted price to 10¹/₈, or having Instinet electronically transmit the 10¹/₈ price to the Nasdaq station, where it will show up as an Instinet quote.

While most people agree that giving investors access to the prices on such private systems is a tremendous boon to investors, some are chagrined that investors won't know precisely what prices they are getting. That's because such private systems often quote prices in increments of 1/16ths of a point or smaller, while on public quotation systems like Nasdaq's workstations, quotes are listed only in increments of ¹/₈.

The SEC's rules allow the Nasdaq quotes to be rounded to the nearest eighth, but require that the quotes have an asterisk attached to them, so that investors know that a better price is available on a private system. But Nasdaq has alerted the SEC that it won't be able to include the asterisk for several months, due to technological constraints. As a result, the SEC has given Nasdaq and others until around July to add the asterisk to rounded stock quotes.

• Investors must be able, for the first time, to have access to the best prices posted by market makers on private systems.

Nasdaq is planning to have investors use a modified version of its SelectNet system, which is now used by dealers to trade privately with one another, as a link to send orders to Instinet or other private systems. Previously, only customers of Instinet could tap those prices.

Nasdaq in 1994: Under Multiple Microscopes

There's little question in retrospect that Nasdaq insiders long knew the market's trading practices were biased against investors. In May of 1994 it became common knowledge among everyone else. That's when two finance professors, William Christie of Vanderbilt University and Paul Schultz of Ohio State University, published an academic study that charged that Nasdaq market makers implicitly agreed with one another to keep an overly wide profit cushion, known as the "spread," on Nasdaq stocks.

The study focused on a strange absence of prices quoted in "odd-eighths." Stocks are traded on U.S. exchanges in multiples of eighths of a point, or 12.5

cents, rather than in some more logical amount, such as tenths of a dollar, or dimes. Silly as it seems, eighths have been a time-honored part of stock trading. The absence of "odd eighths" merely means that the two professors noticed that Nasdaq dealers would routinely offer to sell stocks, even those that traded millions of shares a day, for a quarter-point—25 cents—more than they would pay for the shares when buying from investors or one another. The professors noted that logic would dictate that Nasdaq's most-liquid stocks, which change hands constantly throughout the day, should trade at the minimum 1/8-point, or 12.5 cent, spread. They reasoned that if market makers were indeed independently setting prices, investors would see smaller spreads a much greater percentage of the time. The two professors concluded that Nasdaq dealers "tacitly colluded" to keep spreads unnecessarily wide.

To a great extent, Nasdaq dealers themselves proved that the professors' observations were correct. Soon after the study came to the public's attention, spreads in many of Nasdaq's most-liquid stocks mysteriously narrowed to 12.5 cents. Critics noted, too, that NASD's chief operating officer, Richard Ketchum, convened a 1994 meeting at Bear Stearns offices in midtown Manhattan to urge major market makers to narrow their spreads. Mr. Ketchum characterized the meeting as one of many suggesting they reexamine why their spreads seemed to be overly wide in some stocks. But critics claimed "the Bear Stearns meeting" also coincided with even more decreased spreads.

Even under the intense heat generated by the academic study, NASD officials continued to downplay the issue. "The NASD's response . . . was to engage in public denials, to solicit support from issuers and market makers, and to undertake economic research to discredit what, by June 1994, it should have recognized to be well founded," the SEC later charged.

Fighting a delaying action, NASD began a preemptive effort to implement some changes that might defuse the situation. For guidance, NASD set up a blue-ribbon task force headed by former U.S. Senator Warren Rudman, who was joined by securities lawyer A. A. Sommer Jr.; former SEC regulator Jean W. Gleason; Merrill Lynch's general counsel Stephen L. Hammerman; Salomon Brothers' general counsel Robert H. Mundheim, and former SEC enforcement official Irving M. Pollack.

The Rudman report, released with much fanfare in September of 1995, recommended a long laundry-list of changes, many of which closely tracked what the SEC would later require in its disciplinary settlement. The report noted that NASD had not kept pace with the huge growth in the market, and that it had relied too heavily on the industry it was regulating to help it spot needed changes. The report urged NASD to separate its market-development and market-regulation roles into independent units and see to it that at least half of the units' board and committee members came from outside the securities industry.

But in 1994, the anti-Nasdaq ball was already rolling. Two months after the Christie-Schultz study came out, investors around the country filed a class-action lawsuit alleging price-fixing and seeking repayment of trading over-charges from more than thirty of Nasdaq's biggest trading firms. That lawsuit, which was granted class-action status in the fall of 1996, was settled in 1997 with all but one of the firms agreeing to settle for various sums totaling more than $1 billion—the largest civil anti-trust settlement ever, according to law-yers. None of the firms admitted wrongdoing. BancAmerica Robertson Ste-phens, the lone hold out, said it did nothing wrong.

The Christie-Schultz study also ignited an investigation in October 1994 by the Justice Department's antitrust division into whether there was collusion by traders to keep spreads wider than necessary and whether firms boycotted or refused to deal with traders or firms that tried to insert price quotes that would lower spreads. A month later, the SEC launched its own investigation into whether the self-regulator of Nasdaq, NASD, had failed to spot abuses and punish the offenders.

At the conclusion of those broad investigations in 1996, both the Justice Department and the SEC determined that dealers for at least twenty-four firms had for years settled into an overly cozy relationship with one another in which they set prices to their own advantage; withheld information about recent large transactions that should have been posted within ninety seconds for other in-vestors; and sometimes shared customer trading information that should have been kept confidential. What's more, they used bullying phone calls and other forms of peer pressure to harass those who would upset the arrangement.

"Nasdaq market makers have engaged in a variety of abusive practices to suppress competition and mislead customers," the SEC wrote in its report. Such anticompetitive behavior kept dealers' "spreads" profitably wide, costing their customers millions of dollars, regulators charged.

In 1996, regulators issued damaging reports and announced their sanctions for the dealers and NASD. In July 1996 the Justice Department's antitrust division announced that it had reached a landmark settlement with the twenty-four firms it had been investigating. The firms agreed to tape 3.5 percent of all their Nasdaq trading-desk calls, and permit regulators to make surprise visits and listen to the tapes at any time.

While clearly costly and burdensome to the firms involved, the Justice settlement was criticized as a slap on the wrist by many smaller firms and in-vestor advocates who felt victimized by the past behavior. And the firms them-selves privately felt vindicated that the Justice Department didn't have enough evidence to prove collusion—the original purpose of the investigation. Traders cited the fact that the settlement didn't call for fines or criminal penalties, nor did it require the firms to admit culpability, but rather let them settle without admitting to or denying the charges.

Nonetheless, the settlement seemed likely to prove costly to some of the nation's biggest securities firms, including Merrill Lynch & Co., the largest Wall Street firm; Dean Witter, Discover & Co.; the CS First Boston Inc. unit of CS Holding AG; Lehman Brothers Holdings Inc. and Alex. Brown Inc. None of these firms at that time taped conversations on its over-the-counter desks, though some firms did so before Justice Department lawyers started building their case on hundreds of hours of tapes of trader conversations.

The settlement was almost derailed in January 1997, when attorneys for investors who were separately suing many of the same traders challenged the settlement in court. They contested the insertion into the settlement of a provision that would prevent investors from using those tapes in future lawsuits against the firms, should they later be determined to have incriminating conversations on them. But a few months later, the judge approved the settlement.

The SEC, finalizing its disciplinary case against the NASD in August 1996, accused the organization of failing to investigate "clear indications of possible violations" by Nasdaq market makers, especially spread inflation. The NASD signed the settlement, like many of the firms it had sanctioned over the years, without admitting or denying wrongdoing. But the chastened organization agreed to pay $100 million to improve surveillance and enforcement on Nasdaq and to implement a series of other rules and remedies.

The purpose of the report, SEC Chairman Arthur Levitt Jr. said at the time, was to send a message to other self-regulatory organizations that the SEC expects them to live up to their enforcement responsibilities. "By exposing these events to public scrutiny we will call attention to the potential problems of self-regulation," Mr. Levitt said. The agency also wanted to air Nasdaq's defective "culture" that left investor protection a distant second to profits.

But even more than the punishment, it was the contents of a 157-page supplemental report on the SEC's investigation that became the talk of Wall Street. The so-called 21(a) report was full of transcripts of conversations among Nasdaq traders, both to one another and in sworn testimony, seemingly giving credence to critics' charges that market makers engaged in anticompetitive pricing practices.

The SEC report acknowledged that the NASD had already taken a number of steps the SEC wanted, to correct problems since the May 1994 Christie-Schultz study first accusing Nasdaq dealers of rigging stock prices. Among other improvements, NASD had already beefed up independent representation on NASD's governing boards and split off the enforcement operation into an independent unit called NASD Regulation Inc., headed by former Commodity Futures Trading Commission chairman Mary Schapiro, who was previously an SEC commissioner. A now-separate Nasdaq Stock Market was headed by former Alex. Brown managing director Alfred Berkeley.

Dealer Backlash

Of course, not everyone cheered the reorganization of the NASD. Many of the market-making firms decried the changes on the grounds that the Nasdaq was

SEC Report On Nasdaq Is Full Of Tough Talk

By Jeffrey Taylor
And Deborah Lohse
Staff Reporters of The Wall Street Journal

In a report laden with the rough talk of Nasdaq Stock Market traders, the Securities and Exchange Commission offered its long-awaited diagnosis of the market's ills and how to cure them.

And in one tape transcript unveiled in the report, two traders unwittingly predict what many traders now say will be the result of the SEC's investigation and the remedies it is forcing on the NASD.

"It's the end of your profits," one trader laments to another, explaining that publicity about wide Nasdaq trading spreads forced his firm to narrow them. "If you make 600 a month, you gonna make 400 a month."

In its disciplinary case against the National Association of Securities Dealers, operator and "self-regulator" of the Nasdaq market, the SEC accuses the NASD of failing to investigate "clear indications of possible violations" by Nasdaq market makers. In particular, the NASD didn't do enough to prevent dealers from enriching themselves with artificially wide spreads between their buying and selling prices, the SEC says.

The NASD settled the case without admitting or denying wrongdoing, agreeing to pay $100 million to improve surveillance and enforcement on Nasdaq and to undertake a series of other rules and remedies.

But it was the contents of a 157-page supplemental report on the SEC's investigation that had tongues wagging on Wall Street. The so-called 21(a) report is full of conversations among Nasdaq traders, both to one another and in sworn testimony. Narrowing profitable trading spreads, one veteran of the Nasdaq market told the SEC's lawyers, amounted to "cutting off your nose to spite your face."

Conversely, he explained, trading at wider spreads "allowed you to make up for a multitude of sins."

The purpose of the report, SEC Chairman Arthur Levitt said, is to send a message to other self-regulatory organizations that the SEC expects them to live up to their enforcement responsibilities. "By exposing these events to public scrutiny we will call attention to the potential problems of self-regulation," Mr. Levitt said. The agency also was seeking, he said, to expose defects in the "culture" of Nasdaq in the hope that it can be improved.

Nasdaq dealers counter that the report amounts to a sweeping revision of the SEC's own longstanding policy on their market and their self-regulator. In the past, they assert, the SEC seemed satisfied with the job the NASD was doing, with one official noting in an April 1994 letter that the NASD was reviewing complaints against dealers "expeditiously."

The SEC report does acknowledge that the NASD had taken a number of steps to correct problems since May 1994, when a highly critical academic study accused Nasdaq dealers of rigging stock prices in a system of "tacit collusion." Among other things, these steps included beefing up independent representation on NASD's governing boards and splitting off the enforcement operation into an independent unit called NASD Regulation Inc., headed by former SEC Commissioner Mary Schapiro.

Although she joined the NASD only eight months ago, Ms. Schapiro stepped forward to offer a response to the SEC's case. "We have put in place a tough, experienced, effective enforcement team," she said, "and our boards have committed the resources we need to have a state-of-the-art enforcement program."

The report doesn't identify the traders it quotes or say which Nasdaq firms they work for. The SEC and Ms. Schapiro's NASD unit believe that the tapes and other documents the SEC has gathered prove legal violations by some firms and dealers, and they plan to pursue joint disciplinary cases against them as a follow-up to yesterday's settlement, a person close to the matter said. William McLucas, the SEC's enforcement director, would say only that the investigation is continuing.

These cases, to be filed in coming months, are likely to accuse some Nasdaq firms of "backing away" from trades by refusing to honor their published stock quotes and failing to promptly report trading prices. The report has much to say about these kinds of alleged violations. It says, for instance, that "some market makers have displayed quotations at prices at which they did not intend to trade" to help other market makers and "refused to honor their firm quote obligations . . . as a means of punishing certain market participants."

It says the traders called narrow trading spreads a "Chinese market" and chided those who narrowed spreads by phoning them with phony orders for Chinese food in mock Chinese accents. In one of the many conversations it cites, the report quotes a Nasdaq trader patiently explaining to a retail stockbroker that he can't narrow a spread because it "creates what they call a Chinese market."

What Nasdaq Traders Were Caught Saying

Excerpts from the audio tapes, made by Nasdaq dealer firms, that were reviewed by the government.

COORDINATING QUOTATIONS

One trader holding a position in a stock in spring 1994, Parametric Technology, asked another to move up his bid (what he will pay for it) to $1/4$-point above the selling price.

Trader 1: Are you doing anything in Parametrics?
Trader 2: Running for the hills, bro.
1: Can you go $1/4$ bid for me?
2: Yeah, sure.
1: If you want, I'll sell you two [thousand] at $1/4$, just go up there. I'm 'long' them and I want it going.
2: Yeah.
1: OK, I sold you . . .
2: Two. That would be great.
1: I sold you two at $1/4$. Just go up there, OK?
2: I'm goosing it, cuz.
1: Thank you.

COMPLAINING ABOUT BETTER PRICES

This is traders talking after a Wall Street Journal article in summer 1994 about an academic study on trading spreads (which spurred the government investigation). One trader who had narrowed a spread on Cisco Systems talks about a third firm that tightened the spread in Microsoft:

Trader 1: Hi.
Trader 2: Hi, what's up?
1: Oh, tell me.
2: What, you mean with these spreads?
1. Yeah.

2. Well, (name of a dealer) started it with Microsoft, so . . .
1. Oh, that what happened?
2. Yeah, you know, did you see the Journal today? And all that——that's going on?
1. What? No. I'm sorry. It was all, it was kinda, it had to be done?
2. It doesn't have to be done. It's the end of the business. It's the end of your profits. If you make 600 a month, you gonna make 400 a month.
1. . . . I'm——sitting here with a knot in my stomach you can't imagine.

A MOCKING PHRASE

The SEC says traders use the term "Chinese market" to describe a stock that has only an $1/8$th-point (or 12.5 cents a share) difference between the buying and selling price. Such a tight spread can save money for investors but cost dealers profits. Here, a trader explains to a broker why he avoids $1/8$th-point quotes.

"I really can't do that, 'cause it creates what they call a Chinese market. Stock trades in $1/4$ point (25 cents). I'm on Instinet. If somebody wants to whack at $7/8$, that's where they're gonna whack me."

HARASSMENT

The SEC says that some Nasdaq dealers harassed other dealers who narrowed trading spreads. The SEC said these dealers who narrowed spreads would get calls "in which the caller, in a phony Chinese accent, ordered chop suey, moo goo gai pan, or other Chinese food in an apparent allusion to the understanding among market makers not to make Chinese markets."

The report notes that neither the SEC nor the Justice Department, in a related Nasdaq investigation found evidence of "an express agreement reached among all of the market makers" to rig stockprices. But it says that such a finding of criminal collusion isn't necessary to determine that the behavior of dealers "had anticompetitive consequences and was harmful to the interests of investors."

The report goes on to allege that Nasdaq dealers openly harassed one another to keep spreads wide. Mr. McLucas, in an interview, compared the behavior of Nasdaq dealers with the proverbial schoolyard bully. "You only have to beat up a couple of kids on the first day of school to get lunch money from all the kids for the rest of the semester," he said.

Despite the settlement, the deluge of negative publicity about Nasdaq and the prospect of additional disciplinary cases, some experts aren't confident that the traders' tough talk, or pressure to keep spreads wide, will stop. "You'll get rid of open brow beating, but I'm not sure there won't be some subtle brow beating," said Morris Mendelson, professor emeritus of the University of Pennsylvania's Wharton business school. As long as the big Nasdaq firms are able to identify which firm chooses to narrow spreads, Mr. Mendelson said, they can pressure the firm by withholding the flow of customer orders.

And some Nasdaq traders seem to agree that the report's long-term effect will be less than dramatic. "This is going to make headlines for about a week, but in my opinion, this industry works and it works well," says E.E. Geduld, president of Herzog Heine Geduld, one of the biggest Nasdaq dealers.

The traders said they are already gearing up for order-handling rule changes, as well as increased scrutiny using an improved "audit trail" of trades that is mandated under the SEC settlement. "A lot of the problems that are going to be brought out are already being addressed by NASD," said Jackson Bayer, managing director for OTC trading at Oppenheimer & Co.

NASD spokesman Douglas Parrillo said he didn't know precisely how the NASD would handle an added $20 million a year for five years, but noted "we have plenty of existing resources to deal with the additional expenses." NASD revenues have exceeded expenses in recent years, and the $100 million payout isn't expected to turn that black ink to red.

Nor did NASD Regulation's Ms. Schapiro expect the SEC revelations to force widespread personnel changes at the association. "I believe I have in place now a structure that minimizes the chances for having these kinds of problems arise again," she said. "If I discover that I don't, then I'll make whatever changes are necessary."

becoming more and more like an auction market—which many not-so-subtly attributed to the fact that SEC Chairman Arthur Levitt came from the American Stock Exchange, an auction market that lost its No. 2 status as Nasdaq rose to prominence in the 1980s.

Another pervasive criticism is that the organization is being run more as an SEC annex, rather than a self-regulatory organization that calls on those in the market to decide rules that work in the marketplace. Despite the fact that some would argue NASD's attempt at self-regulation had failed miserably, former NASD chief executive Joseph Hardiman, in a speech he gave during his last week as chief executive of NASD in 1997, complained about the trend of "micromanagement" by outside regulators. "I fear that self-regulation could become dominated by professional regulators," he said, rather than by industry professionals setting rules "that truly work in the real world."

The SEC Mandates Order Handling Rules

One of the biggest changes to hit the market in its twenty-seven-year history is the SEC's order-handling rules. SEC Chairman Arthur Levitt called these rules "among the most significant ever to be considered by the commission," and many investor advocates wholeheartedly agreed. These advocates believe that the rules will go a long way to eliminate the spread problem, because Nasdaq dealers won't be the only people setting the best prices for Nasdaq stocks anymore. And they say these rules will finally give investors who place limit orders for Nasdaq stocks a decent shot of getting those orders filled.

The rules were designed to create far more competition in the pricing of Nasdaq stocks, with small investors who wish to pay different prices than those quoted by Nasdaq dealers finally able to show their "limit" orders to other investors who might want to trade at that price, as well. The new rules have begun to drastically change the way prices are set for Nasdaq stocks, and, regulators hope, improve investors' access to the best prices for Nasdaq stocks.

The rules require four changes that work to the benefit of small investors:

1. Dealers must show the investing public if they are holding customer limit orders of at least 100 shares, with a maximum of just under 10,000 shares or $200,000.

This means if a customer shows up with an order to buy shares of a stock at 20$\frac{1}{8}$, and the dealer had previously quoted a bid price of 20, the customer's limit order must either be filled, or it must be displayed on Nasdaq's computer workstations for other investors to see.

Investors have long complained that when they placed a limit order with their broker, it languished in obscurity while other dealers traded the stock— sometimes even at prices that were worse than those at which the customer was willing to trade. Such unfairness was possible because the only dealer who was required to honor that limit order was the market maker who took the customer's order, not the many other market makers who might be trading that stock.

The SEC's new rules require market makers to put limit orders out in the open, increasing the chance that investors will find those prices more to their liking than what dealers had been offering. Many investor advocates expect that change alone to go a long way toward solving the problem of overly wide price spreads. Where a spread is too wide, customers for the first time will be able to advertise their willingness to buy or sell at better prices than a Nasdaq dealer's price. "You will have hundreds and thousands of potential buyers and sellers competing for the orders through limit orders," predicted Paul Schultz, the Ohio State University professor who coauthored the groundbreaking paper criticizing Nasdaq's trading practices.

2. Dealers must show the public how many shares are available at their customer's limit price.

If a customer is willing to buy 800 shares of a company at 20$\frac{1}{8}$ at a time when market makers are quoting 20, the dealer who took the order must post the fact that his client wants 800 shares at 20$\frac{1}{8}$. And if the dealer had been quoting that he would buy 500 shares at 20$\frac{1}{8}$, then he must increase the number to at least 800 shares.

3. Dealers must show the investing public any better prices they are posting privately.

Although the method of getting there is likely to evolve over time, investor advocates loudly applauded this change, which finally exposed the unfair practice of Nasdaq dealers who would post on a private trading system like Instinet that they are willing to pay 10$\frac{1}{8}$ for a certain stock—even if they were advertising to the average investor on Nasdaq's public system that they would only pay 10. Now, the dealer must let the investing public know about the 10$\frac{1}{8}$ bid.

4. Even better, if a dealer has a better quote on Instinet, investors must be able to trade at that price. That means that investors must be able, for the first time, to have access to the best prices posted by market makers on private systems like Instinet. Previously, only customers of Instinet could tap those prices.

NASD Regulation: Sheriff Schapiro

Mary Schapiro, the president of the newly created regulatory arm, NASD Regulation, hit the ground running after taking office in February 1996, by most accounts. In its first year, NASD Regulation made headlines by finally shutting down the small-stock brokerage firm Stratton Oakmont Inc., which had a seven-year history of disciplinary actions for allegedly bilking investors out of millions of dollars. Ms. Schapiro's unit also worked with criminal authorities to catch fifty-three brokers who were charged with paying impostors to take their broker-licensing examinations.

NASD Regulation quickly got a sense of how much needed changing when a tiny fingerprint-identification company called Comparator Systems began, out of the blue, trading in record-setting volume of more than 150 million shares a day. From pennies a share, its stock price zoomed to nearly $2 over only a few days, as the once-obscure company's stock continued to set records for volume.

Such inexplicable activity in small stocks, Ms. Schapiro knew, frequently indicates manipulation or other improper trading activity on the part of the stock's traders or insiders. But when she went in search of quick answers, she found some of her new colleagues who had been in charge of regulation before she arrived were unresponsive, suggesting time-consuming solutions like an old-style formal investigation.

Instead, Ms. Schapiro got on the phone to find a private investigator to search out Comparator Systems' claims that it had a cutting-edge technology, which was being cited as the reason for the stock's rapid rise. Finding reason to doubt the company's claims, Ms. Schapiro halted trading in the stock within four days—an almost unheard of speed at NASD.

A month later, Comparator Systems' stock had been delisted from Nasdaq after its executives failed to show that its assets were legitimate. The SEC later settled a lawsuit alleging fraud by Comparator executives by getting two of the executives to agree to step down and never run publicly traded companies again.

But the transition hasn't been seamless. The new world under Ms. Schapiro became vividly clear once the SEC's much-anticipated criticisms were published. By then, Ms. Schapiro had been the top cop at NASD for about eight months. Once the controversial SEC report was issued, NASD's president Joseph Hardiman, disgusted with the tone of the SEC's report, issued an edict that the NASD would not comment on the SEC settlement. But Ms. Schapiro, asserting the yet-untested independence of her department, stepped forward to issue a forward-looking response to the SEC's case. "We have put in place a tough, experienced, effective enforcement team," she said, "and our boards have committed the resources we need to have a state-of-the-art enforcement program."

Once the SEC's report was issued, Ms. Schapiro also took a tack clearly divergent from the let's-work-it-out-quietly approach of the old NASD hierarchy. She talked of plans with the SEC to pursue joint disciplinary cases against firms and traders who engaged in violations of the rules and were caught on the tapes. Ms. Schapiro and the SEC indicated they were planning to bring cases against some of the Nasdaq firms for "backing away" from trades by refusing to honor their published stock quotes and failing to promptly report trading prices. The SEC report didn't identify the traders it quoted or say which Nasdaq firms they worked for. But in late 1997, the SEC was preparing civil charges against dozens of traders, people familiar with the SEC told the *Journal*.

The effectiveness of the new regulatory crew that hailed from the SEC became apparent when, in 1996, a little-known brokerage firm by the name of Sterling Foster & Co. was charged by the NASD with illegally making some $51 million by rigging the pricing and sale of three small-stock initial public offerings. The swift action that led to the shuttering of Sterling Foster was in stark contrast with NASD's handling of another allegedly abusive small-stock house, Stratton Oakmont, which took years of local action before the national office, under Mary Schapiro, was finally able to shut Stratton's doors. With Sterling Foster, abuses that allegedly took place in 1995 were included in charges that, while handled in part by local NASD district offices, were orchestrated heavily by the national office and resulted in charges only a year later.

What's more, NASD's actions were backed up by other regulators and authorities, a switch in the NASD's isolationist attitude that had prevailed in previous small-stock cases. In early 1997, the FBI raided Sterling Foster's offices,

Expensive Lesson

Inside a Dubious IPO: Sponsor, It Appears, Held All the Cards

Investors Lost Millions Buying Stock That NASD Says Underwriter Had Rigged

Stuck With Wooden Tickets

By Michael Siconolfi and Deborah Lohse
Staff Reporters of The Wall Street Journal

MELVILLE, N.Y.—When a lawyer for Sterling Foster & Co. proposed that the brokerage firm help bring Advanced Voice Technologies Inc. stock to market, he promised the New York computerized-voice company more than idle talk.

"I work with several underwriters," Alan Novich, the lawyer, wrote in a June 1994 letter to Advanced Voice's then-chairman, James Sparks. "All can get the job done. . . . All are in good standing with the world-at-large."

Not anymore. Last month, the staff of the National Association of Securities Dealers accused Sterling Foster, a one-office firm based here, and 15 of its officials and brokers of making $51 million in illicit profit in just nine months from three rigged underwritings, including $15 million on the Advanced Voice deal. Regulators say the group used manipulative trading and high-pressure sales tactics, including writing up "wooden tickets"—broker parlance for unauthorized trades. It is the largest disciplinary case alleging stock manipulation ever brought by the NASD. A three-member committee of the NASD will weigh the merits of the complaint: any decision could be appealed to the Securities and Exchange Commission and ultimately to a federal court.

Charges Denied

Sterling Foster, President Adam Lieberman and the firm's brokers named in the NASD complaint deny the charges. Advanced Voice denies wrongdoing, and Mr. Novich declines to comment. Neither Advanced Voice nor Mr. Novich was named a respondent in the complaint: the NASD can discipline only its own members. (Mr. Sparks no longer works at Advanced Voice and had no involvement with Sterling Foster or the IPO.)

The case is part of a broader NASD crackdown against brokerage firms that improperly sell small stocks. In just two stock-manipulation cases made public last month, against Sterling Foster and Stratton Oakmont Inc., the NASD alleges that small investors were bilked out of a total of $81 million. (Stratton Oakmont, of Lake Success, N.Y., also denies the charges.)

The two cases are believed to involve more lost money than the NASD has ever alleged in an entire year. It says it now is investigating a dozen similar cases. Regulators link the surge in cases to the bull market, which is making stock manipulation the white-collar crime of choice.

"It's possible in part because of investors' expectations that the market would go up," says Barry Goldsmith, executive vice president of the NASD's enforcement division. Adds Roger Sherman, the NASD's enforcement director: "I can't think of another case where we have alleged so much money has been made over such a short period of time."

Why Little Guys Lose

Beyond its size, the allegation against Sterling Foster illustrates how initial public offerings can be manipulated, usually at the expense of small investors. Although much has been written about stock manipulation—witness the Federal Bureau of Investigation's recent sting involving alleged bribes to brokers by small-stock promoters—few details about Sterling Foster have emerged before. Here is that case, based on an examination of public filings and the NASD complaint, along with interviews with regulators, Sterling Foster investors and brokerage-industry executives.

Prospects for companies whose stocks Sterling Foster underwrote were sketchy.

Advanced Voice's only product is the Homework Hotline, a voice-mail system helping teachers and school officials communicate with parents and students.

The offering's tell-all document, the prospectus—which the NASD says many Sterling Foster clients never received—disclosed that Advanced Voice had a history of operating losses, that it was "delinquent on a significant number of accounts payable" and that several suppliers would deal with the company only on a c.o.d. basis. An independent auditor's report even said the losses raised "substantial doubt about the company's ability to continue as a going concern."

Nestled in a drab tan building next to a vegetable stand on Long Island, Sterling Foster resembles anything but a bustling brokerage firm, despite an NASD membership plaque on the wall. Only the parking lot suggests affluence: The firm's reserved spots are filled with Mercedes-Benz convertibles and BMWs.

But according to the NASD, a client says Sterling Foster broker Brian Kearney, when asked about Advanced Voice's business, told him: "It doesn't matter what the company does. The company could be selling horse manure." What counts, the NASD says Mr. Kearney added, is that the stock would quickly soar as much as 40%. Jerry Selvers, who represents Mr. Kearney and the other brokers, says Mr. Kearney did nothing improper, though he says none of the brokers he represents will comment on specific allegations.

Sterling Foster picked a good time to sell a company's shares to the public for the first time. Initial public offerings are coming out at a record pace. Typically, brokerage firms court a fledgling company to win an underwriting assignment and line up investors for a portion—typically less than half—of the IPO shares. (Other underwriters line up investors for the rest of the IPO shares.) Then the brokerage firm sets a price for the shares—and, in theory, steps back and lets supply and demand take over as the new shares trade in the so-called aftermarket.

That isn't what happened in three IPOs underwritten by Sterling Foster, the NASD says. Instead, the firm first placed a whopping 74% of each of these new issues with its customers. Then, it

relied on a ring of what the NASD terms "affiliated" investors to take advantage of its clients, the NASD says. This was done, it adds, through stock-manipulation maneuvers that allowed Sterling Foster to control trading, artificially inflate prices—and enrich both itself and the affiliated investors. The affiliated investors deny wrongdoing.

The Initial Public Offering

In August 1994, Sterling Foster won the job of heading the group of underwriters handling the Advance Voice IPO. The offering was for 1,150,000 units, each consisting of one common share and one warrant (a tradable security that later could be used to buy stock). In addition, the affiliated investors—some Advanced Voice founders, some outside consultants and others—already owned about 1.5 million shares. So, about 2,650,000 shares would be outstanding after the offering.

Of that total, the NASD says, 57% would thus be held by the affiliated investors—including Mr. Novich, who owned or controlled nearly one-third of the group's 1.5 million shares, and Hartley Bernstein, a well-known lawyer who represents small investors in arbitration cases against brokerage firms. The 1,150,000 shares set for public sale would amount to a 43% stake.

The prospectus contained a significant, though not unusual, "lockup agreement": Affiliated investors couldn't sell their shares for 13 to 24 months unless they sold them at Sterling Foster's discretion.

By the time Advanced Voice filed a registration statement with the SEC for an IPO in November 1994, Sterling Foster had a hammerlock on the deal, controlling the bulk of the shares in the underwriting. This is a necessary element in stock manipulation, regulators say. In addition to effective control over sales of the affiliated group's shares, Sterling Foster got an allocation of about 850,000, or 74%, of the 1,150,000 IPO stock-and-warrant units to sell to its clients. The bottom line for the firm: Immediately after the IPO, about 2,350,000—or 89%—of the 2,650,000 shares outstanding would be in friendly hands.

At this point, Sterling Foster normally would call customers and sell them its allocation of about 850,000 units at $5.50 a unit—the IPO price. The firm did place these shares but, the NASD says, in many cases with favored customers or with people who agreed to "tie-ins"—who promised to buy additional shares after trading began in the aftermarket. Such a tie-in deal violates federal securities law.

Sterling Foster then went further, the NASD says. The firm's brokers, often through cajoling or browbeating, got less-fortunate clients to agree, before trading started, to buy more than two million Advanced Voice shares once trading did begin, the NASD says. Thus, Sterling Foster lined up buyers for more than twice the number of shares it had for sale.

Moreover, the NASD says the brokers gave some of their clients the impression that they would be buying the stock at or very near the initial $5.50 offering price. In reality, they were being committed to pay the far-higher aftermarket price. (When some clients later questioned their brokers, they say they were told their orders were filled on the "first tick" of aftermarket trading.) The brokers had a huge incentive to line up sales. The NASD says Sterling Foster gave them $1.75 for each Advanced Voice share their customers committed to buying in the aftermarket—an outsized 14% commission.

Two hours before the market opened on Tuesday, Feb. 7, 1995, the firm further solidified its control over the issue. It bought back about 200,000 IPO units, or two-thirds of those allocated to other underwriters, the NASD says. It then controlled 91% of the 1,150,000 IPO units, or 96% of all the shares to be outstanding after the IPO. This control helped assure that once trading began, any quick sales by Sterling Foster investors would be unlikely to push down the price; in many cases, the NASD says, the firm wouldn't let clients sell their shares immediately.

The stage was set for trading to pop.

The Aftermarket Trading

Trading in the stock and warrants began around noon, Feb. 7, on the Nasdaq SmallCap Market. Amid heavy demand, the shares opened at an offer price of $11 a share. Within two minutes, the offer price rose to $13; in eight minutes, to $14.

Sterling Foster had kicked into high gear. Between noon and 12:10 p.m., the firm wrote 958 order tickets for small-investor clients whom its busy brokers had lined up before the IPO. The torrent of orders was for some 2.4 million shares, even though only 1,050,000 shares had been allocated to the firm at that time. The orders were filled at $12.25 to $12.75 a share, the NASD says. By day's end, Advanced Voice closed at an offer price of $13.50 a share.

At that point, Sterling Foster had sold 2.1 million more Advanced Voice shares than were then publicly available; the shares owned by the affiliated investors were still locked up. Normally, Sterling Foster would have been in a vulnerable position because it would have had to fill those orders by buying the shares somewhere. Indeed, if Sterling Foster had to buy those shares at $13.50 a share, it would have had to shell out some $28.6 million—more than 10 times its $2.7 million net capital, regulators say.

The Alleged Payoff

In fact, the NASD says, Sterling Foster never faced that risk. That's because it had a prearranged strategy to fill those orders that didn't require it to pay the market price, the NASD alleges. In the days after trading began, Sterling Foster bought back all 1.5 million shares owned by the affiliated-investor group at a steep discount from the prevailing market price of about $13—paying only $2 a share.

The affiliated investors, in many cases, had paid only pennies a share for their stock. Given the choice of risking a wait of as long as two years to cash in or getting a quick $2 a share, they chose to sell. In purchasing those shares from the affiliated investors, Sterling Foster violated NASD rules, regulators say, by buying the shares at a discount and reselling them without notifying the NASD. And the NASD says it never would have approved the transactions.

Meantime, the share price stayed in the $13.50 range for nearly three weeks after the IPO. After Sterling Foster had completed its selling frenzy and nailed down its profits, the NASD says, Advanced Voice fell below $9 a share as buying demand dried up. Yesterday, Advanced Voice closed at $3.875 a share, down 12¹/₂ cents on the day.

The affiliated investors deny wrongdoing. In an interview, Mr. Bernstein says that his investments were small and that the shares he received stemmed from loans he had made to Advanced Voice and other Sterling Foster underwriting clients. "I have no knowledge of any kind of prearrangement, and I was not a party to any kind of prearrangement," he says. He declines to disclose how much money he made on the transactions.

The investors affiliated with Sterling Foster included little-known companies, some controlled either by Mr. Novich or by family members of Advanced Voice founders. Among them were Marketlink Group Ltd., owned by Carole Landau, and Sherbrooke Consulting Inc., owned by Nancy Shalek; both women held founders' stock in Advanced Voice. Ms. Shalek is currently chairman of both Advanced Voice and Com/Tech Communication Technologies Inc., another IPO that the NASD says Sterling Foster manipulated.

James Adelman, a lawyer for Advanced Voice and the Landau and Shalek families, denies any prearranged plan for his clients to sell their stock, which he says they owned as founders' shares. He says Sterling Foster called his clients about a week after the IPO began trading and offered to free them from the lockup agreement if they sold at $2 a share. "Neither my clients nor the companies were involved in any manipulation," he says.

However, several investors affiliated with the Advanced Voice transaction—including Mr. Bernstein, Ms. Shalek and Ms. Landau or their companies—also were involved in at least one other underwriting manipulated by Sterling Foster, the NASD says.

Mr. Novich, who had no comment, seemed to have gotten an especially sweet deal. Sterling Foster paid Bigelow Ventures Inc., a firm he controlled, $450,000 for unspecified "additional consideration and services rendered." That was in addition to $990,000 he got from selling his 495,000 Advanced Voice shares to Sterling Foster.

The NASD says the firm's preferred clients (separate from the affiliated-investor group) didn't fare badly, either. Sterling Foster's Mr. Lieberman personally sold IPO units to 35 clients at $5.50 each, 33 of whom "flipped"—immediately sold back—the units to Sterling Foster in the first five minutes of trading, the NASD says. The price: $12.875 a unit, a 134% profit. Mr. Lieberman apparently did this to please favored clients, regulators say.

The Sales Tactics

Many of Sterling Foster's 175 brokers are inexperienced on Wall Street but are aggressive sellers, regulators say. Regulatory records show some of its brokers had previously sold BMW cars, Calvin Klein cosmetics and Ikea furniture. They seemed to focus their efforts to sell stock on small-business owners, regulators say.

Ronald Ackerman recalls days when one Sterling Foster broker, Robert Paulson, phoned him at home at 6:30 a.m., then several times during the day at his office. "Now's the time to grab some more" Advanced Voice stock, he says Mr. Paulson insisted. Mr. Ackerman, who owns a Boise, Idaho, printing business, says he lost some $50,000 of the $70,000 he invested at Sterling Foster. Mr. Paulson, who was cited in the NASD complaint, denies wrongdoing through his lawyer, Mr. Selvers.

The NASD complaint against Sterling Foster—which alleges specific sales abuses inflicted on 57 clients—coupled with this newspaper's interviews with these and other customers, suggests that some of the salespeople used the following tactics:

The Bait: Many clients say they were lured into trusting their brokers because their first trades were household-name stocks that fared well. In stock-manipulation cases, regulators say, winning investors' confidence with such "opener" stocks is common. For many investors, the opener stocks were their only profitable Sterling Foster ventures.

Terry Balzer, a former Eagle Snacks distributor in Wakeman, Ohio, says Sterling Foster broker Greg Hudgins told him his first foray with the firm, a purchase of Coach USA Inc. stock, will "show you I'm trustworthy." About two weeks later, after shares of the Houston provider of motor-coach tour and sight-seeing services rose, Mr. Hudgins persuaded Mr. Balzer to buy 5,000 shares of Com/Tech Communication; the $35,000 investment is currently worth less than $7,000. Mr. Hudgins, who wasn't named in the NASD complaint, didn't return phone calls.

The Hard Sell: Some clients say their brokers refused to take no for an answer. When Allen Lang told Mr. Kearney, his broker, he wanted to mull over an investment in Advanced Voice, he says the broker demanded an immediate answer, saying: "Nobody ever calls me back when they say they are going to think about it." Mr. Lang, a Chinese immigrant who runs a greenhouse in the Tampa, Fla., area, says, "I'm not the kind of person who will slam the phone down or cut people off—I wasn't brought up that way."

Mr. Lang lost $10,000, leaving him with about $10,000 for his and his wife's retirement and for college expenses of his 15-year-old daughter. Now, he says, he readily hangs up on cold-callers. "That's a $10,000 lesson," he laments. "Hanging up the phone is a lot cheaper."

Unauthorized Trades: Gregory Lambert says broker William Scuteri pressed him to buy shares of another Sterling Foster IPO, Lasergate Systems Inc. Even after refusing to bite, Mr. Lambert says he received a FedEx saying he had purchased about $50,000 of Lasergate shares. An irate Mr. Lambert says he called Mr. Scuteri to complain; he says Mr. Scuteri canceled the trade. Adds Mr. Lambert: "He thought I would come forward with the cash." Mr. Scuteri denies wrongdoing through his lawyer, Mr. Selvers.

Nevertheless, Mr. Lambert, the chief financial officer for a children's-apparel maker in Grand Rapids, Mich., says he lost about $25,000 after buying Advanced Voice from Mr. Scuteri. "You would think a CFO would know better," he says. "It's a little embarrassing to get caught like this."

No Prospectus: Many investors say they never received a prospectus, even after asking for one. Edward Stumm, president of a Zelienople, Pa., lighting company—and a former broker—kicks himself for not demanding more information on Advanced Voice. Despite steep losses, he says he hasn't cashed out of his Advanced Voice position "to remind me what an idiot I was." His broker, Diana Shtainer, denies wrongdoing through Mr. Selvers.

Improper Predictions: Some brokers predicted big, quick profits. Sterling Foster broker Michael Cohn told Thomas Nemic Jr. that Advanced Voice shares would soar to $20 within six months, Mr. Nemic says. "I don't care if they make screen doors for submarines; we're going to make money," he says Mr. Cohn told him. Mr. Cohn did nothing wrong, Mr. Selvers says.

No Commissions: The NASD says many Sterling Foster brokers wrongly told clients they weren't making any commissions. When Mr. Ackerman's broker, Mr. Paulson, said he was forgoing his commission on Advanced Voice, he says he told him: "Give me a break—you're doing this out of the goodness of your heart?" Mr. Ackerman nevertheless bought about $45,000 of the stock.

Can't Get Out: Some clients say their brokers simply refused to execute sell orders. When he pressed, Mr. Lambert says, Mr. Scuteri told him, "You can't sell—the market's not right." He says Mr. Scuteri blamed the weakness in Advanced Voice shares on investors who mistakenly were confusing Sterling Foster with an ailing firm, Hanover Sterling & Co. (Regulators ordered Hanover Sterling to cease operations in February 1995 because of inadequate capital.) Mr. Scuteri denies wrongdoing through Mr. Selvers.

Just as the brokers had an incentive to sell Advanced Voice shares, they had a strong incentive to keep clients in the stock once trading began. If clients sold their shares, brokers would get just 10 cents or less per share on the transaction—and perhaps lose the $1.75-a-share commission they had earned for selling the stock. The whole arrangement is unusual: Typically, brokers keep only one-third to one-half of the 1% to 1.5% commission on either purchases or sales of stock.

Lawyer's Response

To Mr. Selvers, the charges against the Sterling Foster brokers were "instigated by the NASD in their overzealous efforts to bring a far-reaching case."

However, the NASD isn't the first regulator to set its sights on Sterling Foster. The SEC is investigating whether the firm manipulated the underwriting and trading of Lasergate, people familiar with the matter say. The SEC, as is its custom, declines to comment. The Lasergate IPO wasn't cited in the NASD complaint.

At the NASD's market-surveillance center in Rockville, Md., the Sterling Foster case and the pending investigations have put regulators in high gear. And they have a new weapon: a $4.5 million computer system called Radar, which enables them to instantly punch up which dealers traded what, when and how much.

And when regulators wanted to discover the names and status of investors in the IPOs, they sent out inquiry forms, known as "Blue Sheets," to all trade-processing firms involved in the stocks—and compiled and analyzed the responses electronically. This enabled the NASD to interview dozens of Sterling Foster clients and quickly cobble together its case.

Inside the NASD, the Sterling Foster case is being hailed as a triumph. A memorandum tacked up on a wall in the enforcement division's coffee area praises, among others, Jeffrey Stith, an NASD lawyer who handled the Sterling Foster and some other recent fraud cases. The Sterling Foster matter is "evidence of our commitment . . . to ridding the industry of those who defraud the public," according to the memo, signed by John Pinto, an NASD executive vice president.

So far, that commitment hasn't done much for some Sterling Foster clients. Following the NASD action, shares of Advanced Voice, Com/Tech Communications and Embryo Development Corp., the third IPO cited in the complaint, have been hammered. All three plunged from their highs days after their IPOs.

Meanwhile, some investors say they have pulled back from the stock market. Not only did Mr. Stumm lose money on Advanced Voice: he says he was so traumatized he put his other cash in a "nickel-and-dime savings account" getting "chump-change interest rates." He says he missed "one of the greatest bull markets of all time."

November 5, 1996

followed by an SEC lawsuit alleging $75 million in illegal gains from small-stock IPOs, charges the firm denied. While the cases were still pending as 1997 closed, Sterling Foster was no longer doing business.

Ms. Schapiro inherited some snags, as well. In August 1996 and again in February 1997 state regulators complained that NASD Regulation had made a unilateral decision to delete certain data from broker disciplinary files that are jointly maintained by NASD and the states. Seems that in 1995 someone at NASD had set up guidelines that instructed NASD Regulation employees responsible for entering data into the Central Registration Depository—a computerized database of broker disciplinary and employment histories—to delete references to arbitration filings or other complaints that had been withdrawn by investors, arbitration panels, or courts. It was a protocol not approved by states, which tend to give out much more information to investors than NASD ever did. After a brief bout of publicity, Ms. Schapiro's embarrassed unit reinstated the deleted data over two grueling days of work.

NASD Regulation also had to put on hold an ambitious plan dating from 1992 to spend $30 million to overhaul the technology that houses the sixteen-year-old CRD database. After securities firms tested a pilot version of the new CRD software, they criticized the technology as still too outdated. After spending millions already on the software, NASD Regulation put a halt to the program and decided to investigate whether more state-of-the-art technology is needed.

NASD Regulation is struggling to install a multimillion-dollar electronic order-audit trail, which would track every Nasdaq order from the time it arrives at the dealer's desk. This complex and expensive system will ultimately help Nasdaq track such trading violations as backing away or refusing to trade with other traders or customers, although it is not expected to be completed until mid-1998 at the earliest.

The Internet: Regulation's Next Frontier

Ms. Schapiro also has had to grapple with a whole new universe of problems: fraud and stock-touting on the Internet. Investigating events that led up to the wild trading ride of Comparator Systems, Ms. Schapiro and her newly reorganized staff realized that part of the push behind the company came from enthusiastic chatter on Internet bulletin boards. In many of the sites, she noticed, participants in the chatter could use pseudonyms that hid their true identities. A seemingly innocent investor looking to impart information about a new stock find, she realized, could in fact be a promoter, broker or other insider looking to boost interest in a stock so they could reap the profit. And without a subpoena, Ms. Schapiro would have no way to track the identity of some of these crooks.

NASD Regulation staff had to tackle the Internet issue even as staffers freely admitted they didn't precisely know the parameters of the problem they were facing. Ms. Schapiro and her staff homed in on roughly six small stocks that her staff noticed had been the object of much boosting chatter online. Within months, several of those stocks were delisted or had other regulatory actions against them. And the NASD enlisted other agencies as well, resulting in lawsuits against companies like teleconferencing company Systems of Excellence, one of the Internet-touted stocks that was sued by the SEC over allegedly fraudulent claims.

Now, finding out what is happening on the Internet is an integral part of the staff's surveillance activity. NASD Regulation developed a constantly running search engine that reaches out into the Internet and finds mention of stocks that could potentially be the target of manipulators. Looking to the Internet is now also a regular part of the market-surveillance staff's duties. These days, when a stock's trading activity is flagged by surveillance teams as behaving abnormally, surveillance employees log on to the Internet to see what's being said there about the company in question, in addition to searching for news on the company and other efforts to explain the stock's behavior.

SOES on the Ropes

Since the late 1980s, no serious discussion of Nasdaq would be complete without mentioning SOES bandits, the name tacked onto professional day traders who are the biggest users of Nasdaq's Small Order Execution System. These day traders use SOES's unique automatic button to make rapid-fire trades for quick profits in fast-moving stocks. Nasdaq traders see them as profit-leeching gnats, who abuse a system that was supposed to help small investors get trades executed in times of market turmoil. (SOES became a mandatory system for executing up to 1,000 shares of Nasdaq National Market stocks after the 1987 crash, when many investors couldn't get their brokers on the phone to sell tanking shares.)

SOES bandits, naturally, see things quite differently. They say they are legitimately using a system and are putting their own money at risk like any market participant. And they point out, not without reason, that they helped uncover Nasdaq traders' abuses. After all, they experienced problems like refusals to trade, backing away from price quotes and harassment firsthand as unwelcome participants in the Nasdaq trading system, even inviting the Justice Department into their firms to witness such abuses firsthand.

Many market observers say that one reason Nasdaq companies are fleeing to the Big Board is SOES traders, who are blamed for forcing prices up or down to degrees they wouldn't normally swing under normal supply-and-demand conditions. Others argue that by eroding the profits of market makers, SOES traders have caused market makers to stop trading some smaller stocks where they could no longer make a profit. That, they claim, dries up market liquidity for other investors.

Regardless of whether SOES bandits are good or bad for Nasdaq, the landscape is potentially changing drastically for them, thanks to the SEC's order-handling rules. Because the new rules allow additional layers of price quotes from investors to absorb orders, SOES traders have fewer multi-point moves to ride, and less predictability in the market.

SOES traders also hotly complained about a test program Nasdaq hopes to make permanent that lets market makers trade only 100 shares of some stocks at a time with SOES traders, rather than 1,000. The difference is vast: A quarter-point profit on 1,000 shares is $250; on 100 shares it's only $25. And the pilot program includes the top-ten-traded stocks like Microsoft, Intel and Cisco Systems.

Listings: Who Goes, Who Stays

An increasing number of Nasdaq companies have opted to defect from the market, even as it has become a much more visible and liquid market. The companies that leave are often the midsized companies, in the range of $3 billion to $4 billion in market capitalization or less.

These companies say they are leaving largely because the growing volatility in the share prices on Nasdaq affects them to a much greater degree than it affects Nasdaq's giants, like Microsoft and Intel. While Microsoft and Intel might have 2- to 4-point swings in price in a single day—just like shares of the midsized companies—such moves represented a far smaller percentage of a $120 stock than a stock trading in the $25–$40 range.

Why the fluctuations in the first place on Nasdaq more than on the Big Board? Although the facts are in hot dispute, most firms that leave blame, at least partly, costly spreads and SOES day traders for the volatility. They say that as market makers are forced to cede more and more of their profits to such day traders, they decide to stop trading some stocks, decreasing liquidity and, some believe, adding even further to the volatility.

In recent years, Nasdaq has lost some big-name companies like St. Jude Medical; America Online; and Iomega. Experts say Nasdaq is the least appealing to such midsized companies because a $1/8$-point spread is an inordinate share of their price. And such companies don't have the volume to absorb volatility, but they were high-profile enough to attract SOES bandits to trade their shares.

Nasdaq has historically been considered the best market for small, upstart companies that don't trade millions of shares every day. Part of the appeal is practical: Nasdaq, especially its lower-tier SmallCap Market, has far lower listing standards than the rival New York Stock Exchange. Until Nasdaq beefed up its listing standards in 1997, companies needed a relatively small $4 million in assets, $2 million in capital and surplus and 100,000 shares of publicly available shares valued $1 million or more to list on the lower-tier market. The company must be traded by at least two market makers and have a bid price of $3 or more initially and three hundred shareholders. To stay listed on the SmallCap Market, the company has to maintain total assets of $2 million, capital and surplus of $1 million, and market value of at least $200,000 of public float. The bid price can drop to $1 or less, provided the company has $2 million in capital and $1 million in market value of public float.

The ability of ultrasmall companies to find a ready home came into question somewhat when Nasdaq decided to beef up its listing standards in the wake of some high-profile blowups like Comparator Systems, accused by regulators of inflating their financial status to stay listed on Nasdaq. These criteria will get tougher for companies starting in the spring of 1998, however, with many of the financial standards increasing by at least 50 percent and companies being delisted if they drop below the $1 bid price limit. Moreover, companies on the Nasdaq Small-Cap Market have to comply with corporate governance standards that formerly applied only to larger companies on the Nasdaq National Market, including having at least two independent directors, an audit committee and annual shareholder meetings. The Big Board is generally more expensive to list and has stricter profitability requirements.

The impact of the new listing standards on Nasdaq's smallest companies was not immediately apparent. Nasdaq officials said that had the proposed listing standards been in effect between June 1994 and June 1996, more than half of the successful applicants on the SmallCap Market wouldn't have been approved. And more than 10 percent of the successful applications to the Nasdaq National Market would have been denied, they added. But as 1997 ended, many companies had undergone "reverse stock splits" and other tactics to put them in compliance with the new standards by February 23, 1998, when the new standards took full effect.

Nasdaq emphasized that the new listing standards, which hadn't been updated since at least 1991, were necessary to tackle fraud. Alfred Berkeley, Nasdaq's president, cited the new requirement that shareholders approve any stock issuances that would dilute market value by more than 20 percent as a key to preventing companies from flooding the market with stock unbeknownst to public shareholders.

Yet another appeal of Nasdaq for many companies, especially smaller, lesser-known companies, is the dealer market system itself. Nasdaq's market-making firms find that it is worth their while to lend their capital, customers, and research to such shares—knowing that the higher profile they can make such shares, the higher their potential profits from commissions or the trading spread. Many Nasdaq trading firms are also active underwriters, and they bring companies public, trade them on Nasdaq and provide support for them in the form of research and a team of brokers and sales men and women to introduce the stock to potential buyers from among the firm's clients.

Still, in their heart of hearts, Nasdaq officials would have to admit that their crown jewels are the giants, especially top ten companies like Intel, Microsoft, Oracle and Dell Computer, which could easily meet the NYSE's tougher listing standards, but elect to stay on Nasdaq anyway. These firms say they see no difference between the markets; they are highly liquid, trade with $1/8$ spreads or lower, and they have high visibility with investors. And Nasdaq market-making firms are frequently still doing follow-on stock offerings, acquisitions, and other financial services for the firms, so leaving them for the Big Board might rain on the relationship, these firms say.

Icing the cake, too, is the fact that many of these Nasdaq behemoths have corporate relationships with Nasdaq itself. Nasdaq is consulting with many of its technology companies, for instance, to upgrade its outmoded CRD. And Nasdaq-traded Sylvan Learning Systems has for years had an exclusive contract to run the continuing-education testing programs required for NASD's members.

OTC Bulletin Board

Mr. Zarb, by now getting high marks for keeping NASD focused heavily on the welfare of investors in Nasdaq, went a step further in December of 1997 by presiding over some planned improvements to standards on the OTC Bulletin Board. The Bulletin Board is maintained by Nasdaq, but since its inception in 1990, there have been no standards for companies to list there, other than having a market maker willing to post price quotes for a company's shares. The NASD board voted to require companies that list on the OTC Bulletin Board, whose obscurity made it a playground of sorts for unscrupulous promoters or brokers, to file quarterly statements with the SEC, or with banking or insurance regulators. Those that failed to do so—potentially thousands of companies—would get kicked down to the less-automated Pink Sheets, run in a separate system by the National Quotation Bureau. They also voted to require brokers who recommend either Bulletin Board or Pink Sheet stocks to stay apprised of current financial statements of the companies, and to send investors explanations of how such stocks differ from listed stocks on other markets. The NASD, which needs SEC approval to make such changes, also said it was investigating ways to get more authority to de-list Bulletin Board companies or halt trading there.

Nasdaq's People

THE NATIONAL ASSOCIATION OF SECURITIES DEALERS

Frank G. Zarb, chairman, president and chief executive officer, NASD: Mr. Zarb, a longtime businessman with a reputation as a consensus builder and a fixer of troubled organizations, is a former vice chairman at Travelers Corp.'s Smith Barney. He helped revive that firm at a time when it was suffering from heavy debts and money-losing risk-arbitrage trades in the wake of the 1987 market crash, making sharp cuts in Smith Barney's expenses to return the company to profitability. He also reigned over the decision to focus Smith Barney on retail brokerage operations, including a purchase of Drexel Burnham Lambert's offices for a bargain $4 million.

Zarb, Frank
President &
Chairman-NASD

He periodically left Wall Street to work in Washington, as an assistant labor secretary and deputy director of the Office of Management and Budget in the

Nixon Administration, and as head of the Federal Energy Administration under President Ford, as the so-called "energy czar."

Mr. Zarb worked as the back-office operations manager with Sanford Weill at Cogan Berlind Weill & Levitt. Cogan Berlind ultimately became Shearson Lehman Hutton, where Zarb worked in the investment-banking division. He also spent ten years, half as partner, half as senior partner, at Lazard Frères & Co., where he started and ran Lazard's international investment business. In 1988 he left Lazard to run Smith Barney, Harris Upham & Co., at the request of Mr. Weill, who was then chairman of Commercial Credit Group, a Baltimore consumer lending and insurance concern, which had bought Smith Barney's parent company.

After a year as Smith Barney's vice chairman starting in June 1993, Mr. Zarb left to run Alexander & Alexander, one of the world's largest insurance brokers, whose finances had been on a downward slide since 1986, after reinsurance-related losses and other claims began emerging related to its 1982 acquisition of British insurance broker Alexander Howden. Mr. Zarb got his master's degree and his bachelor's degree from Hofstra University, which also granted him an honorary doctor of law degree in 1975.

Richard G. Ketchum, executive vice president and chief operating officer: Mr. Ketchum is the highest-ranking NASD official still at the organization after the wrenching SEC investigation. As COO, Mr. Ketchum helps set Nasdaq policies and develop products for the market. He also manages the office of general counsel, strategic planning, finance, corporate communications, human resources and the congressional and state liaison offices.

Mr. Ketchum, who has been COO since February 1993, is widely credited with having the most expansive knowledge of Nasdaq or NASD of anyone at the place. Ms. Schapiro, NASD Regulation's president, jokes that Mr. Ketchum "forgets more in five minutes" than she expects to learn about the organization.

Mr. Ketchum, a 1975 graduate of NYU Law School, got to NASD in May of 1991, when he was executive vice president of legal, regulatory and market policy. He took the job after fourteen years at the SEC, where his last job was director of market regulation. He was the SEC's market-regulation director during the 1987 crash, when he was responsible for the report on the crash for both the SEC and President Reagan.

NASD REGULATION

Mary L. Schapiro, president: Ms. Schapiro was a logical choice for the first president of NASD Regulation, the unit that was created after NASD was charged with turning a blind eye to dealer misdeeds. Ms. Schapiro, who officially took office in February 1996, spent virtually all of her career as a regulator of the financial markets. She jumped right into finance after graduating from George Washington University Law School in 1980, spending several years as a litigator at the Commodity Futures Trading Commission, the federal agency responsible for regulating the U.S. futures markets. After a brief stint as counsel to the Futures Industry Association, a group representing futures traders, she was tapped for a prestigious SEC commissioner post by President Reagan in 1988.

She arrived at her NASD post from her job as chairman of the CFTC, where she had been only since 1994. An appointee of President Bill Clinton at the CFTC, she had made inroads into overhauling the agency's enforcement division, despite opposition that included one indignant exchange official saying that no "five-foot, two-inch blonde" would ever tell him what to do. Ms. Schapiro participated in the President's Working Group on Financial Markets with the Secretary of the Treasury, the chairmen of the Federal Reserve Board and the SEC.

Elisse Walter, chief operating officer, executive vice president, legal and regulatory policy: Ms. Walter is Ms. Schapiro's longtime trusted deputy, having worked with her at both the CFTC and the SEC. She was recruited to NASD by Ms. Schapiro, joining NASD shortly after her old boss arrived there in February 1996.

Ms. Walter, a graduate of Harvard Law School, was previously general counsel of the CFTC, handling appellate, amicus and defensive litigation for that agency, as well as giving legal advice on CFTC's programs and interpreting the Commodity Exchange Act. Prior to October 1994, she was deputy director of the division of corporate finance at the SEC, having risen from staff attorney in the office of general counsel in 1977 to special counsel and then assistant and associate general counsel.

Linda Fienberg, executive vice president and chief hearing officer: As the person charged with overseeing the NASD's arbitration, mediation and broker dispute-resolution policies, Ms. Fienberg got intimately familiar with her future job as a member of the Ruder Committee, headed by former SEC chairman David Ruder. That group, formally known as the Task Force on Arbitration Policy, was charged with recommending improvement and overhaul of the NASD's notoriously unwieldy and user-unfriendly arbitration system. After the report came out in early 1996, Ms. Schapiro tapped Ms. Fienberg to help implement the controversial changes. She joined NASD Regulation in June 1996.

Ms. Fienberg was formerly a partner at the Washington, DC, law firm of Covington & Burling, and from 1979 to 1990 was executive assistant to two chairmen (including Ms. Schapiro) and associate general counsel in the General Counsel's office in litigation and counseling.

NASDAQ

Alfred R. Berkeley III, president: It would seem appropriate that a man who spent much of his career examining technology from various angles would be tapped as president of a technology-driven stock market. Mr. Berkeley started his career in 1972 fresh out of a four-year stint as an Air Force officer, after spending nearly two dozen years primarily at Baltimore's Alex. Brown & Sons, where he began as a research analyst.

In 1975, Mr. Berkeley, a 1968 graduate of the Wharton School of business at the University of Pennsylvania, joined the research team and started up the firm's software research department.

Mr. Berkeley immersed himself in technology in other ways, too. After seeing what technology could do in the companies he covered, Mr. Berkeley said he decided to try to revamp Alex. Brown's 1960-style computers. From 1985 to 1987 he oversaw the upgrade of Alex. Brown's computer, phone, and video teleconferencing systems. Later he moved to Alex. Brown's mergers-and-acquisitions department, working on software-company mergers.

In early 1989, Mr. Berkeley veered into another corner of technology—this time as a corporate executive at Safeguard Scientifics. Taking a leave of absence from Alex. Brown, he served on Safeguard Scientific's executive committee and was chairman of a number of its subsidiaries including Rabbit Software and Micro Decision Ware.

Although his involvement with Nasdaq until his appointment as president in May of 1996 had been only minimal, Mr. Berkeley said he relished shepherding the market through regulatory changes. Always the technophile, he is busy studying whether Nasdaq's out-of-date huge system of mainframes ought to be transformed into anywhere from one to fifty powerful personal-computer processors that would keep track of the quotes and orders that fly through Nasdaq every weekday, a change he says would simplify the system and cost less for Nasdaq.

Barry R. Goldsmith, executive vice president, Enforcement, NASD Regulation: Mr. Goldsmith, who took office in August of 1996, formulates NASD's national enforcement goals and oversees prosecution of district and national disciplinary proceedings. He was formerly chief litigation counsel of the SEC, handling litigation including those against Drexel Burnham Lambert and junk-bond king Michael Milken, Ivan Boesky and Dennis Levine. In addition, he successfully tried the SEC's stock-parking case against Mark Belzberg and First City Financial Corp. and the securities-fraud case against Victor and Steven Posner. He graduated magna cum laude from the University of Pennsylvania's Wharton School in 1972, and got his law degree from Georgetown University Law Center in 1975.

Salvatore F. Sodano, executive vice president, chief financial officer, NASD: The first person to hold such a title at NASD, Mr. Sodano is responsible for running the organization's corporate financial systems and heads the human resources, administrative services, and service quality areas of NASD. Before joining NASD in June 1997, he was senior vice president, chief manager and principal operating officer at Westpac Banking Corp., Americas Division, in New York, which he joined in 1990 as vice president and deputy controller of its New York branch. He worked from 1983 to 1990 at Bankers Trust Co., in the corporate controllers department, and from 1979 to 1983 at Morgan Guaranty International Finance Corp. as assistant to the treasurer. He got a master's degree in finance and investments in 1983 from Hofstra University, where he also got a bachelor's degree in accounting and economics in 1977.

Mary Alice Brophy, executive vice president, NASD Regulation: Ms. Brophy, formerly senior vice president and compliance director at Dain Bosworth Inc. in Minneapolis, Minnesota, joined NASD Regulation in October 1997. She was also senior vice president of Dain Bosworth's parent company, Interra Financial, where she oversaw compliance for its three broker/dealer subsidiaries and investment advisers. She spent four years as Minnesota's Commissioner of Securities and Real Estate starting in 1979. She was on NASD's Kansas City district business conduct committee, for which she was chairman in 1993. In 1996, during her third year on NASD's board, she was elected chairman of the board of NASD Regulation. She is a graduate of the College of St. Teresa in Winona, Minnesota, and of the Securities Industry Institute at the Wharton School.

J. Patrick Campbell, executive vice president, Market Services, Nasdaq Stock Market: Mr. Campbell took over the newly created market-services job in January 1997 when he moved from the Ohio Company, where he was senior executive vice president. He manages Nasdaq's dealings with market makers who trade Nasdaq stocks, order-entry firms, vendors, private trading systems on Nasdaq, and subscribers to Nasdaq services. He was formerly a member of Nasdaq's board from 1990 to 1993 and a member of the Cincinnati Stock Exchange from 1980 to 1985. He graduated from Ohio University in 1971 and completed the Securities Industry Association's Securities Industry Institute at Wharton School of Finance in 1979.

John M. Hickey, executive vice president, Technology Services, Nasdaq Stock Market, Trumbull, Connecticut: Before joining the NASD in 1984 as vice president in the automation division, Mr. Hickey was at Chemical Bank from 1974 to 1984 as a vice president of corporate-systems development. He was director of SABRE Systems for American Airlines and spent twelve years with General Motors in systems management. Mr. Hickey, who is responsible for all technology services for Nasdaq, graduated from Columbia University business school and St. Francis College with a BAA in accounting.

John T. Wall, president, Nasdaq International Ltd.: Mr. Wall was previously executive vice president of Issuer, Investor and International Services. He handles strategic development and international marketing of Nasdaq products and services and foreign-company listings. He was previously a senior vice president of compliance at NASD, and vice president of NASD's surveillance division. He joined NASD in 1965 as an examiner. He got his BA in economics from University of Notre Dame.

Dean Furbush, chief economist, NASD: Mr. Furbush joined NASD after nearly five years at Economists, Inc., where he was a senior economist until June, 1995. He was economic adviser to the chairman of the Commodity Futures Trading Commission from October 1989 to August 1990; financial economist at the Securities and Exchange Commission's office of economic analysis from June 1987 to October 1989. He has been adjunct professor at Virginia Polytechnic Institute and State University's economics department starting in 1990. He was a consultant and junior economist for the President's Council of Economic Advisers at various times from 1985 to 1987. He got a PhD in economics from the University of Maryland, where he also got an MA in economics. He also has a BA in economics from the University of Washington.

R. Clark Hooper, senior vice president, NASD Regulation: Ms. Hooper directs the office of disclosure and investor protection, which oversees communications between NASD member firms and the public in advertisements on the Internet and elsewhere. Her office also oversees NASD's corporate financing, Internet and investor education, investment companies regulation, and Central Registration Depository/Public Disclosure departments. Ms. Hooper, who worked in various capacities in NASD's corporate financing and advertising/ investment companies divisions, is a graduate of Hollins College.

James M. Cangiano, senior vice president, Market Regulation, NASD Regulation: Mr. Cangiano is responsible for overseeing trading of the thousands of stocks on the Nasdaq Stock Market and for surveillance of activity in other markets operated by Nasdaq such as the OTC Bulletin Board. His department uses automated systems to review trading for unusual trading activity that could indicate insider trading or other abuses. Mr. Cangiano joined NASD in May 1972 as an examiner in the New York district office, joining market regulation as its director in 1986. He graduated from St. Francis College.

I. Grant Callery, senior vice president, general counsel, NASD: Mr Callery joined NASD's general counsel's office in 1979 after five years in private practice.

He is active in NASD disciplinary and rule-making activities like setting corporate-governance and listing standards for Nasdaq-listed companies, and aiding NASD's efforts to get "blue sky" exemptions for certain Nasdaq-listed companies in numerous states. He became general counsel in 1993. He is a graduate of Marietta College and the Georgetown Law School.

Alden S. Adkins, vice president and general counsel, NASD Regulation: Mr. Adkins was formerly vice president of strategic planning and research for NASD and its director of internal review and equal-employment opportunity director. He spent ten years at the SEC as special counsel to the chairman. He graduated in 1981 from Washington College of Law at American University.

Charles Balfour, senior vice president, Nasdaq Stock Market, and managing director, Nasdaq International, London: Mr. Balfour heads Nasdaq's international-services department which assists non-U.S. companies listing on Nasdaq. Before coming to Nasdaq in 1993, he was an executive director of Banque Paribas, handling corporate-finance activities including the leveraged-capital group. At Banque Paribas for thirteen years, Mr. Balfour handled public-sector and export finance. He was educated at Eton and the Sorbonne in Paris, and is a serving member of the Queen's Body Guard for Scotland (the Royal Company of Archers.)

Robert E. Aber, vice president, general counsel, Nasdaq Stock Market, Inc.: Mr. Aber was formerly a vice president and deputy general counsel of NASD, until the organization split into three units: a parent NASD, the Nasdaq Stock Market and NASD Regulation. He began his NASD career as a law clerk in 1972. He is a graduate of Georgetown University Business and Law School.

James R. Allen, senior vice president, treasurer, NASD: Mr. Allen took his current position in 1996. As treasurer, he directs the activities of the finance department, including all financial reporting and accounting operations, treasury management, financial planning and budgeting, tax planning and compliance, risk management and member benefits. He joined NASD in 1983 as controller, before which he was a senior audit manager for Price Waterhouse. He graduated in 1971 from Washington and Lee University.

Michael D. Jones, vice president, Office of Individual Investor Services, NASD: Mr. Jones joined the NASD in 1996 from the SEC, where he was deputy director/counsel with the office of public affairs, policy, evaluation and research. He chairs the NASD's Individual Investor Service Committee, which coordinates NASD's investor policies and initiatives. He was a legislative aide to U.S. Senator Edward W. Brooke, an attorney at Lovett, Ford & Hennessey in Washington, and a national political director for the presidential campaign of John B.

Anderson, among other jobs in law and public relations and public affairs. He got his BA from Boston College and his JD from Boston College law school.

Joan C. Conley, corporate secretary, NASD, Nasdaq, and NASD Regulation: Ms. Conley has been with NASD since 1982 when she was manager of employment and compensation. She was human-resources director from October 1989 to March 1994. She was previously a research assistant at the National Academy of Science in Washington from 1980 to 1982 and a human-resources assistant at the advertising agency of Bently, Barnes & Lynn from 1978 to 1980. She got an MS in industrial and labor relations from Loyola University in Chicago in 1980 and a BA in communications arts and sciences from Rosary College in Chicago in 1978.

Elisabeth P. Owens, director, District No. 1, San Francisco office (Hawaii, and parts of California and Nevada): Ms. Owens joined the NASD in January 1970. Prior to becoming director of the San Francisco office in 1991, she was associate director of the NASD's Chicago district office for more than three years, and before that assistant director of the Philadelphia office for six years. She got her BA degree from Roanoke College in Salem, Virginia, and her JD from Temple University in Philadelphia.

Lani M. Sen Woltmann, director, District No. 2 (Southern California, Southern Nevada and Guam): Ms. Woltmann joined NASD in 1982 and served as regional counsel until her appointment as district director in 1993. She worked previously at the Los Angeles offices of both the Securities and Exchange Commission and the Federal Trade Commission. She has also worked at the National Capitol area office of the American Civil Liberties Union and the Honolulu law firm of Carlsmith, Carlsmith, Wichman and Case. She got her BA from the University of Hawaii and her JD from the University of California at Berkeley's Boalt Hall School of Law.

Frank J. Birgfeld, district director, District No. 3, Denver office (Arizona, Colorado, New Mexico, Utah and Wyoming): Mr. Birgfeld was assigned to his current job in November 1980, after being an assistant director in the NASD's Georgia office. Before that, he was an account executive at E. F. Hutton, after the liquidation of Frances I. Dupont & Co., where he was a branch manager and administrative assistant to the senior vice president. He was an examiner with the NASD in 1969 before leaving for Dupont in 1973. He graduated from Florida State University with a finance degree.

James Dawson, associate director, District No. 3, Seattle office (Alaska, Idaho, Montana, Oregon and Washington): Mr. Dawson is a graduate of the University of Virginia. He was a management analyst with the

U.S. Treasury Department for four years before joining Legg Mason & Co. as a registered representative in 1968. He joined NASD in November 1969 as a securities examiner in the Washington, DC, office and was promoted to supervisor in 1973. He became the associate director of the Seattle office, which was later combined with the Denver office to form District No. 3.

Jack Rosenfield, vice president and district director, District No. 4, Kansas City office (Iowa, Kansas, Minnesota, Missouri, Nebraska, North and South Dakota): Mr. Rosenfield is a former securities salesman for Frances I. Dupont & Co., joining the NASD's New York office in 1970 as an examiner-trainee. He moved to the Washington NASD office in 1973 as a research analyst in the regulatory procedures section of the regulation department. He became assistant director of that department in 1975, and in December 1981 he was promoted to his current job, becoming vice president in January 1992. He's a graduate of the New York University school of commerce.

Warren A. Butler Jr., vice president, director, District No. 5, New Orleans office (Alabama, Arkansas, Kentucky, Louisiana, Mississippi, Oklahoma and Tennessee): Mr. Butler, a father of five, joined NASD as an examiner in 1974, rising to district director in 1987 and vice president in 1995. He was formerly compliance director and partner at a large regional brokerage firm. He was in the Army in Vietnam as an infantry officer.

Thomas M. McNatt, director, District No. 6, Dallas office (State of Texas): Prior to becoming director in April 1995, Mr. McNatt was associate director in the Dallas office for fifteen years. He graduated from the University of North Texas in Denton, Texas, joining NASD's Dallas office in 1970.

Marilyn B. Davis, vice president, director, District No. 7, Atlanta office (North and South Carolina, Georgia, Florida, Puerto Rico, Virgin Islands): Ms. Davis joined the NASD in 1973 after a career as an account executive for Courts & Co. and then Shearson Lehman Brothers. She was appointed in 1972 to President Richard M. Nixon's Presidential Commission on Personnel Interchange, an executive interchange program between industry and government.

Carlotta A. Romano, district director, District No. 8, Chicago office (parts of Illinois, Wisconsin, Michigan and Indiana): Ms. Romano took her current job in June 1995 after beginning her career with the NASD as an examiner in 1980. She got her BA degree from St. Mary's College in Notre Dame, Indiana, and her MBA in finance from DePaul University in Chicago.

William H. Jackson Jr., district director, District No. 8, Cleveland office (Ohio and, parts of Illinois, Indiana, Michigan, Wisconsin and New York):

Mr. Jackson has held his current position since 1986, beginning his NASD career in the Cleveland district office in 1973 as an examiner-trainee. He got his BA in mathematics and economics from Duke University and his JD from the Cleveland-Marshall College of Law of Cleveland State University.

John P. Nocella, vice president, District Director, District No. 9, Philadelphia office (Washington, DC, Delaware, Maryland, Pennsylvania, Virginia, West Virginia, and parts of New Jersey): Mr. Nocella has been with the NASD since 1969, serving in various positions including examiner, supervisor and assistant director. He is a graduate of Temple University.

Martin A. Kuperberg, senior vice president, District Director, District No. 10, New York office (Most of New York, including New York City, and parts of New Jersey): Mr. Kuperberg was formerly senior associate regional director of the SEC's Northeast regional office and responsible for its broker-dealer inspection program, its broker-dealer enforcement program and its full-disclosure program.

Willis H. Riccio, vice president, Director, District No. 11, Boston office (Connecticut, Maine, Massachusetts, New Hampshire, Rhode Island, Vermont, and parts of New York): Mr. Riccio was formerly regional administrator for the New England regional office of the SEC until November 1, 1985, when he left to join the NASD. From 1978 to 1985 he was appointed special assistant U.S. attorney for the district of Rhode Island to criminally prosecute securities fraud cases. He is an adjunct professor of securities law at the New England School of Law. He got his BA degree from Brown University, his JD from Georgetown University Law Center and his Master's Law Degree from Georgetown. He got an honorary degree of Doctor of Laws from the New England School of Law.

THE NEW NASD BOARD MEMBERS

James F. Rothenberg, president, director of Capital Research and Management Co., Los Angeles: Mr. Rothenberg has been with Capital Research since 1970, becoming its president and director in 1994. He has an MBA from Harvard business school and a BA in English from Harvard College.

Bridget A. Macaskill, president, CEO, Oppenheimer Funds, Inc., New York: Ms. Macaskill, also a Nasdaq board member, joined Oppenheimer in 1983 as vice president of marketing, becoming its COO in 1989 and its chief executive in 1995. She has an undergraduate degree from Edinburgh University in Scotland.

Paul H. O'Neill, chairman and CEO, ALCOA, Pittsburgh, Pennsylvania: Before heading ALCOA, Mr. O'Neill was president of International Paper Co., a company he joined in 1977 as vice president of planning. He started his career as an engineer for Morrison-Knudsen, Inc. in Anchorage, Alaska. He worked as a computer systems analyst for the U.S. Veterans Administration from 1961 to 1966 and as a staffer at the U.S. Office of Management and Budget from 1967 to 1977, becoming deputy director of OMB from 1974 to 1977. He has an MA in Public Administration from Indiana University and a BA in economics from Fresno State College.

John D. Markese, president, American Association of Individual Investors, Chicago: Mr. Markese is a former finance professor at Penn State University, Eastern Michigan University and DePaul University in Chicago, where he continues to be an adjunct professor. He started at AAII as their director of research in the summer of 1985. A member of the Nasdaq Stock Market board of directors, he has a PhD from the University of Illinois, which he received in 1971, as well as MS and BS degrees in finance from University of Illinois.

Philip R. Lochner, Jr., senior vice president, Time Warner, Inc., New York: Mr. Lochner spent a year as a commissioner at the Securities and Exchange Commission before taking his current post. Before the SEC, he was general counsel and senior vice president, administration and human resources, and assistant secretary of Time Inc. from 1988 to 1990. He began working at Time in 1978, after being an associate at the law firm Cravath, Swaine & Moore from 1973 to 1978 and associate dean and assistant law professor at the State University of New York from 1971 to 1973. He got a PhD from Stanford University, an LLB from Yale University, and a BA from Yale. Mr. Lochner, a Fulbright Fellow who studied at the University of London from 1967 to 1968, is also on the NASD Regulation board.

Donald J. Kirk, executive-in-residence, Columbia University Graduate School of Business, New York: Mr. Kirk, who has an MBA from New York University and a BA from Yale University, became an accounting professor at Columbia in 1987. He was a member of the Financial Accounting Standards Board from 1973 to 1987, where he was chairman from 1978 to 1986. He began his career at Price Waterhouse in 1959, serving as a partner from 1967 to 1973.

Robert R. Glauber, adjunct lecturer, Harvard University Center for Business and Government, Cambridge, Massachusetts: Mr. Glauber was Under Secretary for Finance at the U.S. Treasury under President George Bush, before which he was a finance professor at Harvard Business School. In 1987, he was executive director of the Brady Commission task force established by President Reagan to study the 1987 market crash. He has a PhD in finance from Harvard and a BA in economics from Harvard College. Mr. Glauber is also on NASD Regulation's board.

Elaine L. Chao, distinguished fellow, the Heritage Foundation, Washington, DC: Ms. Chao was formerly president and CEO of the United Way of America from 1992 to 1996 before joining the Heritage Foundation. She was also once director of the U.S. Peace Corps, deputy secretary of the U.S. Department of Transportation, and chairman of the Federal Maritime Commission. Prior to those positions, she was vice president of the capital markets group at Bank America, from 1984 to 1986, and senior lending officer at Citicorp from 1979 to 1983. She has an MBA from Harvard University and a BA from Mt. Holyoke College.

Nancy Kassebaum Baker, former U.S. Senator, Washington: Ms. Baker served in the U.S. Senate from December 1978 to January 1997, during which time she chaired the Labor and Human Resource Committee, the Foreign Relations Committee's subcommittee on African affairs, and the Commerce Committee's subcommittee on aviation. She has a master's degree in political history from the University of Michigan and a bachelor's degree from the University of Kansas in political science.

Arvind Sodhani, vice president and treasurer, Intel Corp., Santa Clara, California: Mr. Sodhani joined Intel in 1981 as assistant treasurer of Intel Europe. He became assistant treasurer of Intel Corp. in 1984, and treasurer in 1988. He has an MBA from the University of Michigan, an MS from the University of London, and a BS from the University of London. Mr. Sodhani is a member of the Nasdaq Stock Market's board.

Howard Schultz, chairman and CEO, Starbucks Coffee Co., Seattle, Washington: Mr. Schultz joined Starbucks as director of operations and marketing in 1982, leaving the company in 1986, returning in 1987 to buy Starbucks with the help of local investors. He has a BS in business from Northern Michigan University. After graduation, he was in sales and marketing for Xerox Corp., then moved on to become vice president and general manager of Hammarplast U.S.A., a subsidiary of a Swedish housewares company. He is the author of *Pour Your Heart Into It*, his autobiography.

Michael W. Brown, chief financial officer, Microsoft Corp., Redmond, Washington: Mr. Brown spent eighteen years in the public accounting firm of Deloitte & Touche before joining Microsoft in 1989 as treasurer. He has a BA in economics from the University of Washington. Mr. Brown is chairman of the Nasdaq Stock Market board.

James S. Riepe, managing director, T. Rowe Price Associates, Inc., Baltimore, Maryland: Mr. Riepe was formerly executive vice president at T. Rowe Price competitor Vanguard Group, joining T. Rowe Price in 1982. He is chairman of the firm's retail and institutional service subsidiaries and is president of T. Rowe Price Investment Services. He is a member of the executive committee of the Investment Company Institute, the mutual-fund trade group, and was formerly chairman of the board of governors. Mr. Riepe, who has an MBA from the Wharton School, is on the board of NASD Regulation.

Harry P. Kamen, chairman, president and CEO, Metropolitan Life Insurance Co., New York: Mr. Kamen has been with Met Life since 1959, taking his current positions in 1993. From 1979 to 1983, he was the insurance company's vice president, secretary and general counsel, after holding a variety of positions at Met Life. He is a director at the American Council of Life Insurance, and holds an LLB from Harvard University and a BA from the University of Pennsylvania. Mr. Kamen is also on the board of NASD Regulation.

Kenneth J. Wessels, CEO, Wessels, Arnold & Henderson, Minneapolis: Mr. Wessels was formerly executive vice president with Piper, Jaffray & Hopwood, Inc. from 1977 to 1986, after leaving Robertson, Colman, Siebel & Weisel, where he was a partner. He is a former chairman and member of the NASD board. He has a BA in business administration from the University of Missouri. Mr. Wessels is on the board of NASD Regulation, as well.

Todd A. Robinson, chairman and CEO, Linsco/Private Ledger Corp., Boston: Mr. Robinson, who has a BA from Bates College, began in the securities industry at Smith Barney in 1981. He became CEO of Linsco Financial Group in 1985, and merged it with Private Ledger Corp. in 1989. He was an original member on the Securities Industry Task Force on Continuing Education. Mr. Robinson is chairman of NASD Regulation's board, as well.

Donald B. Marron, chairman and CEO, PaineWebber, Inc., New York: After several years as an analyst at several Wall Street firms, Mr. Marron formed his own investment banking firm, D.B. Marron & Co., Inc., in 1959. In 1965 he merged his firm with Mitchell, Hutchins & Co. Inc. and became executive vice president and later president. Mitchell Hutchins merged with PaineWebber Inc. in 1977, and Mr. Marron became president of PaineWebber. In June 1980 he was appointed CEO, and elected chairman in 1981.

James (Jamie) Dimon, co-CEO, Salomon Smith Barney, New York: Mr. Dimon became CEO at Smith Barney in 1996, after having been president, chief operating officer and director of Travelers Group from 1991 to 1996, as well as chief operating officer and executive-committee member at Smith Barney. He was formerly executive vice president and CFO of Primerica Corp., and senior executive vice president and chief administrative officer of Smith Barney from 1986 to 1991. He was vice president of American Express Co. from 1982 to 1985. He has an MBA from Harvard business school, and a BA from Tufts University.

Jon S. Corzine, chairman and CEO, Goldman, Sachs & Co., New York: Mr. Corzine was appointed to his current posts in 1994, before which time he was cohead of the fixed-income division starting in 1988, as well as partner in charge of government, mortgage and money markets trading in that division. He joined Goldman in 1975, becoming a vice president in 1977 and a general partner in 1980. Before Goldman, he worked at Bancohio Corp. and at Continental Illinois National Bank. He is a member of the Bond Market Association, the trade group for bond dealers. He has an MBA from the University of Chicago and a BA from the University of Illinois, and is on Nasdaq's board.

E. David Coolidge III, CEO, William Blair & Co., L.L.C., Chicago: Mr. Coolidge joined William Blair in 1969 as an associate, after spending time in the Peace Corps in Colombia, South America. He became CEO in 1995, after having been a principal and manager of corporate finance. He has an MBA from Harvard business school and a BA from Williams College.

Richard F. Brueckner, managing director, Pershing Division of Donaldson, Lufkin & Jenrette, Jersey City, New Jersey: Mr. Brueckner runs DLJ's Financial Services Group and its Pershing clearing division. Before joining DLJ in 1978, Mr. Brueckner was with the management group of the investment services department of Peat, Marwick, Mitchell & Co. Mr. Brucckner, a certified public accountant, has a BA in economics from Muhlenberg College. Mr. Brueckner is also on the NASD Regulation board.

Frank E. Baxter, chairman, president and CEO, Jefferies & Co., Los Angeles: Mr. Baxter joined Jefferies in 1974, becoming national sales manager in 1983 and managing the London office beginning in 1985. He was elected to his current positions in 1990. Before he joined Jefferies, Mr. Baxter was a vice president at J.S. Strauss & Co., from 1963 to 1974. He has a BA from the University of California, Berkeley. Mr. Baxter also serves on Nasdaq's board.

Herbert M. Allison Jr., president and COO, Merrill Lynch & Co., Inc., New York: Mr. Allison started at Merrill in 1971 as a trainee and investment banking associate, serving stints in the Paris office in 1972, in the Middle East as deputy managing director of a Merrill Lynch joint venture, and London as an executive director of Merill Lynch International Bank. He was elected president and COO in 1997. He has a MBA from Stanford and a BA in philosophy from Yale University. Mr. Allison is on Nasdaq's board.

Even the Ads Were New . . .

During the time period that NASD officials were charged with ignoring market maker's abuses on Nasdaq, they were spending millions of dollars to promote the market as "The Stock Market for the Next 100 Years." Glitzy ads that began running on sports and business TV channels featured quick shots of various household names that listed on Nasdaq. The ad, thick with importance, asked "Where do you find" such big household names and answered, "Actually, there is a list of them printed every day" on Nasdaq.

The Nasdaq Handbook, a nearly four-hundred-page reference, was revised in 1992 to feature essays like "Why Nasdaq?" and "Nasdaq: The Preferred Market for Overseas Companies," extolling Nasdaq's prowess and written by academics, securities professionals, and NASD executives.

The overemphasis on promotion irked the chairman of the SEC, Arthur Levitt. The SEC's famous 21(a) report on Nasdaq made reference to the fact that Nasdaq officials had let its competitive zeal to beat the NYSE—suddenly an attainable goal—overshadow its responsibility to police its members.

Insiders said Mr. Levitt sent word to Nasdaq to clean up its market, including toning down its ads and marketing push and refocusing on investors. The message was clear: Nasdaq shouldn't be spending its budget convincing America it was a ticket to investing nirvana when it was under a barrage of charges of unfair trading practices.

In September of 1996, Nasdaq unveiled its new advertising campaign, focused on the small investor. TV ads featured a cowboy, a white-collar professional, and families as typical individual investors, with investing goals for education, a home, or retirement. Instead of dramatic references to the next hundred years, the ad noted that "nothing is more valuable than information," and pointed investors to the Nasdaq Web site and its charts and graphs on Nasdaq companies.

Wall Street figured Nasdaq made the right choice, considering that pundits had already begun to add a few words of their own to Nasdaq's former motto: "Nasdaq, the stock market for the next 100 years . . . with time off for good behavior."

What's a Spread?

Nasdaq market makers typically buy stocks from investors at one price, known as the "bid" price, and sell them to others for a slightly higher price, known as the "ask" or "offer" price. The difference between the two prices is the spread, and represents profit for a market maker—and a built-in profit hurdle for investors. Because under Nasdaq's system, market makers usually don't simply match up buyer and seller at a mutually

In the Beginning . . .

The National Association of Securities Dealers has been around a lot longer than the Nasdaq Stock Market. NASD was set up under the 1938 Maloney Act amendments to the Securities Exchange Act of 1934. The NASD was created as a "self-regulatory" body for the entire securities industry, under which volunteers from the industry being regulated were elected or appointed to set policy and act as overseer of the industry.

"This Act is designed to effectuate a system of regulation . . . in which the members of the industry will themselves exercise as large a measure of authority as their natural genius will permit," said Francis T. Maloney, sponsor of the 1938 Maloney Act that created the NASD as a national securities association.

One of the first big initiatives by the NASD was in 1943, when NASD's board of governors undertook to set guidelines for how much dealers could mark up stocks they sold to customers. Encountering resistance, the then-executive director of NASD, Wallace H. Fulton, said "The NASD did not and does not seek to regulate, let alone curtail, profits of its members. It is devoted to the principle that its members are in business to make money. Our interest in the individual transaction is only with the fairness of the markup or the commission realized."

The battle between fairness and profits was one that would be repeated over and over in the years to come.

Over time, the NASD's reach has broadened to include registering any broker or brokerage firm that wants to trade securities and ensuring that they keep up their duties of NASD membership, including keeping books and records of trades, taking registration exams, and maintaining a minimum level of net capital to ensure they can stay in business.

In 1945, NASD established informal procedures for arbitrating disputes between members, and in 1981 created the Central Registration Depository, containing the disciplinary histories of NASD member firms and brokers.

The SEC, a federal agency, has power over the self-regulatory organization, including final say over rule-change proposals and power to compel changes at the NASD when it feels the SRO has gone astray.

Nasdaq was launched in February 1971 as a congressionally mandated tool to automate the "over-the-counter" securities market, a hodgepodge of infrequently traded stocks in small companies that couldn't qualify to list on the New York or American stock exchanges. Nasdaq originally stood for the National Association of Securities Dealers Automated Quotation system, although years later the market would put itself in lowercase, as simply the Nasdaq Stock Market. At first Nasdaq was merely an automated version of the over-the-counter "pink sheets"—a place where market makers would indicate their willingness to buy and sell shares at certain prices, which weren't even binding. Nasdaq would display to its member broker-dealers which market makers were trading the shares, and the median bid (or purchase price) and ask (or selling price) prices, a novelty for traders who were used to having to call every market maker on a stock's list to get any picture of a stock's general price range. By late 1971 Nasdaq started providing volume data as well. In 1972, market makers traded 2.2 billion shares in nearly 3,500 securities.

Nasdaq brought the system from its original contractors, Bunker Ramo, in 1976 and in July 1980 started posting the inside spread, or the actual highest bid and lowest ask price being sent in by market makers in a given security. Armed with the knowledge of the best prices, investors sent share volume soaring, to 6.7 billion shares that year.

In 1975, NASD became responsible for regulating municipal-securities dealers, and 246 dealers became members. In 1977, NASD also became responsible for overseeing regulation of its members who were also members of the Boston, Cincinnati, Midwest, Pacific and

Philadelphia exchanges, which had their own staff of self-regulators as well.

By the 1980s, when Nasdaq started making improvements to its system and attracting more and more volume, more and more companies were opting to stay on the upstart market rather than automatically graduating to the American and then New York Stock Exchanges. Companies would often stay because they'd built up relationships with market makers who had helped find investors for their stock, who were increasingly asking for loyalty from the companies they'd nursed from infancy.

Nasdaq's forte continues to be providing a market for small startup companies that need the research and hunt for investors that market markers provided

their shares. Over the years Nasdaq's success stories have included many high-tech startups, lured by the success of Microsoft, which got its start on Nasdaq. And Nasdaq's computer-based system appealed to some, as well. "High-tech companies liked the fact that the market was high-tech," says A. A. Sommer, a longtime NASD board member and head of various NASD committees.

These days, each of the 6,351 securities and 5,538 companies trading on Nasdaq has at least three market makers who show up on the Nasdaq workstation to quote a bid and ask price. Big, highly liquid stocks like Microsoft or Intel might have forty market makers quoting prices, while thinly traded stocks might have only a handful.

desirable price, most shares moved from one investor to another means profit for the Nasdaq trader, even before factoring in any commissions for the firms. And for some stocks that aren't traded a great deal, that spread can get as large as fifty cents per share, or even more.

The actual price that investors get when trading Nasdaq stocks depends on the inside spread, or the best prevailing buying price and the best prevailing selling price, usually set by different dealers or their customers.

An extreme example of the way spreads work came in late May of 1996, in the form of Optical Cable, a maker of durable cable whose president took the company public in an unusual self-underwritten deal, which had an enormous 1996 post-offering run-up from $10 to over $80, prior to two stock splits. On Friday, May 30, when the stock was trading close to its all-time high, the stock had a mind-boggling $7 per share spread between the bid and ask prices. That meant if an investor bought and sold in rapid succession, he would have a built-in $7 loss—without the price budging. (The stock, after two 2-for-1 stock splits, was trading in 1997 with much more modest spreads of 38 cents or so.)

NASD Error Results in a Purge of Broker Data

By Michael Siconolfi
Staff Reporter of The Wall Street Journal

A blunder by the National Association of Securities Dealers has caused the purging of as many as 20,000 pieces of regulatory data on the nation's stockbrokers.

The large-scale deletion, undisclosed until now, could lead to headaches for investors, according to state securities regulators and other people familiar with the situation. The information was purged from the computer system widely used by investors and regulators to track disciplinary histories of stockbrokers and their firms, regulators said.

The NASD, the brokerage industry's self-regulatory organization and the operator of the Nasdaq Stock Market, called the deletions inadvertent; it would confirm only that about 3,000 files have been purged. The state regulators insist it was 20,000.

But the result is the same, whatever the number of purged files turns out to be: Investors can't be sure of the accuracy of the regulatory records of the nation's 535,000 brokers.

"If we can't rely on this information, the public isn't being served," said Denise Crawford, the Texas securities commissioner. "The significance is profound."

And the biggest issue, say some state regulators, is that the blunder has exposed the NASD's practice of allowing some brokers to keep certain settlements of client complaints out of their files to begin with. That practice is a surprise to state regulators.

The Securities and Exchange Commission, which oversees the NASD's activities, declined to comment. However, a senior SEC official said the agency is actively monitoring the matter.

The system involved is called the CRD, or central registration depository. It is investors' first line of defense against bad brokers. Despite the high-tech world of Wall Street, the 16-year-old CRD still works much like a card catalog, with material about brokers and firms entered manually by NASD clerks into computers.

The NASD said it inadvertently issued faulty guidelines that were followed by its clerks. Those guidelines, which the NASD now disavows and says aren't being used, are spelled out in an Oct. 4, 1995, internal memorandum obtained by The Wall Street Journal. In the memo, the NASD told staffers that "revised" guidelines allowed them to excise a broad range of disciplinary data from the CRD system.

These included instances when—before a judgment is entered—a customer, court or arbitration panel withdraws or dismisses a complaint, or dismisses a broker as a named party in a lawsuit or arbitration filing. That is where most of the information was purged.

The problem is that under its contract with state regulators, the NASD isn't allowed to delete any of this information. Why weren't the states told of the revised guidelines? "I don't know," said Linda Fienberg, an executive vice president of NASD's regulatory arm.

"It was an error—a serious error at that," Elisse Walter, chief operating officer at NASD's regulatory arm, said of the purges. But she asserted that the NASD has "put in steps and controls" to ensure the problem won't recur.

"When the mistake came to our attention, we acted very quickly" to clear it up, said Michael Robinson, an NASD spokesman.

The NASD first said the number of deleted filings was only about 1,100. It then amended the number to 1,900 before revising it late yesterday to about 3,000. The NASD said the 20,000 figure repre

---

The problem was discovered by a Colorado investigator looking up information on a stockbroker's past. One day, the files were there. Months later, they had disappeared.

sented only the potential number of purged filings, not the actual ones.

Ms. Fienberg said the NASD is "in the process of putting back" the records and will be finished within 60 days. The purged files are stored in stacks of computer boxes at the NASD's Rockville, Md., warehouse.

Investors can call an NASD hot line to find out about pending and resolved disciplinary cases against either brokers or firms. State securities offices also give investors additional data about pending arbitration and court cases.

Mark Griffin, president of the North American Securities Administrators Association, an organization of state regulators, called the problem and the NASD's response to it "a little bit mind-boggling." But he said his group continues to try to work with the NASD toward an "amicable resolution."

Some lawyers who work with investors aren't satisfied.

"As a self-regulatory organization that disseminates data, the least [the NASD] ought to have said is: 'The information we're providing may not be complete,' " said J. Boyd Page, an Atlanta attorney and former member of the NASD's national arbitration committee.

"It wouldn't have helped an investor to know," Ms. Fienberg countered. "We didn't know, until we did a survey, which records were affected."

The problem was uncovered, by chance, by a sharp-eyed state regulator. About a year ago, John Deden, a Colorado investigator, printed out a CRD report of a stockbroker he was investigating. A few months later, he tapped into the CRD files to update the investigation. To his surprise, two complaints that were on the original printout had vanished from the file.

"Not only was there not more—there was less" on the broker's disciplinary record, Mr. Deden recalled. Intrigued, he began checking other investigatory files and found that a felony conviction on another broker's record had disappeared as well. More digging produced more missing data.

In September at the Snowbird Conference Center near Salt Lake City, a group of NASD executives and state regulators developed "restoration protocol," a code name for fixing the purge mess. The group looked at 300 examples of purged data and discussed what needed to be restored, recalled Renee Erdmann, a Montana state investigator. She said 20,000 pieces of regulatory data were deleted in a sample of records between January 1995 and April 1996 alone.

It isn't easy to figure out what data are missing. For instance, the NASD purged a customer complaint that Joseph Kathrein Jr., a broker for Quick & Reilly Group Inc. in Newport Beach, Calif., had engaged in unauthorized options trading. Mr. Kathrein denied the allegation. The NASD said the complaint was purged because it didn't allege fraud.

Mr. Kathrein says the "case was resolved in arbitration, with no finding of guilt on either side." But he added: "It's part of my record, and I agree that everything should be there" for investors and regulators to view. The NASD promises to restore these types of complaints to the CRD system.

But that won't do anything to get as many as 30 other purges reinstated. These were done with the NASD's blessing, much to regulators' dismay. In these instances, the NASD has taken the extraordinary step of allowing its arbitrators to expunge disciplinary records of brokers as part of private settlement pacts with investors.

"It's unacceptable," said Ms. Crawford, the Texas commissioner. She said the move "raises the issue of whether the states can continue to rely on the CRD" to conduct business.

Such deletions promise to throw a wrench into continuing negotiations between the NASD and state regulators to overhaul the CRD system. The revisions include putting in procedures to erase stale complaints against brokers.

The NASD and the states have agreed that certain complaints—those settled in favor of a broker or that went nowhere after two years—would be excised. A broader overhaul, in which the system would be transformed into an electronic database for investors to view directly on-line, isn't expected to be completed for about two years.

February 7, 1997

Bulletin Board Likely to Remain Wild West of Wall Street

SMALL STOCK
FOCUS

By Deborah Lohse
And John R. Emshwiller
Staff Reporters of The Wall Street Journal

Nestle and Rolls-Royce trade here. But it is also home to stocks like **Dawcin International**, a Garden City, N.Y., financial-services firm whose chairman, William Lucas, has been accused by the Manhattan U.S. Attorney of trying to bribe an undercover federal agent to boost shares of his company. (He denies the allegation.)

Welcome to the OTC Bulletin Board, a hodge-podge of more than 7,000 securities, including sketchy Las Vegas-style companies long on hype but short on substance, uncounted obscure mom-and-pop companies trading infrequently for pennies a share, a couple hundred American depositary receipts of large foreign companies, and hundreds of limited partnerships.

The National Association of Securities Dealers, which runs the Nasdaq Stock Market, last week took steps to beef up the standards for the OTC Bulletin Board, a loosely regulated electronic trade-and-quote-reporting forum, long deemed the Wild West of Wall Street. Though the Bulletin Board is maintained by Nasdaq, it has no listing requirements and has become a haven of sorts for some people seeking to manipulate stocks.

Last week, the NASD announced plans to begin kicking off Bulletin-Board companies that don't file quarterly statements with the Securities and Exchange Commission or with banking or insurance regulators. The NASD also wants to require brokers who recommend these stocks to keep appraised of current financial statements of the companies and to send customers notices explaining the difference between listed stocks and those that trade on the Bulletin Board or the less-automated Pink Sheets. The Pink Sheets is a separate quotation system run by the National Quotation Bureau.

Many analysts figure such changes, which require SEC approval, are a good first step toward taming the unruly forum. For small companies that don't regularly file financial reports, "it is very easy to manipulate the number of shares and the market price" of stocks and very difficult to detect such abuses, says Stuart Allen, a former special investigator for the SEC. Mr. Allen adds that some of these nonreporting "small" companies build up stockmarket values of tens or even hundreds of millions of dollars.

No one believes the NASD's actions are going to rid the market of all of its desperadoes, however. For one thing, companies that fall off the Bulletin Board still will be eligible to trade in the Pink Sheets. And as many as half of the companies slated for removal from the Bulletin Board may start filing SEC documents in order to stay put. Barry Goldsmith, head of enforcement for NASD Regulation, says regulators will have ready ammo to bring enforcement proceedings if those filings are false. Filing would "provide more information to investors, which would be a good thing," Mr. Goldsmith asserts.

The NASD's regulatory reach over the Bulletin Board is largely centered on making sure that brokers don't inappropriately recommend the stocks or that traders don't inappropriately trade them.

One company that says it will start filing financial statements with the SEC early next year is Los Angeles-based **Keystone Energy Services**, an electric-power marketing company that says it wants to move up from the Bulletin Board to the Nasdaq Stock Market. Keystone, which has yet to report any revenue, says it has 14.7 million shares outstanding, which often trade at several hundred thousand shares a day. At a recent share price of nearly $7 a share, the company has a market value of around $100 million.

Keystone isn't short on optimism. The company says it hopes to capture a slice of the electric-utility market by competing with utilities and others to sell power under deregulation, starting next month in California. It has announced contracts valued at more than $8 million a year with some customers.

But Keystone's marketing story is more grandiose: On its Internet Web site, Keystone projects 1998 revenue of more than $177 million and profit of over $12 million, despite the fact that dozens of competitors, including the giant utilities, are vying for a piece of the California market. A spokeswoman calls the company's projections "very realistic." By 2002, moreover, Keystone boldly projects revenue of $1.3 billion and profit of more than $115 million.

NASD's changes also won't deter some of the Bulletin Board's most troubled companies, because many already file with the SEC. Dawcin International, whose chairman Mr. Lucas is fighting the stock-bribing charges brought last year, amended its annual report in May for the year ended June 30, 1996, noting that it originally filed its 10-KSB to the SEC without obtaining a signature from its certified public accountant. The accountant said in a July SEC filing that he didn't do any auditing for the company. Mr. Lucas says that it was a misunderstanding and that he will refile the financial statements to be in compliance with SEC rules.

Some U.S. companies that don't seek active trading in their stock say they aren't unhappy moving to the more-obscure Pink Sheets. **Louisville Bedding**, for one, is a 110-year-old textile concern whose executives consider it largely a privately held company, according to Chief Financial Officer Christian Rapp. Only 15% of the company's 600,000 or so shares are publicly traded, the result of some company-held shares getting into the hands of outsiders over the years, says Mr. Rapp. Because of its small float, the company has no plans to begin filing financial reports to the SEC, Mr. Rapp adds.

"A lot of these companies don't care if they are on the Bulletin Board or not, because they don't have much interest in seeing their stock traded," explains Harry Eisenberg, publisher of Walker's Manual of Unlisted Stocks in Lafayette, Calif.

In fact, many nonreporting companies on the Bulletin Board are well-established small businesses. Some solid, nonreporting Bulletin-Board companies are industrial manufacturer **Conbraco Industries**; **Hydraulic Press Brick** Co., which makes construction products; and **King Cullen Grocery**, according to Mr. Eisenberg, who invests in some of the companies he picks for inclusion in his manuals and doesn't seek to verify all of the claims in the audited financial statements that companies send him.

Whatever the fate of some of the smallest issues, the Bulletin Board already is slated to lose many of the largest foreign companies whose ADRs trade there. That is because the SEC, in giving the seven-year-old Bulletin Board final approval this year, required that Nasdaq kick off ADR issuers that don't comply with certain U.S. disclosure rules by March 31.

December 15, 1997

PART SEVEN

THE REGULATORS

The Securities and Exchange Commission

•

The Federal Reserve

THE SECURITIES AND EXCHANGE COMMISSION

"WORKABLE LAWS" FOR THE MARKETS

The Chairman: Been There, Done That

Arthur Levitt Jr. says that when he was named chairman of the Securities and Exchange Commission in June of 1993 he felt like the "parish priest who became the Pope." But it looks more like he was converted to a new religion. Many of his initiatives as SEC chairman have been designed to stamp out practices that once had been integral parts of Mr. Levitt's life in the securities industry.

The conversion has made Mr. Levitt one of the most aggressive SEC chairmen ever. His pro-investor agenda has included new trading rules and more and simpler disclosure to small investors. But it has also touched off more than a little grumbling on Wall Street. With virtually every initiative he pursued, he has revisited a corner of Wall Street where he either once profited or battled as a competitor.

As the chairman of the American Stock Exchange from 1978 to 1989, for example, he supported initiatives to lower U.S. accounting standards to allow foreign companies to list on U.S. exchanges. As a sales manager early in his career, he was asked to sign off on the hiring of brokers who had great sales records with their prior employers but who, at the same time, had been subject to disciplinary actions—but who were now "clean," they swore.

He admits that although he ran the Amex, essentially an auction market, he probably made more money on Nasdaq, the electronic dealer-based market that he has so harshly criticized and subjected to tough new rules. Perhaps the supreme irony has been his vigorous effort to curb campaign contributions by municipal-bond underwriters. People who knew him on Wall Street say Mr. Levitt himself was a consummate fund-raiser and political contributor. In 1992 he was one of twenty sponsors of a fund-raiser that garnered $3.5 million for a candidate named William Clinton.

"When you come to a job like this, your mind changes about so many issues that, before, you had kind of a proprietary interest in," Mr. Levitt conceded in a 1997 interview with the *Journal*.

The Market's Top Cop

It takes a tough cop to keep tabs on the nation's securities markets, and that's the image that the SEC has shrewdly cultivated since its inception. With offices around the country, the agency responds to more than 42,000 complaints a year regarding possible violations of the nation's securities laws. Many of those complaints involve broker-dealer operations, the firms that buy and sell securities in the public securities markets. The rest of the complaints are made against other institutions that come under the SEC's regulatory mandate, including mutual funds, banks, and registered investment advisers.

Rigorous enforcement of the nation's securities laws has earned the SEC the sobriquet of Wall Street's "Top Cop." Despite battles with Congress over funding, the commission has been able to increase its enforcement staff just in time to absorb the brunt of growing complaints from the swelling pool of first-time investors who have entered the market in recent years. During the past decade, for example, the commission has increased its enforcement staff to a record 934 employees. In the past seven years the number of investigations launched by the enforcement staff has increased 17.6 percent. SEC officials say taxpayers are getting their money's worth; the enforcement staff brought nearly 50 percent more cases in the fiscal year that ended September 30, 1996, than it did in 1990.

But the SEC is responsible for much more than just snagging criminals in the financial industry. Probably the most time-consuming part of the commission's job is the day-to-day regulation of the securities markets, and the various financial entities that fall under its jurisdiction. The commission's chores include everything from keeping an eye on the conduct of brokers, to dealing with potential insider trading cases. Staffers at the commission are required to monitor offerings of new securities issues, as well as the market's self-regulatory organizations, such as the NASD and the Municipal Securities Rulemaking Board, which creates rules for the municipal-bond market.

New areas of regulation open up all the time. With the explosion of computer technology in recent years, the commission has directed increased attention to the Internet and various on-line services that are now offering the public information about a whole slew of investments, from individual stocks to mutual funds. Providing adequate disclosure is another area in flux. The hot disclosure topic of the late 1990s: Soft dollars. Soft dollars are arrangements between brokerage firms and money managers which are used by funds to pay for certain brokerage services, such as research. But what concerns the SEC is that many of these arrangements are done in secret and pay for items that don't directly benefit small investors, such as a money manager's telephone bills and

Regulators Probe Unit Of Barclays

Former Trader Says BZW Covered Losses

BY MICHAEL SICONOLFI
Staff Reporter of THE WALL STREET JOURNAL

Federal regulators are investigating allegations that the U.S. securities unit of Britain's **Barclays Bank** PLC improperly absorbed trading losses caused by client errors.

The investigation, launched by the Securities and Exchange Commission, is specifically examining whether BZW Securities Inc. covered the losses of favored institutional investors in exchange for future business, according to testimony of a former BZW trader taken by the SEC's New York regional office. In two instances alone, the amount of covered losses totaled about $80,000, the former trader testified.

On Wall Street, whatever party is responsible for a trading error is expected to absorb any loss that results from the mishap. Errors, which can range from mistaking a buy for a sell order to the number of shares traded, have become more common in recent years as the volume of trading by big institutional investors has soared. The practice of covering losses for favored clients, although prevalent in Japan, is illegal in the U.S. and is relatively rare.

In the case of BZW, error forms—which the firm uses to account for mistaken trades—"were changed" to show that the firm absorbed the losses, according to Kate Evans, the former BZW senior sales trader, who provided the testimony to the SEC as part of the agency's pending investigation.

BZW officials decline to comment on the investigation. But a spokeswoman says: "It's never been a policy at BZW to absorb losses caused by client errors in placing orders, and we decide this on a case-by-case basis." The SEC, as is its custom, declines to either confirm or deny the existence of a pending investigation. Ms. Evans's lawyer, Bill T. Singer of Singer Zamansky, a New York law firm, also declines to comment.

BZW isn't a big Wall Street player; its capital level ranks the firm No. 57 out of 487 member firms of the Securities Industry Association, a trade group. But the SEC probe underscores concerns by Wall Street regulators about securities firms compensating big institutional clients for trading losses, which violates rules by the New York Stock Exchange and National Association of Securities Dealers. The rules are designed to prevent Wall Street firms from effectively guaranteeing that clients won't lose money and to keep firms from sharing accounts with customers.

"Guarantees could be cast in a lot of different ways," says Barry R. Goldsmith, executive vice president enforcement at NASD Regulation Inc. This includes a situation where for consideration or future business, a firm will make good these kinds of losses." Regulatory activity in this area has been "something that's been fairly constant" in recent years, Mr. Goldsmith says.

It's not the first time the SEC has investigated the issue. In 1991, regulators examined whether the U.S. units of Japan's Big Four securities firms — Nomura Securities Co., Daiwa Securities Co., Nikko Securities Co. and Yamaichi Securities Co.—had, among other things, compensated clients for losses after the four Japanese parents conceded they had paid a total of hundreds of millions of dollars to selected clients to compensate them for losses suffered when Tokyo stock prices plunged in 1990.

That probe led to a 1993 civil administrative proceeding, accusing Yamaichi's U.S. brokerage unit of improperly reimbursing client losses. The unit, Yamaichi International (America) Inc., settled the charges without admitting or denying them. (Neither Nomura, Daiwa or Nikko was charged by the SEC with compensating clients for losses.)

On first blush, the notion of securities firms eating client mistakes seems as odd as, say, supermarkets offering refunds to shoppers who mistakenly buy too much milk that later spoils. But there can be an additional factor at work on Wall Street. In the BZW case, the SEC is investigating whether the firm's clients that were allowed to disavow losing trades later made it up by directing commissions to BZW for an amount equaling the loss, according to testimony.

If, for example, a client error triggered a $50,000 loss to the firm, the client would make up the loss not by placing a $50,000 trade, but a bigger trade that would generate a commission of $50,000, according to testimony presented to the SEC.

In the BZW matter, the SEC is examining, among other things, stock trades BZW made in 1996 for clients including **Sceptre Investment Counsel** Ltd., a Toronto investment-advisory firm, and **Lexington Management** Corp., a Saddle Brook, N.J., investment-advisory concern, according to the SEC testimony provided by Ms. Evans, the former BZW sales trader.

Betty Horton, vice president of finance at Sceptre, declines to comment. Lawrence Kantor, a managing director at Lexington, confirms that Lexington has "a longstanding trading relationship with BZW." But he says Lexington has no knowledge of any quid pro quo arrangement involving trading errors. "You don't operate in an error-free environment," Mr. Kantor says. "If you make the error, you own it; if somebody else makes the error, they own it—that's it."

In her testimony to the SEC staff, Ms. Evans says that clients would pay back BZW for taking customer errors "to keep that relationship good."

How quickly could a client return the favor? Says Ms. Evans in her SEC testimony: "If you were dealing with somebody, for example, like one of the major institutions, one of the Boston-based institutions, they could throw a trade your way 10 minutes after it happened."

July 18, 1997

office supplies. The soft dollar providers have hit back, saying that for the most part they provide services such as information about stocks and other forms of research that benefit investors of all kinds. The debate continues amid the SEC's sweeping examination of the use of soft dollars by brokerage firms, money-management outfits and mutual funds. So far, only a handful of enforcement cases have emerged from the examination program, but SEC officials say more are on the way.

The commission's disclosure mandate extends to many other areas as well, some of which aren't so clearly defined. Take the lucrative business of investment newsletters. Despite a 1985 Supreme Court ruling, which prevents the commission from directly regulating these publications, Wall Street's top cop effectively skirts the Supreme Court by directing its enforcement staff to pursue cases rather than creating regulations that newsletters must follow. Investigators are particularly concerned by newsletter publishers' failures to disclose potential conflicts of interest between what they are recommending, and their own investment decisions as registered investment advisers. In one example, the SEC filed a complaint against a newsletter publisher for allegedly failing to disclose that he received money from publicly traded companies for recommending stocks in his publication.

Where does the SEC go from here? Much of that depends on who becomes the next SEC chairman. Before 1993, the commission paid little attention to activities in the municipal-bond market. All that changed following President Clinton's appointment of Mr. Levitt, who has put the muni-bond market at the top of the SEC's agenda. In recent years, the commission has pushed for a number of rules designed to regulate abuse in the municipal-bond market.

Regulating the Self-regulators

One of the most revolutionary changes the SEC ever imposed came in the mid-1990s in the form of the investigation, censure, and ultimate overhaul of the Nasdaq Stock Market. The SEC charged that Nasdaq's self-regulatory organization, the National Association of Securities Dealers, failed to police abusive trading practices and, worse, even allowed dealers to work in concert in some instances to prop up prices artificially to help each other, rather than their investor clients, make profitable trades.

On paper, a dealer market like Nasdaq is supposed to feature multiple dealers competing with one another to offer the best prices for stocks to be sold or bought. But until around 1994, the Nasdaq Stock Market resembled an old-boy's network where the implicit motto was "you scratch my back and I'll scratch yours." As cited in scathing reports on Nasdaq dealers' practices, some traders routinely engaged in anticompetitive behavior. For example, a trader might do his trader buddy at a competing firm a favor by bumping up the posted "bid" or buying price for a stock temporarily. That way, the upward trend would ensure that his friend could unload his stock at a better price. Left out of that equation: the poor investor who bought at the artificial price, which might drop once the deal was done.

Another common practice was keeping "spreads" wide. That works because market makers act as both buyer and seller of Nasdaq stocks. If the best price at which dealers would sell routinely was twenty-five cents higher than the best price at which they would buy the same stock, other dealers could conceivably cut in and offer to sell at a slightly lower price or offer to buy at a slightly higher price. But for years there was no such competitive pricing. Instead, dealers all moved their prices up or down in a lockstep that kept that twenty-five-cent "spread" intact. Such artificially wide spreads translated into healthy profits for dealers and lost opportunities for investors.

Until the spreads hit the fan, that is. In May 1994 an academic study by two obscure finance professors exposed the apparent collusion to keep spreads wide in the Nasdaq market. The outrage that greeted the study shocked Wall Street and brought the wrath of regulators down on the heads of dealers. Anne Bingaman, the Justice Department's antitrust chief, announced in the fall of 1994 that she was investigating whether dealers had illegally colluded to keep spreads wide. It didn't take the SEC long to join the chase.

For two subsequent years the NASD was under relentless pressure from Washington. NASD President Joe Hardiman and chief operating officer Richard Ketchum took much of the heat. Insiders said the two were forced to play the role of chastened child when they felt more like scapegoats. Mr. Hardiman, for his part, was said to believe the whole spread issue was a red herring raised by disgruntled day traders known as SOES bandits, angry at being snubbed by mainstream trading firms. (SOES stands for the Small Order Execution System, a trading system that many mainstream traders think SOES traders abuse, often at the expense of market makers.) He also blamed the media, believing they had greedily latched onto the issue without understanding how things "really worked" on Nasdaq.

"Joe thought the SOES guys were portraying themselves as the champions of the little guy, when really they were trying to get better prices for themselves," recalled one insider.

And, of course, there were those at the NASD and outside the organization who muttered under their breath that if spreads were such a scandal all those years, why hadn't the SEC, which after all is the ultimate overseer of NASD, caught the problem earlier. Some said that, while he was not blamed, former market-regulation chief Brandon Becker's departure was in part due to his friendly relationship with the NASD, on which the SEC could no longer afford to be seen as "soft."

The point people for the SEC investigation of NASD were enforcement chief William McLucas, Mr. Levitt's then-senior counselor Carrie Dwyer, and Mr. Levitt himself. While trying to keep up a cooperative front, NASD's president, Joseph Hardiman and Richard Ketchum consistently played down the offenses with which the market was being charged, noting hopefully that whatever changes were needed could quietly be implemented, with market forces washing out any other problems.

But the SEC couldn't and wouldn't let that be the end of it. Those involved in the negotiations say that SEC representatives clashed at times bitterly with NASD officials, with the SEC bent on making a public display of the abuses and lack of oversight.

Part of the SEC's antagonistic attitude has been attributed by some to the fact that the Justice Department was first off the mark in launching an investigation. The SEC launched its own inquiry a month after Ms. Bingaman publicly announced the Justice probe.

The SEC and Justice Department ultimately arrived at a workable information-sharing arrangement, they say, but not before some turf uncertainties arose, according to some involved in the negotiations. Whenever NASD had to turn over documents to the SEC or Justice, the other agency would ask for its own copy, people at the NASD recall. That led to internal NASD jokes about "document envy" among the two.

The SEC's report, which Mr. Ketchum, Mr. Hardiman and NASD's lawyers worked overtime to have toned down, was a scathing indictment of the NASD's failure to stop the anticompetitive trading behavior that by 1996 had become well covered in the press. It formally required the NASD to follow up on a vast restructuring that had been recommended by a committee headed by former Senator Warren Rudman of New Hampshire. NASD had convened that committee to head off just such outside punishment.

NASD was obliged to separate its market-regulation and its Nasdaq divisions, each with its own president and boards of governors, and had to insure that each board had 50 percent representation from outside the securities industry. And it had to spend $100 million over the next five years to add compliance personnel and install an electronic "order audit trail" that would track each order from the moment it arrived at trading desks. Ironically, NASD had already begun plans for virtually all such changes, thanks to the Rudman committee and the arrival of Mary Schapiro, a longtime regulator who became the new NASD Regulation chief. But it appeared to the public that the NASD was on a short leash held by Arthur Levitt.

Only a year or so after the changes were imposed, though, Mr. Levitt's choice for NASD president, Frank G. Zarb, took office talking about unraveling some of the structural changes that had been imposed with such fanfare. Mr. Zarb, with the blessing of Mr. Levitt, said initially that he wanted to make the complex NASD organization run more like a corporation with a strong CEO rather than a self-regulator with two autonomous units. While promising that the ultimate structure would retain an independent regulator and 50 percent outside board members, Mr. Zarb's plans were not immediately applauded by some people who worried that Nasdaq would revert to its old ways if the structure were altered. But Mr. Levitt was unperturbed, noting that the NASD's structure had become unwieldy, and that no single board structure could protect against a self-serving NASD.

But even beyond the overhaul of Nasdaq, the SEC's role as watchdog over the self-regulatory markets and organizations got quite a workout during the Levitt regime. "Almost every self-regulatory organization has gone through a period of difficulty ... when they failed to recognize their primary responsibility to the public, and where they confuse their role as an industry cheerleader for their much more important role of protecting our markets and our public," said Mr. Levitt.

The NASD experience probably laid the groundwork for an early 1997 visit by Mr. Levitt to another troubled self-regulator, the Philadelphia Stock Exchange. Mr. Levitt went to the exchange to lay down the law to Philly officials, who were neglecting oversight of the market during a period of bitter political infighting between specialists and market makers. They fought over virtually everything, industry executives recalled, including "new systems and new procedures to specialist assignments to marketing budgets." For example, when the exchange wanted to install a "wheel" to distribute small customer orders, to replace an inefficient manual system, it was delayed at least a year as specialists squabbled with market makers over how orders would be distributed. The system was finally installed in 1997.

Philly's woes were brought to a head when it came to light that two of the members of its thirty-member board had acted inappropriately. In one instance the former chairman invested in a startup technology company that had gotten a contract to develop a new trading system for the exchange. The chairman, Vincent Casella, even requested to be the specialist for the company, Ashton Technology Group, although it didn't list on Philadelphia. He resigned as chairman in October 1996. An SEC investigation of the situation concluded the exchange didn't react quickly to the allegations because its board was mired in political infighting. Similarly, the SEC filed a complaint against Richard B. Feinberg, a member of exchange's board and former head of its conduct committee for allegedly cheating customers for whom he was executing trades on Nasdaq. Mr. Feinberg contested the charges in the case, which was heard by an administrative law judge in February 1997, and is awaiting a ruling.

In his unusual visit to the exchange in March 1997, Mr. Levitt held a closed-door meeting in which he sharply criticized the way the exchange does business, especially its lack of attention to investor's rights on the exchanges. Much as he had done with Nasdaq, Mr. Levitt suggested that the Philadelphia exchange appoint at least 50 percent of its board from the investing public, rather than exchange members or securities-industry representatives. Until then, Philadelphia had the fewest independent directors of any of the five regional exchanges, with only three of its twenty-nine members coming from the public at large. In the spring of 1997, the exchange committed to shrinking its board to twenty-two members, with eleven coming from outside the securities industry. Such measures, and a slew of others, were recommended in a sixty-page report by a special committee led by former SEC Commissioner Irving Pollack.

Curbing "Pay To Play"

In 1993 the municipal-bond market was booming. Bond issuance was reaching historic highs. Interest rates were falling, boosting the value of all fixed-income investments, and Wall Street underwriters were developing new and more profitable ways to help municipalities sell tax-exempt securities. At the same time, state and local politicians were raking in huge campaign contributions from the same Wall Street bond executives they chose to handle the lucrative underwriting assignments.

Everyone seemed happy. Until Arthur Levitt came along.

Since becoming chairman in 1993, Mr. Levitt had taken a keen interest in how business is done in the muni-bond market. He's pushed for more rules and regulations than many of his predecessors. Underwriters are disclosing more information including the once missing details of how a state or city balances its budget.

But where Mr. Levitt has made his biggest mark—and his most enemies— is in the area of "pay-to-play," the practice by which municipalities handed out muni-bond business to underwriters with the best political connections rather than the best market skills. Fueling this system: campaign contributions.

For years, underwriters gladly handed over millions of dollars of donations to state and local officials, all in the hope of winning muni-bond assignments that paid millions more in fees and commissions. The politicians, for their part, put muni-bond executives at the top of the fundraising lists, asking—sometimes demanding—big donations from the executives they selected as underwriters of their debt.

The players included some of the brightest stars in state and local politics, like Elizabeth Holtzman, the feisty New York congresswoman who grilled Gerald Ford over his pardon of President Richard Nixon following the Watergate scandal. Indeed, Ms. Holtzman would build a career on her belief that public officials should be held to the highest ethical standards.

By 1992 Ms. Holtzman, who had been elected New York City comptroller two years earlier, was eyeing the Democratic nomination for U.S. Senate. But as spring became summer that year, her campaign was sagging; state attorney general Robert Abrams and former congresswoman Geraldine Ferraro were locked in a tight race, and by most polls, Ms. Holtzman was far behind. Short of cash and in need of a last-minute advertising barrage, she turned to Fleet Bank, an affiliate of Fleet Financial Services, for a $450,000 loan. The resulting ad campaign targeted Ms. Ferraro and, many political experts say, did nothing more than help Mr. Abrams win the nomination. Ms. Holtzman finished fourth, behind the Rev. Al Sharpton.

Disgraced within her party, Ms. Holtzman's troubles were far from over. She was saddled with a massive campaign debt at a time when she was gearing up to run for reelection as city comptroller. Several months later, Ms. Holtzman promoted Fleet Bank's securities arm to a lucrative post as a city bond underwriter during a time when she had problems repaying the bank loan. At the same time Ms. Holtzman had turned to Wall Street to help finance her campaign for city comptroller. As city comptroller, she helped appoint firms as underwriters of city bond sales, and these same bond underwriters became targets of her fundraising apparatus. Firms like Merrill Lynch, Goldman Sachs and PaineWebber handed over thousands of dollars to the comptroller as she was struggling to win reelection.

In 1993 the issue became public. Newspaper reports detailed her dealing with Fleet and the Wall Street underwriters under her control. Later that year, she was booted from office, losing to Alan Hevesi who vowed to clean up corruption in the city bond sales. Meanwhile an inquiry by the city's Department of Investigation concluded that her "failure to inquire whether Fleet Bank" was seeking business with her office constitutes "gross negligence."

All along, the newly appointed Mr. Levitt was becoming keenly aware of

Ms. Holtzman's troubles, and a series of other muni abuses featured in the national media. He decided to take action, launching a series of high profile investigations into some of the most blantant scandals appearing in the press. When it was all over, major bond underwriters like Merrill Lynch & Co. and Lazard Frères & Co. were forced to pay millions of dollars to settle SEC charges that they were involved in activities that violated the nation's securities law. (Firms neither admitted nor denied wrongdoing.)

At the same time, Mr. Levitt sought to ban the use of campaign contributions to win underwriting assignments. By 1994, the SEC, under his direction, approved a rule that restricted how much money muni-bond executives can give to state and local politicians who hand out underwriting assignments.

The message from the SEC was clear: The era of pay-to-play is over.

Now the muni-bond market is a shadow of what it was when Mr. Levitt first took over. Issuance has dropped significantly. Wall Street firms are closing their muni-bond departments amid the drought in new muni-bond sales. Bankers complain that it's too difficult to comply with Mr. Levitt's new rules and regulations in a market that provides such little room for profit.

Mr. Levitt, for his part, stands by his action. The muni-bond market, he says, is too important to let such practices go unnoticed. Cities and states sell muni-bonds to build roads, bridges, and other infrastructure projects. Big Wall Street firms underwrite the bonds and sell them to legions of small investors who purchase the bonds from their brokers or through tax-exempt mutual funds. In Mr. Levitt's opinion, taxpayers may be getting a raw deal if underwriters are chosen based on their political connections rather than their ability to sell bonds efficiently to the public. Investors could be on the hook, too, since bonds sold by firms violating securities rules could lose their tax-exempt status and plummet in value.

Most of all, Mr. Levitt says he witnessed all these shady dealings firsthand. "Having sold millions of dollars in municipal bonds, and underwritten millions of dollars, I've gone to countless fund-raisers and been asked to attend countless others as a price to being in that business. That was probably my number-one priority, changing the municipal-bond business," he said.

The muni rule has few friends on Wall Street and among state and local officials who have seen a valuable source of campaign cash dry up. In fact, eight state and local groups including the National Conference of State Legislatures and the National Governors Association urged Mr. Levitt and the SEC, as the regulator of the MSRB, to delay the rule change.

And some say the rule is riddled with loopholes. Muni-bond underwriters may be barred from making contributions to state and local officials, but nothing prevents their firms from giving contributions to state and county parties that merely funnel the donations to the politicians. In addition, "pay-to-play" continues unabated among lawyers seeking to earn fees for providing legal opinions on muni-bond deals, as well as from big money management outfits that hand over donations in order to win lucrative assignments from public pension funds.

Ironically, the campaign to clean up municipal finance ran headlong into another of Mr. Levitt's favorite crusades: the promotion of minorities and women on Wall Street. Some African Americans on Wall Street have blamed his crackdown of muni-bond abuses for the slow disintegration of once profitable minority-owned bond firms. Several maintained that unlike big underwriting houses, they needed to use campaign contributions to stay on municipalities' radar screens. Several of the largest, such as Grigsby Brandford Inc., have been forced to close amid the legal pressure imposed by the SEC probes; others, like black-owned Pryor, McClendon, Counts & Co., watched as their capital levels shriveled amid the SEC scrutiny.

Mr. Levitt was said to be personally anguished about how several big minority-owned firms went out of business or saw their franchise crumble during his tenure. Publicly, however, he blamed the firms' troubles on the sharp drop in municipal-bond business in recent years, and refused to concede that his policies had a disparate impact on minority-owned firms. "The notion that this works a hardship on black or minority firms I think denigrates the very important role that is played, by suggesting that the only way to get business is by buying it," Mr. Levitt said.

The Trillion-Pound Gorilla: Mutual Funds

In many ways, the SEC has shed its tough cop image when it comes to regulating the booming business of selling mutual-funds to small investors. Today, more than $3 trillion sits in mutual-fund accounts, and millions more are expected to flood into the business in the years ahead. Likewise, the number of companies peddling mutual funds have increased dramatically—almost 400 percent in the past twenty years.

How has the SEC responded? By increasing routine "examinations" of fund companies, pushing for more investor-friendly initiatives, and working with the fund business's leading trade group, the Investment Company Institute. Mr. Levitt, for his part, has relied on the bully pulpit to get his point across. In speeches to the mutual-fund industry, he has called for restrictions on the common practice of letting mutual-fund managers freely trade for their personal accounts, which regulators say can pit a manager's interests against his clients, the fund shareholders.

Throughout the SEC the message is the same: The mutual-fund companies are among the best-run businesses in the country, and if there's going to be a major scandal, it won't be with the industry's biggest players.

In recent years, the commission has proposed a series of smaller initiatives designed to make fund investing easier for the average person. For example, the SEC proposed that fund companies rewrite their mutual-fund prospectus in plain English, and give investors the choice of receiving a four-page fund "profile" prospectus in addition to the long form, as part of the standard disclosure each fund company has to make to new investors.

The point-man for all this has been Barry Barbash, a former mutual-fund lawyer. As director of investment management, Mr. Barbash is the SEC's eyes and ears when it comes to fund-company regulation, and if his record is any guide, he may be the best listener at the commission. Mr. Barbash, for his part, says there's little evidence that the fund industry is in need of a new set of rules and regulations to prevent scandal; what's on the books will work just fine, he says.

Don't tell that to the millions of small investors who placed their money in bond funds in the early 1990s. The bond market was on a roll; interest rates were falling, and mutual-fund companies were looking for ways to entice those most reluctant to invest in funds—bank depositors—to make the move to bond funds. What they came up with was a series of turbo-charged bond mutual funds, with safe-sounding names that prominently displayed the word "government" to disguise the risky nature of these investments. While the funds did invest in government bonds, they were also laden with risky derivatives of such securities, such as "inverse floaters" and "collateralized mortgage obligations." The banks, eager to ally with the rapidly growing fund industry, jumped headfirst into this frenzy, peddling these investments at the tellers' windows to the elderly and others who had never even heard of mutual funds before.

But in 1994 disaster struck. The bottom fell out of the bond market when the Federal Reserve began a series of interest-rate increases. All those former bank depositors accustomed to earning 3 percent on their money no matter what happened in the securities markets got their first taste of losing money. Many said they lost huge portions of their life savings and joined others in class-action lawsuits against some of the most venerable names in the banking business. In December 1995, NationsBank Corp. of Charlotte, North Carolina, agreed to pay $30 million to settle a Texas state-court lawsuit alleging that it misled investors about the riskiness of two exotic investment funds launched in late 1993 and early 1994.

The controversy continues. In May of 1997, Florida regulators said the brokerage unit of NationsBank will pay $850,000 as part of a settlement that ended the state's wide-ranging review of the company's sales practices. Mutual-fund executives say the bond-fund debacle was isolated among a few fund companies, largely run by banks, that were new to the fund business. The SEC and other regulators are investigating these practices, and will continue to do so as they arise in the future.

But some mutual-fund fund experts say the commission is playing with fire if it doesn't take a more proactive stance in regulating fund companies. Don

Phillips, president of Morningstar Inc., the Chicago-based publisher of mutual-fund information, has emerged as one of the commission's harshest critics when it comes to fund-company regulation. In fact, Mr. Phillip's criticism of the commission's oversight of the fund industry turned into a testy public squabble between himself and Mr. Barbash, after Morningstar posted its concerns in an open letter to the SEC on the company's Web site. Mr. Barbash shot back as well. "What he says we should be doing we're already doing," Mr. Barbash said.

But Mr. Phillips continued with his attack. In many cases, the SEC, he says, is misusing its resources. Plain English disclosures may sound good, but they take pressure off fund companies to serve investor interests in other, more important areas, he said. Of course, Mr. Phillips has an interest in this matter since his company earns its bread-and-butter writing short, plain-English reviews of mutual funds. But his biggest gripe is that the SEC has done next-to-nothing when it comes to forcing the fund companies and their independent boards of directors to treat shareholders like owners. The SEC, he says, should hold fund companies and their independent boards of directors responsible for giving investors complete information rather than easy-to-read information. "If the independent directors were thinking about shareholders as owners, would they really have voted in the number of fee increases" that they have in recent years, Mr. Phillips asked.

The Internet Challenge

Like most government agencies, the SEC's strongest suit is not technology.

When a New York brewery began plans to underwrite and sell its own stock by posting a page on the Internet in the spring of 1996, the SEC had to hastily halt the process while it reviewed the legal issues associated with the system. It finally gave a cautious green light, provided the company, Spring Street Brewing, made some changes to its offering designed to safeguard investors while not choking off innovations like the trading forum, dubbed Wit-Trade, that brought Spring Street Brewing to the public market.

The chief executive of Wit-Trade, Andrew Klein, said at the time that his phone had been ringing off the hook with companies who wanted to know how they could sell their own company's stock over the Internet. Most companies that followed immediately in Wit-Trade's wake were unable to generate the level of interest—$1.6 million—that Mr. Klein managed for Spring Street Brewing. Many early would-be on-line initial public offerings fizzled out after getting investor commitments for a few hundred thousand dollars or less.

Though the Wit-Trade system would ultimately fizzle, orphaning Spring Street shares, Mr. Klein was lucky to have Steven Wallman, an SEC commissioner with an interest in on-line innovations, shepherd the SEC's review.

Then-Commissioner Wallman reassured Mr. Klein that the questions coming from teams of SEC lawyers weren't designed to put his on-line outfit out of business.

The idea was simple. After a self-underwritten public offering, Mr. Klein posted a page on the World Wide Web where investors interested in buying and selling shares could meet and do deals. The SEC agreed to leave the setup largely intact, but required the control of the funds as they passed from investor to investor to be handled by a registered broker-dealer, or processed by a bank or escrow agent.

Mr. Klein also would have been required to warn investors that the shares he was peddling were potentially speculative and illiquid, and to keep a record of recent prices of purchases and sales, a modified version of what stock exchanges are required to do.

Clearly, the issue of regulating on-line upstarts was one for which the SEC had to get up to speed. As SEC deputy director of market regulation Robert Colby said at the time, "Wherever the trading goes, we have to follow." After all, trading stocks over the Internet is a booming business, and most SEC officials believe it is just a matter of time before there is an Internet-based stock exchange.

Some international market participants have also been recommending that U.S. investors be able to use the Internet to finally buy or sell shares of stock directly from foreign stock exchanges. But that idea was getting only lukewarm reception at the SEC. "The Internet doesn't allow any good way to be regulated in terms of access to the United States," Mr. Wallman said. "When you have a system premised on regulating access, I would have questions whether that is a foundation that can be sustained."

The Future of Market Regulation

Picture the SEC in 1997.

It had imposed some of its most sweeping rule changes on the markets, changes destined to make customers more-active players than ever in setting prices for stocks, especially those trading on Nasdaq. Regional exchanges like the Pacific Exchange and the Chicago Exchange were pushing the competitive envelope, with the powerful support of market-regulation director Richard Lindsey, by beating the New York Stock Exchange to committing to quote Big Board stock prices in $1/16$-point increments—something destined to improve prices for investors. Ultimately, the regionals and third-market firms that compete with the NYSE, such as Bernard L. Madoff Investment Securities, put enough pressure on the Big Board that in June of 1997 it finally agreed to break its age-old minimum pricing of $1/8$ point increments, or 12.5 cents—much to the glee of Mr. Lindsey, a free-market economist who wanted exactly such competitive fallout.

Meanwhile, more and more brokerage firms are asking the SEC to let them set up private trading systems much like Reuters Holdings' Instinet, a popular trading forum where dealers or institutional investors like mutual funds can anonymously indicate a desire to buy or sell at specified "limit" prices. If approved, the market for Nasdaq and other stocks will get even more fragmented away from their respective markets and onto scattered systems.

All the various changes added up to a new world, where competition for trading business in the United States is rapidly shifting away from a contest largely between the two biggest markets—New York and its increasingly antiquated open outcry auction market and Nasdaq's dealer market, which is getting more and more driven by customer prices, not dealer quotes. Instead, firms, exchanges, individuals or others with the most convenient, best-priced technological options are going to be the places where stocks are traded in the future.

At the same time, if a foreign stock exchange wanted to invite U.S. investors to trade its stocks in 1997, it would have to set up a base in the United States, complete with all the exchange's reporting requirements and oversight chores, something none opted to do.

Against that rapidly changing backdrop, it became abundantly clear that the SEC was still regulating based on the assumption that trading would take place on an "exchange" like the Big Board, which must police its members for unfair behavior and keep records of the transactions. Upstart systems like Instinet, meanwhile, were awkwardly treated like broker-dealers, forced to follow rules for things like minimum capital requirements that have little relevance for their primary function, but also free to ignore potential abuses of the system since they weren't technically an exchange.

In the spring of 1997, the SEC made its opening move in getting a grip on regulating alternative markets. It posed a slew of questions in a "concept release" sent to market participants on how exchanges should be regulated going into the year 2000. That request for public comment had as its ultimate aim the radical restructuring of how the SEC should supervise markets in the future. The changes under consideration would mark the biggest shift in the way the SEC regulates stock markets since the agency's formation in 1934, said Mr. Lindsey.

Mr. Levitt said, "We are starting down a road I believe will make us more responsive to markets that have changed more in the past five years than they have since they started in this country."

Regulators said their goal in issuing the concept release was to ultimately foster Internet-based stock exchanges, provide a regulation-free incubation period for small upstart stock exchanges, and give the existing large stock markets freedom to create new products without instant regulatory burdens. They also aimed to open up foreign exchanges to U.S. investors. "The fundamental thing underpinning this is that our securities regulations were written in 1934 and in 1934 the world was very different—it was a paper-based world and all the exchanges looked in one way or the other like the New York Stock Exchange," Mr. Lindsey said. "Now, if you can live in Des Moines, Iowa, London or Singapore and trade, maybe we need a different interpretation."

The proposed reforms would reclassify which exchanges should be regulated by the commission and which should not. For instance, Mr. Lindsey said, there may be no need to regulate a small regional stock exchange that has low volume and does not generate prices. That could also be the case with start-up exchanges on the Internet, he said, though as they grew they would become subject to SEC oversight.

One idea in the concept release is to establish a class of exempt exchanges that are regulated by a self-regulatory organization and have limited obligations, such as maintaining an audit trail. If the exchange gathered importance, it would move into the next category of regulated exchange.

The SEC also sought to look at ways to enhance and supervise investors' access to foreign stock markets that want to do business in the United States. There are now no systems to allow that and the SEC is contemplating regulating points of access to those markets. The commission would consider, for instance, allowing large stock exchanges to adopt new trading systems in pilot programs without prior regulatory approval. "Alternative markets have no monopoly on innovation," Mr. Levitt said. "Traditional exchanges should also be able to respond to competitive changes."

Cyber Rogues

While the SEC ponders what role on-line trading may play in the development of future stock and bond exchanges, it is also struggling to deal with a problem here and now: shady brokers or others anonymously or misleadingly touting stocks over the Internet to a potential audience of millions. In congressional testimony, Mr. Levitt conceded that resources were inadequate to police the Internet in 1997. He noted that "the ever-increasing level of securities activities occurring over the Internet will force the commission to expand its activities in order to keep up."

In 1997, the SEC brought what was believed to be its first civil Internet-fraud lawsuit against Theodore Melcher Jr. for allegedly taking payments to promote at least eight stocks over the Internet through his newsletter *SGA Goldstar Research*. Federal criminal prosecutors joined the case against him and others, with Mr. Melcher pleading guilty to conspiracy to commit securities fraud in federal court in Alexandria, Virginia. The SEC's case was pending in early 1998 against Mr. Melcher and his partner, Shannon Terry, with the SEC requesting repayment of allegedly illicit gains made on stocks sold while the newsletter urged subscribers to buy. Mr. Terry denied the allegations.

One of Mr. Melcher's stocks was Systems of Excellence, which had racked up hundreds of mentions in on-line forums. The company's chairman, Charles Huttoe, was sentenced to forty-six months in prison after pleading guilty to securities-fraud and money-laundering charges related to the Melcher case. In addition, a stockbroker, Sheldon Kraft, pleaded guilty in federal court to conspiracy to commit securities fraud and money laundering in connection with the stock, and Merle Finkel, an accountant, pleaded guilty to conspiracy to commit stock and bank fraud to write bogus audit reports.

Clearly the amount of money to be made on the Internet makes it a candidate for further rampant abuse. In another Internet-based fraud case, the SEC also settled fraud allegations against the publisher of several Florida-based on-line investment newsletters—including one called *Hot Stocks Review*—for failing to disclose that he and his companies got $1.1 million and 275,500 shares of stock as payment for recommending companies' securities on the Internet. George Chelekis agreed to pay fines of $162,727 without admitting or denying the charges.

The SEC joined with the Federal Trade Commission's Bureau of Consumer Protection, twenty state attorney generals and five state securities regulators in late 1996 for what was dubbed "Internet Pyramid Surf Day" to search for scams. In one day alone, regulators found hundreds of Web sites making offers that may involve illegal pyramid schemes, regulators said.

Rogue Brokers

For an agency that prides itself on investor protection, a painful thorn in the SEC's side are the countless "rogue brokers" and other scamsters of the industry spawned by the long-running bull market of the 1990s. Overall market success makes it easier for unscrupulous brokers to lure investors into bad investments, buy and sell stocks without their customers' permission, or otherwise cheat customers out of money intended for the stock market.

Although cracking down on such scoundrels is the shared responsibility of a hodgepodge of cops, including the NASD, states, and criminal prosecutors, the SEC aims to be the vortex of all the regulatory bodies. The SEC's enforcement division has powers that rest somewhere between the industry and criminal authorities: unlike such self-regulatory bodies as NASD or the New York Stock Exchange, the SEC can subpoena brokers and firms it is investigating and it can pursue anyone who violates its antifraud or securities rules, whether they are exchange members, registered brokers, or freelance fraudsters. But it doesn't have criminal powers to arrest or prosecute securities criminals, so it tries to work with U.S. attorneys in the states and the Justice Department for bigger cases.

Some of the SEC's longest-running, and most elusive, targets are rogue brokers. A 1994 General Accounting Office report criticized the SEC's efforts to weed out rogue brokers, and results of a two-year-old sweep of firms weren't helping. In that case, the SEC had sent examiners into big brokerage firms to get a picture of how widespread dishonest brokers were in mainstream firms.

The evidence was alarming. In May of 1994, the SEC issued a report that said that nearly 25 percent of such branch-office examinations found violations severe enough to warrant referrals to the SEC's enforcement division, which could bring civil actions against offenders. Shortly thereafter, the SEC, the NASD and the New York Stock Exchange launched a similar sweep of 179 smaller firms, culminating in a 1996 report spelling out a similar degree of lax supervision of brokers with disciplinary histories and other problems. The report found that many firms allow rogue brokers to roam from firm to firm; conduct only minimal reviews of brokers before hiring them; provide scant oversight of brokers' trades with clients; and frequently violate rules regarding unsolicited "cold calls" to customers.

"These findings suggest that many firms' supervisory and compliance systems should be strengthened," the report concluded. The findings suggested that even the SEC's recently stepped-up crackdowns on supervisors could be bolstered.

The initial hoopla over rogue brokers did cause SEC lawyers and the Justice Department to form a joint task force to weed out the industry's bad eggs. In January of 1995 Mr. Levitt and Attorney General Janet Reno announced that charges had been brought against eleven stockbrokers around the country accused of cheating elderly customers out of their savings by stealing money, forging clients' signatures, or selling fake certificates of deposit or other securities. The announcement represented the opening salvo of what was heralded to be a series of federal criminal prosecutions of rogue brokers. Several of the brokers had worked, before getting fired, at such major firms as Merrill Lynch, Prudential Securities, and PaineWebber.

Attorney General Reno said at the time that the prosecutions were meant to show that "brokers who seldom risked more than dismissal and restitution can now expect to be criminally prosecuted and indicted if they cheat their customers." Evidence against the brokers came from SEC civil enforcement investigations and inquiries by stock exchange investigators.

Although all eleven brokers pleaded guilty in that case, regulators have never claimed to have made any sizeable dent in the number of offenders, which seems to grow every day. "We're never going to be able to eliminate this, but we can convey the message that we have no tolerance for this, and we are going to come down very hard," said Mr. Levitt in 1997. "And, we are going to try to enlist other agencies to help us impose criminal penalties."

The SEC and Congress's investigatory arm, the General Accounting Office, both came out with recommendations to crack down on rogue brokers, including beefing up the Central Registration Depository so that brokers' rap sheets are up-to-date and complete. But as recently as 1996 a *Wall Street Journal* search found that there were 112 brokers or securities-firm officials working away in the securities business even after being on the losing side of two or more customer arbitrations from 1991 to 1995—a rogue's gallery that many said only reflected the tip of the iceberg.

Even when the SEC joins forces with other authorities to bring criminal charges, the regulator/prosecutor teams have suffered some painful setbacks. In February 1992 a federal jury in Denver acquitted three firms and eleven defendants who had been netted in an undercover sting, launched by the U.S. Attorney in Denver and the FBI with help from the SEC and NASD, alleging penny-stock manipulation. Nicknamed "Operation Pennycon," the sting used an FBI agent posing as a small-stock promoter inviting brokers to work with him to market his stock, manipulate the prices, then cash out.

Although William McLucas, at the time the SEC's head of enforcement, vowed that the agency wouldn't be sidetracked by such a verdict, observers years later noted some potentially similar problems with another much-heralded joint regulatory effort: the 1996 roundup by regulators and New York criminal authorities of forty-six promoters or brokers accused of trying to bribe undercover FBI agents. Those agents posed as brokers willing to be bribed to get their clients to invest in the promoters' stocks. By the end of 1997, fifteen of the original forty-six defendants in the penny-stock sting had pleaded guilty, with charges pending against twenty-three others and charges dropped against eight others. Prosecutors said, however, that it was likely that many of those dropped charges would later be re-filed. However, some observers noted in the spring of 1997 that prosecutors had found it harder than expected to link the payments, which are not illegal per se, to actual stock-fraud schemes. Sean F. O'Shea, former chief of the business and securities fraud unit of the U.S. attorney's office in Brooklyn, said in March that he foresaw mounting problems for the government. The U.S. Attorney's office in Manhattan in late 1997 brought charges against five additional defendants in the case on related stock-fraud charges stemming from the sting.

Still, the SEC followed up in mid-December 1997 with its own civil complaints in federal court in New York and Salt Lake City charging fifty-five brokers, promoters and small-company officers with fraud in a crackdown related to the FBI sting that occurred fourteen months earlier. The case was pending in late 1997.

One area where the SEC has been able to show action, if not quantifiable results, has been in its push to jack up its penalties for lax supervisors. The SEC is able to fine or suspend sales managers or other bosses who knowingly hire brokers with disciplinary "rap sheets" but who don't keep a tight leash on those brokers, who go on to repeat their sins at the new job. Naturally, Wall

Court Ruling Could Hamper Securities Cases

Panel Scraps SEC Sanctions In California Case, Citing Statute of Limitations

BY MICHAEL SICONOLFI
Staff Reporter of THE WALL STREET JOURNAL

NEW YORK—A recent appellate court decision could make it far more vexing for federal regulators to police the securities industry, some legal specialists say.

A federal appeals court in Washington last week threw out Securities and Exchange Commission sanctions against a former **PaineWebber Group** Inc. branch manager for failing to supervise a broker, saying a five-year statute of limitations applied in such cases. Prior federal court decisions have allowed the SEC to bring such sanctions no matter how old the infractions.

If applied broadly, the decision "would make it more difficult for the SEC to bring cases" punishing offenders in the brokerage business, said Irving Pollack, a securities lawyer in Washington, and a former SEC enforcement chief. "It is very important if you're going to police an industry that the public interest overrides the need of an individual to argue" that the SEC took too long to bring a case, he said.

The controversial decision comes as the SEC seeks to hold brokerage-firm managers more accountable for the actions of brokers under their watch. In recent years, the SEC has filed many more cases than previously, along with tougher penalties, against Wall Street firms and branch managers cited in "failure to supervise" cases. This has raised the ire of the securities industry.

Case of California Broker

What gave rise to the recent ruling was a six-month supervisory suspension of Patricia Johnson. Ms. Johnson supervised a broker in PaineWebber's Beverly Hills, Calif., office who allegedly stole customer funds in 1987 and 1988 by writing unauthorized checks against their accounts. Ms. Johnson had fired the broker in 1988 after receiving complaints from customers; he committed suicide three days later.

In the SEC proceedings, Ms. Johnson acknowledged the thefts, but disputed the allegation that her supervision was lax and claimed the SEC was barred from taking action against her by the statute of limitations.

The case was widely watched. Indeed the Securities Industry Association, a trade group, filed a brief on Ms. Johnson's behalf. "The idea of focusing on failure to supervise is a strong way of getting the most you can from your enforcement dollars, but waiting five years isn't an effective way of enforcing the statute," said Arthur Hahn, a Chicago lawyer who represented Ms. Johnson.

Ms. Johnson, now a broker with Smith Barney Inc., a **Travelers Group** unit, said the decision "was a long time coming."

The SEC hasn't decided whether it will appeal the case to the Supreme Court.

Hurdles to Quick Prosecution

"This seems to fly in the face of any realistic hope to police this market in a real effective manner," an SEC official said. The official said it often is difficult for the agency to quickly prosecute cases because of their complexity, or because the facts sometimes come out years after the alleged wrongdoing.

Besides, the SEC official said, the agency currently carries a case load of nearly 1,500 open investigations. It's unclear how the decision will affect pending cases. "We're now surveying our entire inventory of cases filed," the SEC official said. Among the agency's options is to seek court orders for injunctive relief where the remedy isn't a suspension or bar from the brokerage business.

For his part, Mr. Pollack said the SEC "should have ample time to bring these cases."

He should know. Since 1993, Mr. Pollack has overseen a restitution fund set up by Prudential Securities Inc. stemming from SEC charges that the firm made improper sales of limited partnerships. The case involving the **Prudential Insurance Co. of America** unit took several years to bring because the value of the partnerships for several years weren't accurately reflected on account statements received by investors.

"Pru is a perfect example" of why the SEC should be allowed to pursue supervisory sanctions for cases older than five years, Mr. Pollack said.

June 28, 1996

Street fought such a crackdown every step of the way, with one brokerage-firm attorney calling it a "flawed concept" and saying that "there's only so much a branch manager can do" to stop broker abuses. The SEC disagreed, bringing sixty-three failure-to-supervise cases from 1994 to 1996, compared to fifty-two from 1988 through 1993, according to the agency.

Another Continuing Thorn: Insider Trading

The merger boom of the mid-1990s caused a resurgence of one of the SEC's biggest thorns—insider trading. Those who watched the splashy actions brought in the 1980s by hotshot squads of SEC and criminal authorities against the likes of arbitrager Ivan Boesky and junk-bond king Michael Milken might think that the SEC had put the fear of God in all who might use inside information to their own advantage.

In 1997 the SEC's most powerful tool for prosecuting this crime faced a challenge that would have rendered it toothless. Defense lawyers have long argued that insider trading rules are not hard and fast. In fact, the SEC turns mainly to some simple words in Section 10(b) of the Securities and Exchange Act of 1934, which prohibit using any "manipulative or deceptive device" in connection with "the purchase or sale of any security." During the 1980s the SEC expanded upon that rather vague language and started applying a "misappropriation theory." Under that interpretation, anyone who misappropriates nonpublic information to trade stock in a company, even if that person did not have a legal relationship with or work for that company, becomes guilty of insider trading. Such an expansive interpretation was key to nabbing the likes of Mr. Boesky and his cohorts.

But those were the heydays of insider trading cases. In 1996 a U.S. appeals court for the eighth circuit in St. Louis overturned the conviction of a Minneapolis lawyer who knew that his firm was representing Grand Metropolitan PLC in a nonpublic bid for Pillsbury Co. He used that information to buy options in Pillsbury ahead of the deal, netting $4.3 million. The SEC convinced a lower court that the lawyer had misappropriated confidential, nonpublic information to buy the shares. The appeals court favored the defense's argument that the lawyer had no fiduciary obligation to Pillsbury, since his firm wasn't representing Pillsbury. If that theory of law prevailed, market watchers around the country speculated, an adviser or insider of a company instigating a takeover could trade on the information with impunity, while similar moves by insiders or advisers to a target company would result in jail time.

The SEC argued to the Supreme Court against tossing out the misappropriation definition of insider trading, arguing that the attorney got the information on the pending deal by fraud. "Information is the lifeblood of the securities markets," a Justice Department lawyer representing the SEC told the Supreme Court in April 1997. Investors count on the fact that they aren't trading "with someone who acquired information simply by fraud." The SEC argued that even though the attorney owed no fiduciary duty to Pillsbury, he acquired the pending-acquisition information in a deceitful way, harming his law firm and Grand Metropolitan, to whom he did have a fiduciary duty. Defense attorneys countered that "if Congress wants to get the misappropriation theory into law, it has to write it into law."

Then, at the end of June 1997, the Supreme Court, in a 6–3 vote, surprised many attorneys, who had been expecting the SEC's powers to be curtailed, by upholding the misappropriation theory in the Pillsbury case. In a thirty-five page opinion by Justice Ruth Bader Ginsburg, the court cautioned that investors might "hesitate to venture their capital in a market where trading based on misappropriated nonpublic information is unchecked by law."

Meanwhile, the SEC hasn't taken any apparent enforcement actions in some highly suspicious—and very public—incidents that certainly suggest insider trading. In April 1997, "call options" in Tambrands Inc. soared a week before Procter & Gamble Co. announced it would acquire the company. Options give investors the right, but not the obligation to buy or sell stocks at a certain price by a specified date that might be months or weeks away. But despite the action in Tambrands, no enforcement actions followed. Then, days before Bankers Trust announced that it was buying the Baltimore brokerage of Alex. Brown & Sons Inc., "call options" rose mysteriously, again with no enforcement actions. And in February, "put options," which investors buy anticipating a stock decline, in Scholastic Corp. took off, just days before the company announced that it hadn't set aside enough reserves for book returns and posted a loss of more than sixty cents when the Street had been expecting an equivalent profit. The news sent the stock plunging, garnering a handsome profit for those who'd bought put options.

The Chicago Board Options Exchange said it was conducting a "routine" inquiry into the put-options trading in Scholastic, but the SEC was mum about any inquiries it might have been doing.

Despite anecdotal belief that insider trading has picked up, the number of SEC cases has remained fairly constant. The SEC brought forty-two insider-trading cases in 1996; forty-five in 1995; and forty-five in 1994. Part of the problem is that insider trading can be difficult to both detect and prove, officials have said. Many insider trading cases are spotted by noticeable surges in trading volume around key events. But that method is admittedly imperfect, regulators say. "I have no doubt that there are instances of insider trading that do not get detected," by trading patterns, the SEC's William McLucas said. But he noted that the SEC is often tipped by disgruntled workers or estranged spouses to insider trading.

As the examples cited above suggest, much of the 1990s' insider trading is taking place in the options market. Options cost far less than stocks, offering leverage to the buyer. And since options trade on more than two thousand stocks, up from only 490 in 1986, there are many more vehicles for those looking to use options to trade on insider information. Thus, many believe the instances of insider trading have escalated steeply.

Several high-profile insider-trading cases emerged in 1996 and 1997, including charges against Singaporean businessman Raymond Lum Kwan Sung and another Singaporean, Ong Congqin Bobby, charging that the men used inside information to illegally profit, either through stock shares or call options, from advanced knowledge of the acquisition of APL Ltd. by Neptune Orient Lines Ltd. for $825 million. Both men denied the charges in the case, which was still pending at the end of 1997. Similar charges against London resident Abdul Ismail were dropped. Other cases include a settlement with insiders at Mark IV Industries, which merged with Purolator Products Co., and a complaint filed against the former chairman of haircutting chain Supercuts, alleging that he avoided $621,875 in losses by selling on nonpublic information. The chairman has denied wrongdoing in the case, which was still pending at the end of 1997.

Another problem might be that the nature of insider trading has shifted in some cases from Wall Street to Main Street. Some say any declines in brokerage-firm insider trading is likely due to a 1988 law making brokerage firms liable for damages from insider trading by their employees. Often these days, it's either lawyers or accountants doing the insider trading.

And now insider trading is cropping up in the unlikeliest of places. In April 1997 the SEC brought a unique case against drug researchers. In April 1994, two researchers at Wayne State University in Detroit had leaked that Alpha 1 Biomedicals Inc. and SciClone Pharmaceuticals Inc.'s hepatitis drug had poor clinical trials, passing on the information to friends and associates who sold their shares in advance of the public announcement. Once the news was announced, the two stocks fell by nearly two-thirds, which would have cost the group $300,000 in losses. The SEC reached settlements with eight people charged with insider trading. Four others charged have denied the charges and did not settle in the case, the conclusion of which had not been announced by the end of 1997.

The National Association of Securities Dealers, which oversees trading in Nasdaq stocks, referred 121 cases of suspected insider trading in such stocks to the SEC in 1996, surpassing the record of 115 set in 1986, the time of the Ivan Boeksy scandals. And in the first three months of 1997, the NASD sent a hefty fifty-three cases to the SEC. The New York Stock Exchange similarly sent forty-eight cases of potentially criminal trading to the SEC in 1996, short of the record fifty-seven referrals in 1989, but far exceeding the average of twenty-eight a year for the previous three years.

Another voice calling for a crackdown came from options traders who were losing money on such trades. Options traders are obliged to execute trades for their customers, taking on the opposite side of options and putting up their own capital for 40 to 100 percent of the trades. That's a far greater risk than what stock traders face, since they might only have to put up their own capital for 10 percent of their transactions.

Options traders at the American Stock Exchange were infuriated by unusual buying in Advanta Corp. put options (which bet on a price decline) ahead of news of loan losses at the company; and Philadelphia Stock Exchange traders were riled over losses they suffered after they got sudden demand for call options on Alex. Brown shares before the announced Bankers Trust acquisition of the regional brokerage.

In 1997 options traders got more activist, beginning to clamor for measures that would speed up the process of identifying illegal inside trades or stopping insider trading in its tracks. For instance, most options exchanges will only halt trading in an option that is seeing unusual trading if the underlying stock has already been halted awaiting some disclosure by the company. Some traders said it would be helpful in cases like the APL options if exchanges took more initiative to allow options-trading halts absent stock-trading halts.

Others want the process of recouping their losses speeded up, some fearing that if what appears to them to be a flurry of insider trading cases persist, their capital could be cut to the point that their ability to do their job is impaired.

"This can take a long, long, long time," said one market maker who lost money by selling calls on Alex. Brown stock. "We just hope that the authorities act very quickly, and we see this money again."

Making the World Toe the Line

For the SEC, getting foreign companies to list on the U.S. markets is a high priority. But the invitation comes with a hitch: Foreign companies have to disclose to U.S. investors their finances the same way that U.S. companies must disclose their assets, liabilities, profits, losses and important corporate events and developments that help investors decide whether or not to invest. Currently, the standard is to follow U.S. Generally Accepted Accounting Principles, or GAAP.

Trouble is, not too many foreign companies can meet that standard, so the United States has long been viewed as an impenetrable market for those companies, many of whom are unwilling to take on the additional costs of complying with U.S. rules. Acknowledging that fact, the U.S.'s Financial Accounting Standards Board and the International Accounting Standards Committee have been trying to find some acceptable minimum disclosure level that would open the doors to U.S. markets for foreign companies.

Mr. Levitt became the bad guy to many of his former peers in the U.S. exchanges and investment banking world when he supported the Financial Accounting Standards Board in its push to make international standards mimic the tough U.S. standards. "The number of foreign issuers we have here (in the United States) is proof that we don't need to dilute our standards to compete with foreign markets," he said in a speech to the Economic Club of Detroit.

Despite pressure from foreign companies, U.S. exchange officials, and others eager to attract foreign listings in the United States, Mr. Levitt let it be known that he was opposed to lowering U.S. standards in some areas to allow companies from less-regulated countries to seamlessly list on the U.S. exchanges. Such an approach was in conflict with the position he took as head of the American Stock Exchange, he admitted.

But the SEC realized that U.S. investors could be getting far different, and often inferior, information if accounting standards from foreign countries were used.

"When Daimler-Benz listed a few weeks after I came to the commission, and I realized that using German accounting standards they would have shown a profit almost twice Chrysler's and using U.S. GAAP (Generally Accepted Accounting Principles) they would have shown a substantial loss, I recognized the importance of supporting the FASB and maintaining the integrity of U.S. accounting standards," said Mr. Levitt.

Instead, he decided to tackle the foreign-listing issue by traveling to countries that had largely avoided the U.S. markets, especially Germany, and trying to ease corporations' fears about the bureaucracy and litigation exposure many feared in the United States. He was joined in his travels many times by Richard Grasso, chairman of the New York Stock Exchange, and by Frank Zarb, chairman of the National Association of Securities Dealers, which runs Nasdaq. Mr. Levitt credits such efforts with helping to win over such listings as German car company Daimler-Benz—which agreed to use U.S. standards—and telephone-services giant Deutsche Telekom AG.

As the SEC has meetings and the major markets around the world aim to set international accounting standards, Mr. Levitt says maintaining U.S. standards is still an issue that must be defended. "I regard accounting standards as being a major challenge for the commission as we move toward international standards," he said in an early 1997 interview with the *Journal*. "My hope is that in our drive toward international standards we don't arrive at standards that are less rigorous than our own. That I regard as one of the biggest threats to America's investors: compromise in the quality of information, the quality of the numbers that they must rely upon to make an investment."

An Uneasy Peace with Congress

The SEC is an independent agency governed by Congress—and Congress doesn't let the SEC forget it.

In addition to maintaining constant communication and inquiry by members of congressional banking and commerce subcommittees, Congress's banking committees also control the funding for the SEC, which until recently had to be reauthorized every year. That has in the past required SEC chairmen to walk a delicate tightrope between independent advocate/industry police officer and beseeching constituent. Mr. Levitt, for example, had to lobby to prevent a proposed 20 percent cut in the SEC's fiscal 1996 budget. He and Commissioner Steven Wallman argued that the reduction, proposed by a newly installed antiregulatory Republican majority Congress, would "significantly reduce the agency's ability to police capital markets" by requiring a 35 percent personnel cut and disrupting the SEC's programs.

SEC officials have long argued that the SEC should become a self-funded agency, given that it collects hundreds of millions of dollars for the Treasury in fees, far exceeding the money it gets from Congress.

Budget officials at the SEC did finally succeed in getting Congress to allow it to safeguard its funding for ten years by offsetting its allocated levels by the fees and fines it generates for the Treasury. Thus, SEC officials no longer have to grapple with an annually renewed funding mechanism, although they may from time to time have to argue for increased funding levels. As long as the SEC-generated revenues (nearly $1 billion in 1994) keep coming in as expected, the SEC should be unmolested by congressional budget cutters until 2006 or so. After then, however, the SEC budget-making process could revert back to its annual allocation pleadfest.

One reason that the relationship between the SEC and Congress has been fairly upbeat is the reverence with which the gentlemanly Mr. Levitt is regarded on Capitol Hill. When Mr. Levitt arrives at the hearing rooms to give testimony, the deferential scheduling and his treatment is second only to that of Alan Greenspan, the highly powerful and respected head of the Federal Reserve.

Such relationships can be key. The SEC is also constantly asked to explain securities issues, staff decisions, and constituent problems to members of Congress.

Prior to Mr. Levitt's arrival, staffers of the SEC snidely called "Dingell-grams" the constant barrage of explain-yourself missives from the then-chairman of the House Energy and Commerce Committee, John D. Dingell. Any major move or publicized speech by the commission's executives inevitably brought an inquisitive letter from Rep. Dingell, who remains a veritable SEC backseat driver to this day.

Likewise, Rep. Dingell would request of the SEC explanations of hot press issues, such as 1997's *Business Week* story alleging that organized crime had infiltrated Wall Street. (Chairman Levitt told Rep. Dingell that the mob was not pervasive, but offered to give him a private briefing on SEC initiatives.)

Mr. Levitt also needed every bit of deference he could get with the arrival of the antiregulatory Class of 1994 Republicans. High on the agenda of the new majority led by Speaker of the House Newt Gingrich, and a part of his "Contract with America," was a bill to make it harder for investors to sue companies over performance predictions that later proved untrue.

The SEC was fighting a strong tide when officials spoke up against key provisions of the bill that was proposed in early 1995. That bill sought to stop corporations from being hounded by meritless lawsuits when their stock prices drop unexpectedly. Many such lawsuits accuse companies of defrauding investors by making faulty predictions about earnings or other corporate events. But Mr. Levitt found himself fighting along the way to make sure that the rights of the truly defrauded weren't tossed out in the process.

He was partially successful. He was instrumental in getting removed from an original bill a provision that would make such lawsuits a steep gamble for investors by forcing them to pay the sometimes-exorbitant legal expenses of the corporations they sue if they lost. Lawmakers were also persuaded to drop a controversial provision that investors who sue would have to prove that they "relied on" a false corporate statement in making an investment decision, something that would be extremely difficult to prove and would dissuade investors with legitimate claims from pursuing them.

But critics said the bill ultimately fell short in protecting investors, and blamed the SEC for not taking a harder line by withholding support for the bill. For instance, the bill created a "safe harbor" for companies to make public statements about their earnings and products, with drastically reduced risk of being sued if those statements turned out to be false and their stock prices plummeted as a result. Mr. Levitt had written to Banking Committee Chairman Alfonse D'Amato saying that the bill set a standard of protection for corporate statements that "may be so high as to preclude all but the most obvious frauds" from lawsuits by investors, but he was overruled.

Another provision that critics found objectionable was removal of joint and several liability for accounting firms that audit corporations' financial results. The final bill traded that full liability in cases where investors are defrauded to a standard that limits accounting firms' liability to the proportion of their actual involvement in the fraud, to be determined by a judge.

Lastly, the bill set the statute of limitations for filing a fraud lawsuit at three years after an alleged violation occurs, rather than the five years recommended by the SEC.

Some commentators noted that Mr. Levitt's reputation as an effective consensus builder suffered a heavy blow when President Clinton unexpectedly vetoed the bill, on which Mr. Levitt had worked for months to help forge a compromise acceptable to both Republicans and Democrats.

But Mr. Levitt said the SEC was as effective as it could be at the time, even writing portions of the bill that ultimately passed. "The Congress that came in in 1994 was a somewhat different Congress than we have today, in that almost anything Gingrich wanted during those first five months came through, and he wanted litigation reform," said Mr. Levitt in 1997. "As I saw it, rather than just becoming irrelevant by just baying at the moon, I wanted to be very relevant."

The SEC was credited with a bit more influence in the securities-industry deregulation bill sponsored by Republican Jack Fields of Texas, chairman of the telecommunications and finance subcommittee. Mr. Fields said he wanted the bill, called the Capital Markets Deregulation and Liberalization Act, to eliminate many state securities laws, taking away state regulators' authority to oversee which mutual funds and other securities are sold in their states. It would also curb states' ability to screen stockbrokers, and limit brokers' obligations to judge the suitability of investments sold to big institutional investors such as pension funds and municipalities.

The bill, which ultimately became law in late 1996, had to be stripped of several provisions to appease a skeptical Mr. Levitt. For instance, the final bill did not eliminate the "margin" payments that big investors must post to guarantee their investments; it transferred supervision of those payments to the SEC from the Federal Reserve. Mr. Levitt had considered the margin payments to be an important safeguard that big investors weren't getting in over their heads. The original bill had also sought to relieve Wall Street firms of responsibility for the suitability of investments they sell to big investors, including municipalities such as Orange County, California, which was forced into bankruptcy by losses on risky securities it bought.

The bill, which Mr. Levitt ultimately supported, ended local-level scrutiny of mutual funds and let brokerage firms borrow money from an array of financial institutions, not just banks, saving millions of dollars in financing costs on their securities holdings. It also cut fees that public corporations pay for routine filings with the SEC by $850 million over ten years—in part by imposing a fee on the Nasdaq Stock Market of $1/300$ of 1 percent of the value of trades they execute. The Nasdaq market had been exempt from that requirement, which applied to the American and New York stock exchanges.

And, instead of outright preemption, the bill forced state regulators to standardize within three years their procedures for screening stockbrokers' applications for licenses or face federal preemption of their licensing authority.

The bill also would eliminate states' ability to oversee mutual funds sold to their residents and would require the Securities and Exchange Commission to consider such Wall Street priorities as "capital formation" and "market efficiency" when imposing new regulations.

The SEC's People

Arthur Levitt Jr., chairman: Mr. Levitt prides himself on his wide-ranging business background—a trait not all SEC chairmen have had. Mr. Levitt, who has earned wide bipartisan support as a gentleman negotiator and effective leader, is widely expected to be renominated to another five-year tenure after his chairmanship ends in June of 1998.

Levitt, Arthur
Chairman-SEC

He graduated from Williams College in 1952 and served in the air force for two years. He was an assistant promotion director at Time Inc. for five years, and then sold cattle tax shelters at Oppenheimer Industries in Kansas City. Three years later, he worked at Carter Berlind & Weill, later Cogan Berlind Weill & Levitt, which would ultimately evolve into Shearson Lehman Brothers. Mr. Levitt was president of Shearson Lehman Hayden Stone, a prior incarnation of Shearson Lehman Brothers. In 1975 he was a governor of the American Stock Exchange, then president for eleven years beginning in 1978.

A onetime drama critic for the *Berkshire Eagle*, Mr. Levitt is also an avid disciple of the physical and spiritual challenge organization Outward Bound. The son of Arthur Levitt Sr., the longtime bipartisan-supported New York State Comptroller, Mr. Levitt Jr. is a big proponent of racial and gender diversity in the workplace at the SEC and at securities firms.

Laura Simone Unger, commissioner: The newest SEC commissioner, Ms. Unger is a former counsel to the U.S. Senate Committee on Banking, Housing and Urban Affairs. She was sworn in as commissioner on November 5, 1997, for a term that expires in June 2001. As counsel to the Senate banking committee, she advised Sen. Alfonse D'Amato, the chairman of the committee, and followed legislative issues pertaining to banking and securities. Before joining the banking committee staff, she was a congressional fellow for banking and securities matters in Sen. D'Amato's office. Ms. Unger worked at the SEC in the enforcement division before moving to Capitol Hill. She got a BA in rhetoric from the University of California at Berkeley and a JD from New York Law School.

Paul R. Carey, commissioner: Mr. Carey was nominated to his post by President Clinton and confirmed on October 21, 1997 for a term expiring June 5, 2002. Prior to joining the SEC, he was a special assistant to the president for legislative affairs at the White House, where he'd been since February 1993. Mr. Carey was the liaison to the U.S. Senate for President Clinton, handling banking, financial services, housing, securities and other issues. Before working at the White House, Mr. Carey worked in institutional equity sales at Donaldson, Lufkin & Jenrette and at First Albany Corp. He got his BA in economics from Colgate University.

Norman S. Johnson, commissioner: Commissioner Johnson was appointed by President Clinton and sworn in on February 13, 1996. He previously was a senior partner specializing in securities law with the firm of Van Cott, Bagley, Cornwall & McCarthy. Commissioner Johnson had a stint as an SEC staffer early in his career, from 1965 to 1967, before starting in private practice. He was an assistant attorney general in the Office of the Utah Attorney General from 1959–1965 and also served as a law clerk to the chief justice of the Utah Supreme Court. Commissioner Johnson has not become an outspoken force for major change in the U.S. markets, preferring instead to spend his tenure to date fine-tuning and interpreting some of the intricacies of securities laws, especially professional liability for fiduciaries. In Utah, Commissioner Johnson served on the Governor's Task Force on Officer and Director Liability, State of Utah, and numerous other committees and groups concerned with the application of federal and state securities laws.

Isaac C. Hunt Jr., commissioner: Commissioner Hunt, another President Clinton nominee, took his seat at the SEC on February 29, 1996. He had been dean and law professor at the University of Akron School of Law, a position he held from 1987 to 1995. Before that, he was dean of the Antioch School of Law in Washington, DC, where he also taught securities law.

Mr. Hunt began his tenure acting largely behind the scenes during his tenure as commissioner, representing the commission at international securities conferences and tackling the technical interpretations of securities laws. More recently, he has weighed in on ongoing debates in the securities markets, including "plain English" mutual-fund prospectuses and whether it's appropriate for fund managers to cite their performance at a prior mutual fund when advertising a new one.

Commissioner Hunt worked for the army in the Office of the General Counsel as principal deputy general counsel and as acting general counsel under Presidents Carter and Reagan. He was formerly an associate at the law firm of Jones, Day, Reavis and Pogue, practicing corporate and securities law, government procurement litigation, administrative law, and international trade. He was a staff attorney at the SEC from 1962 to 1967.

He got a BA from Fisk University in Nashville, Tennessee, in 1957, and an LLB from the University of Virginia School of Law in 1962.

Jennifer Scardino, chief of staff: Ms. Scardino is the person to tap if one wants to take the chairman's pulse. Until December 1996 she was the Commission's director of public affairs, policy evaluation and research, a post she took in July of 1993. Prior to working at the SEC, she was press secretary to New York's deputy mayor for Finance and Economic Development, Barry Sullivan, and assistant press secretary to Mayor David N. Dinkins. She graduated, cum laude, from Columbia University's Barnard College in 1989, with a BA in political science and Spanish.

Richard R. Lindsey, director, Market Regulation Division: Mr. Lindsey is the first economist to run the market-regulation division. He administers the SEC's many programs for overseeing securities markets and securities professionals, including broker-dealers, transfer agents, stock and option exchanges, and others. He was formerly chief economist at the SEC, a job he took after being a finance professor at Yale University's School of Management. He was a visiting academic at Nikko Research Institute in Tokyo, Japan, and was a visiting economist at the New York Stock Exchange. He's also a former engineer, working as a research engineer for Owens-Corning Fiberglas and later for CertainTeed Corp., first as manager of process engineering and then the plant manager of the company's manufacturing facility. He has a PhD in finance from the University of California, Berkeley, an MBA from the University of Dallas, and a BS in chemical engineering from Berkeley.

Robert L. D. Colby, deputy director, Market Regulation Division: Mr. Colby is responsible for regulating and overseeing broker-dealers, clearing organizations and the U.S. securities markets. He was named deputy director in 1993, and was previously chief counsel of the market-regulation division and branch chief of the division's office of market structure. He got his law degree, cum laude, from Harvard Law School in 1981. He got his BA, summa cum laude, from Bowdoin College in 1977.

Catherine McGuire, chief counsel, Market Regulation Division: Ms. McGuire has been at the SEC since graduating from law school, serving mostly in market regulation and also acting as counsel to Commissioner Bevis Longstreth in 1982. She has a JD from the University of Kansas School of Law and a BA from the University of Michigan.

Howard L. Kramer, senior associate director, Market Supervision, Market Regulation Division: Mr. Kramer coordinates the SEC's program for overseeing U.S. equity and securities derivatives markets. He was previously senior special counsel in the division, directing the Market 2000 study of the future of U.S. stock markets. He also worked on the SEC's reports on the 1987 market crash and 1989 market break. He got a JD, cum laude, MA, and BA from the University of Michigan.

Larry E. Bergmann, senior associate director for risk management and control, Market Regulation: Mr. Bergmann was previously assistant director, trading practices, in the market-regulation division, and a branch chief in the enforcement division. He got a JD from Boston College in 1975 and an SB in humanities and science in 1971 from the Massachusetts Institute of Technology.

Michael A. Macchiaroli, associate director, Capital Markets, Market Regulation: Mr. Macchiaroli has been with the SEC since 1970 and in market regulation since 1978. His areas of responsibility include broker-dealer record-keeping, reporting capital and customer-protection rules. He is a 1962 graduate of St. Joseph's College in Philadelphia and a 1965 graduate of Villanova College.

William R. McLucas, director, Enforcement Division: Mr. McLucas has been with the SEC since 1977, when he joined as a staff attorney. He's headed the enforcement division since December of 1989. Mr. McLucas oversaw the SEC's case against the NASD, and was responsible for the SEC's action against Bankers Trust Securities for fraud in connection with securities derivatives. He also supervised the SEC's case against Prudential Securities in 1993 that resulted in the firm paying hundreds of millions of dollars to compensate individual investors who bought limited partnerships from the firm. Before joining the SEC, Mr. McLucas was an attorney with the Federal Home Loan Bank Board from 1975 to 1977. He earned a JD from Temple University in 1975 and a BA in political science from Pennsylvania State University in 1972.

Colleen P. Mahoney, deputy director, Enforcement Division: Ms. Mahoney has held her current title since May 1994, joining the SEC in 1983 in the general counsel's office. Previously she was in private practice with Steptoe & Johnson, and was an executive assistant to Chairman Arthur Levitt from 1993 to 1994. She graduated magna cum laude from the American University's School of Government and Public Administration in 1978, and in 1981 she graduated summa cum laude from American University's law school.

Joan Elizabeth McKown, chief counsel, Enforcement Division: Ms. McKown has held the enforcement chief counsel post since November 1993, after joining the SEC general counsel's office in 1986. Before the SEC, Ms. McKown was a clerk for Judge J. Smith Henley of the U.S. appeals court for the eighth circuit. At the SEC, she has worked as assistant director for the branch of regional office assistance in the enforcement division. She graduated from Vanderbilt University in 1980, and from Drake University Law School in 1983, with honors.

Thomas C. Newkirk, associate director, Enforcement Division: Mr. Newkirk took his current job in January 1993, after having been chief litigation counsel for the SEC's enforcement division, where he worked on the junk-bond cases against Michael Milken and Drexel Burnham. He joined the SEC in 1986, before which time he was deputy general counsel with the U.S. Energy Department, which he joined in 1978. Previously, Mr. Newkirk was a senior attorney at the U.S. Justice Department and worked during 1972 and 1973 on a study of commission rates for securities-exchange transactions for the Senate Banking, Housing and Urban Affairs Committee's securities subcommittee. He got an LLB, with distinction, from Cornell Law School in 1966 and a BA from Cornell University in 1964.

William R. Baker III, associate director, Enforcement Division: Mr. Baker has worked at the SEC since 1987 after three years in private practice. At the SEC, he has pursued enforcement actions involving insider trading, market manipulation, financial fraud, sales of unregistered securities, and broker-dealer violations. He coordinates the enforcement division's investigations on municipal securities underwriting and sales. He is a 1983 graduate of Georgetown University Law School.

Paul V. Gerlach, associate director, Enforcement Division: Mr. Gerlach is responsible for supervising an array of investigations, including financial reporting and disclosure, insider trading, market manipulation, broker-dealers, investment advisers and investment companies. He began at the SEC in 1988 as a staff attorney in the enforcement area, becoming associate director in June 1995. He was previously an associate with the Washington law firms of Jenner & Block and Akin, Gump, Strauss, Hauer & Feld. He got his JD, magna cum laude, from Washington & Lee University in 1982. He got his BA, magna cum laude, in 1978 from Boise State University.

Christian J. Mixter, chief litigation counsel, Enforcement Division: Mr. Mixter has argued many of the commission's most known enforcement cases, including the fraud case against First Jersey Securities and its owner, Robert Brennan; the financial fraud case against Comparator Systems Corp., which was settled; and the insider trading cases resulting from transactions related to Rochester Community Savings Bank. Prior to his current position, he was an assistant chief litigation counsel in the same division, and from 1995 to 1996 he was the acting district administrator for the Fort Worth district office. He was formerly an associate counsel to the independent counsel, Lawrence E. Walsh, investigating the Iran/Contra affair. He got a BA, summa cum laude, in history from Ohio State University in 1974 and a JD with distinction in 1977 from Duke University law school.

Brian J. Lane, director, Division of Corporation Finance: Mr. Lane, who has been with the SEC since 1983, heads the division that handles the regulation of most corporate financial disclosures and related activities. He previously worked as a counselor to Mr. Levitt and to former Commissioner Richard Y. Roberts. He coordinated a task force report on simplifying corporate regulations. He spent six years in the corporate-finance division and three years in the market-regulation division. He got a JD from American University's Washington College of Law in 1983 and a BA from Washburn University in Topeka, Kansas, in 1980.

Paul M. Dudek, chief, Office of International Corporate Finance: Mr. Dudek heads the office that develops and implements rules and policies for companies looking to list their shares on U.S. exchanges and register them with the SEC. Mr. Dudek, who has had the position since 1993, joined the SEC in 1990 after practicing law with Cleary, Gottlieb, Steen & Hamilton. As an attorney, he represented foreign and U.S. companies and financial intermediaries in capital-markets transactions. He got his law degree from New York University and his undergraduate degree from Fordham University.

Robert E. Plaze, associate director, Division of Investment Management for Regulation: Until being named associate director, Mr. Plaze was an assistant director in the disclosure and investment-adviser regulation division. He is a graduate of the Georgetown University Law School.

Douglas J. Scheidt, associate director and chief counsel, Division of Investment Management: Mr. Scheidt was previously associate director in the compliance, financial analysis, public utility and investment company regulation department. Before joining the investment management group, Mr. Scheidt was a vice president and associate general counsel of the Boston Company Advisors, Inc. and an attorney with Kirkpatrick & Lockhart in Washington and special counsel in the SEC's general counsel's office. He was law clerk to the Hon. Martin D. Van Oosterhout in the U.S. eighth circuit court of appeals. He got his JD from Drake University and a BA, cum laude, from Northwestern University.

Kenneth J. Berman, associate director, Financial Analysis, Public Utility, and Investment Company Regulation of the Division of Investment Management: Prior to taking his current job, Mr. Berman was assistant director of the division's Office of Regulatory Policy and deputy chief of its Office of Disclosure and Investment Adviser Regulation. He joined the SEC in 1988 after practicing corporate and securities law with a New York firm. He got his JD from the University of Chicago Law School and his BA from Dickinson College in Carlisle, Pennsylvania.

Barry P. Barbash, director, Division of Investment Management: Mr. Barbash has principal oversight for the $3 trillion mutual-fund industry. During his tenure with the investment-management division, Mr. Barbash played a central role in initiatives including making fund prospectuses for investors more useful and easy to read and fine-tuning the ways fund companies communicate their risks to investors. He also had a hand in recent legislative efforts to overhaul federal securities laws. Before taking his current post in September 1993, Mr. Barbash was a partner with the New York City law firm of Wilkie Farr & Gallagher, which he joined in 1981, specializing in institutional investor law. Before that, he was a staff attorney with the investment-management division and the plan-benefits security division of the Office of the Solicitor of the U.S. Labor Department. He has a JD from Cornell Law School and an AB, summa cum laude, from Bowdoin College.

Cer Gladwyn Goins, associate director, Office of Compliance, Inspections and Examinations: Mr. Goins helps coordinate a national program to inspect and examine mutual funds, advisers, brokers, transfer and clearing firms, securities exchanges, and municipal securities dealers. His staff focuses on sales practices, failure to supervise, financial irregularities, and operational risk. He was formerly associate director at the investment-management and enforcement divisions, as well as other positions at the SEC starting in 1979, after getting an LLM in securities regulation from Georgetown University in 1979. He was a captain in the army from 1976 to 1979 in the office of the staff judge advocate. He got a JD from Case Western Reserve University law school in 1976 and a BA, with honors, in 1973.

Gene A. Gohlke, associate director, Investment Company and Adviser Compliance, Office of Compliance, Inspections and Examinations: Mr. Gohlke, a certified public accountant who has been at the SEC since 1975, manages the exam program for mutual funds and other registered investment companies and investment advisers. He was previously acting director of the investment-management division and has held various other financial and accounting positions at the same division. Mr. Gohlke has worked at a management consulting firm, as an adviser for the U.S. Agency for International Development, and as an assistant accounting professor at the University of Wisconsin. He has a PhD in business administration and an MBA from the University of Wisconsin.

Paul S. Maco, director, Office of Municipal Securities: Mr. Maco heads the commission's oversight of the municipal-bond market, ruling on issues like "pay to play" in which participants win government underwriting business by improper contributions, or "yield burning" in which some underwriters erode interest rates on certain bonds through excessive fees. He was previously a partner at the law firm of Mintz, Levin, Cohn, Ferris, Glovsky and Popeo in Boston, an associate at Debevoise & Plimpton and at Hawkins, Delafield & Wood. He was a staff attorney at the SEC's enforcement division from 1977 to 1979. He got a JD from New York University in 1977 and a BA from Lehigh University in 1974.

Kaye F. Williams, director, Office of Legislative Affairs: Ms. Williams monitors legislation and regulation of interest to the securities industry, working with state and federal policy makers. She joined the SEC in 1996 from the Securities Industry Association, where she was assistant general counsel in Washington, DC. She previously was a legal counsel to former SEC Commissioner Richard Y. Roberts and a staff attorney in the SEC's enforcement division. She formerly was a market-surveillance analyst in the legal and compliance division of the National Association of Securities Dealers. She got her JD from Georgetown University in 1986 and a BA in politics and public policy from Goucher College in Towson, Maryland, in 1983.

Nancy M. Smith, director, Office of Investor Education & Assistance: Ms. Smith, a graduate of Georgetown University and its law center, worked on Capitol Hill from 1978 to 1991, serving initially on the staff of Sen. George McGovern and later as deputy director of Sen. Edward Kennedy's political action committee, the Fund for a Democratic Majority. In 1984, she moved to the legislative subcommittee of Rep. Edward J. Markey. There, she handled energy issues, and later became Rep. Markey's senior finance counsel on securities issues for the House Energy and Commerce Committee's Subcommittee on Telecommunications and Finance. In early 1991, Ms. Smith became director of the New Mexico Securities Division.

Gregg W. Corso, counselor to the chairman: Mr. Corso advises Chairman Levitt on corporate-finance and accounting matters. Previously, he held a variety of positions at the SEC, including chief of the office of mergers and acquisitions. He got his BS and JD from Boston University and studied international economics at the London School of Economics. He is an adjunct professor at Georgetown University Law Center, where he teaches a class on mergers and acquisitions.

Belinda A. Blaine, counselor to the chairman: Ms. Blaine was formerly associated with the office of market supervision in the market regulation division.

She has worked on issues like bank securities, automated trading systems, and municipal securities disclosure, and was senior special counsel to the director and the deputy chief counsel in the SEC's office of chief counsel. Before the SEC, she was at the law firm of Kirkpatrick & Lockhart in Washington. She is a graduate of the University of California, Los Angeles, law school and of Pomona College.

Timothy J. Forde, counselor to the chairman: A five-year veteran of Capitol Hill, Mr. Forde advises the chairman on matters affecting the efficiency and integrity of the capital markets and the protection of investors. He represents the chairman in legislative negotiations, including efforts to repeal the Glass Steagall Act and to preempt certain state securities antifraud laws. He was previously a minority counsel in the U.S. House Commerce Committee, and a senior counsel on the U.S. House Energy and Commerce Committee's Subcommittee on Telecommunications and Finance.

Cheryl J. Scarboro, counselor to the chairman: Ms. Scarboro advises the chairman on legal and policy issues relating to enforcement of federal securities law. She was previously a senior counsel in the enforcement division, investigating cases of accounting fraud, insider trading and stock manipulation. Until 1992, she was an associate at Sutherland, Asbill & Brennan in Washington. She got her JD from Duke University in 1989, and her BA, cum laude, in political science from the University of Alabama in Huntsville in 1986.

Susan Ferris Wyderko, counselor to the chairman: Prior to being named to this job, Ms. Wyderko was an assistant general counsel at the SEC with responsibility for filing SEC briefs with the courts of appeal and the Supreme Court. She worked from 1993 to 1995 in the enforcement division as assistant chief litigation counsel, and earlier was an associate with the Washington, DC, law firm of Miller & Chevalier. She is a graduate of Cornell Law School and Wellesley College.

Barbara B. Hannigan, ethics counsel: Ms. Hannigan, who has been with the SEC since 1987, informs the chairman and executive staff on conflict-of-interest and federal ethics rules, including certain equal-employment opportunities matters. Formerly an associate at Shaw, Pittman, Potts and Trowbridge, she got her JD, cum laude, in 1984 at the American University, Washington College of Law after getting a BA in English and MA in English Literature from Georgetown University.

Carmen J. Lawrence, regional director, Northeast Region (Connecticut; Delaware; Washington, DC; Maine; Maryland; Massachusetts; New Hampshire; New Jersey; New York; Pennsylvania; Rhode Island; Vermont;

Virginia; West Virginia): Ms. Lawrence has a tough job as the Northeast's top securities cop, in charge of Boston's mutual-fund industry and Wall Street proper. She has handled many of the SEC's highest profile cases, including the SEC's 1993 civil lawsuit against Towers Financial, in which Steven Hoffenberg settled for $60 million over charges that Towers ran the largest Ponzi scheme in U.S. history. She replaced Richard Walker in her current post in late 1995, after Mr. Walker was promoted to general counsel in Washington SEC headquarters. She is a Long Island, New York, native, who started at the SEC in Washington in 1981, fresh out of the University of Michigan Law School. She got her BA in 1978 from Cornell University. She became head of enforcement division in New York in 1988.

Juan Marcel Marcelino, district administrator, Boston district office of Northeast Region: Mr. Marcelino joined the SEC in June 1984 as a staff attorney after receiving his LLM in securities law from Georgetown University. Before becoming district administrator, he was branch chief and assistant director. He got a JD from Catholic University of America in 1981 and an AB from Brandeis University in 1978.

Ronald Long, district administrator, Philadelphia district office of Northeast Region: Mr. Long took over the Philly district in March of 1997, after being counselor on enforcement matters to Chairman Levitt since 1994. He joined the SEC in 1990 as an attorney in the enforcement division. He was formerly an associate at the law firm of Hoge, Fenton, Jones & Appel, Inc., of San Jose, California, conducting civil litigation in state and federal courts. He got his law degree from Georgetown University in 1983 and graduated from Williams College in 1977.

Randall Fons, Regional Director, Southeast Region (Alabama, Florida, Georgia, Louisiana, Mississippi, North Carolina, Puerto Rico, South Carolina, Tennessee, Virgin Islands): Prior to taking over the Southeast regional office, Mr. Fons was the senior associate regional director for enforcement at the Chicago district of the SEC. He began at the SEC in August of 1988 as a staff attorney. He was previously a law clerk to Judge William R. Moser of the Wisconsin District 1 court of appeals. He got a JD in 1987 from the University of Colorado School of Law, and a bachelor of business administration in accounting in 1984 from the University of Wisconsin School of Business.

Richard P. Wessel, district administrator, Atlanta district office of Southeast Region: Before taking his current position in 1987, Mr. Wessel served in various positions including branch chief for the branch of organized crime and criminal reference and associate director of market regulation. Mr. Wessel started at the SEC in 1973 as a lawyer in the enforcement division. Mr. Wessel got his JD, cum laude, from Boston University law school in 1973 and an undergraduate degree, magna cum laude, in economics from Oberlin College in Ohio.

Mary Keefe, regional director, Midwest Region (Illinois, Indiana, Iowa, Kentucky, Michigan, Minnesota, Missouri, Ohio, Wisconsin): Ms. Keefe was appointed to her post in July 1994, after being at the Midwest regional office since 1982, including a stint as associate regional director in charge of enforcement. She got her BA from Northern Illinois University in 1972 and her JD from DePaul University law school in 1979.

Daniel F. Shea, regional director, Central Region (Arkansas, Colorado, Kansas, Nebraska, New Mexico, North Dakota, Oklahoma, South Dakota, Texas, Utah, Wyoming): Mr. Shea worked as a private attorney in Washington and a trial lawyer for the U.S. Departments of Justice and Energy. He joined the SEC in 1992 and handled the prosecution of California savings and loan figure Charles Keating. Mr. Shea became associate regional director of the office in February 1995, and regional director in March of 1995. He joined the SEC in 1992, holding the title of assistant chief litigation counsel in the enforcement division until early 1995. Previously, he was a partner in a Washington, DC, law firm and was a trial attorney with the U.S. Departments of Justice and Energy. He graduated from the Columbus School of Law at Catholic University in 1975 and from the College of the Holy Cross in 1972.

Harold F. Degenhardt, district administrator, Fort Worth district office of Central Region: Mr. Degenhardt, a former junior high and high school teacher, took his current job in May of 1996. He worked previously at Gibson, Dunn & Crutcher in Dallas in the law firm's litigation department specializing in general commercial, securities, antitrust and product-liability litigation. He worked at Mudge, Rose, Guthrie & Alexander in New York and Coke & Coke in Dallas after getting his JD from Fordham Law School in 1973 and a BA in history from Villanova University in 1968.

Kenneth D. Israel Jr., district administrator, Salt Lake City district office of Central Region: Mr. Israel took his post in June of 1994, after serving as the deputy district administrator of the Salt Lake City office. Mr. Israel joined the SEC in Washington as a staff attorney right out of law school, moving in 1981 to the Denver office. He joined the Salt Lake City office as branch chief in 1987. He got his JD in 1974 from George Washington University law school, and an AB degree from Notre Dame in government and international relations in 1971.

Elaine M. Cacheris, regional director, Pacific Region (Alaska, Arizona, California, Guam, Hawaii, Idaho, Montana, Nevada, Oregon, Washington State): Ms. Cacheris has worked in the SEC's Los Angeles office since 1987, getting the regional director job in 1993. She joined the SEC's Fort Worth, Texas, office as a staff attorney in 1984 after two years in private practice in Dallas and a stint as assistant attorney general for the State of Texas. She got her BA in 1977 from the University of Arizona and her JD from the University of the Pacific law school in 1980.

David Bayless, district administrator, San Francisco district office of Pacific Region: Mr. Bayless has headed the San Francisco office since July 1994, before which he was a litigation partner at the law firm of McDermott, Will & Emery in Chicago, trying cases involving securities fraud and insider trading. He got a PhD from Cambridge University; a JD with honors from University of Chicago, and a BA with high honors from Oberlin College.

Richard H. Walker, general counsel: Mr. Walker, who became general counsel in January 1996, represents the commission in judicial proceedings when the SEC is a party or has filed as "friend of the court." He also drafts Commission comments to Congress on pending and proposed legislation. He was formerly the regional director of the SEC's Northeast Regional Office from 1991 to 1995, supervising investigations and prosecutions including those involving the allegedly fraudulent charity New Era Philanthropy, and the alleged bond-trading abuses by Joseph Jett of Kidder Peabody. He spent fifteen years at Cadwalader, Wickersham & Taft in New York as a litigation partner. He got his JD, cum laude, in 1975 from Temple Law School and an undergraduate degree from Trinity College.

Karen Buck Burgess, associate general counsel, Office of General Counsel: Ms. Burgess advises the general counsel and the SEC on legal and policy issues, managing a group of twenty-four attorneys. Before stints in several other SEC jobs, beginning as an attorney fellow in October 1987 where she contributed to the study on the October market crisis, she was an associate at Milbank, Tweed, Hadley & McCloy in Tokyo, executive assistant at the Office of the United Nations High Commissioner for Refugees in Bangkok, Thailand, and a law clerk for Baker & McKenzie in Hong Kong. She got a JD in 1976 from Antioch School of Law in Washington, DC, and a BA in 1972 from Oberlin College in Ohio.

Richard M. Humes, associate general counsel, Litigation and Administrative Practice Office of General Counsel: Mr. Humes, who joined the SEC in 1977, represents the SEC in district court, appellate and administrative litigation when the SEC or its members or employees are defendants. He also advises the SEC on contracting and leasing issues and directs the SEC's Freedom of Information Act and Confidential Treatment Request programs. He

In the Beginning . . .

Now as much an institution for investors as the New York Stock Exchange itself, the SEC wasn't even on the map until relatively recently.

As unfathomable as it seems now, until 1934 stock investors didn't have an SEC or anything resembling it to worry about. They had more to fear from their postman; until 1934, stock markets had to answer only to U.S. postal laws. (A blatant fraud, of course, could still be prosecuted under state law.) Even commodity markets had rules to follow, from the Agriculture Department.

That was all changed by the great crash of 1929.

The law that created the SEC provided the basis for most of the stock-market rules that apply to the markets today, from bans on market manipulation to free disclosure of information about stock trading.

The SEC wasn't set up to keep investors from losing money, though. As Congress's Office of Technology Assess-ment put it in a report on the evolution of the markets, the 1934 law's consumer-protection clauses were meant to "shield investors against dishonesty, but not incompetence, on the part of brokers."

Later laws, including the formation of the Securities Investor Protection Corp., expanded the government's role in making sure investors' accounts were protected if brokerage firms failed. But there remained a tension between those who believed the markets should basically police themselves, including through the "self-regulatory" organizations like the exchanges, and those who wanted an active, pro-investor SEC.

To many Wall Streeters' surprise, Mr. Levitt blazed into the SEC with more of the latter approach, particularly in his public statements, than the self-policing style that might have been expected from a Wall Street insider. The activist approach immediately drew fire from various quarters.

■

received a JD, cum laude, in 1976 from Howard University law school and a BA in English from Brown University in 1973.

Paul Gonson, solicitor: Mr. Gonson, who joined the SEC in 1961, supervises the SEC's appellate and defense litigation and "friend of the court" filings. He has been solicitor since 1979. He has traveled over the years as a member of U.S. delegations of government and private-sector attorneys advising government and stock-market officials in Moscow, Leningrad, Budapest, Prague, and Warsaw and China. Mr. Gonson got his LLB degree in 1954 from the University of Buffalo, where he also got his undergraduate degree.

Erik Sirri, chief economist: Mr. Sirri advises the SEC and Chairman Levitt on major economic policy issues, heading the office of economic analysis that analyzes the impact of SEC proposals on the capital markets. He was formerly an assistant finance professor at Harvard Business School from 1989 to 1995, and an associate professor of finance at Babson College. Before that, he worked on planetary astronomy missions for NASA and on space surveillance sensors in the aerospace industry. He got a PhD in finance from the University of California, Los

Minority-Run Firms Are Hurt by Crackdown on Munis

BY CHARLES GASPARINO AND
JONATHAN N. AXELROD
Staff Reporters of THE WALL STREET JOURNAL

Several minority-owned securities firms are on the ropes, and some blame Washington for changing the rules in the middle of the municipal-bond game.

As their capital shrivels and legal bills mount, the embattled firms are taking aim at a surprising target: the Securities and Exchange Commission and its chairman, Arthur Levitt, a lifelong Democrat. They charge that the SEC inadvertently crippled a large chunk of their business with its unprecedented three-year assault on abuses in the $1.3 trillion municipal-bond market.

Among those affected are three of the larger, once-prosperous firms owned by African-Americans: New York's WR Lazard & Co. and M.R. Beal & Co. and Atlanta's Pryor, McClendon, Counts & Co., muni-bond executives say. And many smaller firms are waging a day-to-day struggle to survive, although some are doing better outside the muni business.

The SEC's Mr. Levitt says he hasn't targeted minority-owned firms in any way. He knows that many are suffering, but says it's from the same drought of profitability that has stricken larger firms in the muni market, forcing the likes of CS First Boston, Lazard Freres & Co. (unrelated to WR Lazard) and Donaldson, Lufkin & Jenrette Inc. to leave the muni underwriting business.

Painful Fallout
THE SEC'S ACTIONS 'have definitely had an impact' on minority firms, adding costs that 'eat into our profits.'

CLEARED IN A probe that cost him business, Mr. Beal wants to 'put my experience with New York City behind me.'

At the root of the trauma is a sweeping change in the muni-bond business since 1994, when the SEC shrank the amount of political contributions that a would-be muni-bond seller is allowed to make. Mr. Levitt's attack on the past "pay-to-play" climate made it much more difficult to do business. The wind shifted toward "competitive bid" deals that required hefty capital, and away from the "negotiated" deals where a low-capital firm could cut its risk by lining up bond buyers in advance. The SEC's stance affected all firms but hit hardest at the newer, thinly capitalized minority firms.

"People feel that just as African-American businesses began to excel, [the SEC] changed the rules on us," says Tony Chapelle, editor and publisher of Securities Pro newsletter in New York, which has written about the plight of minority firms. But, he says, Mr. Levitt isn't to blame and the firms should be more worried by "a nationwide movement to roll back affirmative action," which in the past had helped them gain a foothold in bond deals.

One minority-firm executive who says the SEC bears some responsibility for the minority firms' plight is Betty Lazard, chairwoman of WR Lazard. In April, an independent auditor's report that reviewed the firm's finances through Dec. 31, 1995 raised "substantial doubt about the company's ability to continue as a going concern." Ms. Lazard, who took over the firm after the 1994 death of her husband Wardell Lazard, says she responded by slashing salaries and costs and by renegotiating office leases. The soft-spoken Ms. Lazard says she doesn't hold any personal animosity for Mr. Levitt. But she says SEC policies "have definitely had an impact" on the company's bottom line, and the ensuing blizzard of regulatory scrutiny has spawned legal bills that "eat into our profits."

Mr. Beal in New York says it is just starting to get back on track. Almost two years ago, the firm was asked to provide information as part of a broader federal probe of political links to Wisconsin's minority set-aside program for bond deals. The firm's chief, Bernard Beal, felt the heat even though neither he nor the firm was ever charged with any misdeeds. New York

City's comptroller's office grew alarmed at the Midwest inquiry and Beal was pushed out of the city's bond underwriting syndicate, ultimately losing business elsewhere as well. Amid the upheaval Beal's net capital fell to around $700,000 today from about $4 million in 1992, people at the firm say.

But things are looking up for Mr. Beal. He and the firm have been cleared in the Wisconsin inquiry, he says; the New York City comptroller's office says it has been told by the U.S. Attorney's office in Wisconsin that Mr. Beal and his company will not likely face charges. New York City has reinstated Beal in its highly sought-after underwriting group. "I'd like to put my experience with New York City behind me and move forward," Mr. Beal says.

Another firm that would like to move forward is Pryor McClendon in Atlanta. By the end of last year, the firm had $675,000 in net capital, according to company filings with the SEC; the firm says the current figure is $1.2 million. Malcolm Pryor, one of the firm's principals, won't forecast the firm's results in the wake of net losses of $520,099 in 1995 and $1,641,396 in 1994. "You make money, you lose money," he says. "We'll be profitable." Mr. Pryor adds, "I can't blame Arthur Levitt. It's economics, not policy."

At the SEC, "we're sensitive to the concerns of minority firms," an agency spokeswoman said in a statement. "Unfortunately, it is difficult at this time for all participants in the municipal-bond market. However, the SEC's overriding goal is to strengthen the market by bolstering public confidence, and to that extent, all firms will benefit." The SEC's Mr. Levitt has called on Wall Street to hire more minorities in sales, trading and banking positions, and has urged Wall Street's larger firms to help minority firms bid competitively on munis.

The profit pinch is sharp. It is reflected in the amount that securities firms get paid to sell a bond, the so-called underwriting spread. The figure has shrunk to a rough average of $8.12 for a $1,000 bond from more than $13 a decade ago. Meanwhile, costs are rising. All of Wall Street is affected, but it is the thinly capitalized minority firms that have been forced to drain their already low capital reserves to pay legal bills and answer a blizzard of subpoenas and requests for information.

Some minority-controlled firms are doing well. Several have backing from strong Wall Street players, including Merrill Lynch & Co. And at least one independently owned firm, San Francisco's Grigsby Brandford & Co., easily dominates the minority-owned underwriting ranks, and regularly beats out big Wall Street firms for bond assignments. Yet even in the bang-up year of 1995, Grigsby produced net earnings of only $598,645, according to an annual report filed with the SEC. Calvin Grigsby, the president, says, "We're not doing that badly," even though "interest rates are up."

"I think it's very sad—I keep track of how the firms are doing and they are not doing well," says Muriel Siebert, president of Muriel Siebert & Co. "For a while it was incredible—there was so much in munis, if you were a minority firm there was a lot of business available to you." Ms. Siebert says her own firm is currently incurring losses in munis, but the stock side of her business is profitable enough to allow her to keep the muni side running.

Angeles, in 1990; an MBA from the University of California, Irvine, in 1984; and a BS in astronomy from the California Institute of Technology in 1979.

Jonathan G. Katz, secretary: Any comment letters on the SEC's proposals come to Mr. Katz, who has held the secretary position since 1986. He also schedules the SEC's meetings and items for consideration and reviews documents issued by the SEC, giving advice to SEC staff on matters of process and procedure. He used to be the SEC's director at what is now called the Office of Investor Education and Assistance. Before joining the SEC in 1983, he worked for eight years at the U.S. Justice Department. He has a JD from the University of Pittsburgh and a BA in economics from Colgate University.

James M. McConnell, executive director: Appointed by former Chairman Richard Breeden in October 1990, Mr. McConnell is responsible for the SEC's internal management policies and budget operations. He was at the Department of Labor from 1970 to 1984 in a variety of positions working on programs for disadvantaged groups. He got a BS in business administration from Virginia Polytechnic Institute and State University in 1970.

Lori A. Richards, director, Office of Compliance, Inspections and Examinations: Ms. Richards was formerly executive assistant and senior adviser to Chairman Levitt, after having been the associate director for enforcement at the SEC's Los Angeles office, where she had started her SEC career in 1985. She got a JD from American University's Washington College of Law and a BA from Northern Illinois University.

THE FEDERAL RESERVE

THE FINANCIAL CENTER OF THE WORLD

When the Fed Speaks, Markets Listen

L ong before the congressional hearing was scheduled to begin, every seat in the cavernous room was filled.

Near the back of the room, a large standing-room-only section formed, packed with Wall Street representatives, lobbyists, journalists, congressional staffers and others just curious to see what the fuss was all about. As television crews busily set up their equipment, congressmen and their aides hovered around an elfin man with thick glasses, who calmly prepared to deliver another in a long series of densely-worded treatises on banking and finance.

A newcomer spotted a friend in the audience, tapped him on the shoulder and asked him how he was lucky enough to get a seat, especially an aisle seat. "Got here real early," replied the man, dressed in a dark pinstriped suit and carrying an expensive attaché case. "This is better than a U2 concert, man."

Not long ago, comparing Federal Reserve Board Chairman Alan Greenspan to a popular rock band might have seemed far-fetched. Indeed, it wasn't so long ago that the words "Federal Reserve" were more likely to conjure up visions in many people's minds of a national forest or a rare old whiskey, rather than the nation's central bank.

No more. While the Fed remains something of a mystery to the vast majority of Americans, they know with certainty that it does something *very* important. Early in 1997, the Fed's role drew especially close attention as it nudged a key short-term interest rate higher in a preemptive strike against inflation. That move sparked intense debate about whether Fed officials were trying to solve a problem that didn't exist.

"There's no inflation to have a preemptive strike against," railed Senator

Paul Sarbanes, a Maryland Democrat. "This is a preemptive strike against economic growth and against jobs."

Jack Kemp, the Republican vice-presidential nominee in 1996, contended that the Fed had "buckled under to big banks and major industrialists" in the absence of any concrete evidence that inflation threatened. Writing in *The Wall Street Journal*, he said the Fed "was taking a shot in the dark at inflation—not only unable to see its quarry, but unsure even that the quarry exists." Referring to the stock-market sell-off that accompanied that first rate hike, he added, "Given the markets' reaction to the Fed's action, many investors probably feel like the victims of a drive-by shooting."

Supporters replied that the Fed merely was administering a small dose of medicine at a very early stage in order to avoid the need for bigger, more painful doses later. They also argued that it's a big mistake to wait to act until the first signs of inflation appear. At that point, it's already too late.

Worries persisted throughout 1997 about the threat of renewed inflation and the possibility that the Fed might raise rates further. But as the year drew to a close, the Fed hadn't made any other moves, the economy still was humming along, inflation remained well behaved, and long-term bond yields had fallen, muting much of the earlier criticism of the central bank and Mr. Greenspan. By mid-December, yields on thirty-year Treasury bonds, which began the year at about 6.6 percent, had fallen below 6 percent. Even so, some Fed officials remained apprehensive that the economy's brisk growth and the falling unemployment rate eventually would lead to higher inflation in 1998.

Even investors who question Mr. Greenspan's judgment or think the central bank has an exaggerated fear of inflation readily concede the enormous power and influence that the Fed Chairman commands. Indeed, since the shy, scholarly New Yorker took over in 1987, replacing Paul A. Volcker, he has become the best known and most powerful figure in world financial markets, capable of making markets around the planet quake merely by hinting, as he once did, that investors were getting a little too "exuberant."

Why should one man, especially one so reserved and modest, command such intense attention and influence in an age when vast, impersonal market forces seem more in command of events than ever?

Part of the explanation lies in the Fed's extraordinary track record during the Greenspan era, especially since 1991. It has helped engineer one of the friendliest economic environments that Americans have enjoyed in decades, a period of modest inflation, relatively low interest rates and continued economic expansion accompanied by booming stock and bond markets. Economists have called this environment the Goldilocks economy: neither too strong nor too weak, but just right.

Another reason for Mr. Greenspan's unquestioned power and popularity is the enormous power that Congress has bestowed upon the central bank. No financial institution on earth commands nearly as much attention as the Fed, and the Chairman's job is widely believed to be the second most important in Washington. Congress has given the Fed the mandate of simultaneously maintaining economic growth, a high level of employment, stable prices and moderate long-term interest rates.

But there are many other powerful forces that have shoved Alan Greenspan and his Fed colleagues onto center stage and are likely to keep them there throughout the late 1990s. One is Washington's growing reliance on the Fed to help manage the economy. With all the focus in recent years on getting the budget deficit under control, economic policymakers can't rely as easily as they once could on big changes in spending or taxes to steer the economy. Investment advisers look increasingly to Mr. Greenspan and the Fed, since they manipulate the powerful levers that control the nation's money-supply growth and key short-term interest rates. This heavy reliance on the central bank makes some Fed insiders uncomfortable. They often insist that interest rates are a blunt instrument that can't be relied upon to steer the world's biggest and most sophisticated economy. Lurking behind these comments is fear that they will be blamed by Congress and voters for the next economic slump. Whatever the case, the Fed is being viewed not only in Washington but also on Wall Street as an extraordinarily important guardian of economic prosperity.

Another factor increasing the Fed's power and focusing more attention on it is Washington's slow but inevitable overhaul of the nation's banking and financial system. Without relief from what they consider to be burdensome restrictions on how they can conduct their business, American banks and other financial institutions say it will be tough to remain competitive in an increasingly tough global marketplace. Many lawmakers and regulators, including Mr. Greenspan, favor demolishing barriers set up during the Depression era between commercial banks and investment banks, but there are significant disagreements over which walls should be pulled down and what the new rules should be.

Under Mr. Greenspan, the Fed also has taken a tougher role as the nation's premier financial regulator, often demonstrating a willingness to take remarkably strong action against offenders. Just ask officials of Daiwa Bank Ltd., a Japanese bank that was expelled from the United States by regulators after pleading guilty to conspiring to conceal huge trading losses.

But perhaps one of the most important sources of Mr. Greenspan's influence is his personality and his remarkably sensitive political antennae. He is unfailingly calm, gentlemanly and a superb listener, which immediately sets him apart from many other Washington leaders. He goes out of his way to seek advice from Fed colleagues and staffers and to resolve conflicts. He is media-savvy, knowing when and how to leak news. He has a rare ability to disagree without sounding disagreeable. He is widely respected within the Fed not only for his genial leadership but also because of his impressive command of economic statistical details and anecdotal evidence.

He uses a deft sense of humor to ward off hostile questions or at least remove the sting from conflicts. During one packed congressional hearing early in 1997, a congressman pointed out that Mr. Greenspan was disagreeing on a vital point with Eugene Ludwig, the Comptroller of the Currency. Mr. Greenspan replied that he was very reluctant to disagree with Mr. Ludwig on any subject because of the possibility that his friend Gene might stop conceding Mr. Greenspan's difficult six-foot putts on the golf course.

His humor often is self-deprecating, such as when he discusses his prowess on the tennis court. Mr. Greenspan took up tennis late in life, and it shows. But he likes to point out that he has improved. He once observed that, as an economist, he is fond of extrapolation, and based upon all the available evidence, he will be ready to join the professional tennis tour when he reaches the age of 104.

Mr. Greenspan also has mastered the fine art of FedSpeak, which means giving lengthy speeches about central banking and Fed policy that reveal little or nothing, leaving him and his Fed colleagues with maximum flexibility. He frequently pokes fun at his own ability in this area, once quipping, "Since I've become a central banker, I've learned to mumble with great incoherence. If I seem unduly clear to you, you must have misunderstood what I said."

Evidence of his success is abundant. Once, after he spoke in Seattle, *The New York Times* reported: GREENSPAN SEES CHANCE OF RECESSION. But *The Wall Street Journal* reported: FED CHAIRMAN DOESN'T SEE RECESSION ON THE HORIZON. These opposing reactions prompted a large financial-services company to run a full-page advertisement with both headlines and the comment: "Confused? Who Wouldn't Be?"

Mr. Greenspan asked for a framed copy.

In the manic-depressive financial markets of the late 1990s, the Fed is as feared as it is trusted. To many people, Alan Greenspan comes across as a stern father figure, constantly warning us of impending disaster unless we improve our behavior, yet also capable of rescuing us from disaster. When the economy is doing fine, it's common to view the Fed as all-powerful. When storm clouds are brewing, it's equally fashionable to blame the Fed. Fed veterans agree there is nothing like a long-running expansion and bull markets to bolster the authority of the central bank and its chairman. Similarly, during periods of recession, there often are cries to overhaul the Fed, keelhaul its Chairman, and reduce the institution's independence from political pressures.

Independence

A photograph of the Federal Reserve Board members of 1914 shows seven distinguished-looking men. Among them were Treasury Secretary W. G. McAdoo and Comptroller of the Currency J. S. Williams.

"I told you the Fed should have tightened."

Today, no members of the President's Cabinet or the Executive Branch are allowed to serve on the Fed. The very idea of letting the Treasury Secretary— or any member of the president's team—have a hand in setting monetary policy would strike most Washington policymakers as heresy. Fed officials pride themselves on their independence, which they view as vital to shelter them from political pressures that might prevent them from taking necessary but unpopular actions.

But that independence is far from complete. Although Fed decisions can't be overturned by the President or anyone else in the executive branch, the President appoints all seven Federal Reserve Board members, subject to Senate approval. And Congress requires periodic reports from the Fed, including a semi-annual report that Mr. Greenspan delivers known as the Humphrey-Hawkins report, after the 1978 law expanding the Fed's responsibilities. Fed officials often point out that the Fed isn't absolutely independent of the government. Rather, it is independent *within* the government.

Granting such extraordinary financial powers to a small group of unelected men and women, who meet in secret, may sound distinctly un-American and certainly undemocratic. But as writer Michael Kinsley once put it, the Federal Reserve is "indefensible in theory—and indispensable in practice."

To carry out its many duties, the modern Fed employs some 25,000 people. The Board and the twelve Federal Reserve Banks also publish mountains of material about the Fed, including comic books about inflation, banks and monetary policy. In 1996, the General Accounting Office, a congressional watchdog agency, concluded that the Fed could "increase its cost consciousness." GAO officials cited "inefficiencies" in such Fed practices as travel costs, personnel benefits, building purchases, contracting and procurement. The report noted pointedly that certain personnel benefits, such as leave policies and savings plans, are "generous compared to those of federal financial regulatory agencies with similar personnel requirements."

The Wall Street Journal ran a page-one article on the subject by staff reporter John R. Wilke on September 12, 1996. The headline read: SHOWING ITS AGE. FED'S HUGE EMPIRE, SET UP YEARS AGO, IS COSTLY AND INEFFICIENT. IT HAS FAR TOO MANY BANKS, OFTEN IN WRONG PLACES; LOSSES IN CHECK-CLEARING. The story reported that the "sprawling Fed empire" had raised concern among some in Congress and at the GAO. The story also reported that Mr. Greenspan had rejected many of the GAO's findings, especially the idea of closing some Fed banks.

First Among Equals

To most Americans, who aren't entirely sure what the Fed does, the nation's central bank is embodied in Mr. Greenspan. While he is only one of seven members of the Board of Governors, the Fed's ruling body, he clearly is First Among Equals.

Just how closely the financial world watches the Fed was evident in December 1996 when Mr. Greenspan, in an apparently innocuous dinner speech, merely asked—and didn't answer—whether there was "irrational exuberance" in the financial markets. The mere hint that the chairman thought there might be such exuberance, coupled with his implied power to curb it, sent traders around the globe scurrying for the nearest sell button. The sell-off only lasted a few days, but served as a reminder to everyone in the financial markets and to Fed officials themselves of the central bank's remarkable power—power that can be exercised without even taking any formal votes or actions.

So far, Mr. Greenspan has earned high marks for using his enormous influence wisely. Indeed, his speedy pledge in 1987 that the Fed would insure that credit was readily available in the wake of the stock market crash is widely credited with stemming the selling tide. One reason for his deft handling of the crisis was that he was well prepared. Before the crash, he had asked the staff to prepare contingency plans for how the central bank could respond to a variety of potential financial mishaps, including a stock-market collapse. Fed officials later said that advance planning helped them react quickly to fast-moving events on Black Monday and Terrible Tuesday.

In view of the huge reaction even a phrase or two can create, it is little wonder that Mr. Greenspan seldom makes straightforward pronouncements of his views. Fed watchers have noted a similar tendency in previous chairmen, nearly all of whom suddenly seem able to explain things much more clearly after their retirements. Still, under Mr. Greenspan's leadership, the Fed has become much less secretive. Now, it routinely announces whatever credit-policy decisions have been taken at its regular meetings shortly after the meeting concludes. Previously, after each meeting, traders had to guess what the Fed was up to, based upon the central bank's fancy feints and maneuvers in the daily credit markets, where it buys and sells government securities.

In the Driver's Seat

In their efforts to explain the seemingly arcane maneuverings of the Federal Reserve, journalists often resort to an analogy that puts the Fed in the driver's seat of an enormous, powerful automobile. Instead of gasoline, this automobile—the nation's economy—runs on money. If the car begins to slow, the Fed steps on the accelerator, providing more money to rev up the economy. If, on the other hand, the car is going too fast for safety, the Fed eases off the accelerator and hits the brakes, cutting the supply of money to the economy. It is a useful analogy, but don't make the mistake of thinking the Fed has anywhere near the control over the economy that a driver has over a modern car. The Fed's tools simply aren't that precise.

Among the things the Fed worries about constantly are the pace of economic growth (is the car going too fast or too slow?), the levels of employment (is the engine running efficiently without backfiring?) and the rate of inflation (is the engine overheating dangerously?). The Fed tries to bring those three factors into perfect equilibrium. The economy should be growing, Americans should be able to find jobs if they want them, and none of that should lead to extreme increases in prices of goods and services. And for several years the Fed (with a little luck) generally has been able to claim success. Remarkably, that success has been achieved without the need for dramatic action by the Fed. During 1996, for example, the Fed changed rates only once: In late January, it pushed the federal funds rate higher by a quarter of a percentage point. (The federal funds rate, which is the rate banks charge each other for short-term loans, strongly influences many other rates.) During 1993, it made no changes at all. As recently as 1991, the Fed made ten changes.

The Fed hasn't always been so fortunate or skillful. During the late 1970s and early 1980s when inflation was soaring, the economy was stumbling and unemployment was rising, the Fed drew heavy criticism as some short-term interest rates rose above 20 percent. Even the harshest Fed critics, though, agreed that the Fed certainly didn't deserve all the blame; indeed, the toughest criticism was aimed at Jimmy Carter's economics team. At one point during that gloomy period, Treasury Secretary Michael Blumenthal coined what he says later became known internationally as "Blumenthal's Law." As he later described it, "The law is very complicated . . . It goes like this: When the curve depicting the prime rate of interest intersects with the curve representing the President's popularity, then it's time for the Secretary of the Treasury to go."

Even before that, the Fed's management of the economy in the late 1920s and early 1930s had been blamed by historians for worsening conditions. They argue that the Fed failed to keep enough money and credit flowing through the veins of the economy. By early 1933, the nation's money supply had fallen by one-third, the largest and longest decline since the end of the Civil War, according to Milton Friedman and Anna Jacobson Schwartz in their 1963 book, *A Monetary History of the United States, 1867–1960*. They concluded that the central bank had enough power to take actions that "would have eased the severity of the contraction and very likely would have brought it to an end at a much earlier date."

Federal Reserve officials have several levers they can pull when they want to take action to expand or shrink the amount of money and credit in the country. While the system may sound complex, it's actually remarkably simple.

Suppose Fed officials are worried that the economy looks dangerously weak, inflation isn't a threat, the money supply is limping along at a very low rate, and Wall Street economists are exhorting the central bank to lift its heavy foot off the economy's throat. The Fed can pump huge amounts of new money into the economy simply by buying U.S. government securities from major financial institutions in the vast financial markets. How does it pay for them? Simply by crediting these institutions' Federal Reserve accounts electronically with the new "money." Nobody needs to crank up the printing presses. In this electronic era, all it takes is a few computer keystrokes, and billions of new dollars have been created. This is known as "open-market" operations.

Reverse this procedure, and the Fed can speedily drain money from the banking system. Suppose Fed officials are deeply concerned that the economy is growing too rapidly and that inflation will surge out of control. It can yank money merely by phoning those same major financial institutions and offering to sell them U.S. Government securities. When the Fed receives payment from the bond dealers for those securities, the money effectively has flowed out of the banking system.

Major decisions on whether—and when— to do all this furious buying and selling are outlined by the Federal Open Market Committee, a twelve-member panel that meets eight or so times a year in Washington. This group consists of all seven Board members plus five of the twelve presidents of Federal Reserve Banks around the country. The president of the Federal Reserve Bank of New York—now William J. McDonough—is a permanent member of this committee, in deference to the major importance of the New York Fed. The other presidents serve one-year terms on a rotating basis. All twelve presidents may participate in discussions at the meeting, but only the five members may vote, along with the seven Board members.

Meetings of the committee are closed to the public. The committee's decisions—either to take action to stimulate or curb the economy or to do nothing—typically have been announced shortly after each meeting concludes. A summary of the FOMC members' discussion is released several weeks later, shortly after the next meeting, along with the outcome of formal votes.

Once a decision is made on whether and when to change monetary policy, directions are given to the Federal Reserve Bank of New York's trading desk. If a policy change is made, the New York Fed executes the decision to drive the federal fund rates to the new target levels. Typically, the New York Fed makes its move between 10:30 and 10:45 A.M., a period that Fed watchers call "Fed time."

Obviously, anyone who knows ahead of time what the Fed will do would be in a position to amass great wealth. And since Wall Street is loath to pass up any opportunity to do that, it employs legions of economists and other "Fed-watchers" to try to figure it out. Many of them have often been wrong. It's said on Wall Street that Fed-watchers have managed to predict at least fourteen of the last three Fed policy changes and more than a dozen of the last four recessions.

To be fair to Fed-watchers, Fed officials often engage in a series of elaborate head-fakes, sometimes as a way to test investor reaction to a move under consideration—in essence, as a financial trial balloon. Indeed, in the summer of 1996 Fed officials began telling journalists that the economy might be too steamy and that perhaps it needed a dose of higher interest rates to calm matters down. "We're at a critical juncture," one official told *The Wall Street Journal*. Another warned ominously that a small rate increase might not be enough. Any rate increase, to be effective, "has to be enough to be convincing." Then came a string of unexpectedly weak economic reports and the picture began to change. Late in the year, some forecasters were even predicting the Fed's next move would be to reduce interest rates.

But hopes for lower rates began to fade in early 1997, as the economy continued expanding at a solid clip and stock prices continued to soar far beyond the point at which Mr. Greenspan had first expressed concern about "irrational exuberance." Mr. Greenspan then began dropping hints that the Fed might launch a preemptive strike against inflation.

That strike came at the Fed's March 25, 1997, meeting, when the Fed decided to nudge the federal funds rate a quarter percentage point higher. Many experts were convinced that the Fed would raise rates again at the May meeting, but it didn't. And the Fed made no further moves for the rest of 1997.

There are other levers the Fed can pull to affect the flow of money, but they are rarely used. For example, the Fed can make direct loans to banks and other financial institutions at what is called the discount rate. That method is seldom used to influence overall monetary policy; rather, the discount window typically serves as a source of seasonal and short-term lending to the banking system, as well as a lender of last resort to individual troubled banks. The Fed also can change bank reserve requirements. If, for instance, the Fed wanted to create more money, it could reduce the amounts of money banks are required to hold in reserve as a sort of safety net. That would free vast amounts of money for re-lending. Or if it wanted to chill lending, it could increase those requirements. But reserve requirements are seldom used as a weapon.

While the Fed's power may be immense, many people, even Wall Street traders, share an exaggerated view of what the Fed can and cannot do. The Fed can, of course, strongly influence short-term interest rates through its daily open-market operations. It can set the discount rate. It can also control the closely watched interest rate on federal funds. But the key word here is "influence." That is very different from the power to set rates. The Fed does not—and cannot—control longer-term interest rates, such as bond yields and home mortgage rates. Those rates are influenced by such factors as investor views of the inflation outlook.

Thus, while the Fed's daily open-market operations play a very important role in the credit markets and command very close attention, many economists focus even more closely on the central bank's longer-term decisions about how rapidly or slowly the nation's money supply should grow. While this is a highly controversial area—practically a religious issue to some economists—this subject also offers insights into what may be the Fed's most significant role in the economy.

An influential school of economists, known as the monetarists, believe fervently that slow and steady money-supply growth is the key to long-term stability in prices and economic health. Monetarists long have urged the Federal Reserve to resist the temptation to adjust its monetary dials frequently in reaction to perceived economic threats. Just set a long-term plan and stick with it. Don't allow the money supply to expand 10 percent one year, then 3 percent the next, and 6 percent the next. Erratic money growth, they say, is like a drunk driver trying to get from Point A to Point B by bouncing off one wall, then the other wall. The driver may reach his destination, but not without doing lots of damage along the way.

Critics of the monetarist approach compare it to a ship captain ordering the crew to put the ship on automatic pilot and steer a straight course, no matter what the weather and seas are like. They insist that monetarists want to tie the Fed's hands and prevent it from being flexible enough to steer around dangerous storms, rocks or shallow water. These critics also say the Fed's money-supply figures, which are released each week, are no longer as reliable as they once were because of vast technological and other changes that have made it much more difficult to answer what might seem like a simple question: What, after all, is money?

"Money" isn't just cash. In fact, all the known cash that we carry around in our wallets and change purses represents only a small portion of what is generally considered the nation's money supply. Reflecting this confusion, the Fed compiles various money-supply measures. For example, the basic measure, known as M1, consists basically of currency, traveler's checks, and checking deposits.

That may sound like a pretty broad definition, but it actually omits many other sources of money, such as savings deposits and money-market deposit accounts. They are part of a broader definition, known as M2, which includes everything in M1 plus other important sources of buying power, such as savings deposits. An even broader measure, M3, takes the entire M2 measure and adds a few other items. In addition, the Fed publishes a broad measure of credit.

In the early 1980s, when inflation was running at double-digit levels, the Fed's weekly money-supply and banking statistics commanded extraordinarily close attention around the world. The main reason for all this attention was that Fed officials, trying to conquer inflation, were paying close attention themselves. This produced a cottage industry of money-supply watchers, sometimes with tragic or comic results.

In the 1990s, it has been hard to get anyone to focus on the money-supply numbers. Instead, the search is intensifying for a new magic bullet—some economic report or concept that will help investors predict what the Fed will do next and thus get an advantage over their competitors.

Ask traders what they think will move the Fed most quickly, and the answer usually is an unexpected trend in the employment reports released each month by the Labor Department. The employment reports often hit page one of major newspapers around the nation, and snippets often are carried by network television news reports.

But it isn't likely that the Fed would rely so heavily on a single report. When Mr. Greenspan testifies before Congress or speaks publicly he often cites a wide variety of useful statistics, including the value of the dollar, the size of the trade deficit and the price of gold and other commodities. He even notes arcane details such as how long it takes for raw materials to reach factories, known more formally as the diffusion index of supplier-delivery lags.

International factors can also play important roles in the Fed's decision-making processes. For example, Fed officials late in 1997 were keeping an especially close watch on Asia's turbulent financial markets and troubled economies. At the time, Mr. Greenspan said the impact on the United States still looks "modest though not negligible." Even so, there was speculation that Asian currency devaluations, the dollar's strength and softer exports to Asia would combine to help slow the U.S. economy in 1998.

Anthony Solomon, a former president of the New York Fed, sums it up nicely: "We watch everything."

A Tough Cop

Another of the Fed's jobs is to monitor the health of the U.S. government securities markets. Although the stock markets long have dominated financial headlines and investor attention, the Treasury securities markets are much larger and far more important to the economy than the stock markets. For better or worse, the U.S. economy in the late twentieth century is floating on a vast sea of credit, making the health of the credit markets central to the health of the overall economy. The Federal Reserve Bank of New York, the Fed's most important outpost, carefully tracks the daily twitches of the vast credit markets, watching for signs of problems among the nation's major financial powerhouses. Fed officials also are constantly on the alert for any evidence of market mishaps.

The Fed's vast power and toughness was vividly displayed in 1991 when a scandal erupted involving Salomon Brothers, which admitted that it had repeatedly violated rules of the Treasury's multibillion-dollar note auctions.

The message from the Salomon bond scandal (which is summarized in the chapter on Salomon Smith Barney Holdings Inc.) came through clearly: Fed officials take their role very seriously as manager of the auctions of U.S. Treasury bills, notes and bonds. Without successful auctions, the government wouldn't have the cash to pay its bills.

The Fed doesn't have much sympathy for a financial institution that tries to conceal problems. The best example involved Daiwa Bank Ltd. after disclosures late in 1995 that a trader at the Japanese bank had amassed losses of $1.1 billion over eleven years. Daiwa executives knew of the trader's losses before telling U.S. and Japanese authorities. After months of denials, Daiwa Bank pleaded guilty to conspiring to conceal the trading losses from U.S. regulators and agreed to pay a $340 million fine, one of the biggest ever imposed by the United States. The Fed and other regulators later "terminated" the bank's U.S. operations.

Mr. Greenspan later explained that this action was "stern" but vital because actions such as Daiwa's "carried the threat of significant damage to a major asset of our nation, the integrity of our financial system." He said trust is a key element of all smoothly running financial systems. "When confidence in the integrity of a financial institution is shaken or its commitment to the honest conduct of business is in doubt, public trust erodes and the entire system is weakened," he told a House subcommittee in December 1995. "Indeed, there is no set of statutes that can ensure the effective functioning of a market if a critical mass of financial counterparties is deemed untrustworthy." The potential costs to the U.S. financial system and hence to the economy are "too large."

The Fed's roles in the Salomon and Daiwa episodes illuminate only a small part of the central bank's vast powers. Fed officials have enormous regulatory powers over a wide variety of financial institutions. For example, the Fed has the primary responsibility for regulating bank-holding companies, including those companies' nonbank and foreign units. Fed officials also are responsible for state-chartered banks that are members of the Federal Reserve System, as well as their foreign branches and subsidiaries. And they are responsible for certain other types of corporations through which U.S. banking oganizations conduct operations abroad. Some of the Fed's powers are shared with other agencies, both federal and state.

Among the Fed's other roles are to regulate margin requirements on securities transactions and to implement laws protecting consumers in credit and deposit transactions. The Fed also monitors compliance with money-laundering provisions contained in the Bank Secrecy Act. And Fed officials also can decide the fate of many proposed mergers.

Reshaping Banking and Finance

Alan Greenspan, other federal regulators and many lawmakers agree enthusiastically on the need to overhaul Depression-era banking restrictions to adapt to modern-day changes and to help American financial institutions compete more effectively with international financial behemoths.

But how? Here, there is widespread disagreement among regulators and lawmakers, raising doubts about whether new legislation will be enacted anytime soon. Even so, officials at J. P. Morgan & Co. say the likelihood of Congress enacting broad financial services modernization legislation is greater than ever before.

Chief among those ancient restrictions under attack is the Glass-Steagall Act, which long has prohibited mergers of commercial banks with investment banking firms. In recent years, more and more cracks have been opening up in the once-impenetrable walls separating commercial banking, investment banking and other types of businesses. As Mr. Greenspan once put it, modern technology "already is altering the nature of what constitutes finance."

But what kinds of new businesses should banks be permitted to dive into? How should financial regulation be changed? Should banks be allowed to merge with major industrial corporations? For example, should banks own and be owned by such commercial and industrial giants as Microsoft, General Motors, or General Electric? And how should insurance be regulated?

Mr. Greenspan argues enthusiastically in favor of removing some barriers set up by the Glass-Steagall Act because he says such changes would provide improved financial services. "We strongly urge an extensive increase in the activities permitted to banking organizations and other financial institutions," he explained at a House banking subcommittee hearing in early 1997. Indeed, Fed officials already have taken steps to make it easier for banks to sell and underwrite securities. Several of those steps came during 1997, and more are expected.

But Mr. Greenspan also urges a go-slow approach. He is especially opposed to handing over the benefits of federal deposit insurance to the securities industry, insurance companies and other industries. "We must, I think, be continually on guard that the subsidy provided by the safety net does not leak outside the institutions for which it was intended and provide a broad subsidy to other kinds of activities," he says.

Ultimately, though, the financial service business will undergo huge changes no matter what Congress does, Mr. Greenspan predicts. "Indeed, just as the lines between banking and other financial institutions are often already difficult to discern, the boundaries between finance and nonfinance are likely to become increasingly indistinct as we move into the twenty-first century," he says. For example, he says, computer and software firms will surely be offering ever more sophisticated financial products. And financial firms will be offering an increasingly sophisticated variety of nonfinancial services.

Banker to the Banks

The twelve Federal Reserve Banks provide a wide range of banking services to banks and other financial institutions around the nation, as well as to the federal government. For example, the Fed plays a major role in operating the nation's delicate payments system, making sure that checks move through the financial pipeline on time and without glitches.

Another big job is making sure enough currency and coins are circulating around the country to meet public demand. Glance at those dollars in your wallet, and you will notice they are "Federal Reserve Notes." These notes are printed by the Treasury Department's Bureau of Engraving and Printing and delivered to Reserve Banks for circulation.

The Fed also plays an important role in collecting checks and electronically processing funds. It is officially the government's "fiscal agent," which means it serves as the federal government's bank and performs vital services for the Treasury. For example, it maintains the Treasury's funds account, clears Treasury checks drawn on that account and conducts regular public auctions of new Treasury bills, notes and bonds. The Fed also issues, services and redeems U.S. government securities.

Moreover, the Fed is responsible for implementing many laws designed to protect consumers in credit and other financial transactions. Among these are transactions involving charge and credit cards, automated teller machines, automobile leases and mortgages. Each Reserve Bank has on its staff specially trained examiners who are supposed to evaluate the performance of banks in that District in enforcing consumer-protection laws.

In short, the Federal Reserve Banks serve as the operating arms of the central bank. The twelve banks also are an important source of intelligence for Washington. They regularly provide news and analysis of local economic conditions and trends, and Wall Street economists monitor their publications closely for clues to where the Fed is heading.

Fed Diplomacy

Since foreign-exchange rates began to float more than two decades ago, governments and central banks around the globe often intervene in the currency markets in an attempt to stabilize conditions. The U.S. Treasury has the overall responsibility for managing U.S. international financial policy, but it works closely with the Fed. Should officials decide that the dollar is too weak or too strong, instructions would be sent to the Federal Reserve Bank of New York to intervene in the markets. Most of the transactions done by the Fed involve exchanging dollars for either German marks or Japanese yen.

Currency market developments can play a major role in the U.S. economy, just as Fed actions in the U.S. credit markets play prominent roles in currency markets. The dollar's foreign-exchange value in terms of other currencies is one of the channels through which U.S. monetary policy affects the U.S. economy. For example, suppose the Fed raises U.S. interest rates, which in turn could help make the dollar look more attractive to investors. A stronger dollar, in turn, would raise the foreign price of U.S. goods trading in world markets, while cutting the price of goods imported into the United States. Thus, these developments could have important impacts throughout the U.S. economy.

Over the past few years, the Fed hasn't done nearly as much intervention in the foreign-exchange markets as it used to do, in part because the currency markets generally have been much calmer than they were in the roller-coaster days of the early 1980s. Even so, the Fed's enormous clout commands respect throughout world financial markets, and the Fed's regular reports on how much or how little intervention it has done are avidly read by currency traders.

Fed officials work closely with representatives of central banks of other countries through the Bank for International Settlements, an organization based in Basel, Switzerland. Fed representatives also participate in activities of the International Monetary Fund, as well as with representatives of other industrial nations at the Organization for Economic Cooperation and Development in Paris, known as the OECD.

The Fed has been conducting currency operations—buying and selling dollars in exchange for foreign currency—for customers since the 1950s and for its own account since 1962.

There's Gold in Them Thar Vaults

Heard of Fort Knox? Forget about it. The Fed is the world's largest known repository of gold. Stored in vast vaults under the Federal Reserve Bank of New York, located eighty feet below street level on the bedrock of Manhattan island, are billions of dollars' worth of gold bars, owned by the various nations and international monetary organizations. (Fed officials won't tell you which nations stash their gold there. That is a closely guarded secret.) Safety and convenience are the main reasons so much gold is stored there. The Fed's gold vaults are a popular tourist attraction, drawing more than 22,000 visitors a year. The gold vaults have even caught Hollywood's imagination. The movie *Die Hard With a Vengence* includes a sensational—but fictional, only—attempt to smash into the vaults. A New York Fed spokesman solemnly emphasizes that no attempt, outside of film, has ever been made to break into the well-protected gold vaults.

The Federal Reserve's People

FEDERAL RESERVE BOARD OF GOVERNORS

Alan Greenspan, chairman: At the helm of the Federal Reserve is Alan Greenspan, a longtime Republican who once served as chairman of President Gerald Ford's Council of Economic Advisers. Curiously, Mr. Greenspan's artful monetary management in the 1990s has been credited by many observers with being one of the most important factors in helping Bill Clinton become the first Democrat since World War II to win a second term.

Greenspan, Alan
Chairman-Federal
Reserve Board

Mr. Greenspan is a close student not only of economics but also of politics. Before he came to the Fed, he would often remind friends that Fed officials follow election returns, just like everyone else. He also once reminded a reporter for *The Wall Street Journal* to forget about the silly textbook theory that the Fed is totally above politics and doesn't pay any attention to such mundane issues as presidential primaries. Nearly a year before one presidential election, he told the reporter that the Fed had only a limited amount of time to act to raise interest rates. The reason, he explained, is that once the presidential primary season kicked into high gear, the central bank probably would feel compelled to refrain from anything that might drag it into the spotlight.

At the Fed, Mr. Greenspan has gone out of his way to be as collegial as possible and to avoid the image of being a dictatorial chairman, as some Fed officials accused his predecessor, Paul Volcker, of being. Mr. Greenspan has a much milder, softer approach than Mr. Volcker, whose more direct and occasionally abrasive style rubbed some colleagues the wrong way.

In view of the bipartisan support that Mr. Greenspan enjoys today, it may be startling to remember how badly the financial markets reacted when President Ronald Reagan announced his appointment in June 1987. At the time, many people assumed Paul Volcker would continue at the helm. Instead, the President said Mr. Volcker had declined a third term and that he would nominate Mr. Greenspan to replace him. Bond prices took their worst pounding in years, the dollar plunged against all major currencies, and commodity prices rose sharply. Supply-side publicist Jude Wanniski called the Greenspan appointment "the worst decision to come out of the Ronald Reagan White House," saying that Mr. Greenspan is "one of the ringleaders of the austerity gang."

But Mr. Greenspan shrugged aside such criticism and now has been named chairman by three Presidents: Reagan, Bush and Clinton. He long has enjoyed superb relations with reporters, who enjoy his dry sense of humor and his fine eye for revealing anecdotes, both economic and political. He has close friends in both political parties. The Senate vote to approve his nomination for a third term was revealing: 91–7.

Alan Greenspan was born in New York City on March 6, 1926. He studied economics as an undergraduate at New York University, receiving a BS, summa cum laude, in 1948. He later received a masters in economics in 1950 and a doctorate in 1977, also from NYU. He also has done advanced graduate work at Columbia University. He was a devoted and early disciple of Ayn Rand, the late author and philosopher who favored freeing capitalism from government constraints.

Before coming to the Fed, Mr. Greenspan headed his own economic-consulting firm, Townsend-Greenspan & Co., based in New York City. He worked at the firm from 1954 to 1974, when he left to join the Ford Administration, and then again from 1977 to 1987. From 1981 to 1983, he served as Chairman of the National Commission on Social Security Reform.

As a youngster, Mr. Greenspan was a talented musician, playing the clarinet. He continues to have a keen interest in music. Once, he was asked by a friend to name his favorite story in *The Wall Street Journal* that year. His surprise answer: a story by Joanne Lipman, then a twenty-two-year-old staff reporter and a violist who played on various New York City street corners with a violinist friend and earned $40 an hour in loose change from passersby. Ms. Lipman recalls that she actually made more money per hour as a street musician than as a reporter.

In April of 1997, Mr. Greenspan married NBC-TV News correspondent Andrea Mitchell in a ceremony presided over by Supreme Court Justice Ruth

Bader Ginsburg. After the couple became engaged, Ms. Mitchell was asked what impact the merger might have on Wall Street. She replied, "I hope they will not become irrationally exuberant."

Alice M. Rivlin, vice chair: In some circles, she is known jokingly as "Landslide Alice." Ms. Rivlin didn't exactly win overwhelming approval from Congress when she came up for confirmation in June 1996. On the same day the Senate overwhelmingly confirmed Alan Greenspan for his third term, it narrowly voted 57–41 for Ms. Rivlin, who at the time was White House budget chief. The votes against her came largely as a protest against Clinton fiscal policy.

Born on March 4, 1931, in Philadelphia, Ms. Rivlin received her BA in economics from Bryn Mawr College in 1952. She received a masters in economics in 1955 and a doctorate in economics in 1958, both from Radcliffe College. She was the founding head of the Congressional Budget Office, serving there from 1975 to 1983. She also served as a member of the staff at the Brookings Institute, a Washington think tank, for many years. From 1968 to 1969, she served as Assistant Secretary for Planning and Evaluation at the Department of Health, Education and Welfare.

Among her awards: a prestigious MacArthur Foundation Prize Fellowship, sometimes referred to as the genius awards. She also has taught at Harvard University, served on the boards of directors of several corporations and served as President of the American Economic Association. She is married to another economist, Professor Sidney G. Winter, and has three children as well as three grandchildren.

OTHER FEDERAL RESERVE BOARD GOVERNORS

Edward W. Kelley Jr.: Mr. Kelley was born January 27, 1932, in Eugene, Oregon. He received a BA in history from Rice University in 1954 and an MBA from Harvard Business School in 1959. Before joining the Board, Mr. Kelley was chairman of Investment Advisors Inc. in Houston, Texas.

Susan M. Phillips: Ms. Phillips joined the Fed on December 2, 1991. She was born December 23, 1944, in Richmond, Virginia. She received a BA in mathematics from Agnes Scott College in 1967, an MS in finance and insurance from Louisiana State University in 1971 and a PhD in finance and economics from LSU in 1973. Before joining the Fed, she was at the University of Iowa, serving as vice president for Finance and University Services. She was also a finance professor in the College of Business Administration. A Fed publication says her areas of specialization include options and commodity futures, financial management and economic theory of regulation. In 1981, she was named a member of the Commodity Futures Trading Commission and became chairman in 1983. She was reappointed as Commissioner and Chairman of the CFTC in 1985, serving there until her resignation in 1987 to return to the University of Iowa as vice president.

Laurence H. Meyer: Mr. Meyer won Senate confirmation by a 98–0 vote in mid-1996. Born March 8, 1944, in the Bronx, New York, he received a BA degree, magna cum laude, from Yale in 1965 and a PhD in economics from Massachusetts Institute of Technology in 1970. Prior to joining the Fed, he was president of a St. Louis-based economic consulting company bearing his name. He cofounded the firm in 1982 with partners Joel Prakken and Chris Varvares. He also was a professor of economics at Washington University. He once received an annual economic-forecasting award for the most accurate forecasts among leading analysts polled each month by the *Blue Chip Economic Indicators* newsletter.

Edward M. Gramlich: President Clinton nominated Dr. Gramlich in 1997. At the time, Dr. Gramlich was an economics professor and dean of the University of Michigan's public-policy school. From 1994 to 1996, he was chairman of a federal advisory council on Social Security. In 1986 and 1987, he served as the Deputy Director and then the Acting Director of the Congressional Budget Office. He also previously worked at the Federal Reserve and the Brookings Institute. He earned a BA from Williams College, as well as an MA and PhD in economics from Yale. At the time of his nomination, he had written nine books and numerous journal articles. He was confirmed by the Senate in late 1997.

Roger W. Ferguson Jr.: Dr. Ferguson also was nominated by President Clinton and confirmed by the Senate in 1997. Previously he was a partner and director of research and information systems at McKinsey & Company, the large New York City consultant. He was born October 28, 1951 and grew up in Washington, DC. He earned an undergraduate degree in economics, magna cum laude, at Harvard, and spent two years on a fellowship at Cambridge University in England before returning to Harvard, where he earned a law degree, cum laude, as well as a PhD in economics. His doctorate dissertation was "Joint Ventures in the American Manufacturing Sector." In 1981, he joined the law firm of Davis Polk & Wardwell, where he worked with investment banks and commercial banks on public offerings, mergers and acquisitions and new product development. He joined McKinsey in 1984, specializing in financial issues. He is only the third African-American to serve on the Federal Reserve Board. The first was Andrew F. Brimmer, who as of late 1997 was heading the federally appointed control board overseeing the tangled finances of Washington, DC. The other was Emmett J. Rice.

FEDERAL RESERVE BANK PRESIDENTS

Cathy E. Minehan, president, First District, Boston (covers all of Maine, Massachusetts, New Hampshire, Rhode Island, Vermont and all but Fairfield County in Connecticut): Ms. Minehan took office July 13, 1994, as the twelfth chief executive of the Federal Reserve Bank of Boston. Born February 15, 1947, in Jersey City, New Jersey, she earned a master's degree in business administration from New York University in 1977. She graduated from the University of Rochester in 1968 with a BA in political science. She began her career with the Fed in 1968, holding various staff positions at the New York Fed, including bank examiner, analyst, and supervisory posts in Public Information and Accounting Control. In 1978, she served as visiting assistant secretary to the Federal Reserve Board of Governors. Upon returning to the New York Fed in 1979, she was named an assistant vice president, with responsibilities in data processing and, later, as a senior aide to the president. She was named vice president in 1982 and over the next five years served in the accounting, check processing and funds and securities areas. In 1987, she was named senior vice president, with responsibility for the funds, securities and accounts group. In 1991, she became first vice president of Federal Reserve Bank of Boston and held that post until she was named President in 1994.

William J. McDonough, president, Second District, New York (covers all of New York, Fairfield County in Connecticut, and twelve counties in northern New Jersey): Mr. McDonough took office July 19, 1993, replacing E. Gerald Corrigan. Prior to that, Mr. McDonough was executive vice president and head of the financial markets group at the New York Fed. He joined the New York Fed in January 1992. Previously, he had worked at First Chicago Corp. and its bank, First National Bank of Chicago. He left there in 1989, after a twenty-two-year career, having risen to vice chairman. He is the first New York Fed president in decades to have spent most of his career in the private sector.

Prior to his First Chicago career, he worked at the State Department from 1961 to 1967 and was in the Navy from 1956 to 1961. He was born April 21, 1934, in Chicago and earned a bachelor's degree from Holy Cross College in Worcester, Massachusetts, in 1956, as well as a master's degree in economics from Georgetown University in 1962.

Edward G. Boehne, president, Third District, Philadelphia (covers Delaware, nine counties in southern New Jersey, and forty-eight counties in the eastern two-thirds of Pennsylvania): Mr. Boehne took office February 1, 1981. He is the longest-serving of all the current twelve Fed presidents. Born May 15, 1940, in Evansville, Indiana, he joined the Philadelphia Fed in 1968 as an economist and has served in a number of posts, including vice president and director of research, beginning in 1971, and senior vice president in 1973. Prior to becoming president, he had wide-ranging responsibilities in supervision and regulation, the discount window, monetary policy, economic research, consumer affairs and bank and public relations. He is a graduate of Indiana University; he also holds an MBA, MA and PhD in economics from Indiana. While teaching economics at Indiana, he received an award for outstanding teaching.

Jerry L. Jordan, president, Fourth District, Cleveland (covers Ohio, parts of eastern Kentucky, western Pennsylvania and northern West Virginia): Mr. Jordan took office March 9, 1992. Born November 12, 1941 in Los Angeles, he received a BA from California State University in Northridge, California, and a PhD in economics from the University of California at Los Angeles (UCLA) in 1969. He is highly regarded for his dry wit and ability to translate complex economic theories into plain English. Prior to becoming president of the Cleveland Fed, he was senior vice president and chief economist at First Interstate Bancorp in Los Angeles. Among his other prior posts were dean and professor at the Robert O. Anderson School of Management at the University of New Mexico, a member of President Reagan's Council of Economic Advisers, a member of the U.S. Gold Commission, and senior vice president and chief economist of Pittsburgh National Bank. He also worked at the Federal Reserve Bank of St. Louis from 1967 to 1975, rising to senior vice president and director of research. From November 1971 to May 1972, while on leave from the St. Louis Fed, he served as economic consultant to Germany's Bundesbank in Frankfurt. Before joining the Fed, Mr. Jordan served for many years as a member of the Shadow Open Market Committee, a group of private-sector economists who meet regularly to critique economic policy—and often are highly critical of the Federal Reserve. Members of the "Shadow" long have urged the Fed to focus on maintaining slow and steady growth of the nation's money supply, which they argue is the key to long-term economic prosperity and low inflation.

J. Alfred Broaddus Jr., president, Fifth District, Richmond, Virginia, (covers Maryland, Virginia, North Carolina and South Carolina; forty-nine counties comprising most of West Virginia; and Washington DC): Mr. Broaddus took office January 1, 1993. Born July 8, 1939, in Richmond, he received his BA from Washington and Lee University, where he was elected to Phi Beta Kappa and Omicron Delta Kappa. Following graduation, he studied in France under a Fulbright, receiving a graduate degree from the Center for Advanced European Studies at the University of Strasbourg. After military service, he got MA and PhD degrees in economics from Indiana University. He joined the Richmond Fed research staff as an economist in 1970, was named assistant vice president in 1972, vice president in 1975, and senior vice president and director of research in 1985.

Jack Guynn, president, Sixth District, Atlanta (covers Alabama, Florida and Georgia; parts of Tennessee, Louisiana and Mississippi): Mr. Guynn (pronounced gwinn) took office January 1, 1996. Born December 10, 1942, in Staunton, Virginia, he earned his bachelor's degree in industrial engineering in 1964 at Virginia Polytechnic Institute and State University. He received a master's degree in industrial management from Georgia Institute of Technology in 1969 and completed Harvard Business School's program for management development in 1974. He joined the Atlanta Fed in 1964 as a systems analyst and, in 1970, was picked to help develop plans for the bank's new office in Miami and assisted with the start-up of those operations. For seven years, he was vice president in charge of the New Orleans office. In 1979, he was named senior vice president, with responsibility for bank supervision and regulation, discount and credit, human resources, and legal. In 1984, he was named first vice president and chief operating officer. While keeping those posts, Mr. Guynn was named in 1994 to serve as chairman of the Federal Reserve System's newly formed Financial Services Management Committee, which is responsible for "developing and implementing an integrated business plan for Federal Reserve payments services as well as coordinating national Federal Reserve activities that support the plan."

Michael H. Moskow, president, Seventh District, Chicago (covers all of Iowa; parts of Indiana, Illinois, Michigan and Wisconsin): Mr. Moskow took office September 1, 1994. Born January 7, 1938, in Paterson, New Jersey, he received a BA in economics from Lafayette College in Easton, Pennsylvania, in 1959, an MA in economics in 1962 and a PhD in business and applied economics in 1965 from the University of Pennsylvania. He began his career teaching economics, labor relations and management at Temple University, Lafayette College and Drexel University. From 1969 to 1977, he held a number of senior U.S. government posts, including senior staff economist at the Council of Economic Advisers; Assistant Secretary for Policy Development and Research at the U.S. Department of Housing and Urban Development; Director, Council on Wage and Price Stability; and Under Secretary of Labor. He joined Esmark Inc. in Chicago in 1977 as vice president of corporate development and planning, and was named executive vice president of Estronics Inc., a subsidiary, in 1980. Later, he served as president and chief executive officer of Velsicol Chemical Corp., a subsidiary of Northwest Industries Inc. of Chicago; vice president of corporate development for Dart and Kraft Inc., of Northbrook, Illinois; and vice president of strategy and business development for Premark International Inc. of Deerfield, Illinois. In 1991, he was named by then-President Bush as Deputy U.S. Trade Representative. In 1993, he became a professor of strategy and international management at the J. L. Kellogg Graduate School of Management at Northwestern University.

Thomas C. Melzer, president, Eighth District, St. Louis (covers all of Arkansas; parts of Illinois, Indiana, Kentucky, Mississippi, Missouri and the city of St. Louis, and part of Tennessee): Mr. Melzer took office June 1, 1985, as the tenth chief executive of the Federal Reserve Bank of St. Louis. Born October 23, 1944, in Philadelphia, he received a BS in electrical engineering in 1966 and an MBA in finance in 1968 from Stanford University. Prior to joining the St. Louis Fed, he worked at Morgan Stanley & Co., where he was involved in a wide variety of management activities, including corporate finance, real estate finance and investment, and securities sales and trading. The St. Louis Fed long has been known for its advocacy of "monetarism," a theory that emphasizes the importance of slow and steady growth in the nation's money supply. Late in 1997, Mr. Melzer announced his plan to resign as of January 31, 1998.

Gary H. Stern, president, Ninth District, Minneapolis (covers all of Minnesota, Montana, North Dakota and South Dakota, the Upper Peninsula of Michigan and part of northern Wisconsin): Mr. Stern took office March 16, 1985, as the eleventh chief executive of the Federal Reserve Bank of Minneapolis. Born November 3, 1944, in San Luis Obispo, California, he holds an AB in economics from Washington University in St. Louis and a PhD in economics from Rice University in Houston. He joined the Minneapolis Fed in January 1982 as senior vice president and director of research. In August 1983, he was given the additional post of chief financial officer. He has also served on the faculties of Columbia University, Washington University and New York University. Earlier in his career, he worked for seven years at the Federal Reserve Bank of New York, where his last assignment was as manager of the domestic research department. In 1981, he wrote a book with Paul DeRosa called, *In the Name of Money, A Professional's Guide to the Federal Reserve, Interest Rates and Money*.

Thomas M. Hoenig, president, Tenth District, Kansas City, Missouri (covers all of Colorado, Kansas, Nebraska, Oklahoma and Wyoming, parts of Missouri and New Mexico): Mr. Hoenig took office October 1, 1991, as the eighth chief executive of the Federal Reserve Bank of Kansas City. He was born September 6, 1946, in Fort Madison, Iowa. He earned a BA in economics and mathematics at Benedictine College in Atchison, Kansas, and received MA and PhD degrees in economics from Iowa State University. In 1973, he joined the Kansas City Fed as an economist in the banking supervision area. He was named a vice president in 1981 and senior vice president in 1986.

Robert D. McTeer Jr., president, Eleventh District, Dallas (covers all of Texas; parts of Louisiana and New Mexico): Mr. McTeer took office February 1, 1991, as the tenth chief executive of the Federal Reserve Bank of Dallas.

Born October 22, 1942, in Ranger, Georgia, he received BBA and PhD degrees in economics from the University of Georgia and served on its faculty for two years prior to joining the Federal Reserve System. He joined the Richmond Fed in 1968 as an economist in the research department. He was promoted to assistant vice president and given administrative responsibility for the research department in 1971. He was promoted to vice president in 1975 and was made special assistant to the bank's president and first vice president. In 1978, he was assigned official responsibilities for the bank's fiscal agency and securities departments. In 1980, he was promoted to senior vice president in charge of the Baltimore branch of the Richmond Fed, a post he held until he took over the Dallas Fed.

Robert T. Parry, president, Twelfth District, San Francisco (covers Alaska, Arizona, California, Hawaii, Idaho, Nevada, Oregon, Utah and Washington): Mr. Parry took office February 4, 1986, as the tenth chief executive of the Federal Reserve Bank of San Francisco. Born May 16, 1939, in Harrisburg, Pennsylvania, he received a BA from Gettysburg College in 1960 and was elected to Phi Beta Kappa. He received an MA in economics from the University of Pennsylvania in 1961 and a PhD in 1967. He served as research economist at the Federal Reserve Board in Washington starting in 1965. He served at the Board until 1970 and helped build a financial model of the U.S. economy. In 1970, he joined Security Pacific National Bank as a vice president and became chief economist in 1973. Later, he was promoted to senior vice president and executive vice president of Security Pacific Corp. and its main unit, Security Pacific National Bank. Mr. Parry is a past president of the National Association of Business Economists.

OTHER FEDERAL RESERVE OFFICIALS

Donald L. Kohn, director, Division of Monetary Affairs, and secretary of the Federal Open Market Committee: Mr. Kohn is rarely quoted but is considered one of the most influential people at the Federal Reserve Board. His lengthy official title doesn't come close to indicating the enormous influence he commands at the Fed. He is in charge of a large staff of economists who analyze monetary policy and related issues and help frame policy options to be considered by senior Fed policymakers. He graduated in 1964 from the College of Wooster in Wooster, Ohio, and received his MA and PhD from the University of Michigan. From 1970 to 1975, he worked as an economist at the Federal Reserve Bank of Kansas City. From 1975 to 1978, he was an economist at the Federal Reserve Board's government finance section. From 1978 to 1981, he was chief of the capital markets section; from 1981 to 1983, he was an officer in the division of research and statistics. From September 1983 to June 1987, he was deputy staff director in the Office of the Staff Director for Monetary and Financial Policy. And from June 1987 to October 1987, he was deputy director, monetary policy and financial markets, in the division of research and statistics. He was named Director in the Division of Monetary Affairs in late October 1987.

Richard Spillenkothen, director, Division of Banking Supervision and Regulation: He oversees supervision and regulation of such areas as state member banks, bank holding companies, and foreign banking institutions operating in the United States. Mr. Spillenkothen coordinates supervisory policy with Reserve Bank officials, as well as with other federal, state and foreign banking authorities. He also is responsible for overseeing the process of applications submitted to the Federal Reserve System and for supervising state member banks and bank holding companies.

J. Virgil Mattingly Jr., general counsel: Serving as General Counsel since 1989, Mr. Mattingly joined the Fed in 1974 after several years as an attorney in the U.S. Army Judge Advocate General Corps. He received a BBA degree in accounting from George Washington University, a JD degree from George Washington University and also went to Judge Advocate General School. Under his direction, the Fed's legal division provides legal counsel on a wide range of supervisory, regulatory, monetary, legislative, litigation and other matters. He also shares in responsibility for preparing congressional testimony and speeches made by the Fed Chairman and other Board members.

Edwin M. Truman, staff director, Division of International Finance: Mr. Truman has a wide-ranging job that includes helping to manage the Third World debt crisis. His division is one of three research divisions at the Board, with a staff of about 110, including more than fifty PhD-level economists. The division does research and prepares forecasts and analyses for the Board and Federal Open Market Committee on what the Fed refers to the "external sector" of the U.S. economy, foreign exchange, and financial markets, and the global economy. Mr. Truman is a former associate professor of economics at Yale University, where he received his PhD in economics. He received his BA from Amherst College and an LLD (hon.) from Amherst.

Michael J. Prell, director, Division of Research and Statistics: This division, which has about 275 people, is responsible for a wide range of activities, including providing forecasts and other analyses to the Board and Federal Open Market Committee, to help them with monetary policy and financial regulation. Before joining the Board staff in 1973, he served for almost three years as a financial economist at the Federal Reserve Bank of Kansas City. Mr. Prell began his career at the Board in the Capital Markets Section of the Research Division and then worked in the Government Finance section. In 1977, he was named chief of the Capital Markets Section. He was appointed an officer of the Board in 1978 and held various posts before being named Director of the Research Division in 1987. He received his AB (1966), his MA (1967) and his PhD (1971) in economics from the University of California, Berkeley.

Clyde H. Farnsworth Jr., director, Division of Reserve Bank Operations and Payment Systems: Mr. Farnsworth is responsible for the smooth operation of the Fed's electronic payment system, which is designed to allow the Fed and depository institutions to transmit funds and securities quickly and efficiently. He also is responsible for financial planning and control of the various Federal Reserve Banks. That includes oversight of annual operating and capital budgets. Prior to joining the Board in 1975, he was Assistant Vice President and economist at the Federal Reserve Bank of Richmond. He has also held teaching posts at Virginia Tech and Clemson University. He received his BA and MA degrees from East Tennessee State University and his PhD from the University of Missouri.

Joseph R. Coyne, assistant to the Federal Reserve Board and assistant secretary, Federal Open Market Committee: Mr. Coyne is the veteran spokesman for both the Federal Reserve Board and the FOMC. Having worked at the Fed since 1968, he has an impressive, first-hand knowledge of the Fed's history, characters and operations. Once, when asked when he finally will write his tell-all book, he replied with a chuckle: "Never! I know too much! There will be no book." Mr. Coyne was born July 25, 1928, in Scranton, Pennsylvania. He graduated from the University of Scranton with an AB magna cum laude. He also went to Fordham University and received an MFA in communications arts.

OTHER TOP OFFICIALS OF THE FEDERAL RESERVE
BANK OF NEW YORK

Ernest T. Patrikis, first vice president: He also is an alternate member of the FOMC. A graduate of Cornell Law School, he joined the New York Fed in 1968. Since then, he has held a wide range of major posts, including general counsel and executive vice president of the legal group, and head of the bank's corporate group. He also served as deputy general counsel of the FOMC for five years.

Peter R. Fisher, executive vice president and manager, System Open Market Account: Mr. Fisher is one of the most important staffers in the entire Federal Reserve System. Not only is he head of the Fed's markets group, he also manages the "System Open Market Account" for the Federal Open Market Committee, the Federal Reserve's monetary policy-making unit. And he oversees all domestic "open market" operations, which involve buying and selling U.S. Government securities on behalf of the New York Fed, as directed by the

FOMC. In addition, he oversees foreign-exchange trading operations at the New York Fed and is a member of the bank's management committee. He also serves on the Gold and Foreign Exchange Committee of the G-10 central banks. Mr. Fisher is a graduate of Harvard College, with a BA in history, in 1980. He also has a degree from Harvard Law School. In September 1985, he joined the New York Fed in the legal department and was named an assistant counsel in October 1988. In May 1989, he was given a leave of absence to work at the Bank for International Settlements in Basel, Switzerland, on a special study for the G-10 nations on "netting arrangements and interbank payments." While on leave, he was appointed counsel. Upon his return in October 1990, he was assigned to foreign exchange as an assistant vice president. In July 1992, he was named a vice president, while continuing in the foreign-exchange job. In September 1993, he was named senior vice president in charge of foreign exchange.

Thomas C. Baxter Jr., general counsel and executive vice president, Legal Group: Mr. Baxter has held his post since March 1995. He also serves as deputy general counsel of the FOMC. His principal job is to supervise the day-to-day operations of the New York Fed's legal group, and he also serves on the bank's management committee. He received his law degree from the Georgetown University Law Center.

Stephen G. Cecchetti, executive vice president and director of the research and Market Analysis Group: He joined the New York Fed in August 1997. Before that, he had been a professor of economics at Ohio State University. He earned his undergraduate degree in economics from MIT and a PhD degree in economics from the University of California at Berkeley.

Terrence J. Checki, executive vice president, Emerging Markets and International Affairs Group: During his career at the bank, he has held key posts in the corporate, bank supervision, foreign and international affairs areas. He hold a master's degree in business from Columbia University.

Suzanne Cutler, executive vice president, Banking Services Group: Her post includes responsibility for bank services, cash, central bank services, check, electronic payments and fiscal services, as well as the bank's East Rutherford, New Jersey, operations center and the Buffalo branch. She has been an executive vice president since October 1987. She joined the bank in 1970 as an economist in the banking studies department. She holds a doctor of philosophy degree in economics from New York University's Graduate School of Arts and Sciences, as well as a master of business administration degree from Wharton.

In the Beginning . . .

The idea of creating a central bank was debated intensely during the early years of the United States. The very notion of handing over such vast financial power to a single institution struck many Americans as frightening. After all, wasn't the American Revolution all about escaping from central authority?

During the presidency of George Washington, a struggle erupted between Treasury Secretary Alexander Hamilton, who favored a central bank, and Secretary of State Thomas Jefferson, who hated the idea. Hamilton won. The First Bank of the United States was born in 1791.

According to a Fed publication, only 20 percent of the bank's capital came from the federal government. The rest came from private individuals. Only five of the twenty-five directors were appointed by the U.S. government, and the rest by the private investors. It was the largest corporation in the new nation. Based in Philadelphia, it had branches in other major cities, and it performed such basic banking jobs as accepting deposits, issuing bank notes, making loans and transacting in securities.

Although the bank drew praise for helping the new nation get started, many Americans remained deeply suspicious of such a vast financial empire. After the bank's charter expired twenty years later, Congress decided not to renew it. State-chartered private banks grew rapidly, and so did a wide variety of bank notes. Several years later, Congress narrowly approved a bill chartering the Second Bank of the United States, and President James Madison signed it. This was very much like the first, only much larger and more powerful—and, like the first, it soon became a lightning rod for criticism. Among its toughest critics was Andrew Jackson. When the bank's charter expired in 1836,

it died. Once again, state-chartered banks flourished.

During the Civil War, Washington approved a national banking act that set up nationally chartered banks. This legislation effectively provided that only the national banks could issue bank notes, a Fed publication recalls. But there was still no central bank.

Financial panics in the late 1880s and early 1900s helped build support for the idea of a new central bank. Many Americans blamed the economy's terrifying boom-bust cycle on the lack of a sensitive national financial thermostat. Momentum for a central bank grew especially rapidly after a severe financial panic in 1907. The historic Federal Reserve Act was signed at 6:02 P.M. by President Woodrow Wilson on December 23, 1913.

The severity of the Great Depression reshaped the thinking of many analysts about the American economic system and the role of its central bank. After absorbing heavy criticism for not acting more aggressively during the late 1920s and 1930s, the Fed underwent enormous changes in its structure and authority. In subsequent years, the Fed's authority rapidly expanded, such as through the Employment Act of 1946 and the Humphrey-Hawkins Act of 1978, which spelled out a wide variety of objectives. Among them: a high level of employment, stable prices, and moderate long-term interest rates.

In short, Congress wants the Fed to give Americans the best of all possible worlds, with the least amount of pain.

But perhaps the best-known definition of the Fed's job comes from William McChesney Martin, who was Fed Chairman from April 2, 1951, through January 31, 1970. Mr. Martin once said the Fed's unenviable job is to remove the punch bowl just as the party gets going.

Chester B. Feldberg, executive vice president, Bank Supervision Group:
This group is responsible for supervising all state member banks, bank holding companies and foreign bank offices in the district. It also processes applications

by banking organizations to expand their activities, and it participates in the development and implementation of supervisory policies and procedures. Mr. Feldberg joined the New York Fed in the legal department in 1964. He graduated from Harvard Law School in 1963.

Kathleen A. O'Neil, executive vice president, Corporate Group: She is responsible for overseeing the credit and risk management, human resources, planning and control, and public information areas. She also is responsible for internal communications and multimedia services, and accounting and services functions. As the bank's "senior risk officer," she is also responsible for coordinating response to "financial system dysfunction," as the New York Fed delicately phrases it. She earned a BS degree in economics from John Carroll University and an MBA degree in finance from Wharton.

Israel Sendrovic, executive vice president, Automation and Systems Services Group: This includes technical but highly important areas of the New York Fed, such as systems development, data processing and security control. This group also is responsible for facilities management, data collection and administrative services. Mr. Sendrovic earned a master of science degree in operations research from New York University in 1970 and a bachelor of science degree in mathematics from Brooklyn College.

THE FEDERAL RESERVE SYSTEM

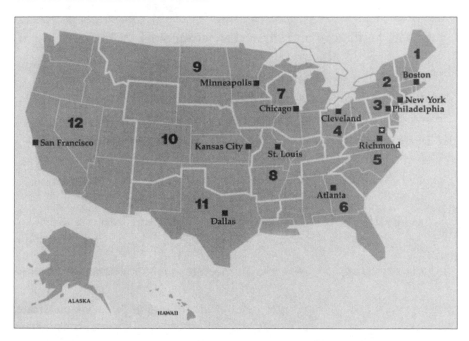

INDEX

ABOUT THE AUTHORS

 **Douglas R. Sease** is Deputy Editor of *The Wall Street Journal*'s Money and Investing section.

Michael Siconolfi is a Senior Special Writer covering Wall Street.

 **R. Thomas Herman** is a Senior Special Writer covering taxes and personal finance.

Stephen E. Frank covers banking.

 **Deborah Lohse** covers small stocks and the National Association of Securities Dealers.

Gregory Ip covers stocks and the New York Stock Exchange.

 **Suzanne McGee** covers the stock market.

Charles Gasparino covers mutual funds and municipal finance.